Handbook of Research on Advanced Practical Approaches to Deepfake Detection and Applications

Ahmed J. Obaid
University of Kufa, Iraq

Ghassan H. Abdul-Majeed
University of Baghdad, Iraq

Adriana Burlea-Schiopoiu
University of Craiova, Romania

Parul Aggarwal
Jamia Hamdard, India

IGI Global
PUBLISHER of TIMELY KNOWLEDGE

A volume in the Advances in Multimedia and
Interactive Technologies (AMIT) Book Series

Published in the United States of America by
IGI Global
Information Science Reference (an imprint of IGI Global)
701 E. Chocolate Avenue
Hershey PA, USA 17033
Tel: 717-533-8845
Fax: 717-533-8661
E-mail: cust@igi-global.com
Web site: http://www.igi-global.com

Library of Congress Cataloging-in-Publication Data

Names: Obaid, Ahmed J., editor.
Title: Handbook of research on advanced practical approaches to deepfake detection and applications / Ahmed J. Obaid, Ghassan Abdul-Majeed, Adriana Burlea-Schiopoiu, and Parul Agarwal, editors.
Description: Hershey, PA : Engineering Science Reference, [2023] | Includes bibliographical references and index. | Summary: "This book provides an introduction to deepfakes and the challenges and difficulties identifying them as a potentially devastating consequence of counterfeiting to our society"-- Provided by publisher.
Identifiers: LCCN 2022039843 (print) | LCCN 2022039844 (ebook) | ISBN 9781668460603 (hardcover) | ISBN 9781668460627 (ebook)
Subjects: LCSH: Online manipulation--Prevention. | Deepfakes. | Computer security.
Classification: LCC TK5105.878 .H36 2023 (print) | LCC TK5105.878 (ebook) | DDC 004.67/8--dc23/eng/20221017
LC record available at https://lccn.loc.gov/2022039843
LC ebook record available at https://lccn.loc.gov/2022039844

This book is published in the IGI Global book series Advances in Multimedia and Interactive Technologies (AMIT) (ISSN: 2327-929X; eISSN: 2327-9303)

British Cataloguing in Publication Data
A Cataloguing in Publication record for this book is available from the British Library.

For electronic access to this publication, please contact: eresources@igi-global.com.

Advances in Multimedia and Interactive Technologies (AMIT) Book Series

Joel J.P.C. Rodrigues
Senac Faculty of Ceará, Fortaleza-CE, Brazil; Instituto de Telecomunicações, Portugal

ISSN:2327-929X
EISSN:2327-9303

Mission

Traditional forms of media communications are continuously being challenged. The emergence of user-friendly web-based applications such as social media and Web 2.0 has expanded into everyday society, providing an interactive structure to media content such as images, audio, video, and text.

The **Advances in Multimedia and Interactive Technologies (AMIT) Book Series** investigates the relationship between multimedia technology and the usability of web applications. This series aims to highlight evolving research on interactive communication systems, tools, applications, and techniques to provide researchers, practitioners, and students of information technology, communication science, media studies, and many more with a comprehensive examination of these multimedia technology trends.

Coverage

- Web Technologies
- Audio Signals
- Multimedia Services
- Multimedia Technology
- Internet Technologies
- Digital Communications
- Digital Images
- Social Networking
- Digital Games
- Multimedia Streaming

IGI Global is currently accepting manuscripts for publication within this series. To submit a proposal for a volume in this series, please contact our Acquisition Editors at Acquisitions@igi-global.com or visit: http://www.igi-global.com/publish/.

The Advances in Multimedia and Interactive Technologies (AMIT) Book Series (ISSN 2327-929X) is published by IGI Global, 701 E. Chocolate Avenue, Hershey, PA 17033-1240, USA, www.igi-global.com. This series is composed of titles available for purchase individually; each title is edited to be contextually exclusive from any other title within the series. For pricing and ordering information please visit http://www.igi-global.com/book-series/advances-multimedia-interactive-technologies/73683. Postmaster: Send all address changes to above address.

Titles in this Series

For a list of additional titles in this series, please visit: http://www.igi-global.com/book-series/advances-multimedia-interactive-technologies/73683

Dynamics of Dialogue, Cultural Development, and Peace in theMetaverse
Swati Chakraborty (GLA University, India)
Information Science Reference • © 2023 • 236pp • H/C (ISBN: 9781668459072) • US $240.00

Handbook of Research on New Media, Training, and Skill Development for the Modern Workforce
Dominic Mentor (Teachers College, Columbia University, USA)
Business Science Reference • © 2022 • 439pp • H/C (ISBN: 9781668439968) • US $295.00

Handbook of Research on New Media Applications in Public Relations and Advertising
Elif Esiyok (Atilim University, Turkey)
Information Science Reference • © 2021 • 572pp • H/C (ISBN: 9781799832010) • US $295.00

Multidisciplinary Perspectives on Narrative Aesthetics in Video Games
Deniz Denizel (Bahcesehir University, Turkey) and Deniz Eyüce Şansal (Bahcesehir University, Turkey)
Information Science Reference • © 2021 • 300pp • H/C (ISBN: 9781799851103) • US $195.00

Recent Advances in 3D Imaging, Modeling, and Reconstruction
Athanasios Voulodimos (University of West Attica, Athens, Greece) and Anastasios Doulamis (National Technical University of Athens, Athens, Greece)
Information Science Reference • © 2020 • 396pp • H/C (ISBN: 9781522552949) • US $215.00

Handbook of Research on Recent Developments in Image Processing and Applications
Suresh Kumar Nagarajan (VIT University, India) and R. Mohanasundaram (VIT University, India)
Information Science Reference • © 2020 • 1700pp • H/C (ISBN: 9781799802228) • US $565.00

Graphical Thinking for Science and Technology Through Knowledge Visualization
Anna Ursyn (University of Northern Colorado, USA)
Information Science Reference • © 2020 • 374pp • H/C (ISBN: 9781799816515) • US $250.00

New Media and Visual Communication in Social Networks
Serpil Kır (Hatay Mustafa Kemal University, Turkey)
Information Science Reference • © 2020 • 345pp • H/C (ISBN: 9781799810414) • US $215.00

IGI Global
PUBLISHER of TIMELY KNOWLEDGE

701 East Chocolate Avenue, Hershey, PA 17033, USA
Tel: 717-533-8845 x100 • Fax: 717-533-8661
E-Mail: cust@igi-global.com • www.igi-global.com

List of Contributors

Table of Contents

Preface xxiii

Section 1
Advanced Practical Approaches to Deepfake Detection

Chapter 1
An Overview of Fraud Applications and Software on Social Media 1
Nadia Mahmood Hussien, Mustansiriyah University, Iraq
Yasmin Makki Mohialden, Mustansiriyah University, Iraq

Chapter 2
An Overview of Rumor and Fake News Detection Approaches 12
Zainab Ali Jawad, University of Kufa, Iraq
Ahmed J. Obaid, University of Kufa, Iraq

Chapter 3
Deepfakes Spark Implementation for Big Data Analytics 32
A. Muruganantham, Kristu Jayanti College, India
Ayshwarya Balakumar, Kristu Jayanti College, India
N. Srinivas, KG Reddy College of Engineering and Technology, India
C. Srinivas Gupta, Mallareddy Engineering College, India
Vinod Desai, BLDEA's P.G.H. College of Engineering and Technology, Vijayapur, India
K. Saikumar, KL University, India

Chapter 4
Experimental Work and Discussion of Results on Deepfakes in Stock Prices Using Sentiment Analysis and Machine Learning 44
Anbarasu N., Nandha Engineering College, India
S. Karuppusamy, Nandha Engineering College, India
S. Prabhu, Nandha Engineering College, India
P. Sobana, Nandha Engineering College, India

Chapter 5
An Overview of Available Deepfake Datasets in Neural Network-Based Soil and Weather Prediction Models for High Quality Crops 55
A. Anisha Sanjeetha, Nandha Engineering College, India
R. Sivaraj, Nandha Engineering College, India
P. Uma, Nandha Engineering College, India

Chapter 6
An Introduction to Deepfakes on Cryptographic Image Security 72
P. Boobalan, Nandha Engineering College, India
K. Gunasekar, Nandha Engineering College, India
P. Thirumoorthy, Nandha Engineering College, India
J. Senthil, Nandha Engineering College, India

Chapter 7
Deepfakes on Smart Devices in Stock Price Prediction Using Machine Learning 82
P. Sobana, Nandha Engineering College, India
S. Prabhu, Nandha Engineering College, India
S. Karuppusamy, Nandha Engineering College, India
N. Anbarasu, Nandha Engineering College, India

Chapter 8
Machine Learning Algorithms to Detect Deepfakes Fine Tuned for Anomaly Detection of IoT 95
N. Sridhar, Nandha Engineering College, India
K. Shanmugapriya, Nandha Engineering College, India
C. N. Marimuthu, Nandha Engineering College, India

Chapter 9
Data Storage, Data Forwarding, Data Retrieval With Big Data Deepfakes in Secure Cloud Storage 106
K. Vinitha, Nandha Engineering College, India
P. Thirumoorthy, Nandha Engineering College, India
S. Hemalatha, Nandha Engineering College, India

Chapter 10
A Privacy Protection Method for Deepfake Hybrid Cloud Computing 120
L. Subhashini, Nandha Engineering College, India
S. Maheswari, Nandha Engineering College, India
S. Prabhu, Nandha Engineering College, India

Section 2
Advanced Practical Approaches to Applications

Chapter 11
Enhancing the Protection of Information in Digital Voting Using the Fraud Application of Blockchain Technology 134
P. Ganesan, BMS Institute of Technology and Management, India
D. Rosy Salomi Victoria, St. Joseph's College of Engineering, India
Arun Singh Chouhan, Malla Reddy University, India
D. Saravanan, IFET College of Engineering, India
Rekha Baghel, Ajay Kumar Garg Engineering College, Ghaziabad, India
K. Saikumar, Koneru Lakshmaiah Education Foundation, India

Chapter 12
A Machine Learning-Based Image Segmentation for Real-Time Images in Smart Intelligent Transportation Systems 147
S. Jayalakshmi, Ramachandra College of Engineering, India
Aswin Kumer S. V., Koneru Lakshmaiah Education Foundation, India
Jarabala Ranga, Ramachandra College of Engineering, India
K. Venkatasubramanian, Ramachandra College of Engineering, India
V. N. S. L. Narayana A., University of Technology, Jaipur, India
Y. Lavanya, Ramachandra College of Engineering, India

Chapter 13
Techniques and Applications of Optimal Cluster Head Selection With Trusted Multipath Routing and MANET Intrusion Detection 162
Venkatasubramanian Srinivasan, Saranathan College of Engineering, India
P. L. Rajarajeswari, Saranathan College of Engineering, India
T. Sathis Kumar, Saranathan College of Engineering, India

Chapter 14
Deep Learning Algorithms in Cluster Analysis on an E-Learning System in Data Mining 183
S. Keerthana, Nandha Engineering College, India
P. Thirumoorthy, Nandha Engineering College, India
S. Maheswari, Nandha Engineering College, India
S. Karuppusamy, Nandha Engineering College, India

Chapter 15
COVID-19 Diagnosis Using Transfer Learning Techniques and Applications on Chest X-Ray Images 194
E. Manimehalai, Nandha Engineering College, India
D. Vanathi, Nandha Engineering College, India
C. Navamani, Nandha Engineering College, India

Chapter 16
Features Manipulation of Classification and Recognition of Images Under Artificial Intelligence Using CNN Algorithm and LSTM 207
J. Priyadharshini, Nandha Engineering College, India
E. Padma, Nandha Engineering College, India
S. Prabhadevi, Nandha Engineering College, India

Chapter 17
Security Enhancement in Cloud Computing Using CBC Technique 221
V. Gunasundhari, Nandha Engineering College, India
M. Parvathi, Nandha Engineering College, India
S. Prabhu, Nandha Engineering College, India

Chapter 18
Techniques and Applications of Demographic Determinants of Mobile Phone Brand Switching in Attitude Towards Switching and Switching Intentions 233
Binit Patel, Charotar University of Science and Technology, India

Chapter 19
Recent Application of Deep Neural Network and Data Augmentation for Classifying Leaf Diseases 245
R. Angeline, SRM Institute of Science and Technology, India
Raunak Agarwal, SRM Institute of Science and Technology, India
Sidhant Kumar Sidharth, SRM Institute of Science and Technology, India
Pratik Raj Biresh, SRM Institute of Science and Technology, India

Chapter 20
Implementation of Dynamic Gesture Interpretation of Sign Language for Impact on Hearing and Speech Impairment 257
Judy Flavia B., SRM Institute of Science and Technology, India
Aarthi B., SRM Institute of Science and Technology, India
P. Charitharyan, SRM Institute of Science and Technology, India
Renuka Thanmai, SRM Institute of Science and Technology, India
Meghana Kesana, SRM Institute of Science and Technology, India

Chapter 21
Adapting Multi-Temporal Information for Optimized Ship Detection From SAR Image Dataset Using Transfer Learning Application 275
Deva Hema D., SRM Institute of Science and Technology, Ramapuram, India
Agnes Faustina, SRM Institute of Science and Technology, Ramapuram, India
E. Aravindhan, SRM Institute of Science and Technology, Ramapuram, India

Chapter 22
YOLO v5 and Faster R-CNN Performance Evaluation of Solid Waste in Object Detection Application ... 288
Pradeep Kumar T., Adhiyamaan College of Engineering, India
Lilly Florence M., Adhiyamaan College of Engineering, India
Fathima G., Adhiyamaan College of Engineering, India

Chapter 23
Professional Career Planning and Decision Making Based on SQL Server Data Mining Techniques ... 305
Nandhini S., Sathyabama Institute of Science and Technology, India
S. Parthasarathy, Sathyabama Institute of Science and Technology, India
V. Marimuthu, SRM Institute of Science and Technology, India

Chapter 24
An Introduction to Audio Manipulation and Generation of a Unified High Performance Recommendation Framework for Netflix ... 319
R. Angeline, SRM Institute of Science and Technology, India
Harish Babu M., SRM Institute of Science and Technology, India
Rehith B., SRM Institute of Science and Technology, India
Pranav B., SRM Institute of Science and Technology, India

Chapter 25
Practical Approaches to Machine Learning for 5G and Beyond Wireless Network ... 333
M. M. Kamruzzaman, Jouf University, Saudi Arabia
Md Altab Hossin, Chengdu University, China
Ibrahim Alrashdi, Jouf University, Saudi Arabia

Compilation of References ... 345

About the Contributors ... 373

Index ... 377

Detailed Table of Contents

Preface xxiii

Section 1
Advanced Practical Approaches to Deepfake Detection

Chapter 1
An Overview of Fraud Applications and Software on Social Media 1
Nadia Mahmood Hussien, Mustansiriyah University, Iraq
Yasmin Makki Mohialden, Mustansiriyah University, Iraq

Fraud involves intentional deception. While the victim's rights are violated, the criminal profits from the situation. Fraud can be committed by individuals, groups, or even entire companies. The importance of social media cannot be overstated. The management of natural disasters and medical difficulties are both handled through social media. The use of social media has resulted in the establishment of a marketplace for goods and services. Because social networking has evolved into a money-making opportunity, dishonest users now cheat in many ways. Fraud on social media platforms has been on the rise. Cybercriminals exploit unethical social engineering to steal data. Indicators of fraud include excessive pressure, a broad scope, honey traps, and justification. People who are unaware of something lose both money and information. In the current environment, information technology professionals are unable to protect social media users from being scammed or spammed.

Chapter 2
An Overview of Rumor and Fake News Detection Approaches 12
Zainab Ali Jawad, University of Kufa, Iraq
Ahmed J. Obaid, University of Kufa, Iraq

People in this day and age like to keep up with the most recent news on social media since it is economical, simple, and can be obtained in a short amount of time. However, social media can be a double-edged sword, since it may propagate fake news or information that cannot be relied upon. The dissemination of false information could adversely affect both individuals and society as a whole. Therefore, researchers gave their all to devise a system that could identify fake news before its publication. This article gives an overview of the most major attempts that have been made to construct a system that can filter online news and detect false news with a decent amount of accuracy. Data mining approaches were reviewed in the detection phase, including feature extraction and model construction.

Chapter 3
Deepfakes Spark Implementation for Big Data Analytics 32
A. Muruganantham, Kristu Jayanti College, India
Ayshwarya Balakumar, Kristu Jayanti College, India
N. Srinivas, KG Reddy College of Engineering and Technology, India
C. Srinivas Gupta, Mallareddy Engineering College, India
Vinod Desai, BLDEA's P.G.H. College of Engineering and Technology, Vijayapur, India
K. Saikumar, KL University, India

One of the most significant challenges we have in the context of today's big data world is the fact that we are unable to process enormous amounts of data in a timely manner. In this piece, the authors will use drive HQ cloud to analyse and evaluate two different supervised multiplication systems that are built on service cluster applications. Spark, on the other hand, provides a framework for managing data that is more dependable, and also has the ability to address concerns such as the loss of nodes and the duplication of data. Although it comes at the expense of insufficient failure organization, this study issue has the ability to considerably increase pace effectiveness, which is something many research/industry companies are interested in. A soon-to-be-released study will examine the methods on bigger datasets, especially in cases where the data cannot be totally stored in memory.

Chapter 4
Experimental Work and Discussion of Results on Deepfakes in Stock Prices Using Sentiment Analysis and Machine Learning 44
Anbarasu N., Nandha Engineering College, India
S. Karuppusamy, Nandha Engineering College, India
S. Prabhu, Nandha Engineering College, India
P. Sobana, Nandha Engineering College, India

In the field of artificial intelligence, the employment of computer algorithms that develop themselves mechanically as they get more and more experience in experimental work and discussion of results on deepfakes is essential to the research process. It is frequently thought of as being in close proximity to artificial intelligence. Machine learning is a set of techniques that generates a model by making use of sample data, commonly referred to as training data, in order to make predictions about the future without actively attempting to do so, by separating the various types of tweets taken from the data on Twitter regarding a number of different companies. A classification algorithm was applied to the data that was collected and used in order to categorise the tweets. In addition, the OHLCV of the data from a number of different organisations is taken into account in order to improve efficiency.

Transportation, the environment, business, and agriculture are just a few areas where IoT and DL-based solutions are profoundly impacting. Soil nutrient insufficiency is a prevalent problem that can spread and harm plants if not addressed right away. An IoT-based system that monitors soil and weather conditions for nutrient deficiencies can help increase crop yields. One of the most crucial factors to include in existing deepfakes datasets is soil temperature when modelling terrestrial ecosystems. From January 1, 2010, through December 31, 2018, the Baker, Beach, Cando, Crary, and Fingal weather stations in North Dakota recorded daily weather and soil temperature readings. This study presents an enhanced convolutional neural network-based approach to soil and weather forecasting (CNN). In order to enhance the classification accuracy of the pre-trained CNN architecture, the slime mold algorithm is employed to optimise the model weight.

The level of protection afforded to the encryption key is directly proportional to the level of security afforded to the data being encrypted. Data transmission via networks is the primary application for encryption use. There have been many different methods developed and put into use, all of which are utilized for safeguarding sensitive image data from any kind of illegal access. Text, audio, video, graphics, and still photos are some of the numerous types of data that can be included within multimedia files. A rise in the use of multimedia content transmitted over the internet has resulted in an increase in the sortage for the content. The vast majority of current encryption algorithms are typically reserved for use with informations since they are mismatched with digitalized data. A block-based transformation technique was utilized for this project.

The stock market is a widely used investment scheme promising high returns, but it has some risks. It is an act to forecast the future value of the stock market. The change in the stock market is explosive, and there are multiple sophisticated financial indicators. Still, the enhancement in technology provides a

Chapter 10
A Privacy Protection Method for Deepfake Hybrid Cloud Computing.. 120
L. Subhashini, Nandha Engineering College, India
S. Maheswari, Nandha Engineering College, India
S. Prabhu, Nandha Engineering College, India

Cloud computing developed the world rapidly, so in our lifetimes, other cloud services are entered, and the security protection in our cloud services, particularly the protection against data sequestration, is gaining importance. Still, the protection separation implementation causes a huge drain. Therefore, it is difficult to implement the most appropriate product to reduce consumption power while protecting separation. The proposal proposes a full-scale sequestration scheme (PPPS) to provide usable sequestration protection that satisfies stone sequestration requirements while system performance can be maintained. First, the separation is unidentified by the drugs they carry, and they quantify the degree of security and perform the TripleDES standard and AES standard encrypts algorithms. The safety formulation is also derived from analysis results and professional data. Finally, similar results display that PPPS also meets the request sequestration from stones and maintains the performance in various cloud environments.

Section 2
Advanced Practical Approaches to Applications

Chapter 11
Enhancing the Protection of Information in Digital Voting Using the Fraud Application of Blockchain Technology... 134
P. Ganesan, BMS Institute of Technology and Management, India
D. Rosy Salomi Victoria, St. Joseph's College of Engineering, India
Arun Singh Chouhan, Malla Reddy University, India
D. Saravanan, IFET College of Engineering, India
Rekha Baghel, Ajay Kumar Garg Engineering College, Ghaziabad, India
K. Saikumar, Koneru Lakshmaiah Education Foundation, India

Elections are conducted electronically instead of using paper ballots to cut down on mistakes and discrepancies. Recently, it has been discovered that paper-based balloting fails owing to security and privacy difficulties, and the electronic balloting approach has been recommended as a replacement. For the sake of keeping your data safe, the authors have designed and developed a hashing algorithm based on SHA-256. The blockchain's adaptability is aided by the sealing of the block concept's incorporation. Consortium blockchain technology is employed to ensure that only the election commission has access to the blockchain database, which candidates and other outside parties cannot modify. When used in the polling method, the methodology discussed in this chapter can yield reliable findings. The authors used a hashing algorithm (SHA-256), block generation, data collection, and result declaration to get to this point.

In the ever-evolving world of computer vision, image recognition is critical task including using image processing to solve real-world problems like reducing human involvement in the art of driving. We face many challenges in completing this mission, including object detection and segmentation. By integrating Keras and TensorFlow with instance segmentation and binary masks, the challenges are effectively overcome by the method proposed in this chapter. The technique instantaneous segmentation is adopted for separating and detecting each individual object of interest in an image based on their pixel characteristics. The Mask RCNN model outperforms the current CNN models in terms of object detection accuracy and performance. Also, the objects of interest are classified using regional proposal networks (RPN) instead of selective search algorithm by CNN. The instance segmentation system is conceptually clear, versatile, and general. The method successfully finds items in acquired input and also produces good results by masking for each case.

A MANET (mobile ad hoc network) is a self-constituted wireless setup that operates independently of existing infrastructure and centralized control. In various daily uses, such as automotive, military, and other field networks, it is possible to find MANET on wireless systems. In contrast with MANET, a fixed or cable data and computer connectivity system are required for many networks. The WiFi, satellite networking, and smartphone network include fixed infrastructure technology. Moreover, MANET is a dynamic energy and security vulnerable system. The fundamental problem of energy efficiency optimization has been addressed effectively by Routing Protocols (R.P.) among the most extant techniques. This work, therefore, offers an efficient multi-track routing in a MANET-based optimization procedure. The intrusion detection and optimal cluster head (C.H.) selection approach, namely firefly algorithm (FFA) based fuzzy clustering and Random Forest (R.F.), is used to address the energy and security crises in the MANET effectively. The multipath routing is then carried out using secure nodes based on the R.P., Bird swarm with Mayfly algorithm (BS-MFA). The best routes are chosen founded on fitness features such as trust, energy connectivity, and throughput. The approaches are compared using existing techniques and various performance metrics such as energy consumption, Delay, and detection rate.

Chapter 14
Deep Learning Algorithms in Cluster Analysis on an E-Learning System in Data Mining 183
S. Keerthana, Nandha Engineering College, India
P. Thirumoorthy, Nandha Engineering College, India
S. Maheswari, Nandha Engineering College, India
S. Karuppusamy, Nandha Engineering College, India

Data mining is one space that helps in churning out helpful data from the abounding knowledge offered. Mining is gaining immense quality currently. To perform data processing, a majority of techniques exist. Agglomeration approach relies on the scholar performance and activities allotted as a district of process. Clusters are accustomed realize the relation between the attributes. The cluster analysis was performed by organizing collections of patterns into team-supported student behavior. In this chapter, several agglomeration approaches of area unit are used including agglomerated hierarchal agglomeration, K means, and C means.

Chapter 15
COVID-19 Diagnosis Using Transfer Learning Techniques and Applications on Chest X-Ray Images 194
E. Manimehalai, Nandha Engineering College, India
D. Vanathi, Nandha Engineering College, India
C. Navamani, Nandha Engineering College, India

COVID-19 is a viral disease caused by a new type of coronavirus called SARS-CoV-2. The World Health Organization (WHO) declared it a pandemic due to this disease spreading over many countries. Currently, there is no medicine available to prevent or cure infectious diseases. COVID-19 samples are commonly tested using reverse transcription polymerase chain reactions (RT-PCR), which are more expensive and take 24 hours to deliver either a positive or negative result. This chapter aims to develop a rapid and accurate medical diagnosis support system for COVID-19 in chest x-ray images by combining transfer learning techniques with the KNN algorithm. There are multiple approaches to building a classification system for analyzing radiographic images in deep learning. In this way, the knowledge acquired from a pre-trained convolutional neural network can be used to solve a new problem. Stacking is a machine learning method that combines the performances of the many transfer learning-based models to ensure the robustness of the proposed system.

Chapter 16
Features Manipulation of Classification and Recognition of Images Under Artificial Intelligence Using CNN Algorithm and LSTM 207
J. Priyadharshini, Nandha Engineering College, India
E. Padma, Nandha Engineering College, India
S. Prabhadevi, Nandha Engineering College, India

The established model provides appropriate picture pixel gaining knowledge in image detection. Additionally, it also affords an alternative solution for item tracking and predicting the usage of deep gaining knowledge of strategies. The proposed technique offers a fine overall performance in photo recognition issues or even outperforms humans in positive cases. Deep learning architectures containing dispensed techniques will become more critical as the scale of datasets increases. Then, it is important to understand which are the most green approaches to carry out distributed education, so as to maximize the throughput of the gadget, while minimizing the accuracy and model regression. This chapter explores features manipulation of classification and recognition of images under artificial intelligence using CNN algorithm and LSTM.

Chapter 17
Security Enhancement in Cloud Computing Using CBC Technique 221
V. Gunasundhari, Nandha Engineering College, India
M. Parvathi, Nandha Engineering College, India
S. Prabhu, Nandha Engineering College, India

The data protection mechanism in cloud storage systems is based on two-way factored inversion. With the authors' solution, users can store encrypted communications in the cloud and distribute them to their intended recipients. There is no requirement for the sender to have any other information (public key, certificate, etc.) except from the name of the receiver. There are two things the decoder needs in order to decipher the ciphertext. Your computer's private key is the first. The second is a one-of-a-kind computer-based security system for the individual. The ciphertext cannot be cracked without both keys. The loss or theft of your security device will also cause it to become inoperable. In other words, it can't be utilised to read encrypted messages. A cloud server is an option for this. The sender will not be aware of any of this activity. In the same vein, cloud server reads encrypted Chrome content. The system's practicability is supported by analyses of its safety and efficiency.

Chapter 18
Techniques and Applications of Demographic Determinants of Mobile Phone Brand Switching in Attitude Towards Switching and Switching Intentions 233
Binit Patel, Charotar University of Science and Technology, India

The Indian telecom industry is growing at a very rapid pace. Both networking and handset-related technologies are refining day by day and year by year. Even the routine activities are executed by the use of mobile phones. Hence, mobile phones nowadays have become a necessity and not a luxury. Switching has now become a trend. There are demographics that actually suggest the switching behaviour; hence, they need to be identified. The descriptive study was used with a total of 1502 respondents across the state of Gujarat, wherein the respondents were selected using the hybrid sampling method. A structured questionnaire was designed using different items, constructs, and dimensions found in the literature review. The study has developed a regression model that can further help in predicting the switching behaviour of mobile phone users. There are demographics that moderate the relationship between 'switching intention' and 'attitude towards switching'.

Chapter 19
Recent Application of Deep Neural Network and Data Augmentation for Classifying Leaf Diseases........ 245
R. Angeline, SRM Institute of Science and Technology, India
Raunak Agarwal, SRM Institute of Science and Technology, India
Sidhant Kumar Sidharth, SRM Institute of Science and Technology, India
Pratik Raj Biresh, SRM Institute of Science and Technology, India

Vegetable leaves are the main part of the plant and the main source for production of vegetables. The vegetable is high in energy and a superb wellspring of Vitamin C, Vitamin B, potassium-folate, magnesium, and many other nutrients. It also gives iron, phosphorus, and niacin. This natural product has low cholesterol and sodium, which is great for human wellbeing. The species originated in almost all the parts of India but mainly in the northern states. In this chapter, the authors give an overview of leaf boundary examination; recognition of solid, debilitated, or impacted areas of the leaf; and arrangement of leaf sicknesses by involving various techniques for the vegetable plants. It is pivotal and hard for natural eyes to distinguish the specific kind of leaf infection with unaided eyes. Each plant leaf has various side effects of different infections. The calculation intended for one plant doesn't work precisely with another plant's leaf. Particular calculations for the vegetable leaves plant are expected to identify leaf sicknesses alongside the leaf boundary analyzer.

Chapter 20
Implementation of Dynamic Gesture Interpretation of Sign Language for Impact on Hearing and Speech Impairment 257
Judy Flavia B., SRM Institute of Science and Technology, India
Aarthi B., SRM Institute of Science and Technology, India
P. Charitharyan, SRM Institute of Science and Technology, India
Renuka Thanmai, SRM Institute of Science and Technology, India
Meghana Kesana, SRM Institute of Science and Technology, India

Expression of languages is a basic survival skill to make conversations in this world. To convey thoughts and express themselves vocally and nonverbally, mankind relies on a variety of languages. Hearing-impaired people, on the other hand, are unable to communicate verbally with others. Because sign language communicates one's message through signs using fingers, arms, head, and body, as well as mannerisms, it has become the major means of nonverbal communication for the deaf. Sign recognition is an ideal step in communicating in this non-verbal communication. Much research on languages that signers use and study have been conducted based on their respective regional sign languages such as the American (ASL) and Indian (ISL). Identifying patterns in the nuances of these different non-verbal languages helps us understand what a person is trying to communicate via signs. Since not all gesticulations are universally centralized, a few of them are single-handed; a few others, particularly the majority, use both the hands (or a mix of both).

Synthetic aperture radar (SAR) can be reasonably mobile or area-based 2D high-resolution imaging radar. Unlike optical remote sensing, which can add bad climatic conditions and nights, SAR works day and night regardless of climatic conditions and can be used for military and civilian purposes. However, unlike natural images, SAR images duplicate the intensity of electromagnetic backscatter and require specialists to interpret the SAR images. In addition, finding interesting targets in huge human SAR images is tedious and very difficult, justifying the demand for low-cost automated SAR target recognition (ATR). Ways of supporting headed-oriented bounding boxes (OBB) have received progressive attention from researchers. However, most of the recently planned deep learning-based methods for OBB detection meet with the boundary separation downside in angle or aim for regression to attenuate this downside.

Object detection is a booming technology that is on par with computer vision and image processing in which an object of a specific type is detected in an image or video. Object detection consists of several approaches like Retina-Net, Single Shot MultiBox Detector (SSD), and Faster R-CNN. These approaches are used in object detection with limited data, but these approaches either run in two algorithms or has high execution time; to overcome these limitations, the authors have used the latest version of Yolo with the custom dataset of solid waste. In this algorithm, an image in the solid waste dataset, which was annotated, labelled, pre-processed, and segmented and a build version is created with the yolo model; this version can either be used directly in the code for online execution or downloaded in the local system for offline execution.

The world today is facing the fourth industrial revolution – a "revolution of skills." The demand for completely new sets of skills is unprecedented, with the advent of and rapid change in digital technologies. On the other hand, a large population of graduates and professional are struggling to empower themselves with newer skillsets and develop capabilities to achieve competitive edge in building a successful career. There is a need for a platform to bridge the gap between these two market forces so that "the supply meets the demand." This chapter seeks to provide a predictive solution using SQL server data mining techniques that implements Microsoft decision tree data mining algorithm.

Individual users within the Netflix environment demand flexible and appropriate Netflix operations. In real-time, digital Netflix should be willing to supply appropriate Netflix objects to a user. Collaborative filtering algorithm is used in a large portion of digital recommender systems. These techniques are held back by means of real-time adaptation and need pupils to have prior information. Hence, this proposed research provides an instant recommendation system that is appropriate for complex and changeable contexts. The proposed solution is based on the problem of reinforcement Netflix. The existing method approach can explore the domain to collect information (data) and make use of that information to obtain a judgment. The built strategy is tested by making use of real-world information (data). The suggested system showcases an improved approach called Adaptive Recommendation depending upon digital Netflix style, which uses learners' behavioural data to implement Netflix resource adaption.

Wireless communication is now the market segment that is expanding the fastest, and this is because it can offer ubiquitous access to a wide range of applications and services at very low costs. This issue makes it difficult to analyze energy consumption and maximize that energy. Additionally, it might raise certain financial and environmental issues. Modern energy service companies are working to develop and implement energy solutions using cutting-edge technologies. Machine learning is overemphasized by all data scientists while being a widely used technology in the fields of advanced sciences. Automated decision-making is the foundation for advanced machine learning features. It has been noted that every industry is attempting to adopt and utilize machine learning and artificial intelligence in order to reduce reliance on humans. As the field of information technology continues to advance quickly, developers are working to incorporate machine learning for energy management in wireless systems.

Preface

In recent years, falsification and digital modification of video clips, images, and textual contents have become widespread and numerous, especially when DeepFake technologies have been adopted in many sources. Due to the adoption of DeepFake Techniques, much current content cannot be recognized from origin sources. "DeepFake" refers to a method based on deep learning that produces content such as films in which one person's face is swapped for another, facial expressions are exported for another or identity is replaced from one person to another. The levels are up to humor and entertainment only. The phrase gained popularity in late 2017 when a Reddit user claimed to have created a machine-learning algorithm to convert celebrity appearances into pornographic films. Besides false pornography, some malicious applications of this type of material are fake news, fraud, forgery in economic and financial matters, political news, and some of the posts displayed on social networking sites and other applications intended for personal use on mobile phones for humor. As a result, the field of study previously devoted to general multimedia forensics has been revived.

This book aims to study the recent techniques and application of illustration, generation, and detection DeepFake Content in Multimedia (e.g., Videos, Images, Textual Contents, etc.). The technology of deep forgery came and spread quickly and left great and dangerous effects. It is no secret that violation of privacy and impersonation are among the crimes and dangerous practices this technology causes, in addition to other social, economic, and political effects. Therefore, it became necessary to provide a counter to this technology or a court to verify the contents published on Sites that claim the validity of the data. We will work in this research to find a way to distinguish fraud and deep forgeries in some media content, such as images, which are the most prevalent on social networking sites and the most vulnerable to manipulation. The search will be dedicated to detecting fraud in pictures of people's faces, specifically using some advanced learning algorithms, where many advances and deep learning algorithms can generate very accurate face images or replace some faces in videos or even text content to be very close the real one. We cannot even recognize the original content in many of these content. However, this project aims to give brighter about this sensitive field of study by illustrating, discussing, and specifying All the Deep Fake techniques and applications that are used mostly in Images, Videos, and Textual content, which are the most content that we use or watch every time on our life. Also, this project will focus on the techniques used to generate the DeepFake content. Currently, many applications and techniques use very advanced or non-believable processes to generate DeepFake that are very close to real or original.

With this accuracy of DeepFakes content, we cannot know if certain content could be original or fake. However, this book will focus on this thing; also, it will become the main source for people who would like to learn much and much about DeepFakes to protect themself and even to understand how

DeepFakes can be worked, where the perception of DeepFakes scenarios can bring much attention to a lot of applications and software that we use on our smartphones and PCs. These could become DeepFakes softwares that are used or private content to generate DeepFakes media. This book will receive much attention from Cyber Security Centres and other agencies. DeepFakes became very challenging to identify and validate or even recognize origin content than fake ones. This book will also differ from all other books. It will become the main source to know recent techniques and applications of DeepFakes, which most published papers do not list all these contents deeply and do not focus on the wide applications of how DeepFakes could be worked. This book also will be the main source from all computer science, security, information theory, bio-metrics, bio-medical, information centers, data analysis, data understanding, cyber security, ..etc. Departments in universities, general government and government agencies, research centers, companies, organizations, Courts, and Information Originality focus on understanding and recognizing the origin and fake content. We trust this book is instructive yet much more than it is provocative. We trust it moves, driving per user to examine different inquiries, applications, and potential arrangements in making sheltered and secure plans for all.

ORGANIZATION OF THE BOOK

The book is organized into 25 chapters. A brief description of each of the chapters follows:

Chapter 1 involves intentional deception of fraud. Criminals profit from violating victims' rights. Individuals, groups, and companies can commit fraud. Social media is crucial. Social media handles natural disasters and medical issues. Social media has created a goods-and-services marketplace. Dishonest users cheat in many ways because social networking can make money. Increased social media fraud. Data thieves use unethical social engineering. Extra pressure, a wide scope, honey traps, and justification are fraud indicators. Uninformed people lose money and knowledge. IT pros can't protect social media users from scams and spam in the current climate. This chapter discusses social media fraud apps and software. It ends with fraud prevention solutions.

Chapter 2 identifies people in this day and age who like to keep up with the most recent news on social media since it is economical, simple, and can be obtained quickly. Social media can spread fake news or unreliable information. False information can harm individuals and society. Researchers worked hard to identify fake news before publication. This article describes major attempts to build a system that can accurately filter online news and detect fake news. Detection included feature extraction and model construction.

Chapter 3 analytics is a major challenge in today's big data world because we can't process huge amounts of data quickly. We'll use the drive HQ cloud to evaluate two supervised multiplication systems built on service cluster apps. Spark provides a more reliable data management framework to address node loss and duplication. This study issue can increase pace effectiveness, which many research/industries companies want. A forthcoming study will test the methods on larger datasets, especially when the data can't be stored in memory.

Chapter 4 discusses how computer algorithms that develop themselves mechanically as they gain experience are essential to the research process in artificial intelligence. It's often grouped with AI. Machine learning generates a model from sample data, called training data, to make future predictions without actively trying to separate Twitter data on various companies' tweets. A classification algorithm was used to categorize the tweets. To improve efficiency, the OHLCV of data from multiple organizations is considered. When forecasting stock prices, daily firm-specific events are also considered. We used historical data and public opinion to improve our experiments.

Chapter 5 reviews transportation, the environment, business, and agriculture using IoT and DL-based solutions. Soil nutrient deficiency can spread and harm plants if not corrected. An IoT-based system that monitors soil and weather can boost crop yields. Modeling terrestrial ecosystems with DeepFakes requires including soil temperature. North Dakota weather stations Baker, Beach, Cando, Crary, and Fingal recorded daily weather and soil temperatures from 2010 to 2018. This study uses convolutional neural networks to forecast soil and weather (CNN). Slime Mold Algorithm optimises model weight to improve CNN classification accuracy. Current classifier performance is compared to the proposed model using RMS, MAE, and SD.

Chapter 6 introduces DeepFakes, the encryption key's security determines the data's security. Encryption is primarily used for network data transmission. There are many methods for protecting sensitive image data from illegal access. Multimedia files can include text, audio, video, graphics, and photos. A rise in Internet-transmitted multimedia content has increased content shortages. Most current encryption algorithms are reserved for use with pieces of information, not digitalized data. The project used block-based transformation. This algorithm blocks the image. These blocks are transformed before encryption. Repositioning the blocks after decryption on the receiving end yields the original image. No information is lost during encryption or decryption with this method. This strategy's benefit is this.

Chapter 7 predicts the stock market as a high-return investment with risks. Stock market forecasting is an act. Multiple sophisticated financial indicators show explosive stock market change. The advancement of technology provides a chance to grow wealth from the stock market and helps experts detect the most insightful indicators to make better predictions. Machine Learning algorithms accurately predict stocks. This chapter proposed a Multiple Regression algorithm for stock valuation. First, Apple and Microsoft's datasets were analysed. Yahoo finance provides live historical data. The dataset was prepped for analysis. This paper also addressed raw dataset preprocessing. After preprocessing the data, Momentum, Volatility, Index Volatility, Stock Momentum, and Sector Momentum were calculated. Multiple regression uses the generated results to accurately predict a stock's future value.

Chapter 8 explains that the Internet of Things (IoT) is a global network of interconnected gadgets that share data. Anomalies are deviations from the norm that may signal a problem. We differentiate ourselves from previous tactics by implementing machine learning algorithms while running the program. This effort aims to create an anomaly detection system that can screen IoT flaws, alert the CEO, and help the network. We use KNN and RF to fine-tune the spreading network's parameters. This framework improves model performance without overfitting, allowing cross-validation to yield a fit and a measure score (CV). Examine the dataset's substitute components for discrepancies. A binary and multi-class machine learning classification model can identify Internet of Things dangers and abnormalities. Anomaly detection, abnormal patterns, privacy, machine learning, cross-validation, classification algorithm.

Chapter 9 is about distributed storage management of deduplication to reduce space and transfer rate needs by eliminating redundant information and storing only its single replica. Redistributing comparable data to a shared repository is ideal for deduplication but raises ownership and confidentiality concerns. Each data owner can show a distributed storage service they own a piece of data via holding plans. Many clients encrypt data before transferring it to distributed storage, unlike the state. Encryption's unpredictability prevents data duplication. Deduplication systems allow multiple owners to share the same encryption key for identical data. Most plans lack security because they don't account for unique shifts in data responsibility in distributed storage management. This study provides a server-side deduplication graph for encoded data. Using random concatenated encryption and secure distribution of ownership group keys, the cloud server can control who can access revalued data even if ownership has changed. No one can access the data, including a genuine but nosy distributed storage server, even if a surrendering client owns it. The proposed layout protects data from labelling errors. The efficiency analysis shows that the suggested layout is nearly as effective as prior schemes with minimal computational complexity.

Chapter 10 develops Cloud computing is growing rapidly, so other cloud services are entering our lives, and data sequestration protection is gaining importance. Protection separation implementation drains resources. Choosing the best product to reduce power consumption and maintain separation is difficult. The proposal proposes a full-scale sequestration scheme (PPPS) to meet stone sequestration requirements while maintaining system performance. First, the separation isn't based on the drugs they carry; they use Triple DES and AES to encrypt algorithms. Analysis results and professional data also inform the safety formulation. PPPS displays similar results. It shows PPPS, sequestration from stones, and cloud performance.

Chapter 11 shows how electronic elections reduce mistakes and discrepancies. Electronic balloting has been recommended as a replacement for paper-based balloting due to security and privacy issues. We designed a SHA-256-based hashing algorithm to protect your data. Sealing the block concept helps blockchain's adaptability. Consortium blockchain technology prevents candidates and outside parties from modifying the blockchain database. This article's polling method yields reliable results. SHA-256, block generation, data collection, and result declaration got us here. All procedures will use blockchain. Electronic voting improves information security with blockchain and manages sensitive data easily.

Chapter 12 talks about the ever-evolving world of computer vision; image processing is used to solve real-world problems like reducing human involvement in driving. Object detection and segmentation are among our challenges. The proposed method overcomes challenges by combining Keras, TensorFlow, instance segmentation, and binary masks. Instantaneous segmentation is used to separate and detect images based on pixel characteristics. Mask RCNN outperforms current CNN models in accuracy and performance. CNN uses Regional Proposal Networks (RPN) to classify objects of interest instead of a selective search algorithm. Simple, versatile, and general describe the instance segmentation system. Our method masks each case to find items in an input.

Chapter 13 detects that bearing faults become crucial in electrical machines, particularly induction motors. Using vibration sensors, temperature sensors, and other traditional monitoring methods is expensive and requires additional testing. In many sectors, current monitoring ensures constant tracking. FFT is used to analyse stator current for motor problems. Due to issues with conventional FFT analysis, fault diagnosis will be incorrect. The cutting-edge spectrum techniques include wavelet transform, matrix pencil method, MUSIC algorithm, and s-Transform. Each technique needs individual attention to be successful. Induction motor problems can be categorised as bearing-, rotor- and stator-, and eccentricity-related. Bearing damage causes 40-90% of failures and is difficult to assess. Progressive faults like misaligned bearings and roughness are common. This work uses the S-Transform to cancel out unaffected frequencies in a three-phase induction motor. The proposed architecture is tested on a 2 HP motor.

Chapter 14 analyzes Data Mining and extracts useful information from vast amounts of data. Mining quality is improving. The agglomeration strategy, a common way to process data, depends on the student's performance and the activities assigned. Cluster members are trained to see the connections. Before cluster analysis, student behaviour patterns were grouped into teams. This process investigates information in academic settings using data processing techniques. Large databases store educational knowledge. This study used hierarchical agglomeration, K Means, and C Means.

Chapter 15 diagnosis of SARS virus causes COVID-19 disease. WHO has declared this virus disease widespread. At the time of the virus's spread, there was no antiviral medication. COVID-19 test samples were evaluated using costly RT-PCR, which takes 24 hours to provide a positive or negative result. This paper develops a fast and accurate clinical analysis assist system for COVID-19 in chest X-ray images using transfer learning and KNN. Deep learning classifies radiographs. CNN's pre-trained staff solved a problem. Stacking integrates transfer learning-based models to ensure the proposed system's high robustness for diagnosing COVID-19 using chest X-ray images. These models use healthy, COVID-19-affected, and pneumonia data. The proposed system's performance was then evaluated using common measures. Compared to previous techniques, our system is accurate.

Chapter 16 discusses hybrid image recognition. Using CNN and LSTM, which has massive effects on identifying image reputation based on the CIFAR-10 picture dataset, will produce the best results. LSTM technology is used to research image representation features. The established model provides accurate picture pixel learning for image identification and a deep learning-based solution for item tracking. In some cases, the suggested method performs better than humans at photo recognition. As datasets grow, dispensed deep learning architectures will become more important. Then, it's important to know the most environmentally friendly methods for dispersed education to optimize device throughput while reducing accuracy and model regression.

Chapter 17 addresses two-way factored inversion-based cloud data protection. Our solution stores encrypted communications in the cloud and distribute them. The sender doesn't need the recipient's public key, certificate, etc. Decoding ciphertext requires two things. First, your private key. Second, an individual computer-based security system. Without both keys, the ciphertext is unbreakable. Loss or theft will disable your security device. It can't decrypt messages. A cloud server can help. The sender won't know about this. Cloud servers read Chrome's encrypted content. System practicability is supported by safety and efficiency analyses.

Chapter 18 shows that Indian telecom is growing quickly. Daily and annually, networking and handset technologies improve. Mobile phones perform routine tasks. Mobile phones are no longer a luxury. Switching is trending. Some demographics suggest switching; identify them. The descriptive study used 1502 hybrid-sampled respondents from Gujarat. Using the literature review, a structured questionnaire was created. The study's regression model can predict mobile phone users' switching behavior. Demographics moderate 'Switching Intention' and 'Attitude towards Switching.'

Chapter 19 classifies vegetable leaves as the main plant part and vegetable source. The vegetable is full of vitamin C, B, potassium-folate, magnesium, and other nutrients. Contains iron, phosphorus, and niacin. Low cholesterol and sodium make this natural product healthy. The species originated in India's northern states. In this paper, we'll discuss leaf boundary examination, recognising solid, debilitated, or impacted leaf areas, and arranging leaf diseases using various techniques for vegetable plants. Unaided eyes can't distinguish the specific leaf infection. Each leaf has different infections. Calculations for one plant's leaf don't work for another's. Along with the leaf boundary analyzer, vegetable leaf calculations should identify leaf diseases. Images help AI and process strategies distinguish vegetable leaf infections. Recent computer upgrades through deep learning have made it possible to identify and analyse plant diseases by using a camera to take pictures. This study identifies various plant diseases. The framework was meant to distinguish vegetable, corn, grapes, potato, sugarcane, and vegetable. The system can detect plant diseases.

Chapter 20 discusses how language is a basic survival skill for making conversations. Mankind uses languages to communicate vocally and nonverbally. Hearing-impaired people can't speak. Sign language uses fingers, arms, head, body, and mannerisms to communicate with the deaf. Non-verbal communication requires sign recognition. Much research on sign languages, such as American (ASL) and Indian, has been done (ISL). Identifying patterns in non-verbal languages helps us interpret signs. Some gestures are single-handed, but most use both hands (or a mix of both). Fingerspelling is used by most signers to represent words. We run detection datasets through a model to build this keypoint detection system. We'll decode and separate key point patterns into sentences to improve communication.

Chapter 21 adapts SAR as mobile or area-based 2D high-resolution imaging radar. Optic remote sensing can add bad weather and nights. SAR can be used for military and civilian purposes day and night, regardless of the weather. SAR images duplicate electromagnetic backscatter intensity and require experts to interpret. Finding interesting targets in large human SAR images is tedious and difficult, necessitating low-cost automated SAR target recognition (ATR). Researchers have studied ways to support headed-oriented bounding boxes (OBB). Most recently planned deep learning-based methods for OBB detection meet the boundary separation problem in angle or aim for regression to attenuate it. Researchers propose manually setting parameters or adding network branches to identify boundary cases that make training harder and degrade performance. The previous model trains and tests data using CNN in the training model. The new model data set will have CNN-trained image data classified for transfer learning. A flexible and easy transfer algorithm is introduced. Using fewer layers and parameters, the algorithm detects and recognises features. Transmission learning algorithms reduce training time and improve accuracy. According to experiments, the proposed method outperforms modern algorithms even with fewer options.

Chapter 22, Object detection, which detects a specific type of object in an image or video, is a booming technology. Object detection uses Retina-Net, SSD, and Faster R-CNN. To overcome these limitations, the author used the latest version of Yolo with a custom solid waste dataset. In this algorithm, an image in the solid waste dataset is annotated, labelled, pre-processed, and segmented, and a build version is created with the yolo model. This version can be used directly in the code for online execution or downloaded locally for offline execution. The rob flow dataset is trained in a single neural network using the yolo algorithm, and then grids are used to predict, weight, and bias bounding boxes by expected probability. Later respected weights are inferences along with a test set of data in the Tensor board with metrics, recall, mAP, etc. Similarly, with the same dataset but using deception2 model configuration for Faster R-CNN are trained. Tensor board accuracy curves. Comparing yolo with training curves.

Chapter 23 plans that today, the entire globe is in the midst of the fourth industrial revolution, sometimes known as the "Revolution of Skills." With digital technologies' rapid evolution, there's never been a greater need for new skills. On the other hand, many graduates and professionals struggle to gain new skills and build successful careers. To ensure "supply meets demand," a platform must connect these two competing market forces. We'll implement the Microsoft Decision Tree Data Mining Algorithm in this work using SQL Server Data Mining Techniques. The mining model built using the SQL Server Decision Tree Algorithm has higher realistic prediction accuracy, providing the best possible career guidance.

Chapter 24 discusses how Netflix users want flexible operations. Digital Netflix should provide appropriate objects in real time. Many digital recommender systems use collaborative Filtering. These techniques require prior knowledge and real-time adaptation. This research proposes an instant recommendation system for complex and changing contexts. The solution uses Netflix Reinforcement. The current method can explore the domain to collect data and make a judgement. Real-world data tests the built strategy (data). The suggested system uses behavioural data from students to implement Netflix resource adaptation. First, it groups students by Netflix preferences. Second, Collaborative Filtering and AR mining extract each cluster's preferences and behaviours. It creates a variable-size, personalised suggestion list. The proposed system suggests films to viewers based on their previous viewing habits and movie patterns. Data mining is suggested.

Chapter 25 presents wireless communication is the fastest-growing market segment because it offers ubiquitous access to many applications and services at low cost. This makes it hard to analyse and maximise energy consumption. Financial and environmental issues may arise. Modern energy service companies develop and implement cutting-edge energy solutions. Data scientists overemphasise machine learning, despite its use in advanced sciences. Advanced machine learning relies on automated decision-making. Every industry is adopting machine learning and AI to reduce human reliance. Developers are using machine learning to manage energy in wireless systems as IT advances. While machine learning opens up many opportunities, it also presents challenges, such as service quality, vulnerable procedures, ineffective energy management, centralised data management, and deployment. This chapter analyses wireless machine learning using two use cases. Machine learning can be used to manage energy in wireless mobile networks.

Ahmed J. Obaid
University of Kufa, Iraq

Ghassan H. Abdul-Majeed
University of Baghdad, Iraq

Adriana Burlea-Schiopoiu
University of Craiova, Romania

Parul Agarwal
Jamia Hamdard, India

Section 1

Advanced Practical Approaches to Deepfake Detection

Chapter 1
An Overview of Fraud Applications and Software on Social Media

Nadia Mahmood Hussien
Mustansiriyah University, Iraq

Yasmin Makki Mohialden
Mustansiriyah University, Iraq

ABSTRACT

Fraud involves intentional deception. While the victim's rights are violated, the criminal profits from the situation. Fraud can be committed by individuals, groups, or even entire companies. The importance of social media cannot be overstated. The management of natural disasters and medical difficulties are both handled through social media. The use of social media has resulted in the establishment of a marketplace for goods and services. Because social networking has evolved into a money-making opportunity, dishonest users now cheat in many ways. Fraud on social media platforms has been on the rise. Cybercriminals exploit unethical social engineering to steal data. Indicators of fraud include excessive pressure, a broad scope, honey traps, and justification. People who are unaware of something lose both money and information. In the current environment, information technology professionals are unable to protect social media users from being scammed or spammed.

INTRODUCTION

This chapter explains insider computer fraud (ICF) to academics and practitioners. The second goal of the inquiry is to provide them with background information on a number of pertinent subjects so that they may more effectively frame the issue with the ICF. To give a paradigm for thinking about ICF detection from the perspective of risk mitigation is the third and last objective. There is no way to halt the action of the ICF. The ICF Defense in Depth Model is broken down and explained using the examples in this book. It results in fewer errors. As the owner of a business, you'll notice it more often. The greatest

DOI: 10.4018/978-1-6684-6060-3.ch001

obstacle we face is preventing businesses from spending more money on fraud protection and detection than they actually lose due to fraudulent activity. In the event that we get a threatening phone call or letter, we will never accuse the wrong person or act on a tip for the wrong reasons. Lying has long-lasting repercussions. When a company discovers that it has been a victim of fraud, it is responsible for paying the costs associated with determining what went wrong, correcting the error, and preventing future instances of the fraud (Silverstone and Davia, 2005a). People who have been given permission to access the network, system, or application are considered to be insiders.

It's possible that one of your employees or a third-party contractor providing your business services or software is a reliable company insider. According to this concept, all parties involved (stakeholders) should be consulted during risk and threat assessments. It is hard to do business in today's environment without utilising social media in some capacity. It is commonly held that the collective intelligence of a population can be put to use to detect fraudulent activity in commercial enterprises (Xiong et al., 2018). Because of the volume and variety of transaction data, financial institutions like banks and credit card companies have a difficult time discovering illegal activity involving money. In recent years, the use of crowdsourcing for things like breaking news, marketing, and flu surveillance has been demonstrated to be effective as a result of the innovative uses that have been made possible by social media (Matti et al., 2014). The amount of content that was created by users and posted on the internet has exploded since the early 2000s. Blogs, forums, social networking websites, and video-sharing websites all encourage users to contribute original content. The focus of this statistics is on the connections that exist within the community. The data collected from social media platforms disclose a great deal about the creators of such platforms and the social networks they use. The information can be exploited to discover illegal or fraudulent behaviour on the part of a person. The authorities and insurance firms are both looking into this matter at the moment (Diaz-Granados et al., 2015).

RELATED WORK

According to Khan et al. (2021), Beetle Antenna Search (BAS) is a meta-heuristic method that finds corporate malfeasance. Financial specialists and auditing teams employ financial and nonfinancial signs to uncover fraud. It is difficult. They propose an optimization problem to maximize recall while minimizing loss (sensitivity and specificity). We iterated this using BAS. In a simulation of beetle foraging, one particle finds the optimal three-dimensional answer. The simulation used SEC AAER benchmark data, and indicators from 1991 to 2008 were analyzed. BAS was compared to RUSBoost. SVM-FK vs. Logit BAS processing time is equal or better.

Xiong et al. (2018) examine social media's ability to detect corporate fraud (i.e., Empowered Products Inc.). This article compares social media to traditional media to highlight its relevance. Twitter uses public information to improve company knowledge. We teach managers about social media data management.

Matti and Timothy (2014) look at how tweets, retweets, and comments on Twitter can be used to find examples of financial fraud.

Glazer et al. (2021) address fraud in 55-year-old Internet-based insomnia studies. Flyers, health providers, Craigslist, and social media (Facebook, Twitter, and LinkedIn) were used to recruit candidates for the study. Data-filled interest forms (name, date of birth, and address) were sent to them. TransUnion's TLOxp was used to determine the applications' status. Either application details matched that in TLOxp, or they were bogus (i.e., confirmed discrepancy). Out of 1766 interest forms, 78% were bogus. The candidates who sought to join fraudulently were 12.22% of those who applied on the internet, 7.04% of those who applied on social media, 4.58% of those who applied through conventional methods, and 4.27% of the remaining candidates. Online trial researchers should beware of candidates' false information. Online clinical trials need to screen all participants' applications.

Zhao et al. (2018) suggest analyzing call content to spot telecom fraud. Complex calls complicate this. Internet news helps people interpret call content. We collected Internet fraud descriptions. A total of 12,368 Sina Weibo and Baidu telephone fraud examples were gathered in 2017. They eradicated fraudsters. Machine learning picks up textual data. The machine learning model's dataset prediction accuracy is 98.53%. Then NLP extracts data traits. They design fraud-detection criteria for SMS. They built an Android app to identify telecom fraud using the offered algorithms. Call content identifies telecom fraud rather than a blacklist. No user data is uploaded. Locally-based.

Andreassen (2021) examines Danish asylum judgments from 2015 to 2019. How does social media impact the trustworthiness of LGBTQ refugees (asylum seekers who claim asylum based on sexual orientation or gender identity)? Officials use social media to confirm or reject LGBTQ identification and expect refugees' online behaviors to match that of "real" LGBTQ people. The magazine stated that asylum processes employ social media postings.

Diaz-Granados et al. (2015) utilize social media data to detect insurance fraud. The group discusses and analyzes our CometCloud-based solution. They show how our data-driven technology may find investigator-relevant data.

FUNDAMENTAL ELEMENTS OF COMPUTER FRAUD

Before computer fraud is considered, the following essential conditions must be met while consciously using a computer:

- Use of a computer without permission.
- Illegal computer usage or accessing a computer to commit a crime.

Title 18, Section 1030 addresses computer fraud and related acts. In the year 1994, the Computer Abuse Amendments Act was amended. First passed in 1986, Section 1030 sanctions unauthorized computer access for obtaining critical national security data and confidential financial data using a government computer, committing fraud, or deleting computer data. The following must be true for a computer to be protected: it is used only by financial organizations and the US government. It's a phrase used in interstate or international commerce or communication if its use impacts a financial institution or the federal government. Computer fraud comprises unlawful access (or going beyond what's permitted), a scheme to fool someone, and gaining anything of value, such as money or software.

Fraud Classification

Only a few methods are appropriate for classifying fraud. The most common are origin, magnitude, and frequency. Frauds are -

- Internal, when committed by corporation employees.
- External, when fraud occurs outside of the corporation
- Both internal and external, when there is a collaboration

The magnitude and frequency of frauds are used to categorize them as -

- Occupational: minor, ongoing internal fraud committed by employees
- Significant: infrequent internal frauds committed by management
- Endemism: external scams that are usually small in scale and occur frequently.

Figure 1. shows how the fraud is classified by origin.

Figure 1. Fraud classified by origin

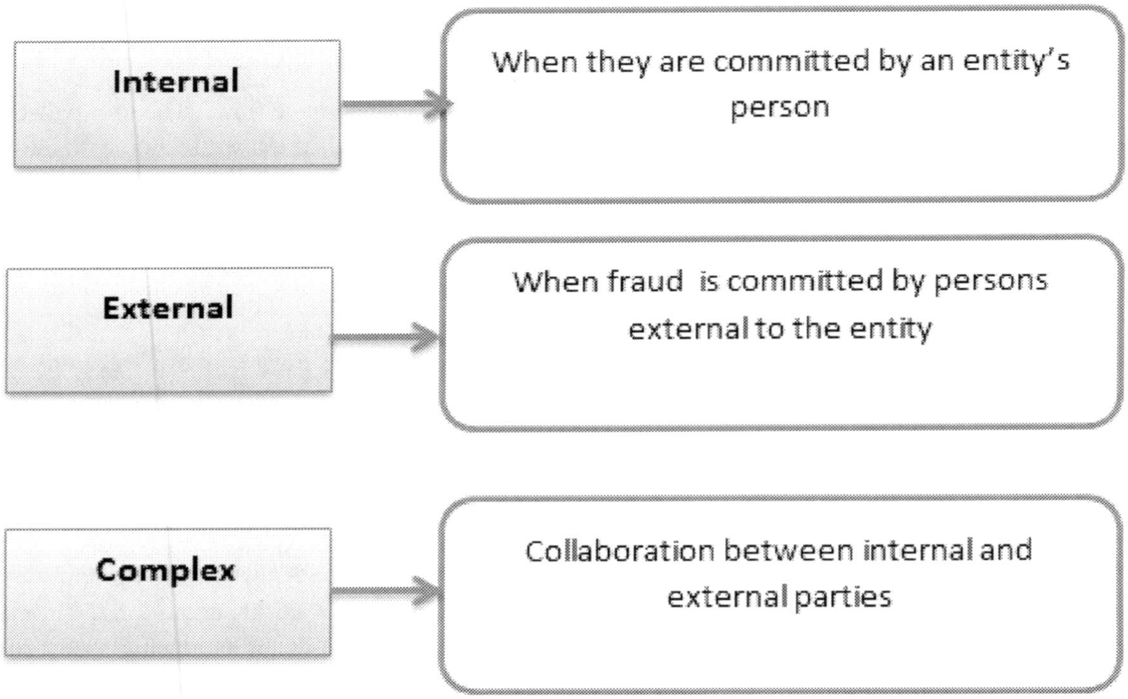

Elements of Fraud

Silverstone and Davia (2005b) describe three frauds. They are straightforward to understand and popular with fraudsters with limited opportunities. The frauds are duplicate payment fraud, multiple payee fraud, and shell fraud.

In these three easy scams, duplicate creditors' payments are caught. These three types of fraud are easy to conduct but hard to detect, requiring distinct processes. However, all of them may be recognized using acceptable techniques. Below are instances of detecting approaches and issues of identifying fraud.

Duplicate Payment Fraud

In this type of fraud, identical checks are used to satisfy the same debt. One of the checks pays the creditor, while the others are recovered. Fraud occurs when an employee, with a criminal motive, creates excessive debt payments to a vendor or contractor. The employee may perform the fraud alone or with suppliers or contractual workers. The crook cashes the second check and the others.

Multiple Payee Fraud

The difference between multiple payee fraud and duplicate payment fraud is in the checks themselves. This type of fraud occurs when one or more vendors or contractors are paid twice for the same debt. The goods or services are often delivered by one of the payees. Someone else is either being mislead or is helping to spread the lie. Multiple payee fraud is not as easily discovered as duplicate payment fraud, hence someone acquainted with fraud detection procedures likely came up with it.

Shell Fraud

Payment to third-party vendors or contractors for bogus work, materials, or services constitutes shell fraud. There is a complete fabrication of evidence. It is conceivable for contractors and suppliers to collude together. The crooks keep all the money they are paid.

FRAUD ON SOCIAL MEDIA

Social media is used to communicate, make friends, shop, and have fun. Fraudsters utilize social media too. As per the FTC, in 2021, one in four fraud victims said that it started with a social media advertisement, post, or communication. Social media fraud was 2021's most lucrative fraud. In 2021, 95,000 individuals lost $770 million online. These losses account for 25% of fraud losses in 2021 and are 18 times higher than that in 2017. In 2021, young people were twice as likely to report fraud losses. Social media attracts convicts. Getting billions is inexpensive on social media. Frauds can create a fake profile or hack an existing one to swindle "friends." They can tweak their tactics by scouring social media for personal details. Scammers may target users with fake advertisements based on their ages, hobbies, or past purchases using social network advertisements. Social media is used in investment fraud too, especially in cryptocurrency scams. The victims say more than half of the investment scams in 2021 originated on social media. The FTC says fraudsters use social media to promote fake investment opportunities and seek "friendly" investments. People transfer money, often bitcoin, hoping for significant profits. After investment scams, romance scams are the most lucrative. Romance scams lead to huge losses. A third of the romance scam victims in 2021 lost their money on Facebook or Instagram. Scams start with a buddy request, smooth talk, and then a money request. Investment and romance scams cost the most, yet most victims buy online. Online fraud accounted former content of social media money losses in 2021.

In 70% of cases, buyers placed a purchase after viewing an advertisement but never received anything. Complaints say the advertisements impersonated online retailers and led users to similar sites. Nine out of ten undeliverable-goods reports cite Facebook or Instagram.

Application Fraud

Application fraud occurs when a criminal applies for a loan or line of credit using a fake or stolen identity with no intention of repaying the money borrowed. To qualify for more credit and loans, the con artist creates a credit history and account activities that look completely legitimate. Bust-out fraud refers to several instances of application fraud committed by a single criminal. A long-term fraudster will open a wide variety of credit accounts. The perpetrator of the fraud reaches his or her credit limit at the optimal time and then vanishes.

WAYS FRAUDSTER FIND TO COMMIT APPLICATION FRAUD

Data Breaches

More than six million records are lost or stolen every day, giving fraudsters easy access to a treasure trove of private information. Identity thieves use stolen personal information to construct fake identities, impersonate victims, and take over their accounts. Criminals also resort to application fraud and strategies like compromised credentials to gain access to sensitive information. Information security breaches are the second most distressing part of application fraud for financial organisations. First-party fraud causes the most heartache.

Synthetic Identity Theft

As a result of the more than six million data records that are lost or stolen every day, con artists have access to a plethora of personal information. Fraudsters use stolen personal information to construct fictitious identities, impersonate actual customers, and take control of their accounts. Fraudsters who have stolen data may also resort to application fraud and other approaches, such as using compromised passwords. When it comes to application fraud, the second most difficult part for financial institutions is having their data compromised. The most excruciating aspect is the first-party deception.

Call Center Attacks

Fraudsters frequently concentrate their efforts on contacting call centres. According to the Aite Group, 61 percent of fraudulent activity in the United States may be traced back to contact centres. People are able to submit applications for loans and lines of credit at a variety of financial institutions, including credit unions and banks, online and over the phone. Call centre workers are unable to catch fraudsters who use fake or stolen identities to fill out loan or credit card applications. Traditional call centre security measures are not designed to catch fake identities or coordinated fraud patterns, so call centre workers are also unable to catch fraudsters who use fake identities.

Intercepted Mail

Some con artists commit fraud by applying for identification cards using stolen personal information and the USPS Informed Delivery system, and then stealing the actual cards from people's mailboxes after they have been sent. Informed Delivery is a service offered by the United States Postal Service (USPS), which offers customers with the ability to get a preview of their upcoming mail and parcels. A con artist can sign up for informed delivery using a different name and address than they actually use. A notification is sent to the fraudster whenever a credit card is anticipated to arrive at the provided address. After then, the con artist can remove the credit card from the mailbox before the rightful owner has a chance to retrieve it.

Scams Targeting Seniors

Cons that prey on individuals who may be more susceptible to being taken advantage of, such as senior folks, are among the most problematic types of application fraud for financial institutions. It is easy to take advantage of elderly people because it is commonly believed that they lack technical knowledge, they are more likely to respond to requests that seem plausible, and they have less time to check with trusted sources before giving out personal information. This makes them an easy target.

Advanced Tools of Fraud

The perpetrators of large-scale application fraud have access to a diverse arsenal of tools.

Cloud Infrastructure

The cloud services and infrastructure that are available to businesses are also accessible to criminals who commit fraud. Con artists will pay for cloud computing services so that they can execute scripts and bots that are fully automated in order to carry out large-scale fraud schemes.

Bots / Botnets

Criminals who commit fraud often make use of bots. Email addresses for Gmail and Outlook can be produced automatically by bots. Hacking bots are used by those who commit fraud. An attack using brute force requires the user to repeatedly enter a password or PIN, and bots help to accelerate the hacking process. Bots are used in the fraudulent activities of credential stuffing and attacking ticketing platforms.

Virtual Machines

A virtual machine creates a virtualized interface to physical hardware, such as a CPU or RAM, and uses the CPU's own self-virtualization capabilities. Virtual machines for Windows, Android, iOS, and Linux are all available to those who commit fraud.

Device Emulators

Fraudsters use device emulators to reset mobile device IDs to avoid fingerprinting. Emulators emulate device hardware entirely in software, unlike virtual machines.

Device Obfuscation

Fraudsters use device obfuscation to make it appear that the website and the app logins are coming from different devices.

IP Obfuscation

Fraudsters hide IP addresses through cloud services, VPNs, or proxies. IP obfuscation bypasses blacklists and rules-based systems.

Location/GPS Spoofing

Using proxies, VPNs, or data centers, fraudsters may impersonate the geolocation of devices.

Web Scraping Software

Scammers find personal information online, especially on social networks. Personal data is stolen through web scrapers and data extraction apps. This personal information can be then used to create fake identities and trick KBA call centers.

FORMS OF APPLICATION FRAUD

Credit Card Application Fraud

Data breaches and viruses steal credit card numbers. On the dark web, they get credit card numbers. Sometimes, criminals get credit cards to max them out and never pay them back.

Bust-Out Fraud

Digital fraudsters use stolen or synthetic identities to borrow money. The fraudster creates credit and credit lines. The fraudster then maxes out the credit card and disappears.

First-Party Fraud

First-party fraud involves the account holder. First-party fraud happens when someone takes out a loan or line of credit without intending to repay it.

How Can You be Secure on Social Media?

Here are some account security suggestions (Mergel & Greeves 2012).

- Close the accounts you are not using. Forgotten social media accounts may be hacked without warning. Hackers can use them to access other accounts, including your email.
- Check what applications are connected to your social media accounts. Do you use Facebook or Google to sign in to other apps? Assess if this sort of access is needed.
- Practice proper password hygiene. Use multiple passwords for your social media accounts, and make each one complicated and interesting. Enabling 2FA for all your accounts helps prevent illegal access.
- Keep the applications updated. Check that your platform is up-to-date. Security fixes stop new threats.
- Use a distinct email for your social media profiles. If you can, make a separate email address for your social media accounts so that hackers can't get to important information.

SECURING CORPORATE ACCOUNTS

Social media is also utilized as the public face of businesses or entrepreneurs that use it as a marketing tool or to create their brand. Hackers can take over a company's social media accounts to promote their own brand, get followers, or convey a certain message. Such hacking activism is a concern, especially with Twitter accounts.

Tips for keeping business social media accounts secure:

- It is important to keep an eye on all of your social media accounts.
- Limit access to only the required people—the fewer the better. That way, it's easy to regulate the posts and avoid sabotage.
- Keep your personal and work lives separate; you don't want to mistakenly publish something personal on a business account.
- Conduct an audit of the tools that have access to your accounts; restrict posting assistance tools since they may be susceptible to assaults.
- Keep up with the latest security measures. Some platforms may be getting rid of passwords or adding new security features that you may want to use.
- Maintain proper password hygiene and enforce stringent patching and updating rules.

Protecting Yourself from Fake News and Misinformation

False news is a serious problem for online communities to tackle. While some platforms have begun addressing the problem and making efforts to curb it, there are still numerous opportunities for the spread of disinformation. Although hackers have been able to influence public opinion through cyber propaganda for some time, the advent of 24/7 social media platforms has made it much easier for them to do so. Bots programmed to post false tweets can influence public opinion when they share widely shared hoaxes on Facebook. Common international websites use the same methods of success. It's easy to make up news, but it's hard to check. Users have become the first line of defence against fake news while platforms struggle to do so. To combat fake news, they need to stop spreading misinformation themselves. They must fulfil the following conditions to achieve this:

- Check out the story on other credible media outlets.
- Check the article's sources and links for legitimacy.
- Research author, publication date, and place
- Check if the comments are from actual individuals or bots. Are they copied? Is the message specific or generic?
- Read news from a variety of sources—similar outlets may share articles.

Even with the best procedures, you might be hacked. Multilayered security for social media accounts and effective and complete security solutions can keep you secure online. Trend Micro Maximum Security protects numerous devices and passwords against online dangers.

CONCLUSION

The number of Internet users is growing, and a significant proportion of them are active social network members. People rely on various social media networks for news, information, and the opinions of others on many topics. Users, therefore, have many accounts on various social media networks. In social networks, individuals disclose a large quantity of personal information. However, it can result in several privacy risks. As an example, a fraudster may utilize these publicly available personal details to construct a phony account. The prevalence of fraudulent behavior on social media platforms is on the rise. To accomplish their crimes, cybercriminals engage in unethical social engineering to acquire access to private and sensitive data. Several symptoms hint at the probability of fraud, such as scale, pressure, honey traps, and justification. Those who do not pay attention to their surroundings are more prone to falling into a trap, resulting in the loss of both money and knowledge. In the current situation, it would be a big job for IT professionals to keep social media users safe from online fraud and raise awareness of spamming behavior. Some fraudsters engage in "bust-out fraud," a comprehensive approach that includes several instances of application fraud. Over time, the fraudster cultivates many credit lines. When the moment is right, the fraudster quickly maxes up all available credit lines and then vanishes.

This chapter discusses the definition of fraud in computers and networks, the classification of fraud in computers, and the three categories of fraud elements (Multiple Payee Fraud, Duplicate Payment Fraud, and Shell Fraud). This chapter provides an overview of the numerous programs and technologies that may be utilized to conduct fraud on social media platforms. Also, the following types of fraud happen on social media: By the end of this chapter, you will learn several ways to avoid becoming a victim of fraud or other types of fraud.

REFERENCES

Andreassen, R. (2021). Social media surveillance, LGBTQ refugees and asylum: How migration authorities use social media profiles to determine refugees as "genuine" or "fraud". *First Monday*, *26*, 1–4. doi:10.5210/fm.v26i1.10653

Brancik, K.C. *Insider computer fraud: an in-depth framework for detecting and defending against insider attacks.* CRC Press.

Coderre, D. (2009). *Fraud analysis techniques using ACL.* John Wiley & Sons.

Diaz-Granados, M., Diaz-Montes, J., & Parashar, M. (2015). Investigating insurance fraud using social media. *Big Data*, 1344–1349.

Glazer, J. V., MacDonnell, K., Frederick, C., Ingersoll, K., & Ritterband, L. M. (2021, September 25). Liar! Liar! Identifying eligibility fraud by applicants in digital health research. *Internet Interventions: the Application of Information Technology in Mental and Behavioural Health*, *25*, 100401. doi:10.1016/j.invent.2021.100401 PMID:34094883

Khan, A. T., Cao, X., Li, S., Katsikis, V. N., Brajevic, I., & Stanimirovic, P. S. (2021). Fraud detection in publicly traded US firms using beetle antennae search: A machine learning approach. *Expert Systems with Applications*, 116–148.

Matti, T. (2014). Financial fraud detection using social media crowdsourcing. *33rd International Performance Computing and Communications Conference, IPCCC 2014.* (pp. 2). IEEE. 10.1109/PCCC.2014.7017023

Mergel, I., & Greeves, B. (2012). *Social media in the public sector field guide: Designing and implementing strategies and policies*. John Wiley & Sons.

Silverstone, H., & Davia, H. R. (2005a). Techniques and Strategies for Detection (2nd ed.). John Wiley & Sons, Inc.

Silverstone, H., & Davia, H. R. (2005b). *Fraud 101: Techniques and strategies for detection*. John Wiley & Sons.

Xiong, F., Chapple, L., & Yin, H. (2018). The use of social media to detect corporate fraud: A case study approach. *Business Horizons*, *61*(4), 623–633. doi:10.1016/j.bushor.2018.04.002

Zhao Q., Chen K., Li T., et al., (2018). Detecting telecommunication fraud by understanding the contents of a call. *Cybersecurity, 1*(8).

Chapter 2
An Overview of Rumor and Fake News Detection Approaches

Zainab Ali Jawad
University of Kufa, Iraq

Ahmed J. Obaid
https://orcid.org/0000-0003-0376-5546
University of Kufa, Iraq

ABSTRACT

People in this day and age like to keep up with the most recent news on social media since it is economical, simple, and can be obtained in a short amount of time. However, social media can be a double-edged sword, since it may propagate fake news or information that cannot be relied upon. The dissemination of false information could adversely affect both individuals and society as a whole. Therefore, researchers gave their all to devise a system that could identify fake news before its publication. This article gives an overview of the most major attempts that have been made to construct a system that can filter online news and detect false news with a decent amount of accuracy. Data mining approaches were reviewed in the detection phase, including feature extraction and model construction.

INTRODUCTION

Define the problem broadly, discuss it in depth, and add other people's perspectives (literature review) to the conversation to prove, disprove, or illustrate your position. social media is increasingly influencing our daily lives, and people often get their news from social media more than traditional news outlets. Several factors contribute to this change in consumption behaviors on social media platforms: For example, different internet platforms often provide more well-timed and cheaper news than traditional media. Additionally, it is simpler to share, comment on, and discuss the information with groups and other people on the internet (Shu et al., 2017). According to a study (Wakefield, J., 2016), social media outlets outperform television as the most important news source. Despite the advantages of social media, the value of news on the internet is lesser than in traditional media. However, it is cheaper and faster

DOI: 10.4018/978-1-6684-6060-3.ch002

to offer news to distribute, which leads to large volumes of fake news. By the end of the presidential election, over 1 million tweets referred to the fake news "Pizzagate" (Wikipedia contributors, 2022). In 2016, the Macquarie dictionary named "Fake news" the word of the year based on the prevalence of this new phenomenon.

Fake news spreads widely and can seriously affect individuals and society. Firstly, fake news damages the credibility of the news ecosystem. For example, the most popular fake news during the 2016 U.S. presidential election spread more widely on Facebook than the most popular authentic mainstream news (Buzzfeed, 2022), (Figure 1). Secondly, fake news intentionally misleads consumers. Usually, misinformation content is created by publicists to increase governmental influence or convey political messages. According to some reports, Russia has created fake accounts and social bots to spread misleading news (Time, 2022). Thirdly, misinformation content changes how people interpret and react to real news. In some cases, fake contents is intended to make people distrustful and confused, hindering their ability to detect what is real from what is not (Nytimes, 2022).

Figure 1. Example of Fake News in U.S Presidential Election (Higgins et al., 2016)

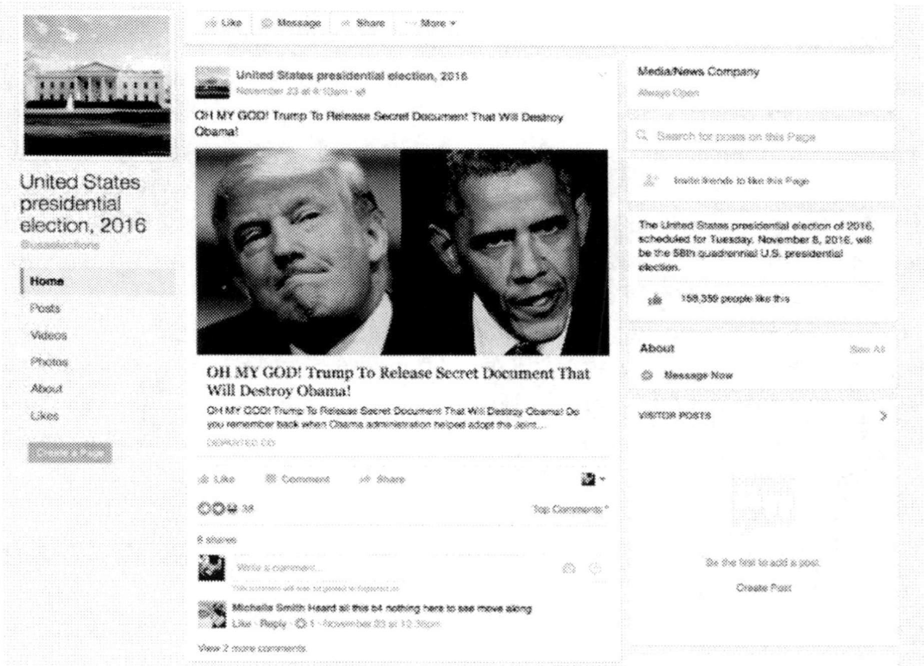

To help mitigate the negative effects of fake news to gain the general public and the information ecosystem. Many studies tried to increase methods to automatically discover fake information on social media. Detecting fake information on social media poses several challenges. However, fake information itself isn't always a brand-new problem. The rise of net-generated information on social media makes fake information a more powerful force that challenges traditional journalistic norms. Numerous traits of this hassle make it uniquely challenging for automatic detection. This problem has numerous characteristics that make it uniquely difficult for automatic detection. First, fake information is intentionally written to misinform readers, making it challenging to discover based on information content. Second, exploiting this auxiliary information results in another critical challenge, i.e., the quality of the information itself.

Fake news is generally associated with newly emerging, time-essential events, which might not have been proven effectively through current information stands due to the lack of corroborating indication or claims. Powerful strategies to differentiate credible users, extract beneficial post features, and take advantage of network interactions are an open region of research and need additional investigations.

AN OVERVIEW OF FAKE NEWS

This section will illustrate the most fundamental social and psychological concepts of fake news and explore added complex forms presented by different platform of the internet. Here, we describe several definitions of misleading contents and distinguish related misunderstood hypotheses. After that, we discuss the different aspects of fake news in traditional media and the new patterns found on social media.

Fake News Definitions

Historically, fake news has existed almost as long as news has circulated widely since the printing press was invented in 1439 (Soll, 2016). Fake news does not have an agreed definition. However, we review and compare some widely used definitions of fake news in the existing literature. In a narrow definition, fake news is articles containing intentional and verifiable false information (Allcott and Gentzkow, 2017). This definition is characterized by two features: authenticity and intent. According to this definition, fake news includes false information that is verifiable. In addition, fake news is intentionally created to mislead people (see figure.2). Recent studies generally agree with this definition (Mustafaraj and Metaxas, 2017; Conroy et al., 2015; Potthast et al., 2018; Klein and Wueller, 2018). A broader definition of fake news focuses on the content's authenticity or intention. The contents of some satire papers are regarded as fake news since they are false, even though the satire is often entertainment-oriented and reveals its deceptiveness to consumers (Rubin et al., 2016; Balmas, 2014; Jin et al., 2016; Brewer et al., 2013). Several sources refer to deceptive news directly as fake news (Rubin et al., 2015), including serious fabrications, hoaxes, and satires (Figure.3). For these purposes, we use the narrow definition of fake news. In summary, we state this definition as follows:

Definition 1 (Fake News) fake news is an article that contains intentionally false and verifiable statements.

Figure 2. Network Journalism of Social Networking Service (SNS) News (Park, and Choi, 2015a)

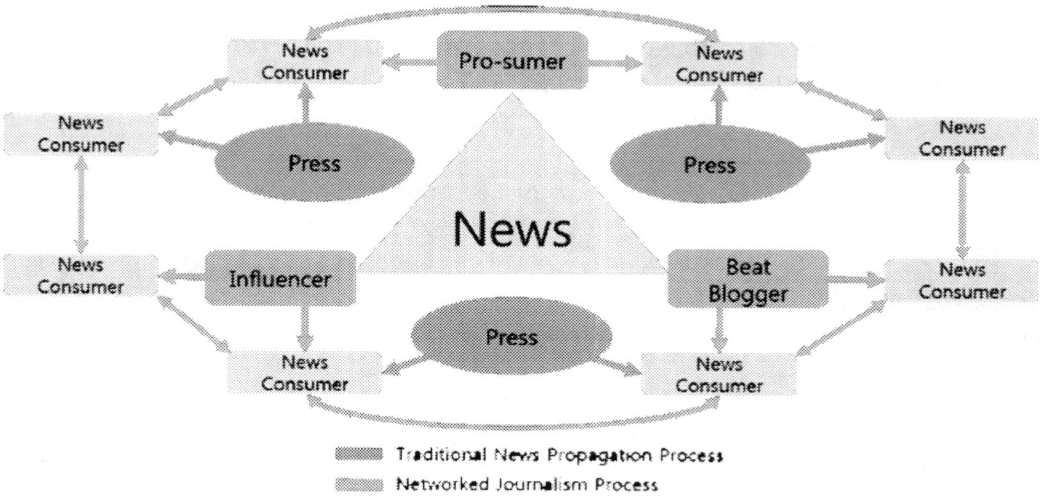

There are three reasons for choosing this narrow definition. Firstly, learning about the underlying intent of fake news allows us to understand and analyze this topic. Secondly, any truth-verification techniques that employ to the contracted concept of misinformation content also applied to the broad concept. Thirdly, definition can remove uncertainties among misinformation content and other theories not covered in this section. According to this definition, the following concepts are not fake news (Shu et al., 2017):

- Satire news in context, with no intent to deceive or mislead consumers, and unlikely to be misinterpreted as factual.
- Rumours have nothing to do with current news events.
- Conspiracy theories that are difficult to prove, true or false.
- Unintentionally created misinformation.
- Hoaxes are motivated solely by amusement or to defraud specific individuals.

Fake News on Traditional News Media

The issue of fake news is not new. The fake news media ecology has developed over time, from newsprint to radio/television and, more recently, online news and social media. We define "traditional fake news" as the fake news problem before the impact of social media on its generation and sharing. Following that, we will discuss several psychological and social science foundations for describing the impact of fake news at the personal and societal information environment levels.

Psychological Foundations of Fake News

Humans are naturally not good at distinguishing between true and false news. Several psychological and cognitive theories exist to explain this phenomenon. Traditional fake news primarily exploits consumers' vulnerabilities. Consumers are naturally vulnerable to fake news due to two major factors:

I. Naïve Réalisme: Ward, A. et al., 1997 argue that consumer often view their conceptions of reality as the only correct ones (Ward, A. et al., 1997).
II. Confirmation Bias: It has been proven that consumers prefer information that supports their beliefs (Nickerson, 1998). Human nature makes it easy for consumers to mistake fake news for true news. Further, correcting a mistake after it has been committed is extremely challenging.

According to psychology studies, correcting false information (e.g., misinformation content) by presenting true, factual information is ineffective in reducing misperceptions and increasing them, particularly among ideological groups (Nyhan and Reifler, 2010).

Social Foundations of the Fake News Ecosystem

We describe some social dynamics that contribute to the spread of fake news if we consider the entire news consumption ecosystem. According to prospect theory, individuals create choices centered on virtual improvements and costs associated to their current state (Kahneman and Tversky, 2013; Tversky and Kahneman, 2016). This desire to maximize the reward of a decision also applies to social gains. This favorite for social acceptance and confirmation is critical to an individual's identity and confidence, leading consumers to select "socially safe" options when consuming and disseminating news information, adhering to community norms even if the news being shared is fake news. We assume there are two types of key players in the information ecosystem to explain fake news: publisher and consumer (Shu et al., 2017).
The publisher utility is divided into two perspectives:

- Short-term utility: the motivation to increase profits, which is positively proportional to the number of users reached.
- Long-term utility: their reputation for news accuracy.

Consumer utility is divided into two categories:

- Information utility: obtaining accurate and unbiased information (usually at an additional cost).
- Psychology utility: receiving news that meets their prior beliefs and social needs.

Fake News on Social Media

This section will discuss some of the unique characteristics of misinformation content on social media. We'll focus on the key characteristics of fake news made possible by social media. The characteristics of traditional fake news might also apply to misinformation content on social media.

Propaganda-Focused Accounts on Social Media

While many social media users are legitimate, some are malicious, and some are not real. The low cost of creating social media accounts encourages malicious users such as bots, cyborgs, and trolls. Bots are social media accounts operated by computers, which generate content and interact with people (or other bot users) on social media (Figure.3).

Social bots can evolve into malicious entities designed to cause harm, such as manipulating and spreading false information on social media. On the other hand, Trolls, real human users who seek to disrupt online communities and elicit emotional responses from consumers, also play a key role in spreading misinformation content on social media.

Figure 3. Total Facebook Engagement for Top 20 Election Stories (B, J. M., 2018)

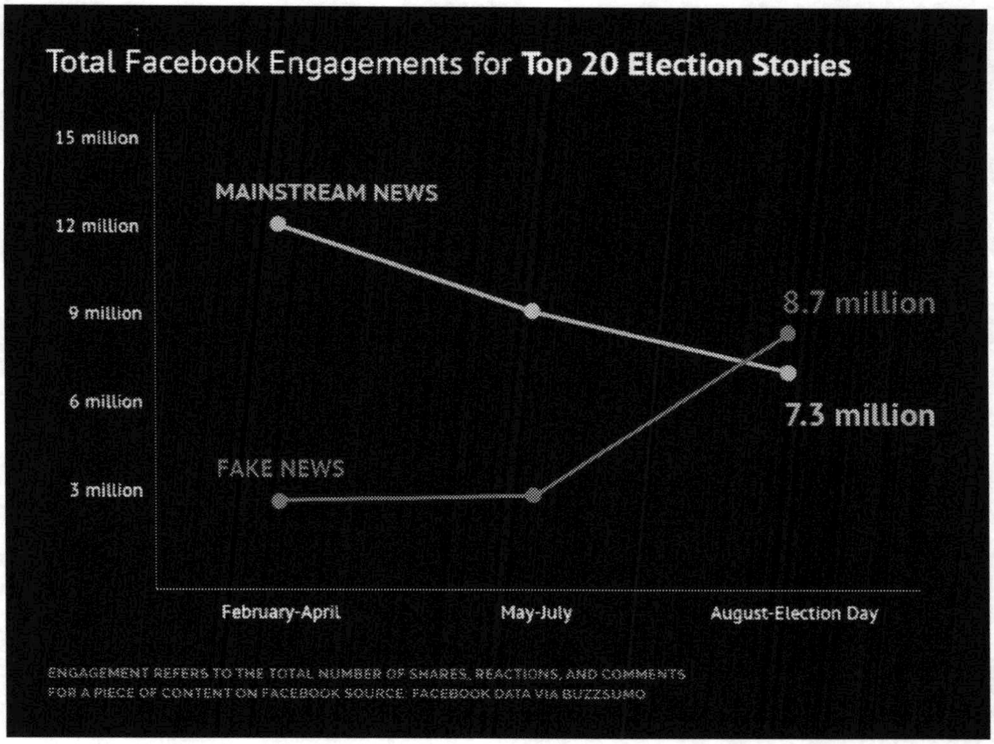

The Effect of the Echo Chamber

Users can create and consume information in new ways thanks to social media. The process of seeking and consuming information is shifting from being mediated (e.g., by journalists) to being more disintermediated (Del Vicario et al., 2016). Because the news feeds appear on people's Facebook homepages, consumers are selectively exposed to certain types of news, exacerbating the psychological challenges of spotting misinformation content. For example, Facebook users always follow like-minded people and thus receive news that supports their preferred narratives (Quattrociocchi et al., 2016). Due to this phenomenon, people on social media often form groups of friends where their opinions are polarized, leading to an echo chamber effect. Based on the following psychological factors (Paul and Matthews, 2016). (Figure.4), the echo chamber effect facilitates people's consumption and belief in misinformation content:

- Social credibility implies people perceive a source as credible if they perceive others to be credible, especially in circumstances where the truthfulness of the source is difficult to quantify.
- The frequency heuristic implies users favour information they often hear, even if it is incorrect. According to studies, increasing exposure to an idea can result in a positive opinion (Zajonc, 1968; Zajonc, 2001).

Figure 4. Fake Election Stories by Facebook Engagement (B, J. M., 2018)

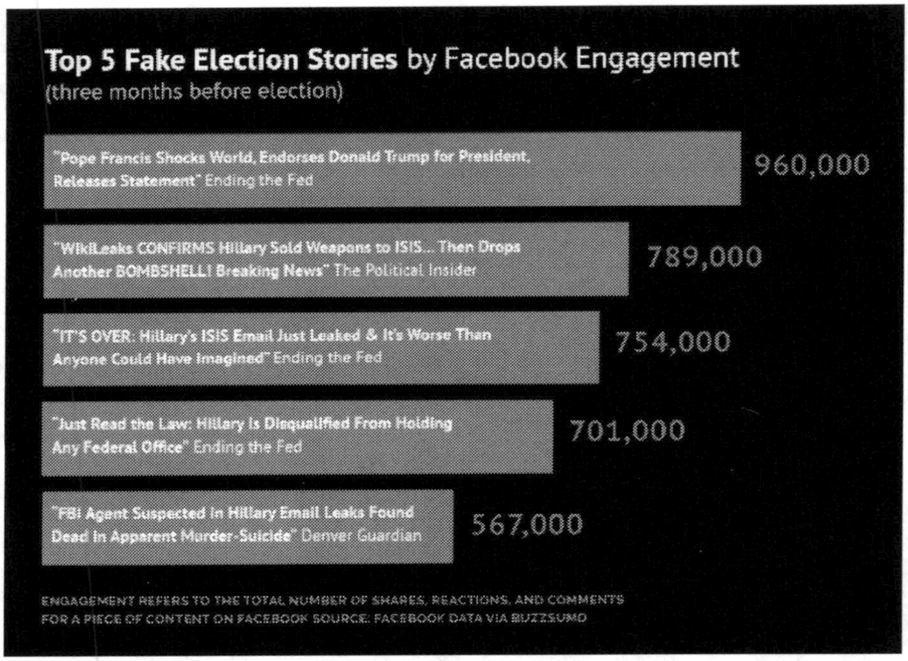

FAKE NEWS DETECTION

In the previous section, we described the conceptual characterization of traditional fake and misinformation content on social media. Based on this characterization, we explore the problem definition and propose methods for detecting fake news (Figure 5).

Figure 5. Fake news: from characterization to detection (Shu et al., 2017)

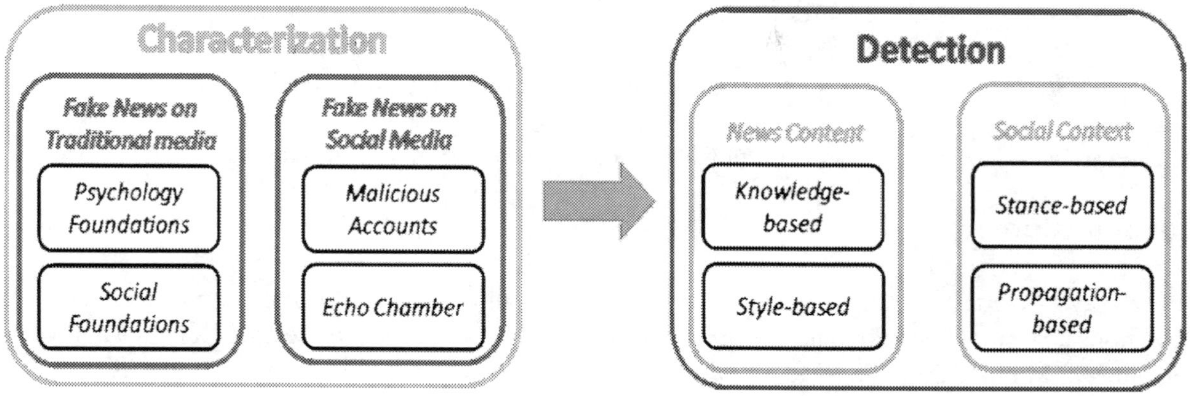

Definition 2 (Misinformation Content Detection):

Define misinformation content detection as a binary classification problem because The definition of fake news is that it consists of manipulated information that has been distorted by the publisher. Traditionally, distortion bias has been modeled as a binary classification problem in media bias theory (Gentzkow et al., 2015). Then, we propose a general data mining framework for fake news detection that includes two phases:

- Feature Extraction
- Model Construction

The feature extraction phase describes news content and additional related data in a mathematical structure. In contrast, the model construction phase builds machine learning methods to better distinguish misinformation content from real news using feature representations.

Preprocessing

In any natural language processing (NLP) system, text preprocessing is crucial, as characters, words, and sentences identified serve as the inputs for all subsequent processing stages, including morphological analyzers and part-of-speech taggers, information retrieval, and information retrieval translation systems. Preprocessing text documents is a collection of activities. It is necessary to eliminate some of the most common words that are unlikely to aid text mining, such as prepositions, articles, and pronouns. Since text data usually contains several special formats, such as number formats, date formats, and most common words (Feldman and Sanger, 2006).

Benefit of Text Preprocessing in NLP System

1. Text document indexing (or data) file size reduction:
   - Approximately 20%-30% of documents contain stop words.
   - Index sizes may be reduced by 40-50% upon stemming.

2. To increase information retrieval (IR) effectiveness and efficiency, we must do the following:
   - Stop words are not useful when searching or using text mining, and they may confuse retrieval system.
   - Stemming is used to match words in a document that are similar.

There are several types of preprocessing techniques, such as (Feldman and Sanger, 2006):

Tokenization

When a text stream is tokenized, it is divided into words, phrases, symbols, or other meaningful words or phrases. Tokenization allows us to explore words within a text. Earlier processing steps, such as parsing and text mining, are based on a list of tokens. The use of tokenization as part of linguistic analysis and text segmentation benefits both computer science and linguistics. A text file usually begins with a few characters. There must be words in the data set to retrieve information. Thus, a parser requires the tokenization of documents. Since the text is already saved in machine-readable formats, it can appear unimportant. There are still some problems, such the omission of punctuation.

There are more characters that must be processed in addition to brackets and hyphens. Consistency in documents can also be taken into account by tokenizers. The main purpose of tokenization is to find useful keywords. Inconsistencies can arise from varying number and time formats. The conversion of acronyms and abbreviations into a standard form is another problem.

STOP WORD REMOVAL

Several words frequently appear in documents, but they are broadly unimportant because they are used to connect words in a sentence. Stop words, and it is widely accepted, do not donate to the context or content of textual documents. Their presence in text mining builds a barrier to understanding the matter of the documents due to their high frequency of occurrence. Stop words, such as 'and,' 'are,' 'this,' and others, are frequently used. They are ineffective in document classification. As a result, they must be removed. However, compiling a list of stop words is difficult and inconsistent across textual sources. This method also reduces text data and enhances system performance. These words appear in every text document and are not required for text-mining applications.

Stemming

By using the stemming technique, the multiple word formulae are combined into a single statement, the stem. The term "present" can be used to represent the terms "presentation," "presented," and "presenting." It is a typical text processing method for IR, and it is based on the idea that asking a question with the word "presenting" in it implies that the documents it appears in have been given some attention.

Feature Selection

There are three main paradigms for feature selection: Filter techniques rank all features and analyze each one independently of the training set's class labels before selecting the top-ranked features (Forman,

2003). Wrapper approaches continually evaluate several feature subsets using cross-validation with a particular induction algorithm to find the "optimal" subset of features using traditional AI search techniques like greedy hill-climbing or simulated annealing. Embedded techniques provide a linear prediction model that reduces the amount of input features while increasing the model's goodness of fit (Guyon & Elisseeff, 2003). Some variations use the complete data set to create a classifier, then progressively eliminate the attributes the classifier depends on (Guyon, 2002). Since they begin with the complete data collection, they are the least scalable. To actualize the entire feature vectors with all conceivable features, huge feature spaces may require more memory than is available. The most user-friendly and scalable filtering techniques are available. They are the focus of this study since they are suitable for treating very large feature spaces.

Additionally, this method does not scale well when dealing with the numerous characteristics needed for text categorization. Cross-validation chooses amongst feature generators, much like a wrapper method does. Although it optimizes other parameters, it uses the induction process far less frequently than the standard wrapper feature selection (Kyriakopoulou & Kalamboukis, 2007).

FEATURE EXTRACTION

Misinformation content detection is established primarily on news content in traditional news media. However, the increased auxiliary information in the social context uses as extra knowledge to assist discover misinformation content. As a result, we'll go through how to take information from news articles and social context and extract and visualize valuable aspects. Features for News Content explain the meta-data associated with a piece of news. Here is a list of typical characteristics of news content:

- Writer or producer of the news posts as the source
- A headline that states the main topic of the article in a brief paragraph to capture readers' attention.
- The central text explains the story of news; a main claim is usually underlined and contours the publisher's perspective, which is defined as the body text.
- Image/Video: A visual cue to frame the story that is part of the body content of a news article.

The news content will typically be visual-based and linguistic-based, as explained further below:

Linguistic-Based

Fake news is produced for personal or political gain rather than to report objective information, so it often contains opinionated and inflammatory content. Clickbait (i.e., to entice readers to read the full article) or confusion is often used by fake news authors (Chen et al., 2015). Language can work as a useful tool for detecting fake news by capturing sensational headlines. In terms of document organization, linguistic features are extracted from text content at various levels, including characters, words, sentences, and documents. Existing work used common and domain-specific features to capture the different aspects of fake and real news. Common linguistic features in NLP are regularly used to represent documents for various tasks.

(i) lexical characteristics, including the number of words, characters per word, frequency of big words, and unique words;
(ii) syntactic features For example, sentence-level characteristics, the regularity of function words and phrases (also known as "n-grams"), bag-of-words methods (Fürnkranz, 1998), or punctuation and parts-of-speech (POS) tagging.
(iii) Domain-specific linguistic features, like quoted words and the typical length of graphs, these attributes all correspond to the news domain (Potthast et al., 2018). Other features, such lying-detection features, can be made particularly to identify false information content by detecting misleading indicators in writing styles (Afroz et al., 2012).

Visual-based are a powerful manipulator in the spread of misinformation content propaganda. As previously stated, misinformation content preys on people's vulnerabilities, relying on misinformation images to elicit consumers' anger or other emotional responses. Visual-based features are extracted from visual parts (such as images and videos) to take the various features of misinformation content. Using a classification framework, fake images are identified based on user-level and tweet-level hand-crafted features (Gupta, 2013). For news authentication, special visual and numerical features lately extract (Jin et al., 2017).

Social Content Features

Besides features related to the content of the news articles, additional social context features can also be derived from users' interactions with the social media platforms related to news consumption. News articles copy from social engagements by tracing the propagation process over time and using it to infer their credibility. A limited number of studies deal with detecting fake news using social context features in the literature. Since this aspect is a critical factor in successful fake news detection, we present common features also used in similar research areas, such as rumor veracity classification on social media. We explore how social context features extract and represent to support fake news detection using these three aspects (see figure.6).

Figure 6. Fake news: How to Spot Fake News (B, J. M. (2018)

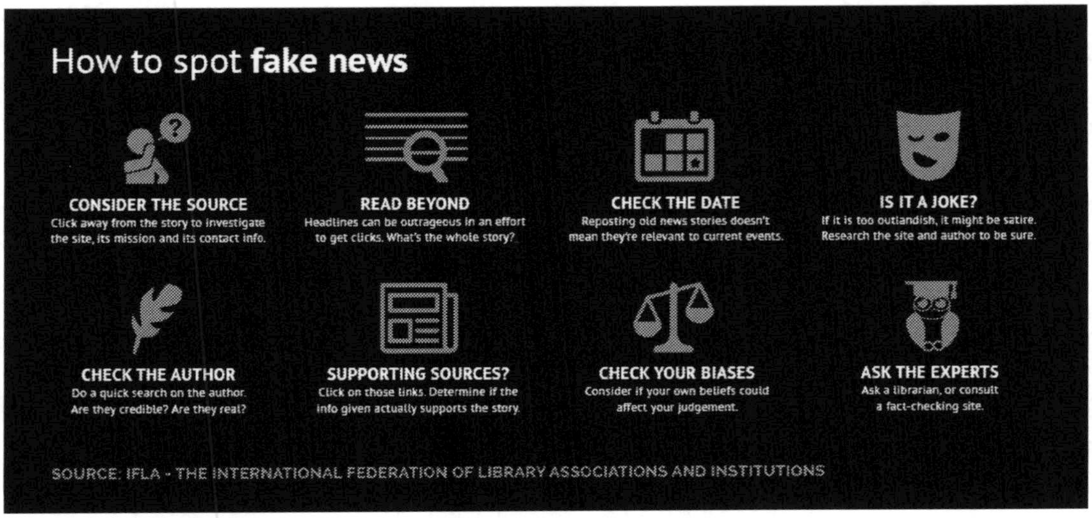

How to spot **fake news**
CONSIDER THE SOURCE
Click away from the story to investigate the site, its mission and its contact info.
READ BEYOND
Headlines can be outrageous in an effort to get clicks. What's the whole story?
CHECK THE DATE
Reposting old news stories doesn't mean they're relevant to current events.
IS IT A JOKE?
If it is too outlandish, it might be satire. Research the site and author to be sure.
CHECK THE AUTHOR
Do a quick search on the author. Are they credible? Are they real?
SUPPORTING SOURCES?
Click on those links. Determine if the info given actually supports the story.
CHECK YOUR BIASES
Consider if your own beliefs could affect your judgement.
ASK THE EXPERTS
Ask a librarian, or consult a fact-checking site.
SOURCE: IFLA - THE INTERNATIONAL FEDERATION OF LIBRARY ASSOCIATIONS AND INSTITUTIONS

User-Based

User-based features in social media indicate the aspects of individuals whom connect with articles. We can divide these features into individual features and group features. By using a variety of demographic attributes, such as a user's registration age, the number of followers/followers, the number of tweets they have authored, etc., individual-level features are extracted to infer the reliability and credibility of each user. Group-level features were collected to describe the general features of consumers associated to the news (Yang et al., 2012). According to this hypothesis, fake news and real news spreaders may form different communities with unique characteristics represented as group-level attributes. The most commonly used group-level features are the aggregation (e.g., averaging and weighting) of individual-level features, including 'the percentage of verified users' and 'average followers' (Ma et al., 2015; Kwon et al., 2013).

Post-Based

Social media posts can express emotions about fake news, such as skeptical opinions, sensational reactions, etc. Therefore, it is reasonable to extract post-based features to help detect fake news using public reactions expressed in posts. We attempt to identify relevant information from social media posts to infer the integrity of the news based on post-based. Post-level features, group-level features, and time-level features can be categorized. Each post is assigned feature values at the post level. In furthermore to the linguistic features mentioned previous paragraph, a few embedding methods can be implemented to individual posts. In particular, posts with unique aspects such as stance, topic, and credibility represent the social response from the public. A user's stance (or viewpoint) indicates their opinion of the news, such as supporting it, disagreeing with it, etc. (Jin et al., 2016).

Network-Based

Social media users from various networks are classified based on their interests, topics, and relationships. Network-based features form specific networks among users who share similar social media posts. Various types of networks can be created. The stance network can be constructed with nodes representing all relevant tweets and edges (Tacchini et al., 2017; Jin et al., 2017). The concurrence network is created by user engagement and calculating posts that consumers created about the similar news objects (Ruchansky et al., 2017). Furthermore, the relationship network shows the undermentioned/followers' arrangement of users who tweet about the same thing (Kwon et al., 2013).

Why Text Fake News is Challenging?

Raw data sets obtained to detect fake news frequently contain noise, such as missing values. Preprocessing data should be done in a modern way to improve the efficiency of fake news recognition based on ML (Kotteti et al., 2018). The data structure must be correct to get well effects from the process used in Deep Learning and Machine technique initiatives. Random Forest algorithms, for example, do not accept null values. Some defined ML models, for example, require data in a specific format. NLP techniques can perform all of the Preprocessing. Which tasks break down words into smaller, more understandable parts to see if the components work together to found value. Stemming and Tokenizing are typically required during Preprocessing.

Information categorization, subject exploration and modelling, meaning retrieval, and emotion analysis are performed using NLP strategies such as Word2Vec and TF-IDF Vectorizer. Language processing is the process of processing raw language and converting or attaching meaning to it using linguistic structures and algorithms. Pre-learned Word Embedding Vectors such as word2vec (Mikolov et al., 2013) and Glove (Pennington et al., 2014) are commonly used for word sequences. If the input is a complete article, other preprocessing stages are required to extract the central idea from raw texts. Thorne et al. (2018) ranked the sentences using TF-IDF and the DrQA system (Chen et al., 2017). Detecting fake news by using incorrect information. The absence of any other news articles requires a thorough collection of indication and detailed checking of information. They investigated how AL technology, specifically ML and NLP, can detect fake information. Even professional experts find it difficult to determine the integrity of a news story (see figure.7). In this case, Stance Detection could be a useful component of an Artificial Intelligence-powered fact-checking system. The Stance Detection (Ferreira and Vlachos, 2016) method evaluates the relative perception (or place) of two pieces of text on a subject, topic, or question (Merryton and Augasta, 2020).

Figure 7. Example of Text Fake News (Brookings, 2022)

Fake News Detection Techniques

Online misleading information is detected using several methods by researchers worldwide. By using ML algorithms, the documents can be represented easily after being feature selected and transformed. Text classification has been developed using Machine Learning techniques, Probabilistic models, Deep Learning, and so on. As a result of their research, Decision Trees, Naive Bayes, Neural Networks, and Nearest Neighbors have been studied, as have Support Vector Machines and Nearest Neighbors. Automated text classification remains in the research spotlight despite numerous approaches being proposed; currently, automatic text classifiers do not operate flawlessly and need to be improved (Ikonomakis et al., 2005).

- Naive-Bayes: Several text classification applications and experiments use Naive Bayes to classify texts (Kim et al., 2002) for its simplicity and effectiveness. Unfortunately, it performs poorly when modeling text because it doesn't model it well. According to Schneider (Schneider, 2005), simple changes could resolve the problems. A Bayesian Multi-Net classification system based on a content learning process for huge tree-like Bayesian networks was evaluated empirically by Klopotek and Woch (2003). The results show that tree-like Bayesian networks can be used to classify texts with 100,000 variables quickly and accurately.
- Support vector machines (SVM): Its precision is excellent, but its recall is poor when applied to text classification. Adding a threshold to an SVM can improve its recall by customizing it. The thresholds of generic SVMs can be automatically improved by a process described by Shanahan and Roma (2003).
- Decision Tree: Through a rule simplification method and utilizing sparse text data, Johnson et al. (2002) developed a fast decision tree construction algorithm that uses sparse text data and logically equivalent rules.
- Logistic Regression: Data are classified by logistic regression using predictor variables. By converting the categorical dependent variable into a probability score, it is possible to determine the probability relationship between the categorical dependent variable and the continuous independent variable. (Kamath et al., 2018) classified logistic regression into binary and multinomial types.
- Multi-layer Perceptron (MLP): Are an artificial neural network that uses backpropagation as a supervised learning method for classification (Rosenblatt, 1961; Leudar, 1989). Input features are represented by neurons in the input layer. Following the first layer, the hidden layer employs a weighted linear summation and a nonlinear activation function to solve the problem (Pedregosa et al., 2012).
- Recurrent neural networks (RNNs): Natural language processing and text generation use process inputs that use "memory" (Mikolov et al., 2010). As the term suggests, long short-term memory relies on "gates" to "forget" input at each stage of a particular learning process (Bharadwaj and Shao, 2019).

Evaluation Metrics

Several valuation metrics used to assess the performance of processes for detecting misinformation contents. This section will look at the most commonly used metrics for detecting fake news. The majority of existing approaches regard the fake news problem as a classification problem that predicts whether or not a news article is fake (Shu et al., 2017):

- The True Positive (TP) flags fake news items when they are predicted.
- An annotation of true news is a True Negative.
- Real information is annotated are misinformation contents, it is called a False Negative.

- Annotating misinformation contents are true is known as a false positive (FP).

We can define the following metrics by resolving this as a classification problem.

- Precision $= \frac{\text{true positive}}{\text{true positive} + \text{ false positive}}$
- Recall $= \frac{\text{true positive}}{\text{true positive} + \text{ false negatine}}$
- $\text{F1} = 2.\frac{\text{precision} + \text{Recall}}{\text{precision} + \text{Recall}}$
- Accuracy $= \frac{\text{true positive} + \text{true negative}}{\text{true positive} + \text{true negative} + \text{false negative} + \text{false positive}}$

We can evaluate a classifier's performance from many angles using these metrics, which are widespread in the machine learning community. When comparing predictability to actual misleading content, accuracy is determined. Precision is the fraction of all detected misinformation contents addressing the critical issue of determining which news is fake that has been annotated as fake news.

CONCLUSION

Because of the rise in popularity of social media, an increasing number of people are choosing to get their news through social media platforms rather than traditional ones. In addition, bogus news has been disseminated via social media, which has the potential to have a harmful influence not just on individual users but also on society. As part of this investigation, we combed through the previous studies on identifying fake news and classifying it into several categories. During the process of characterization, both traditional media and social media were brought up and discussed. During the detection phase, methods of data mining, such as feature extraction and model creation, were examined. In addition, we reviewed evaluation measures as well as potential future avenues for research on the detection of fake news.

REFERENCES

Shu, K., Sliva, A., Wang, S., Tang, J., & Liu, H. (2017). Fake news detection on social media: A data mining perspective. *SIGKDD Explorations: Newsletter of the Special Interest Group (SIG) on Knowledge Discovery & Data Mining, 19*(1), 22–36. doi:10.1145/3137597.3137600

Wakefield, J. (2016, June 14). Social media "outstrips TV" as news source for young people. *BBC News*. https://www.bbc.com/news/uk-36528256

Wikipedia contributors. (2022, November 18). Pizzagate conspiracy theory. *Wikipedia*. http://en.wikipedia.org/w/index.php?title=Pizzagate_conspiracy_theory&oldid=1122678316

Higgins, A., McIntire, M., & Dance, G. J. (2016, November 25). Inside a fake news sausage factory: 'this is all about income.' *The New York Times*. https://www.nytimes.com/2016/11/25/world/europe/fake-news-donald-trump-hillary-clinton-georgia.html

Soll, J. (2016, December 18). The long and brutal history of fake news. *POLITICO Magazine*. https://www.politico.com/magazine/story/2016/12/fake-news-history-long-violent-214535/

Allcott, H., & Gentzkow, M. (2017). Social media and fake news in the 2016 election. *The Journal of Economic Perspectives: A Journal of the American Economic Association, 31*(2), 211–236. . doi:10.1257/jep.31.2.211

Mustafaraj, E., & Metaxas, P. T. (2017). The fake news spreading plague: Was it preventable? *Proceedings of the 2017 ACM on Web Science Conference*. ACM. 10.1145/3091478.3091523

Conroy, N. K., Rubin, V. L., & Chen, Y. (2015). Automatic deception detection: Methods for finding fake news: Automatic Deception Detection: Methods for Finding Fake News. *Proceedings of the Association for Information Science and Technology, 52*(1), 1–4. doi:10.1002/pra2.2015.145052010082

Potthast, M., Kiesel, J., Reinartz, K., Bevendorff, J., & Stein, B. (2018). A stylometric inquiry into hyperpartisan and fake news. *Proceedings of the 56th Annual Meeting of the Association for Computational Linguistics* (Volume 1: Long Papers). Association for Computational Linguistics. 10.18653/v1/P18-1022

Klein, D. O., & Wueller, J. R. (2018). Fake News: A legal perspective. *Australasian Policing, 10*(2). doi:10.3316/informit.807638896756480

Rubin, V., Conroy, N., Chen, Y., & Cornwell, S. (2016). Fake news or truth? Using satirical cues to detect potentially misleading news. *Proceedings of the Second Workshop on Computational Approaches to Deception Detection*. Association for Computational Linguistics. 10.18653/v1/W16-0802

Balmas, M. (2014). When fake news becomes real: Combined exposure to multiple news sources and political attitudes of inefficacy, alienation, and cynicism. *Communication Research, 41*(3), 430–454. doi:10.1177/0093650212453600

Jin, Z., Cao, J., Zhang, Y., & Luo, J. (2016). News Verification by Exploiting Conflicting Social Viewpoints in Microblogs. *Proceedings of the AAAI Conference on Artificial Intelligence, 30*(1). doi:10.1609/aaai.v30i1.10382

Brewer, P. R., Young, D. G., & Morreale, M. (2013). The impact of real news about "fake news": Intertextual processes and political satire. *International Journal of Public Opinion Research, 25*(3), 323–343. doi:10.1093/ijpor/edt015

Rubin, V. L., Chen, Y., & Conroy, N. K. (2015). Deception detection for news: Three types of fakes: Deception Detection for News: Three Types of Fakes. *Proceedings of the Association for Information Science and Technology, 52*(1), 1–4. doi:10.1002/pra2.2015.145052010083

Park, Y.-H., & Choi, H.-S. (2015a). A trend and prospect of news media through mobile news application. *International Journal of Multimedia and Ubiquitous Engineering, 10*(7), 11–22. doi:10.14257/ijmue.2015.10.7.02

Ward, A., & … . (1997). *Naive realism in everyday life: Implications for social conflict and misunderstanding. Values and knowledge, Publisher: Lawrence Erlbaum AssociatesEditors: Terrance Brown, Edward S.* Reed, Elliot Turiel.

Nickerson, R. S. (1998). Confirmation bias: A ubiquitous phenomenon in many guises. *Review of General Psychology, 2*(2), 175–220. . doi:10.1037/1089-2680.2.2.175

Nyhan, B., & Reifler, J. (2010). When corrections fail: The persistence of political misperceptions. *Political Behavior*, *32*(2), 303–330. doi:10.100711109-010-9112-2

Kahneman, D., & Tversky, A. (2013). Prospect theory: An analysis of decision under risk. In *Handbook of the Fundamentals of Financial Decision Making* (pp. 99–127). World Scientific. doi:10.1142/9789814417358_0006

Tversky, A., & Kahneman, D. (2016). Advances in prospect theory: Cumulative representation of uncertainty. In *Readings in Formal Epistemology* (pp. 493–519). Springer International Publishing. doi:10.1007/978-3-319-20451-2_24

Ferrara, E., Varol, O., Davis, C., Menczer, F., & Flammini, A. (2016). The rise of social bots. *Communications of the ACM*, *59*(7), 96–104. doi:10.1145/2818717

B, J. M. (2018). *Fake news: Real lies, affecting real people*. Createspace Independent Publishing Platform.

Del Vicario, M., Vivaldo, G., Bessi, A., Zollo, F., Scala, A., Caldarelli, G., & Quattrociocchi, W. (2016). Echo chambers: Emotional contagion and group polarization on Facebook. *Scientific Reports*, *6*(1), 37825. doi:10.1038rep37825 PMID:27905402

Quattrociocchi, W., Scala, A., & Sunstein, C. R. (2016). Echo chambers on Facebook. SSRN Electronic Journal. doi:10.2139/ssrn.2795110

Paul, C., & Matthews, M. (2016). The Russian “firehose of falsehood” propaganda model. *Rand Corporation*, *2*(7), 1–10.

Zajonc, R. B. (1968). Attitudinal effects of mere exposure. *Journal of Personality and Social Psychology*, *9*(2, Pt.2), 1–27. doi:10.1037/h0025848

Zajonc, R. B. (2001). Mere exposure: A gateway to the subliminal. *Current Directions in Psychological Science*, *10*(6), 224–228. doi:10.1111/1467-8721.00154

Gentzkow, M., Shapiro, J. M., & Stone, D. F. (2015). Media bias in the marketplace: Theory, in Handbook of media economics. Elsevier, 623-645.

Feldman, R., & Sanger, J. (2006). Text Mining Preprocessing Techniques. In *The Text Mining Handbook* (pp. 57–63). Cambridge University Press. doi:10.1017/CBO9780511546914.004

Forman, G. (2003). An extensive empirical study of feature selection metrics for text classification. *Journal of Machine Learning Research*, *3*, 1289–1305.

Guyon, I., & Elisseeff, A. (2003). An introduction to variable and feature selection. *Journal of Machine Learning Research*, *3*, 1157–1182.

Guyon, I., Weston, J., Barnhill, S., & Vapnik, V. (2002). Gene selection for cancer classification using support vector machines. *Machine Learning*, *46*(1/3), 389–422. doi:10.1023/A:1012487302797

Kyriakopoulou, A., & Kalamboukis, T. (2007). Using clustering to enhance text classification. *Proceedings of the 30th Annual International ACM SIGIR Conference on Research and Development in Information*. ACM Press. 10.1145/1277741.1277918

Chen, Y., Conroy, N. J., & Rubin, V. L. (2015). Misleading online content: recognizing clickbait as "false news". In *Proceedings of the 2015 ACM on workshop on multimodal deception detection*. ACM. 10.1145/2823465.2823467

Fürnkranz, J. (1998). A study using n-gram features for text categorization. Austrian Research Institute for Artificial Intelligence, 1–10.

Afroz, S., Brennan, M., & Greenstadt, R. (2012). Detecting hoaxes, frauds, and deception in writing style online. *Symposium on Security and Privacy*. IEEE. 10.1109/SP.2012.34

Gupta, A. (2013). Faking sandy: characterizing and identifying fake images on twitter during hurricane sandy. In *Proceedings of the 22nd international conference on World Wide Web*. ACM. 10.1145/2487788.2488033

Jin, Z., Cao, J., Zhang, Y., Zhou, J., & Tian, Q. (2017). Novel visual and statistical image features for microblogs news verification. *IEEE Transactions on Multimedia*, *19*(3), 598–608. doi:10.1109/TMM.2016.2617078

Yang, F., Liu, Y., Yu, X., & Yang, M. (2012). Automatic detection of rumor on Sina Weibo. *Proceedings of the ACM SIGKDD Workshop on Mining Data Semantics*. ACM Press. 10.1145/2350190.2350203

Ma, J., Gao, W., Wei, Z., Lu, Y., & Wong, K.-F. (2015). Detect rumors using time series of social context information on microblogging websites. *Proceedings of the 24th ACM International on Conference on Information and Knowledge Management*. ACM Press. 10.1145/2806416.2806607

Kwon, S., Cha, M., Jung, K., Chen, W., & Wang, Y. (2013). Prominent features of rumor propagation in online social media. *13th International Conference on Data Mining*. IEEE.

Tacchini, E., Ballarin, G., Della Vedova, M. L., Moret, S., & de Alfaro, L. (2017). Some like it hoax: Automated fake news detection in social networks. https://arxiv.org/abs/1704.07506

Ruchansky, N., Seo, S., & Liu, Y. (2017). CSI: A hybrid deep model for fake news detection. https://arxiv.org/abs/1703.06959 doi:10.1145/3132847.3132877

Kotteti, C. M. M., Dong, X., Li, N., & Qian, L. (2018). Fake news detection enhancement with data imputation. *2018 IEEE 16th Intl Conf on Dependable, Autonomic and Secure Computing, 16th Intl Conf on Pervasive Intelligence and Computing, 4th Intl Conf on Big Data Intelligence and Computing and Cyber Science and Technology Congress(DASC/PiCom/DataCom/CyberSciTech)*. IEEE.

Mikolov, T., Chen, K., Corrado, G., & Dean, J. (2013). Efficient estimation of word representations in vector space. https://arxiv.org/abs/1301.3781

Pennington, J., Socher, R., & Manning, C. (2014). Glove: Global vectors for 356 word representation. In *Proceedings of the 2014 conference on empirical methods in natural*. ACL Anthology. 10.3115/v1/D14-1162

Thorne, J. (2018). Fever: a large-scale data-set for fact extraction and verification.

Chen, D., Fisch, A., Weston, J., & Bordes, A. (2017). Reading Wikipedia to answer open-domain questions. *Proceedings of the 55th Annual Meeting of the Association for Computational Linguistics* (Volume 1: Long Papers). Association for Computational Linguistics. 10.18653/v1/P17-1171

Ferreira, W., & Vlachos, A. (2016). Emergent: a novel data-set for stance classification. *Proceedings of the 2016 Conference of the North American Chapter of the Association for Computational Linguistics: Human Language Technologies*. Association for Computational Linguistics. 10.18653/v1/N16-1138

Merryton, A. R., & Augasta, G. (2020). A survey on recent advances in machine learning techniques for fake news detection. *Test Eng. Manag*, *83*, 11572–11582.

Meserole, C. (2022). *How Misinformation Spreads on Social Media—and What to Do About It*. Brookings. https://www.brookings.edu/blog/order-from-chaos/2018/05/09/how-misinformation-spreads-on-social-media-and-what-to-do-about-it/

Ikonomakis, M., Kotsiantis, S., & Tampakas, V. (2005). Text classification using machine learning techniques. *WSEAS Transactions on Computers*, *4*(8), 966–974.

Kim, S.-B., Rim, H.-C., Yook, D., & Lim, H.-S. (2002). Effective methods for improving naive Bayes text classifiers. In *Lecture Notes in Computer Science* (pp. 414–423). Springer Berlin Heidelberg.

Schneider, K.-M. (2005). Techniques for improving the performance of naive Bayes for text classification. In *Computational Linguistics and Intelligent Text Processing* (pp. 682–693). Springer Berlin Heidelberg. doi:10.1007/978-3-540-30586-6_76

Kłopotek, M. A., & Woch, M. (2003). Very large Bayesian networks in text classification. *International Conference on Computational Science*. Springer 10.1007/3-540-44860-8_41

Shanahan, J. G., & Roma, N. (2003). Improving SVM text classification performance through threshold adjustment. In *Machine Learning: ECML 2003* (pp. 361–372). Springer Berlin Heidelberg. doi:10.1007/978-3-540-39857-8_33

Johnson, D. E., Oles, F. J., Zhang, T., & Goetz, T. (2002). A decision-tree-based symbolic rule induction system for text categorization. *IBM Systems Journal*, *41*(3), 428–437. doi:10.1147j.413.0428

Kamath, C. N., Bukhari, S. S., & Dengel, A. (2018). Comparative study between traditional machine learning and deep learning approaches for text classification. *Proceedings of the ACM Symposium on Document Engineering*. ACM. 10.1145/3209280.3209526

Rosenblatt, F. (1961). *Principles of neurodynamics. perceptrons and the theory of brain mechanisms.* Armed Services Technical Information Agency.

Leudar, I. (1989). James L. McClelland, David Rumelhart and the PDP Research Group, Parallel distributed processing: explorations in the microstructure of cognition. Vol. 1. Foundations. Vol. 2. Psychological and biological models. Cambridge MA: M.I.T. Press, 1987. *Journal of Child Language*, *16*(2), 467–470. doi:10.1017/S0305000900010631

Pedregosa, F., Varoquaux, G., Gramfort, A., Michel, V., Thirion, B., Grisel, O., & Duchesnay, É. (2012). Scikit-learn: Machine Learning in Python. https://arxiv.org/abs/1201.0490

Bharadwaj, P., & Shao, Z. (2019). Fake news detection with semantic features and text mining. *International Journal on Natural Language Computing*, *8*(3), 17–22. doi:10.5121/ijnlc.2019.8302

Chapter 3
Deepfakes Spark Implementation for Big Data Analytics

A. Muruganantham
Kristu Jayanti College, India

Ayshwarya Balakumar
Kristu Jayanti College, India

N. Srinivas
KG Reddy College of Engineering and Technology, India

C. Srinivas Gupta
Mallareddy Engineering College, India

Vinod Desai
BLDEA's P.G.H. College of Engineering and Technology, Vijayapur, India

K. Saikumar
https://orcid.org/0000-0001-9836-3683
KL University, India

ABSTRACT

One of the most significant challenges we have in the context of today's big data world is the fact that we are unable to process enormous amounts of data in a timely manner. In this piece, the authors will use drive HQ cloud to analyse and evaluate two different supervised multiplication systems that are built on service cluster applications. Spark, on the other hand, provides a framework for managing data that is more dependable, and also has the ability to address concerns such as the loss of nodes and the duplication of data. Although it comes at the expense of insufficient failure organization, this study issue has the ability to considerably increase pace effectiveness, which is something many research/industry companies are interested in. A soon-to-be-released study will examine the methods on bigger datasets, especially in cases where the data cannot be totally stored in memory.

DOI: 10.4018/978-1-6684-6060-3.ch003

INTRODUCTION

The advent of the information age has resulted in a flood of big data from many walks of life, including, but not limited to, human activity alerts via wearable devices, scientific research from the field of particle detection, & stock market data structures. (Silva et.al., 2021). Samples of these activities are data processing, real-time analysis, data extraction, & classical conceptual production. Recent advances in the area suggest that the rate of information expansion will only accelerate in the years ahead, making it imperative to find effective ways to deal with the problem.

There are presently several relevant techniques that take advantage of numerous types of correspondence, e.g., multi-core, various-core, GPU, cluster, etc. To provide clarity, they are unique to each submission; they weigh many criteria, such as efficiency, cost, failure administration, data recovery, repair, and accessibility.

The primary distinctions between the 2 implementations lie in the availability of fault-tolerance features as well as the use of redundant data. Spark is capable of working with them successfully. However, it slows things down noticeably. Alternatively, closed/AMPI provides a solution optimized for HPC, although it has several drawbacks, mainly when used with commodity hardware. As of yet, no attempt has been made to differentiate between the 2 approaches.

Hardware & software costs may add up quickly when using conventional in-house technology. (Ahmed et al., 2020) & it is everything that must be put to utilize for the business to succeed. However, Information Technology companies like Google, Amazon, & Microsoft host cloud systems that rent out their infrastructure to individuals & businesses for a monthly fee that varies according to the user's requirements (in terms of time, number of servers, size of the systems, & so on).

The portions of the article are as follows: In Part 2, we discuss the use of the RFO & Pegasos Convolution Neural Network learning methods in tandem. Spark & ClosedMP/AMPI are each described in Part 3 & 4, respectively. Its experimental procedures & findings are presented & discussed in Part 5. They conclude with a summary of our findings & some suggestions for further study in Part 6 (Chi et.al., 2021).

Hadoop & Spark are 2 of the more well frameworks for building massive data models. Both provide a wide variety of open-source tools for preparing, analyzing, & managing large amounts of data and running analytics programs on that data.

Whether huge information environments must be tailored for consignment or real-time dispensation is at the heart of most Hadoop vs. Spark debates. Furthermore, doing so misrepresents the distinction between the 2 frameworks, Apache Hadoop and Apache Spark. Whereas Hadoop was first limited to batch applications, it is now possible to utilize it for intuitive questioning & continuous investigations duties. In contrast, Spark is developed to process batch workloads faster than Hadoop.

It's not always a black-and-white choice, either. Sparkle applications are typically built on top of the Hadoop Distributed File Scheme and the YARN assets the boards innovations, both of which were widely adopted by organizations for a wide range of big data applications (HDFS). Because Spark does not have its repository or file system, HDFS remains a viable option for storing data. (Karagiorgi et.al., 2022).

One key differentiation is Hadoop, precisely the MapReduce programming paradigm and engine for handling large data sets. While HDFS is integral to early versions of Hadoop, Spark is developed to replace MapReduce. Hadoop is no longer dependent entirely on MapReduce, but the 2 remain closely related. According to Erik Gfesser, chief of architecture at SPR, an Information Technology services consulting firm, most people associate Hadoop with MapReduce.

Matei Zaharia, then a Ph.D. candidate at UC Berkeley, developed Spark in 2009. His primary focus with this technology was to improve data integration to scale in-memory training over distributed team hubs. Sparkle, like Hadoop, could manage large data sets by dividing up processing among multiple nodes, but it does so at an astonishingly higher rate. (Ketu et.al., 2020). Flash will now be able to handle use situations that MapReduce in Hadoop can't, making it anything other than a handling motor that is always useful.

Spark relies primarily on the following techniques:

- Spark's central processing unit. This core execution engine schedules jobs and handles basic Input/output operations using Spark's core Application programming interface.
- The Spark SQL modules allow for the efficient processing of structured information by merely consecutively SQL queries or using Spark's Dataset Application programming interface to access the SQL executing motor.
- Spark Streaming & the more recent Structured Streaming. These components enable the processing of data streams. Sparkle Streaming divides data from several streaming services, such as HDFS, Kafka, and Kinesis, into manageable chunks to simulate a continuous stream. The goal of the enhanced method known as Organized Streaming, based on Spark SQL, is to enhance sleep & simplify programming.
- MLlib is a foundational Artificial Intelligence package that provides several Artificial Intelligence calculations and tools for feature selection & pipeline design.

Architecture

Data preparation is where Hadoop & Spark diverge significantly. Hadoop stores data in frames replicated across the hard drives of all the computers in a cluster, providing a great deal of redundancy and the ability to withstand hardware failure (Peng, 2019, pp 309-312). An application written for Hadoop might thus be executed either as a single process or as a DAG with several tasks.

Hadoop 1.0 featured a centralized Job Tracker facility for distributing Map Reduce jobs to nodes that might function self-sufficiently of one additional and a decentralized Task Tracker service for monitoring the executions of operations on individual nodes. Hadoop 2.0 supplanted Job Tracker & Task Tracker using the following YARN features:

- Resource Manager, a daemon that acts as a worldwide job planner & arbitrator of available resources
- Node Manager, The agents installed on every node in the cluster to keep tabs on its resources consumption;
- Application Masters, a daemon set up for every application that negotiates needed resources with Resource Managers and coordinates processing activities by Node Managers; &
- Containers for storing application-specific resources when they're required.

A spark might operate independently or on clusters controlled by YARN, Mesos, or Kubernetes. Spark may access HDFS, a cloud object storage similar Amazon Simple Storage Service, or other data warehouses & data sources. Whenever data indexes become too large to fit into RAM, the system "spills" the data to a circular buffer, where it might be accessed & processed. (Ameer & Shah 2018). Similarly, with Hadoop, Spark's architecture is changed significantly since its inception. Spark Core was utilized to organize data hooked on a flexible disseminated dataset (RDD), an in-memory data store distributed crossways many nodes in a cluster. It also built DAGs to aid in scheduling & preparation. RDD API is always accessible.

The RDD API is still readily accessible. But following the 2016 launch of Spark 2.0, the Dataset API replaced it as the advised programming interface. In 2016, with Spark 2.0, the Dataset API became the preferred API. In the same way, as RDDs are distributed collections of data with solid type characteristics, datasets are also, though they benefit from additional optimizations made possible by Spark SQL. In R and Python, the equivalent of work in a relational database were called "data frames," which contain datasets with named columns. Structured Streaming & MLlib employ the Dataset/Data Frame technique.

Big Data Analytics

Single of the more active investigate areas, big data analytics presents several obstacles & calls for discoveries that have implications for many different sectors. Effective frameworks are required for the development, construction, & management of the pipelines & algorithms required for large-scale data processing. Apache Spark is a powerful unifying engine for large-scale data analytics. It could process many different types of data & processes them quickly and efficiently. Using a unified dispensation engine & overall-purpose programming language, data scientists & engineers have developed a groundbreaking approach to addressing a wide range of data problems. Apache Spark's high level of sophistication has earned it widespread support from academics and professionals. One of the most widely used open source projects overall, & the best widely used project of its kind in the sample data space, both developed by the Apache Software Foundations.

Deliberate the supervised also conventional machine learning scheme, in which a sequence. of data $D_n = \left\{ \left(x_1, y_1\right), \ldots, \left(x_n, y_n\right) \right\}$ is verified i.i.d. as of an unnamed circulation concluded $x \times y$, where $x \in R^d$ be an input space $x \in X$ and $y \in R$ is an output space $\left(y \in Y\right)$. In this paper, we concentrate on binary arrangement difficulties with $y \in \left\{ \pm 1 \right\}$. The 2 main goals of the learning strategies classes are Lazy learning (LL) & eager knowledge (AE), which were the 2 central tenets of the educational system (EL). (Rivas-Gomez et.al., 2019). The main problem with LL is that it does not do any abstractions prior to predictions, which makes it challenging to use for classification tasks. However, LL approaches are popular due to their simplicity & potential for parallelization. Instead of keeping individual data examples, EL uses global representations known as a battered model f. Past cannot develop explicit models f until a study sample is categorized; then, it merely duplicates the spreading in the area. A higher computationally expensive learning process is required to achieve these memory savings, but with these abstractions, this is no longer the case.

One of the most often used LL machine learning-ML models is K-Nearest Neighbors, mainly because of how simple it is to create & how well it performs (AKNN). Using a distance metric, K-Nearest Neighbors finds the k samples most similar to the test sample & collects their labels. The key is found using the method Algorithm 1 depicts the pseudocode for AKNN classifications, showing the parallelizable parts and the serialization bottlenecks. To tune AKNN, you could adjust the distance metric & the hyperparameter k. With d kept within reasonable bounds, the Euclidean Distance is the default metric. (Morán-Fernández et.al., 2020). However, k plays a crucial role in determining how generalizable an algorithm is.

$$w : arg\ min_{w} \frac{\lambda}{2} w^{2} + \frac{1}{n} \sum_{i=1}^{n} max \left| 0, 1 - y_{i} w^{T} x_{i} \right|$$

where w^2 is the regularizer & $l\left(w^{T}x_{i}, y_{i}\right) = max\left[0, 1 - y_{i}w^{T}x_{i}\right]$ Whence Comes to the Regularizer, & The hinge loss function represents a loss of a hinge. As a CP, Eq. (1) has a continuous and complex solution. As with k in AKNN, it must be adjusted to maximize f's simplification ability in ASVM (x). Pegasos is one of only a handful of feasible parallel approaches to solving the CP. Pegasos is an automated support vector machine (ASVM) approach that we introduce here and in Algorithm (2). It is a deterministic sub-gradient descent learning process. The method must be executed sequentially because each iteration builds on the previous one.

On the other hand, we must look at the processes happening inside. Although the classifications step in this technique is so straightforward & computationally negligible compared to the preceding preparations phase, we report on the learning process. Pegasus has a second hyperparameter that's worth mentioning. (Guo et.al., 2022).

Algorithm 1: AAKNN

Input: $D_{n}, k\, and \left\{x_{1}^{c}, \ldots, x_{n_{c}}^{c}\right\}$

Output: $\left\{y_{1}^{c}, \ldots, y_{n_{c}}^{c}\right\}$ /* serial */

1 Read D_{n} ; /* serial */

2 Read $\left\{x_{1}^{c}, \ldots, x_{n_{c}}^{c}\right\}$ /* serial */

3 for K $\leftarrow$ 1 to n_{c} do /* serial */

4 | for L $\leftarrow$ 1 to n do /* serial */

5 | | d_{i} = length $\left(x_{1}^{c}, x_{i}\right)$; /* classical */

6 | z = nearest k features in d ; /* classical */

7 | y_{1}^{c} = mode $\left(\left\{y_{i} : i \in x\right\}\right)$;

8 return $\left\{y_{1}^{c}, \ldots, y_{n_{c}}^{c}\right\}$;

Algorithm 2: AASVM

source: D_{n}, λ and no if loops T

destination: W

1 Read D_{n} ;

2 W =0 ; /* serial */

3 while T $\leftarrow$ 1 to T do

4 | $I = \left\{i : i \epsilon \left\{1, \ldots, n\right\}, y_{i} w^{T} x_{i} < 1\right\}$; /* classical */

5 | $\eta_t = 1 / \lambda t$; /* Parallelizable */

6 | $w = \left(1 - \eta_t \lambda\right) w$;

7 | $w + = \eta_t / n \sum_i \epsilon \, x y_i x_i)$;

8 return w ; /* Parallelizable /Bottleneck */

LITERATURE SURVEY

In this section clear notes of literature survey have been placed according problem definition shown in figure 1.

Figure 1. Literature Survey

S.No	Author	Technique	Key point	Advanced model
1	Agarwal et.al [2014]	A technique is based on linear predictors and convex losses	Also, for these vast issues, it may be claimed that multicore solutions designed for single machines are preferable.	Machine learning
2	Divyakant Agrawal et.al [2011]	A technique is based on DBMS design development	This method introduces about the MapReduce paradiagram	Deep learning
3	D. Anguita et.al [2012]	Enable vector machine model selection and error calculation using in-sample methods	Our plan for converting them is one step toward enhancing their acceptance.	Neural learning

High-energy particle colliders have traditionally observed exotic particles. Deep-learning algorithms will aid collider search for unusual particles. Figure 1: Deep learning.

SPARK-HADOOP MODELLING

Spark is a state-of-the-art parallel computing architecture created to handle calculations that repeat themselves, such as the supervised AAKNN & AASVM techniques. In contrast to more popular methods like Apache Mahout, which necessitate data reloading & have extensive redundancy, it continues to be constructed around keeping data in memory rather than on disc. Spark is more efficient than the standard Map. Experiments suggest you can cut the speed at which tasks must be completed by as much as 2 orders of magnitude. (Padmini et.al., 2021).

Spark's primary information structures are called Resilient Distributed Datasets (RDDs). Spark may be operated with a number of different cluster management choices, from the Spark Standalone Scheduler to more complex systems like Apache Mesos & Hadoop YARN. Spark will be deployed in a Hadoop cluster for this undertaking. Hadoop is an open-source framework for processing massive datasets distributed using commodity cluster designs.

As an alternative to entirely distributed algorithms, which present new challenges owing to the necessity of network connections, it is possible to argue that multicore techniques optimized for single machines with lots of fast storage & memory were better for these central issues. We argue that distributed ML on a cluster has strong advantages. Such data sets include recordings of user clicks or search queries and are grouped across numerous industry-scale systems. To eliminate the bottleneck of data transport to a single effective computer, it is still desirable to process data in a clustered method. In this study, we improve on previous methods by discussing design decisions that affect large-scale linear learning interactions and computing speeds. This section analyses the plan. We outline the datasets to be used, then analyse our design from a systems and ML standpoint. Next, we'll assess our plan academically. It blends real-time and background processes. They discuss online and batch learning's merits and limitations. Online learning algorithms can attain rough precision after a few rounds by using target details.

The HDFS (name node) & resource planning were handled by separate master computers in the chosen Hadoop architecture. Through serialization, they had improved network output (o/p)(Kryo). Every machine has been outfitted with Hadoop 2.4.1 and Spark 1.1.1. To control parallelism & simultaneously operate all devices & cores, they overrode Spark's default settings by increasing the number of storage partitions from the default of NM to NM NC. To prevent slowdowns, we often rechecked the device's memory settings to verify that all train information was being kept in memory without spills or recalculations.

Data is retrieved from HDFS stores, transformed, & acted upon by RDD norms. Spark operations merely entail passing function objects to carry out distributed computations over results, which explains why the map-reducing algorithm shown here does not involve any iterations, in contrast to Algorithms 1 & 2. To create a prediction, the K-Nearest Neighbors model takes each training sample as well as a test sample & converts the Euclidean distance among them into the names of their k-nearest neighbors. The predicted grade is the mode of these grades, thanks to the magic of computers. In contrast, Pegasos adaptive learning employs a filter feature to choose train samples that pass the criterion and then uses targeted gradient projections to arrive at g. At last, a g-multiplier is applied to the weights. Because of its recursive nature, such methods store the classification models in memory for future usage.

Algorithm 3: Spark AKNN

Input: $D_n, k\, and \left\{x_1^c, \ldots, x_{n_c}^c\right\}$

Output: $\left\{y_1^c, \ldots, y_{n_c}^c\right\}$

1 Read D_n ;

2 Read $\left\{x_1^c, \ldots, x_{n_c}^c\right\}$

3 for j $\leftarrow$ to n_c do

4 | $\{(y_1, d_1), \ldots, (y_k, d_k)\} = D_n.map(Euclidean\,Distance(x_j))$. Take ordered (k, Distance Comparator ())

5 | $y_1^c = mode(\{y_i\})$

6 | return $\{y_1^c, \ldots, y_{n_c}^c\}$;

Algorithm 4: Spark Pegasos ASVM

Input: D_n, λ and number if iterations T

Output: w

1 Read D_n ;

2 Set w=0:

3 for j ← 1 to T do

4 | $g = D_n$. Filter (Gradient Condition (w)).map(Gradient()).reduce (Sum()) ;

5 | $\eta_t = 1 / \lambda t$;

6 | $w = (1 - \eta_t \lambda) w + g$

7 | reappearance w;

SPARK-HADOOP COMPATIBILITY

Hadoop's framework is implemented in Java, although it is possible to use Python or C++ to create applications for the framework. Programs for MapReduce could be created in Python without the need for jar file translation.

To facilitate Python with Spark, the Apache Spark community developed a Python application programming interface (API) called PySpark. Inside the Python environment, using PySpark makes it simple to include & interact with RDDs. (Saba et.al., 2020).

The interactive Python shell, PySpark shell, is included with Spark. This PySpark shell is responsible for creating the connections among the Python API as well as the Spark core & for initializing the spark context. If you give it some interactive instructions, PySpark may similarly be launched from the command line shown in Fig 2.

Figure 2. Hadoop & Spark compatibility (Data-flair.training.)

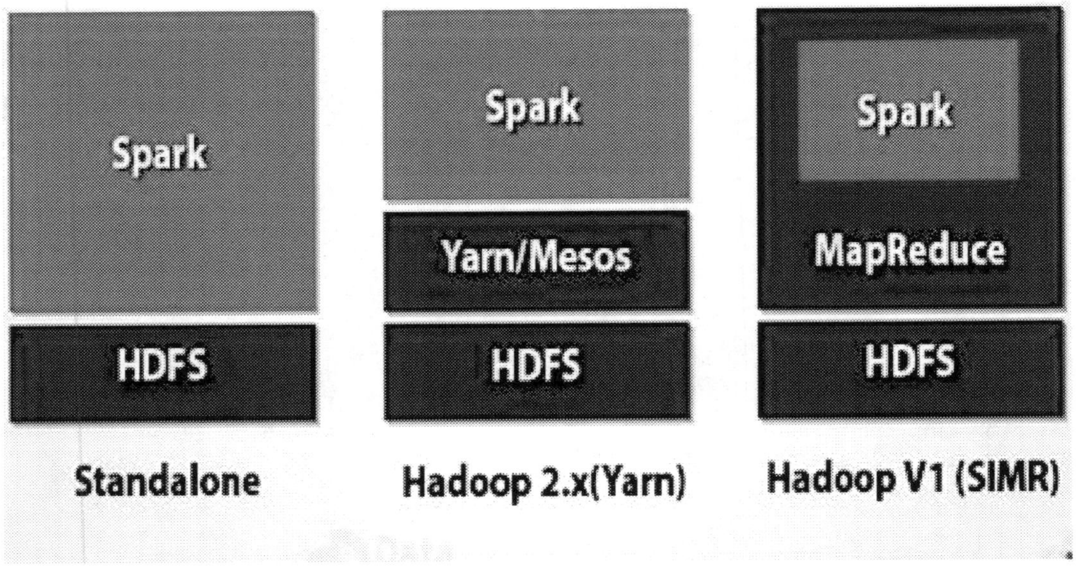

Hadoop

Hadoop is great for storing and analysing Big Data since it may preserve crucial files in HDFS without a schema.

This system is very scalable since as many nodes as needed can be added to increase performance. Hadoop makes data very accessible despite hardware failure.

Spark

A spark is a good option for analyzing many structured or unstructured information even though the data is stored in clusters. Spark will explain how to keep as much data as possible in memory before writing any of it to disc. A subset of the datasets would be stored in memory, while the rest would remain on disc. (Yasmeen & Uddin, 2022).

Hadoop & Spark both offer Pythons application programming interfaces (APIs) for processing big data & getting a connection to big data platforms, making Python the language of choice for numerous data scientists.

AAMPI / closed MP on cloud

Point-to-point and two-way communications are supported by AAMPI, a networking protocol for parallel computing independent of programming languages. AAMPI is designed to be fast, scalable, and movable. The Advanced Message Passing Interface (AAMPI) has become the standard networking protocol for concurrent programming using distributed memory architectures. Due to its focus on High-Performance Computing (HPC), the standard does not currently offer automatic failover. Machines store the entire dataset D_n in equal bits, resulting in n/ N_M data samples per computer $\left(D^M_{n/N_M}, i\epsilon\ \{1,\ldots,N_M\}\right)$. For optimum architecture utilization, Each AAMPI process releases one or more ClosedMP threads, and the processes run in parallel. Given the preceding, Algorithms 5 & 6 provide the AAMPI/closedMP system based on AKNN and Pegasos. AAMPI is based on the idea that multiple processes can be executed simultaneously with minimal coordination. Synchronization of the devices follows. $O\left(\log\left(N_M\right)\right)$ Time utilizing a three-step reduction technique that maximizes throughput in the record. Both Pegasos and k-nearest-neighbors undergo a reduction process during their respective climbing and discovery phases. Similarly, the closed MP threads use procedures. It's worth noting that reading D^M_{n/N_M} from disk can't take advantage of the multi-core architecture given that there is a bottleneck during disc readings, the severity of which varies based on the physical implementations in the data center.

Evaluation

Here we look into how Spark's new AKNN and Pegasus ASVM algorithms perform on Hadoop & Beowulf using AMPI/ClosedMP & open MPI, respectively. To build complete Linux shell script frameworks for deploying applications & operating systems (the latest version of CentOS 6) on virtual servers, they use Google Cloud Platform's Linux scripting procedures. Dependent upon the many forms of machinery. Each machine preinstalled one 500 GB solid-state drive (SSD) disc for persistent data storage. Every system update was triple-checked. Furthermore, Algorithms 4 and 6 of the Pegasos family were tried, with hyper parameters set to T = 100.

The UCI Machine Learning Repository necessitates using the HIGGS Data Sets to distinguish among sign and foundation Higgs boson-radiating cycles. A total of 11,000,000,000 samples in 28 dimensions were generated using Monte Carlo simulations. The previous 500,000 examples served as a data set of comparison. Seven gigabytes of space were devoted to the study, all comprising text files containing the training data. Thanks to the massive dataset, we could identify that one of the technologies (Spark) had reached its scaling limit. Also, the virtual machines' preferences are considered while selecting a dataset size to fit entirely within the capacity of the shortest bunch arrangement. We avoided capacity reloading and circle spill since they would not have resulted in an entirely in-memory program and would have increased execution time shown in figure 3.

Figure 3. Spark Evaluation (Professional Education, 2021)

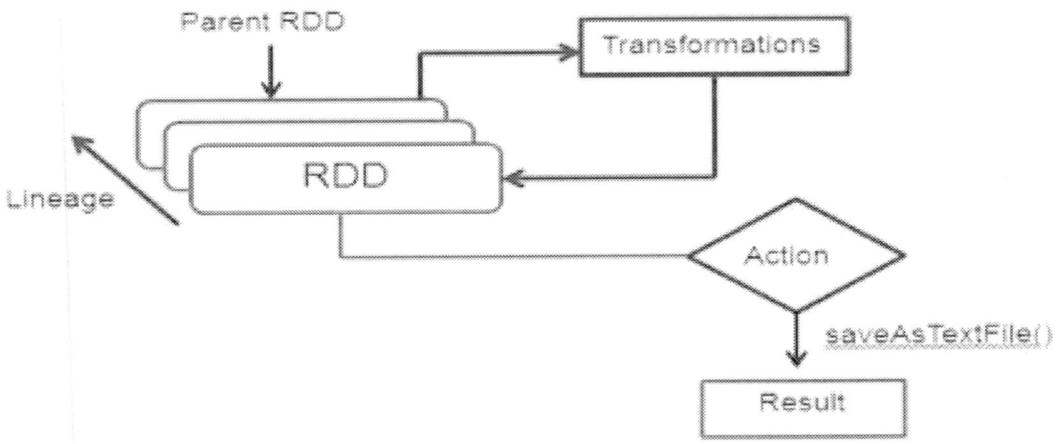

Due to Spark's LE architecture, the time needed to read data from the disc was combined with the time needed to accomplish the first operation across RDDs. in this agrees with the declining train statistics. Therefore, we employed a two-period estimation in our testing & compared the results to those obtained using AMPI/ClosedMP. In the above stage displays the outcomes of implementing AKNN. There are no surprises when it comes to the following sums shown in Fig 3.

CONCLUSION

While the efficiency gap between Hadoop MapReduce and high-performance computing (HPC) for machine learning has shrunk thanks to Spark on Hadoop's in-memory data processing, we still can't quite match the efficiency of the most modern HPC systems. On the other hand, Spark on Hadoop may be the better choice due to the following characteristics. At this time, Hadoop is not scheduled to be combined with AMPI or Closed MP. Many research/industry firms are interested in this area of study because of the potential for greatly higher speed efficiency, which makes up for the expense of insufficient failures organisation. Analyzing the technologies on larger datasets would allow for more immediate research, especially when the data could be stored entirely in memory.

REFERENCES

Ahmed, N., Barczak, A. L., Susnjak, T., & Rashid, M. A. (2020). A comprehensive performance analysis of Apache Hadoop and Apache Spark for large scale data sets using HiBench. *Journal of Big Data*, *7*(1), 1–18. doi:10.118640537-020-00388-5

Ameer, S., & Shah, M. A. (2018, August). Exploiting big data analytics for smart urban planning. In *88th Vehicular Technology Conference (VTC-Fall)* (pp. 1-5). IEEE. 10.1109/VTCFall.2018.8691036

Chi, D., Tang, C., & Yin, C. (2021). Design and Implementation of Hotel Big Data Analysis Platform Based on Hadoop and Spark. *Journal of Physics: Conference Series*, *2010*(1), 012079. doi:10.1088/1742-6596/2010/1/012079

Data-flair. (2022). Apache Spark Compatibility with Hadoop. Data flair. https://data-flair.training/blogs/apache-spark-hadoop-compatibility.

Guo, J., Huang, C., & Hou, J. (2022). A Scalable Computing Resources System for Remote Sensing Big Data Processing Using GeoPySpark Based on Spark on K8s. *Remote Sensing*, *14*(3), 521. doi:10.3390/rs14030521

Karagiorgi, G., Kasieczka, G., Kravitz, S., Nachman, B., & Shih, D. (2022). Machine learning in the search for new fundamental physics. *Nature Reviews Physics*, *4*(6), 399–412. doi:10.103842254-022-00455-1

Ketu, S., Mishra, P. K., & Agarwal, S. (2020). Performance analysis of distributed computing frameworks for big data analytics: Hadoop vs spark. *Computación y Sistemas*, *24*(2), 669–686. doi:10.13053/cys-24-2-3401

Morán-Fernández, L., Bolón-Canedo, V., & Alonso-Betanzos, A. (2020). Do we need hundreds of classifiers or a good feature selection? In ESANN (pp. 399-404).

Padmini, G. R., Rajesh, O., Raghu, K., Sree, N. M., & Apurva, C. (2021, March). Design and Analysis of 8-bit ripple Carry Adder using nine Transistor Full Adder. In *7th International Conference on Advanced Computing and Communication Systems (ICACCS)* (*Vol. 1*, pp. 1982-1987). IEEE.

Peng, Z. (2019, January). Stocks analysis and prediction using big data analytics. In *International conference on intelligent transportation, big data & smart City (ICITBS)* (pp. 309-312). IEEE.

Professional Education. (2021) *What is Apache spark RDD*. Pro-edu. https://proedu.co/spark/what-is-apache-spark-rdd-resilient-distributed-dataset/ .

Rivas-Gomez, S., Fanfarillo, A., Narasimhamurthy, S., & Markidis, S. (2019, September). Persistent coarrays: integrating mpi storage windows in coarray fortran. In *Proceedings of the 26th European MPI Users' Group Meeting* (pp. 1-8). ACM. 10.1145/3343211.3343214

Silva, N., Barros, J., Santos, M. Y., Costa, C., Cortez, P., Carvalho, M. S., & Gonçalves, J. N. (2021). Advancing logistics 4.0 with the implementation of a big data warehouse: A demonstration case for the automotive industry. *Electronics (Basel)*, *10*(18), 2221. doi:10.3390/electronics10182221

Yasmeen, F., & Uddin, M. S. (2022). A novel watermarking scheme based on discrete wavelet transform-singular value decomposition. *Security and Privacy*, *5*(3), e216. doi:10.1002py2.216

Chapter 4
Experimental Work and Discussion of Results on Deepfakes in Stock Prices Using Sentiment Analysis and Machine Learning

Anbarasu N.
Nandha Engineering College, India

S. Karuppusamy
Nandha Engineering College, India

S. Prabhu
Nandha Engineering College, India

P. Sobana
Nandha Engineering College, India

ABSTRACT

In the field of artificial intelligence, the employment of computer algorithms that develop themselves mechanically as they get more and more experience in experimental work and discussion of results on deepfakes is essential to the research process. It is frequently thought of as being in close proximity to artificial intelligence. Machine learning is a set of techniques that generates a model by making use of sample data, commonly referred to as training data, in order to make predictions about the future without actively attempting to do so, by separating the various types of tweets taken from the data on Twitter regarding a number of different companies. A classification algorithm was applied to the data that was collected and used in order to categorise the tweets. In addition, the OHLCV of the data from a number of different organisations is taken into account in order to improve efficiency.

DOI: 10.4018/978-1-6684-6060-3.ch004

INTRODUCTION

Predicting the value of a company's stock is something that people have been doing for years because it may result in significant gains (Abulkasim et al., 2019). Elementary and technical analysis are the two methods that are used the most frequently when attempting to forecast stock values (Adil et al., 2021a). It is possible for the economy of a country to improve or worsen as a direct result of the performance of the stock exchange (Adil et al., 2022a). In a number of studies, it has been demonstrated that the news that is reported in news reports serves as crucial signals that cause market volatility (Adil et al., 2022b). Prediction of the stock market confers significant benefits on businesses and sectors. Accurate predictions allow investors to not only make profitable stock market decisions but also profit from the market overall (Adil et al., 2021b).

In addition, market forecasting is challenging due to the complexity of the components involved in the economy and politics. Learning stock movement patterns and trading behaviours requires the acquisition of relevant data, which is an essential component of any profitable market trading strategy (Adil et al., 2021c). As methods of machine learning, a shallow neural network and a support vector machine were utilised in order to solve this challenge (Adil et al., 2021d). Because their answer incorporates the generalisation mistake implicitly, Support Vector Machines were seen to be a more suitable contender for the job (Farouk et al., 2020). Even when working with financial data, Deep Learning methods are excellent for time series forecasting because, in addition to being able to model extremely nonlinear and complicated data, they can also predict the course of time series (Aoudni et al., 2022); (Abu-Rumman, 2021); (Khaled et al., 2018).

The key contribution that it makes is an extremely in-depth study on how to estimate the movement of stocks' mid prices using the data that is provided by the limit order book (Naseri et al., 2018a). This is its primary contribution (Farouk et al., 2018). There is evidence to suggest that emotions and news can influence the performance of the stock market and also function as indicators (Farouk et al., 2015); (Al Shraah et al., 2013). We collected and evaluated data as well as tweets from a number of different companies (Heidari et al., 2019). The supervised-based strategy that makes use of TextBlob was also investigated as a potential method for the extraction of sentiment features (Mendonça et al., 2021). A forecasting model that can generate accurate forecasts can be developed by factoring in sentiments and public opinions in connection to actual changes in stock prices (Metwaly et al., 2014).

LITERATURE SURVEY

Gurav, and Sidnal (2018) in view of the fact that reducing one's exposure to risk in the stock market is closely connected with reducing one's level of error in one's forecasts, this article presents the findings of a study that investigates several topics pertaining to dynamic stock market forecasting. The EMH, which is the foundation of a large portion of economic theory, has yielded encouraging results in the predicting of stock values based on financial news (Naseri et al., 2018b). The goal of developing a model for a time series is to research and learn about how the series evolves over the course of time so that the changes in the series may be predicted (Naseri et al., 2017).

According to Ishita Parmar, Navanshu Agarwal, Sheirsh Saxena, Ridam Arora, Shikhin Gupta, Himanshu Dhiman, and Lokesh Chouhan (Khan et al., 2022), increasing accuracy can be achieved by estimating a value that is relatively near to the actual tangible value. Machine learning has been applied in studies to the task of predicting stock prices due to the effectiveness and precision of the measurements it provides (Zhu et al., 2021). These hypotheses are supported by regression models and LSTM models in their own right. The suggested model is tested using data acquired from Yahoo Finance, which is also used to train the model. The combination of the two approaches led to enhanced predictions, which indicates that the outcomes are also favourable (Zhou et al., 2016).

Reshma et al. (2021) Predicting the future is a task that has always held a great deal of allure for people due to the fact that it is both thrilling and fascinating. Examining the differences between single and multi-layer perceptrons (Al Shraah et al., 2022). The method that is given in this study for modelling the market involves making use of several aspects of the market as input qualities. The model generates two distinct classes of output, which are referred to respectively as Positive Market and Negative Market. The Multi-Layer Perceptron algorithms were successful in predicting 77 percent of the outcomes of market developments thanks to the application of machine learning (Naseri et al., 2015).

Devani and Patel (2022), During the course of this research project, the suggested model was put to use and assessed using 13 different financial benchmark datasets in comparison to the Levenberg-Marquardt (LM) method for artificial neural networks. According to the findings that were obtained, the model that was provided was both extremely accurate and capable of optimising the LS-SVM algorithm using PSO. The over-fitting issue that ANNs cause can be fixed with an approach called LS-SVM, which is a reformulated version of the conventional SVM methodology that makes use of the least squares-support vector machines (LS-SVM) method (Abu-Rumman and Qawasmeh, 2021). As a direct consequence of this, the least squares function is computed with the help of regularised least squares. The supervised learning algorithms connected to LS-SVM search for patterns inside data and perform analysis on those patterns. With the help of this method, accurate stock price forecasting is significantly accelerated.

Guo et al. (2018) provides light on this challenge by studying the application of deep learning in automatically building usable features from massive data sets. Deep learning has captured the attention of researchers in a variety of domains, including machine learning and pattern analysis, amongst others. Implementing a deep recurrent neural network would be a step forward in the process of finding a solution to these problems. This network is capable of intuitively identifying benefits from a wide variety of texts and taking secular aspects into consideration. Recurrent neural networks, which can also be represented as hierarchically stacked RBMs, are the typical choice for modelling time-series data. Input data for news articles are word vectors, and this is accomplished by employing a representation known as a bag of words.

Reshma et al. (2021), In particular, this study looks at the data collected from Twitter. In addition to that, this research offers a model that is intended to improve the accuracy of classification. The objective of this research is to develop Hybrid Naive Bayes Classifiers (HNBCs), which will be used for the classification of stock market data using machine learning techniques. Investing, businesses and researchers will all gain from the conclusion since it will make it possible to make strategies that take into account the feelings of individuals. The method that was proposed resulted in an accuracy of 90.38 percent being reached by it.

According to Karuppusamy and Singaravel (2019), the most common application of SVR is for forecasting. So as to arrive at the most precise projections possible on future stock prices. We determined the SVR by calculating it using the penalty coefficient C and the distribution parameter. In this research, an adaptive SVR based on PSO is proposed with the intention of providing greater versatility with no need to alter the SVR parameters. The results of a study that compared adaptive SVR, traditional SVR, and BPNN revealed that adaptive SVR was superior in terms of its ability to adapt to new information and make correct predictions.

Abdolmaleky et al., (2017) the raw order book data is used as a starting point for handmade features, which are then extracted from this data by machine learning techniques, resulting in extremely varied aspect aims. These feature sets are merged in order to conduct an evaluation of three different classifiers using three different prediction scenarios for two distinct evaluation settings. This study provides a comprehensive examination of the data provided by the high prevalence limit order book for the purpose of forecasting future changes in the midprice. The fact that the extracted and handmade feature representations combined give a better forecast, as was anticipated, demonstrates that the feature extraction models are able to reveal previously hidden information.

Abulkasim et al., (2019) a new algorithm was devised by attempting to forecast the moment at which a specific stock exchange would close. According to the findings of this research, techniques involving machine learning may properly forecast how the stock market will perform. The method that is suggested as a result of this research is to make use of the numerous aspects that have an effect on the market as input qualities for the model.

Abulkasim et al., (2018) utilising the fundamental methods for identifying mistakes in software systems, flaws inside the code segment are found. As a result of the software programme development lifecycle model, the data set is acquired, and then it is combined with a reliability-finding set of rules, specifically the Bayesian choice concept, in order to determine mistake chances and to anticipate software problems all through the prediction.

PROPOSED METHODOLOGY

The construction of supervised machine learning models requires the usage of large amounts of labelled text or sentence examples. Naive Bayes and Support Vector Machines are the methods that are utilised, and the problem that they solve is modelled as a classification issue. In addition, SVMs are utilised extensively in the process of stock classification. It has been ensured that there will be no overfitting, which will finally lead to positive generalisation findings. Artificial neural networks (ANNs) that are inspired by biological neurons are quickly becoming one of the most important methods for predicting the stock market. This is due to the fact that ANNs are able to handle uncertainties, noise, a lack of complete data, and subtle functional relationships between the data. LS-SVM is a new method that was presented that improved the traditional SVM method by reducing the large number of parameters to fix. Additionally, the user did not need any prior knowledge about the relevant inputs in the problem that was to be studied. This was accomplished by reworking the traditional algorithm of the SVM in order to counteract the overfitting effect caused by ANNs. Calculating a regularised least squares function is accomplished by the use of equality constraints in a regularised least squares (LS-SVM) approach. A group of supervised learning techniques known as an LS-SVM is used for data analysis and optimisation with the purpose of improving classification and analysis.

MODULES AND DESCRIPTION

It has been discovered that LS-SVM reworks the traditional algorithm of SVM in order to counteract the overfitting effect that artificial neural networks (ANNs) have. This is accomplished by reducing the number of parameters that need to be adjusted and minimising the prior knowledge that the user needs to have about the relevant inputs in the problem being analysed. The least squares function is computed in a regularised least squares (LS-SVM) approach by imposing equality restrictions on the calculation results. In the context of supervised learning, there are numerous variants of the LS-SVM model to choose from. They are utilised to classify and analyse data, as well as evaluating and optimise said data.

The first thing I do is scrape two sets of securities details from connected sources, the one being information about OHLCV taken from finance databases and the second being a Twitter feed including public tweets about these firms. Next, I extract numerous attributes from the tweets by performing data pre-processing using a variety of natural language processing approaches. In the following section, we will put some machine learning models to use, and then we will assess how excellent those models are. The subsequent phase will be carried out after the exactness reaches a level lower than a predetermined threshold known as T. After the features have been chosen and altered, the next step is to incorporate them into the various machine learning models. In this stage, the correctness of the models developed in the previous step is evaluated. In the end, I decided to employ regularised model stacking to enhance categorisation performance.

In order to conduct a noise-free analysis of social media posts, tweets first need to be cleaned and standardised. Only then can they be evaluated. It is crucial to begin by removing tweets that contain spam, tweets that were written in a language other than English, and tweets that are not pertinent to the stock or the company. Tweets that were found to contain identical content to other tweets were deleted. Using the NLTK vocabulary, stop words were removed from the document. Twitter posts will no longer include punctuation, URLs, hashtags, or user IDs.

I've utilised Python's TextBlob API for Natural Language Processing (NLP) to conduct sentiment analysis. It gives the subjectivity score as well as the polarity score for each tweet. This sentiment indicator is compiled each day, and then tweets are matched to the stock return data for each day in order to depict the market sentiment for that particular day. During process optimisation, the value extracted is transformed into the information or value that is the most beneficial in terms of its cost-effectiveness by utilising a high-performance solution.

RESULT ANALYSIS

In order to conduct a more accurate sentiment analysis, the tweets were converted into a more easily useable format using NLP. After that, the OHLCV was studied similarly to contrast the accuracy of real and forecast stock (figure 1).

Figure 1. Analysis of characters of tweeter data of Amazon and Facebook (a,b & c)

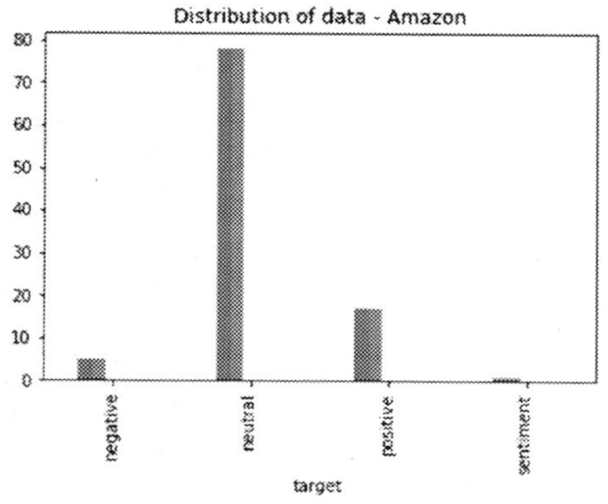

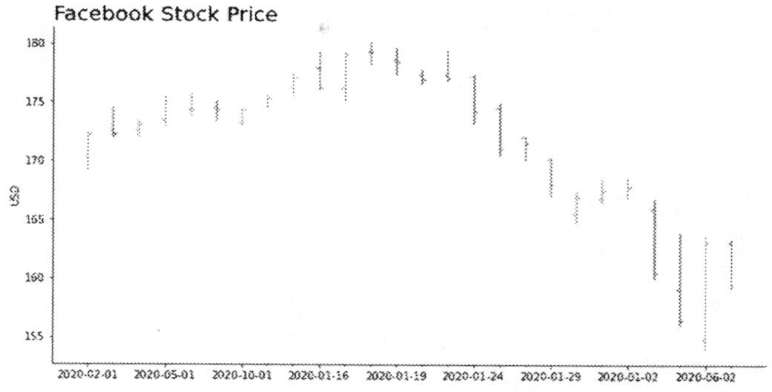

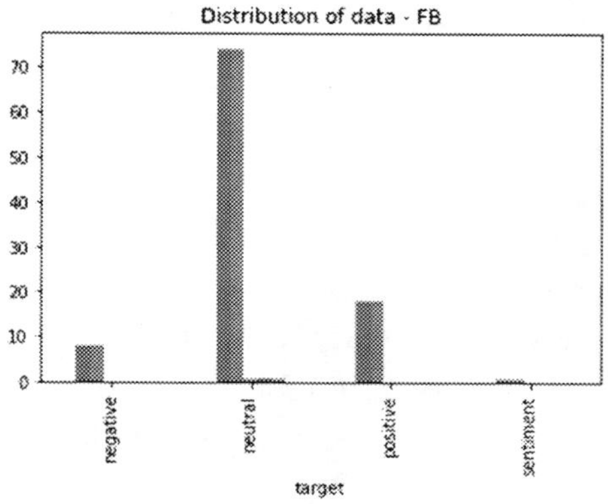

With the assistance of TextBlob, the chart presents an examination of a user's tweet following the removal of any symbols, special characters, repetitive comments, and URLs that were deemed unnecessary. It displays the number of positive, negative, or neutral comments towards the particular company (figure 2).

Figure 2. Analysis of Open, High, Low, and Close, Volume of Amazon and Facebook

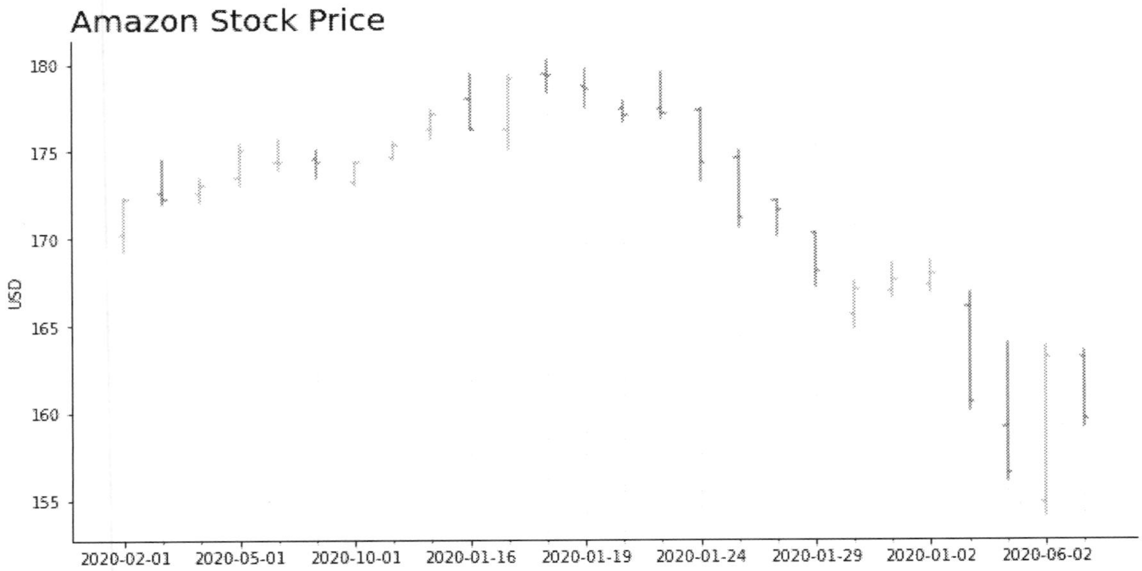

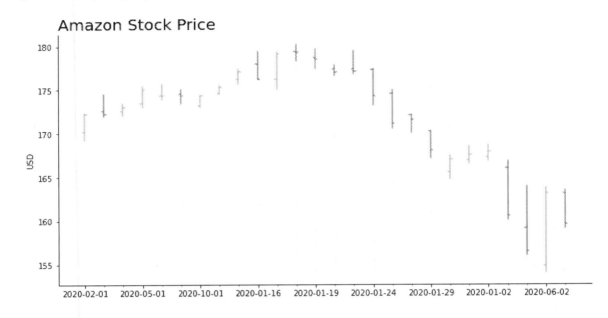

The graph shown above illustrates how the growth or decline of a given stock's share price is dependent on that stock's OHLCV (figure 3). By contrasting this value with the results of our analysis of sentiment, it is possible to determine how accurate this sentiment prediction is (table 1).

Table 1. Shows that the stock's correctness has improved by 60 per cent

Stock	Accuracy
Amazon	0.672
Facebook	0.58

Figure 3. Plot between Actual and Predicted

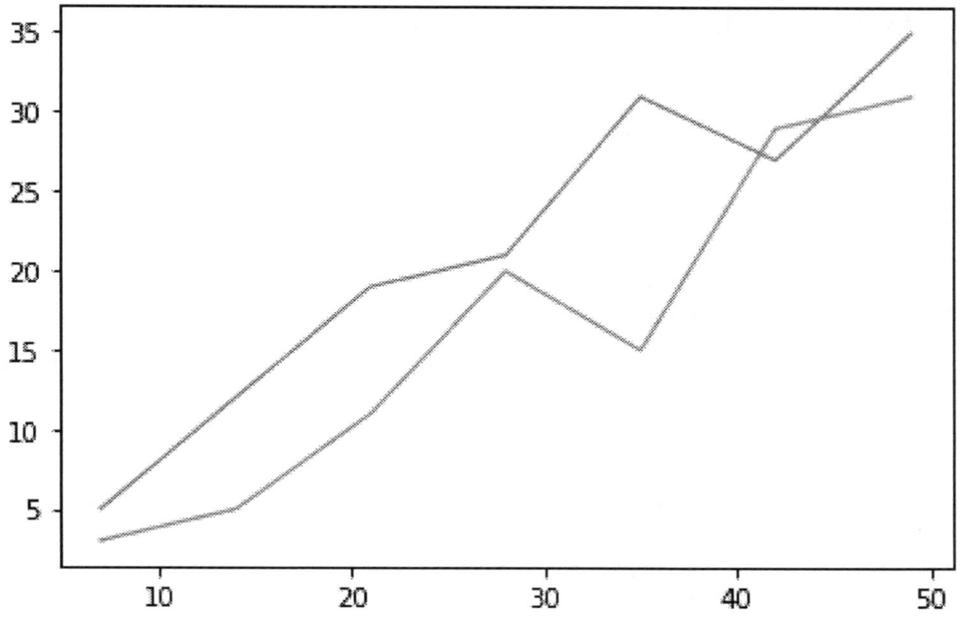

This graph provides a visual representation of a comparison between the actual stock and the expected stock. On the other hand, the orange line indicates the prediction, while the blue line depicts the actual stock. When a trend has been seen for an extended length of time, then predictions can get close to predicting the actual trend. As the training continues, the trainee will eventually achieve higher precision.

CONCLUSION AND FUTURE WORK

In this research, we propose a method for improving the representation of sentiments based on a variety of text-based elements. After this step, a variety of feature selection algorithms are applied to make a contextual determination regarding which feature sets are the most appropriate during various seasons. Finally, an individual pattern is assembled to create the most effective stock direction classifier that is possible. My hypothesis states that the price of a company's stock will either go up or down in direct proportion to the sentiment or opinion communicated on Twitter. The only thing that must be done is to perfect the collection of textual features that indicate sentiment and mature sentiment analysis through machine learning algorithms. Because of the dynamic and complicated nature of stock time series data, the upcoming focus of my study will be on applying deep learning techniques not only to construct sentiment characteristics for stock movement but also to model it in a predictive manner. Embedded words and stock aspects will be extracted; however, this depends on the approach taken.

REFERENCES

Abdolmaleky, M., Naseri, M., Batle, J., Farouk, A., & Gong, L. H. (2017). Red-Green-Blue multi-channel quantum representation of digital images. *Optik (Stuttgart)*, *128*, 121–132. doi:10.1016/j.ijleo.2016.09.123

Abu-Rumman, A. (2021). Effective Knowledge Sharing: A Guide to the Key Enablers and Inhibitors. In D. Tessier (Ed.), *Handbook of Research on Organizational Culture Strategies for Effective Knowledge Management and Performance* (pp. 133–156). IGI Global. doi:10.4018/978-1-7998-7422-5.ch008

Abu-Rumman, A., & Qawasmeh, R. (2022, December 06). And Qawasmeh, R (2021). "Assessing international students' satisfaction of a Jordanian university using the service quality model. *Journal of Applied Research in Higher Education*, *14*(4), 1742–1760. doi:10.1108/JARHE-05-2021-0166

Abulkasim, H., Alsuqaih, H. N., Hamdan, W. F., Hamad, S., Farouk, A., Mashatan, A., & Ghose, S. (2019). Improved dynamic multiparty quantum private comparison for next-generation mobile network. *IEEE Access: Practical Innovations, Open Solutions*, *7*, 17917–17926. doi:10.1109/ACCESS.2019.2894101

Abulkasim, H., Farouk, A., Alsuqaih, H., Hamdan, W., Hamad, S., & Ghose, S. (2018). Improving the security of quantum key agreement protocols with single photon in both polarisation and spatial-mode degrees of freedom. *Quantum Information Processing*, *17*(11), 1–11. doi:10.100711128-018-2091-7

Abulkasim, H., Farouk, A., Hamad, S., Mashatan, A., & Ghose, S. (2019). Secure dynamic multiparty quantum private comparison. *Scientific Reports*, *9*(1), 1–16. doi:10.103841598-019-53967-9 PMID:31780675

Adil, M., Ali, J., Attique, M., Jadoon, M. M., Abbas, S., Alotaibi, S. R., & Farouk, A. (2021a). Three Byte-Based Mutual Authentication Scheme for Autonomous Internet of Vehicles. *IEEE Transactions on Intelligent Transportation Systems*.

Adil, M., Attique, M., Khan, M. M., Ali, J., Farouk, A., & Song, H. (2022a). HOPCTP: A Robust Channel Categorization Data Preservation Scheme for Industrial Healthcare Internet of Things. *IEEE Transactions on Industrial Informatics*, *18*(10), 7151–7161. doi:10.1109/TII.2022.3148287

Adil, M., Jan, M. A., Mastorakis, S., Song, H., Jadoon, M. M., Abbas, S., & Farouk, A. (2021b). Hash-MAC-DSDV: Mutual Authentication for Intelligent IoT-Based Cyber-Physical Systems. *IEEE Internet of Things Journal*.

Adil, M., Khan, M. K., Jadoon, M. M., Attique, M., Song, H., & Farouk, A. (2022b). An AI-enabled Hybrid lightweight Authentication Scheme for Intelligent IoMT based Cyber-Physical Systems. *IEEE Transactions on Network Science and Engineering*, 1. doi:10.1109/TNSE.2022.3159526

Adil, M., Khan, M. K., Jamjoom, M., & Farouk, A. (2021c). MHADBOR: AI-enabled Administrative Distance based Opportunistic Load Balancing Scheme for an Agriculture Internet of Things Network. *IEEE Micro*.

Adil, M., Song, H., Ali, J., Jan, M. A., Attique, M., Abbas, S., & Farouk, A. (2021d). EnhancedAODV: A Robust Three Phase Priority-based Traffic Load Balancing Scheme for Internet of Things. *IEEE Internet of Things Journal*.

Al-Naif, K. L. & Al Shraah A. E. M. (2018). Working capital management and profitability: Evidence from Jordanian mining and extraction industry sector. *IUG Journal of Economics and Business, 2*(1), pp 42-60.

Al Shraah, A., Abu-Rumman, A., Alqhaiwi, L. A., & Alsha'ar, H. (2022). The impact of sourcing strategies and logistics capabilities on organizational performance during the COVID-19 pandemic: Evidence from Jordanian pharmaceutical industries. *Uncertain Supply Chain Management, 10*(3), 1077–1090. doi:10.5267/j.uscm.2022.2.004

Al Shraah, A., Irtaimeh, H. J., & Rumman, M. A. (2013). The Strategic Human Resource Management Practices in Implying Total Quality Management (TQM): An Empirical Study on Jordanian Banking Sector. *International Journal of Management, 4*(5), 179–190.

Aoudni, Y., Donald, C., Farouk, A., Sahay, K. B., Babu, D. V., Tripathi, V., & Dhabliya, D. (2022). Cloud security based attack detection using transductive learning integrated with Hidden Markov Model. *Pattern Recognition Letters, 157*, 16–26. doi:10.1016/j.patrec.2022.02.012

Devani, D., & Patel, M. (2022). Stock market (BSE) prediction using unsupervised sentiment analysis and LSTM: A hybrid approach,. in *Proceedings of the 2nd International Conference on Recent Trends in Machine Learning, IoT, Smart Cities and Applications. Singapore: Springer Nature Singapore,* pp. 79–87. Springer. 10.1007/978-981-16-6407-6_8

Farouk, A., Alahmadi, A., Ghose, S., & Mashatan, A. (2020). Blockchain platform for industrial healthcare: Vision and future opportunities. *Computer Communications, 154*, 223–235. doi:10.1016/j.comcom.2020.02.058

Farouk, A., Batle, J., Elhoseny, M., Naseri, M., Lone, M., Fedorov, A., & Abdel-Aty, M. (2018). Robust general N user authentication scheme in a centralised quantum communication network via generalised GHZ states. *Frontiers in Physics, 13*(2), 1–18.

Farouk, A., Zakaria, M., Megahed, A., & Omara, F. A. (2015). A generalised architecture of quantum secure direct communication for N disjointed users with authentication. *Scientific Reports, 5*(1), 1–17. doi:10.1038rep16080 PMID:26577473

Guo, Y., Han, S., Shen, C., Li, Y., Yin, X., & Bai, Y. (2018). An adaptive SVR for high-frequency stock price forecasting. *IEEE Access: Practical Innovations, Open Solutions, 6*, 11397–11404. doi:10.1109/ACCESS.2018.2806180

Gurav, U., & Sidnal, N. (2018). Predict stock market behavior: Role of machine learning algorithms. In Intelligent Computing and Information and Communication. Springer.

Heidari, S., Abutalib, M. M., Alkhambashi, M., Farouk, A., & Naseri, M. (2019). A new general model for quantum image histogram (QIH). *Quantum Information Processing, 18*(6), 1–20. doi:10.100711128-019-2295-5

Karuppusamy, S., & Singaravel, G. (2019). *Investigation Analysis for Software Fault Prediction using Error Probabilities and Integral Methods* (Vol. 13). Applied Mathematics & Information Sciences An International Journal.

Khan, W., Ghazanfar, M. A., Azam, M. A., Karami, A., Alyoubi, K. H., & Alfakeeh, A. S. (2022). Stock market prediction using machine learning classifiers and social media, news. *Journal of Ambient Intelligence and Humanized Computing*, *13*(7), 3433–3456. doi:10.100712652-020-01839-w

Mendonça, R. V., Silva, J. C., Rosa, R. L., Saadi, M., Rodriguez, D. Z., & Farouk, A. (2021). A lightweight intelligent intrusion detection system for industrial internet of things using deep learning algorithm. *Expert Systems: International Journal of Knowledge Engineering and Neural Networks*, 12917.

Metwaly, A. F., Rashad, M. Z., Omara, F. A., & Megahed, A. A. (2014). Architecture of multicast centralised key management scheme using quantum key distribution and classical symmetric encryption. *The European Physical Journal. Special Topics*, *223*(8), 1711–1728. doi:10.1140/epjst/e2014-02118-x

Naseri, M., Abdolmaleky, M., Laref, A., Parandin, F., Celik, T., Farouk, A., Mohamadi, M., & Jalalian, H. (2018a). A new cryptography algorithm for quantum images. *Optik (Stuttgart)*, *171*, 947–959. doi:10.1016/j.ijleo.2018.06.113

Naseri, M., Abdolmaleky, M., Parandin, F., Fatahi, N., Farouk, A., & Nazari, R. (2018b). A new quantum gray-scale image encoding scheme. *Communications in Theoretical Physics*, *69*(2), 215. doi:10.1088/0253-6102/69/2/215

Naseri, M., Heidari, S., Baghfalaki, M., Gheibi, R., Batle, J., Farouk, A., & Habibi, A. (2017). A new secure quantum watermarking scheme. *Optik (Stuttgart)*, *139*, 77–86. doi:10.1016/j.ijleo.2017.03.091

Naseri, M., Raji, M. A., Hantehzadeh, M. R., Farouk, A., Boochani, A., & Solaymani, S. (2015). A scheme for secure quantum communication network with authentication using GHZ-like states and cluster states controlled teleportation. *Quantum Information Processing*, *14*(11), 4279–4295. doi:10.100711128-015-1107-9

Reshma, R. (2021). Stock market prediction using machine learning techniques. In Advances in Parallel Computing Technologies and Applications. IOS Press.

Zhou, N. R., Liang, X. R., Zhou, Z. H., & Farouk, A. (2016). Relay selection scheme for amplify-and-forward cooperative communication system with artificial noise. *Security and Communication Networks*, *9*(11), 1398–1404. doi:10.1002ec.1425

Zhu, F., Zhang, C., Zheng, Z., & Farouk, A. (2021). Practical Network Coding Technologies and Softwarization in Wireless Networks. *IEEE Internet of Things Journal*, *8*(7), 5211–5218. doi:10.1109/JIOT.2021.3056580

Chapter 5
An Overview of Available Deepfake Datasets in Neural Network-Based Soil and Weather Prediction Models for High Quality Crops

A. Anisha Sanjeetha
Nandha Engineering College, India

R. Sivaraj
Nandha Engineering College, India

P. Uma
Nandha Engineering College, India

ABSTRACT

Transportation, the environment, business, and agriculture are just a few areas where IoT and DL-based solutions are profoundly impacting. Soil nutrient insufficiency is a prevalent problem that can spread and harm plants if not addressed right away. An IoT-based system that monitors soil and weather conditions for nutrient deficiencies can help increase crop yields. One of the most crucial factors to include in existing deepfakes datasets is soil temperature when modelling terrestrial ecosystems. From January 1, 2010, through December 31, 2018, the Baker, Beach, Cando, Crary, and Fingal weather stations in North Dakota recorded daily weather and soil temperature readings. This study presents an enhanced convolutional neural network-based approach to soil and weather forecasting (CNN). In order to enhance the classification accuracy of the pre-trained CNN architecture, the slime mold algorithm is employed to optimise the model weight.

DOI: 10.4018/978-1-6684-6060-3.ch005

INTRODUCTION

If crops are not chosen properly, yields will suffer. How to interpret soil test results is a big difficulty for farmers trying to decide which crops to plant (Rehman et al., 2020). In light of this, the question of how to predict crop yields is fascinating (Ruxandra et al., 2018). Early attempts at estimating agricultural yields relied on the farmer's familiarity with a certain land and crop (Barbedo, 2013). Additionally, it will be easier to decide on additional steps if moisture, water level, and current temperature are all monitored often (Saddik et al., 2021). In addition, the system needs to know what nutrients are already present in the soil and conduct research to see if the crop needs more nutrients (Wiréhn, L., 2018). Keeping an eye on nutrient levels is essential for producing the best harvest possible (Mee et al., 2017).

Plants' capacity to take in water, sunlight, and nutrients is crucial to the success of this system. Macronutrients and micronutrients are needed by plants in various proportions (Ray et al., 2018). More abundant than micronutrients, macronutrients are essential to a plant's cells and tissues (Semary et al., 2015). Nitrogen, phosphorus, potassium, calcium, sulfur, and magnesium (Mn) are all macronutrients that a plant need (Asfarian et al., 2014). When leaves aren't getting enough macronutrients, crop production suffers. Lack of nutrition can result in stunted growth, reduced flowering, and fewer fruits produced. The symptoms of nutritional deficiencies, such as altered leaf coloration and stunted development, are listed in Table 1.

Table 1. Macronutrient deficiency symptoms

Macronutrients	Symptoms
Magnesium (Mg)	Yellow between the leaf veins with red-brown tints and early leaves fall
Nitrogen (N)	Light green of upper leaves and yellow of lower leaves.
Phosphorus (P)	Slow growth and yellow foliage.
Potassium (K)	Yellow and purple leaves with brown at leaves edge and poor flower and fruit.

Historically, deficiency shadowing has been performed by hand. Farmers frequently inspect crops to ensure they are receiving adequate nourishment (Prasad et al., 2016). The massive size of the agricultural sector presents a challenge to this strategy (Zhang et al., 2015). Researching a big area requires more time and energy (Carvajal-Yepes et al., 2019). Several strategies for the automated measurement and management of crop soil nutrient levels have been proposed by researchers in the past. Lettuce calcium deficiency in greenhouses can be detected using machine vision approaches based on temporal, colour, and morphological changes in plants (Story et al., 2020).

Applying machine learning has led to tremendous progress in recent years in the diagnosis and quantification of a wide variety of diseases. SVM, K-Nearest Neighbors (KNN), and Discriminant Analysis are some of the most widely used disease diagnosis approaches. Several studies have described automated methods for diagnosing rice diseases utilising digital images, support vector machines, pattern recognition, and computer vision (Tian et al., 2010).

Although machine learning approaches have been tremendously successful in the field of image identification, they do have some drawbacks, such as the necessity for segmentation and feature extraction (Chen et al., 2019). (Chen, & Yuan, 2019). Unhealthy area segmentation is not a simple process for all agricultural photographs (Lu et al., 2017). Consequently, current machine learning approaches fail when trying to correctly categorise images of agricultural diseases. As machine learning has progressed, deep learning techniques have proven particularly useful for processing massive datasets and developing intricate models. Deep learning methods can immediately be applied to the task of classifying photographs of agricultural distress without the need for preparatory stages such as segmentation and feature extraction.

In this research, a convolutional neural network (CNN) was used to anticipate optimal growing conditions based on soil and weather data. In Section 2, the author provides a review of the existing strategies, while Section 3 details the proposed method. Section 4 includes the results of a comprehensive validation investigation of the proposed model. Part 5 provides a brief overview of the final results of the study.

RELATED WORKS

Xing et al. (2018) applied the SVM model with AT and solar radiation as predictors throughout the course of numerous seasons across a variety of climate zones in the United States. We tested the SVM model and found that it was up to the challenge (Jian & Wei, 2010). Samadianfard et al. (2018) used wavelet transformations in tandem with ANN and GEP models to predict ST at a range of depths in Tabriz, Iran. Predictions were made using a variety of factors, such as solar radiation and the absence of air conditioning. Soil temperature (ST) at different depths in Turkey was predicted using this model by Sanikhani et al. (2018), who employed it as a non-tuned prediction model. In comparison to artificial neural network and M5 Tree models, it performed exceptionally well. We estimated the result of this experiment using several different factors. Parameters such as temperature, solar radiation, relative humidity, and wind speed were measured.

For instance, precision agriculture enabled by the internet of things (IoT) enables farmers to make more informed decisions about the care of their crops (Salam et al., 2019). (Ahmed et al., 2018). In this article, Raj et al. (2019) describe how IoT can be used to automatically collect data in a sustainable environment. There is also real-time analysis for detecting calmness (Vijayakumar and Vinothkanna, 2020).

The use of a genetic algorithm and a back propagation neural network for irrigation scheduling in litchi orchards was investigated (BPNN). When to water was dependent on the soil's moisture content. Despite this, there is zero information available regarding the influence of soil moisture on litchi development at any time. In order to forecast soil moisture one day in advance, Adeyemi et al. (2018) used data from three weather stations to create an LSTM-based dynamic network model. Weather and soil moisture information were also included in the input items. When comparing the predicted and real soil moisture levels, we were only able to obtain an R2 value of 0.99. However, the model was not tested in this investigation across several growth seasons.

Soil moisture and electrical conductivity were predicted using a bidirectional LSTM model created by Gao et al. (2021) for a citrus grove. Air temperature, humidity, wind speed, and precipitation were among the variables acquired by the five Internet of Things nodes used in the model. These factors were crucial in shaping the final design. Results showed that the bidirectional LSTM model performed well in forecasting soil moisture. Values predicted and observed had a correlation of 0.964. The model was validated at five IoT nodes, but all of the citrus trees we looked at bore fruit every year, despite the fact that their watering needs would likely change with the seasons.

PROPOSED METHODOLOGY

Dataset Explanation

Due to its central location in North America, North Dakota (ND) experiences both harsh winters and scorching summers. The climate is marked by dramatic temperature shifts for each of the four seasons, resulting in distinct weather patterns. The climate in the eastern and western sections of North Dakota is very distinct from each other. North Dakota is classified as having humid continental and semi-arid climates by the Köppen–Geiger classification system. ND has seen an average temperature increase of 3 °C since 2000, according to the US Global Change Research Program. Crary station's soil fever fluctuations over nine years were more pronounced and long-lasting than those observed at other sites. Baker and Fingal stations' STs have generally remained consistent over the years.

On the other hand, Cando station had the greatest range of ST during the nine years. There were no significant differences between the lowest and highest ST between 2010 and 2012, and 2014 and 2018 were the slowest risers until 2018. Overall, the ST differences appeared to be more pronounced for each year except for 2012 and 2015, when they were the smallest during this period.

Baker and Fingal were the least reliable stations in 2012, while Beach and Cando were the least reliables 2012. Baker, Beach, Cando, and Fingal all had lower ST values throughout the nine years, whereas Crary had lower ST values more than three times.

Table 2. Statistical analysis of the ST dataset at the meteorological station

	Minimum	Average	Maximum	Skewness	SD
Baker	31.0	47433.2	82379.0	0.32	17770.0
Beach	53.0	48494.0	82713.0	0.29	17117.0
Fingal	30.0	48349.0	87334.0	0.20	19019.0
Cando	29.0	46328.0	83643.0	0.30	17006.5
Crary	8513.0	46465.0	86404.0	0.20	19870.3

Various soil properties have been measured using a systematic approach. Data from sensors can be displayed on a digital screen or transmitted as serial input to the cloud system. The system can also be used to remotely monitor soil conditions and to keep tabs on crops. The 2000 × 1000 sq. ft. space is used to gather data in real-time. The entire field is divided into three sections, one of which is 1000 × 1000 square feet and receives direct morning sunlight. The other two sections, 500 x 500 square feet, receive indirect morning sunlight exclusively. Then there's the other side, which is shielded from the sun. Sensors connected to a Raspberry Pi 3 continuously monitor moisture, temperature, and water level. From this, the cloud environment can analyze the soil's necessary properties. Periodic measurements of the nutrients in the soil are used to assess its progress.

Hybrid Classification

In this section, hybrid Classification includes learning rate optimization for CNN using Slime Mold optimization is described briefly. Initially, the CNN is explained as follows:

Classification Using CNN

CNN is a feed-forward neural network with numerous layers containing convolution, ReLU, and fully connected output layers of the convolutional neural network (CNN). CNN can recognize image elements such as edges and shapes.

Convolutional Layer

A convolutional layer is always the initial layer in a CNN design. A CNN's input layer typically accepts MxNx1 as input. It's the two-dimensional size of a single-layer image in MxN. Using the same depth parameters as the input image, CNN utilizes a filter that is convolved with that image. Image processing software uses a filter to alter an image into another image. Convolution raises the value of the shape that mimics the input image's curve, represented by the filter. An equation can be used to express a convolution procedure (1).

$$s(t) = (x^{*}w)(t) \tag{1}$$

Pooling Layer

Using the pooling layer, you can reduce the amount of data you have. Pooling is the process of grouping the matrix data into distinct segments and then substituting the entire segment with a single value, thus lowering the metrics data dimensions. Maximum and average values of all the values within the current segment can be used as replacements for the segmented matrices in popular pooling algorithms like Maxpooling and Average-pooling (as shown in Figure 1).

Figure 1. Some of the pre-trained deep CNN

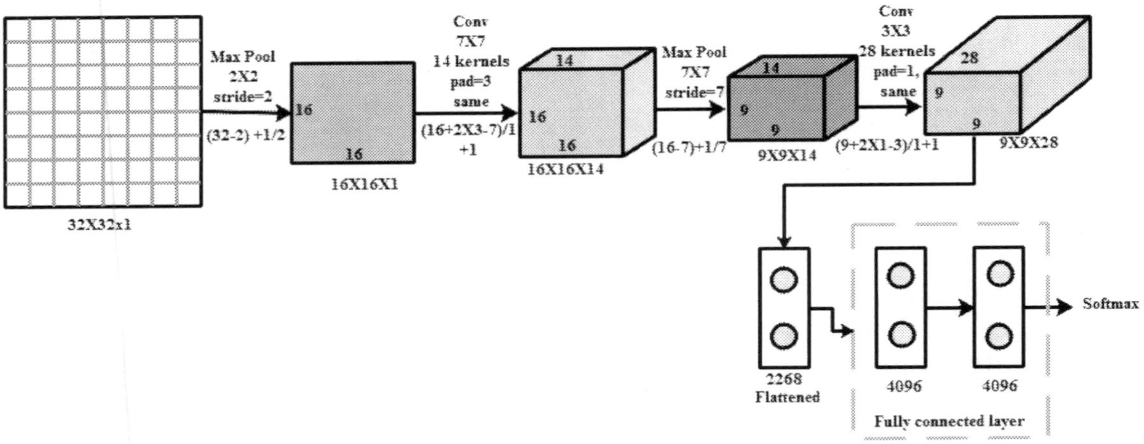

Fully Connected Layer

The dimensionality of layers in a fully linked layer is changed to meet the network layer architecture. A function operation with connected m or n input and output dimensions is called a fully connected layer. As in a normal artificial neural network, all the activations from the preceding layer are connected to the following layer by a completely connected layer.

Soft-Max Layer

For each class, the Soft-max function calculates a probability for the sum of the probabilities from the input from the preceding layers. Because the anticipated output class has the highest likelihood based on the supplied input data, this layer is crucial. Classifying photos using deep neural networks is possible. This study's first deep network was pre-trained to categorize other photos. Still, we may use transfer learning to adapt it to our classification task by adjusting key parameters: linear networks. The proposed model's parameters are shown in Table 2.

The networks' training hyperparameters have been held at a constant value. We've broken down the data into a maximum of 25 epochs. Model internal parameters are changed after a certain number of samples, called the mini-batch size. In our experiment, we kept the number of mini-batches at seven and the initial learning rate at 0.0001.

Table 2. 1D multi-scale Main parameters of convolution layer

Layer name	Output Shape	Kernel size	Numbers of kernel	Stride	Padding
Max pooling1-1	16X16X1	2	--	2	--
Convolution1-1	16X16X14	2	14	Same	3
Max pooling1-2	9X9X14	7	--	7	--
Convolution1-2	9X9X28	3	28	Same	1
Flattened	9X9X28	--	--	--	--
Fully connected layer (2)	4096	--	--	--	--
Output (softmax)	2	--	--	--	--

Optimization using Slime Mold Algorithm (SMA)

As a relatively new meta-heuristic algorithm, the slime mold algorithm (SMA) draws inspiration from slime mold's foraging behaviour, which has variable feedback characteristics depending on the quality of its prey. Approaching food, wrapping food and finally grabbing food are mathematically defined in the slime mold's SMA. Approaching food can be described as the first step in the process.

$$Xi(t+1)=\begin{cases} Xb(t)+vb.(W.XA(t)-XB(t)), e=r1<p \\ vc.Xi(t), r1\geq p \end{cases} \tag{2}$$

Iteration number is t, Xi(t+1) is a new position, Xb(t) is the best location found by slime mold in iteration t, XA(t) and (t+1), two random positions taken from the population of slime mold, and r1 is a random value in [0, 1].

Each time an iteration occurs, the coefficient vc decreases linearly from one to zero to imitate slime mold's oscillation and contraction modes. A's computational formula is vb's range, and vb's range is a to a

$$a = arctanh\left(1-\frac{t}{T}\right) \tag{3}$$

In this case, the maximum number of iterations is T. In Equations 2 and 3, it can be shown that as the number of iterations grows, the slime mold will wrap around the meal.

The following formula is used to compute W, an important indicator of slime mold weight:

$$W(SmellIndex(i))=\begin{cases} 1+rand.log\left(\frac{bF-S(i)}{bF-\omega F}+1\right), i\leq N/2 \\ 1-rand.log\left(\frac{bF-S(i)}{bF-\omega F}+1\right), i>N/2 \end{cases} \tag{4}$$

$$SmellIndex(i) = sort(S(i)) \tag{5}$$

A random value between zero and one is called a rand; bF and wF are the best and worst fitness values found so far; S(i) is a slime mold's fitness value, N is the population's size, and SmellIndex is a ranking of the fitness values of the population's members in order of decreasing size.

According to Equation 2, in which slime mold's fitness values and food's fitness values are used, p is the chance of finding the slime mold's updated location:

$$p = \tanh\left|S(i) - DF\right| \tag{6}$$

where DF stands for the population's best fitness.

It is also possible for the slime mold to look for new food (z) after it has located the food (i.e., grabble food).

$$X(t+1) = rand.(UB - LB) + LB, r2 < z \tag{7}$$

To put it another way, r2 represents a random value within the range of [0, 1] for UB and LB.

So, z is set to 0.03 in SMA as a general rule of thumb. Algorithm 1 concludes with the pseudocode for SMA.

Initialize the parameters popsize(N) and maximum iterations(T)

Initialize the positions of all slime mold Xi(i = 1, 2, ..., N)

While(t ≤ T)

Calculate the fitness of all slime mold

Update bestFitness, Xb

Calculate the weight W by Equation(4) and (5)

For each search agent

If r2 < z

Update position by Equation(7)

$Else$

$Update\ p, vb, and\ vc$

$Update\ position\ by\ Equation(2)$

$End\ if$

$End\ for$

$t = t + 1$

$End\ While$

$Return\ bestFitness, Xb$

RESULTS AND DISCUSSION

Performance Metrics

The proposed predictive models were assessed using four performance indicators.

- **Root mean square error (RMSE):** It is calculated by the next equation:

$$RMSE = \sqrt{\frac{1}{n}\sum_{i=1}^{n}\left(a_i - p_i\right)^2} \tag{8}$$

- **Standard deviation (STD):** It is calculated by the subsequent equation:

$$STD = \sqrt{\frac{1}{n}\sum_{i=1}^{n}\left(RMSE_i - \mu\right)^2} \tag{9}$$

where μ is the mean value of the RMSE.

- Mean Absolute Error (MAE):

$$MAE = \frac{1}{n}\sum_{i=1}^{n}\left|a_i - p_i\right| \quad (10)$$

Root Mean Squared Relative Error (RMSRE)

$$RMSRE = \sqrt{\frac{1}{n}\sum_{i=1}^{n}\left(\left|\frac{a_i - p_i}{a_i}\right|\right)^2} \quad (11)$$

Validation of Proposed model

Figure 2 shows the scatter plots of the proposed methodology for various stations.

Figure 2. Scatted Plots of the Proposed model for five different stations ((a) Baker, b) Beach, c) Cando, d) Crary, and e) Fingal stations)

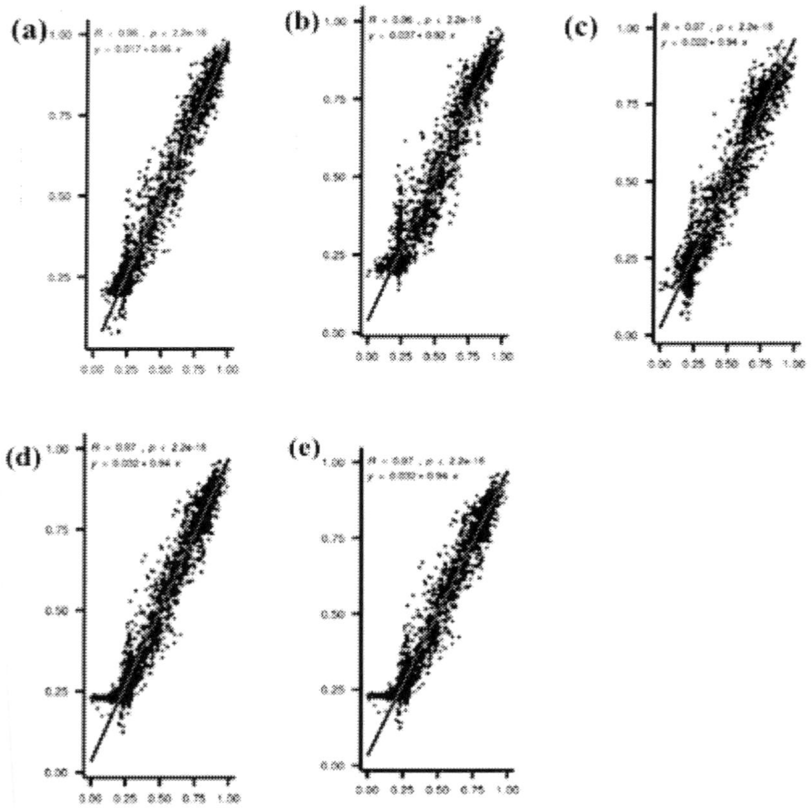

The proposed model's performance is compared to another meta-heuristic strategy for increasing the rate at which a CNN model learns. The suggested CNN-SMA is being compared to the normal CNN, the CNN with Genetic Algorithm (GA), and the CNN with Particle Swarm Optimization (PSO). Tables 3 to 7 show the performance of approaches in terms of various metrics for five metrological stations (figures 3 to 7).

Table 3. Statistical performance of predictive models at Baker meteorological station in the testing phase

Technique	RMSE	MAE	STD	RMSRE
CNN-SMA	0.058	0.044	0.0014	0.483
CNN-GA	0.112	0.091	0.0165	0.487
CNN-PSO	0.059	0.045	0.0013	0.552
CNN	0.215	0.182	0.1123	2.063

Figure 3. Graphical Representation of the proposed model for Baker station

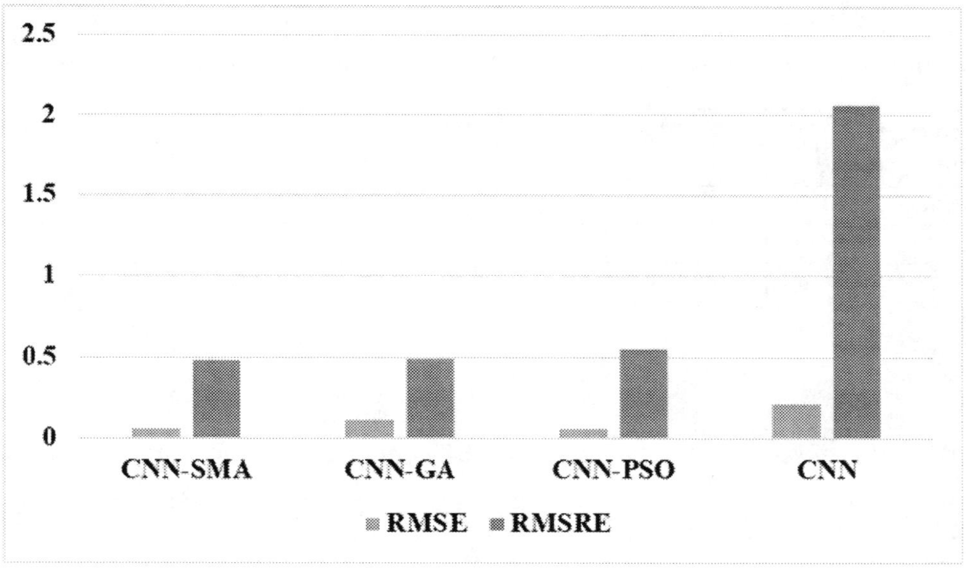

Figure 4. Graphical Representation of Proposed model with existing techniques at Baker Station

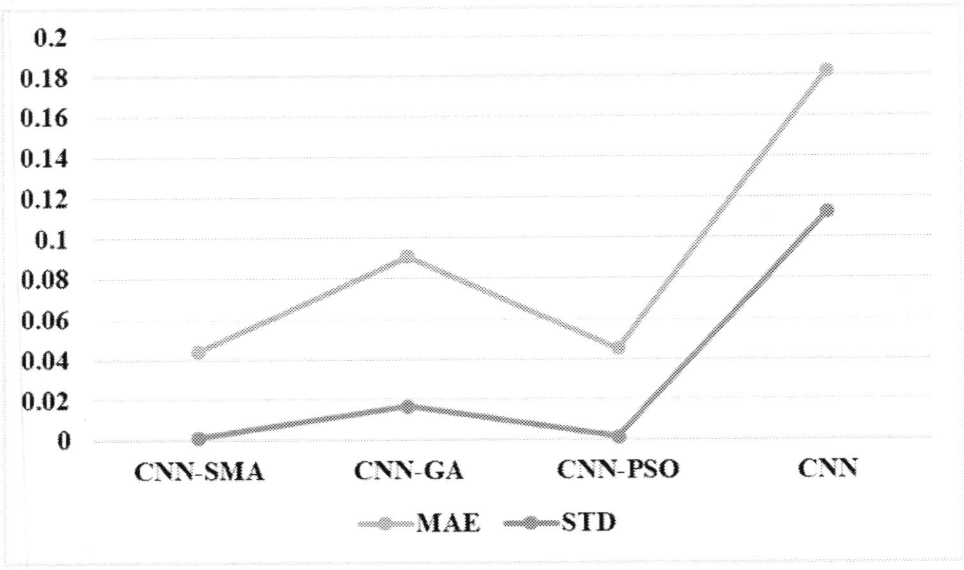

Table 4. Statistical performance of predictive models at Beach meteorological station in the testing phase

Technique	RMSE	MAE	STD	RMSRE
CNN-SMA	0.067	0.052	0.0022	0.034
CNN-GA	0.144	0.152	0.0614	0.703
CNN-PSO	0.274	0.160	0.0824	0.729
CNN	0.262	0.218	0.2094	0.402

Table 5. Statistical performance of predictive models at Cando meteorological station in the testing phase

Technique	RMSE	MAE	STD	RMSRE
CNN-SMA	0.067	0.052	0.0022	0.034
CNN-GA	0.215	0.152	0.0614	0.703
CNN-PSO	0.224	0.160	0.0824	0.729
CNN	0.262	0.218	0.2094	0.403

Table 6. Statistical performance of predictive models at Crary meteorological station in the testing phase

Technique	RMSE	MAE	STD	RMSRE
CNN-SMA	0.0556	0.044	0.0003	0.070
CNN-GA	0.0690	0.055	0.0066	0.082
CNN-PSO	0.0638	0.050	0.0030	0.079
CNN	0.2378	0.195	0.1428	0.330

Table 7. Statistical performance of predictive replicas at Fingal meteorological station in the testing phase

Technique	RMSE	MAE	STD	RMSRE
CNN-SMA	0.057	0.045	0.0011	0.027
CNN-GA	0.0230	0.164	0.0565	0.782
CNN-PSO	0.323	0.153	0.0912	0.924
CNN	0.296	0.256	0.1732	0.420

Figure 5. Graphical Representation of the proposed model with existing techniques in terms of RMSE for different stations

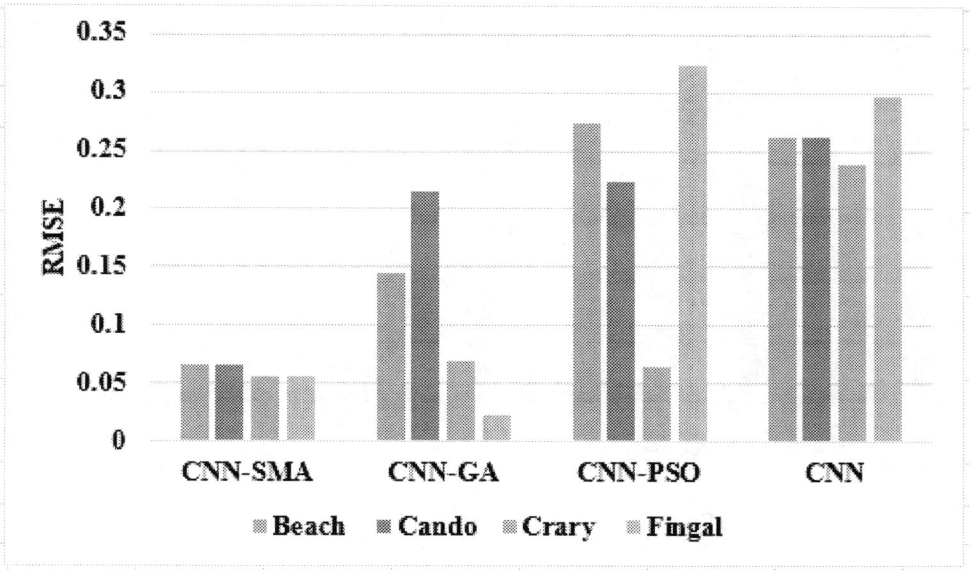

Figure 6. Overall Output Snap of soil and weather conditions for nutrient deficiencies of crop yields

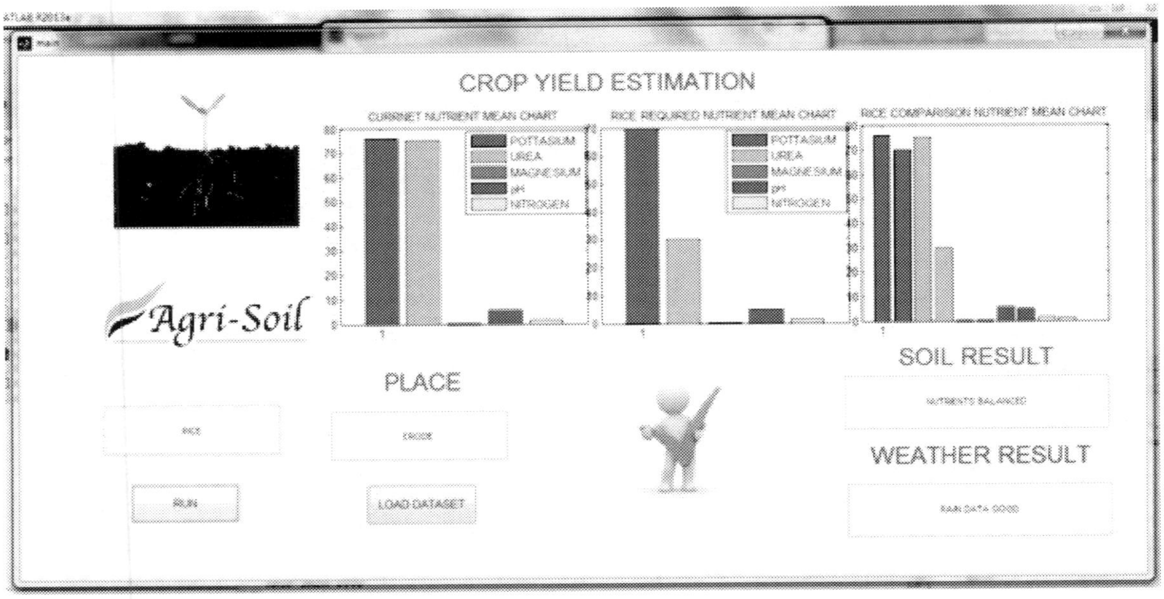

Figure 7. Wheather Data Input Snap

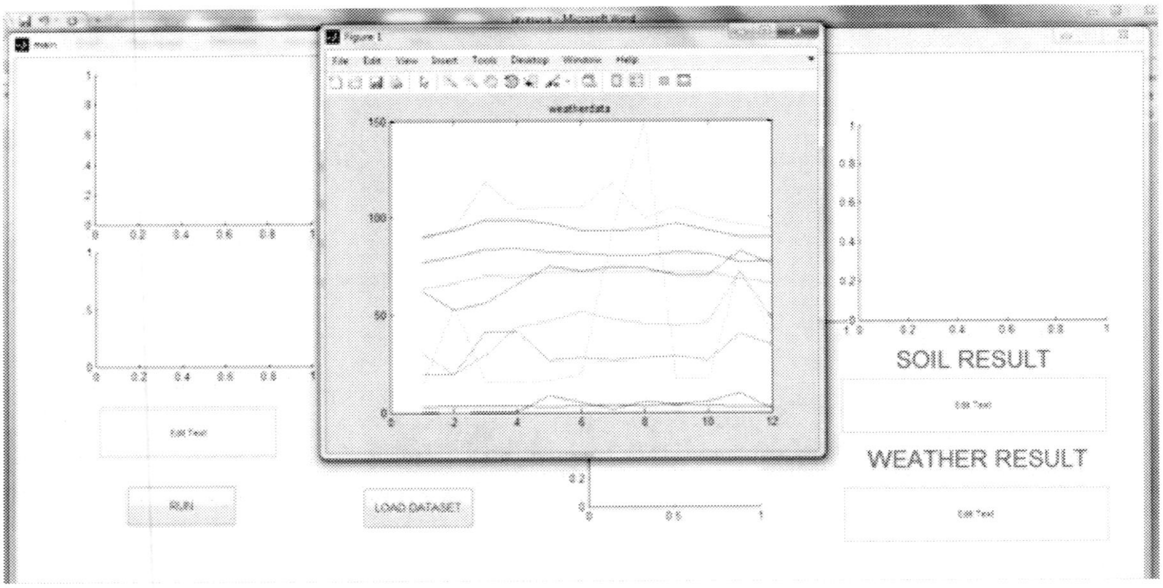

There were no significant differences between CNN, CNN-GA, and CNN-PSO in terms of RMSE and MAE between the CNN-SMA model and all other stations, except for Fingal, where CNN-SMG had the greatest performance, exhibiting an 81% improvement in MAE and an 82% improvement in

RMSE. The proposed CNN-SMA showed the greatest improvement in performance at Cando Station (0.067 RMSE and 0.052 MAE) compared to the least-performed model (i.e., CNN). However, CNN's model had the greatest MAE and RMSE values for every station except Cando (See Tables 3-7). This can be attributed to the most fluctuating soil and air temperatures from 2010 to 2018. Station-specific analyses of the mean absolute error (a) and root mean squared error (b) of predictive models throughout the testing phase. This model and all of the stations confirmed the existence of the erratic fluctuation. The CNN-GA model was the second-best performer across all stations except the Crary one, where CNN-PSO scored higher based on the same values of the performance matrices. The genetic algorithm and particle swarm optimization, two optimization methods inspired by the resilience of nature, may provide an explanation for this phenomenon. It's also feasible that, over the course of a year, all weather stations monitored the extreme soil temperature and AT showed increasingly cold temperatures as time went on. A potential alternative to CNN's model is CNN-PSO, with the exception of the Beach station, where it performed worse in terms of RMSE and MAE. AT showed the lowest year-to-year variance of all the meteorological stations, possibly due to the wide variations in Beach's geographical location among all the sites. One of the reasons for CNN's poor performance is that it is tested using a standard model, but alternative models are improved using various techniques that demonstrate superior performance.

CONCLUSION

A univariate modelling approach was used to predict soil and weather using only data on air temperature. The proposed intelligence model (i.e., CNN-SMA) was tested against the objective soil and weather conditions at various meteorological stations in North Dakota (ND), USA. Based on three other models, the hybrid intelligence model was tested against the new one (i.e., CNN, CNN-GA and CNN-PSO). Daily records of maximum, mean, and lowest air temperature for a period of nine years were used in both the training and testing phases of the modelling process (January 1 2010 - December 31 2018). The predictive models were tested in a number of ways, one of which was through the use of statistical data. The findings suggest that a CNN model equipped with optimization methods can provide reasonably accurate estimates of soil temperatures (SMA). The estimated performance of the hybrid models built for Crary station varies slightly. Across a range of RMSE values, the CNN-SMA model performed better than the standalone CNN model in tests conducted at the Baker, Beach, Cando, Crary, and Fingal weather stations by between 73% and 87%. For forecasting soil temperatures from single-variable air-temperature situations, the CNN-SMA model performed admirably.

REFERENCE

Adeyemi, O., Grove, I., Peets, S., Domun, Y., & Norton, T. (2018). Dynamic Neural Network Modelling of Soil Moisture Content for Predictive Irrigation Scheduling. *Sensors (Basel), 18*(10), 3408. doi:10.339018103408 PMID:30314346

Ahmed, N., De, D., & Hussain, I. (2018). Internet of Things (IoT) for smart precision agriculture and farming in rural areas. *IEEE Internet of Things Journal, 5*(6), 4890–4899. doi:10.1109/JIOT.2018.2879579

Ana Ruxandra, M. I. C. U., Tudor, V., & Dumitru, E. A. (2018). *Researches on the Capacity of Marketing Agricultural Crop Production in the South-West Oltenia Region*. SCIENTIFIC PAPERS.

Asfarian, A., Herdiyeni, Y., Rauf, A., & Mutaqin, K. H. (2014). A computer vision for rice disease identification to support integrated pest management Crop. *Prot*, *61*, 103–104.

Barbedo, J. G. A. (2013). Digital image processing techniques for detecting, quantifying and classifying plant diseases. *SpringerPlus*, *2*(1), 660–672. doi:10.1186/2193-1801-2-660 PMID:24349961

Carvajal-Yepes, M., Cardwell, K., Nelson, A., Garrett, K. A., Giovani, B., Saunders, D. G., Kamoun, S., Legg, J. P., Verdier, V., Lessel, J., Neher, R. A., Day, R., Pardey, P., Gullino, M. L., Records, A. R., Bextine, B., Leach, J. E., Staiger, S., & Tohme, J. (2019). A global surveillance system for crop diseases. *Science*, *364*(6447), 1237–1239. doi:10.1126cience.aaw1572 PMID:31249049

Chen, L., & Yuan, Y. (2019). Agricultural disease image dataset for disease identification based on machine learning. In J. Li, X. Meng, Y. Zhang, W. Cui, & Z. Du (Eds.), Lecture Notes in Computer Science: Vol. 11473. *Big scientific data management. BigSDM 2018*. Springer. doi:10.1007/978-3-030-28061-1_26

Chen, Y., Wang, J., Xia, R., Zhang, Q., Cao, Z., & Yang, K. (2019). The visual object tracking algorithm research based on adaptive combination kernel. *Journal of Ambient Intelligence and Humanized Computing*, *10*(12), 4855–4867. doi:10.100712652-018-01171-4

Gao, P., Xie, J., Yang, M., Zhou, P., Chen, W., Liang, G., Chen, Y., Han, X., & Wang, W. (2021). Improved Soil Moisture and Electrical Conductivity Prediction of Citrus Orchards Based on IoT Using Deep Bidirectional LSTM. *Agriculture*, *11*(7), 635. doi:10.3390/agriculture11070635

Jian, Z., & Wei, Z. (2010). Support vector machine for recognition of cucumber leaf diseases. In*: Proceedings of the international conference on advanced computer control (ICACC),* Patiala, India, pp 264–266.

Lu, Y., Yi, S., Zeng, N., Liu, Y., & Zhang, Y. (2017). Identification of rice diseases using deep convolutional neural networks. *Neurocomputing*, *267*, 378–384. doi:10.1016/j.neucom.2017.06.023

Mee, C. Y., Balasundram, S. K., & Hanif, A. H. M. (2017). Detecting and monitoring plant nutrient stress using remote sensing approaches: A review. *Asian Journal of Plant Sciences*, *16*, 1–8.

Prasad, S., Peddoju, S. K., & Ghosh, D. (2016). Multi-resolution mobile vision system for plant leaf disease diagnosis. *Signal, Image and Video Processing*, *10*(2), 379–388. doi:10.100711760-015-0751-y

Raj, J. S., & Vijitha Ananthi, J. (2019). Automation using IoT in greenhouse environment. *Journal of Information Technology*, *1*(01), 38–47.

Ray, R. L., Fares, A., & Risch, E. (2018). Effects of drought on crop production and cropping areas in Texas. *Agricultural & Environmental Letters*, *3*(1), 170037. doi:10.2134/ael2017.11.0037

Rehman, F. U., Kalsoom, M., Adnan, M., Toor, M., & Zulfiqar, A. (2020). "Plant growth promoting rhizobacteria and their mechanisms involved in agricultural crop production: A review." SunText Rev. *Biotechnol*, *1*(2), 1–6.

Saddik, A., Latif, R., El Ouardi, A., & Elhoseney, M. (2021). VSSAgri: A Vegetation Surveillance System for precision Agriculture application. In *E3S Web of Conferences* (Vol. 297, p. 01054). EDP Sciences. doi:10.1051/e3sconf/202129701054

Salam, A., & Shah, S. (2019). Internet of things in smart agriculture: Enabling technologies. In *5th World Forum on Internet of Things (WF-IoT),* pp. 692-695. IEEE.

Samadianfard, S., Asadi, E., Jarhan, S., Kazemi, H., Kheshtgar, S., Kisi, O., Sajjadi, S., & Manaf, A. A. (2018). Wavelet neural networks and gene expression programming models to predict short-term soil temperature at different depths. *Soil & Tillage Research, 175*, 37–50. doi:10.1016/j.still.2017.08.012

Sanikhani, H., Deo, R. C., Yaseen, Z. M., Eray, O., & Kisi, O. (2018). Non-tuned data intelligent model for soil temperature estimation: A new approach. *Geoderma, 330*, 52–64. doi:10.1016/j.geoderma.2018.05.030

Semary, N. A., Tharwat, A., Elhariri, E., & Hassanien, A. E. (2015). Fruitbased tomato grading system using features fusion and support vector machine. In D. Filev, (Ed.), *Intelligent Systems'(2014). AISC* (Vol. 323, pp. 401–410). Springer. doi:10.1007/978-3-319-11310-4_35

Story, D., Kacira, M., Kubota, C., Akoglu, A., & An, L. (2010). Lettuce calcium deficiency detection with machine vision computed plant features in controlled environments. *Computers and Electronics in Agriculture, 74*(2), 238–243. doi:10.1016/j.compag.2010.08.010

Tian, Y. W., Li, T. L., Zhang, L., & Wang, X. J. (2010). Diagnosis method of cucumber disease with hyperspectral imaging in green house. *Nongye Gongcheng Xuebao (Beijing), 26*(5), 202–206.

Vijayakumar, T., & Vinothkanna, R. (2020). Mellowness Detection of Dragon Fruit Using Deep Learning Strategy [JIIP]. *Journal of Innovative Image Processing, 2*(01), 35–43. doi:10.36548/jiip.2020.1.004

Wiréhn, L. (2018). Nordic agriculture under climate change: A systematic review of challenges, opportunities and adaptation strategies for crop production. *Land Use Policy, 77*, 63–74. doi:10.1016/j.landusepol.2018.04.059

Xing, L., Li, L., Gong, J., Ren, C., Liu, J., & Chen, H. (2018). Daily soil temperatures predictions for various climates in united states using data-driven model. *Energy, 160*, 430–440. doi:10.1016/j.energy.2018.07.004

Zhang, S. W., Shang, Y. J., & Wang, L. (2015). Plant disease recognition based on plant leaf image. *J Anim Plant Sci, 25*(3), 42–45.

Chapter 6
An Introduction to Deepfakes on Cryptographic Image Security

P. Boobalan
Nandha Engineering College, India

K. Gunasekar
Nandha Engineering College, India

P. Thirumoorthy
Nandha Engineering College, India

J. Senthil
Nandha Engineering College, India

ABSTRACT

The level of protection afforded to the encryption key is directly proportional to the level of security afforded to the data being encrypted. Data transmission via networks is the primary application for encryption use. There have been many different methods developed and put into use, all of which are utilized for safeguarding sensitive image data from any kind of illegal access. Text, audio, video, graphics, and still photos are some of the numerous types of data that can be included within multimedia files. A rise in the use of multimedia content transmitted over the internet has resulted in an increase in the sortage for the content. The vast majority of current encryption algorithms are typically reserved for use with informations since they are mismatched with digitalized data. A block-based transformation technique was utilized for this project.

DOI: 10.4018/978-1-6684-6060-3.ch006

INTRODUCTION

Image Security, in our rapidly developing world, where the Internet allows critical communicates with entire peoples anong worldwide and is being progressively used as an application for e-commerce, security becomes a major issue that needs to be addressed. Image Security. Information security has evolved into an extremely important component of modern computing systems. As a result of the widespread adoption of the Internet, virtually every computer in the world is now connected to each other; however, this connectivity has also resulted in the emergence of new security threats. Therefore, there is an urgent need for security, and one component that is vital for ensuring the security of communications is cryptography (Ishaq et al., 2021).

Data in the form of digital photographs is widely communicated, stored, and utilised. Because of the importance of protecting the privacy of individuals, it is essential that biometric pictures such as fingerprints, faces, and irises not be shared outside of authorised channels. Some applications of picture encryption include the Internet, multimedia systems, medical imaging, telemedicine, and military communications. When dealing with extremely large image sizes, traditional encryption methods such as data encryption standard (DES), international data encryption algorithm (IDEA), and advanced encryption standard (RSA) are inefficient (Yousaf et al., 2021). Existing methods for text encryption are inadequate for securing digital images for a number of reasons, including the fact that an image's size is nearly always larger than that of a text message and that standard algorithms require a very long time to encrypt digital images. The goal of this research is to use this approach to create and develop new methods for image encryption, which together offer a very high level of protection.

Images undergo a SCANNING pattern that is applied to each pixel as part of the Block-Transformation procedure, where the matrix is essentially ignored. As a result, this image seems very different from the original. SCAN generates scan patterns to shuffle the blocks around, and a simple substitution rule is used to change the pixel values within each block to get the desired permutation (Rupapara et al., 2021). The final stage in producing the encrypted image is to conduct an Ex-OR operation between the block transmitted image and the carrier image, the image formed by the random numbers (Sadiq et al., 2021). The standard approach of image encryption, which employs the Blumblum algorithm to create random integers, is contrasted with the suggested system.

Cryptography

In todays digitalized world, cryptography plays a vital role in data security, It contains many terminologies like Encryption and Decryption, by using this major techniques all data datas are secured as per highy preffered mathematical and logical methodologies.

Security Requirements

- Authentication: It is a process of providing users or any accessing persons identity.
- Confidentiality: Ensuring that no intruder can able to access the resource.
- Integrity: Ensure the destination data and source data were same, without any alteration.
- Non-repudiation: The technique to confirm, if the received data is original and source data.

Symmetric Key Cryptography

In methodis also known as private-key cryptography, a secret key can either with a member or traded between the source and destination of a message (Rupapara et al., 2021). This makes the communication securely. If private key cryptography is employed to communicate confidential data between two parties, then both the sender user and the receiver user of the message are required to possess a copy of the secret key. However, there is a risk that the key will be compromised while it is en-route. You are able to give the key to the other party in advance if you are familiar with the person with whom you are exchanging communications. If, on the other hand, you need to transmit a message that is encrypted to a person that you have never met, then you will need to figure out a way to exchange keys in a secure manner. Sending information via a different channel that is also secure is one option (Rustam et al., 2021).

Asymmetric Key Cryptography

Its is like two step verification process in current day aplications, if the send to the receivers side, first the user uses the secrete key and then public key of the sender. It is the highly securable key crypto mechanism that is most used in now a days majorly. The both sender and the receiver are highly confidential in this methodology.

Existing Encryption Algorithms

S.S. Maniccam and N.G. Bourbakis (2021) have developed a technique that uses just two-dimensional ideas, requires less multitasking and processing encryption than the prior system, and can only read binary and grayscale image formats (Joseph & Auwatanamongkol, 2016).

Once standard practise for protecting digital information, the Data Encryption Standard algorithm is now widely believed to be vulnerable to brute-force attacks. The Blowfish crypto technique was discovered by Aman Jantan and Mohammad Ali ban Younes, two very technically savvy and accomplished individuals. By employing this method, we discovered that there is a negative link between block count and entropy and a direct correlation between block count and entropy (Joseph, 2022c).

It consists of numerous techniques of new algorithms and codings with the highly complex starategies. It makes the end user as securable and effective data transaction. The data that sended to the end user has the specific key, this key plays a vital role in the accessing of the original data. The key will shared to the end user as confidential message via any mode of communication. This lines clearly explains the concept of cryptology and the related procedures.

Scan Patterns

At runtime, the data will be scanned using whichever built-in mechanism happens to be available. The rows and columns of the cells used to group comparable pieces of information together make up the "two-dimensional" scanning. SCAN is a programming language that supports four different types of scan patterns: the spiral S, the continuous raster C, the continuous diagonal D, and the continuous orthogonal O. The SCAN algorithm's primary benefit is not its rapid throughput, but rather the strength of its encryption.

Rearranging the image blocks and repositioning the pixel are at the heart of the SCAN pattern-based block transformation. The pixel transactions will restore the image to its original quality, nearly identical to the source file, so there is little to no loss of quality during the process.

Using a technique called "confusion," the cypher text and the symmetric key have an intricate and convoluted relationship. The goal of the diffusion approach is to create a relationship between the plain-text and the cypher text that is as intricate and involved as possible.

Table 1. Scan pattern 1: Continuous raster (C)

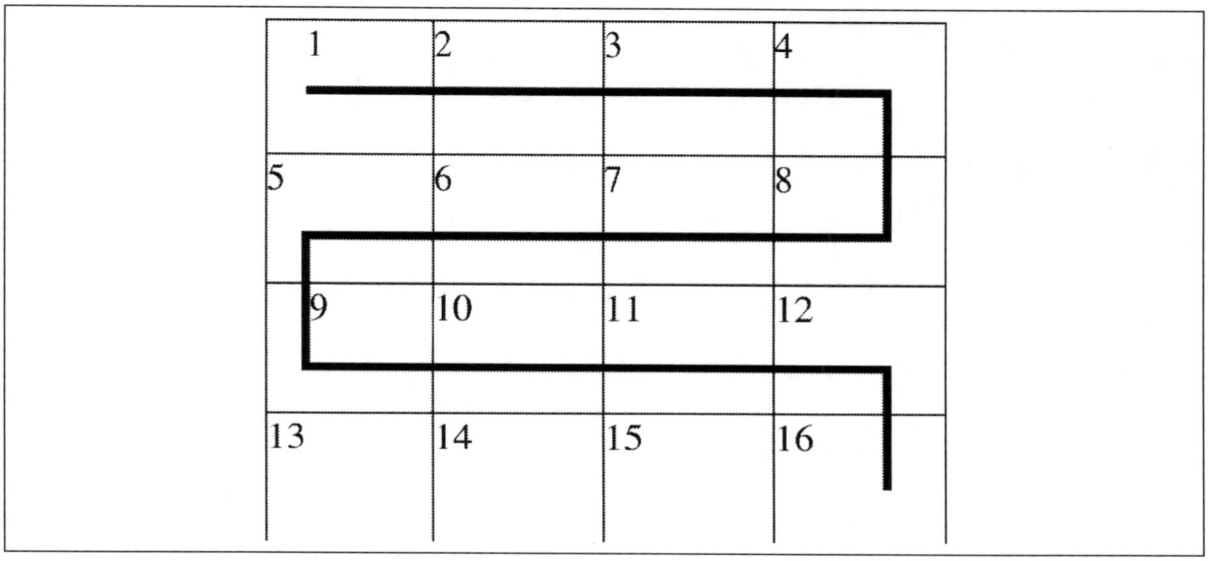

Table 2. Scan pattern 2: Continuous diagonal (D)

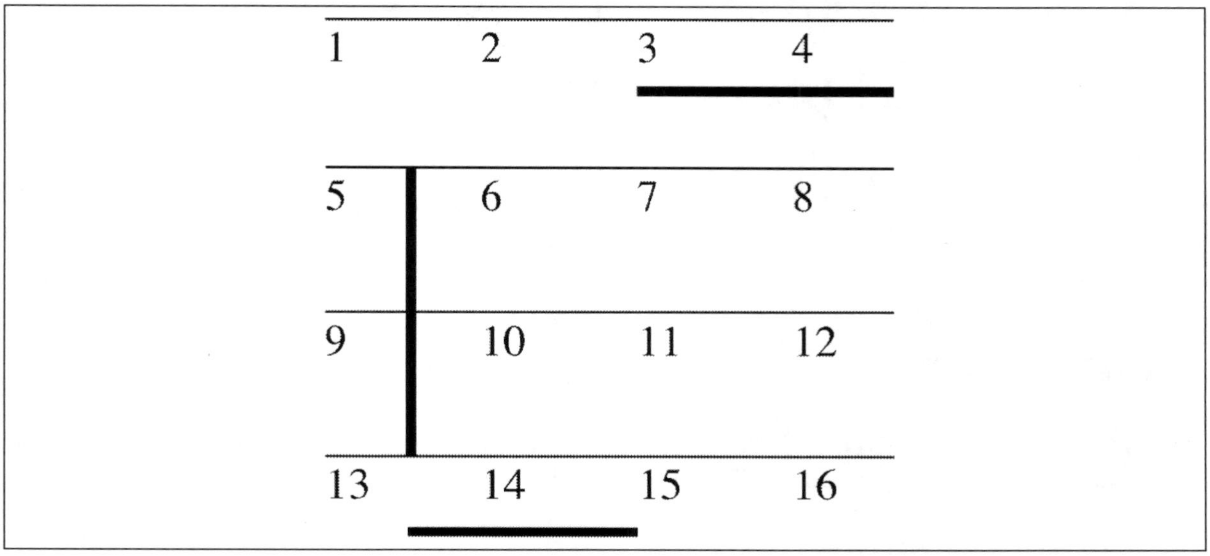

Table 3. Scan pattern 3: Continuous orthogonal (O)

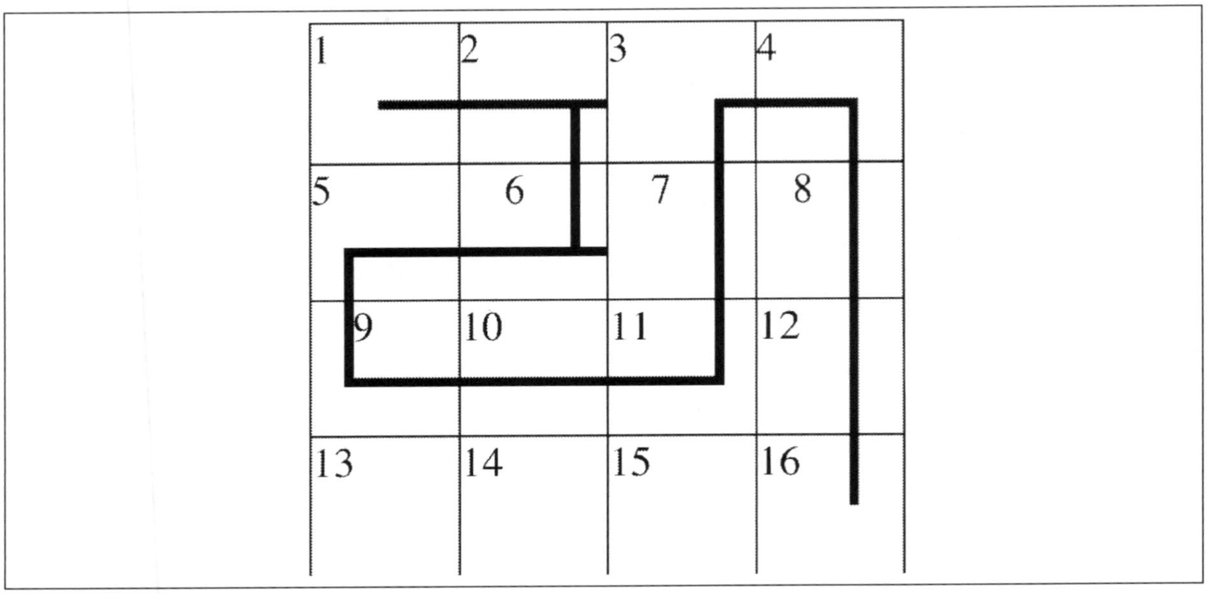

Table 4. Scan pattern 4: Continuous spiral (S)

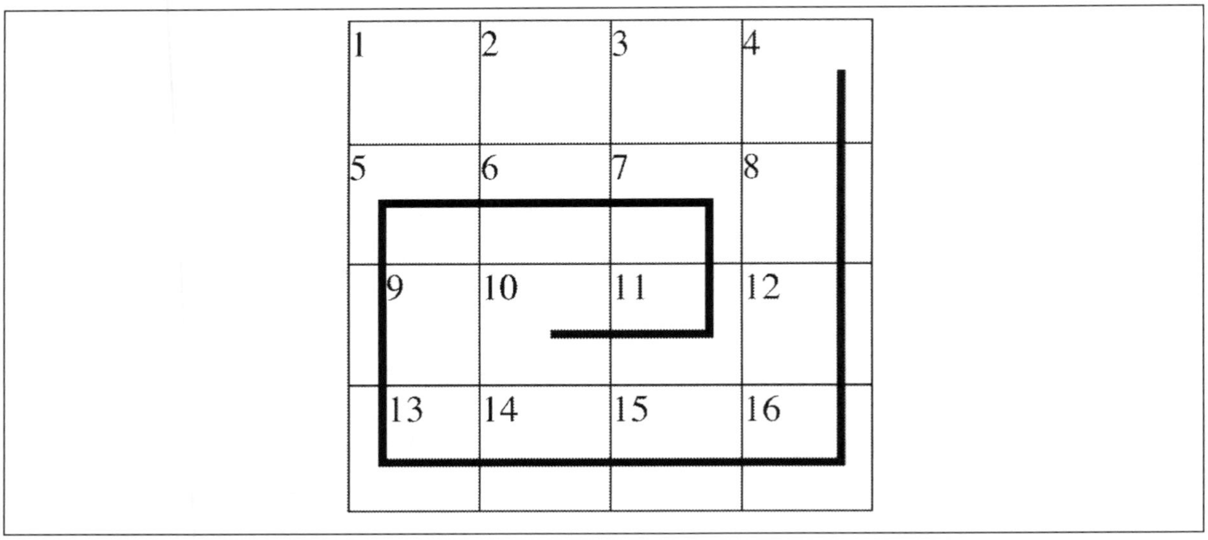

LITERATURE SURVEY

Data security, often known as cryptography, is the field that studies how to keep sensitive information secret (Maniccam & Bourbakis, 2004). The fields of cryptology and cryptanalysis are inextricably linked to the term "cryptography." The history of cryptography is rooted in the practise of secret communication. Regardless, in today's PC-driven world, cryptography is commonly associated with the process of encrypting and decrypting plaintext (standard text, sometimes referred to as cleartext) into ciphertext (known as decoding). Cryptographers are the specialists who work in this area.

Calculations of this kind encrypt and decrypt communications with a key, making it difficult to read or understand the content without the key. Keys used for encryption and decryption in a symmetric cryptosystem share the same secret (Upadhyay et al., 2016).

These equations use two distinct keys to scramble and unscramble data, making understanding them difficult or impossible (Ma et al., 2019). Safe key distribution. Since the private key decodes messages, it's termed the public key. Due to the difference between encryption and decoding keys, public-key cryptosystems are often called "unbalanced." This idea came from (Joseph, 2022b). Public-key cryptosystems give unbreakable, easy-to-manage security. Sometimes they're even more secure than secret-key cryptosystems, but they're usually much slower. The encryption key can be shared, so parties don't have to agree on a secret key. They're often employed with secret-key cryptosystems to gain speed without knowing secret information.

This uses two different keys to "sign" and verify messages, making it impossible to counterfeit a signature without the original key (Dhanush et al., 2022). In public-key cryptosystems, the marking key is a private key and the check key is a public key. Brand plans build trust and approval. They're slower than secret-key cryptosystems and cryptographic hashing, but they share certain advantages of public-key cryptosystems, such as not requiring participants to agree on a mysterious key (Pattana-anake & Joseph, 2022).

Through a data transaction, the keys used to monitor private attributes were kept secret. Groups agree on a concealed secret after the exchange. Without inferred private qualities, determining the secret key from exchanged texts is difficult.

These characteristics compress arbitrary-sized notes into short codes, making it difficult to find a note with a given hash code and, in some situations, to observe two messages with the same hash code. Keyless lock (Joseph, 2023). Message digests and alternate acknowledgement codes are hash functions. 128- or 160-bit hash codes are prevalent. If an attacker just performs the beast power attack, it takes 212* preliminary tests to verify if a message with a given hash code exists (128-bit hash) and 2M to see if two messages have a similar hash code. Without the secret key, it's hard to compute an authentication code or find a new message with one. These codes compress arbitrary-length messages into compact codes under a secret key. Authentication codes hide messages' origins. Security isn't needed.

Combining picture transformation and encryption and unscrambling calculations, we present Blowfish (Joseph et al., 2022a). First, the original image was separated into blocks, which were subsequently reworked using a change computation given in this study. Finally, the modified image was scrambled using the Blowfish technique.

You suggest a hybrid technique for encrypting images based on transporter pictures and SCAN designs (Srisook et al., 2022). SCAN is a language-based, two-layered spatial getting-to method that can generate an endless number of investigating ways. Filter language has four output types. Ever-present slant C, skew D, symmetry O, and twisting S. The Watchword completes the transporter image.

The 4 out of 8-code will generate a unique 8-bit value for each alphabetic key. By combining it with a different image, the new transporter picture has become encoded (Joseph, 2019). Either a unique picture or a transporter picture is subjected to the output philosophy, with both pictures being expanded to yield an extraordinarily misshaped jumbled picture. In the crossover process, the next image is perceived to be even more warped than the one before it. By using the inverse interaction, we may reveal the hidden meaning.

The original image is divided into a specified number of squares, which are then rearranged to form an encrypted image (Pattana-Anake et al., 2021). The generated (or modified) image is utilised in blowfish encryption, creating a squares game. Blowfish, a symmetric square code scheme, secures communication and storage. The key length ranges from 32 to 448 pieces, making it ideal for data retrieval. Blowfish Algorithm is a Feistel Network that emphasises encryption. Keys can be up to 448 pieces long, and squares are 64. Such a technique provides suitable for projects where the key won't change much, like a correspondence connection or pre-programmed record encryptor.

PROBLEM STATEMENT

This problem statement describes the various security issues in the image transactions and ditital mode of images. By implementing this method the image is highly confidential in the markets and the source node and the destination node will be highly secured. If the intruder interacts the original data or in the in between transactions, entire business get collapsed.

PROPOSED SYSTEM

The proposal system splits the images into various blocks and follows a SCAN methodology for rearranging the position of blocks, which results in less possibility of finding the original image. Thus the system provides an efficient cryptosystem using block transformation to provide confidentiality service for data transmitted over a public network. Then the key image is generated with the given initial seed value. The resulting block-transferred image is encrypted using the key, which is generated using random numbers. At the destination, these blocks are retransformed into their original state and makes a decryption process which gives the real image. The usage of this project is that it reproduces the original picture with no loss of data for the cryptographic process.

Proposed System Algorithm

Algorithm:

The following steps are followed for sending images from one user to another for secure communication.

Block Transformation Algorithm Encryption

INPUT: Original image OUTPUT: Block transferred image

Step 1: Load the Original image

Step 2: Get the Image width (w) and Image height (h) Step 3: Resize the image into n × n size

Step 4: Get the block size as m × m

Step 4.1: Calculate Low Horizontal No. of blocks = (Image width) / m Step 4.2: Calculate Low Vertical No. of blocks = (Image Height) / m

Step 5: No. of blocks (k) = Horizontal No. of blocks × Vertical No. of blocks Step 6: Rearrange the pixel of the plain image into a vector I of size k × m2

Step 7: Using continuous diagonal SCAN pattern, rearrange the blocks in the matrix I Step 8: For B = 0 to k – 1

Step 8.1: Get the new location of block B from the transformation table Step 8.2: Set block B in its new location

Step 9: Convert the vector I into the image of size n × n Step 10: Store the block transferred image

Step 11: End

Decryption

INPUT: Decrypted block transferred image OUTPUT: Original image

Step 1: Load the Decrypted block transferred image Step 2: Get the Image width (w) and Image height (h) Step 3: Resize the image into n × n size

Step 4: Get the block size as m × m

Step 4.1: Calculate Low Horizontal No. of blocks = (Image width) / m Step 4.2: Calculate Low Vertical No. of blocks = (Image Height) / m

Step 5: No. of blocks (k) = Horizontal No. of blocks × Vertical No. of blocks Step 6: Rearrange the pixel of the image into a vector I of size k × m2

Step 7: Using continuous diagonal SCAN pattern, rearrange the blocks in the matrix I Step 8: For B = 0 to k – 1

Step 8.1: Get the new location of block B from the transformation table Step 8.2: Set block B in its new location

Step 9: Convert the vector I into the image of size n × n Step 10: Store the block transferred image

Step 11: End

Carrier Image Generation Algorithm

Step 1: Set the image size as m × m

Step 2: Get the seed value (n) and prime number (p) Step 3: for each r = 1 to m, do step (4) to (12)

Step 4: for each c = 1 to m, do step (5) to (11) Step 5: Convert the number n into binary Step 6: Count the No. of 1's in the number n

Step 6.1: count ← Number of 1's in n

Step 7: Find the next highest number (h) with the same number of 1's in n Step 7.1: While count != count_h

Step 7.2: Increment the number n

n ← n+1

Step 7.3: count_h ← Number of 1's in n Step 7.4: End while

Step 8: Multiply the number (n) with prime number (p) and add the multiplication value of row index and column index.

Step 8.1: n ← ((n × p) + (r × c)) % 256

Step 9: Store the number as the pixel value in the position (r, c) Step 9.1: Key_image (r, c) ← n

Step 10: If c is not equal to m then go to step (5) else go to step (11) Step 11: If r is not equal to m then go to step (4) else go to step (12) Step 12: Store the matrix as Key_image.jpg

Step 13: End

CONCLUSION

An efficient cryptosystem that produces random numbers and uses a method called Block Transformation was presented by us in this paper. This system's primary purpose is to maintain the confidentiality of communications carried out via public networks. Because it takes a different technique to generate random numbers than the Blum Blum algorithm does, the encryption that this algorithm provides is superior to that of the Blum Blum algorithm. This is due to the fact that this algorithm uses a novel approach to generate random numbers. This method of developing a cryptosystem is also superior for usage with short communications that are intended to be kept completely confidential. The proposed method produces the best results when compared to other available options in terms of the interacts between the encrypted picture and the original picture as well as the correlation of pixels in the encrypted format of images. This is the case regardless of whether the original picture was encrypted or not. When compared side by side, the histograms of the original image and the encrypted version reveal clear distinctions between one another.

REFERENCES

Dhanush, S., Mohanraj, S. C., Sruthi, V. S., Cloudin, S., & Joseph, F. J. J. (2022). CODEDJ-Private Permissioned Blockchain Based Digital Wallet with Enhanced Security. *International Conference on Bio-Neuro Informatics Models and Algorithms*. IEEE.

Ishaq, A., Sadiq, S., Umer, M., Ullah, S., Mirjalili, S., Rupapara, V., & Nappi, M. (2021). Improving the Prediction of Heart Failure Patients' Survival Using SMOTE and Effective Data Mining Techniques. *IEEE Access: Practical Innovations, Open Solutions*, *9*, 39707–39716. doi:10.1109/ACCESS.2021.3064084

Joseph, A. J. J., Joseph, F. J. J., Stanislaus, O. M., & Das, D. (2022a). *Classification methodologies in healthcare, Evolving Predictive Analytics in Healthcare: New AI techniques for real-time interventions*. IET.

Joseph, F. J. J. (2019). Twitter based outcome predictions of 2019 indian general elections using decision tree. In *4th International Conference on Information Technology (InCIT)* (pp. 50-53). IEEE. 10.1109/INCIT.2019.8911975

Joseph, F. J. J. (2022b). IoT Based Aquarium Water Quality Monitoring and Predictive Analytics Using Parameter Optimized Stack LSTM. In *International Conference on Information Technology (InCIT)*. IEEE

Joseph, F. J. J. (2022c). IoT-Based Unified Approach to Predict Particulate Matter Pollution in Thailand. *The Role of IoT and Blockchain: Techniques and Applications*, 145-151.

Joseph, F.J.J (2023). Time series forecast of Covid 19 Pandemic Using Auto Recurrent Linear Regression. *Journal of Engineering Research*.

Joseph, F. J. J., & Auwatanamongkol, S. (2016). A crowding multi-objective genetic algorithm for image parsing. *Neural Computing & Applications*, *27*(8), 2217–2227. doi:10.100700521-015-2000-2

Ma, C., Yan, Z., & Chen, C. W. (2019). Scalable access control for privacy-aware media sharing. *IEEE Transactions on Multimedia*, *21*(1), 173–183. doi:10.1109/TMM.2018.2851446

Maniccam, S. S., & Bourbakis, N. G. (2004). Image and video encryption using SCAN patterns. *Pattern Recognition*, *37*(4), 725–737. doi:10.1016/j.patcog.2003.08.011

Pattana-Anake, V., Danphitsanuparn, P., & Joseph, F. J. J. (2021, February). BettaNet: A Deep Learning Architecture for Classification of Wild Siamese Betta Species. *IOP Conference Series. Materials Science and Engineering*, *1055*(1), 012104. doi:10.1088/1757-899X/1055/1/012104

Pattana-anake, V., & Joseph, F. J. J. (2022). Hyper Parameter Optimization of Stack LSTM Based Regression for PM 2.5 Data in Bangkok, In *International Conference on Business and Industrial Research (ICBIR)*. IEEE 10.1109/ICBIR54589.2022.9786465

Rupapara, V., Narra, M., Gunda, N. K., Gandhi, S., & Thipparthy, K. R. (2021). Maintaining social distancing in pandemic using smartphones with acoustic waves. *IEEE Transactions on Computational Social Systems*, 1–7. doi:10.1109/TCSS.2021.3092942

Rupapara, V., Rustam, F., Shahzad, H. F., Mehmood, A., Ashraf, I., & Choi, G. S. (2021). Impact of SMOTE on Imbalanced Text Features for Toxic Comments Classification using RVVC Model. *IEEE Access: Practical Innovations, Open Solutions*, *9*, 1–1. doi:10.1109/ACCESS.2021.3083638

Rustam, F., Khalid, M., Aslam, W., Rupapara, V., Mehmood, A., & Choi, G. S. (2021). A performance comparison of supervised machine learning models for Covid-19 tweets sentiment analysis. *PLoS One*, *16*(2), e0245909. doi:10.1371/journal.pone.0245909 PMID:33630869

Sadiq, S., Umer, M., Ullah, S., Mirjalili, S., Rupapara, V., & Nappi, M. (2021). Discrepancy detection between actual user reviews and numeric ratings of Google App store using deep learning. *Expert Systems with Applications*, *115111*, 115111. doi:10.1016/j.eswa.2021.115111

Srisook, N., Tuntoolavest, O., Danphitsanuparn, P., Pattana-anake, V., & Joseph, F. J. J. (2022). Convolutional Neural Network Based Nutrient Deficiency Classification in Leaves of Elaeis guineensis Jacq. *International Journal of Computer Information Systems and Industrial Management Applications*, *14*, 19–27.

Upadhyay, S., Dave, D., & Sharma, G. (2016). *"Image encryption by using block-based symmetric transformation algorithm (international data encryption algorithm)," in Advances in Intelligent Systems and Computing*. Springer Singapore.

Yousaf, A., Umer, M., Sadiq, S., Ullah, S., Mirjalili, S., Rupapara, V., & Nappi, M. (2021). Emotion Recognition by Textual Tweets Classification Using Voting Classifier (LR-SGD). *IEEE Access: Practical Innovations, Open Solutions*, *9*, 6286–6295. doi:10.1109/ACCESS.2020.3047831

Chapter 7
Deepfakes on Smart Devices in Stock Price Prediction Using Machine Learning

P. Sobana
Nandha Engineering College, India

S. Prabhu
Nandha Engineering College, India

S. Karuppusamy
Nandha Engineering College, India

N. Anbarasu
Nandha Engineering College, India

ABSTRACT

The stock market is a widely used investment scheme promising high returns, but it has some risks. It is an act to forecast the future value of the stock market. The change in the stock market is explosive, and there are multiple sophisticated financial indicators. Still, the enhancement in technology provides a chance to grow constant fortune from the stock market and so helps experts to detect the most enlightening indicators to produce better predictions. Machine learning algorithms have made a magnificent effect in determining stocks precisely. This paper proposed a multiple regression algorithm for determining the future value of a stock. The first thing that was taken into account is the dataset of the companies Apple and Microsoft. Live historical data has been collected from yahoo finance. The dataset was pre-processed and tuned up for real analysis. Hence, this paper also focused on preprocessing of the raw dataset. After preprocessing the data, some forecasting measures are suggested, such as momentum, volatility, index volatility, and stock.

DOI: 10.4018/978-1-6684-6060-3.ch007

INTRODUCTION

The buying and selling of shares in publicly traded corporations takes place on a stock market, also known as an equity market or a share market. Related terms include share market. A stock, which may also be referred to as "offers" or "value," is a type of protection that indicates proportionate ownership in a responsible economic enterprise. Other names for stocks include "offers" and "value." The stock market acts as an arbitrator to facilitate the buying and selling of various offerings. Companies are able to increase their capital through the use of the stock market. With the help of stock markets, businesses are afforded the opportunity to launch an initial public offering (IPO) and collect significant sums of capital without having to be overly concerned about their ability to make payments. Additionally, the stock market contributes to individual investors' ability to amass personal wealth. The stock market provides opportunities to invest previously earned gains and to take ownership of those profits. People are known to put their money into the stock market, which is commonly considered to be one of the most popular types of investments. The effects of market forces continually drive price fluctuations in stocks.

A stock market prediction is able to determine the future value of an organization's shares as well as the value of other financial instruments that are traded on an exchange. It is extremely challenging to forecast with a high degree of precision the prices of stocks (Maniraj et al., 2021). Therefore, methods of machine learning are utilized in order to make predictions regarding the stock values of various organizations. An approach called multiple regression is suggested for determining the value of a stock before it is born. When attempting to forecast future stock prices, the data sets of the businesses Apple and Microsoft were utilized. The algorithm for multiple regression was built so that a more accurate prediction of the results could be made. The characteristics of open, close, high, low, adjacent close, and volume were taken into consideration during the data collection process. After that, the data were analyzed, and multiple regression techniques were performed in order to make a prediction about the future value.

LITERATURE SURVEY

Kanade (2020) presented a structure by the usage of various boundaries assembled from the historical information for a chosen organization utilizing Long Short Term Memory Machine Learning Algorithm and Adaptive Stock technical indicator for proficient estimating. Information is acquired from Yahoo Finance for working on this algorithm. There are two modules at the expectation of stock cost utilizing Long Short Term Memory, such as training sessions and forecasting values based on previously trained data. The stock development was anticipated by considering the end cost of the stock as input and news heading. It was inferred that Stock market development could be anticipated all the more unequivocally by utilizing Machine Learning calculations.

Torres et al., (2019) makes sense of the fact that it is so conceivable to involve PC as an instrument to consequently deal with the information gathered from financial activities. The fundamental goal is to consequently deal with the information utilizing Artificial Intelligence procedures, especially the utilization of Machine Learning algorithms.Random Trees and Multilayer Perceptron algorithms were utilized to foresee the end cost of a chosen organization (Deepika & Prabhu, 2019). The forecast has been performed with the stock exchange information of Apple Inc, with elements like opening cost, closing cost, highest cost, least cost and volume. WEKA software was utilized to execute the Machine

Learning algorithms. Both the algorithms were tried on similar arrangements of information of Apple Inc. Henceforth, it was inferred that the two executions fit the genuine historical cost information as 0.998 for the Random tree and 0.9976 for Multilayer Perceptron. Additionally, mistakes are recognizable.

Irfan et al., (2020) support Vector Machine, Logistic Regression and Perceptron calculation are the three machine learning algorithms utilized to foresee the following day's trend of the stocks. The primary point is to play out the prediction with higher precision than the strategies used in the existing framework. Different specialized pointers, in particular Exponential Moving Average (EMA), Moving Average Convergence divergence (MACD), Average True Range (ATR) and Relative Strength Index (RSI), were utilized for the stock forecast. In light of the end value, these indicators were determined. Therefore, SVM gives a higher exactness among the calculations utilized.

The examination work (Jai et al., 2019) makes a framework in light of the Machine Learning algorithms to foresee the stock cost. Moreover, the proposed work additionally oversees stocks for a specific user with functionalities like add, update and erase share. It is done in view of the current costs of the market. Pattern- Based Customized approach was utilized for the Stock Market price forecast. Forecast plans, looking as well as following the stocks are the modules utilized in the algorithm. The forecast model, which depends on a Pattern-based customized algorithm, produces higher precision.

Focused on (Umer et al., 2019) the utilization of Machine Learning algorithms such as Linear Regression (LR). The Linear Regression (LR) algorithm has been carried out on the different facts gathered from Yahoo Finance. Amazon (AMZN) and Apple (AAPL) informational indexes are utilized in this exploration. Stock exchange Trends for both items were investigated, and later AMZN informational index was utilized to apply Linear Regression (LR). Then, at that point, a three-month moving average (3MMA) strategy was applied to foresee the stock upsides of AMZN. The equivalent was completed for APPL too. At long last, Exponential Smoothing (ES) was applied for predictions. The outcome has shown that fewer mistakes and higher precision wereobtained while utilizing Exponential Smoothing (ES).

Nabipour et al. (2020) predicts the stock exchange price with usage of deep learning (DL) and machine learning (ML) algorithms, decision tree, random forest, adaboost, XG boost, SVC, Naïve Bayes, KNN, logistics regression and ANN are the machine learning models thought about in this examination. Likewise, deep learning strategies, for example, RNN and LSTM, were additionally considered for the examination. The info values are the ten signs of a decade of verifiable information. The correlation results show that deep learning techniques are the most incredible in binary data evaluation.

The assessment works out (Prabhu et al., 2019) the likelihood of scattering data analytics in the huge capacity of information in a cloud computing environment by the self-adaptive group forming procedure which is assisted through data analysis mapping, with the given instructive assortments as info. The methodology is organized into four sorts, explicitly traditional methodology, relative methodology, subjective methodology, and conditional methodology. The input data indexes are changed over into approaches, then similar traits are perceived, and the probability of the occasion of that event is supported. The Map Reduce is the course of arrangement in this investigation to have load impact close by the better show approach for cluster utilization by handling probability distribution.

Centres around the test of anticipating future upsides of a stock market index (Shubham & Mark, 2018). Two records explicitly, Dow Jones Industrial Average and NYTimes, are picked for test investigation. Tests are principally founded on 10 years of historical information on these two indices. The paper introduced how to anticipate stock values in light of the information fromthe NY Times of 10 years utilizing machine learning algorithms: logistic regression, random forest and multilayer perceptron (MLP). It reasons that MLP is superior to the next two algorithms in light of the fact that, inside a specific reach, the distinction between the actual price and predicted cost is minuscule when contrasted with those in Logistic Regression and Random Forest. Additionally, in foreseeing stock values, Random Forest is superior to Logistic Regression, yet the second rate compared to MLP.

Sentiment analysis is utilized in this paper to work out the extremity scoreand then use it comparatively to figure out the kind of article has an exceptional or horrible impact towards the stock and people is probablyutilized with the evaluation (Kompella & Chilukuri (2019). To cipher the charges of stock, the attained evaluations are employed, and to complete the intakes as a constant, the exponential moving average methodology was used and saved due to the fact the impact of stock is efficiently determined. The data subsequent to working out is refreshed and proven to the purchaser as a diagram. At last, Random Forest Algorithm is executed and in correlation with logistic regression for execution.

Different algorithms were utilized via social media and economic news information to figure out the impact of these statistics on stock market prediction exactness for ten days from now (Khan et al., 2022). For upgrading in general execution and nature of predictions, feature selection and spam tweets decrease are made at the informational indexes. Additionally, tests were completed to find such stock markets which are difficult to foresee and individuals who are extra stimulated through methods for online entertainment and financial data. The authors assess the results of different algorithms to find a consistent classifier. At last, to arrive at the most forecast accuracy, deep learning is utilized, and a couple of classifiers are ensembled.

PROBLEM STATEMENT

People have become much more dependent on data and information in society over the course of the past twenty years, and with this appearance improvement, advancements have proceeded for their capacity, evaluation, and taking care of a much larger scope. The fields of data mining and machine learning have not only taken advantage of them to speculate on the outcomes of future events, which are difficult to guarantee. In addition, one of the difficult things to forecast that caught our attention is stock, which is more commonly referred to as shares. When it comes to research that is analytical and deals with money, one of the most important topics to explore is probably how to anticipate stock prices. In order to address this issue, a variety of data mining methodologies are typically coupled with assessments. However, a method that makes use of machine learning will provide a more thorough, accurate, and crucial strategy for settling such concerns as those relating to stock and market prices.

METHODOLOGIES

Multiple Regression

Multiple regression is a statistical technique that can be used to dissect the connection between a single dependent variable (criterion) and many independent variables (predictors). The idea of multiple regression is to use the independentvariables (whose values are known before) to predict the dependent variable. Generally, a regression model is written as follows:

$Y=\alpha + \beta_1 X_1 + \beta_2 X_2 + B_n X_n + \varepsilon$ (1)

Where,

- Y is Dependent variable,
- α is intercept, which is likewise called constant;
- β is regression coefficient
- X is unbiased (independent) variable, also calleda predictive variable;
- E is referred to asan error term.

Python programming has been utilized to construct the prediction model by utilizing the Multiple Regression algorithm. The fundamental goal is to utilize the historical information to anticipate a stock's consistently high by considering the characteristics stock's opening and the market's open. The multiple Regression model,which is most comprehensively involved in stock market prediction, is utilized here. In accounting, the persuasive thought about the financial exchange, a particular day's basic cost is phenomenally subject to a lot of components. Subsequently, observingthe hidden cost of a stock as an independent part of the prediction model will give a blend of that huge number of components. The market's underlying worth gives a more expansive enthusiasm for the instances of the stock, particularly if there should arise an occurrence of a phenomenal contrast in the whole market (figure1).

Figure 1. Stock prediction model

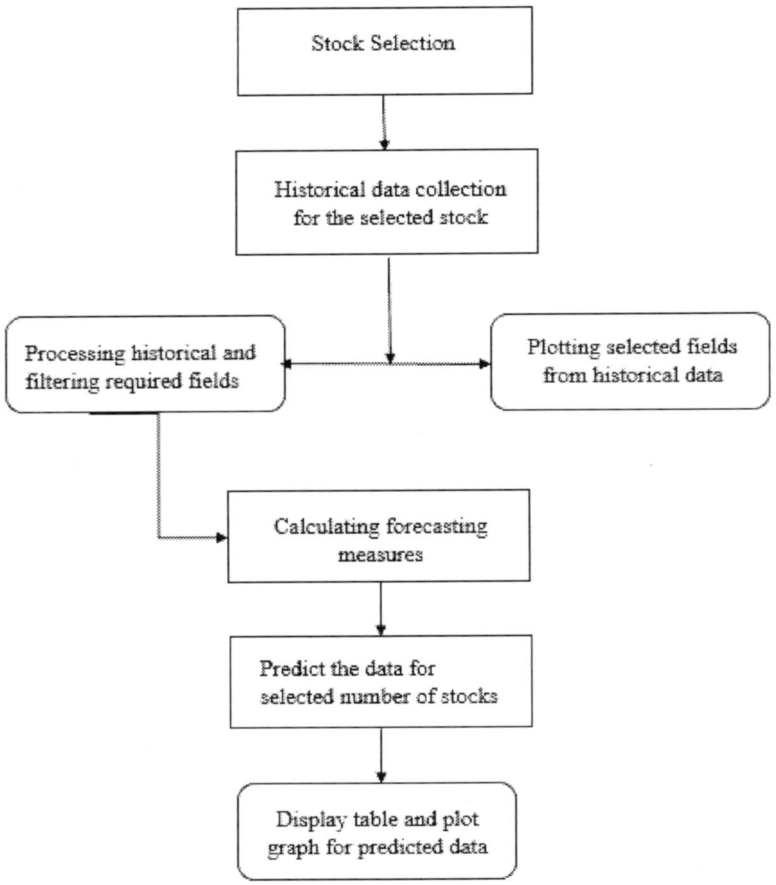

Data Collection

Apple (AAPL) and Microsoft (MSFT) are the stocks taken for prediction. The data accumulated utilizing the Yahoo Finance Developer API, based on which the prediction model is developed. The Yahoo API gives different strategies which work with data procurement. Utilizing the API, the accompanying data boundaries are assembled:

- Stock's Day Open Price
- Stock's Day Close Price
- Stock's Day High Price

Further, since the stock costs don't change throughout the end of the week, it is great to remove them. Yahoo API gives a component that gets just the workday's stock costs. The Yahoo finance API gets the beginning date and end date as input and gives the chosen stocks historical data between those days.

Data Preprocessing

Following the development of the necessary information, it is essential to proceed with the preprocessing of the information. The records that have been accumulated are transferred to Panda's Data-frame, and the frame is then indexed so that the interaction can go more smoothly. In addition, it's clear to peers that the Data-values include some exceptional NAN (Not A Number) values in their very own right. The presence of a Not A Number esteem in a Panda's Data-body indicates that a value has been lost. As a result of the missing values, the Stock Price Trend prediction based on the use of Multiple Linear Regression is incoherent, which assists in the functioning of any prophetic models based on them. For this reason, the fill() function is applied to the Data-frame in order to forward fill the data and fill in the NAN values. Additionally, data from weekends have been ignored, which may be an example of redundant data and may have an impact on the prediction model. As a result, the data have been cleansed of any and all redundant information as well as discrepancies.

Calculating Forecasting Measures

When the fields from the input are taken into consideration, a few transitory forecast metrics are devised. These measures include momentum, volatility, index momentum, index volatility, sector momentum, stock momentum, and stock price volatility. When the additional attributes are taken into account, it is possible to create a prediction model that is more definitive and accurate. The multiple linear regression method is what is used to construct the prediction model. This method is a pretty established statistical approach that is employed in the evaluation of the inventory market. It makes it possible for the analyst to take into consideration multiple dependency variables, each of which has an impact on the quantity that is to be anticipated. Following is a list of the mathematical formulae that are utilized in the calculation of the predictive measures.

- **momentum(a)** $= \begin{cases} 1 & closing(a) > closing(a-1) \\ 0 & closing(a) \le closing(a-1) \end{cases}$ (2)

- **volatality(a)** $=\frac{1}{5}\sum_{k=a-4}^{a} V_k$, where V is the volatility (3)
- **indexVolatality(a)** $=\frac{1}{5}\sum_{k=a-4}^{a} I_k$, where I is the index (4)
- **sectorMomentum(a)** $=\frac{1}{5}\sum_{k=a-4}^{a} M_k$, (5)

  where I is the index and provided k has the same sector of a

- **stockMomentum(a)** $=\frac{1}{5}\sum_{k=a-4}^{a} M_k$, (6)

  where I is the index

The calculations are done programmatically and are added to the processed data as extra columns. After the addition of predictive measures columns rather than open, close and predictive measures, values can be dropped from Data Frame. So, the final processed data contains the Open and Close columns obtained from yahoo finance and the Predictive measures as individual columns in the format of pandas Data Frame.

Splitting Train and Test Data

The data is split into train data and test data in order to get a predictive model using the train data and use the predictive model on test data and compare the results acquired with the test data in order to find the prediction score of our model and to find the accuracy obtained. Here we have chosen to split the train data and split data in the ratio of 75:25; thus, 75% of the historical data obtained is used to obtain the prediction model, and the remaining 25% is used to calculate the accuracy of the model.

Data Forecasting

Python Programming was used during the construction of the Prediction Model. Utilizing a stock's past performance in order to forecast its daily close is the goal of this activity. The data that is used is the stock's open, and predictive measures are computed by making use of the historical data that is readily available. The multi-linear regression model, which is one of the models that is used most frequently in the evaluation of the stock market, is the one that is used here. Due to the very volatile and unpredictable nature of the stock market, the initial price of a share of stock on any given day is extremely dependent on a large number of different factors. The subsequent step involves taking into account the starting cost of a stock as an independent variable for the purpose of developing a model that will provide a combination of those many different components. The starting price of the market offers a more comprehensive understanding of the patterns of the stock, particularly in the event of a significant gyration in the market as a whole.

Plot Forecast Data

The comparison of test data and forecast data is represented in graphical format as a trend distribution graph. Using a trend distribution graph, it is easy to compare the difference between the actual test data and the predicted data. Thus, after processing the data, this project graphs the trend of the daily close of the selected Stock's actual and predicted data, which can observe the precision of our prediction.

RESULT AND ANALYSIS

Apple and Microsoft are the companies whose datasets can be selected for the purpose of prediction within the scope of this project. The start date, from which the historical data for the chosen stock can be selected using a glider that takes into consideration the numbers as years, is one of the options. Data is retrieved from Yahoo Finance, which offers live historical data based on the stock that was chosen and the date range that was specified (figure 2).

Figure 2. Raw Data

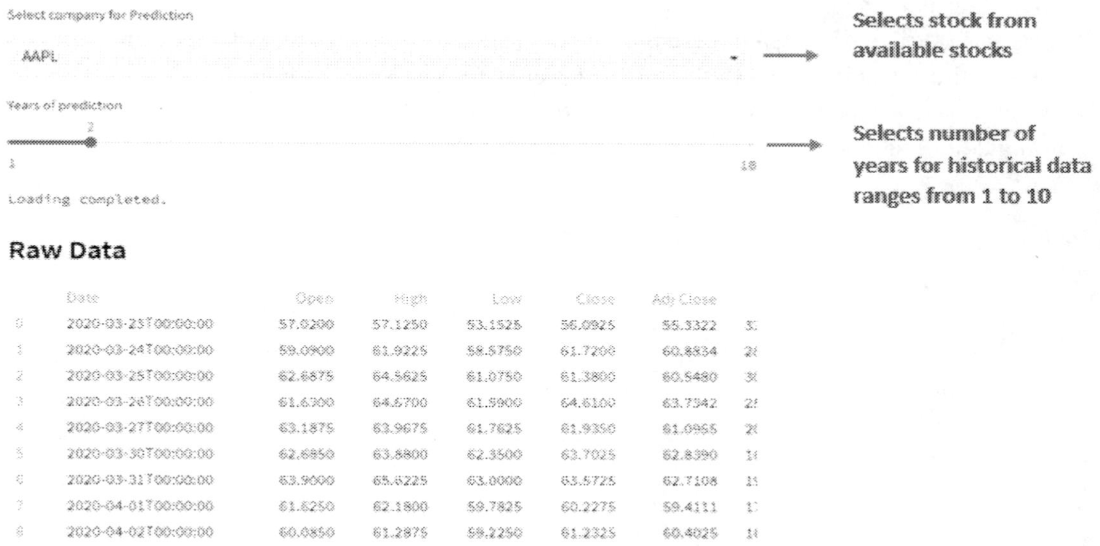

	Date	Open	High	Low	Close	Adj Close
0	2020-03-23T00:00:00	57.0200	57.1250	53.1525	56.0925	55.3322
1	2020-03-24T00:00:00	59.0900	61.9225	58.5750	61.7200	60.8834
2	2020-03-25T00:00:00	62.6875	64.5625	61.0750	61.3800	60.5480
3	2020-03-26T00:00:00	61.6300	64.6700	61.5900	64.6100	63.7342
4	2020-03-27T00:00:00	63.1875	63.9675	61.7625	61.9350	61.0965
5	2020-03-30T00:00:00	62.6850	63.8800	62.3500	63.7025	62.8390
6	2020-03-31T00:00:00	63.9000	65.6225	63.0000	63.5725	62.7108
7	2020-04-01T00:00:00	61.6250	62.1800	59.7825	60.2275	59.4111
8	2020-04-02T00:00:00	60.0850	61.2875	59.2250	61.2325	60.4025

The data will be preprocessed before they are going to be used. The filtered data will then be populated in a table and plotted on graphs for better understanding. The open and close value of the historical data or plotted on a graph considering the date on the X column and the open and close value on the Y value. The library used for graph plotting is plot.ly (figure 3).

Figure 3. Time Series Data

The data that is undesired or redundant is removed from the raw data, and then the data that has been processed is utilized to create predictive metrics such as momentum, volatility, index momentum and index volatility, stock momentum, and sector momentum. The formulas for all of the metrics are presented up top where they can be found. After that, these predictive metrics are added to the data, and the resulting combination is presented in table format (figure 4).

Figure 4. Processed data with calculative measures

	Open	Close	Moment...	Volatality	Index Volatality	Stock Momentum
5	62.6850	63.7025	1	-0.0285	-0.0269	0.6000
6	63.9000	63.5725	0	0.0020	-0.0064	0.4000
7	61.6250	60.2275	0	0.0526	0.0030	0.4000
8	60.0850	61.2325	1	-0.0167	0.0102	0.4000
9	60.7000	60.3525	0	0.0144	0.0048	0.4000
10	62.7250	65.6175	1	-0.0872	-0.0070	0.4000
11	67.7000	64.8575	0	0.0116	-0.0051	0.4000
12	65.6850	66.5175	1	-0.0256	-0.0207	0.6000
13	67.1750	66.9975	1	-0.0072	-0.0188	0.6000
14	67.0775	68.3125	1	-0.0196	-0.0256	0.8000

The data is further split into train data and test data. The training data is used for building the prediction model, and the test data will be used to evaluate the model. After splitting, train data is used to build the prediction model, which considers columns open, momentum, volatility, index momentum, index volatility, stock momentum and sector momentum as its input to calculate the close value.

The multiple linear regression method is used to fit the train data. The linear regression Module available from Sklearn is used for regression. The regression coefficients are as follows (figure 5).

Figure 5. Intercept and Co-efficient

Intercept: 0.45422632157576004

Coefficients:

	0
0	0.9961
1	-0.2156
2	-109.5316
3	1.0543
4	0.4471
5	1.0543

The regression model that was built is used on the test data to predict the close values on each test date. After prediction, the actual close value of the test data and the predicted close value of the test data are displayed as a table and plotted as a graph to compare the values (figure 6).

Figure 6. Actual data vs Predicted data

	Actual	Predicted
0	175.6400	174.4621
1	176.2800	176.0535
2	180.3300	179.4830
3	179.2900	179.6074
4	179.3800	179.2595
5	178.2000	178.7589
6	177.5700	177.6313
7	182.0100	180.2818
8	179.7000	181.1526

Figure 7. Graph for Trained data vs Predicted data

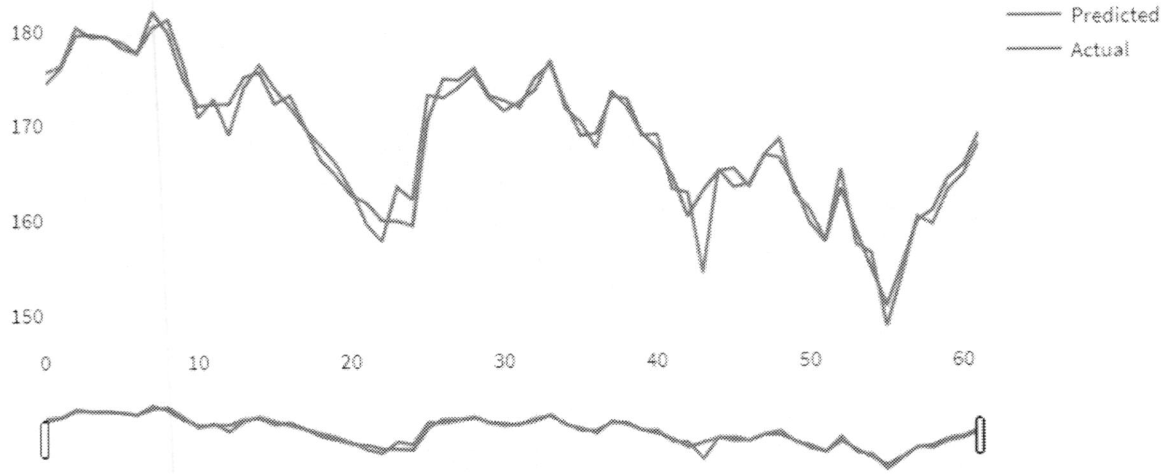

Contrasting the predicted close value and the actual close, the prediction score and the RSME (Root mean square blunder) is determined and shown (figure 7). This model delivers 0.9388 asthe R2 value and 3.22127 as RMSE (Root Mean Square Error). The R2 rating, otherwise referred to as the coefficient of guarantee, is the volume of alternate inside the reliant variable that can be expected from the impartial variables. The RMSE is a habitually applied percentage of the differences among values anticipated through a version or an assessor and the values honestly noticed (figure 8).

Figure 8. Prediction details

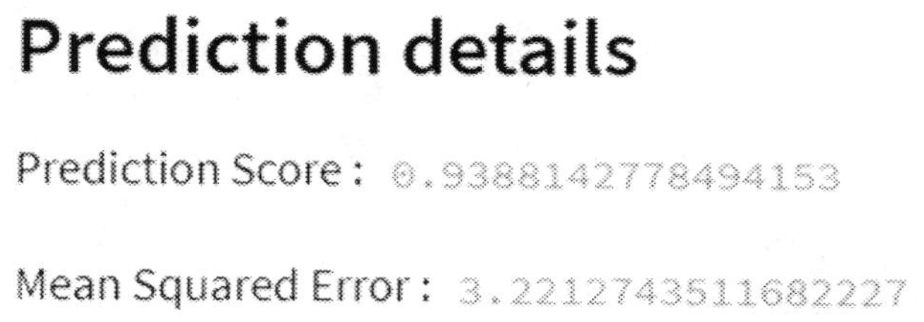

Finally, the current day's Expected stock close value is printed in distinct, which is again predicted from our prediction model (figure 9).

Figure 9. Forecast Data

CONCLUSION

This study made use of the Multiple Linear Regression approach, which is the method that is employed in the financial market forecasting process more frequently than any other. The starting price of a share of stock is taken into account as an independent variable, which eliminates the need to keep track of a variety of different aspects while attempting to forecast how high the stock price will go. Knowledge of the variations in stock costs across the full market can be obtained by looking at the open value of the marketplace. The precision of the model is built using the predictive measures that were determined and taken into consideration. When all of these factors were taken into consideration, the number that the linear regression model produced for the RMSE was 3.22127. The performance measurements that were obtained here have the potential to be improved further through the application of many other supporting measures. The scope of the model could be expanded through the consideration of a diverse collection of interesting stocks as well as the NASDAQ market.

REFERENCES

Deepika, S. (2019). Cloud Task Scheduling Based on a Two Stage Strategy using KNN Classifier. *International Journal of Latest Engineering Science, 2*(6), 33-39.

Jain, S. & Kain, M. (2018). Prediction for Stock Marketing Using Machine Learning. *International Journal IJRITCC, 6*(4).

Kanade, P. A. (2020). Machine learning model for stock market prediction. *International Journal for Research in Applied Science and Engineering Technology, 8*(6), 209–216. doi:10.22214/ijraset.2020.6030

Khan, W., Ghazanfar, M. A., Azam, M. A., Karami, A., Alyoubi, K. H., & Alfakeeh, A. S. (2022). Stock market prediction using machine learning classifiers and social media, news. *Journal of Ambient Intelligence and Humanized Computing, 13*(7), 3433–3456. doi:10.100712652-020-01839-w

Kompella, S., & Chilukuri, K. C. (2019). Stock market prediction using machine learning methods. *International Journal Of Computer Engineering And Technology, 10*(3). doi:10.34218/IJCET.10.3.2019.003

Maniraj S. P, Shettigar, R., Kannadasan, B., & Prabhu, S. (2021). Artificial Intelligence Application in Human Resource Development. *International Journal of Biology, Pharmacy and Allied Sciences, 10*(11), 1089-1100.

Nabipour, M., Nayyeri, P., Jabani, H., S, S., & Mosavi, A. (2020). Predicting stock market trends using machine learning and deep learning algorithms via continuous and binary data; A comparative analysis. *IEEE Access: Practical Innovations, Open Solutions, 8*, 150199–150212. doi:10.1109/ACCESS.2020.3015966

Irfan Ramzan Parry, Surinder Singh Khurana, Munish Kumar, Ali A. Altalbe (2020). Time Series Data Analytics of Stock Price Movement using Machine Learning Techniques. *Time.*

Prabhu, S., Sengottaiyan, N., & And Geetha, B. G. (2019). Self Adaptive Approaches to Probability Distribution of Data Analytics in Cloud Computing Resource Services for Infrastructure Hybrid Models. *Applied Mathematics & Information Sciences, 13*(S1, No: S1), 437–446. doi:10.18576/amis/13S147

Torres, P. E. P. (2019). Stock market data prediction using machine learning techniques. In Advances in Intelligent Systems and Computing. Springer International Publishing.

Umer, M., Awais, M., & Muzammul, M. (2019). Stock market prediction using machine learning(ML) algorithms. *Adcaij Advances In Distributed Computing And Artificial Intelligence Journal, 8*(4), 97–116. doi:10.14201/ADCAIJ20198497116

Verma, J. P, Tanwar, S., Garg, S., Gandhi, I., & Bachani, N. (2019). Evaluation of Pattern Based Customized Approach for Stock Market Trend Prediction With Big Data and Machine Learning Techniques. *International Journal of Business Analytics (IJBAN), 6*(3), pages 1-15.

Chapter 8
Machine Learning Algorithms to Detect Deepfakes Fine Tuned for Anomaly Detection of IoT

N. Sridhar
Nandha Engineering College, India

K. Shanmugapriya
Nandha Engineering College, India

C. N. Marimuthu
Nandha Engineering College, India

ABSTRACT

The internet of things (IoT) is a worldwide network of interconnected gadgets that enables devices to communicate with one another and share data in a continuous manner. Any deviation from the typical course of events is referred to as an anomaly, and it might serve as an early indicator that there is a problem. The authors differentiate themselves from previous tactics by requiring less time to identify and respond to attacks since they implement a variety of machine learning algorithms while the programme is running. This effort intends to establish a system for anomaly detection that is capable of screening IoT flaws and alerting the organization's CEO as well as the help network. The authors make use of a machine learning approach called k-nearest neighbor (KNN) in conjunction with a random forest (RF) algorithm in order to fine-tune the parameters of the spreading network. As a result, this framework improves the performance of the model without causing it to overfit.

INTRODUCTION

Internet of Things refers to the network of physical objects that are capable of exchanging and requesting data from one another or in relation to the external environment through the utilization of technology that is incorporated into the design of the object. People will be able to take care of daily routines in different ways and give more complex administrations as a result of developments based on the Internet

DOI: 10.4018/978-1-6684-6060-3.ch008

of Things in the years to come. Among the most evident domains in which IoT has been unquestionably established are the pharmaceutical business, the electricity sector, the production of high-quality pharmaceuticals, agriculture, sophisticated urban networks, and sophisticated residences (Farouk, et al., 2018). There are approximately 9 billion 'Things' (real-world, living items) that are connected to the internet at this same moment. It is anticipated that by the end of this decade, this number will have skyrocketed to a staggering 20 billion (Farouk, et al., 2020). When compared to the entire planet for a tiny town that is universally related by just going from one side of the globe to the other, the definition of the Internet of Things consists of just two words that clearly clarify what it means (Aoudni et al., 2022). There has been a significant increase in the use of the Internet of Things across many different areas, including the medical field, the information technology sector, and the agricultural sector (Farouk et al., 2015). The ability to provide assurance of safety is likely the most important factor, given that it is the factor that is at the heart of a variety of problems, including government enterprise (Adil et al., 2021).

Any deviation from the norm, often known as an anomaly, might serve as an early warning sign for impending trouble (Heidari, et al., 2019). A problem in a manufacturing unit, for instance, may be indicated by abnormalities in the time-series data collected by an Internet of Things sensor (Mendonça, et al., 2021). Despite this, the process of spotting anomalies has become significantly more difficult over time. The application of techniques from machine learning allows for the detection of anomalies in data. Unsupervised, semi-supervised, and supervised anomaly detection methods are the three categories that make up the overall anomaly detection landscape (Naseri, et al., 2018). Labels in a dataset indicate the most appropriate detection strategy. In this paper, a methodology for finding irregularities in IoT devices is proposed in order to identify them and alert the top management or senior managers in a business. This approach is proposed in order to identify them and bring them to the attention of the readers. We make use of a machine learning approach called K-Nearest Neighbor (KNN) in conjunction with a Random Forest (RF) algorithm in order to fine-tune the parameters of the spreading network. As a result, this framework improves the performance of the model without causing it to overfit, and it makes it possible to get a fit and a measure score by making use of cross-validation (CV). After that, look into the many discrepancies that are caused by the dataset's use of substitute components. It is possible to utilize both a binary and a multi-class machine learning classification model to recognize dangers and abnormalities that may be present in an Internet of Things environment (Zhu, et al., 2021). After then, the study that is being proposed would test the model by attempting to predict the class of provided data points contained in the dataset. When this step is complete, the accuracy of the classifier is determined by dividing the total number of test models by the number of correct selections (Metwaly, et al., 2014). Finally, with the help of this research, we will be able to prevent attacks by identifying new dangers and anomalies in the Internet of Things configurations and smart devices. Following that, a description of the literature review that was carried out for this paper is presented. Following that, the following section of this study will detail our proposed approach and module. At this point, the report comes to an end with a succinct conclusion about an analysis of the results.

LITERATURE SURVEY

Ramapatruni, S. et al. (2019) proposed the usage of machine learning and big data in a shrewd home environment to recognize anomalous activities. On network-level sensor data, a Hidden Markov Model (HMM) is created utilizing a proving ground with various sensors and smart devices. The created HMM model has been found to have a precision of 97 percent in identifying probable abnormalities that suggest signs of attacks.

Sahu and Mukherjee, (2020), proposed a design to find various anomalies based on the alternate element in the dataset. Logistic regression and artificial neural network aretwo machine learning classification models utilized, and correlationsof these models are shown. In the main case, the arrangement calculation expressed above is applied overall 3.5 lakh dataset, and in the subsequent case, all the order calculations are applied in the wake of overlooking the element "esteem" having information as 0 and 1. This work can be utilized for recognizing dangers and abnormalities happening in savvy gadgets and IoT arrangements and forestall assaults.

Alrashdi, I. et al. (2019) proposed an Anomaly Detection IoT system, which is intelligent anomaly detection dependent on Random Forest machine learning algorithm for the IoT cyber-security dangers in a shrewd city. The proposed setup can successfully distinguish compromised IoT gadgets at conveyed vapour hubs. The model was tested using the current dataset. In the AD-IoT, they work toward the achievement of the most noteworthy characterization precision of 99.34% with the least false positives.

Priya et al. (2021) proposed a two-stage anomaly detection model to redesign the trustworthiness of an IIoT association. SVM and Nave Bayes are merged in the main stage employing a company blending approach. For instance, an Artificial Neural Network (ANN) classifier that leverages the Adam enhancer to improve accuracy is utilized. The end outcome is considered the model's gathering unit and the most significant accuracy concern. WUSTL IIOT-2018, N BaIoT, and Bot IoT were among the IoT attack datasets included in the model. An overall assessment of the suggested model is conducted utilizing top-tier data collection approaches in order to demonstrate the prevalence of the findings and, as a result, to undermine the reliability of an IIoT association.

Savic, M. et al. (2021) in order to assist 3GPP's versatile cell network planning, examined 5G IoT transparency and anomaly detection.As such, this configuration inserts an autoencoder-based irregularity recognition mechanism and an adjustable focus association, changing the responsiveness and precision of the structure as necessary. Construct, fabricate, demonstrate and analyze a testbed that demonstrates actual sending as part of a 3GPP Narrow-Band IoT (NBIoT) flexible director association.

Aversano, L. et al. (2021) proposed a deep learning approach to evaluate five datasets of unusual IoT traffic with a view to identifying both fraudulent and legitimate behavior. A proper hyperparameter optimization phase has enriched the deep learning approach. This study focuses on the smartest deep neural networks with noise removal through some of the characteristics under consideration, particularly during the selecting features stage with an auto-encoder neural network.Based on the results obtained, it can be shown that the IoT dataset may also be used to detect anomalies in noisy settings, owing to its deep learning capabilities.

Reddy, et al. (2021) suggested a novel framework for identifying and categorizing anomalous behaviours from regular activity in the Internet of Things regarding the type of assault that uses deep learning and a layered random neural network technique.The study gives a complete performance evaluation of deep learning neural network architecture for the recognition of seven sorts of attacks using data from the Distributed Smart Space Orchestration System traffic trace data set. By using a simulation model, the empirical results indicated a notable improvement in most categorical attacks using deep neural network architecture.

Rashid, et al. (2020) proposed an approach for identifying assaults and abnormalities in IoT networks that uses machine learning algorithms (LR, SVM, DT, RF, KNN, and ANN) to protect against and filter out IoT network security threats in smart cities. Additionally, to improve the visibility of the recognition framework, consider using gathering tactics like bagging, boosting, and stacking. This method is viable for differentiating cyber-attacks, according to findings presented with the new assault dataset, and the stacking troupe model beats other similar models in terms of accuracy, review, and False alarm rate, demonstrating the benefits of stacking in this field.

Chen and Chen, (2022) explored Smart Urban Traffic Monitoring (SurMon); drones are employed through an edge computing paradigm to monitor urban traffic. This framework suggests applying multidimensional Singular Spectrum Analysis (mSSA) to space in order to recognizedistinct cars on roadways in real time to detect abnormal vehicle behavior. Instead of developing a database of regular activity patterns of vehicles on the road, anomaly detection gets restructured as an outlier identifying challenges. A cascaded capsule network is designed to determine if such behavior seems to be in violation. The feasibility and efficiency of a SurMon (Smart Urban Traffic Monitoring) method have been demonstrated through experimental experiments.

Shakya and Smys (2020) developed a platform of dispersed streaming as part of the fog paradigm for the Internet of Things. As a condition of maintaining the network's and application's efficiency, anomalies are supposed to be removed. The deep learning framework is used to identify anomalies in fog paradigms via hardware techniques. An experimental study revealed that deep learning models were more accurate, false alarm-free, and elastic than other basic detection structures.

PROPOSED METHODOLOGY

An anomaly detection framework is proposed in this work that is intended to detect IoT vulnerabilities and alert an organization's executive or service administrators. Based on the K-Nearest Neighbor (KNN) algorithm for unsupervised learning and the Random Forest (RF) algorithm for supervised learning, the proposed system can get fine-tuned parameter settings.Hence, this framework boosts the model's performance without over-fitting and facilitates a fit and a measure score by using Cross Validation (CV). Then, examine various inconsistencies based on substitute components used in the dataset. A binary and multi-class machine learning classification model can be used to identify risks and anomalies occurring in an IoT environment (figure 1).

Contributions tothis work include the following:

- In this paper, anomaly detection based on machine learning techniques is used to determine attacks on the dataset, including modern attacks assumed in networks associated with IoT botnets (Peter, et al., 2011).
- Using real-time attack behaviours as input, the proposed system works.
- In this system, use a dataset from UNSW-NB15 to address the lack of modern normal and attack network traffic.
- Then use K-Nearest Neighbor (KNN) and Random Forest (RF) algorithms to analyze the proposed framework system to predict benign or malicious data (Karthikeswaranet al., 2012).
- Utilizing the Scikit-Learns CV method, characterize a network of hyper-parameter ranges and randomly sample from the grid, performing K-Fold CV with every combination ofvalues.
- Optimizing the model's performance without over-fitting or creating an excessive variance by tuning the machine learning algorithm.

- After that, a binary and a multi-class machine learning classification model are created to categorize a given dataset into classes.
- Afterwards, the process predicts the class of each data point. Finally, evaluate model accuracy by comparing it with the standardized dataset.

Figure 1. Evaluation of parameter turning using machine leraning algoritham

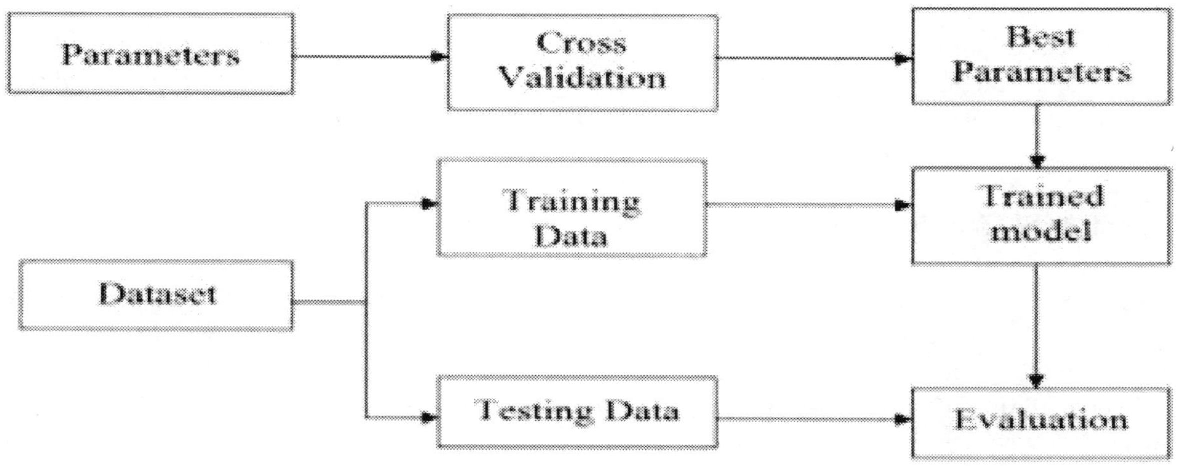

MODULES AND DESCRIPTION

The proposed method for anomaly detection was based on two machine learning models: K-nearest neighbour and Random Forest.

With the real-time attack behaviours taken into account, this module creates a dataset using UNSW-NB15. It includes both a testing set (82,332) as well as a training set (1,75,341) for the process. Different vulnerabilities are present in this package, including normal bugs, DoS vulnerabilities, fuzzes, exploits, backdoors, and reconnaissance.

The KNN algorithm may be considered a supervised machine learning algorithm, but this module adopts an unsupervised method of anomaly detection. All things being equal, the process is completely based on limited values due to the fact that there is no real learning happening during the process and that there is no predetermined labelling of anomalous data. Ultimately, information researchers believe that past the threshold, all perceptions are considered anomalies.

A Random Forest is made up of many individual decision trees working together. Each tree represents a class prediction, and the category receiving the most votes is considered the predictioncategory. As well as hyper-parameters, there are parameters, which are particulars and limitations that are utilized during preparedness to part every hub. Hyper-parameters are trees in the forest, as well as how many factors each tree considers while parting a hub. For every model, Scikit-Learn creates a handful of reasonable default hyper-parameters, but these are not intended to be optimal.

In the field of Data Science, there is a proverb that emphasizes the value of Cross-Validation over domain knowledge. In cross-validation, an algorithm is used called K-Fold CV. Whenever a machine learning issue arises, it is necessary to divide our data into a training set and a testing set. Each training set is divided into K subsets. Then the data validation is carried out every time the training K-1 folds are iterated, and with the proposed model, the split is random and approximately equal on ten occasions. As part of the first iteration, nine folds are used for constructing training datasets and assessing test sets on the first fold. This process is repeated nine more times, each time assessing on a new fold. A one-time validation of each part and a K-time development of trained data were made available. This technique has the advantage that every perception is used both for training and validation, and each perception is validated exactly one time.

For the most part, binary classifications are utilized for errands that give both two class labels as a result. One is ordinarily viewed as the normal state, and the other is thought of as abnormal. For most notations, the values of 0 are assigned to the normal state and 1 to the abnormal state.

EXPERIMENTAL RESULTS

Using Scikit-Learn's Randomized Search CV method and Tensor-Flow tool, we performed experiments using the Python Programming Language. This work obtained data from the UNSW-NB15 dataset [2] on the GitHub platform. Different vulnerabilities are present in this package, including normal bugs, DoS vulnerabilities, fuzzes, exploits, backdoors, and reconnaissance.The KNN algorithm, even though it consists of supervised machine learning features, adopts an unsupervised approach with regard to anomaly detection. This experiment was run using Scikit-Learn. Using the train_test_split aide, random sets could be divided into training and testing by using sklearn. Metrics to import the accuracy of the score, cross-validation is the most straightforward way to use it. In order to cluster unlabeled data, sklearn. Cluster is called. Next, read the test CSV file and the training CSV file from the UNSW-NB15 data set to fit a KNN. Then we will create an odd list of K for the KNN and an empty list to hold the cross-validation scores. Afterwards, calculate the accuracy score for neighbours by performing ten-fold cross-validation.The UNSW-NB15 was also loaded to run an experiment for a supervised machine learning algorithm using a Random Forest to read training CSV files and testing CSV files. Then an empty list will be created to keep cross-validation scores and the number of estimators list for Random Forest. Now,calculate the number of estimators' accuracy scores by performing 10-fold cross-validation. After that,a binary machine learning classification model is created to categorize a given dataset into classes. This experiment utilized tensor-flow Keras. Models to create the model and compile the model for binary classification. The model creation includes kernel initialize and activation functions. The model compilation includes binary cross-entropy to calculate a deviation from actual and predicted classes. Then the proposed work evaluatesthe model by predicting the class of given data points in the dataset. At that point, decides classifier's accuracy by isolating the number of right choices by the total number of test models.

Figure 2. Accuracy metrics percentage for various attack types using a binary classification algorithm

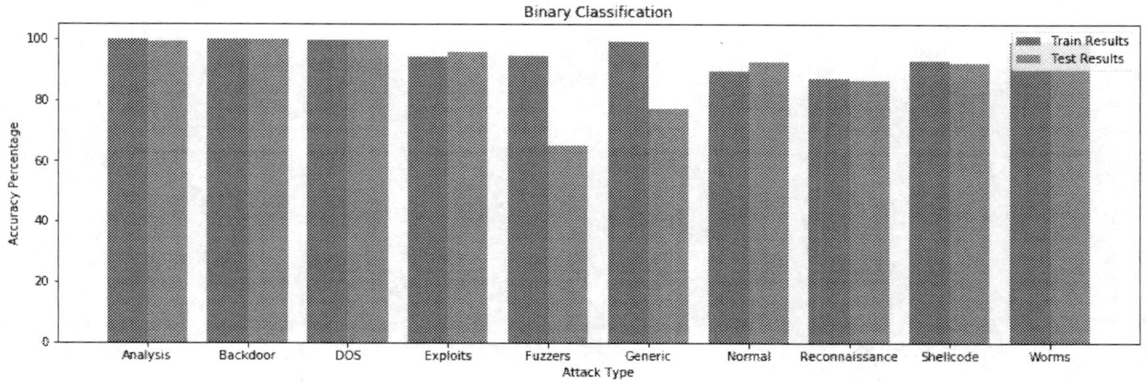

In figure 2, the bar chart shows the Accuracy metrics percentage for various attack types using a binary classification algorithm. The prediction shows the training and test results for the different attack types with accuracy metrics scores.In the experiment for top-performing variants of the proposed method, the observations made for respective classifiers and machine learning ensembles were examined. As seen in Figure 2, performance metrics used for classification score accuracy yield such top-performing outcomes.

Figure 3. Train results accuracy score for various attack types using a binary classification algorithm

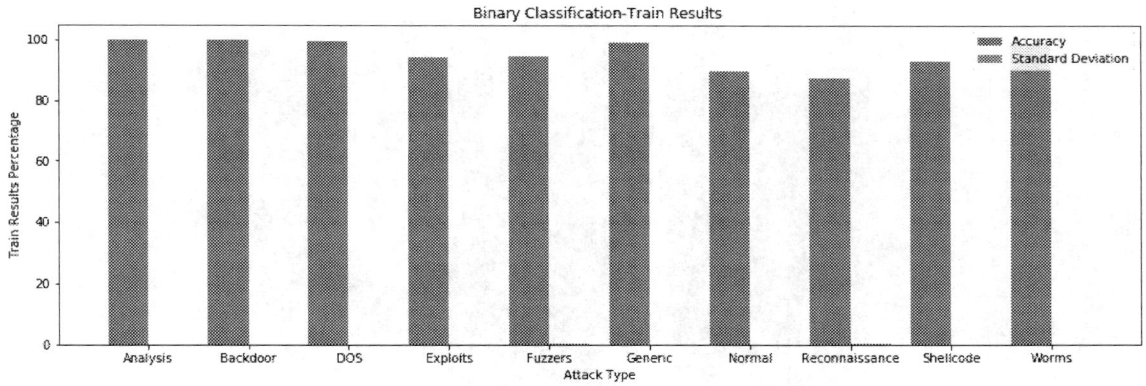

In figure 3, the bar chart train results accuracy score for various attack types using a binary classification algorithm. The prediction shows the accuracy and standard deviation for the different attack types with accuracy metrics scores for train results.

Figure 4. Test results accuracy score for various attack types using a binary classification algorithm

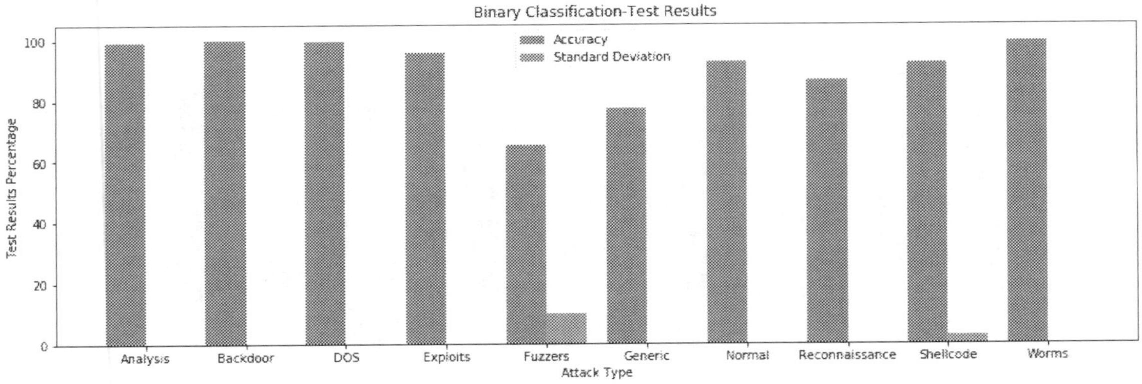

In figure 4, the bar chart test results accuracy score for various attack types using a binary classification algorithm. The prediction shows the accuracy and standard deviation for the different attack types with accuracy metrics scores for test results.

Figure 5. The Performance for binary classification algorithm from uniform distribution ranges between 0 and 1

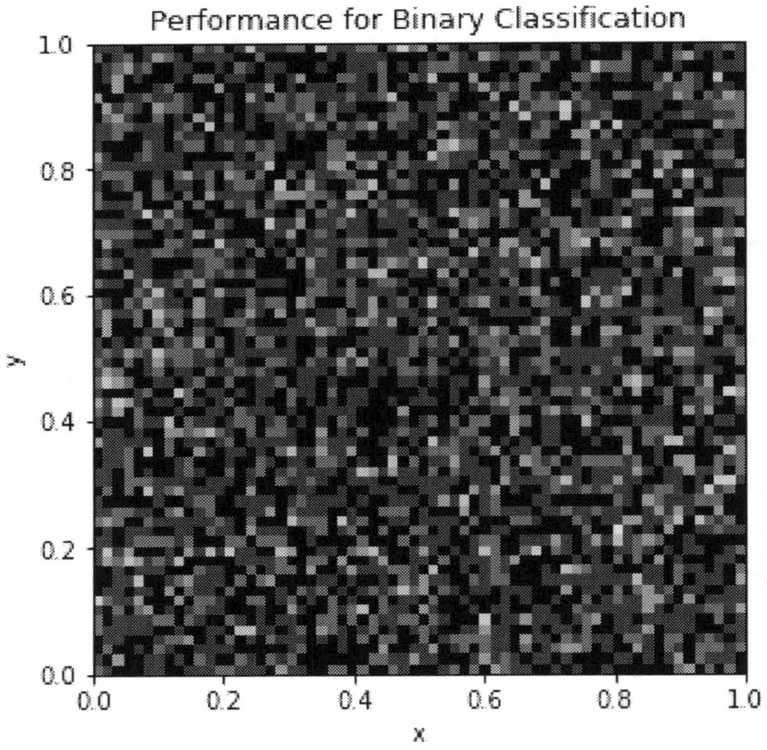

In figure 5, the heat map shows the performance ofthe binary classification algorithm. The prediction shows the samples from uniform distribution ranges between 0 and 1.Observations were made during experiments to identify top-performing variants of the proposed method using the respective classifiers and machine learning ensembles. Figure 5 gives such top-performing observations regarding the performance metrics used in uniform distribution.A tuned machine learning algorithm ensures that the models do not overfit or make an excessively high difference.A binary classification model and an ensemble of those were used to identify anomalies in the retrained dataset by determining classifier accuracy through isolation.This section discussed the observed results of the experiments conducted.

CONCLUSION

This paper outlines a method for detecting anomalies in IoT using datasets, including the results of various attacks. In order to extract the various features, UNSW-NB 15 was used to examine some of the vulnerability types, namely Normal, DoS, Fuzzers, Exploits, Backdoors, and Reconnaissance. The ensembles of machine learning models with cross-validation as their ensemble type were trained using KNN in unsupervised and Random Forest in supervised learning. Afterwards, the performance was evaluated using the KNN and RF validation scores and accuracy. Taking into account these experimental results, we found that tuning machine learning was best done by maximizing the models'performance and also monitoring the nodes without over-fitting by using Scikit-Learn.For attack identification, a binary machine learning classification model is created using tensor flow to categorize a given dataset into classes. Afterwards, the process predicts the class of each data point. Then the proposed work compares model accuracy by evaluating with a standardized dataset and shows the accuracy metric score as a result. This made it comparable to other classes in that field. Finally, by utilizing this work, this model can detect risks and abnormalities emerging in an IoT arrangement and smart gadgets and prevent attacks.

REFERENCES

Adil, M., Song, H., Ali, J., Jan, M. A., Attique, M., Abbas, S., & Farouk, A. (2021). EnhancedAODV: A Robust Three Phase Priority-based Traffic Load Balancing Scheme for Internet of Things. *IEEE Internet of Things Journal.*

Alrashdi, I. (2019). AD-IoT: Anomaly detection of IoT cyberattacks in smart city using machine learning. In *2019 IEEE 9th Annual Computing and Communication Workshop and Conference (CCWC).* IEEE. 10.1109/CCWC.2019.8666450

Aoudni, Y., Donald, C., Farouk, A., Sahay, K. B., Babu, D. V., Tripathi, V., & Dhabliya, D. (2022). Cloud security based attack detection using transductive learning integrated with Hidden Markov Model. *Pattern Recognition Letters, 157,* 16–26. doi:10.1016/j.patrec.2022.02.012

Aversano, L., Bernardi, M. L., Cimitile, M., Pecori, R., & Veltri, L. (2021). Effective anomaly detection using deep learning in IoT systems. *Wireless Communications and Mobile Computing, 2021,* 1–14. doi:10.1155/2021/9054336

Chen, N., & Chen, Y. (2022). Anomalous vehicle recognition in Smart Urban traffic monitoring as an edge service. *Future Internet, 14*(2), 54. doi:10.3390/fi14020054

Farouk, A., Alahmadi, A., Ghose, S., & Mashatan, A. (2020). Blockchain platform for industrial healthcare: Vision and future opportunities. *Computer Communications*, *154*, 223–235. doi:10.1016/j.comcom.2020.02.058

Farouk, A., Batle, J., Elhoseny, M., Naseri, M., Lone, M., Fedorov, A., ... Abdel-Aty, M. (2018). Robust general N user authentication scheme in a centralized quantum communication network via generalized GHZ states. *Frontiers in Physics*, *13*(2), 1–18.

Farouk, A., Zakaria, M., Megahed, A., & Omara, F. A. (2015). A generalized architecture of quantum secure direct communication for N disjointed users with authentication. *Scientific Reports*, *5*(1), 1–17. doi:10.1038rep16080 PMID:26577473

Heidari, S., Abutalib, M. M., Alkhambashi, M., Farouk, A., & Naseri, M. (2019). A new general model for quantum image histogram (QIH). *Quantum Information Processing*, *18*(6), 1–20. doi:10.100711128-019-2295-5

Karthikeswaran, D. (2012). A pattern based framework for privacy preservation through association rule mining. *IEEE-International Conference On Advances In Engineering, Science And Management (ICAESM -2012),* 816–821.

Mendonça, R. V., Silva, J. C., Rosa, R. L., Saadi, M., Rodriguez, D. Z., & Farouk, A. (2021). A lightweight intelligent intrusion detection system for industrial internet of things using deep learning algorithm. *Expert Systems: International Journal of Knowledge Engineering and Neural Networks*, 12917

Metwaly, A. F., Rashad, M. Z., Omara, F. A., & Megahed, A. A. (2014). Architecture of multicast centralized key management scheme using quantum key distribution and classical symmetric encryption. *The European Physical Journal. Special Topics*, *223*(8), 1711–1728. doi:10.1140/epjst/e2014-02118-x

Naseri, M., Abdolmaleky, M., Laref, A., Parandin, F., Celik, T., Farouk, A., Mohamadi, M., & Jalalian, H. (2018). A new cryptography algorithm for quantum images. *Optik (Stuttgart)*, *171*, 947–959. doi:10.1016/j.ijleo.2018.06.113

Peter, K. J. (2011). Improving ATM security via face recognition. In *2011 3rd International Conference on Electronics Computer Technology*. IEEE. 10.1109/ICECTECH.2011.5942118

Priya. (2021). Robust attack detection approach for IIoT using ensemble classifier. *Computers, Materials & Continua, 66*(3), 2457–2470. . doi:10.32604/cmc.2021.013852

Ramapatruni, S. (2019). Anomaly detection models for smart home security. In *2019 IEEE 5th Intl Conference on Big Data Security on Cloud (BigDataSecurity), IEEE Intl Conference on High Performance and Smart Computing, (HPSC) and IEEE Intl Conference on Intelligent Data and Security (IDS).* IEEE. 10.1109/BigDataSecurity-HPSC-IDS.2019.00015

Rashid, M. M., Kamruzzaman, J., Hassan, M. M., Imam, T., & Gordon, S. (2020). Cyberattacks detection in IoT-based smart city applications using machine learning techniques. *International Journal of Environmental Research and Public Health*, *17*(24), 9347. doi:10.3390/ijerph17249347 PMID:33327468

Reddy, D. K., Behera, H. S., Nayak, J., Vijayakumar, P., Naik, B., & Singh, P. K. (2021). Deep neural network based anomaly detection in Internet of Things network traffic tracking for the applications of future smart cities. *Transactions on Emerging Telecommunications Technologies*, *32*(7). Advance online publication. doi:10.1002/ett.4121

Sahu, N. K., & Mukherjee, I. (2020). Machine Learning based anomaly detection for IoT Network: (Anomaly detection in IoT Network). In *2020 4th International Conference on Trends in Electronics and Informatics (ICOEI)*. IEEE. 10.1109/ICOEI48184.2020.9142921

Savic, M., Lukic, M., Danilovic, D., Bodroski, Z., Bajovic, D., Mezei, I., Vukobratovic, D., Skrbic, S., & Jakovetic, D. (2021). Deep learning anomaly detection for cellular IoT with applications in smart logistics. *IEEE Access: Practical Innovations, Open Solutions*, *9*, 59406–59419. doi:10.1109/ACCESS.2021.3072916

Shakya, D. S., & Smys, D. (2020). Anomalies detection in fog computing architectures using deep learning. *Journal of Trends in Computer Science and Smart Technology*, *2*(1), 46–55. doi:10.36548/jtcsst.2020.1.005

Zhu, F., Zhang, C., Zheng, Z., & Farouk, A. (2021). Practical Network Coding Technologies and Softwarization in Wireless Networks. *IEEE Internet of Things Journal*, *8*(7), 5211–5218. doi:10.1109/JIOT.2021.3056580

Chapter 9
Data Storage, Data Forwarding, Data Retrieval With Big Data Deepfakes in Secure Cloud Storage

K. Vinitha
Nandha Engineering College, India

P. Thirumoorthy
Nandha Engineering College, India

S. Hemalatha
Nandha Engineering College, India

ABSTRACT

Deduplication technologies are extensively used in distributed storage management to lower the space and transfer rate needs of services by eliminating redundant information and storing only its single replica. Many clients redistributing comparable data to a shared repository is ideal for deduplication; however, this practise raises concerns about data ownership and confidentiality. Each data owner can confidently show a distributed storage server that they are the rightful owner of a piece of data via confirmation of holding plans. In contrast to state, many clients would encrypt data before re-appropriating it to distributed storage for added safety. Due to the unpredictable nature of encryption, this prevents data duplication. Some recent deduplication systems have been proposed to solve this issue by allowing multiple owners to share the same encryption key for identical data.

DOI: 10.4018/978-1-6684-6060-3.ch009

INTRODUCTION

Distributed computing is a term that is commonly used in the IT industry. An authentic depiction of what awaits registrants in the future from a specialised and based on societal perspectives forms the backdrop of this extravagantly beautiful presentation (Abdolmaleky, et al., 2017). It wasn't until much later that the term "distributed computing" was invented, but the idea of housing data and processing capacity in remote data centres owned and operated by private enterprises isn't novel (Abulkasim, et al., 2019). Regaining favour wasn't possible until the 1990s, when it was used in conjunction with other distributed registering providing mechanisms like matrix processing. Distributed computing's original intent was to use a utility pricing model to offer IT as a service to businesses and individuals via cloud computing on-demand (Adil, et al., 2021a). The developments in matrix processing might be seen as the earliest examples of distributed computing (Adil, et al., 2021b). In late 2006, Eric Schmidt, CEO of Google, was the first to offer a concrete definition to the term "cloud processing" (Aoudni, et al., 2022). Thus, the evolution of distributed computing is a highly remarkable quirk, despite the fact that its basis is built on some outmoded principles that have been modified to integrate new business, specialised, and social viewpoints (Farouk, et al., 2018). Technically speaking, the cloud is an extension of a preexisting network-based design (Harnik et al., 2010) that makes use of the framework's administrations while also incorporating some novelties, such as virtualization and different approaches (Farouk, et al., 2020).

Deployment Models

Access to the cloud might be public, private, hybrid, or community, and is defined by organisational structures (Farouk, et al., 2015). The Public Cloud has made it possible to efficiently release previously inaccessible frameworks and administrations to the broad public (Naseri, et al., 2018). Due to its dynamic nature, public cloud services like email may not be as secure as their more immobile private counterparts (Vijayalakshmi, C. 2020). Access to a company's own frameworks and management is made available through the deployment of a private cloud (Kaaniche and Laurent, 2014). There is an added layer of security thanks to the fact that it is hidden (Naseri, et al., 2015). As a result of the Community Cloud, numerous organisations can work together to create shared infrastructures and administration structures (Heidari et al., 2019). However, private clouds are used for the more fundamental types of training, while public clouds are used for the more advanced types of training (Wang, C. et al., 2010).

Service Models

Model management the models are reliable with Cloud Computing is based. They are arranged into 3 essential assistance models for recorded beneath:

- Foundation as a Service (IaaS)
- Stage as a Service (PaaS)
- Programming as a Service (SaaS)

IaaS platforms provide extraordinarily adaptable assets that may be modified on demand. Because of this, IaaS is suitable for tasks that are transient, exploratory, or subject to sudden shifts. The automation of management assignments, dynamic scaling, work area virtualisation, and strategy-based administrations are some of the different features of IaaS circumstances. IaaS customers typically pay on a per-use, hourly, weekly, or monthly basis, depending on the plane. The upfront expenditures of purchasing in-house equipment and programming are eliminated thanks to this strategy, which calls for additional payments only when those costs are incurred. IaaS providers their own frameworks, executive monitoring, and other monitoring tasks may become more difficult for customers to perform. In a similar vein, in the event that an IaaS provider goes on vacation, it is possible that customers' responsibilities will be altered (Naseri et al., 2015). For instance, if we take into consideration that a company is pushing another product, it may be quite advantageous to host and analyse an application with a supplier of infrastructure as a service (IaaS) (Zhu et al., 2021). It is possible that once the new code has test and improved, that can be removed in IaaS environment also and replaced with a traditional in-house setup. This may be done to save money or make resources available for other initiatives. Amazon Web Services (AWS), Microsoft Windows Azure, Google Compute Engine, Rackspace Open Cloud, and IBM Smart Cloud Enterprise are among the top IaaS providers.

Platform as A Service (PAAS)

PaaS provides the runtime climate for the applications, advancement and organization devices. In PaaS model the cloud supplier change the equipment and programming apparatuses. Those who saw an enhanced client-facing application as a necessity. Components of a PaaS provider's infrastructure. Customers can develop and launch more applications without investing in costly infrastructure and complex code with PaaS. In most cases, a company's whole infrastructure can't be replaced by a PaaS service. Businesses typically rely on PaaS providers for critical administrations like Java development and application support. For on-premises provisioning of a typical office building, the IT department, for instance, may have to acquire and deploy hardware, frameworks, and middleware (such as data storage systems and application programming interfaces).

Software as A Service (SAAS)

The SaaS model allows for the participation of programming programmes as a means of providing support to end users. The use of SaaS removes the necessity for organisations to install and execute apps on their very own personal computers or within their very own server farms. This eliminates the cost of purchasing equipment, providing for its upkeep, and maintaining it, as well as the cost of obtaining programming authorisation, establishing it, and providing support. The following are some of the many advantages offered by the SaaS model: Adaptable instalments: Customers opt to subscribe to a SaaS product rather than purchasing additional programming or hardware to facilitate its implementation. They pay for this support in most cases using a methodology that requires additional payments to be made only when those costs are incurred. Several different types of businesses are able to engage in more effective and less unpredictable planning as a result of the use of escalating costs for recurrent labour expenses. Customers have the ability to cancel their subscriptions to SaaS at any time in order to get rid of those recurring costs (Zhou, et al., 2016). Versatile use: Customers have option can acquire to extra or fewer services or elements whenever they choose when using cloud-based services like SaaS because these kinds of services offer a great degree of flexibility. Programmable Updates: Instead of buying entirely new software, customers can rely on a SaaS provider to automatically update and fix issues. This saves customer money in the long run. Additionally, this lessens the workload for the IT workers located internally.

LITERATURE SURVEY

Recent years have seen an uptick in the consideration of pressure as a notable method for encouraging adaptability among managers in distributed computing. Data compression is a general term for the process of reducing the size of digital files without sacrificing quality. The process improves storage efficiency and can organise data transfers to lessen the total number of necessary bytes transmitted. When there are multiple copies of the same piece of data, pressure eliminates the unnecessary copies, leaving behind only the real copy and directing all other repetitions to it. The manifestation of pressure can take place either on the level of the document or the square. Gets rid of all copies of a record that are essentially identical in order to maintain maximum pressure. Similar pressure can act on the square level, wiping out duplicates of information squares that appear in similar data.

The private information deduplication convention was introduced by Metwaly et al., 2014, and is a codified presentation of a deduplication technique for storing private data. As one might expect, the private data deduplication standard enables a client to demonstrate to the information server's contour chain that it is the rightful owner of a piece of private information without the server disclosing any further information. In this way, our proposal can be seen as supplementary to the cutting-edge public information deduplication norms of Mendonça et al., 2021). In a two-party computing scenario, the safety of private information deduplication conventions is codified in a reenactment-based framework. Finally, the development of private deduplication protocols is described and analysed in the context of common cryptographic presumptions. Assuming the underlying hashing work is collision-versatile, the discrete logarithm is hard, and the computation of the time the encoding can remove up to -part of Bitcoin, in the presence of malicious adversaries, we demonstrate that the proposed private information deduplication convention is provably secure. As far as we are aware, this is the first deduplication standard for securing confidential data.

PROPOSED SYSTEM

With the goal of enforcing information classification and making effective use of pressure, joint encryption was developed. Duplicate data can be encoded and decoded with the help of a single key (ECDH), which can be obtained by computing the cryptographic hash value of the data's essence. The clients keep the keys and send the encrypted message to the cloud when the key has been aged and the information has been encrypted. Due to the fact that the encryption process is predicated on the information's content, identical copies of the data will generate the same uniform key and a similarly crafted coded message. Furthermore, a thorough validation of the ownership convention is anticipated to provide proof that the client really owns a comparable document when a copy is located, which is important for preventing unwanted access. After the record has been validated, the server will offer a reference to any subsequent clients with the same record so that they do not need to retransmit the same document. The server can provide the client with an encrypted document that can be accessed via a pointer; the document can then be decrypted by comparing the keys of the document's rightful owners. In this way, the cloud can push the code texts thanks to the integrated encryption, and an unauthorised client can't get to the document thanks to the evidence of ownership. Differential copy permission checks are useful in many scenarios, but previous push systems lacked the infrastructure to handle them. And within this accepted system of pressure.

Many privileges are granted during the framework declaration, and further privileges are applied to each record when it is uploaded to the cloud, limiting access to only the types of users for whom the document was intended.

Proposed Methodology

The proposed timestamp-based plot is an augmentation of the plan proposed by Li, J. et al. (2015). It is utilised for secure distributed storage, information recovery and information sent. The ideas like encryption, eradication codes, and intermediary re-encryption ideas are utilised for distributed storage security. The information of cloud clients is put away on different servers. The comparing security keys are put away in key servers. The usefulness of the proposed conspire is perceived as far as arrangement, information capacity, information recovery and information sending with trustworthiness.

Setup

This is the primary stage where framework supervisors set required boundaries. A short time later, every client is allocated a couple of keys as a feature of public-key cryptography. A short time later, the client's mystery key is put away in the key server.

Data Storage

This stage is designed to ensure the confidentiality of any information that may be present. Clients who use the cloud play out this movement. When a cloud customer has to re-appropriate a record to the cloud, he will first break the record into a particular number of squares. Then, each square is given its own unique code. The encoded blocks are then saved to a large number of different capacity servers within the cloud. The figure text is received by the servers, where it is then converted into code words and stored. The capacity interaction is related to two important actions altogether. They are currently encoding, calculating encryption, and registering the character token. The following is how the calculation of tokens should be done.

$$\mathcal{T} = h^{f(a_3, \mathrm{ID})}$$

$$C_i = \left(0, \propto_i, \beta, \gamma_i\right) = \left(0, g^{r_i}, \tau, m_i e\left(g^{a_1}, \tau^{r_i}\right)\right), \tag{2}$$

$$C' = \left(0, \prod_{i=1}^{k}\left(\propto_i^{g_i}\right), \beta, \prod_{i=1}^{k}\left(\gamma_i^{g_i}\right)\right)$$

$$= \left(0, g\sum_{i=1}^{k} g_{i^{r_i}}, \tau\prod_{i=1}^{k} m_i^{g_i} e\left(g^{a_1}, \tau\right)\sum_{i=1}^{k} g_{i^{r_i}}\right)$$

$$= \left(0, g^{r'}, \tau, We\left(g, \tau\right)^{a_1 r'}\right), \quad (3)$$

Data Forwarding

Clients of the cloud can advance their information to different clients. It happens with public key cryptography. At the point when client A needs to send information to client B, client A scrambles information with the public key of client B and sends the information. On getting information, client B can decode it with his own private key. The information sending is done through servers. Before information is sent to the beneficiary, the servers re-encode the information utilising the public key of B. Then, at that point, the information is sent to B. There are three calculations associated with the information-sending process. They are known as KeyRecover(.), ReKeyGen(.), and ReEnc(.). Whenever the client needs the first part's mystery key, KeyRecover(.) calculation is summoned. It proceeded as follows.

$$a_1 = \sum_{s\epsilon T}\left(fA,1\left(s\right)\prod_{\substack{s'\epsilon T \\ \{s\}}}\frac{-s'}{s-s'}\right) mod\, p.$$

For producing a re-encryption key, the ReKeyGen(.) is summoned. This calculation thus conjureReEnc(.) calculation. The ReKeyGen(.)proceeded as follows.

For creating re-scrambled code word images, the ReEnc(.) calculation plays out the accompanying.

$$R, K_{A\rightarrow B}^{ID} = \left(\left(h^{b_2}\right)^{a_1\left(f\left(a_3.ID\right)+e\right)}, h^{a_1 e}\right). \quad (5)$$

$$C" = \left(1, \propto, h^{b_2 a_1\left(f\left(a_3.ID\right)+e\right)}, {}^{3}\cdot e\left(\propto, h^{a_1 e}\right)\right)$$

$$= \left(1, g^{r'}, h^{b_2 a_1\left(f\left(a_3.ID\right)+e\right)}, We\left(g, h\right)^{a_1 r'\left(f\left(a_3.ID\right)+e\right)}\right). \quad (6)$$

Data Retrieval

It is a course of recovering information with complete trustworthiness. Whenever a client sends information recovery demand, the client is confirmed by key servers. Then the capacity servers do incomplete decoding of the accessible information and afterwards consolidate the entire information prior to sending it to the cloud client. More subtleties on information capacity, recovery and sending can be found. Data and Combine(.) are the two calculations engaged with information recovery. Information is conjured by a vital server subsequent to acquiring unique codeword images to perform incomplete unscrambling. Then, at that point, the incomplete decoding happens at various servers where bits of information are put away. Then, at that point, combine(.) calculation is summoned to the club for every one of the pieces to get the unique record.

Fault Tolerance

Adaptation to non-critical failure is incorporated into the structure of the cloud framework. At the point when a server is down under any circumstance, different servers will keep handling demands. Later on advances can be taken to recuperate the server which neglected to handle demand.

MODULES

User Module

In this module, users have confirmation and security to access the details that are introduced in the cosmological framework. Before clients get to the nitty-gritty or view it, they should have a record of how they should log in first.

Secure

An outsider can simultaneously deal with many inspecting appointments in response to diverse clients' requests in this module, which is the core of protection safeguarding in cloud computing. The individual assessing of these activities for an outsider might be a very tedious and time-consuming process. Clump testing not only enables an outsider to carry out numerous evaluating chores at the same time, but it also results in a large reduction in the amount of money that an outsider must spend on calculations.

Data Dynamics Module

Therefore, supporting information elements for protection ensuring the control of public gambling are also crucial. We are currently showing how our basic plan can be modified to extend the current work to help information elements, including block-level change, cancellation, and inclusion tasks. This procedure can include in our plan to achieve the safety security of the public control of gambling by means of informational elements.

Security of Duplicate Check Token

He considers several kinds of security that require protection, that is unforgeability of the copy, really look at the token: There are two kinds of enemies, or at least the external enemy and the internal enemy. An external enemy can be considered an internal enemy with virtually no honor. Assuming that the client has honor p, it expects that an adversary cannot produce and originate from a substantial copy of a token with some other honor p′ on any entry F where p does not match p′. Likewise, it requires that unless an adversary requests a token with its own honor from a private cloud server, it could not create a legitimate copy of the token with P in any F requested.

Experimental Setup

The execution of the proposed plot is as per the following. The execution of arrangement, secure distributed storage, information sending and information recovery are compared and investigated. This paper centers around timestamp-based participation among the vital servers and capacity servers. This participation among the servers guarantees consistency in information elements. Information consistency and fair treatment of solicitation are considered in the proposed conspire. The information irregularities because of correspondence delays in the current frameworks are defeated here by utilising the timestamp-based instrument. The new plan utilises a worldwide time stamp which is trailed by capacity and key servers. As numerous servers are associated with the tasks, the information elements are to be completed with consistency and security.

At all times, even when storing information, retrieving information, and sending information, you should maintain an upright posture. For instance, capacity interaction occurs when customers transmit information to the cloud, which involves a number of different servers. The timestamp-based setup both monitors the transaction and ensures that it takes place correctly in accordance with its specifications. In the event that there are issues with communication, the new method has to require extra time in order to ensure consistency. This method is carried on through the process of information recovery as well as the conveying of information. For the purpose of evaluating the viability of the suggested configuration, a sample application was developed by our team. The results of the preliminary research indicated that the timestamp-based structure had the potential to prevent abnormalities in distributed storage.

As a matter of fact, in all activities like Encode, KeyRecover, ReKeyGen, ReEnc, Share Dec and Combine, a timestamp is related to the respectability of tasks related to a solitary exchange. The timestamp is some way or another, connected with the ID of the current exchange. The point of the timestamp-based tasks is to guarantee that all activities in a solitary exchange, where numerous servers are involved, are executed as a unit. In this manner, more participation and hearty respectability of the activities can be accomplished.

We have made tests in a custom test system that worked in the Java stage. The cloud servers, cloud server suppliers and the information proprietors, the tasks included are reenacted. The recreation results uncover that the proposed timestamp approach beats the current methodology.

RESULT

We compare the proposed model with an accuracy of 94% in efficiency, whereas the existing model is 79%. This comparison graph is the representation for the theoretical purpose only (figs. 1 to 5).

Figure 1. Secure Cloud

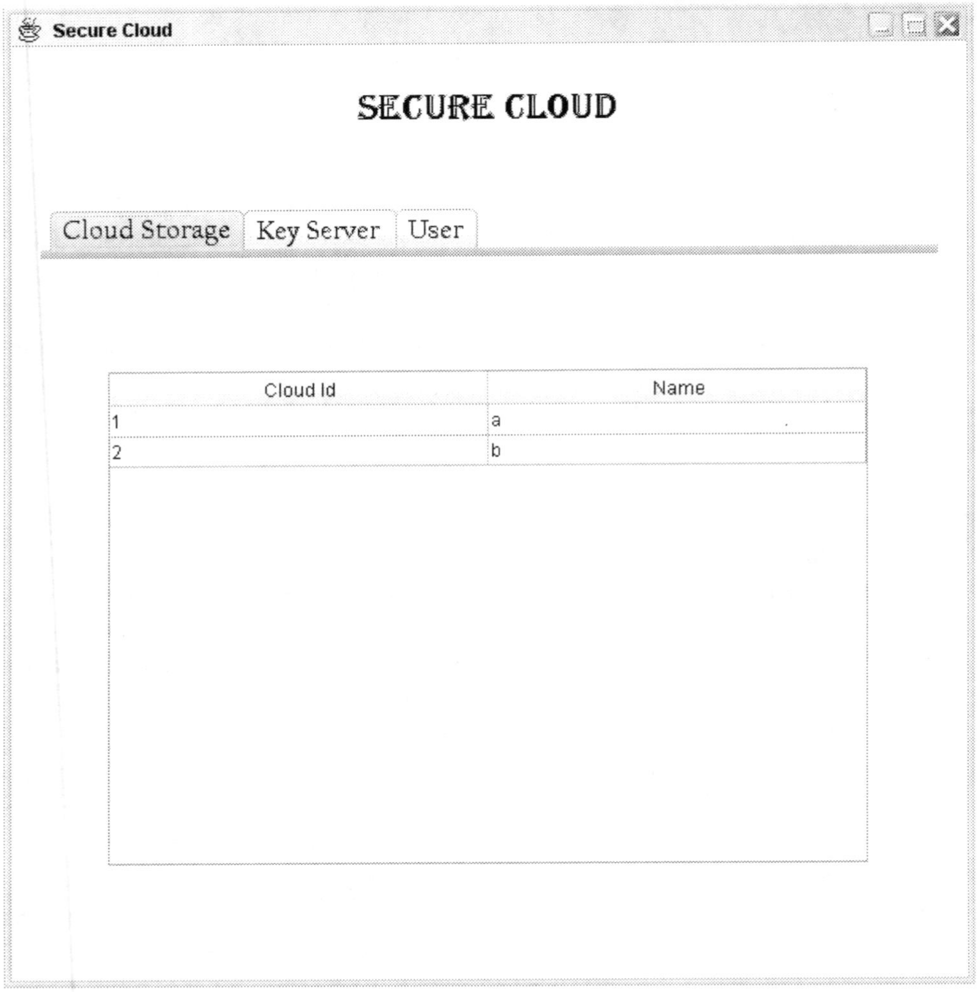

Figure 2. Key Server

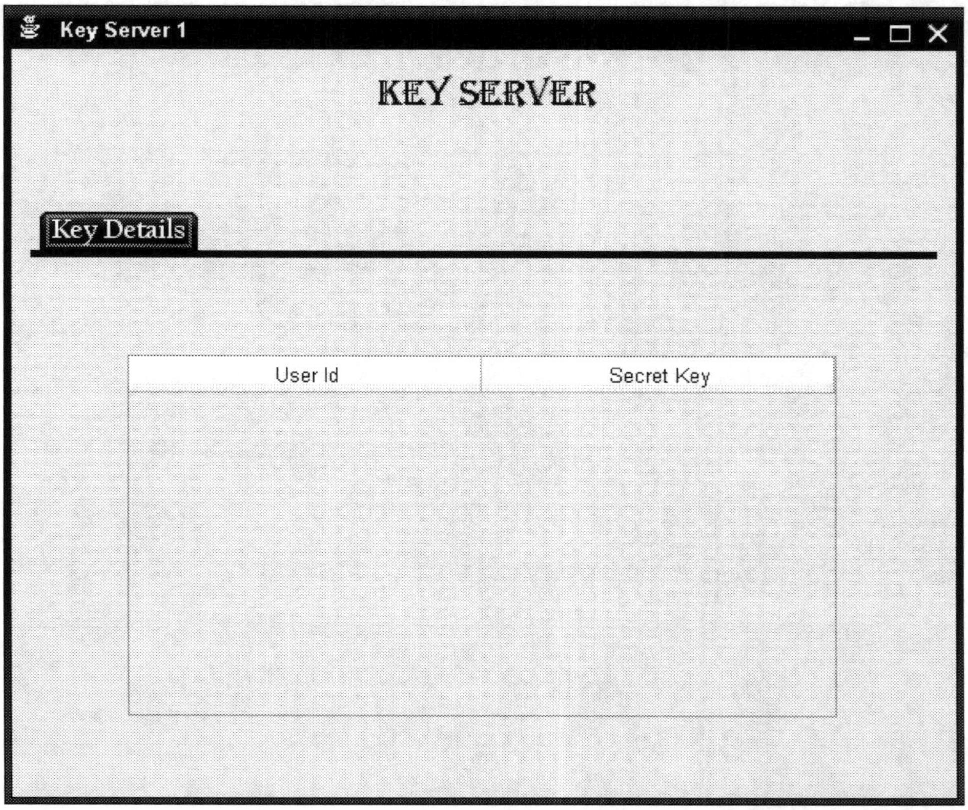

Figure 3. User Key Generation, Data Storage, Forwarding, Retrieval Forms

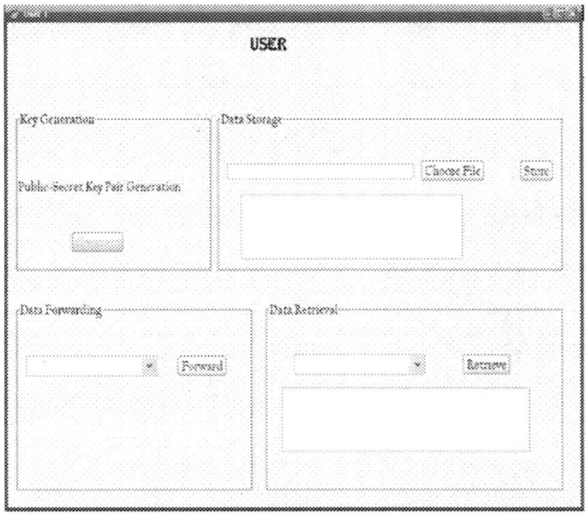

Figure 4. User Key Generation, Data Storage, Forwarding, Retrieval Forms

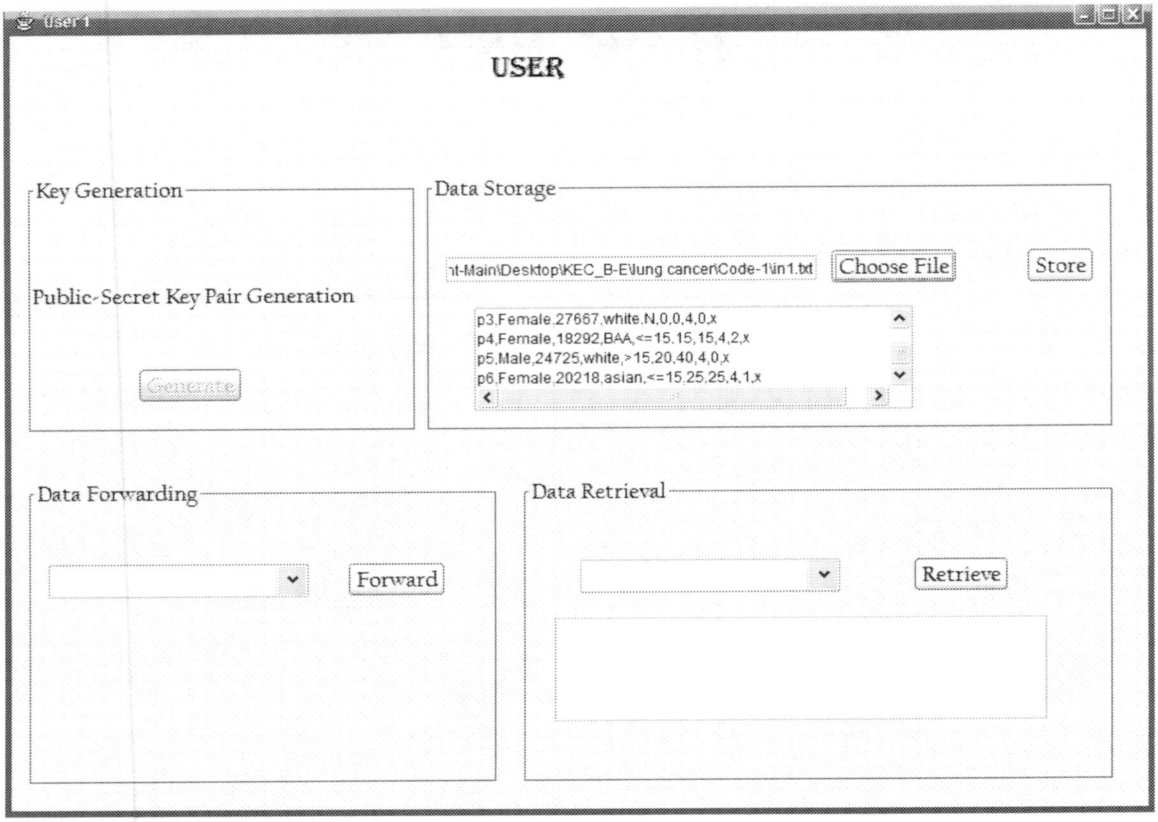

Figure 5. User Key Generation, Data Storage, Forwarding, Retrieval Forms

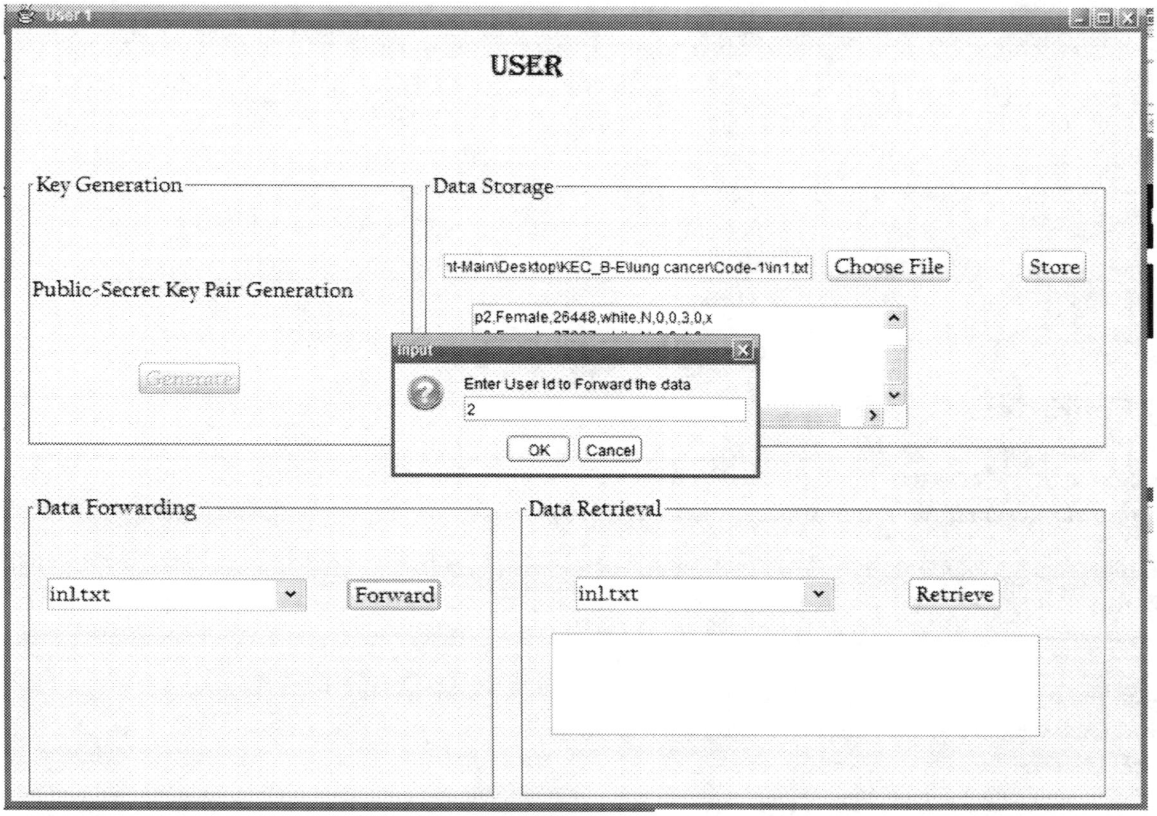

CONCLUSION

By keeping track of various clients' valuations for copy control, the concept of allowed information pressure was presented in this SVT employing ECDH project to guarantee data security. Using a record copy control badge to generate a private cloud server with private keys, we also provided various new innovations in information pressure enabling approved copy controls in crossover cloud engineering. After doing a thorough security analysis, we have concluded that our plans are safe from both insider and unreachable assaults using the recommended security paradigm. To demonstrate the viability of our proposed approved copy control scheme, we developed a sandbox environment and invited key stakeholders to experiment with it. To demonstrate that, in comparison to simultaneous encryption and organisational shift, the impact of our approved copy control is minor. By compressing data, we may reduce the amount of data being transferred and conserve valuable storage space. This programme is useful for quickly backing up data in the cloud environment. The client is unaware of the cost savings made possible by cloud storage for documents that are not printed. Any lost file or piece of data can be easily retrieved for the customer. The cloud controller's spare space is where information pressure is carried out. The informational load can be symmetrically distributed across clients in this implementation. We also revealed various new information pressure advancements in support of the approved design of a hybrid cloud for copy clearance, wherein tokens for controlling copies of documents are generated by a private cloud server using private keys. Security analysis demonstrates that our strategies are safe from the types of insider and external assaults outlined in the security framework we've developed. We tested this theory with a poll using a copy we had prepared and approved specifically to address the conspiracy. To show that, in comparison to simultaneous encryption and network relocation, our preferred method of copy control imposes only negligible extra burden. It is possible to reduce the need for both storage and data transmission by applying pressure to the information. The app provides basic cloud-based support data and is therefore useful. The customer doesn't care that no backup files are being kept on the cloud, which costs money. If the client loses something, they can get it back in a jiffy. Information compression is performed in the cloud regulator's spare space. Customers may be able to balance out their data pressure with this release of the app.

REFERENCES

Abdolmaleky, M., Naseri, M., Batle, J., Farouk, A., & Gong, L. H. (2017). Red-Green-Blue multi-channel quantum representation of digital images. *Optik (Stuttgart)*, *128*, 121–132. doi:10.1016/j.ijleo.2016.09.123

Abulkasim, H., Alsuqaih, H. N., Hamdan, W. F., Hamad, S., Farouk, A., Mashatan, A., & Ghose, S. (2019). Improved dynamic multi-party quantum private comparison for next-generation mobile network. *IEEE Access: Practical Innovations, Open Solutions*, *7*, 17917–17926. doi:10.1109/ACCESS.2019.2894101

Adil, M., Khan, M. K., Jamjoom, M., & Farouk, A. (2021a). MHADBOR: AI-enabled Administrative Distance based Opportunistic Load Balancing Scheme for an Agriculture Internet of Things Network. *IEEE Micro*.

Adil, M., Song, H., Ali, J., Jan, M. A., Attique, M., Abbas, S., & Farouk, A. (2021b). EnhancedAODV: A Robust Three Phase Priority-based Traffic Load Balancing Scheme for Internet of Things. *IEEE Internet of Things Journal*.

Aoudni, Y., Donald, C., Farouk, A., Sahay, K. B., Babu, D. V., Tripathi, V., & Dhabliya, D. (2022). Cloud security based attack detection using transductive learning integrated with Hidden Markov Model. *Pattern Recognition Letters*, *157*, 16–26. doi:10.1016/j.patrec.2022.02.012

Farouk, A., Alahmadi, A., Ghose, S., & Mashatan, A. (2020). Blockchain platform for industrial healthcare: Vision and future opportunities. *Computer Communications*, *154*, 223–235. doi:10.1016/j.comcom.2020.02.058

Farouk, A., Batle, J., Elhoseny, M., Naseri, M., Lone, M., Fedorov, A., ... Abdel-Aty, M. (2018). Robust general N user authentication scheme in a centralized quantum communication network via generalized GHZ states. *Frontiers in Physics*, *13*(2), 1–18.

Farouk, A., Zakaria, M., Megahed, A., & Omara, F. A. (2015). A generalized architecture of quantum secure direct communication for N disjointed users with authentication. *Scientific Reports*, *5*(1), 1–17. doi:10.1038rep16080 PMID:26577473

Harnik, D., Pinkas, B., & Shulman-Peleg, A. (2010). Side channels in cloud services: Deduplication in cloud storage. *IEEE Security and Privacy*, *8*(6), 40–47. doi:10.1109/MSP.2010.187

Heidari, S., Abutalib, M. M., Alkhambashi, M., Farouk, A., & Naseri, M. (2019). A new general model for quantum image histogram (QIH). *Quantum Information Processing*, *18*(6), 1–20. doi:10.100711128-019-2295-5

Kaaniche, N., & Laurent, M. (2014). A secure client side deduplication scheme in cloud storage environments. In *2014 6th International Conference on New Technologies, Mobility and Security (NTMS)*. IEEE. 10.1109/NTMS.2014.6814002

Li, J., Chen, X., Huang, X., Tang, S., Xiang, Y., Hassan, M. M., & Alelaiwi, A. (2015). Secure distributed deduplication systems with improved reliability. *IEEE Transactions on Computers*, *64*(12), 3569–3579. doi:10.1109/TC.2015.2401017

Mendonça, R. V., Silva, J. C., Rosa, R. L., Saadi, M., Rodriguez, D. Z., & Farouk, A. (2021). A lightweight intelligent intrusion detection system for industrial internet of things using deep learning algorithm. *Expert Systems: International Journal of Knowledge Engineering and Neural Networks*, 12917.

Metwaly, A. F., Rashad, M. Z., Omara, F. A., & Megahed, A. A. (2014). Architecture of multicast centralized key management scheme using quantum key distribution and classical symmetric encryption. *The European Physical Journal. Special Topics*, *223*(8), 1711–1728. doi:10.1140/epjst/e2014-02118-x

Naseri, M., Abdolmaleky, M., Laref, A., Parandin, F., Celik, T., Farouk, A., Mohamadi, M., & Jalalian, H. (2018). A new cryptography algorithm for quantum images. *Optik (Stuttgart)*, *171*, 947–959. doi:10.1016/j.ijleo.2018.06.113

Naseri, M., Raji, M. A., Hantehzadeh, M. R., Farouk, A., Boochani, A., & Solaymani, S. (2015). A scheme for secure quantum communication network with authentication using GHZ-like states and cluster states controlled teleportation. *Quantum Information Processing*, *14*(11), 4279–4295. doi:10.100711128-015-1107-9

Rafaeli, S., & Hutchison, D. (2003). A survey of key management for secure group communication. *ACM Computing Surveys*, *35*(3), 309–329. doi:10.1145/937503.937506

Vijayalakshmi, C. (2020). Convergent dispersal: Toward storage-efficient security in a cloud-of-clouds. *International Journal for Research in Applied Science and Engineering Technology*, *8*(4), 541–547. doi:10.22214/ijraset.2020.4087

Wang, C. (2010). A novel encryption scheme for data deduplication system. In *2010 International Conference on Communications, Circuits and Systems (ICCCAS)*. IEEE. 10.1109/ICCCAS.2010.5581996

Zhou, N. R., Liang, X. R., Zhou, Z. H., & Farouk, A. (2016). Relay selection scheme for amplify-and-forward cooperative communication system with artificial noise. *Security and Communication Networks*, *9*(11), 1398–1404. doi:10.1002ec.1425

Zhu, F., Zhang, C., Zheng, Z., & Farouk, A. (2021). Practical Network Coding Technologies and Softwarization in Wireless Networks. *IEEE Internet of Things Journal*, *8*(7), 5211–5218. doi:10.1109/JIOT.2021.3056580

Chapter 10
A Privacy Protection Method for Deepfake Hybrid Cloud Computing

L. Subhashini
Nandha Engineering College, India

S. Maheswari
Nandha Engineering College, India

S. Prabhu
Nandha Engineering College, India

ABSTRACT

Cloud computing developed the world rapidly, so in our lifetimes, other cloud services are entered, and the security protection in our cloud services, particularly the protection against data sequestration, is gaining importance. Still, the protection separation implementation causes a huge drain. Therefore, it is difficult to implement the most appropriate product to reduce consumption power while protecting separation. The proposal proposes a full-scale sequestration scheme (PPPS) to provide usable sequestration protection that satisfies stone sequestration requirements while system performance can be maintained. First, the separation is unidentified by the drugs they carry, and they quantify the degree of security and perform the TripleDES standard and AES standard encrypts algorithms. The safety formulation is also derived from analysis results and professional data. Finally, similar results display that PPPS also meets the request sequestration from stones and maintains the performance in various cloud environments.

INTRODUCTION

Cloud computing is the most suitable pattern for individuals and is related to penetrating affordable and on-request computing checkouts and scalable operations and storing data services. The cloud storage systems, related to Google Drive, Microsoft OneDrive, Dropbox etc., allow a large amount of data to be stored from druggies that penetrate and participate between drugs, time regardless and constrained

DOI: 10.4018/978-1-6684-6060-3.ch010

position. Cloud computing of growing vogue, and the amount of businesses and separate moving towards using the cloud continues to increase.

The ordinary businesses association and individuals cloud services are using. The data owners move the sensitive data to the lobby, and the element of control over the data is lost. They have no guarantee for cloud druggies of how cloud providers will handle and protect this sensitive data.

The cloud gives druggists the comfort of accessing data over many biases, using the cloud services to make the data from the unsafe number of cruel attacks and traps. Security events happen all the time. Even worse, cloud service providers can falsify data to an unapproved reality of profiteers.

One possible outcome is the use of Cryptography to overcome these problems. Various data owners must shift the sensitive data before being stored in a potentially untrusted field. The encryption scheme strength was largely depending on the decoding operation strength method. The encryption security scheme lies in the secrecy keys, identified only for narcotics permits to study the individual data, and the encryption algorithm is used not only in the secrecy.

Due to the number of documents that are saved and the cloud is connected, and added amount of stored data drugs, cloud storage wants a cryptographic scheme design that encounters the security conditions, efficiency, inflexibility, and ease to use is an exhausting task. The home results are generally suffering from limited applicability in encryption operations operate. The data owners manually encrypt their documents before uploading them to the palette.

Operating railway systems better enforce encrypting media. A customer operation interacts with the original encrypted train system, and the translated data is stored in back-end cloud storage. The design includes hybrid, speed, and safety views.

The following are explained in detail.

1. Speed - The sensitive information data does not position in demand. The weak composition takes advantage to gain additional performance in Druggies cloud services.
2. Hybrid – The data contain sensitive information for the position with demand. The partial data need weak encryption for particular data (e.g., address and business id), and the remaining data have strong encryption (e.g., account balances).
3. Security - The data have more wanted information. The other privileged drug addicts see the maximum amount of data and less privileged drug users view limited data.
    - Encrypt/decrypt less important data using a weak encryption system to make communication fast.
    - Encrypt/decrypt using a weak encryption system in partial data and a strong encryption system in other partial data so we have fast communication and increased security position.
    - Encrypt/decrypt using a strong encryption system in a particular field and some weak encryption system used in another field to show high-privilege drugs and low-privilege drugs in the partial fields.
    - Encrypt/decrypt weak encryption systems have watermarked content, and strong encryption systems have unwatermarked content.

LITERATURE SURVEY

Domingo-Ferrer et al. (2019) are developing the extent of personal and sensitive records amassed by facts managers increases the need to use the cloud not handiest to save facts but also to method it in cloud environments. However, safety concerns against common statistics breaches and superior criminal statistics protection necessities (including the EU Union's preferred records safety law) discourage extracting touchy unprotected records from public clouds. To resolve this hassle, this research includes technologies that enable the external storage of private records and processing of touchy records in public clouds. More specifically, and as a novelty, we overview methods to cover external information based on statistics classification and anonymity, further to the cryptographic strategies included in different surveys. We then compared those methods in phrases of ambulatory statistics operations, overhead, accuracy retention, and effect on statistics control. In addition, we listed several studies projects and to be had products that use some established answers. Subsequently, we identify the final studies' challenges.

Hassija et al. (2019), the internet of things (IoT) is the following technology of conversation. Via IoT, the fabric can seamlessly create, acquire and alternate information. Extraordinary IoT focuses on performing unique duties and tries to empower inanimate items to do something without human intervention. Existing and cutting-edge IoT applications promise to grow the extent of comfort, efficiency and automation of customers. The intention to use such land sustainably calls for excessive tiers of protection, privacy, assurance and assault recovery. In this regard, it's vital to make important changes within the layout of IoT applications to gain extra relaxed IoT environments. This document presents an in-depth evaluation of security challenges and threats to IoT systems. After discussing protection issues, various rising and present technologies aim to acquire an excessive belief in IoT structures. It discusses four unique technology, blockchain, fog computing, facet computing and device-gaining knowledge, to increase the level of safety in IoT.

Deng et al. (2020) protect the privacy of records saved within the cloud. The information owner generally encrypts its information in this manner so that positive, precise customers of the records can decrypt it. This increases a critical problem while encrypted statistics wish to be shared with greater human beings than those at first unique by using the information owner. To resolve this hassle, we introduce and formalize an identity-primarily based encryption transformation (IBET) model by seamlessly integrating two well-hooked-up encryption mechanisms, particularly identification-primarily based encryption (IBE) and identity-primarily based broadcast encryption (IBBE). In IBET, records users are recognized and licensed to get the right of entry to information primarily based on their visual identification, which avoids complex certificate management throughout trendy dispensed systems. Extra importantly, IBET provides a conversion method that converts IBE ciphertext to IBBE ciphertext so that a new group of unidentified customers can enter the underlying facts at some point of IBE encryption. We build a strong-sided IBET scheme and display its safety towards competitive assaults. Complete theoretical evaluation and evaluation reveal the effectiveness and efficiency of the proposed gadget.

Eurostat (2022) presents the latest data on the commercial use of cloud computing services within the EU Union (EU). Cloud computing includes components, cloud infrastructure and software packages. The primary contains the hardware assets needed to aid the cloud offerings supplied and commonly consists of a server, garage and community additives. The second element relates to software program applications and laptop structures for jogging commercial enterprise programs as provided using the internet to 0.33 events.

Alliance (2019) was distributed to more than 165 IT and security professionals in the US and globally, representing various industries and business sizes. The goal was to understand their vision for how their businesses use cloud applications, what kind of data they stream through those applications, and what that means for risks.

T. Haeberlen, and L. Dupre (2014), is developed a new manner to supply computing offerings, not new technology. Pc services, from facts storage and processing to software programs, including email control, are effortlessly available, free and on demand. With time to tighten our belts, this new model of the computing economy has found fertile ground and is experiencing big international funding. Cloud Computing: advantages, dangers, and statistics security Recommendations3 that brings cloud economies of scale and safety flexibility to friends and foes alike. Extra attention to sources and facts exposes targets which can be extra attractive to attackers, but cloud defences can be sturdy, scalable and much less luxurious. The ENISA record permits a complete evaluation of the security dangers and advantages of using cloud computing – imparting a security guide for ability customers of cloud computing.

A. Westin, A (1967) explains within the statistic society is information self-determination, i.e. "the right of people, agencies or establishment to decide for herself how, while and to what quantity statistics approximately disseminated to others.

Ramirez, Every day, purchasers engage in the diffusion of online and offline sports that display personal statistics approximately them. Different, not unusual sports encompass using a cell telephone, buying a residence or car, subscribing to a magazine, buying a catalogue, browsing the net, taking a survey to get a chit, and using social media. Subscribing to online news websites or setting bets. As purchasers interact in those everyday sports, business companions accumulate facts approximately themselves and, in many cases, provide or promote that information to fact providers.

Khan, M. A. (2016) can dispose of the want to set up costly computing structure solutions and IT-primarily-based offerings utilized by enterprises. They promise to offer bendy, online accessible IT architectures for lighter portable devices. This will allow doubling the capacity or capabilities of existing software and youth. In the case of cloud computing, all data is stored on fixed community sources, permitting admission to record through digital machines. Since the information might lie in some other us of a past the user's management and control, they have numerous safety and privacy issues to understand and maintain. Also, it can never be denied that there could have been a server crash, which has been proven quite often recently. Various issues need to be addressed in terms of security and privacy in the case of cloud computing. This comprehensive survey aims to expand and analyze the many outstanding issues that threaten cloud computing and distribution and affect the various stakeholders associated with it.

Singh et al. (2016) demonstrate the incredible power of providing much-needed services to consumers in a highly flexible and inexpensive manner. As we approach the concept of much-needed services, resource integration, and transformation of everything in our distribution landscape, protection impedes this latest dream of overall computing performance. The overview affords a complete evaluation of the safety problem of various cloud computing issues. In addition, in-depth dialogue on numerous important subjects about the embedded device, utility, garage gadget, integration associate trouble and must extra. So this document covers other public and private cloud authorities and security concerns. In addition, it integrates requirements for better security management and proposes a three-layer security structure. Open conversation issues as new security concepts and recommendations are also presented.

A. Singh, and K. Chatterjee (2017), present many needed online services with the help of large amounts of the digital garage. The main capabilities of cloud computing are that the person does now not must install an expensive computer infrastructure, and the price of its offerings is minimal. In recent years, cloud computing has incorporated the industry with many different fields, which has recommended the researcher discover new related technologies. Due to the supply of its offerings and measurement of computing strategies, personal customers and agencies switch their requests, records and offerings to the cloud storage server. Like the benefits, changing a neighbourhood computer to a far-flung laptop has brought many protection issues and challenges to clients and providers. Many cloud offerings are provided with the aid of a dependent on 0.33-party enterprise, which brings new safety threats. The cloud issuer offers its services online and uses a wide range of web technology that increases new protection troubles. This article discusses the primary features of cloud computing, security issues, threats and answers. Further, this paper outlines numerous key subjects associated with the cloud: cloud structure, service and deployment version, cloud technology, cloud safety concepts, threats and assaults. This paper also discusses many open research questions related to cloud protection.

Praveen-Kumar et al. (2018) help shop and get the right to enter statistics remotely online. However, records storage on an unreliable cloud server leads to privateness and control in getting the right of entry to the cloud. Traditional encryption schemes, which include symmetric and uneven schemes, are not appropriate to offer to get entry to manipulation because of the shortage of flexibility. Pleasant-grained get right of entry to manipulate. one of the fantastic cryptographic techniques of providing privacy and fine-grained get right of entry to manage to cloud computing is Encrypted. on this paper, we take a closer take look at current key policies and ciphertext-based characteristics policy schemes primarily based on access shape and multi-authority schemes. Similarly, this evaluation examines, in addition, ciphertext-based total encryption for diverse capabilities such as encrypted coverage, proxy encryption, withdrawal technique, and hierarchical characteristic-based encryption. In addition, this paper compares different ABE schemes based on features, protection, and efficiency. This paper also identifies the validity of attribute-based encryption in real-time programs. Ultimately, this paper analyzes the diverse ABE programs, which will identify the research hole and demanding situations that must be similarly investigated in Qualification-based Encryption. Highlights discuss the primary standards of ABE and its variations from KPABE and CPABE based totally on getting the right of entry to structure with extra authority. check out more about CPABE with encrypted coverage, proxy reset, withdrawal approach and HABE. Examine various ABE schemes based on overall performance, safety, and performance to release open demanding situations. Discover appropriate applications and future steering primarily based on an attribute of cloud computing.

Kaaniche, N., & Laurent, M. (2017) have led to storms and successes. The new pattern increasing the new para was gaining increasing hobby as it offers a less expensive infrastructure that helps transmission, garage, and deep computing performance. But these promising garage offerings present many difficult layout challenges because of the lack of management over information and the invisible cloud environment. This survey aims. This survey provides an important comparative evaluation of cryptographic security measures and, in addition, explores research guidelines and technological approaches to address the protection of data extracted from cloud infrastructure.

Tang et al. (2017) summarize and analyzes modern-day defence experts. We introduce the safety threats and requirements for eliminating streaming records and comply with this with a complete overview of well-suited protection technologies. The awareness of existing security answers for secure, dependable and secure cloud facts services, which include facts retrieval, information computation, information sharing, facts garage and facts get entry to. Subsequently, we recommend open calls and ability studies guides for the rapid development of cloud computing that support broad data transfer and computing deployment to cloud service providers through limited liability companies. Based on each payment model, a client that lacks sufficient integration capabilities can easily perform large cloud computing tasks. The research suggests certain secure programs to exclude people from various computer applications. This study aims to design and implement state-of-the-art technologies in the field. It introduces security threats and requirements, followed by other factors to consider when creating secure computer hacking programs. We have systematically focused on the existing security solutions for various computational tasks such as matrix computation, mathematical precision, etc., data confidentiality management, and integrity computation. Finally, we provide a literature discussion and a list of open challenges in the area.ch solution section.

Shan et al. (2019) support the widespread use of data and computer deployment for cloud service providers by enterprises with limited resources. Based on each payment model, a client that lacks sufficient integration capabilities can easily perform large cloud computing tasks. Recently, more publish proposed to research and suggest certain secure programs to exclude people from various computer applications. This study aims to design and implement state-of-the-art technologies in the field. It introduces security threats and requirements, followed by other factors to consider when creating secure computer hacking programs. We have systematically focused on the existing security solutions for various computational tasks such as matrix computation, mathematical precision, etc., data confidentiality management, and integrity computation. Finally, we offer a book discussion and a list of open calls in the field.

Geetha et al. (2019) give a higher answer with distributed resources and offer customers with better facts get right of entry to ability. Building a network to provide services with excessive velocity gets the right of entry while keeping security and communication between software programs is known as cloud computing. The cloud computing platform can provide an answer for massive facts centres and assemble consumer desires. Maximum software builders have provided the spirit of open supply cloud, which include Google, Microsoft, Amazon and so on. The rules editing feature needs a one-of-a-kind multi-impact technique advanced based on state-of-the-art strategies. In this, look at the opportunity of dispensing facts and information to a massive records garage space within the cloud computing in the form of a customer organization made out of editing data evaluation maps become calculated, and datasets were provided as input. In this study, map reduction is a design process to change the load and improve the performance of group use by controlling the distribution of opportunities.

PROPOSED METHODOLOGY

Cloud computing is an arise computing model that gives flexible, pay-as-you-go services and is scalable. Cloud computing and other computing models differ in participatory service-driven applications and data collection in an outsourced warehouse. Service sharing streamlines work with computer hardware and offers economic benefits to users to reduce costs and overheads.

The position of sequestration breaks into three situations because it's considered that druggies cannot easily be divided between their sequestration conditions at further than three situations. The tiers can have types of hybrid, security and speed. They are as follows.

- **Speed:** This position's requirements include non-sensitive data. Druggies who desire better cloud performance utilize poor encryption. Then TripleDES is utilized.

- **Hybrid:** The Requirements contain some sensitive data presented in the levels. The requirements that partial data for strong encryption and other data with strong encryption. They have both TripleDES and AES encrypt fashion used.
- **Security:** In the insulation position contains the important data. The process to convert the data is secure farther the privileged view the ultimate of data, and druggies view limited data in weak privileges. Then TripleDES encrypt fashion is used.
- A disadvantage of cloud computing was the shared resource construct stores and reuses druggist data that it does not own; druggist data can be exposed or manipulated by other cloud brutes.
- Because encryption and media increase processing and drain, they reduce overall efficiency.
- Strict security cannot be maintained if equal honour is given to all kinds of drugs.

In the proposed system, the existing levels of privacy protection are implemented; they have three processing levels security, speed and hybrid. The content and safety are ensured. Some documents already have images and audio content watermarked, providing lower security and being accessible to most users, while strong cryptography contains normal content with higher security. Security breaches are not concerned with watermark content.

Algorithm

AES: The AES is otherwise known as the name of Rijndael. The full form is Advanced Encryption Standard. The Rijndael is a euphemism for electronic information developed in 2001 by US Nation Institution.

It is a stand-alone version of AES block cypher composed of 2 cryptography Belgian and Vincent Rijmen, and they submitted a request to the NIST during the AES Process tender. The various key and block sizes came from the Rijndael family.

The AES select three members in the family from Rijndael by NIST that each block contains three block sizes with 128 bits, so the various key size is 128 bit, 192 bit and 256 bits. This symmetric key algorithm is defined from the AES algorithm, meaning that both encrypted and decrypted data have the same key.

3DES: The rate of full key find against the DES algorithm after 1990 commenced to purpose soreness among DES customers. But, customers no longer need to change DES due to changing broadly typical encrypt embedded huge system calls of money and time. The logical method is not to desert DES altogether; however, DES is used in an alternate method.

It caused a revised version of 3DES. After all, they have two versions of 3DES referred to as 2-key Triple DES as 2TDES and 3-key Triple-DES as 3TDES. Three-Key Triple DES Previously. The Triple Key Triple DES uses a key value as k for a customer in distribution and first generatesincludingde three special keys in DES K1, K2, and K3 (figure 1).

Figure 1. 3DES Process

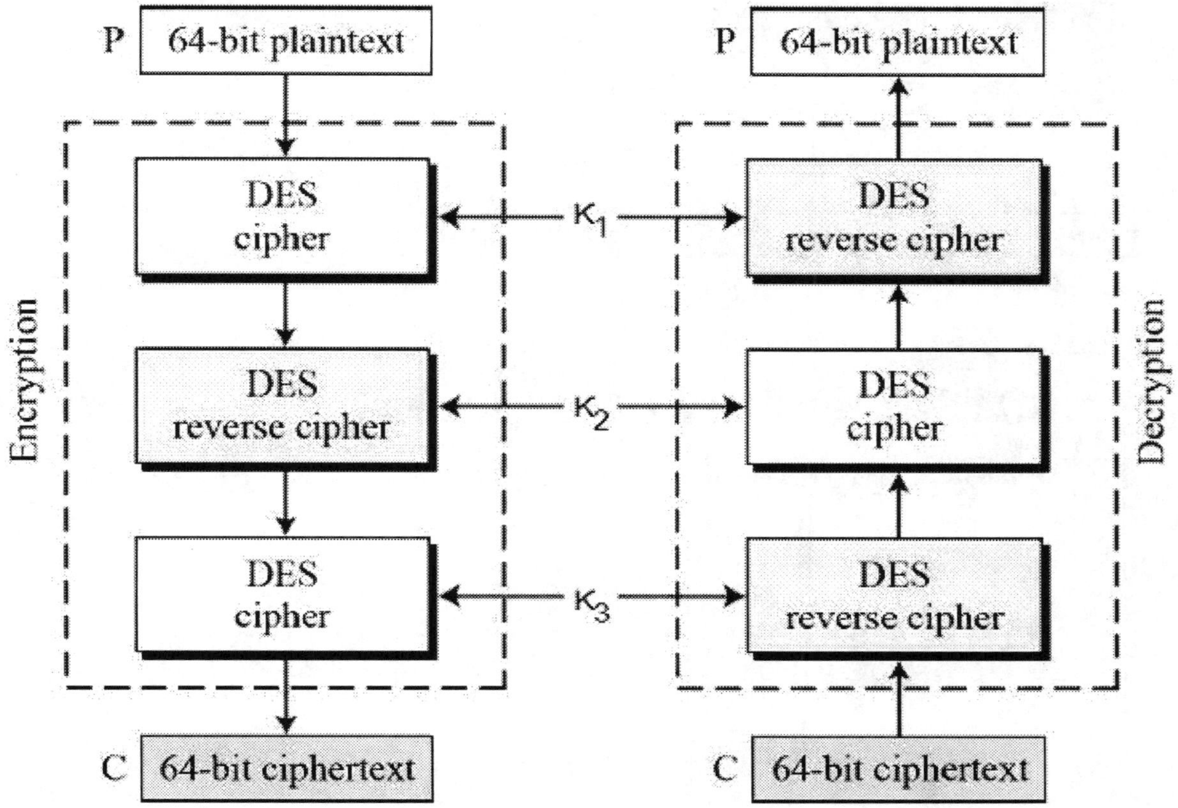

DENTIFING

- The different levels of encrypt and decrypt mechanisms are used; the storage overhead and processing are different and suitable with the reduction.
- Communication is reduced when the different data are handled using the same mechanical protection.
- The different kinds of users are granted different privileges, so there is no need to maintain strict security.
- Different levels of security accessed from different types of content to increase the speed.
- Security is high when the encrypt is used in a single text message in both TripleDES and partial AES (figure 2).

Figure 2. Messages List in Encryption (a & b)

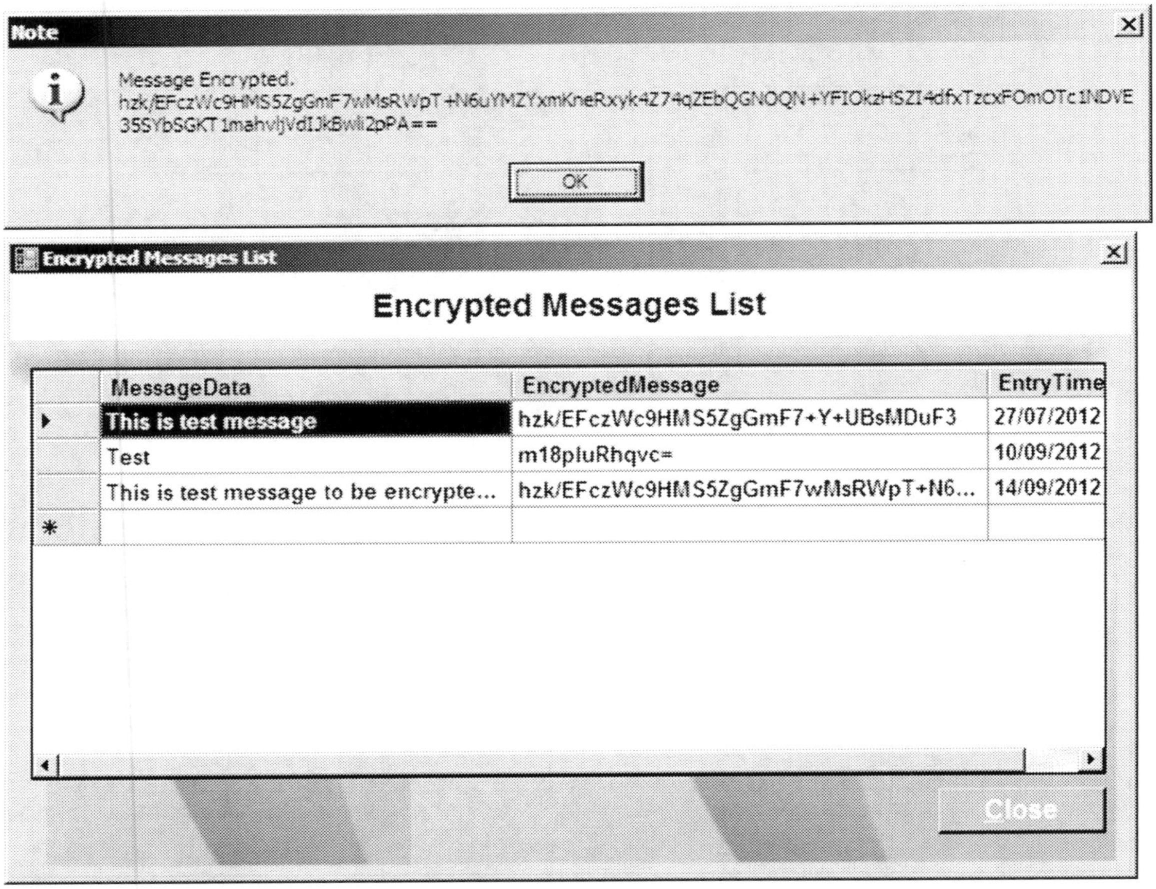

RESULT

Based on this work, a privacy protection method for deepfake hybrid cloud computing has resulted below (figures 3 to 6)

Figure 3. Analyzing 3DES, AES and Hybrid Process

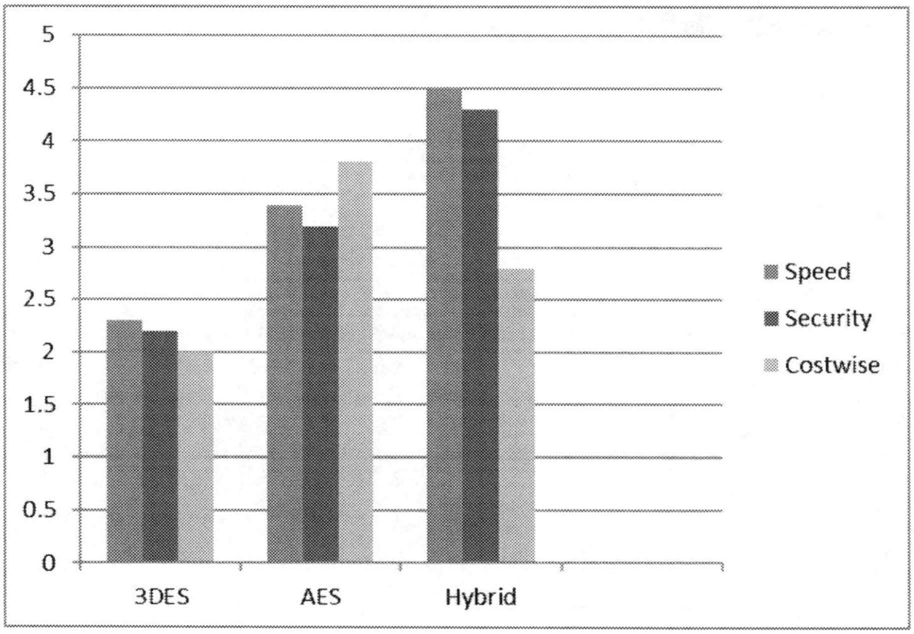

Figure 4. Encrypt Block (Hybrid)

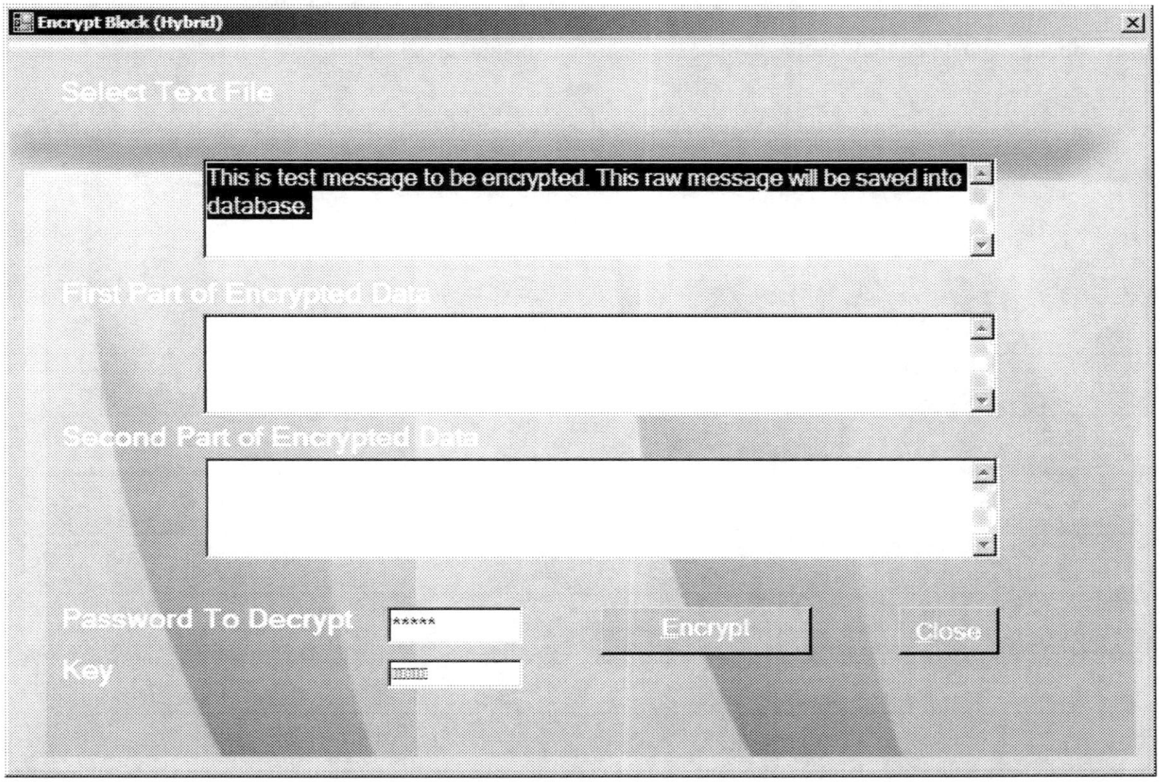

Figure 5. After Hybrid Encryption

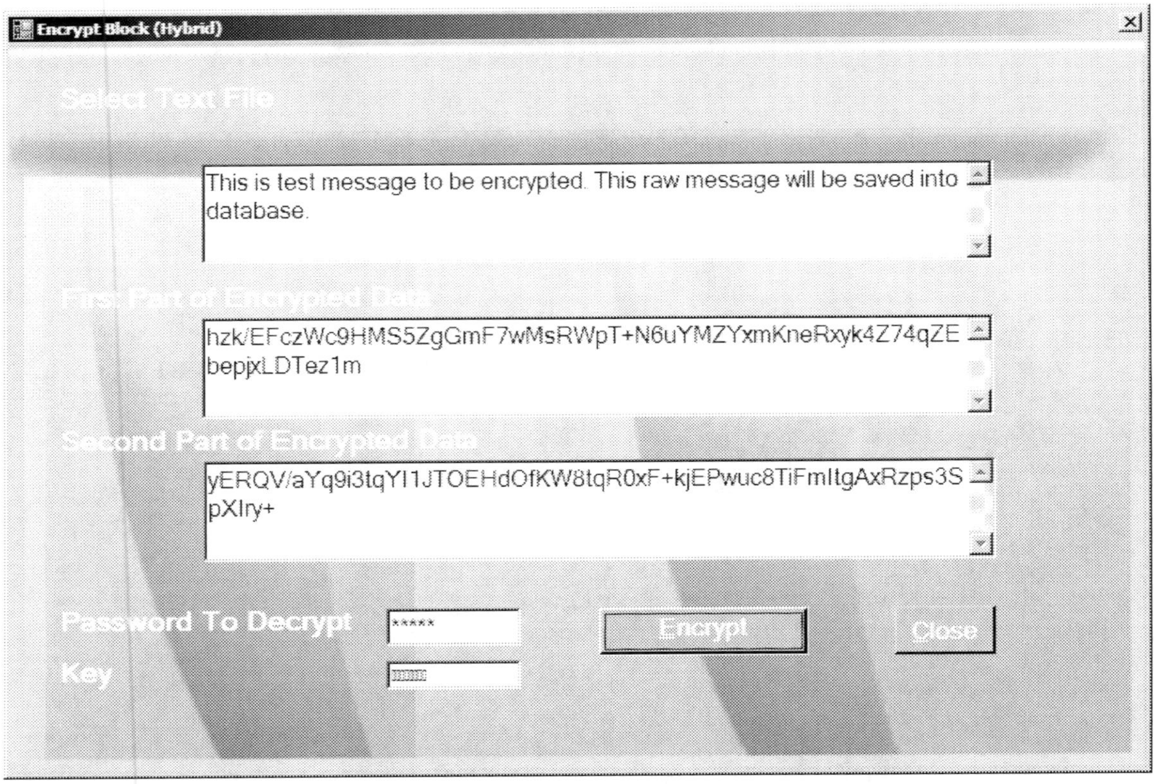

Figure 6. Decrypt Block (Hybrid)

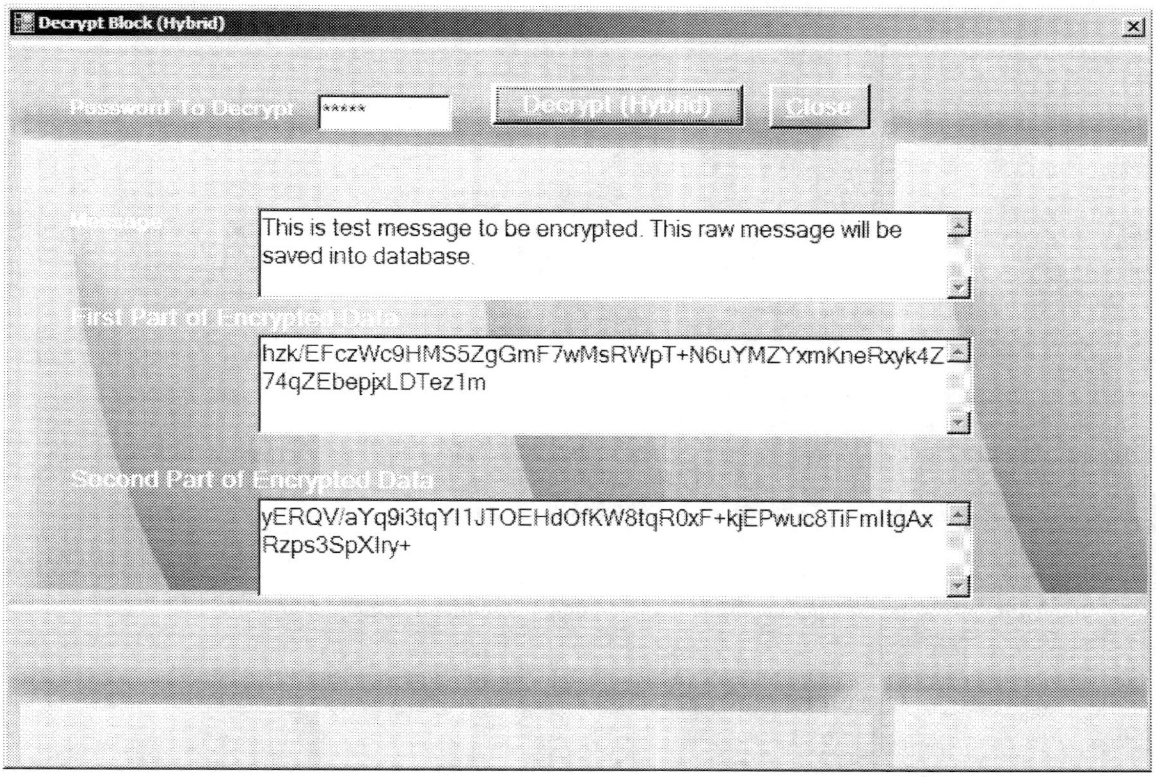

CONCLUSION

This architecture eliminates secure communication. Software operation requires less system familiarity. End consumers use well-tested software. Nearly all system objects planned at the start of software development have been connected, and design implementation is complete. The application's testing run yielded good results and straightforward, correct processing. No method existed to prepare plans for operational evaluation. The design stores and retrieves cloud database records efficiently. Translating and decrypting records protects them. Future development should include the following. The operation uses web services; records can employ many operations. Cloud computing ignores data integrity. Mismatches restore error situations. Web app and database can be implemented in a real cloud.

REFERENCES

Alliance, C. S. (2014). *Cloud usage: Risks and opportunities report* https://downloads.cloudsecurityalliance.org/initiatives/collaborate/netskope/Cloud_Usage_Risks_and_ Opportunities _Survey_Report.pdf

Cloud computing - statistics on the use by enterprises. (n.d.). Retrieved November 2, 2022, from Europa.eu website: https://ec.europa.eu/eurostat/statistics-explained/index.php /Cloud_computing_-_statistics_on_the_use_by_enterprises

Deng, H., Qin, Z., Wu, Q., Guan, Z., Deng, R. H., Wang, Y., & Zhou, Y. (2020). 'Identity-based encryption transformation for flexible sharing of encrypted data in public cloud. *Trans. Inf. Forensics Security*, *15*, 3168–3180. doi:10.1109/TIFS.2020.2985532

Domingo-Ferrer, J., Farràs, O., Ribes-González, J., & Sánchez, D. (2019). Privacy-preserving cloud computing on sensitive data: A survey of methods, products and challenges. *Computer Communications*, *140–141*, 38–60. doi:10.1016/j.comcom.2019.04.011

Haeberlen & Dupre. (2012). *Cloud computing. benefits, risks and recommendations for information security (rev. b).* European Network and Information Security Agency.

Hassija, V., Chamola, V., Saxena, V., Jain, D., Goyal, P., & Sikdar, B. (2019). A survey on IoT security: Application areas, security threats, and solution architectures. *IEEE Access: Practical Innovations, Open Solutions*, *7*, 82721–82743. doi:10.1109/ACCESS.2019.2924045

Kaaniche, N., & Laurent, M. (2017). Data security and privacy preservation in cloud storage environments based on cryptographic mechanisms. *Computer Communications*, *111*, 120–141. doi:10.1016/j.comcom.2017.07.006

Khan, M. A. (2016). A survey of security issues for cloud computing. *Journal of Network and Computer Applications*, *71*, 11–29. doi:10.1016/j.jnca.2016.05.010

Kumar, P., & Kumar, S., & Alphonse. (2018). Attribute based encryption in cloud computing: A survey, gap analysis, and future directions. *Journal of Network and Computer Applications*, *108*, 37–52. doi:10.1016/j.jnca.2018.02.009

Prabhu, S., Sengottaiyan, N., & Geetha, B. G. (2019). Self-adaptive approaches to probability distribution of data analytics in cloud computing resource services for infrastructure hybrids models. Applied Mathematics &. *Information Sciences*, *13*(S1), 437–446. doi:10.18576/amis/13s147 1

Ramirez, Brill, Ohlhausen, Wright, & McSweeny. (2014). *Data brokers: A call for transparency and accountability*. US Federal Trade Commission.

Shan, Z., Ren, K., Blanton, M., & Wang, C. (2019). Practical secure computation outsourcing: A survey. *ACM Computing Surveys*, *51*(2), 1–40. doi:10.1145/3158363

Singh, A., & Chatterjee, K. (2017). Cloud security issues and challenges: A survey. *Journal of Network and Computer Applications*, *79*, 88–115. doi:10.1016/j.jnca.2016.11.027

Singh, S., Jeong, Y.-S., & Park, J. H. (2016). A survey on cloud computing security: Issues, threats, and solutions. *Journal of Network and Computer Applications*, *75*, 200–222. doi:10.1016/j.jnca.2016.09.002

Tang, J., Cui, Y., Li, Q., Ren, K., Liu, J., & Buyya, R. (2017). Ensuring security and privacy preservation for cloud data services. *ACM Computing Surveys*, *49*(1), 1–39. doi:10.1145/2906153

Westin, A. (1967). *Privacy and Freedom*. Atheneum.

Section 2

Advanced Practical Approaches to Applications

Chapter 11
Enhancing the Protection of Information in Digital Voting Using the Fraud Application of Blockchain Technology

P. Ganesan
BMS Institute of Technology and Management, India

D. Rosy Salomi Victoria
St. Joseph's College of Engineering, India

Arun Singh Chouhan
Malla Reddy University, India

D. Saravanan
IFET College of Engineering, India

Rekha Baghel
Ajay Kumar Garg Engineering College, Ghaziabad, India

K. Saikumar
https://orcid.org/0000-0001-9836-3683
Koneru Lakshmaiah Education Foundation, India

ABSTRACT

Elections are conducted electronically instead of using paper ballots to cut down on mistakes and discrepancies. Recently, it has been discovered that paper-based balloting fails owing to security and privacy difficulties, and the electronic balloting approach has been recommended as a replacement. For the sake of keeping your data safe, the authors have designed and developed a hashing algorithm based on SHA-256. The blockchain's adaptability is aided by the sealing of the block concept's incorporation. Consortium blockchain technology is employed to ensure that only the election commission has access to the blockchain database, which candidates and other outside parties cannot modify. When used in the polling method, the methodology discussed in this chapter can yield reliable findings. The authors used a hashing algorithm (SHA-256), block generation, data collection, and result declaration to get to this point.

DOI: 10.4018/978-1-6684-6060-3.ch011

INTRODUCTION

Using an electronic voting scheme could help with the organization & transparency of voting processes. Votes cast with this method are valid in all elections, whether hosted by a university, a private club, or any other group. Anywhere the voter has internet access where he can cast his ballot with this approach. Voter apathy about the electoral process can be traced back to the following problems: To begin, pre-poll rigging refers to illegally coordinating an election to produce the desired outcome. Voters in the outlying villages might choose not to vote or have their ballots altered if they travel a long distance to cast their ballot. They were second, manipulating the vote tally to favor one party over another, registering multiple votes in an election that spans more than one jurisdiction, etc.

From the beginning, secrecy in the voting process has been a top priority. Voting was not a transparent process and was fraught with issues, as evidenced by several indicators. Voting by paper is inefficient because it may be easily manipulated, wastes paper, and takes a long time to declare the consequences. Several new organizations, such as the "Electoral Commission," emerged intending to improve the electoral system. Primary responsibilities of the election commission include setting guidelines for elections, creating electoral districts, and organizing the voting and counting processes. Connecting systems to the blockchain-BC provide immutability, preventing any data changes (Avgerou et.al., 2019).

Information can only be added to the blockchain-BC; it cannot be altered or removed. It consists of more and more roadblocks all the time. The hash value of the prior blocks is included in each block after the first one. This initial building block is often called the "genesis block." Every vote on the blockchain-BC is connected to the one before it. Each block contains the previous block's voter ID, timestamp, & digest (hash) (Hardwick et.al., 2018). Distributed ledger technology refers to the underlying infrastructure for blockchain (DLT). All information can be stored safely & precisely thanks to cryptography. It may be possible to increase data security while using blockchain-BC in voting systems by consuming the SHA-256 hashing algorithm. (Shown in figure 1)

Figure 1. Block Chain

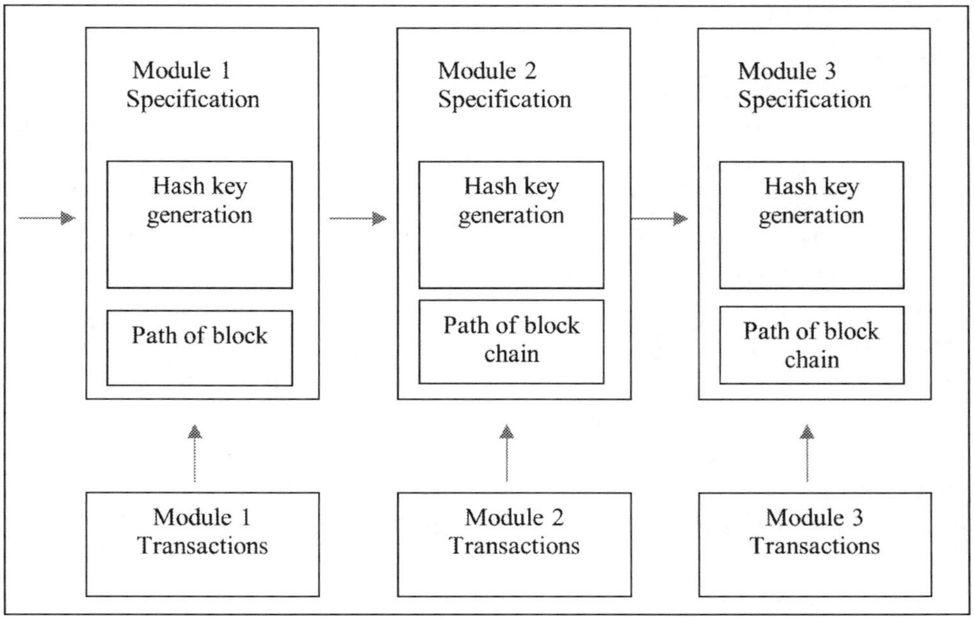

Since the 1970s, electronic voting, frequently known as e-casting a ballot, has been used in numerous structures with key benefits over paper-based frameworks, including improved productivity and decreased blunders. Notwithstanding, there are still hindrances to the broad reception of such frameworks, particularly in enhancing their resistance to potential defects. Blockchain-BC is a promising new technology that may increase the general strength of electronic democratic frameworks. This investigation aims to utilize the highlights of blockchain, for example, cryptographic underpinnings and straightforwardness, to make a successful e-voting instrument. The proposed approach meets the fundamental prerequisites for electronic democratic frameworks and accomplishes start-to-finish certainty. E-voting and its implementation on the Multichain platform are discussed in great detail in this white paper. E-voting schemes that are verifiable from beginning to finish may be achieved using this technology, according to new research (Risnanto et.al., 2022).

Because elections enable the whole people to voice their views, they are an essential part of a democratic society. For the sake of our democracy, elections must be open and reliable to ensure that participants have faith in their legality. Voting methods in this setting have evolved throughout time. This shift is motivated by a desire to make the system more secure, verifiable, & open. Due to its relevance, work continues to improve the voting system's overall efficiency and long-term durability. The widespread adoption of electronic voting (or "e-voting") has significant implications. Although its punched-card voting systems were first introduced in the 1960s, electronic voting systems have come a long way (Hjálmarsson et al, 2018). If an e-voting system is to gain widespread acceptance, it must meet a minimum bar of requirements. Prior to voting, specific requirements must be completed. These include maintaining voters' confidentiality, verifying their identities, & not rejecting their ballots.

This developing technology has strong cryptographic underpinnings, which may be used to build safe arrangements on the Blockchain. In a sense, the Blockchain is an information structure that preserves and provides access to all of the transactions that have taken place since its start. We have a distributed, decentralized database that keeps tabs on an ever-expanding set of data records that are protected from unauthorized interference. Every block in the blockchain-BC is allocated a cryptographic confusion (which might be thought of as a square's distinctive mark) which remains stable as extended as the content in the block is not transformed (Kshetri & Voas 2018). If there are improvements to the square, the cryptographic hash will swiftly change, representing that the information has altered, maybe due to malicious action. Because of its solid cryptographic foundations, blockchain-BC is quickly used to avoid fraudulent transactions in many settings.

Aside from Bitcoin, academics are interested in exploring how blockchain technology might aid applications in a wide range of fields, using properties like non-repudiation and anonymity to aid their research. We use blockchain technology to examine how e-voting systems might benefit from anonymity, integrity, and end-to-end validation. Our theory is that the self-cryptographic authentication erection between exchanges (via hashes) & openness of the circulated record of archives may be used for electronic balloting on the Blockchain itself. Because of its essential nature of keeping up with secrecy and keeping a decentralized and openly circulated record of exchanges across all hubs, the sphere of electronic democracy could greatly benefit from blockchain-BC technology. Therefore, blockchain innovation is profoundly viable in managing the danger of utilizing a democratic token on various occasions and endeavors to influence the result's straightforwardness (Kulkarni, 2021).

The employment of computers & other electronic voting devices to project polling forms & provide high-quality, accurate results that reflect voters' preferences has been a focus of study for quite some time. Various approaches have been used. Practically speaking to help the constituent cycle. From the outset, the PC tallying framework allowed citizens to decide on paper voting forms. Afterward, those cards were filtered and counted at individually graphing cell on a focal worker. In the long run, despite the resistance of PC researchers, Direct Recording Electronic (DRE) casting ballot strategies were executed, which were immensely enjoyed and recognized by the citizens. In order to increase the framework's convenience, the electors must understand the democratic framework properly. DRE frameworks, in particular, have had great success in teaching voters about innovation (Shahzad & Crowcroft 2019). These frameworks work likewise to conventional political decision frameworks. With the use of DRE, an elector begins his journey by traveling to the surveying site and acquiring an e-voting token that he then uses at the democratic terminal to vote in favor of the candidate of his or her choice. After the up-and-comer determination stage is done, DRE frameworks offer the last choice to the citizen prior to projecting the polling form (on the off chance that the elector wishes to modify his brain), and the voting form projecting is finished after the last choice. (Shown in figure 2)

Figure 2. Electronic voting System

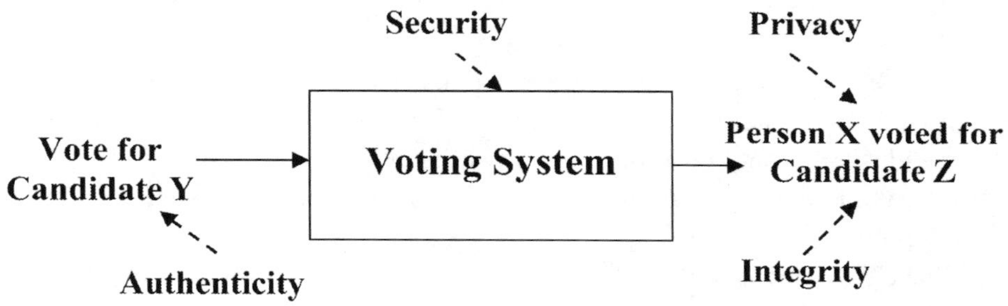

Dispersed record innovations, for example, blockchain, have recently been utilized to make e-casting ballot frameworks, inferable from its advantages as far as start-to-finish evidence. A blockchain is a desirable option in contrast to the current e-casting a ballot framework, with characteristics like namelessness, security assurance, and non-renouncement. This article also offerings an exertion to leverage such blockchain-BC characteristics to develop a superior e-voting system. The following section provides a comprehensive analysis of these types of systems, as well as a comparison of various methods (Fusco et.al., 2018).

LITERATURE SURVEY

To meet the project's objectives & conduct in-depth study on the methods used in blockchain methodology, a literature review was continued by looking at a number of publications based on related methodologies.

As suggested in "Waiting in Line to Vote" (Shaheen et al., 2017), in order to complete the project's objectives & conduct an in-depth learning on the procedures used in the idea of blockchain-BC skill, a literature review was undertaken through investigating many publications depending on related methodologies.

There was no need to stand in line for hours just to cast one vote, as was recommended in "Waiting in Line to Vote," an essay detailing the challenges voters experience throughout an election & how this impacts voter turnout. Electoral malpractices like rigging, bribery, hacking, data manipulation, & misconduct were common during general elections, a study titled "Trusting e-voting among experiences of electoral malpractice: The instance of Indian elections" explains.

Freya Sheer Hardwick's research paper "E-Voting with Blockchain: An E-Voting Protocol with Decentralization and Voter Privacy" When related to the traditional opaque one-sided voting scheme (Hussain et.al., 2021) Study by Freya Sheer Hardwick entitled "E-Voting with Blockchain: An Electronic Voting Protocol with Decentralization and Voter Privacy" Recommend a democratic convention that considers blockchain to be little more than a simple polling station used to cast a ballot; this was an inspiring attempt, but it lacked adequately for long-period usage with complex features. In their analysis of where electronic voting systems are at the moment.

The blockchain employs decentralized consensus techniques to maintain each voter as a node, and the person receiving the most votes will be the leader. We only enable matching people to vote for district leaders when they are announced, as stated by (Saba et.al., 2020), the blockchain-BC employs distributed consensus mechanisms to ensure that each voter remains a node, & the leader is elected through a majority vote. According to the rules in counting votes, only registered voters in a particular district will be eligible to cast ballots for the newly appointed district leader. When that time comes, there will be no evidence of falsified votes. The blockchain records all the votes and guarantees that none have been changed or withdrawn. With blockchain-BC, voters can leave verifiable audit trails of their ballots that cannot be altered in any way. Due to the accessibility provided by this architecture, this platform can be considered public.

Adjustable blockchain with hashing methodology was a server-side validation method utilized by Basit Shahzad & Jon Crowcroft. The blockchain-BC notion of mutable node property allows for correct results storage by having the voter's aadhaar number one unique attribute. The hashing method eliminates the possibility of further chain-breaking procedures by drastically decreasing the amount of duplicate data. After collecting voter information, that data is immediately saved in our Oracle database MySQL. Hashing is used in the database to verify that two blocks in a blockchain are identical, with each voter linking via their unique hash (hash). Francesco Fusco, Maria IlariaLunesu, Filippo Eros Pani, & Andrea Pinna employed side chain technology in their research paper "Crypto-voting, a Blockchain-based e-Voting System" to ensure that voters' ballots remained private. Voters have no access to or ability to change the information of other voters, protecting their privacy. Through blockchain-BC technology, they can make sure no malware will compromise our system or app. Using blockchain-BC technologies, they can confirm that no malware determination compromise our scheme or applications. For an electronic voting system to continue to function reliably, all pertinent data must be made available to the public to protect both the integrity of the system and the confidentiality of voters' personal information. Because of this feature of blockchain-BC technology, the integrity of the stored data is immune to manipulation. Since they are developing this framework, not only is the expense of holding a nationwide election reduced but so is the risk to our personal information.

Voting Process

We present a run-of-the-mill client communication with the proposed technique based on our existing system implementation. An elector frequently signs into the framework by having its thumb effect. If a match is distinguished, the citizen is given a rundown of possibilities to browse, with the alternative of casting a ballot against them. Then again, if the match fizzles, further access will be impeded. This design is refined by the appropriate execution of the confirmation method (in this model, fingerprinting) and job-based admittance control of the board. Besides, it is imagined that every citizen is relegated to a specific electorate. This data is used to assemble a rundown of possibilities for whom they can cast a ballot. Since citizen task to supporters is a disconnected activity, it is outside the extent of this examination.

Following a fruitful vote cast, it is approved by different diggers, and substantial and checked votes are transferred to the public record. The votes' security depends on blockchain innovation, which utilizes cryptographic hashes to guarantee start-to-finish confirmation. To this point, a compelling vote cast is treated as an exchange in the democratic application's blockchain. Therefore, a vote cast is put away in information tables at the backend of the data set and transferred to the blockchain as another square (after practical mining). The framework guarantees that casting a ballot framework sticks to the one-individual, one-vote (majority rule government) rule. This is cultivated by coordinating with the elector's particular thumbprint toward the beginning of each casting a ballot endeavor to abstain from twofold democracy. When the diggers mine the vote, a particular exchange is created for each cast ballot. Miners will reject a vote if it is deemed to be malicious.

WORKING PRINCIPLE OF BLOCK CHAIN

The infrastructure for mixing blockchain-BC with e-voting can be helpful because it provides redundancy. This is because security risks associated with paper-based voting are not mitigated by employing the concept of blockchain-BC. A voter could cast duplicate ballots using traditional methods. However, the secure hashing method SHA-256 generated at the voting time makes this impossible. Individual voters will have less sway over electoral commission procedures. Voters would only be allowed to cast their ballots & check to see if their ballots went to their preferred candidates. That means everyone can see what is going on at every step. After the polls have closed, the electoral commission can finally reveal the winning candidates. The blockchain-BC system can help guarantee honest elections. This means they can prevent vote-buying, voter-count manipulation, & vote duplicates before the polls even open. The election commissioner would announce the election results once the votes for each candidate have been tallied. (Shown in figure 3)

Figure 3. Blockchain working principle

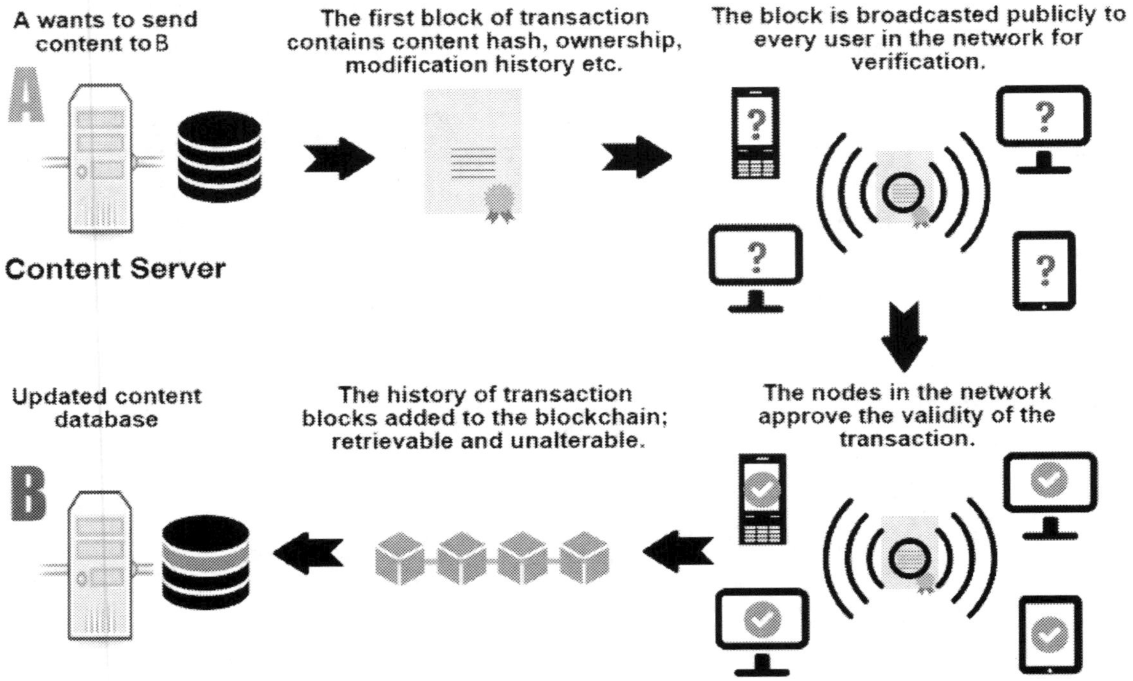

Working of Blockchain

The graphic below shows a sequence of 3 consecutive blocks. Each block includes both its hash and the hash of the previous block. The third building block is identical to the second, while the second building block is identical to the first. The "Genesis" building block comes first. (Demonstrated in figure. 4) If even one block is altered, the hash value will change, putting the entire chain at risk. The distributed nature of blockchain, along with its novel hashing and proof-of-work procedures, ensures its security. Instead of relying on a central authority to oversee the network, blockchain uses a decentralized, open-access system of computers. Any new network participant will be provided with a full, verifiable copy of the blockchain-BC. Using this, the node may verify the integrity of its components and ensure that nothing has been tampered with. A newly generated block will continue to be broadcast to all nodes in the network. Every node then confirms that the block has not been altered by performing a rectification. A consensus is reached once all of the nodes have finished their checks. A blockchain-BC cannot be altered by altering every block in the chain, which is computationally demanding.

Figure 4. Basic working of Block chain

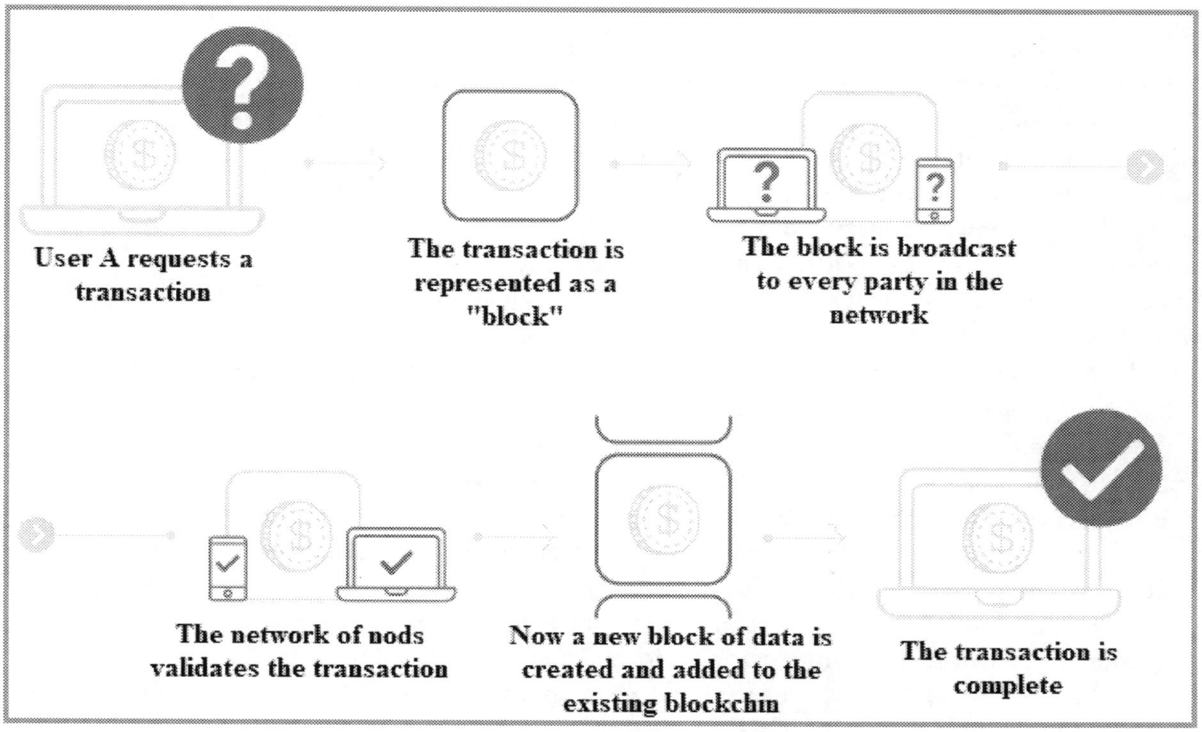

Hashing is a method for generating a checksum hash from the unprocessed text. Data integrity checks rely on it. Thus, we may employ this tactic to guard against the corruption and tampering of our data. With this hashing algorithm, you could ensure that rows in a database table always reference the same block. In this setup, the hash is derived from a combination of a person's phone number & voter id. A 256-bit hash could be generated with the help of the SHA-256 algorithm. We are employing SHA-256, considering it is harder to crack.

The quantity of information necessitates the use of a database for storage. MySQL is highly adaptable to other database management systems and features a user-friendly interface for managing database tables. In this framework, they construct numerous tables for candidates, election commissions, users, election commission validation, & voter information. New candidates' information for an election is kept in the candidate table, while voters' voting ability is verified in the election commission database. The election table is where a voter's information is saved once he has known how he or she voted, while the user table is where a voter is registered to cast an unauthenticated ballot. The information in the "Voter Details" table is comprehensive.

Implementation

An open election is the focus of this piece. There are 2 primary sections to this study.

- Election Commissioner

- User / Voter

In order to have an election, candidates & the general public must first be registered, according to the Election Commissioner. One authorized person, in this case, the election commissioner, must ensure that all information is accurate and up to date. In light of this, we must develop a separate component known as an election commissioner or administrator.

In order to prove his identity as the official election commissioner, the commissioner must first register himself using the unique code and key given to him. This one-of-a-kind combination of code & key will not allow anybody else to access the system in the capacity of an election official. The election commissioner will now need to register by entering his details such as name, phone number, email address, & password. After he registers, his email address will serve as his username in the electoral commission module. After checking in, he can enhance a new user/candidate. He may view the final tally for each political party, but he has no control over the tally itself.

The Election Commissioner's role encompasses the following responsibilities.:

The election commissioner has the critical duty of recruiting new candidates to run in the elections. Upon a voter's arrival at the polls, this component would communicate to the database & conduct read/write operations, like retrieving information about the voter's registered candidates. (shown in figure 5).

Registration to Vote: Second, the election commissioner needs to enter the details of each voter, including their name, date of birth, gender, and maybe a photograph. After those prerequisites have been completed, their names will remain additional to the list of eligible voters. The voter's age will be verified after he receives all of the necessary information from the voter. When voters select candidates, the module instantly verifies their state and electoral district.

Reviewing & Making a Statement the election commissioner would declare the results after the deadline. The results are presented visually employing several charts (bar chart, area chart, pie chart, etc.). For the same reason that a voter's district & state would coincide through that of the candidates, the consequences would remain broken down in the same method, according to the voter's district & state, in the graphical representations of the election.

Figure 5. Anticipated e-voting scheme for election commission part

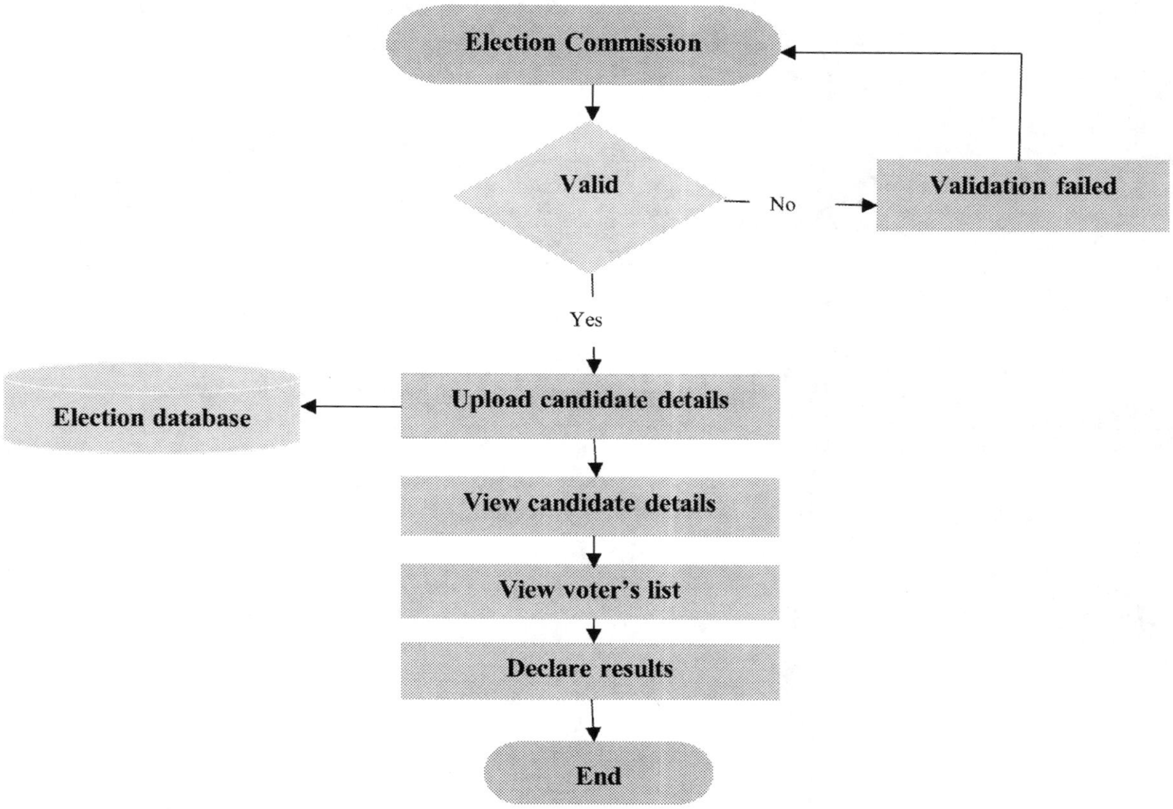

The user / Voter, an elector, has only the right to vote if his name appears on the list of eligible candidates, & only if those credentials are blank.

Figure 6. Anticipated e-voting scheme for user/voter role

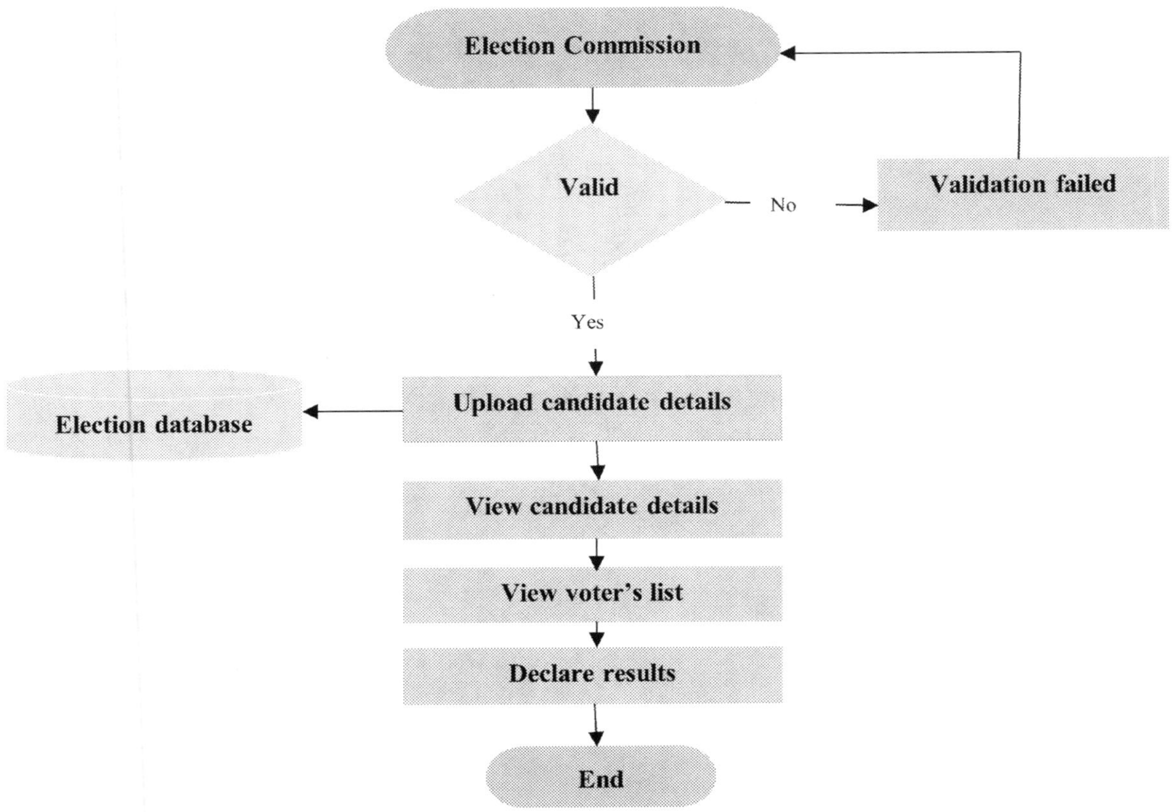

The election commissioner now checks the voter's eligibility to cast a ballot. He has a unique number attached to his phone number or Aadhaar card number; he may log in to the portal and update his credentials. Voters in his district can then see which political parties are represented. (As demonstrated by figure 6. Block containing his or her vote is added to the blockchain when the SHA-256 algorithm is employed to produce a hash value founded on his or her single identification and the unique number of the party for which he or she voted. An individual's ballot may be restricted to only those candidates running for office in his home district. After that, the voter can see if his ballot was cast for a legitimate candidate and check the results. When āvoters are blocked from casting a ballot in an election, they are prevented from casting additional ballots for that election.

Results

When combined with electronic voting, blockchain technology can provide a more secure and trustworthy system with multiple layers of redundancy. Paper ballots could be vulnerable to hacking if the blockchain-BC concept is not implemented. A voter could cast several ballots in paper-based voting, but the robust hashing mechanism designed for this election makes that impossible. Voters will have less leeway to challenge the election commission's procedures. The voter's only options are to cast a ballot and verify that it went to the party of his or her choice. This will ensure that everyone involved in the process may rest easy. This might be a time limit on when the Election Commissioner can make the results public following the election. The blockchain system can help guarantee honest elections. This means they can effectively counter pre-poll fraud, voter manipulation, & vote duplication.

A unique hash created in the backend using the SHA-256 method will be chained on the blockchain for each election vote cast. As a result, the next block of the vote is the hash of the block that came before it in the blockchain. Because of this, if a person tries to cast a ballot again, this method will not grant them a second chance, thereby restricting them to voting only once. As a result, by utilizing this blockchain-BC technique, vote duplication would be impossible.

The hash value for the prior voter is equal to the hash value for the present voter, as shown in the following figure 7. The SHA-256 algorithm is used to generate hash codes. By producing these hash values for each voter, we can ensure that people will only vote once and will not vote multiple times.

Figure 7. Table showing the creation of blocks for the user

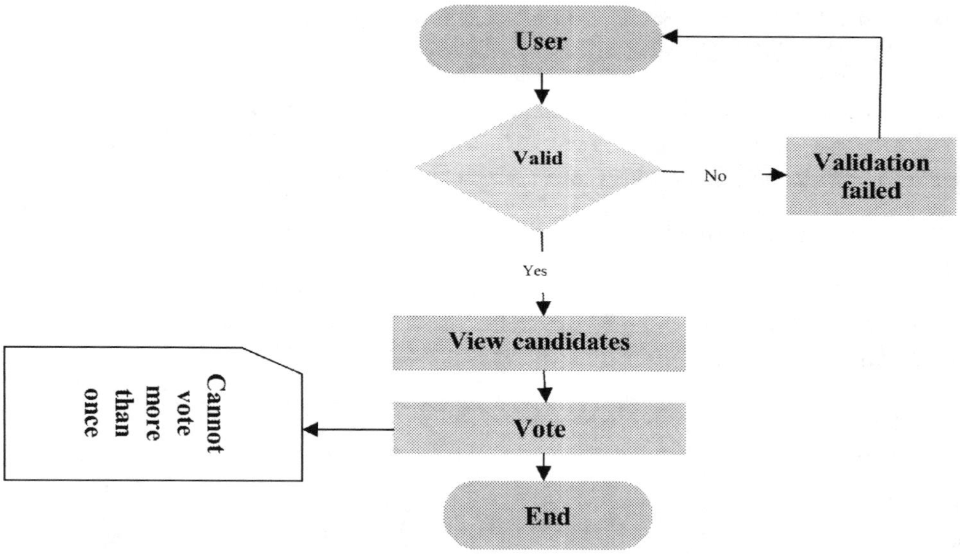

CONCLUSION

Whereas electronic voting is possible, data security & voting procedural worries prevent widespread usage in many countries. Information was made more secure & unnecessary steps were cut out by integrating the blockchain-BC idea into the electronic voting process. Therefore, it can fulfil the needs of the electoral commission. Voting procedure verifiability is guaranteed by choice of hash methods. Based on the findings of this research, a blockchain-based architecture has been developed with the potential to solve polling issues. When tested with accurate data, the results of our proposed models are striking. Our future success depends on implementing this idea into the live voting process. An enhanced electronic voting system can remain achieved in the impending by using hybrid encryption technologies.

REFERENCES

Avgerou, C., Masiero, S., & Poulymenakou, A. (2019). Trusting e-voting amid experiences of electoral malpractice: The case of Indian elections. *Journal of Information Technology, 34*(3), 263–289. doi:10.1177/0268396218816199

Fusco, F., Lunesu, M. I., Pani, F. E., & Pinna, A. (2018). Crypto-voting, a Blockchain based e-Voting System. In KMIS (pp. 221-225). doi:10.5220/0006962102230227

Hardwick, F. S., Gioulis, A., Akram, R. N., & Markantonakis, K. (2018). E-voting with blockchain: An e-voting protocol with decentralisation and voter privacy. In *2018 IEEE International Conference on Internet of Things (iThings) and IEEE Green Computing and Communications (GreenCom) and IEEE Cyber, Physical and Social Computing (CPSCom) and IEEE Smart Data (SmartData)* (pp. 1561-1567). IEEE.

Hjálmarsson, F. Þ., Hreiðarsson, G. K., Hamdaqa, M., & Hjálmtýsson, G. (2018). Blockchain-based e-voting system. In *2018 IEEE 11th international conference on cloud computing (CLOUD)* (pp. 983-986). IEEE. 10.1109/CLOUD.2018.00151

Hussain, S. S., Reddy, E. S. C., Akshay, K. G., & Akanksha, T. (2021). Fraud Detection in Credit Card Transactions Using SVM and Random Forest Algorithms. In *2021 Fifth International Conference on I-SMAC (IoT in Social, Mobile, Analytics and Cloud) (I-SMAC)* (pp. 1013-1017). IEEE.

Kshetri, N., & Voas, J. (2018). Blockchain-enabled e-voting. *IEEE Software, 35*(4), 95–99. doi:10.1109/MS.2018.2801546

Kulkarni, D. (2021). Leveraging blockchain technology in the education sector. *Turkish Journal of Computer and Mathematics Education, 12*(10), 4578–4583.

Risnanto, S., Abd Rahim, Y., Mohd, O., & Abdurrohman, A. (2022). *E-Voting: Technology Requirements Mapping*. Academic Press.

Shaheen, S. H., Yousaf, M., & Jalil, M. (2017). Temper proof data distribution for universal verifiability and accuracy in electoral process using blockchain. In *2017 13th International Conference on Emerging Technologies (ICET)* (pp. 1-6). IEEE. 10.1109/ICET.2017.8281747

Shahzad, B., & Crowcroft, J. (2019). Trustworthy electronic voting using adjusted blockchain technology. *IEEE Access: Practical Innovations, Open Solutions, 7*, 24477–24488. doi:10.1109/ACCESS.2019.2895670

Chapter 12
A Machine Learning-Based Image Segmentation for Real-Time Images in Smart Intelligent Transportation Systems

S. Jayalakshmi
Ramachandra College of Engineering, India

Aswin Kumer S. V.
Koneru Lakshmaiah Education Foundation, India

Jarabala Ranga
Ramachandra College of Engineering, India

K. Venkatasubramanian
Ramachandra College of Engineering, India

V. N. S. L. Narayana A.
University of Technology, Jaipur, India

Y. Lavanya
Ramachandra College of Engineering, India

ABSTRACT

In the ever-evolving world of computer vision, image recognition is critical task including using image processing to solve real-world problems like reducing human involvement in the art of driving. We face many challenges in completing this mission, including object detection and segmentation. By integrating Keras and TensorFlow with instance segmentation and binary masks, the challenges are effectively overcome by the method proposed in this chapter. The technique instantaneous segmentation is adopted for separating and detecting each individual object of interest in an image based on their pixel characteristics. The Mask RCNN model outperforms the current CNN models in terms of object detection accuracy and performance. Also, the objects of interest are classified using regional proposal networks (RPN) instead of selective search algorithm by CNN. The instance segmentation system is conceptually clear, versatile, and general. The method successfully finds items in acquired input and also produces good results by masking for each case.

DOI: 10.4018/978-1-6684-6060-3.ch012

INTRODUCTION

Image segmentation-IS is the procedure of identifying pixels in an image as being part of a particular categories. (Bhavana et.al., 2019). Usually, image segmentation will be implemented by using the input image features to correlate and grouping the pixels founded on the center pixel as the conventional method. Once the pixels are grouped, then the process of segmentation will be easy with the help of a suitable and efficient algorithm used to process the segmentation. The algorithm's efficiency can be measured by observing the output image quality and comparing it with the algorithms used in the existing methods. The algorithm's accuracy can also be observed in the output image based on the edge preserving and pixel handling capabilities processed in the input images. Despite the fact that there were many different image segmentation-IS techniques, the 2 most common in the context of deep learning-DL (Hemasundara et.al., 2019) are:

Open CV

This is a free open-source platform. It is a feature collection specially designed for real-time computer viewing (Aswin Kumer & Srivatsa 2019). Its main interface is c++ and still retains a less complex but wide older c interface. All the newest developments and algorithms are on the Python interface. It is a central library for computer vision, machine learning, and image processing (Inthiyaz et.al., 2018) and now plays an essential role in today's systems in real-time activity. We will use this to process photos and videos to identify people, faces, and handwriting (Sastry et.al., 2019). In addition to the pillow, SciPy, and NumPy, Python may implement the computer vision library. In order to recognize the image pattern, the vector space is used, and its various characteristics calculate the characteristics arithmetically. The Python, C++, C, and Java interfaces can be accessed on Windows, Linux, iOS, etc.

Python

It is primarily known for its reusability and simplicity of programming. While it is slower, it includes a key python feature that can easily be extended within c. Due to this trait, intrinsic computational programs can be written in C++/C. Python supports various programming styles, such as procedural and object-oriented programming. It consists of the library NumPy. NumPy is mighty and mathematics operation optimized. All items are written in optimized C or C++ to take advantage of multi-core computation.

RELATED WORK

The conventional image segmentation method starts with image acquisition, followed by extracting region proposals using the selective search algorithm. Based on the output generated by the region extraction process, the warped region can be formed to apply the computation to extract the features using the pre-trained CNN (Raja & Balaji 2019). Based on the output generated by the CNN, it will be classified using the SVM classifier (fig.1).

Figure 1. Sequence Diagram of the CNN Based Segmentation

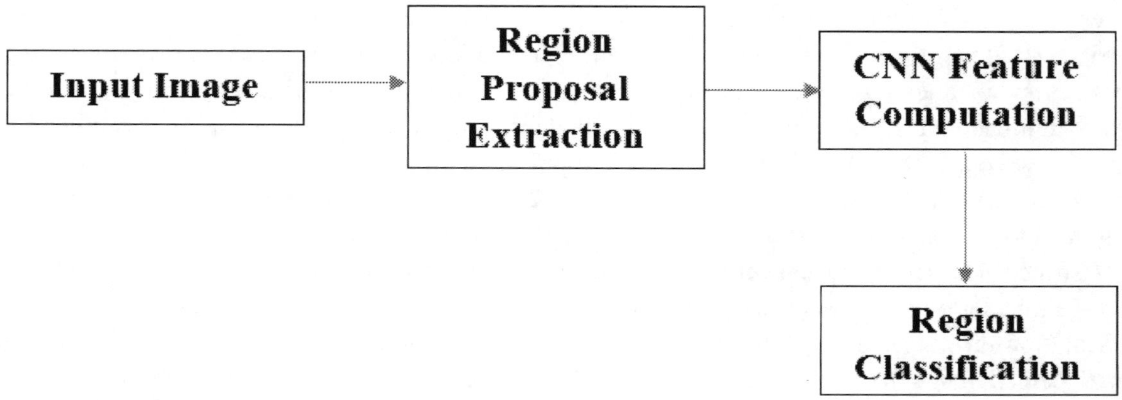

PROPOSED METHOD

The bounded alignment of the Region of Interest supplies the data to the two convolutional layers to form the output mask. The regions can be created by the RPN, which the R-CNN adopts. The ranks are provided to the objects based on the N regions for optimization purposes to indicate the region has the object (Nayak et.al., 2018). The value of N ranges from a maximum of 2K to a minimum of 0.01K, 0.1K, 0.2K, and 0.3K to achieve the best results. The proposed method uses 0.3K as an N Value to connect the ROIs as same as the N value to predict the mask, bounding box, and label (fig.2).

Figure 2. Block Diagram of the CNN Feature Computation

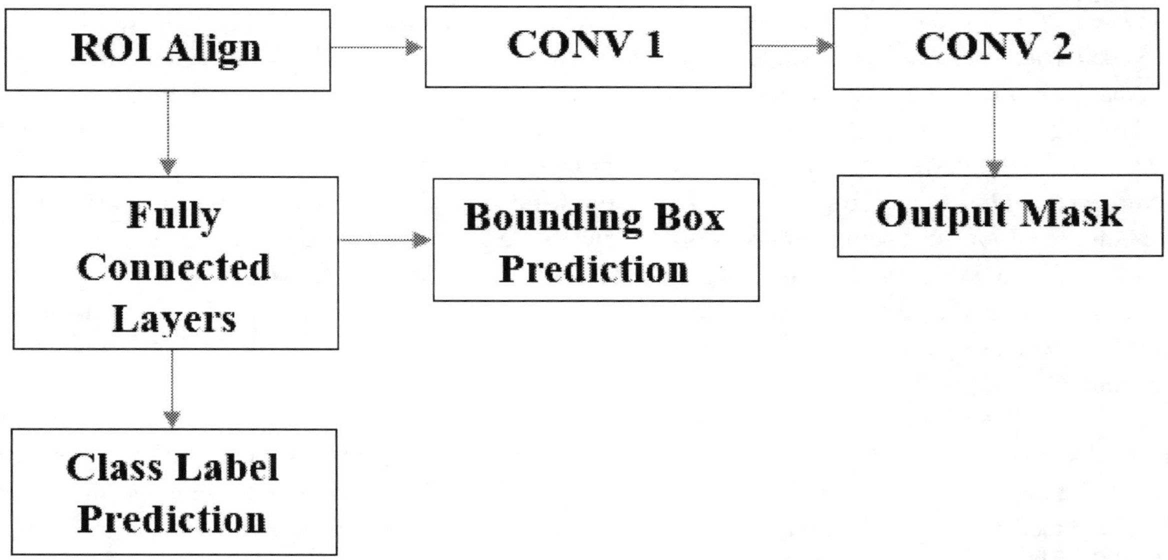

A medical image segmentation to recognize organ pixels or lesions from background pictures such as CT One of the most difficult obstacles to providing crucial information in the processing of medical images regarding the shapes & volumes of this organ is MRI scans. Using those tools at their disposal, numerous academics proposed several automatic segmentations strategies. Dated innovations like edge filters & mathematics algorithms have been created in former systems. Then, learning algorithms to extract handmade traits has been a prominent method for many years. The design and extraction of these properties were always the main priority in developing as a system. The complexity of these methods were regarded to be a substantial restriction. In the 2000s, deep learning algorithms were developed due to technological advancement, and their significant strengths in image processing jobs began to be demonstrated. The successful capacity of deep learning algorithms has made them the dominant choice for the segmentation of images, particularly for medical images. In the last several years, especially, the segmentation of images depending on deep learning-DL methodologies have received a lot of attentions & demonstrates the need for a thorough review. The utmost that we can tell, there is no extensive examination of the segmentation of medical images utilizing deep learning approaches. Some recent survey articles on the segmentation of medical images, such as Shen et al. explored many types of medical image analysis (Ramaiah et.al., 2021) but did not concentrate on technological aspects of the segmentation of medical images. Several other parts categorization, detection, & registrations methods of medical image analysis were also explored, which does not include a specific medical picture segmentation survey. Medical image analysis Because of this article's extensive coverage, information on networks, capacity, and deficiencies remain lacking. This inspired us to develop this piece to acquire an overview of cutting-edge methods. This review focuses more on machine learning approaches, analyzes their structures and procedures in detail and analyses their strengths and inconveniences during the latest medical segmentation study. This article covers three main aspects, methodologies, ways of training and difficulties (network structures). The network structure section provides the major architecture, advantages and weaknesses of the network's image segmentation. It covers the emerging structural sequence. Here, we are trying to deal with the most prominent organizations that dominate forebears.

The Challenges section addresses various challenges linked to the segmentation of medical images using deep learning algorithms. These problems pertain mostly to network architecture, data & training. This section also proposes feasible literature-based solutions for network design, data and training issues.

A CNN is a neural network branch collected of a set of coats, apiece of which accomplishes a particular operation, like convolution, bundling, loss estimation, etc. The input from the preceding layers is received by each layer. The first layer is an input layer that is straightly associated to a neuron count picture input with an equal number of pixels. The following layers are convolutions showing the results of combining the input data with several filters and functioning as an extractor. The filters generally referred to as kernels, are arbitrary, designed, and dependent on the size of the core. The receptive arena of the preceding layer is the region to which each neuron solely reacts. The output-O/p of every convolution layer is viewed as an instigation map that emphasizes the influence that a particular filter is applied to the input. Evolutionary layers generally follow activation.

The main idea is to segment with a image with a 2D input-i/p & 2D filters. Throughout the experiment, Zhang et al. sent numerous data sources (T1, T2, and the FA) in the procedure of 2D images to the CNN input layer on various picture stations (e.g., R, G, B). Their results were more accurate than those obtained with a single input-i/p modality. A transfer learning techniques is used in a different experiment by Bar et al. to acquire low-level properties from an Imagenet models that has already been trained. PiCoDes (Mohammad et.al., 2021) takes the high-level features and fuses all of these elements.

The fact that 3D medical imagery is available and computer technology has improved considerably have led to the idea of using 3D information to divide spatial information to its most significant potential. The complete information in all directions may be provided by volumetric photographs, not only in 2D view and in 3 orthogonal views in 2.5D methods. One of the first 3 dimensional models for a segment of arbitrary size in a brain tumour was introduced. Following that approach, Kamnitsas (Padmini et.al., 2021) constructed a cross-section, double-group 3D CNN. The receptive field had two equal-size parallel routes, and the second received patches on the image from one sub-sample picture. This enables processing more significant areas in a multi-scale context around the voxel. This adjustment with the usage of a smaller 3 by 3 kernel size led to greater accuracy (an average Dice coefficient of 0.66). Moreover, comparing to its original designs, the processing time were decreased (3 min aimed at a 3D scan through 4 modalities).

In order to extract essential properties, we generally require a deep model to divide the organ from inappropriate, volumetric images. Training a Deep network-D is still viewed as a significant issue for 3D modelling.

Dou et al. argued for a sequence of 3D kernels to handle the problem of dimensionality and to improve processing time, thus spatially reducing the number of parameters. 3D max pooling is done to stabilize the learning features in a constrained cubic neighborhood against local 3D translation. Implementing the convolution masks through the similar input volume size contributed to a much quicker convergence than pure 3D CNN. In (Saba et.al., 2020) the formidable challenge of Kleesiek et al. was to recognize the 3D CNN borders of the brain. With a cut-off threshold function, binary segmentation was used, and the products were mapped to the desired design and improved by about 6 percentover more traditional techniques. Since the kernels had mastered more accurate & structured volume representations, information in the 3D receptive field of the Kleesiek models can be more discriminatory than in 2D and 2.5. It is helpful for dividing large organs into a small number of picture regions that include more volumetric information than tiny organs.

One of the more widely utilized medical picture segmentation schemes is the U-Net, which Ronneberg et al. first developed and which is based on. This design is depending on FCN's beautiful architectures. Superior skip connection architecture in U-Net uses many network phases. and enlarges network depth to 19 layers. It uses several adjustments to overcome the compromise between location and context use. This adjustment grows as large parts require more pooling layers and thus decreases location accuracy.

On the further hand, only minor input contexts can be seen by small patches. The presented construction comprises of 2 methods of examination & synthesis. The study is based on the construction of the CNN (see Fig. 3).

The synthesis path is a sampling and a deconvolution layer typically referred to as the expansion phase. The essential attribute in U-analysis Net's path to expansion is the shortcut connections between the equal resolution layers. These connections offer deconvolution layers with critical high-resolution properties. This new structure has garnered a great deal of attention in the segmentation of medical images and has led to several variants. Gordienko et al., for example, explored the segmentation by a U-network of the lung in x-ray imaging. The results reveal that U-Net can segment images quickly and accurately. The same study assessed a single CPU and evaluated the influence of equipment with several CPUs and GPUs on classification accuracy. The results showed a speed of 3 and 9.5 times.

Utilizing sophisticated computing techniques, picture segmentation automatically finds image sections. With the development of more powerful computers, segmentations algorithms' complexities have grown tremendously in past years. Techniques like Saliency Otsu thresholds of combines are now included in

Otsu segmentation with automatic thresholds altered. Algorithms for region-based picture segmentations have evolved into iterative, supervised processes. A cutting-edge region segmentation approach for natural & floral photos called Graph Cuts has converted single-scale to multiscale.

All of the recently mentioned supervised techniques are computationally slow. Initializations of graph cuts presented a challenge by use of seed pixels. Unverified graph cuts through spectral meshes, textures, linear & non-linear shape priors, as well as conditional rand fields are also included discovering graph cut were now widely employed for complex picture segmentations due to the development of graphics processing units-GPU.

Active contours-based image segmentations are another paradigm that has gained enormous popularity among scientists studying image processing—initially presented as Geodesic Active contours, which drove the contour on the boundary of the images using image gradients. However, when statistical models of form prior control the contour movements shortly after, the curve evolutions are governed by shape priors. Since image gradients favor pixel modifications, the contour is susceptible to pixel fluctuations. By creating the level set models, which depends on picture regions & are insensitive to edges, Active Chan Vese-CV contour models overcame the issue. The Expectation Maximization-EM algorithm's convex optimizations form the basis of the CV models, a global energy minimizations problems. Furthermore, the models are well-liked for traditional applications of shape priors in medical picture segmentations.

The methods are supervised since they already have information about the divided areas of the images. The most popular models for picture segmentations with both active contours & graph cuts are shape priors. In addition to shape, which can be manually segmented or via any other models, the procedure should once more be supervised. Pre-information extractions are suggested in supervised segmentation models with unsupervised color or texture. Graph cuts might be used to supervise the as recommended, a knowledge foundation for the active contour segmentations.

The sophisticated raw image segmentation procedure incorporates supervised Extraction of colour & texture data using active contours in unsupervised picture segmentations models. Machine learning-ML, which uses classifications techniques like support vector machines & neural networks (NN), is now reviving the field of segmentation. Convolutional neural networks-CNN with deep learning-DL are recommended for segmenting cancers in medical imaging.

All the techniques mentioned above are iterative, yet they are generally accurate. Clustering is gradually becoming a feature of natural picture segmentations because iterative natural image segmentation is straightforward. Active contour models and machine learning-ML algorithms work together to precisely segment unfamiliar regions by establishing a setting where the contour can learn. K-Means is a simple but efficient iterative technique for segmenting images that relies on the standard for computing distances among region centroids. Another model that adds fuzziness to segmentations and adapts it to the human visual system is fuzzy C-Means.

For contour propagation and extracting local segments, varying techniques use fuzzy rule bases. To achieve nearly perfect segmentations, modest bias corrections must be incorporated into each model because they are all image-specific. Flower image segmentations have been explored using simple image processing methods and sophisticated segmentation techniques. Describes the classification of 103 types of floral photos using four separate criteria. Color, texture, form, & general spatial distribution of the petals are the 4 features utilized. With an accuracy of 72.8%, Support Vector Machine-SVM identified the various kernel characteristics. Similar strategies were used to segment floral images; graph cut-based methods minimize an energy function with terms for data constraint & gradient border.

Grab cuts are another well-liked segmentation method for flower images that minimize the cut energy between two sections. However, these methods are very dynamic and produce incorrect segmentation in photos of chaotic flowers. The authors extract flowers using textural features & floral skeletal features. In situations Using those approaches autonomously resulted in poor flower segmentations because of things similar object constrictions & changes in spatial illumination throughout recording. Mean shift segmentations isolated the required region using a K-means-like method to compute the distance among the area of interest as well as the average of all the image's collective segments. Using mathematical morphology & pyramidal decompositions, the segmentation accuracy for 40 floral pictures was 83%. Scale Invariant Feature Transform (SIFT) & Histogram of Oriented Gradient (HOG) structures was used to extract relevant data from floral photographs as they are sensitive to the bulk of the image characteristics contained in flower images.

The skeleton features, which have been highly popular recently, provide additional data to forecast actions. The works offered a variety of features-based skeletal action recognition techniques. Convolutional neural networks-CNN were utilized by Wang et al. to represent the Spatio-temporal data to joint trajectory mappings (JTMs) for action recognition. A joint angular characteristic indicating the relationship among the spatial joints of an action sequence was first developed by Kumar et al. Motion (MJ) & non-motion joints are 2 subsets of the joints in the Motionless Ensemble Model. (NMJ). For instance, only the right or left-hand joints are used when "hand waving."

Each body joint's models were used to obtain the combined relative detachments & angle features among the motion & non-motion joints as MJ & NMJ, also adaptive kernel-founded classifications were originated to classify human activity. According to past studies, taking into account a number of 3-dimensional skeleton features improved action recognition accuracy. Along with joint positions, joint relative distances, angles, velocities, & angular distances of joints, as well as a grouping of these structures, has revealed complete exactness for AR. The authors emphasised geometrical elements such joint surfaces. The skeleton's two straight edges create the surface. Zhang et al. made use of additional geometrical elements.

The authors of combined 10 distinct geometrical elements that relate joints & lines. Recently, algorithms like Convolution Neural Networks, LSTMs, & RNNs have been frequently utilized in AR. Even though they consistently completed large training sets, they still had exceptional performance. Kernel-based similarity techniques might partially solve these issues. The kernel-based approaches recently demonstrated exemplary performance and classified the kernel using a Support Vector Machine. Only GAKs are employed in AR. Here, we propose a novel fusion model that, in contrast to other earlier techniques, uses alignment kernel checking to attain more excellent recognition rates.

Applications for Wireless Communications Networks (WSNs) are expanding dramatically every day, & their breadth draws academics and development authorities. Advancements in cognitive radio-CR approaches have provided solutions to critical problems in wireless communications. Cognitive radio-CR can boost spectrum efficiency and power consumption at the reception section thanks to dynamic spectrum analyses. Advanced cognitive radios are compatible with the 5G technologies that will power future wireless networks. This paper suggests teaching & learning-based optimizations for use in communications in the future. The study's primary goal is to reduce energy usage and spectral efficiency. The prior techniques could only target network complexity and transmission rate. The suggested adaptive teaching and learning-based WCN could increase the data rate by 47% & energy efficiency by 78% (fig.3).

Figure 3. classifier

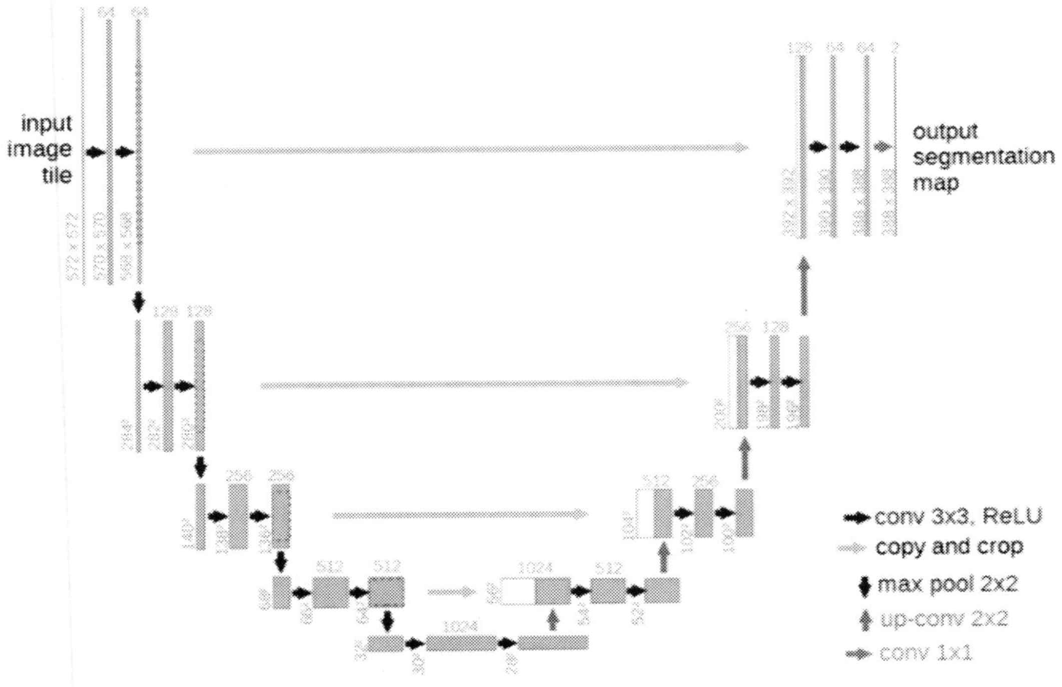

RESULTS AND DISCUSSIONS

The main principle of deep supervision is to supervise the hidden levels directly and transmit them to lower layers rather than do so on the output layer. For non-medical usage, the notion was applied in adding the supplementary objective function to the layers that are covered. For the segment of 3D liver volumes, Dou et al. employed thoroughly monitored techniques. Two hidden layers of the 22-layer network were also monitored at GoogLeNet (figs. 4 to 14).

Figure 4. Input Image to the Proposed Method

Figure 5. Output Image of stage 1 of FC Layer

Figure 6. Output Image of stage 2 of FC Layer

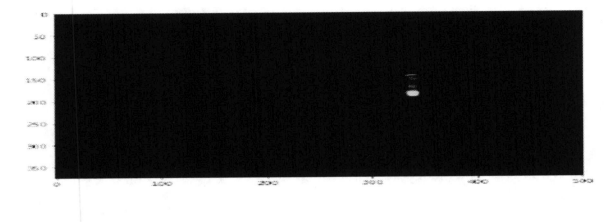

Figure 7. Output Image of stage 3 of FC Layer

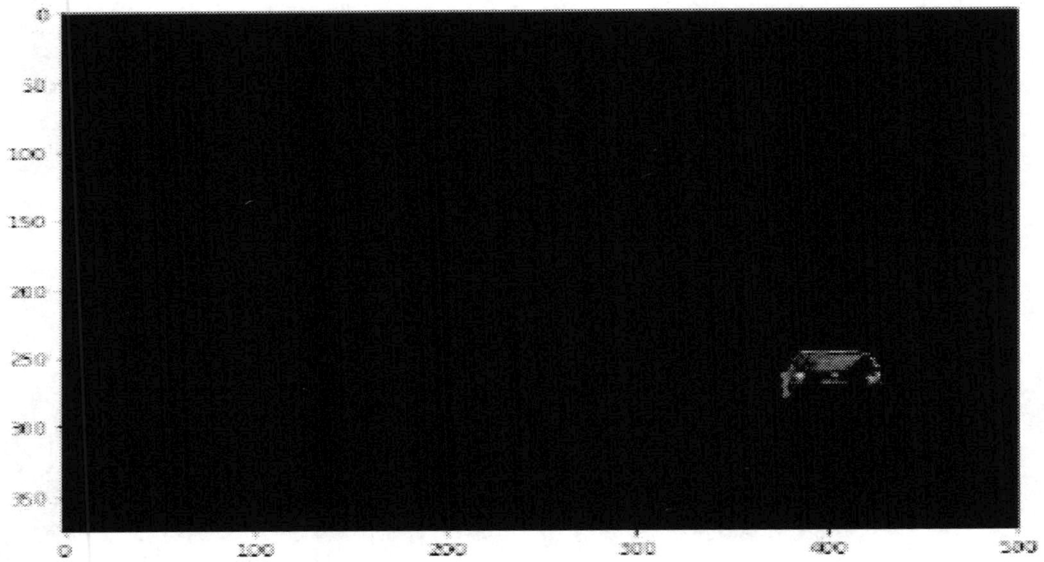

Figure 8. Output Image of stage 4 of FC Layer

Figure 9. Frame Slot 1 of Input Video

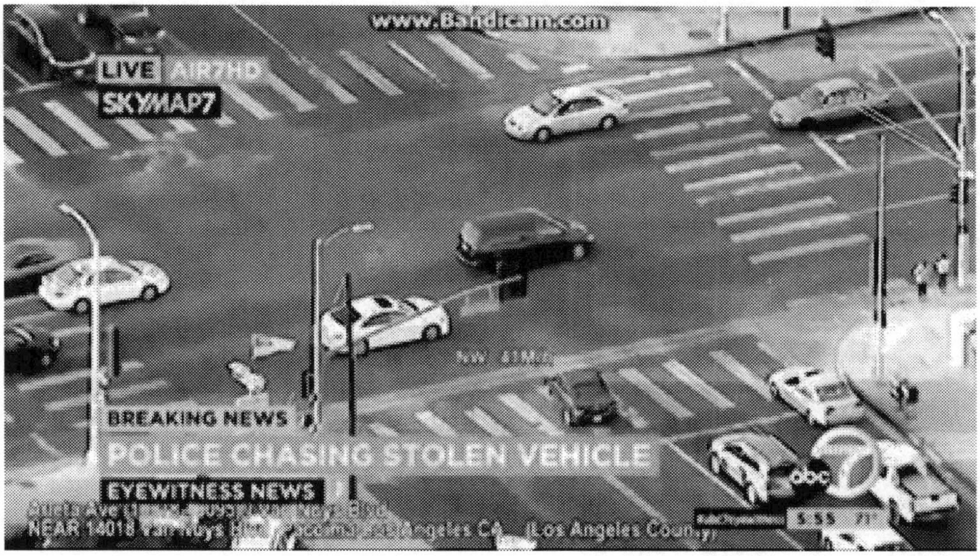

Figure 10. Frame Slot 2 of Input Video

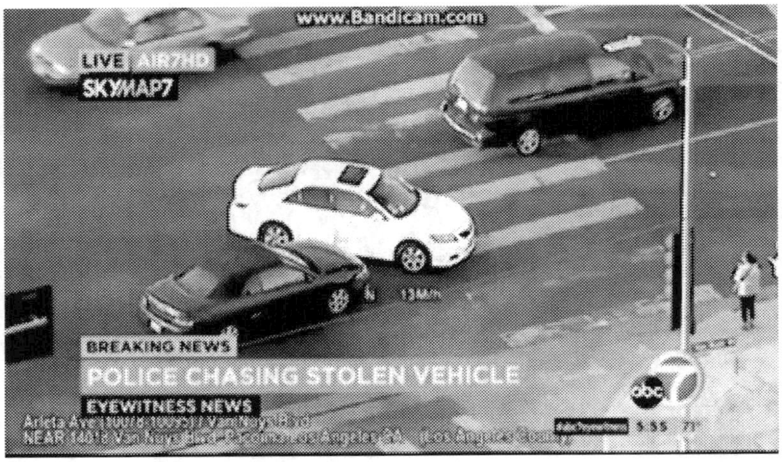

Figure 11. Frame Slot 3 of Input Video

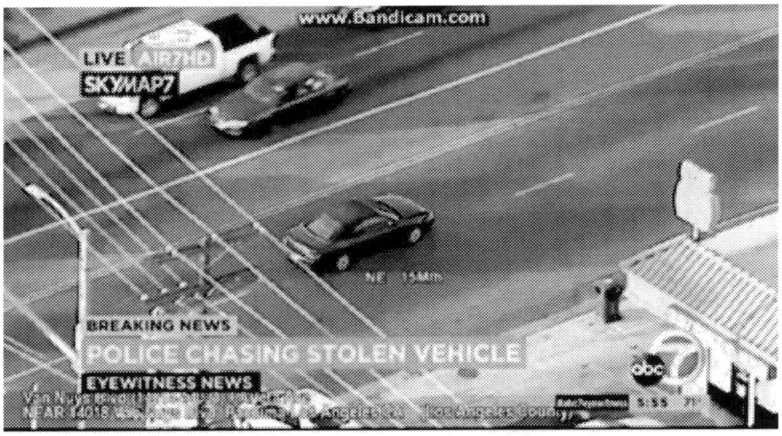

Figure 12. Frame Slot 1 of Output Video

Figure 13. Frame Slot 2 of Output Video

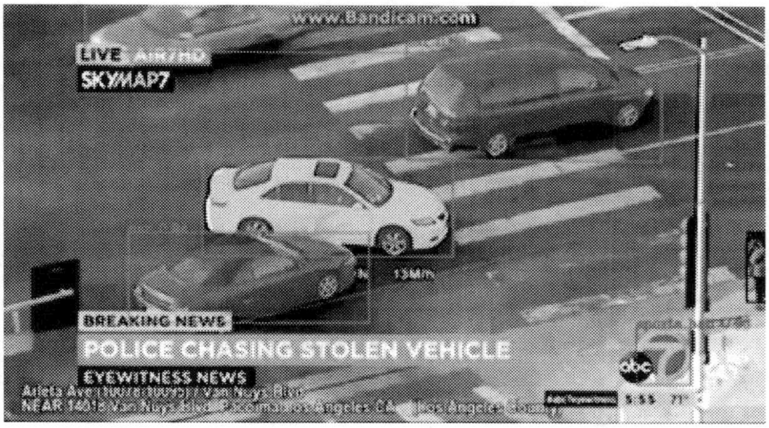

Figure 14. Frame Slot 3 of Output Video

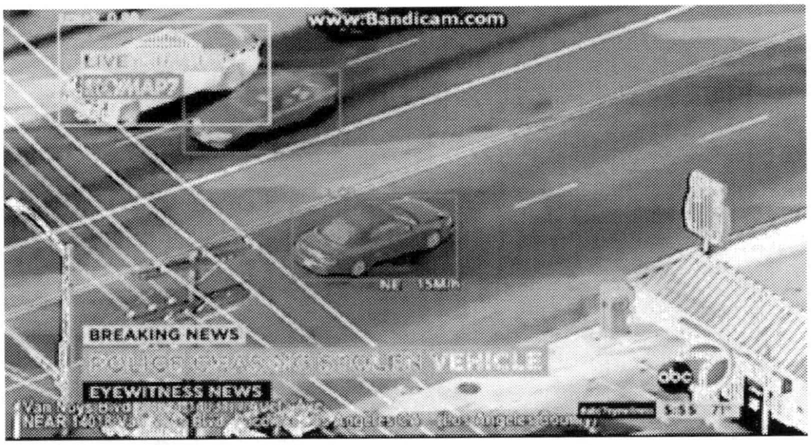

CONCLUSION

The proposed method generated pixel-wise masks and object classes for all the objects in an acquired image using MASK R-CNN. The bounding boxes are also generated in this paper, which results in the easy separation of the foreground object in the acquired image. Instance segmentation applies to all types of technologies and fields; real-time self-driving cars can detect the objects in front of them and make a safe step to avoid causing harm to the vehicle, as well as other people and objects in the area. This form of segmentation is used in various fields, including face recognition and identifying a required vehicle in traffic footage. The MASK R-CNN was implemented for real-time images for object detection.

REFERENCES

Bhavana, D., Kishore Kumar, K., Rajesh, V., Swetha Sree, M., Mounika, D., & Bhavana, N. (2019). Deep learning for pixel-level image fusion using CSR technique. *International Journal of Recent Technology and Engineering, 8*(2), 792-797.

Hemasundara Rao, C., Naganjaneyulu, P.V., & Satyaprasad, K. (2019). Automatic classification breast masses in mammograms using fusion technique and FLDA analysis. *International Journal of Innovative Technology and Exploring Engineering, 8*(5), 1061-1071.

Inthiyaz, S., Madhav, B. T. P., & Kishore, P. V. V. (2018). Flower image segmentation with PCA fused colored covariance and gabor texture features based level sets. *Ain Shams Engineering Journal, 9*(4), 3277–3291. doi:10.1016/j.asej.2017.12.007

Kumer, S. A., & Srivatsa, S. K. (2019). An implementation of futuristic deep learning neural network in satellite images for hybrid image fusion. *International Journal of Recent Technology and Engineering, 8*(1), 484–487.

Nayak, S. R., Mishra, J., & Palai, G. (2018). A modified approach to estimate fractal dimension of gray scale images. *Optik (Stuttgart)*, *161*, 136–145. doi:10.1016/j.ijleo.2018.02.024

Padmini, G. R., Rajesh, O., Raghu, K., Sree, N. M., & Apurva, C. (2021, March). Design and Analysis of 8-bit ripple Carry Adder using nine Transistor Full Adder. In *2021 7th International Conference on Advanced Computing and Communication Systems (ICACCS)* (Vol. 1, pp. 1982-1987). IEEE.

Raja, C., & Balaji, L. (2019). An automatic detection of blood vessel in retinal images using convolution neural network for diabetic retinopathy detection. *Pattern Recognition and Image Analysis*, *29*(3), 533–545. doi:10.1134/S1054661819030180

Saba, S. S., Sreelakshmi, D., Sampath Kumar, P., Sai Kumar, K., & Saba, S. R. (2020). Logistic regression machine learning algorithm on MRI brain image for fast and accurate diagnosis. *International Journal of Scientific and Technology Research.*

Sastry, A. S. C. S., Geetesh, S., Sandeep, A., Varenya, V. V., Kishore, P. V. V., Kumar, D. A., & Kumar, M. T. K. (2019). Fusing spatio-temporal joint features for adequate skeleton based action recognition using global alignment kernel. *International Journal of Engineering and Advanced Technology*, *8*(4), 749–754.

Chapter 13
Techniques and Applications of Optimal Cluster Head Selection With Trusted Multipath Routing and MANET Intrusion Detection

Venkatasubramanian Srinivasan
https://orcid.org/0000-0001-7560-0164
Saranathan College of Engineering, India

P. L. Rajarajeswari
Saranathan College of Engineering, India

T. Sathis Kumar
Saranathan College of Engineering, India

ABSTRACT

A MANET (mobile ad hoc network) is a self-constituted wireless setup that operates independently of existing infrastructure and centralized control. In various daily uses, such as automotive, military, and other field networks, it is possible to find MANET on wireless systems. In contrast with MANET, a fixed or cable data and computer connectivity system are required for many networks. The WiFi, satellite networking, and smartphone network include fixed infrastructure technology. Moreover, MANET is a dynamic energy and security vulnerable system. The fundamental problem of energy efficiency optimization has been addressed effectively by Routing Protocols (R.P.) among the most extant techniques. This work, therefore, offers an efficient multi-track routing in a MANET-based optimization procedure. The intrusion detection and optimal cluster head (C.H.) selection approach, namely firefly algorithm (FFA) based fuzzy clustering and Random Forest (R.F.), is used to address the energy and security crises in the MANET effectively. The multipath routing is then carried out using secure nodes based on the R.P., Bird swarm with Mayfly algorithm (BS-MFA). The best routes are chosen founded on fitness features such as trust, energy connectivity, and throughput. The approaches are compared using existing techniques and various performance metrics such as energy consumption, Delay, and detection rate.

DOI: 10.4018/978-1-6684-6060-3.ch013

INTRODUCTION

A MANET is a network of mobile nodes that do not have centralized administration. MANET topology can be dynamic. Furthermore, each mobile node has partial resources such as a battery, computing power, and RAM (Huiyao. A et al., 2004; Goyal, P et al., 2014). Mobile nodes in MANETs interact with one another n a multi-hop way.

This indicates that a mobile node routes a packet to a target via intermediary nodes. As a result, each node's availability is equally essential. Otherwise, the network's complete performance may suffer. An efficient R.P. is required for MANET to fulfill these unique features and design restrictions (Hinds. A et al., 2013). Designing an effective R.P. for MANETs is a complex challenge that has been the subject of ongoing study. There are many proposed R.P., which could be split into two categories: proactive and reactive. Mobile Nodes often update their router databases with proactive routing techniques such as destination sequence distance vectors (DSDV) (Uddin, M et al., 2012). A proactive routing system creates a high number of control mails in the network as a result of frequent information exchanges. As a result, proactive R.P. is not deemed appropriate for MANET (Venkatesan T.P. et al., 2014).

Reactive R.P. methods such as ad hoc on-demand distance vector routing (AODV) and dynamic source routing (DSR) have been suggested for MANET to address the constraints of proactive R.P. (Karthikeyan B et al., 2014). A route is identified in a reactive routing system only when needed. The reactive routing protocol is made up of two major tools: (a) route discovery and (b) route keep. The route discovery method is used by a source node to find a path to an endpoint. A source node detects any topological change in the network using the route preservation method (Patel, D.N et al., 2014). The route discovery method employs a global search technique in which a source node employs a flooding mechanism to identify all possible pathways to a destination. Once all routes have been found, a source node selects the shortest way.

When the shortest route method is employed, nodes situated towards the core of a network transport more traffic than nodes placed around the network's periphery. When numerous connections are put up in a network, the wireless links at the network's core carry more traffic and might therefore get overloaded (Cheng. H, Yang.S, and Wang.X., 2012). This sort of congestion can have an impact on network performance in terms of latency and throughput. The shortest path may be broken in mobility circumstances owing to node movement. Furthermore, communication through a wireless medium is inherently unstable and prone to connection failures. Researchers have proposed multipath routing to address the constraints of shortest-path routing methods (Robinson, Y. & Rajaram.M.. 2015). However, achieving both energy economy and network security at the same time is a difficult task because maximum security techniques in the collected works are demanding (Sarkar S, Datta R, 2013). It is critical to meet MANET security demands since these networks are required to handle a large number of sensitive communications in applications linked to surveillance and warfare operations. Such sensitive transactions occur between appreciation units and the communiqué range's border (Yavuz, A.A., 2010; Marina MK, Das SR,2001). As a result, safe and energy-efficient multipath protocols are required. As a result, the R.P. should be designed to resist widely used attacks such as network data interception, hijacking, and jamming (Sarkar et al., 2015; Anderegg et al., 2003).

BS-MFA is a protocol for energy-efficient multipath routing in long-lived networks. The MANET environment and nodes' trust energy are simulated before transmission. Energy restriction is managed using fuzzy clustering-based optimum C.H. selection. MANET security is provided by R.F. IDS's refusal of intruder nodes. Secure nodes are then used for network broadcast. Multipath is established when network transmission begins and is picked using BS-MFA. Energy, connectivity, and latency are used to determine the optimum multipath. The study of assaults shows the technique's effectiveness.

RELATED WORKS

This part offers an analysis of the literature articles with the requirement for establishing a procedure. ABC-SD, a new cluster-based routing system, was introduced (Abba Ari, A et al., 2016). The suggested approach is based on the ABC meta-heuristics and quick searching features to create low-power consumption clusters. A fitness function has been developed to choose the best Cluster Head. At the sink, the centralized location-unaware clustering algorithm is run, with energy stages and the S.N.'s adjacency info as input parameters. The suggested protocol has been widely used in a variety of network topologies and situations. The results were compared to those of other well-known bio-inspired based cluster-based routing algorithms. In terms of network lifespan and the number of packets distributed at the sink, the acquired results exceeded the competitors. A two-phase clustering technique based was suggested (Jabeur, Nafaâ. 2016), which is based on fireflies. Sensors were automatically clustered during the micro-clustering phase. Clusters are refined by a competition to combine tiny adjacent clusters during the second phase. Another meta-heuristics-based approach for clustering suggested (Anandamurugan, S., &Abirami T, 2017) for WSNs with the anti-predator ability, which evades the algorithm from being trapped in the local optima. Results approved local optima evading if compared with original SFLA and PSO in clustering of WSNs.

A novel idea suggested (Zahedi et al., 2016) that employs a swarm intelligence-based method to create R.P. with fuzzy rule-based decision-making that overcomes the constraints of cluster-based R.P. This is required since there is no mechanism on cluster head distributions, and they create imbalanced clusters. The authors utilized FCM approach to create balanced groups into clusters, and then C.H.s were chosen using a fuzzy inference scheme. Agreeing with them because the fuzzy rules are written manually, and the system's performance suffers as a result. As a result, they combined the firefly and imitation annealing methods to improve the excellence of fuzzy rules. They also enhanced the performance of their fuzzy scheme using this method, and the authors stated that the combination of swarm intelligence with fuzzy logic extended network longevity. A meta-heuristic-based clustering strategy based on FFA (G. Gupta & S. Jha, 2018) and simulated annealing to increase network lifespan in heterogeneous WSNs by lowering total energy consumption are developed. The program first attempts to identify the best clustering across the network using the FFA and then uses the simulated annealing approach to determine the best chain inside each clusterIt uses an objective function to distribute C.H.s equitably over the network. Fuzzy SFLA (FSFLA) uses SFLA in combination (Fanian & Rafsanjani,2018). A MANET multi-level IDS uses a cluster technique to assess external and internal intruder patterns and identify black hole attacks (Bala et al., 2019). TNK-CIDS was proposed to improve data transport without interruption (Yannam A, Prasad, 2019). Attacks slowed data flow. Fitness Function-based AFF-AOMDV (Taha A et al., 2017). The network chose the best energy-saving path. The method is low-energy and long-lasting. However, QoS restrictions weren't solved.

PROPOSED SYSTEM

In this section, two different types of processes are carried out. The first step is to detect the attacks using a machine learning algorithm, and the second step is multipath routing using optimization techniques.

Proposed IDS and Multipath Routing in MANET

MANET is a mobile system in which nodes are spread across the atmosphere, and, as a result of the energy problem, the nodes are clustered into clusters using the first of the clustering methods. Consider the network to be made up of n nodes and let *Ni* designate the *ith* node that is assumed as

$$N = \left\{N_1, N_2, \ldots . N_i, \ldots N_n\right\} \tag{1}$$

Let's name S and D, respectively, source and destination nodes. A network is launched, and the belief of the nodes is calculated and rationalized in the trust table so that the network can only communicate nodes that have effective trust factors. The CH is picked using fuzzy clustering once the table of trust has been established. Consequently, I represented the C.H.s in the network as,

$$C = \left\{C_1, C_2, \ldots . C_j, \ldots C_m\right\} \tag{2}$$

Where m represents C.Hs. Then, IDS select secure nodes for future MANET connectivity. Lastly, multipath selection is conducted using a path based on safe C.H.s and established optimization. Figure 1 depicts multipath routing flow.

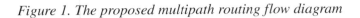

Figure 1. The proposed multipath routing flow diagram

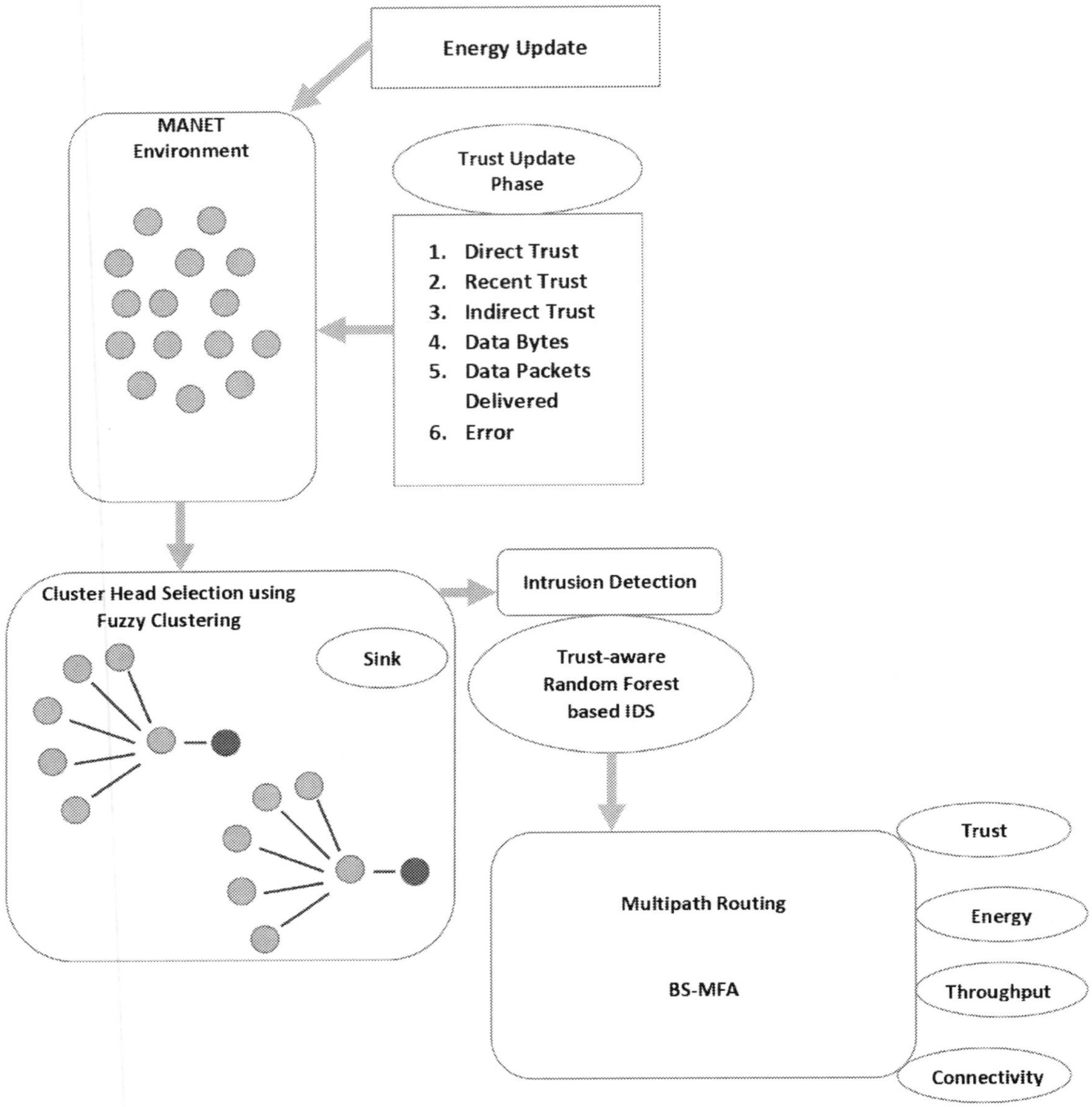

Establish the MANET Nodes Trust Table

A confidence component prevents communication by harsh nodes. It has six trust factors: direct trust, recent trust, indirect trust, data bytes trust, error, and D.P. Before communicating, nodes construct a trust table set to '1' Nodule table ensures MANET intrusion detection before multipath communication. Shadows of confidence:

DT

The D.T. is calculated using the estimated communiqué time among the ith and the dth endpoint. The difference between the actual and expected time for the ith node to validate the public key provided by the dth endpoint is measured as D.T. Thus, the distance between ith node and dth endpoint is denoted as,

$$DT_i^d\left(\tau\right)=\frac{1}{3}\left[DT_i^d\left(\tau-1\right)-\left(\frac{\tau_{appx}-\tau_{est}}{\tau_{appx}}\right)+\omega\right] \tag{3}$$

Where τ_{appx} is the estimated time and τ_{est} is the estimated time for validating the public key. In, τ_{appx} and τ_{est} are the approximate and estimated times for the destination and node to send and receive the public key, respectively. ω represents the node's witness factor

IDT

It is well known that the witness feature is authentic using D.T. The node deprived of a witness factor, on the other hand, is authentic using the IDT (Singh O, Singh J, Singh R, 2018), which is provided by,

$$IDT_i^d\left(\tau\right)=\frac{1}{r}\sum_{i=r}^{r}DT_i^d\left(d\right) \tag{4}$$

Where *I* and *d* are represented as the destination, *r* identifies the total node neighbors.

RT

RT (Subba B et al., 2016) is calculated by combining the D.T. and IDT, as well as the key authenticity and recognizing the sink or endpoint, and is displayed as a function of time. The R.T. is written as,

$$RT_i^d\left(\tau\right)=a*DT_i^d\left(\tau\right)+\left(1-a\right)*IDT_i^d\left(\tau\right) \tag{5}$$

where $a=0.3$.

DB

The trust is computed based on the data transmission in bytes among the ith node and the dth endpoint. The trusted formula based on the D.B. is expressed as,

$$DB_i^d\left(\tau\right)=\frac{1}{2}*\left[\frac{DB^i}{\ell}+\frac{DB^d}{\ell}\right] \tag{6}$$

where DB^i and DB^d denote the total number of bytes transferred and expected at node i and dth destination node, respectively, and ℓ denote the data limitations of the packet at the time of transfer and reception.

Error Based Trust

The communication error describes the trust using the error that is well-definite as, $\mathcal{E}$ designates the total transactions and

$$\mathcal{E}_i^d = \frac{1}{T} * \sum_{\blacklozenge=1}^{T} \mathcal{E}_{\blacklozenge} \tag{7}$$

Where $\mathcal{E}_{\blacklozenge}$ mentions to the error, which is each '0' or '1' found on the error in the linking.

Trust by the D.P. Delivery

Lastly, trust is calculated using the D.P.s distributed as the ratio of entire packets conventional to packets sent by the node. The D.P. delivery is represented by DP_i^d, which is calculated for all T transactions that occur among the node and the endpoint. As a result, the trust of node I am denoted as

$$t^i = \left\{DT_i^d\left(\tau\right) + IDT_i^d\left(\tau\right) + RT_i^d\left(\tau\right) + DB_i^d\left(\tau\right) + PD_i^d\left(\tau\right) + \mathcal{E}_i^d\right\} \tag{8}$$

Where *ti* represents the thrust vector of $the\, ith$ node.

Initialize the Nodes' Energy

At the end of every communication, the power of the MANET nodes is updated, and the residual energy in the nodes is simulated accordingly:

$$e_{i,\tau}^{remain} = e_{i,\tau}^{remain} * s\left(\tau - 1, \tau\right) - e_{i\tau}^{trans} * s\left(\tau - 1, \tau\right) \tag{9}$$

Where $e_{i\tau}^{trans}$ and $e_{i,\tau}^{remain}$ are the required energy for communicating a single bit of info. Though, energy is expended in the initialization of network connectivity. The remaining energy in the nodes is governed by the energy ratio, which is the ratio of energy left at the start of communication to maximum energy. If the energy ratio goes below the upper boundary of the lower range, the node's residual energy is insufficient for network data packet transmission. If the ratio exceeds the upper threshold, the node's residual energy is sufficient. 0.2 is the user-selected threshold (Yadav AK, Tripathi S, 2017).

Optimal CH selection firefly based Fuzzy based clustering

Fuzzy C Means Algorithm

FCM system segregates the input $\left\{x_k\right\}_{k=1}^{N}$ into c the number of groups constructed on the succeeding neutral function Eq. (10).

$$J_m = \sum_{i-1}^{c}\sum_{k-1}^{N} u_{ik}^{p}\left\|x_k - v_i\right\|^2 \tag{10}$$

Where p denotes the real sum, u_{ik}^{p} the link of the data point x_k belongs to the cluster, which satisf $\sum_{i=1}^{c} u_{ik} = 1$ ies and v_i is the centroid of the cluster. The number of concept records is indicated by the above equation 10, where is the full digit of clusters. In FCM, the extrication is accomplished by iteratively informing the affiliation ideals and mass centroids. The membership value of each data point to each centroid is obtained after updating each time of centroids that may be completed by Equation (11).

$$u_{ik} \frac{1}{\sum_{j-1}^{c}\left(\frac{\left\|x_k - v_i\right\|^2}{\left\|x_k - v_j\right\|^2}\right)^{\frac{1}{p-1}}} \tag{11}$$

The distance between a data point and the cluster centroid is used to update the cluster centroid. The Firefly Algorithm optimization is used to select the best C.H., as described in the section below.

Firefly Algorithm

The flame retardant algorithm is used in the first cluster (FFA). In the FFA, the Firefly bug produced short-term bursts is reliant on the bioluminescence phenomenon. In this approach, the distance of the flash is a powerful parameter. Three rules must be observed while using the firefly approach: To begin with, the beauty of each firefly is gender-specific. Second, the capacity to attract fireflies is controlled by the brightness of the flash. Third, the brightness of the firefly is calculated using the objective function. The appealing element of lightning is its brightness. The intensity of the light is determined by this factor. The most prevalent variables in this method are attraction and light intensity. The FFA creates a firefly population at random at first. The next stage is to fitness repeatedly and updates the population to the maximum sum of iterations. During the population-updating phase, firefly j using Eq. (12):

$$x_i = x_i + \beta e^{-\gamma d_{ij}^2}\left(x_j - x_i\right) + \alpha\left(r - 0.5\right) \tag{12}$$

Where the first phrase is the current firefly location, the second term concerns the appeal of the firefly j; the third term is a random shift. d j is a Euclidean fireflies distance I to j. Random numbers are three constant parameters in the range [0,1] and α,β. Once the optimal C.H. is selected, the next step is to notice the malicious nodes using a machine learning algorithm.

Random Forest classifier for sensing the Malicious Nodes

When calculating the ideal C.H.s, the network intrusion is calculated based on the trust factors of the network nodes, and the information of the nodes transmitted to the sink via the C.H.s indicates that the intruder is identified by the sink node. The intruder node is excluded from advanced network infrastructures once the intruders have been identified. The sink node has the R.F. classifier (Rodriguez-Galiano et al., 2012) for forecasting intruders, which is based on the tree structure theory. The rationale for selecting the R.F. is because:

- It performs well on huge databases.
- It can handle hundreds of input variables without deleting any of them.
- It is less computationally demanding than other tree ensemble approaches (e.g. Boosting).
- It computes an unbiased internal estimate of the generalization error.
- It provides estimates of which variables are significant in the classification.
- It computes proximities between examples that can be used to find outliers.
- It is fairly resistant to outliers and noise.

Proposed BS-MFA Optimal Selection

Multipath communiqué in MANETs guarantees safe network transmission by selecting legitimate nodes to construct a path between the source and endpoint nodes. The optimum path is picked based on energy, throughput, trust, and connection in the path. The path is first established using RPL routing to create multipath between source node S and endpoint node D. BS-MFA chooses the best produced path.

Solution Encoding

This section shows the illustration of the solution to be resolute by the proposed BS-MFA. The multipath between S and D nodes is calculated here, and the communication multipath is definite on the basis of the maximum fitness measurement value.

Fitness Measure

The fitness is determined by the maximum confidence of the nodes, the maximum energy in the nodes, maximum output, and excellent communication between the nodes. The fitness is hence a maximizing function that is provided as,

$$FF = \frac{1}{4}\left\{t + \varepsilon + u + y\right\} \tag{13}$$

where t,ε,u, and y are path confidence, energy, transduction, and connection, calculated using path nodes. As in Equations (8) and (9), respectively, the confidence and energy in the node are calculated. The measured output is calculated by way of a track as the ratio of the whole bits sent throughout the network each second.,

$$u = \frac{v}{\tau} bps \tag{14}$$

Where v refers to the communicated sum of bits and Ţ mentions the transmitted time in secs. Connectivity [17] is founded on two-directional connections which join two nodes,

$$y = \frac{1}{g}\left[\sum_{i=1}^{g} \frac{y_i}{cc}\right] \tag{15}$$

Where *cc* signifies total connections and *yi* means the connectivity of *the i*th node.

Algorithmic steps of BSA

The BSA proposal is followed by a swarm-based intelligence procedure, the optimization process. The BSA is based on birds' social connections and is structured into three conducts, such as fuelling, alertness, and flight. BSA's key benefits are the diversity of the world and the prematureness. In addition, effective balance is achieved with an effective global optimum convergence ability between exploration and exploitation. However, it is a tough issue to decide on the optimization settings and also to improve the search functionality for an ideal solution. The above concerns are solved by utilizing the MFA, which improves optimization convergence.

The BSA's basis is limited to the following rules of decision: Between the fodder properties and alertness, a bird may jump. At the same time, the birds maintain a record of the bird's past knowledge in food search and the record of where the food has previously been found, which gives the efficient search capacity for the global solution. Similarly, the birds migrate to the center at the time of their wakefulness behavior because of the interference as a consequence of the swarm competition. In contrast, the birds migrate elsewhere, quickly switching between their production and their scrounging throughout this period. The manufacturer has the biggest reserves, while the scrounger has the lowest reserves. But birds pick arbitrarily between producers and scroungers among the highest and the lowest reserves. It should be noted that the producers seek their food, whilst the scroungers follow the creators for food.

Vigilance activities

The bird looks for food based on the knowledge of the swarm that is shaped like,

$$B_{b,c}^{\tau+1} = B_{b,c}^{\tau} + \left(\rho_{b,c} - B_{b,c}^{\tau}\right) \times p \times rand\left(0,1\right) + \left(X_{c} - B_{b,c}^{\tau}\right) \times q \times rand\left(0.1\right) \tag{16}$$

$$B_{b.c}^{\tau+1} = B_{b.c}^{\tau} + \rho_{b.c} \times p \times rand(0,1) - B_{b.c}^{\tau} \times p \times rand(0,1) + X_{c} \times q \times rand(0,1) - B_{b.c}^{\tau} \times q \times rand(0,1) \quad (17)$$

$$B_{b.c}^{\tau+1} = B_{b.c}^{\tau}\left[1 - p \times rand(0,1) - q \times rand(0,1)\right] + \rho_{b.c} \times prand(0,1) + X_{c} \times q \times rand(0,1) \quad (18)$$

Eq. (18) is the typical BSA equation in the vigilance properties, and BSA delivers an effective convergence to the best solution worldwide.

Flight behavior

In case of forages or dangers, the birds travel to other locations, and when the birds reach a new place, they are fed, where just a few birds are the producers, while other birds are the scrotum makers. The conduct is as defined,

$$B_{b.c}^{\tau+1} = B_{b.c}^{\tau+1} + randn(0,1) \times B_{bc}^{\tau} \quad (19)$$

$$B_{b.c}^{\tau+1} = B_{b.c}^{\tau+1} + \left(B_{h.c}^{\tau} - B_{b.c}^{\tau}\right) \times fl \times randn(0,1) \quad (20)$$

Where *randn*(0, 1) mentions the Gaussian distribution numeral, the next section will explain the MFA.

Mayfly Algorithm

In the Mayfly algorithm (Zervoudakis et al.,2020) two sets of mayflies are first produced randomly, demonstrating the population of men and women, respectively. In short, each magic can be placed randomly in the issue space as a candidate solution that is signified by a vector of the d dimension $x = (x_1, \ldots, x_d)$, A fly's speed $v = (v_1, \ldots, v_d)$ is distinct as an alteration of position, and dynamic interaction between separate and social flying involvements is the flying direction of each fly. In particular, everyone can adapt their paths to their own best position (pbest) to date and to the best position achieved by any swarm up to now (gbest)

Male *Mayflies Movement*

The assembling of men in swarms means that every male fly's position is adapted both according to his own and his neighbor's experience.

Female may fly movement

Disparate males, mayflies are not collected in swarms by females. Instead, they fly to males to raise.

Mayflies Mating

The crossover operator describes the combination of two magazines as follows: One of the males and one of the female population is chosen. The selection of parents is the same as the attraction of women by men. The assortment can be random or founded on the fitness function in particular. The second is the best woman, the second best woman, the second best male, etc. The second is the best female. The results of the crossing are the following two offspring:

$$offspring1 = L * male + \left(1 - L\right) * female \tag{21}$$

$$offspring2 = L * female + \left(1 - L\right) * male \tag{22}$$

Where the male parent is male, the female parent is female, and L is an alleged value in a certain range. The initial offspring speeds are set to nil. In the pseudo-code can be summarized the basic processes of the MFA

Algorithm 1: Pseudo Code of MFA

$Objective\, function\, f\left(x\right), x = \left(x1, \ldots, xd\right)^T$

$Initialize\, the\, male\, mayfly\, population\, x_i \left(i = 1, 2, \ldots, N\right) and\, velocities\, v_{mi}$

$Initialize\, the\, female\, mayfly\, population\, y_i \left(i = 1, 2, \ldots, M\right) and\, velocities\, v_{fi}$

$Evaluate\, solutions$

$Find\, global\, best\, gbest$

DoWhile $stopping\, criteria\, are\, not\, met$

$Update\, velocities\, and\, solutions\, of\, males\, and\, females$

$Evaluate\, solutions$

$Rank\, the\, mayflies$

$Mate\, the\, mayflies$

$Evaluate\, the\, offspring$

$Separate\, offspring\, to\, male\, and\, female\, randomly$

$Replace\, the\, worst\, solutions\, with\, the\, best\, new\, ones$

$Update\, pbest\, and\, gbest$

End while

$Post - process\, results\, and\, visualization$

RESULTS AND DISCUSSION

The method is introduced for optimum clustering and routing for the MANETs in MATLAB version R2018b. The entire process is performed with the 8 GB RAM I7 structure. The MANET parameters are labeled in the section already. The factors such as performance, energy use, detection rate, and latency predict whether the malicious node is in the network or not. Table 1 displays the MANET parameter.

Table 1. Parameters of MANET

Network Parameters	Value
Area of Interest (M×M)	200m×200m
Sum of sensor nodes (N) setup	30. 60, 90, 120, 150
The initial energy of S.N.	0.3J
Sum of sensor nodes (N) setup	30, 60, 90, 120, 150
d0	87.0m
Maximum No. of Rounds	6000
Sum of clusters (C)	0.1×N
Packet Size	4000 bits
E_{elec}	50 nJ/bit
E_{mp}	0.013 pJ/bit/m^4
E_{fs}	100 pJ/bit/m^2
R_{agg}	0.3
E_{DA}	5 nJ/bit

Evaluation Metrics

In this part, we use the presentation indicators to approximate our modeling results:

- The energy used by the complete S.N. network on Jules (J) experiments is called energy use. We assess the energy intake of the node on the basis of the proposed energy model.
- Network bandwidth is the quantity of bandwidth for all targets. Target output is the number of messages received per second. Disrupting the network and providing extra energy can lead to organizational costs.
- The standard divergence (SED) in all nodes is the regular differential among the energy used.
- The distribution of the network defines the distribution of energy. The distribution of energy. Low average nodes suggest that a similar volume of power is used while the communiqué charge is equally spread between more significant standard deviation nodes.

This definition uses a modest S.D. to utilise residual mean node size. Root time determines paths between source and target nodes. To assess travel detection software and heuristic local update methodologies for the proposed road operation, we built various dynamic networks of varying sizes. Effective procedures should have a high detection rate for high-precision malicious nodes. For an efficient approach and delay, the time between Source and Destination Notes should be minimal.

Proposed Method Delay Performance

Table 2 and Figure 2 demonstrate the validation of the proposed BS-MFA with existing methods in terms of Delay.

Table 2. Comparative Analysis of Proposed Methods in terms of Delay

Methodology	Delay (ms)				
	30 nodes	60 nodes	90 nodes	120 nodes	150 nodes
Naive Bayes	0.051	0.102	0.138	0.165	0.192
Decision Tree	0.049	0.98	0.127	0.152	0.183
Proposed RF	0.032	0.68	0.103	0.128	0.154
ACO	0.047	0.95	0.142	0.178	0.200
WOA	0.039	0.89	0.132	0.164	0.198
Proposed BS-MFA	0.029	0.60	0.93	0.119	0.140

Figure 2. Graphical Representation of Proposed Methodology based on delay

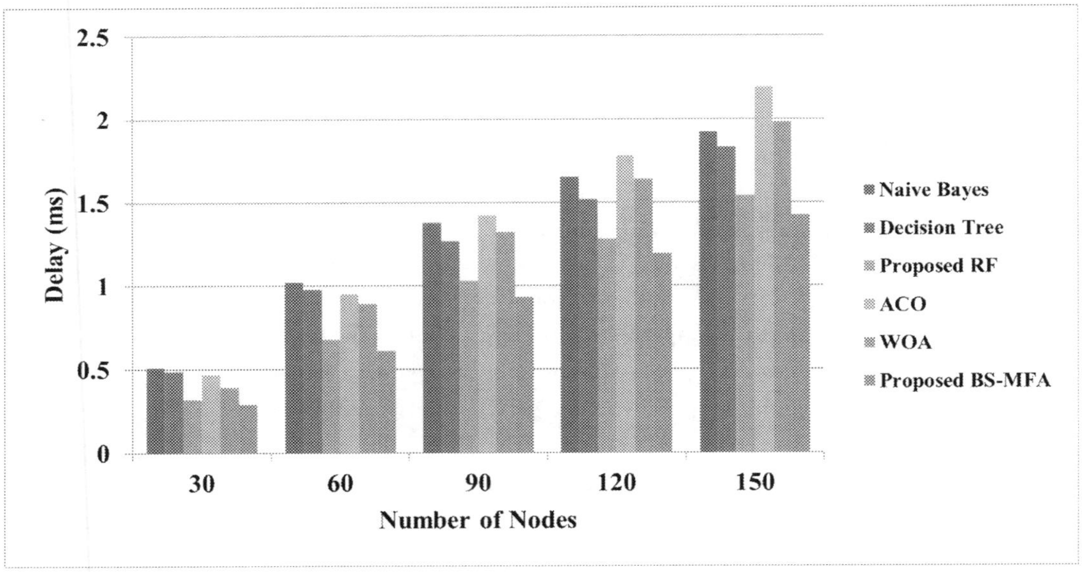

When the number of nodes upsurges, the delay of proposed and existing techniques also increases. When the node is 60, the delay time of NB, DT, proposed RF, ACO, WOA and proposed BS-MFA are 0.102ms, 0.98ms, 0.68ms, 0.95ms, 0.89ms and 0.60ms. At the same time, when the node is 150, the delay time of NB, DT, proposed RF, ACO, WOA and proposed BS-MFA are 0.192ms, 0.183ms, 0.154ms, 0.200ms, 0.198ms and 0.140ms. This proves that the proposed RF and BS-MFA have less delay time than existing techniques.

Performance Analysis of Proposed Scheme in Terms of Detection Rate

Table 3 and Figure 3 show the validation of proposed BS-MFA with existing practices regarding the detection rate.

Table 3. Comparative Analysis of Detection Rate of Proposed Techniques

Methodology	Detection Rate (%)				
	30 nodes	60 nodes	90 nodes	120 nodes	150 nodes
Naive Bayes	5	25	38	59	71
Decision Tree	0	8	26	41	67
Proposed RF	8	29	68	86	91
ACO	0	14	26	46	65
WOA	3	9	18	38	54
Proposed BS-MFA	15	32	70	89	94

Figure 3. Graphical Illustration of Proposed Methodology based on Detection Rate

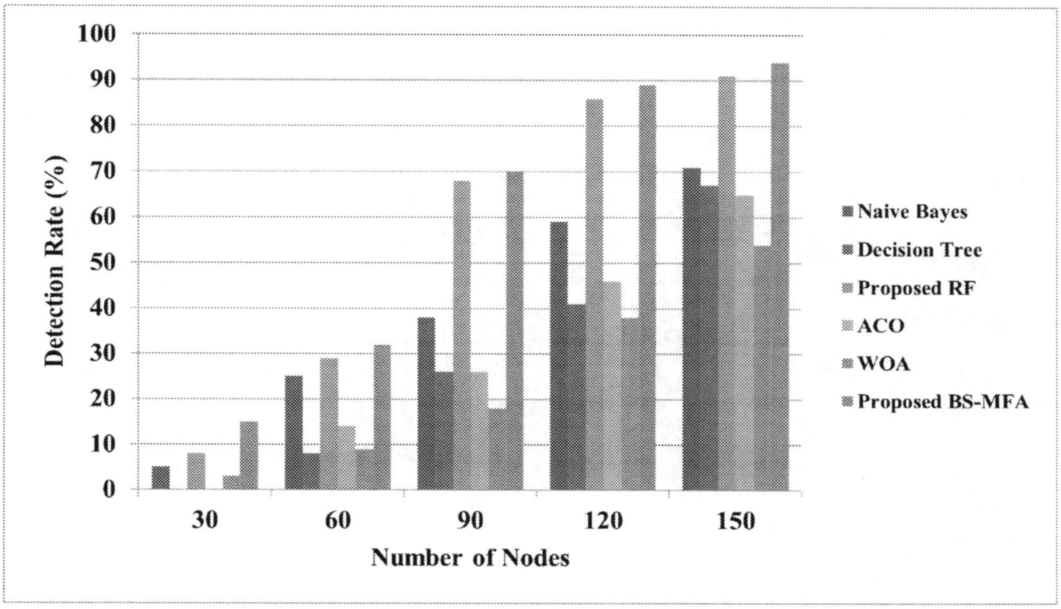

When the number of nodes increases, the detection rate of proposed and existing techniques also increases. When the node is 30, the detection rate of NB, proposed RF, WOA and proposed BS-MFA are 5%, 8%, 3% and 15%, whereas the DT and ACO have no detection rate for the 30th nodes. At the same time, when the node is 120, the detection rate of NB, DT, proposed RF, ACO, WOA and proposed BS-MFA are 59%, 41%, 86%, 46%, 38% and 89%. This proves that the BS-MFA has a higher detection rate than the proposed RF and existing techniques. The detection rate of BS-MFA and RF reaches above 90% only when they reach the 150th node.

Performance Analysis of Proposed Method in terms of Energy Consumption

Table 4 and Figure 4 show the validation of projected BS-MFA with existing systems in terms of energy consumption. The number nodes varied from 30 to 150.

Table 4. Comparative Analysis of Energy Consumption of Proposed Techniques

Methodology	Energy Consumption(Joule)				
	30 nodes	60 nodes	90 nodes	120 nodes	150 nodes
Naive Bayes	9.8	10.4	11.9	12.8	13.7
Decision Tree	9.7	10.8	12.9	13.7	14.7
Proposed RF	8.6	9.1	9.7	10.8	11.8
ACO	9.8	11.9	13.4	14.9	16.0
WOA	9.6	11.1	12.6	14.9	16.5
Proposed BS-MFA	8.1	8.8	9.3	9.9	10.4

Figure 4. Graphical Representation of Proposed Methodology based on Energy Consumption

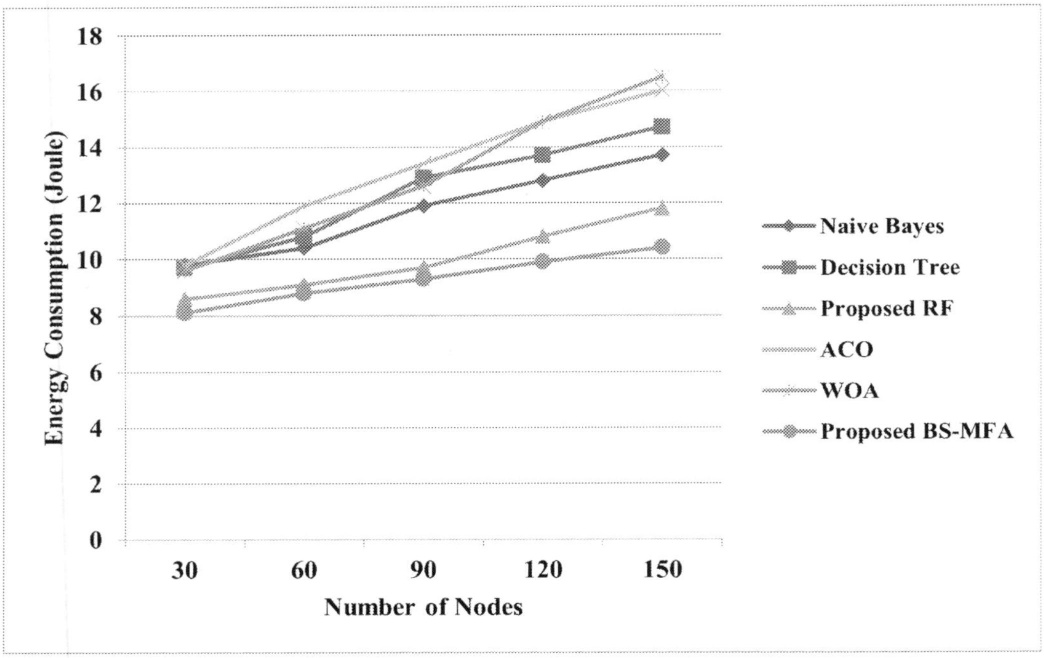

When the node is 90, the energy consumption of NB, DT, proposed RF, ACO, WOA and BS-MFA are 11.9J, 112.9J, 9.7J, 13.4J, 12.6J and 9.3J. At the same time, when the node is 30, the energy consumption of NB, DT, proposed RF, ACO, WOA and BS-MFA are 9.8J, 9.7J, 8.6J, 9.8J, 9.6J and 8.1J. This proves that the BS-MFA consume less energy than the proposed RF and existing techniques. BS-MFA and RF energy consumption reaches above 10J only when they reach the 150th node. The RF reaches 10J when it touches the 120th node, and BS-MFA reaches 10J when it touches the 150th node.

Proposed Method Throughput Performance

Table 5 and Figure 5 demonstrate the validation of the proposed BS-MFA with existing procedures in terms of throughput.

Table 5. Proposed Techniques Throughput Analysis

Methodology	Throughput(kbps)				
	30 nodes	60 nodes	90 nodes	120 nodes	150 nodes
Naive Bayes	0.55	0.60	0.65	0.69	0.80
Decision Tree	0.57	0.66	0.68	0.77	0.87
Proposed RF	0.64	0.70	0.80	0.87	0.96
ACO	0.51	0.61	0.74	0.84	0.90
WOA	0.58	0.67	0.79	0.81	0.89
Proposed BS-MFA	0.67	0.76	0.81	0.89	0.98

Figure 5. Graphical Representation of Proposed Methodology based on throughput

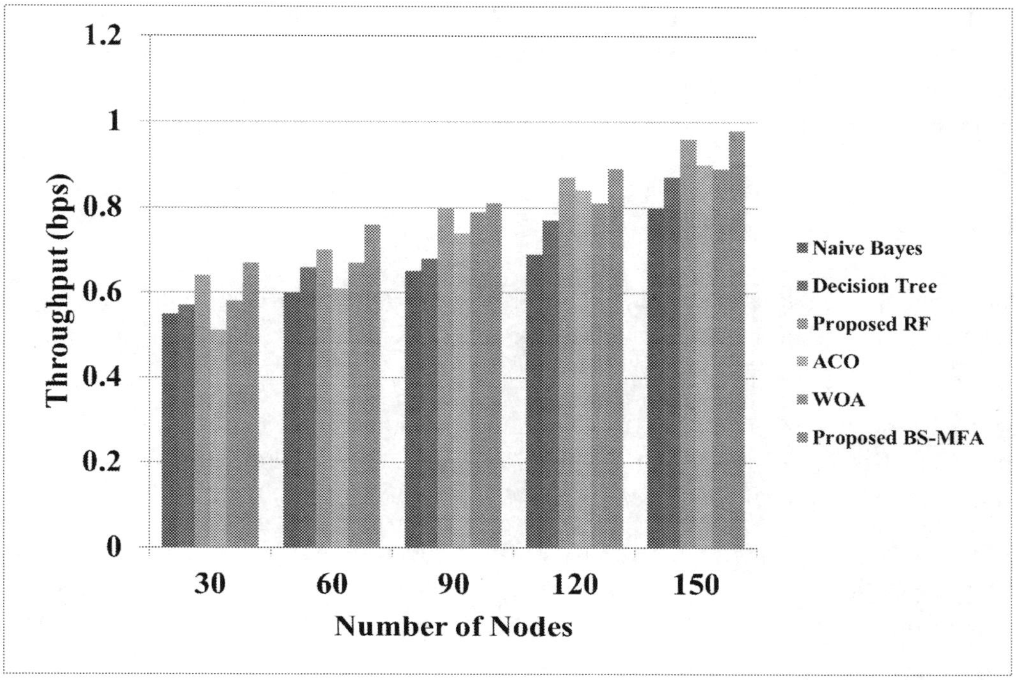

When the node is 30, the throughput (bps) of NB, DT, proposed RF, ACO, WOA and BS-MFA are 0.55, 0.57, 0.64, 0.51, 0.58 and 0.67. At the same time, when the node is 90, the throughput (bps) of NB, DT, proposed RF, ACO, WOA and proposed BS-MFA are 0.65, 0.68, 0.80, 0.74, 0.79 and 0.81. When the techniques reach the 150th node, the throughput of NB, DT, proposed RF, ACO, WOA and proposed BS-MFA are 0.80, 0.87, 0.96, 0.90, 0.89 and 0.98. This proves that the BS-MFA achieved high throughput than the proposed RF and existing techniques. The throughput of BS-MFA and RF reaches above 0.85 only when they reach the 120th node. The table above discusses the comparative discussion of the routing strategies. According to a clear overview of figures 2 to 5, it is observed that the suggested strategy in the event of attacks acquires the maximum throughput, detection rate, energy and shortest delay.

CONCLUSION

In this study, the BS-MFA suggested that multi-track routing overcomes the major disadvantages of the current multi-track routing systems. Initially, the nodes in the network are initialized in such a mode that the efficient routing of multipath based on optimization is guaranteed. The selection of the CH is based on the fuzzy cluster strategy based on the FFA, in which the optimum CH is indomitable. The optimal routing in the network, which filters the hostile nodes out using the RF classification, is enabled once the CH is detected. The communiqué in the network is thus launched by secure nodes so that energy efficiency and safety are efficiently enabled. The BS-MFA, which inherits the advantages of BS MFA, provides safe routing. The simulated method analysis shows that the suggested approach beat previous methods with a maximum power output of 0.98 bps and 10.4 jule. In contrast, for the 150th node, the maximum detection rate and minimum delay were 94 percent. This approach can still be enhanced in future by adding delay tolerance in routing to increase system performance in the network. The package has to be divided into real-time and non-real-time flows that can be programmed with various paths depending on road delay tolerance.

REFERENCES

Anandamurugan, S., & Abirami, T. (2017). Anti-predator adaptation shuffled frog leap algorithm to improve network lifetime in wireless sensor network. *Wireless Personal Communications*, *94*(4), 2031–2042. doi:10.100711277-016-3354-1

Anderegg, L., & Eidenbenz, S. (2003). Ad hoc-VCG: A Truthful and Cost-Efficient Routing Protocol for Mobile ad hoc Networks with Selfish Agents. *Proceedings of the Annual International Conference on Mobile Computing and Networking, MOBICOM*, 245–259. 10.1145/938985.939011

Ari, A. A. A., Yenke, B. O., Labraoui, N., Damakoa, I., & Gueroui, A. (2016). A power efficient cluster-based routing algorithm for wireless sensor networks: Honeybees swarm intelligence based approach. *Journal of Network and Computer Applications*, *69*, 77–97. doi:10.1016/j.jnca.2016.04.020

Bala, K., Chandra Sekar, A., Baskar, M., & Paramesh, J. (2019). An efficient multi- level intrusion detection system for mobile ad-hoc network using clustering technique. *International Journal of Engineering and Advanced Technology*, *8*(6), 1977–1985. doi:10.35940/ijeat.F8291.088619

Cheng, H., Yang, S., & Wang, X. (2012). Immigrants-enhanced multi-population genetic algorithms for dynamic shortest path routing problems in mobile ad hoc networks. *Applied Artificial Intelligence*, *26*(7), 673–695. doi:10.1080/08839514.2012.701449

Fanian, F., & Kuchaki Rafsanjani, M. (2018). Memetic fuzzy clustering protocol for wireless sensor networks: Shuffled frog leaping algorithm. *Applied Soft Computing*, *71*, 568–590. doi:10.1016/j.asoc.2018.07.012

Goyal, P., Parmar, V., & Rishi, R. (2011). Manet: Vulnerabilities, challenges, attacks, application. *IJCEM International Journal of Computational Engineering & Management*, *11*, 32–37.

Gupta, G. P., & Jha, S. (2018). Integrated Clustering and routing protocol for wireless sensor networks using cuckoo and harmony search based meta-heuristic techniques. *Engineering Applications of Artificial Intelligence*, *68*, 101–109. doi:10.1016/j.engappai.2017.11.003

Hinds, A., Ngulube, M., Zhu, S., & Al-Aqrabi, H. (2013). A review of routing protocols for mobile ad-hoc networks (manet). *International Journal of Information and Education Technology (IJIET)*, *3*(1), 1–5. doi:10.7763/IJIET.2013.V3.223

Huiyao, A., Xicheng, L., & Wei, P. (2004). *A cluster-based multipath routing for MANET*. Computer School, National University of Defense Technology.

Jabeur, N. (2016). A firefly-inspired micro and macro clustering approach for wireless sensor networks. *Procedia Computer Science*, *98*, 132–139. doi:10.1016/j.procs.2016.09.021

Karthikeyan, B., Kanimozhi, N., & Ganesh, S. H. (2014). Analysis of reactive AODV routing protocol for MANET. *World Congress on Computing and Communication Technologies*, 264–267 10.1109/WCCCT.2014.70

Marina, M. K., & Das, S. R. (2001). On-demand multipath distance vector routing in ad hoc networks. *Proceedings of the Ninth International Conference on Network Protocols (ICNP)*, 14–23. 10.1109/ICNP.2001.992756

Patel, D. N., Patel, S. B., Kothadiya, H. R., Jethwa, P. D., & Jhaveri, R. H. (2014). A survey of reactive routing protocols in MANET. *International Conference on Information Communication and Embedded Systems (ICICES2014)*, 1–6. 10.1109/ICICES.2014.7033833

Robinson, Y. H., & Rajaram, M. (2015). Energy-aware multipath routing scheme based on particle swarm optimization in mobile ad hoc networks. *TheScientificWorldJournal*, *284276*, 1–9. Advance online publication. doi:10.1155/2015/284276 PMID:26819966

Rodriguez-Galiano, V. F., Ghimire, B., Rogan, J., Chica-Olmo, M., & Rigol-Sanchez, J. P. (2012). An assessment of the effectiveness of a random forest classifier for land-cover classification. *ISPRS Journal of Photogrammetry and Remote Sensing*, *67*, 93–104. doi:10.1016/j.isprsjprs.2011.11.002

Sarkar, S., & Datta, R. (2013). A game theoretic model for stochastic routing in self-organized MANETs. *Proceedings of the IEEE Wireless Communications and Networking Conference (WCNC)*, 1962–1967. 10.1109/WCNC.2013.6554865

Sarkar, S., & Datta, R. (2016). A secure and energy-efficient stochastic multipath routing for self-organized mobile ad hoc networks. *Ad Hoc Networks*, *37*, 209–227. doi:10.1016/j.adhoc.2015.08.020

Singh, O., Singh, J., & Singh, R. (2018). Multi-level trust based intelligence intrusion detection system to detect the malicious nodes using elliptic curve cryptography in MANET. *Cluster Computing*, *21*(1), 51–63. doi:10.100710586-017-0927-z

Subba, B., Biswas, S., & Karmakar, S. (2016). "Intrusion detection in mobile ad hoc Networks: Bayesian game formulation. *EngSciTechnol. Engineering Science and Technology, an International Journal*, *19*(2), 782–799. doi:10.1016/j.jestch.2015.11.001

Taha, A., Alsaqour, R., Uddin, M., Abdelhaq, M., & Saba, T. (2017). Energy efficient multipath routing protocol for mobile ad-hoc network using the ftness function. *IEEE Access: Practical Innovations, Open Solutions*, *5*, 10369–10381. doi:10.1109/ACCESS.2017.2707537

Uddin, M., Rahman, A. A., Alarifi, A., Talha, M., Shah, A., Iftikhar, M., & Zomaya, A. (2012). Improving performance of mobile ad hoc networks using efficient tactical on demand distance vector (TAODV) routing algorithm. *International Journal of Innovative Computing, Information, & Control*, *8*(6), 4375–4389.

Venkatesan, T. P., Rajakumar, P., & Pitchaikkannu, A. (2014). Overview of Proactive Routing protocols in MANET. *Fourth International Conference on Communication Systems and Network Technologies*, 173–177. 10.1109/CSNT.2014.42

Yadav, A. K., & Tripathi, S. (2017). QMRPRNS: Design of QoS multicast routing protocol using reliable node selection scheme for MANETs. *Peer-to-Peer Networking and Applications*, *10*(4), 897–909. doi:10.100712083-016-0441-8

Yannam, A. (2019). Trust aware intrustion detection system to defend attacks in MANET. *International Journal of Innovative Technology and Exploring Engineering*, *8*(6), 1298–1306.

Yavuz, A. A., Alagöz, F., & Anarim, E. (2010). A new Multi-Tier adaptive military MANET security protocol using hybrid cryptography and signcryption. *Turkish Journal of Electrical Engineering and Computer Sciences*, *18*, 1–22. doi:10.3906/elk-0904-6

Zahedi, Z. M., Akbari, R., Shokouhifar, M., Safaei, F., & Jalali, A. (2016). Swarm intelligence based fuzzy routing protocol for clustered wireless sensor networks. *Expert Systems with Applications*, *55*, 313–328. doi:10.1016/j.eswa.2016.02.016

Zervoudakis, K., & Tsafarakis, S. (2020). A mayfly optimization algorithm. *Computers & Industrial Engineering*, *145*, 106559. doi:10.1016/j.cie.2020.106559

Chapter 14
Deep Learning Algorithms in Cluster Analysis on an E-Learning System in Data Mining

S. Keerthana
Nandha Engineering College, India

P. Thirumoorthy
Nandha Engineering College, India

S. Maheswari
Nandha Engineering College, India

S. Karuppusamy
Nandha Engineering College, India

ABSTRACT

Data mining is one space that helps in churning out helpful data from the abounding knowledge offered. Mining is gaining immense quality currently. To perform data processing, a majority of techniques exist. Agglomeration approach relies on the scholar performance and activities allotted as a district of process. Clusters are accustomed realize the relation between the attributes. The cluster analysis was performed by organizing collections of patterns into team-supported student behavior. In this chapter, several agglomeration approaches of area unit are used including agglomerated hierarchal agglomeration, K means, and C means.

DOI: 10.4018/978-1-6684-6060-3.ch014

INTRODUCTION

It unearths information that has been buried inside the data, which can either be connected to machine learning or exploratory information analysis, both of which are becoming increasingly common in today's world (Guiamalon, et al., 2022b). Agglomeration is a method that can be used in processing that assembles information of similar types into clusters (Guiamalon, T. S., 2022a). It is a method of learning that occurs without a teacher present. Unsupervised learning is supposed to have occurred when the clusters formed for a number of classes that were not known. As a result, this region is considered to be one in which unsupervised learning took place. The most important goal of agglomeration is to minimise the degree to which different classes are alike and maximise the degree to which individual classes are alike, with the criteria for this determination being printed on the factor of characteristics (Raja and Priya, 2021b).

The machine learning technique known as "deep learning" will be among the options under consideration (Demeter, et al., 2021). It's a discipline where experts can study computer algorithms to learn on their own. Deep learning involves artificial neural networks that are meant to mimic the way humans think and learn, whereas machine learning sticks to more simplistic approaches (Balas-Timar and Lile, 2015). In the recent past, computational power constraints capped the complexity of neural networks. Thanks to developments in big data analytics, however, computers now have access to larger, more sophisticated neural networks, allowing them to analyse, understand, and respond to complex information at a rate that exceeds that of humans. Speech recognition, language translation, and image categorization are just few of the areas where deep learning has proven useful (Raja and Lakshmi, 2022). As such, it can be used to remedy any issue with pattern recognition that arises without the need for human intervention (Lumapenet, et al., 2022).

Comparable to the neurons that make up the human brain, neural networks consist of layers of nodes. Adjacent nodes on different layers are linked together (Rad, et al., 2020). The greater number of layers in the network is used as evidence that it is more complex (Raja and Priya, 2021a). A single human brain nerve cell is constantly bombarded by millions of impulses from other neurons (Roman et al., 2020). Signals are transmitted between the nodes of a synthetic neural network, where weights are then assigned based on the information conveyed. A node with a higher weight has a great deal of influence over the nodes below it (Rad and Balas 2020). A final layer aggregates the inputs and generates an output based on their relative importance (Raja, and Lakshmi, 2020). Due to the large amount of data they collect and the complexity of the arithmetic they employ, deep learning systems can only run on high-end computers. However, it will take weeks to train a neural network, even with this cutting-edge gear (Rad, et al., 2019).

Educational Data-Mining (Edm)

A wide range of data mining methods is utilised in order to perform an analysis of the knowledge. Students' human capacities to explore and extract the most useful information from student databases are far above their ability to do so without the assistance of machine-controlled analytical methods. This is a result of the vast amount of information that is stored in student databases. Knowledge discovery is the process of being able to search through enormous amounts of data and locate information that is either explicit or previously unknown, as well as potentially useful (KD). Processing the data in KD allows for the discovery of patterns that are based on the requirements of users. A set of information that is defined as a pattern is one that is described by an expression in language.

The EDM method has four main phases. The drawback definition is that the initial phase in that a particular problem is translated into a knowledge mining downside. During this part, the project goal and objectives area unit developed similarly because of the main analysis queries. The foremost long part is the second part, the information preparation and gathering part. It will take up to 80 you look after all the analysis time. Information quality may be a major challenge in the data processing. During this part, source information should be known, clean and formatted in a prespecified format (Raja, et al., 2019). After that, there's a Modeling and Evaluating introduction where the parameters are set to the best values, and completely different modelling techniques are chosen and applied. The preparation part is the last phase in that the results of the data mining area unit are organised and given through graphs and reports. It's necessary to indicate that the data mining method is a repetitive method which implies that the method doesn't stop once a selected resolution is deployed. It may be simply a replacement input for a new process.

The proliferation of technological tools utilised in educational settings has resulted in an excessive amount of information being made accessible to users. EDM gives a significant quantity of information that is pertinent and presents a more accurate picture of learners and the learning activities that they engage in. Researching instructional information and finding solutions to instructional issues are accomplished through the application of DM approaches. In a manner that is analogous to that of various DM strategies, the EDM methodology gleans information from instructional expertise that is fascinating, explicable, helpful, and unique. EDM, on the other hand, places its primary emphasis on the creation of educational systems that make use of many forms of knowledge. Therefore, these methods are utilised to improve data relating to instructional phenomena, students, and, therefore, the contexts in which they are instructed. By establishing machine approaches that combine knowledge and theory, it is possible to increase the overall quality of T&L operations.

Cluster Analysis

Cluster analysis is often thought about as a tool for beta knowledge analysis that's aimed toward sorting completely different objects into purposeful teams in such the simplest way that the degree by which these objects are unit associated is at the utmost if they belong to an equivalent cluster and at the minimum if they are doing not. Cluster analysis is employed to get the hidden structures or relationships inside knowledge while not having the requirement to clarify or interpret what this relationship is. In essence, cluster analysis is barely wont to discover the structures found in knowledge while not explaining why those structures or relationships exist.

Hierarchical Cluster Analysis

In this technique, first, a cluster is formed and so added to a different cluster (the most similar and nearest one) to make one single cluster. This method is recurrent till all subjects area units in one cluster. This explicit technique is thought of as clustered technique. Clustered bunch starts with single objects and starts grouping them into clusters. The divisive technique is another reasonably graded technique during which the bunch starts with the whole information set and so starts dividing into partitions.

Centroid-Based Clustering

This style of clustering clusters area units portrayed by a central entity, which can or might not be a section of the given information set. K-Means technique of bunch is employed during this technique, wherever k area unit the cluster centres and objects area unit appointed to the closest cluster centers.

Distribution-Based Clustering

It is a sort of cluster model closely associated with statistics supported by the models of distribution. Objects that belong to an equivalent distribution are placed into one cluster. This type of cluster will capture some complicated properties of objects, like correlation and dependence between attributes.

Density-Based Clustering

In this variety of clusters, clusters square measure outlined by the square measures of density that are more than the remaining of the information set. Objects in thin square measures are sometimes needed to separate clusters. The objects within these thin points area unit sometimes noise and border points in the graph. The most common methodology during this variety of clusters is DBSCAN.

LITERATURE SURVEY

Dutt, A. (2015), the goal of the degree programme in Educational Data Mining is to develop models for enhancing students' learning experiences and the efficiency of educational institutions by conducting an analysis of the various interconnected and unconnected systems that produce information in an educational environment. Although the term is frequently used in association with knowledge discovery in databases (KDD), the practice of information mining is rarely utilised in educational settings.

Kiran, R. et al. (2020), E-learning may be a field that is trending in terms of analysis given the high quality of e-learning systems and the growing trend in data mining. Learning using e-learning systems offers a more comprehensive educational experience in addition to being more practical and adaptable. Clumping algorithms such as K-Means clump and DBSCAN algorithms were used to separate the learners into distinct groups in order to support the learners' performance during this test. This was done in order to help the learners' performance. The portal is meant to support the performance of a group of learners whenever a new cluster of learners is generated.

Gushchina and Ochepovsky, (2020), among others, Educational methods teach students how to make adjustments to feedback, determine personal needs, and provide additional individualised attention to student profiles by dynamically observing and following up on the student's behaviour while they are using the system. These are all attempts to increase the efficiency of e-learning. In addition, the following methods are recommended: cluster analysis, which can be used to establish the most productive time to make each session; data analysis and visualisation, which can be used to discover the academic resources that are most suitable for finishing courses.

Chugh, and Baweja, (2020) the massive and multifaceted nature of databases creates a difficult environment for the management of information in online retailers. The information of customers is required to be kept private, and a two-phase clustering strategy is utilised in order to accomplish this goal. In the first step of the process, a heuristic technique is used to vary the k-means formula. When we use collective clustering, we see instances of outliers. This method provides an efficient means of knowledge analysis, making it possible to prevent consumer failure in online shopping.

Kousiga, and Shanmuga (2019), Data mining is a process that can be used to convert raw data into more usable information. Extracting meaningful information from large data sets often requires the use of a number of distinct methods and algorithms. In the realm of data processing, agglomeration can be counted as one of the many different types of analytic procedures. It's a system for organising related pieces of data and information together in one place. The process of agglomeration makes use of a number of different algorithms. A survey of ranked agglomeration algorithms and a few linked analysis methods have been mentioned throughout this study.

Khor, (2021) Cluster processing was used to learn typologies based on educational records and the behaviour of learners interacting with e-learning platforms so that patterns could be discovered. Given that cluster learners tend to achieve results that are comparable to other cluster members, it may be possible to provide them with learning help and strategies. The outcomes of this study can assist in understanding how students would react to various options in an online learning environment. This is in addition to providing information regarding the effects that different options have on the performance of tutorials.

Goel, (2019), Each day, more data is being collected. On the other hand, in order for this knowledge to be used for strategic decision-making, it must first be converted into data. The processing of data is one of these areas that assist in the generation of useful data from the information that is provided. It's the process of finding interesting patterns or pieces of information hidden inside a vast body of data. The quality of mining is currently improving significantly. There is a multitude of different approaches that can be taken to process data. There is a possibility that a clump is a mining approach that functions according to the principle of comprehending the differences and similarities between the information.

Faizan, M. et al. (2020), Clustering is an important component of information processing that plays a vital role. Unattended learning is acknowledged as being a part of the process of clustering, which is the process of segmenting information structures inside a single unknown in order to figure out more. The most popular clustering technique involves locating information patterns through the examination of representative samples of data.

Qiu, F. et al. (2022) education and data technology are closely intertwined in order to enhance learning, and they are crucial components in ensuring that all students receive an equivalent level of education. To keep up with the expanding user teams and application domains, it has become increasingly vital to make certain that the quality of e-learning is assured. This is because of the growing competition in this space. Currently, one of the ways in which e-learning standards are validated is by employing the knowledge of reciprocal freelance e-learning behaviour to build a learning performance predictor. This learning performance predictor is then used to direct and evaluate education while it is being gained.

Kaur, M. (2013), E-learning is a relatively new kind of education that eliminates the need for face-to-face interaction between teachers and their pupils. E-learners enrol in instructional courses that are offered via the internet and have the ability to study online during this type of internet-based or online learning. This study suggests doing an investigation into the ways in which students make use of various data processing tools and methods. In order to investigate the connection between students' participation in courses and their overall performance, classification and clustering methods are utilised. The performance of students is dependent on their grades, the amount of time they spend learning, their utilisation of facts, as well as the richness of the quality of the course.

PROPOSED SYSTEM

The proposed system addresses educational data "processing" techniques with the goal of improving the efficiency of the e-learning process. This is accomplished through the implementation of a plan to reconcile feedback, individual assessment, and additional personalised attention to each student's profile. Academic system to assist them in improving their methods of decision-making. The knowledge of the students will be put to better use in this manner for the purpose of performance analysis through the appropriate selection of the cluster algorithmic programme that justifies the students' analysis questions. Students are able to have their academic behaviour figured out by using the kernel fuzzy clump methodology, which allows for the classification of students into categories according to the most signs of their activity.

Data Preprocessing

The transformation of information into a format that can be read is what's known as "data preparation." It is also an essential stage in the processing of data, as, without it, we would be unable to work with the information. Before implementing any machine learning or data processing techniques, it is important to make sure that the quality of the information has been verified. The positive information preprocessing approach is reacting because it creates information that is unspecified and ready for examination, there is no feedback, and it communicates for the operation of data collection. This is because it creates information that is ready for examination. The variance in the information that exists between different information sets is the most significant drawback of the information preparation.

During the preprocessing stage of information, distinct processes work to uncontaminated the data by filling in missing values, smoothing noisy information, identifying and either rejecting or keeping outliers, and deciding inconsistencies. Knowledge purification is a method that costs $64,000 and may involve eradicating craft errors or authenticating accurate values against a significant list of entities. Both of these activities may be performed against the list.

Tutorial process (EDM) point information Sets are responsible for performing information preprocessing as the first stage in the process. The dataset has a total of 4362 instances and seven decisions, which are referred to as ID, Course 1, Course 2, Sex, Pearson Correlation, Pval, and Students, respectively. The essential decisions are which course to take first, which course to take second, and whether or not to use the Pearson correlation.

The preprocessing of knowledge is very important when considering the quality of the information. The ensuing measures ensure that the criterion is met.

Accuracy: to envision whether or not the information entered is correct or not.

Completeness: to envision whether or not the information is accessible or not recorded.

Consistency: to envision whether or not constant information is unbroken, all told the places that do or don't match.

Timeliness: the information ought to be updated properly.

Believability: the information ought to be trustable.

Interpretability: The comprehensibility of the information.

Cluster Assignment

Cluster assignment is used to allocate knowledge to the clusters that were antecedently formed by some cluster methods such as K-means, DBSCAN (Density-Based abstraction cluster of Applications with Noise), and several other cluster methods (Self-Organizing Maps). This algorithmic rule requires that the associated cluster procedures preserve cluster information, also known as a cluster model, which also includes the management parameters in order to maintain consistency. It makes the assumption that fresh information comes from the same distribution as previous information and hence is unable to update the cluster information.

Fuzzy Clustering

The main purpose of fuzzy c-means cluster is the partitioning of knowledge into a set of clusters, wherever every datum is allotted a membership price for every cluster. Consequently, fuzzy classification is the method of grouping people having identical characteristics into a fuzzy set. A fuzzy classification corresponds to a membership operation that indicates whether or not an individual could be a member of a category, given its fuzzy classification predicate ~Π. The fuzzy c-means formula has a higher performance than the k-means. The fuzzy c-means formula features a weakness in terms of procedure time needed, and fuzzy c-means are longer than k-means. The main advantage of fuzzy c – suggests that bunch is that it permits gradual memberships of knowledge points to clusters measured as degrees in [0, 1]. This offers the pliability to specify that information points will belong to over one cluster.

Kernel-Based Fuzzy Clustering Technique

The upgraded kernel-primarily based Fuzzy agglomeration (EKFC) is an extended version of the fuzzy clustering method (FCM) algorithmic rule, and the convergence qualities of the projected method are recapitulated. Instead of making use of a feature-weight linkage vector that is predetermined, the projected technique's coaching portion makes use of dynamic feature-weight vector updates. Because the feature-weight linkage vector of the standard fuzzy c-means algorithmic rule stays fixed all through the agglomeration procedure, the significance of certain options to the dynamical cluster data cannot be properly manifested. This is because the rule is part of the standard fuzzy c-means algorithmic rule.

Cluster Assessment

Calculate the cluster assessment by utilising a distance matrix that takes a fixed number of multiple places and involves entirely complexes that have an adequate amount of variety in nearby networks. This is something that can be obtained based on the descriptor that was chosen in the stage before this one. The use of geometric measures as resemblance actions is a frequent practice in the process of calculating the degree of similarity between different chemical compounds. The Euclidean expanse is the similarity live that is favoured, and this preference is based on the distinction between the constellations. The Euclidean life is chosen because it hints that it would have been enjoyable to utilize in a shared-neighbor cluster.

RESULT

However, based on this theory and concepts in Deep Learning Algorithms in Cluster Analysis on an E-Learning System in Data Mining have been performed based on these results (figures 1 to 3)

Figure 1. Consensus Neighbour Clustering Result

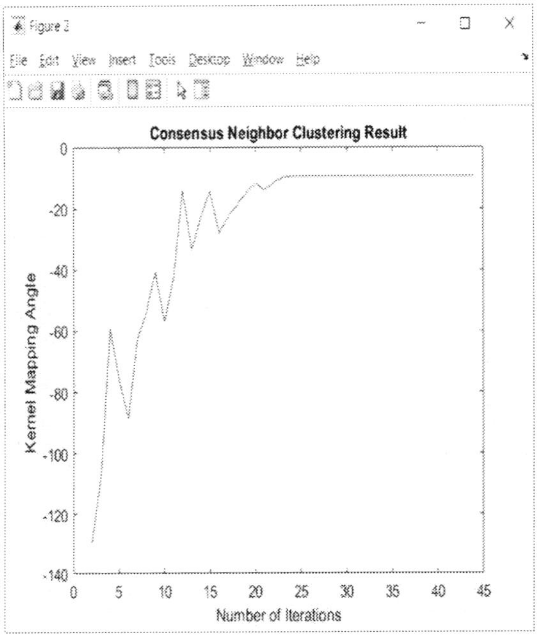

Figure 2. Fuzzy Clustering Result

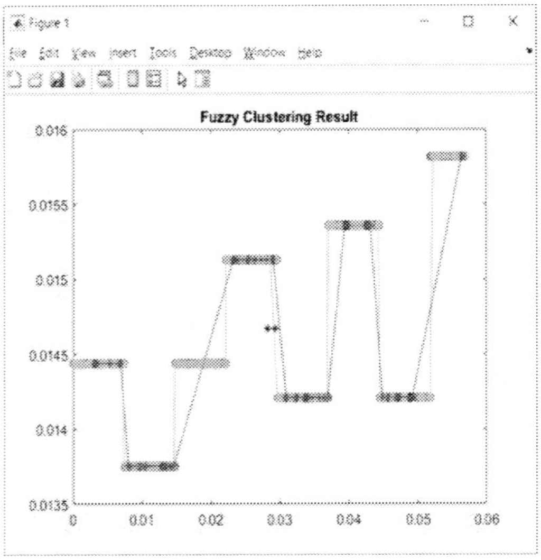

Figure 3. Kernel Mapping Angel of Edm Lab Data Set Connectivity Clustering Result

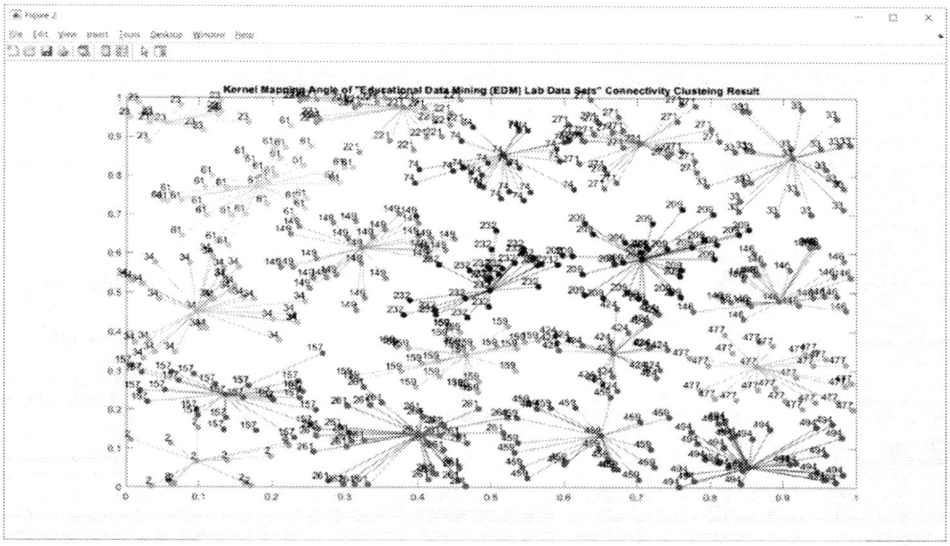

CONCLUSION AND FUTURE ENHANCEMENT

The Educational data mining tools that are available in the E-learning system, one is able to investigate the educational behaviour of students in order to ascertain the level of interest that students have in educational content as well as the educational contents themselves. It was found that students' academic behaviour in an online environment varied according to their academic levels and degrees of performance. This finding suggests that students at different academic levels distribute their online activity differently. Validate simulation results by deploying failure recovery techniques on a medium-sized cluster for which public data is available. Analyse concerns with high-dimensional data clustering usage in our testbed cluster through the use of profiling data. It is also possible to employ applied deep learning algorithms to do analysis on high-dimensional data.

REFERENCES

Balas-Timar, D., & Lile, R. (2015). The story of Goldilocks told by organisational psychologists. *Procedia: Social and Behavioral Sciences*, *203*, 239–243. doi:10.1016/j.sbspro.2015.08.288

Chugh, S., & Baweja, V. R. (2020). Data mining application in segmenting customers with clustering. In *2020 International Conference on Emerging Trends in Information Technology and Engineering (ic-ETITE)*. IEEE. 10.1109/ic-ETITE47903.2020.259

Demeter, E., Rad, D., & Balas, E. (2021). Schadenfreude and General Anti-Social Behaviours: The Role of Violent Content Preferences and Life Satisfaction. BRAIN. *Broad Research in Artificial Intelligence and Neuroscience*, *12*(2), 98–111. doi:10.18662/brain/12.2/194

Dutt, A. (2015). Clustering algorithms applied in educational data mining. *International Journal of Information and Electronics Engineering*. . doi:10.7763/IJIEE.2015.V5.513

Faizan, M., F, M., Ismail, S., & Sultan, S. (2020). Applications of clustering techniques in data mining: A comparative study. *IJACSA*, *11*(12). Advance online publication. doi:10.14569/IJACSA.2020.0111218

Goel, N. (2019). Implementing cluster analysis on an E-learning website. *Vivekananda Journal of Research*, *8*(2), 158–170.

Guiamalon, T., Sandigan, D. A., & Dilna, S. G. (2022b). The impact of Alternative Learning System in Cotabato Division: A case study. *International Journal of Scientific Research and Management, 10*(4), 1–5. . doi:10.18535/ijsrm/v10i4.el01

Guiamalon, T. S. (2022a). Social And Economic Development: State Universities And Colleges' (Suc's) Contribution Creativity Skills Of The Students In Recycling. *Globus Journal of Progressive Education: A Refereed Research Journal, 12*(1), 104-110.

Gushchina, O. M., & Ochepovsky, A. V. (2020). Data mining of students' behavior in E-learning system. *Journal of Physics: Conference Series*, *1553*(1), 012027. doi:10.1088/1742-6596/1553/1/012027

Kaur, M. (2013). Cluster analysis of behavior of E-learners. *International Journal of Soft Computing and Engineering*, *3*(2), 344–346.

Khor, E. T. (2021). A learning analytics approach using clustering data mining for learners profiling to extrapolate e-learning behaviours. In T. Bastiaens (Ed.), *Proceedings of Innovate Learning Summit 2021 Online* (pp. 59-64). Association for the Advancement of Computing in Education (AACE). https://www.learntechlib.org/primary/p/220271

Kiran, R., & Kumar, D. K. R. A. (2020). Adaptive upgradation of personalized E-learning portal using data mining. *International Journal of Innovative Technology and Exploring Engineering*, *10*(1), 224–227. doi:10.35940/ijitee.A8167.1110120

Kousiga, T., & Shanmuga Vadivu, R. (2019). Survey on hierarchical clustering algorithms in data mining. *International Journal of Scientific Development and Research*, *4*(9), 1–3.

Lumapenet, H. T., & Usop, M. P. (2022). School Readiness towards the Delivery of Learning in the New Normal. *International Journal of Early Childhood Special Education, 14*(3), 2629-2637.

Qiu, F., Zhang, G., Sheng, X., Jiang, L., Zhu, L., Xiang, Q., Jiang, B., & Chen, P. (2022). Predicting students' performance in e-learning using learning process and behaviour data. *Scientific Reports*, *12*(1), 453. doi:10.103841598-021-03867-8 PMID:35013396

Rad, D., Balas, E., Ignat, S., Rad, G., & Dixon, D. (2020). A Predictive Model of Youth Bystanders' Helping Attitudes. *Revista romaneasca pentru educatie multidimensionala-Journal for Multidimensional Education, 12*(1Sup2), 136-150.

Rad, D., & Balas, V. E. (2020). A Novel Fuzzy Scoring Approach of Behavioural Interviews in Personnel Selection. BRAIN. *Broad Research in Artificial Intelligence and Neuroscience*, *11*(2), 178–188. doi:10.18662/brain/11.2/81

Rad, D., Dughi, T., & Demeter, E. (2019). The Dynamics of the Relationship between Humor and Benevolence as Values. *Revista romaneasca pentru educatie multidimensionala-Journal for Multidimensional Education, 11*(3), 201-212.

Raja, M., & Lakshmi Priya, G. G. (2020). Factors Affecting the Intention to Use Virtual Reality in Education. *Psychology and Education, 57*(9), 2014–2022.

Raja, M., & Lakshmi Priya, G. G. (2022). Using Virtual Reality and Augmented Reality with ICT Tools for Enhancing quality in the Changing Academic Environment in COVID-19 Pandemic: An Empirical Study. *Studies in Computational Intelligence, 1019*, 467–482. doi:10.1007/978-3-030-93921-2_26

Raja, M., & Priya, G. G. L. (2021a). An Analysis of Virtual Reality Usage through a Descriptive Research Analysis on School Students' Experiences: A Study from India. *International Journal of Early Childhood Special Education, 13*(2), 990–1005. doi:10.9756/INT-JECSE/V13I2.211142

Raja, M., & Priya, G. G. L. (2021b). Conceptual Origins, Technological Advancements, and Impacts of Using Virtual Reality Technology in Education. *Webology, 18*(2), 116–134. doi:10.14704/WEB/V18I2/WEB18311

Raja, M., Srinivasan, K., & Syed-Abdul, S. (2019). Preoperative Virtual Reality Based Intelligent Approach for Minimising Patient Anxiety Levels. *2019 IEEE International Conference on Consumer Electronics - Taiwan, ICCE-TW 2019*, art.no. 8991754.

Roman, A., Rad, D., Egerau, A., Dixon, D., Dughi, T., Kelemen, G., Balas, E., & Rad, G. (2020). Physical Self-Schema Acceptance and Perceived Severity of Online Aggressiveness in Cyberbullying Incidents. *Journal of Interdisciplinary Studies in Education, 9*(1), 100–116. doi:10.32674/jise.v9i1.1961

Chapter 15
COVID-19 Diagnosis Using Transfer Learning Techniques and Applications on Chest X-Ray Images

E. Manimehalai
Nandha Engineering College, India

D. Vanathi
Nandha Engineering College, India

C. Navamani
Nandha Engineering College, India

ABSTRACT

COVID-19 is a viral disease caused by a new type of coronavirus called SARS-CoV-2. The World Health Organization (WHO) declared it a pandemic due to this disease spreading over many countries. Currently, there is no medicine available to prevent or cure infectious diseases. COVID-19 samples are commonly tested using reverse transcription polymerase chain reactions (RT-PCR), which are more expensive and take 24 hours to deliver either a positive or negative result. This chapter aims to develop a rapid and accurate medical diagnosis support system for COVID-19 in chest x-ray images by combining transfer learning techniques with the KNN algorithm. There are multiple approaches to building a classification system for analyzing radiographic images in deep learning. In this way, the knowledge acquired from a pre-trained convolutional neural network can be used to solve a new problem. Stacking is a machine learning method that combines the performances of the many transfer learning-based models to ensure the robustness of the proposed system.

DOI: 10.4018/978-1-6684-6060-3.ch015

INTRODUCTION

Covid-19, an epidemic that impacts the breathing system of human beings, become first identified in Wuhan city in China on December-2019. The sickness is effortlessly spread from one man or woman to any other via droplets released from an infected man or woman while coughing, sneezing or exhaling. Nearly all nations are operating tough to reduce the quantity of COVID infections (Aoudni, Y. et al. 2022). The possibility of decreasing the rate of covid-19 contamination through preventive movement depends on knowing the actual quantity of covid-19 cases in a given location, and this may most effective be done through proper covid testing (Naseri, M. et al. 2017). Tests for the Covid-19 virus should be selected based on their accuracy in detecting positive cases, the time required to obtain a result, and the cost of the test (Metwaly, A. F. et al. 2014). World Health Organization has encouraged RT-PCR test because the gold general for testing for Covid-19. This test provides excessive accuracy in diagnosing sicknesses. The downside is the cost and time it takes to complete the test. Early analysis of patients with covid-19 can be carried out by computed tomography (CT) test of the chest (Li and Xia, 2020). an advantage of this approach is its speedy with diagnostic rate.

However, the accuracy is decrease in comparison to RT-PCR tests. Loop-mediated isothermal amplification (LAMP) (Liu et al., 2016) amplifies the target genetic material and offers outcomes within an hour. But it produces much less accuracy, so it isn't commonly used. Cases of COVID are diagnosed using antibody tests based on antibodies produced by the immune system. It has worked well to identify people infected with Covid in the past, but it cannot identify people who are currently infected and has a low accuracy problem. using deep learning, Covid-19 turned into distinguished from other various pneumonia instances with an AUC of 0.87 (Wang, S. et al., 2020). We used social optimization to extracting the efficient features from X-ray of chest images the usage of a CNN model to come across Covid-19 cases (Toğaçar et al., 2020). Covid-Net is a deep convolutional neural network developed for cancer detection from X-ray images (Wang et al., 2020). A convolutional neural network with a transfer learning approach was used to detect disease from X-ray and CT scan images (Alom, M. Z. et al. 2020). When CT scans had been used, accuracy turned into higher (Naseri, M. et al. 2015). With the assist of X-ray images, darknet has been used to hit upon corona instances and non-corona instances (Ozturk, T. et al. 2020).

By using darknet model, accuracy was achieved for several classes, including covid, non-covid and pneumonia (Farouk, A. et al. 2018). The usage of the Fractional Multichannel Exponent Moments (FrMEMs) method (Elaziz, M. A. et al. 2020), we extracted the features from X-ray of chest images and labeled the Covid instances primarily based on machine learning techniques (Naseri, M. et al. 2018). We advanced a deep learning- depended system, the usage of VB-net neural network to come across and quantify the infected region in CT images (Shan, F. et al. (2020). Type of coronavirus instances and non-coronavirus instances from chest X-rays changed into done using 2-d and 3-d deep learning models. Transfer learning became used to classify covid and non-covid instances using pre-trained CNN models (Gozes, O. et al. 2020). The following is a list of some of the critical issues associated with current methods of diagnosing patients with Covid-19.

i. Health professionals should collect breath samples. Nasopharyngeal swab sampling is a not unusual approach in which the nurse is in near contact with the affected person. This could increase the danger of cross-infection.

ii. The WHO has recommended the use of RT-PCR kits to screen for Covid cases, but the availability of these kits in developing countries is insufficient for large populations. Therefore, developing countries must find ways to develop cost-effective solutions for testing.
iii. The sensitivity of rapid antigen tests means that they cannot be used exclusively for initial screening.
iv. It takes a long time to get the result, which delays the process of tracing the contacts of an infected person with non-infected persons.

This paper proposes a new Coronavirus detection architecture. This method uses chest X-ray datasets (Chowdhury, M. E. H. et al. 2020). To make a new radiographic image, use these datasets: healthy, pneumonia, and COVID. Image processing software standardizes images and improves model learning (Asif, S. et al. 2020). Improve COVID-19 prediction accuracy. The proposed system includes DenseNet121, DenseNet169, MobileNetV2, VGG19, and VGG16. Using transfer learning, these models extracted X-ray features (Qian, Y. et al. 2020). Then, the stacking and KNN algorithms were used to combine the five classifier models' predictions. These methods can be used to find COVID-infected patients (Farouk, A. et al. 2015). The proposed system was trained and tested on healthy, COVID-19-affected, and pneumonia datasets.

MATERIALS AND METHODS

The proposed system is to detect COVID-19-infected patients using stacking techniques with different transfer learning models (Farouk, A. et al. 2020). Those all-switch learning models are present in the Kera's library. The dataset turned into derived from databases containing the X-ray of chest images. Those datasets generated three classes: healthy, COVID-19- affected, and pneumonia (Farfan, M. J. et al. 2020). The dataset was divided into training, testing, and validation sets. The images were preprocessed. Each chest X-ray image is 224 224 3. Two-level training creates the final model. In training, the base version uses DenseNet121, DenseNet169, MobileNetV2, VGG19, and VGG16 (Zhou, N. R. et al. 2016). These models use 224*224*3 input dimensions. Using a validation set to avoid overfitting and underfitting (Scohy, A. et al. 2020). Follow that, using a testing set for predicting and identifying classes. Based on the training level the output prediction would be used as input at the meta-level. In the next phase of training, combined the predictions made by different classifiers using the stacking methodology. The algorithm of KNN is used to make contributions to the performance of Base-models to make the very last prediction. Afterward, the model generation was saved, and the model proposed became evaluated.

A Method of Stacking Things Up

Stacking Technique is one of the ensemble methods in machine learning. This stacking method is to construct many models with unique algorithmic kinds to provide a final prediction. This model requires n classification models as input. Therefore, the input of this base algorithm is to incorporated with the output of the final algorithm (Naseri, M. et al. 2018).

Dataset

Several X-ray of chest image datasets were analyzed in this proposed system. due to the variety, it'll increase the dimensions of the dataset. Additionally, this can enhance detection performance as properly. All datasets are explored and generate a final outcome dataset with 3 training: healthy, pneumonia, and COVID-affected. Afterward, these datasets might be divided into three segments as 80% of training, 10% of validation, and 10% of testing. Then, all of the X-ray images are resized and normalized to 1024 ×1024.

Pre-Trained Models Were Tuned Using Transfer Learning Techniques

DenseNet121-based TL Model

DenseNet is a system that makes deep learning networks more efficient to train using short connections between layers. It contains 120 Convolutions layers and 4 AvgPools layers. Transform layers spread the weights across multiple inputs to make use of the previously extracted features for all layers in the dense block. 70381444 out of 70525188 architecture parameters are trainable.

DenseNet169-Based TL Model

The descent-169 model is a part of the DenseNet group, designed to classify the images. within the DenseNet- 169 structure that removes the final fully connected layer, to begin with, 256 nodes completely related layer changed into created, observed through a 128-node FLC, and in the end, a 10 class FLC with the SoftMax activation for an output. Most effective the final layer used ReLU activation. The architecture carries 54820100 general parameters, with 97664 nontrainable parameters and 54722436 trainable parameters (Heidari, S. et al. 2019).

MobileNet_V2-based TL model

The MobileNetV2 version is a convolutional neural network with 53 layers with a intensity of 88. It turned into trained on 10 lakh images from the database of ImageNet and carried out an accuracy of 90.1% for this dataset. The architecture has 13665092 total parameters, 34112 untrainable parameters and 13930680 trainable parameters.

VGG_16-based TL Model

A team of Oxford University researchers proposed the VGG16 CNN model, which achieves 90.1% accuracy by training on ImageNet data. VGG16 has 17469508 total parameters, 0 non-trainable, and 17460508 trainable.

VGG_19-based TL model

CNN's 2015 VGG19 model the model was trained on 1 million depth 26 images from ImageNet and achieved 90% accuracy. VGG-19 has 227,204 trainable and 0 non-trainable parameters.

RESULTS

Confusion Matrix and OPAM

A confusion matrix is used to classify classifier predictions. It has two dimensions: reference and prediction. This matrix's rows have identical classes. These lessons allow us to test for confounding by calculating true positive, true negative, false positive, and false negative (FN). Class X chaos element equations:

$$\mathrm{TPclassX} = \mathrm{C}_{\mathrm{i,j}}$$

$$\mathrm{FNclassX} = \sum_{\mathrm{l=1}}^{4} \mathrm{C}_{\mathrm{i,l}} - \mathrm{TPclassX}_{.}$$

$$\mathrm{FPclassX} = \sum_{\mathrm{l=1}}^{4} \mathrm{C}_{\mathrm{l,i}} - \mathrm{TPclassX}_{.}$$

$$\mathrm{FPclassX} = \sum_{\mathrm{l=1}}^{4} \sum_{\mathrm{k=1}}^{4} \mathrm{C}_{\mathrm{l,k}} - \left(\mathrm{FPclassX} + \mathrm{FNclassX} + \mathrm{TPclassX}\right)$$

where Ci,j is the number of correctly classified samples and Ci,l is the number of negative samples, we calculated five score metrics: accuracy, precision, sensitivity, specificity, and negative predictive value (NPV). Matrix equations:

$$\text{Accuracy} = \frac{\mathrm{TP} + \mathrm{TN}}{\mathrm{TP} + \mathrm{TN} + \mathrm{FP} + \mathrm{FN}}$$

$$\text{Sensitivity} = \frac{\mathrm{TP}}{\mathrm{TP} + \mathrm{FN}}$$

$$\text{Precision} = \frac{\mathrm{TP}}{\mathrm{TP} + \mathrm{FP}}$$

$$\text{NPV} = \frac{\mathrm{TN}}{\mathrm{TN} + \mathrm{FN}}$$

$$\text{Specificity} = \frac{\mathrm{TN}}{\mathrm{TN} + \mathrm{FP}}$$

Experimental Results

Training of CNN Method

TensorFlow 2.1 turned into used to import the unique pre-trained models into this proposed model and put into the effect of the proposed tuned models primarily based on transfer getting to know techniques. It is used by the default Python library's API. Models had been generated immediately by the use of Kera's default implementation. It implemented the stacking method in Python to integrate the overall performance of various different models. It used the Scikit-learn Library for the KNN model.

The Python experiments were analyzed using the Jupyter library. Google Colab was used to train TL-based models. Google Collab is a cloud-based application for training and researching machine learning and deep learning algorithms. All algorithms were trained with Adam and cross-entropy loss. All arrays have 224-*-224 input images. This study's baseline models were hyperparameter-tuned. DenseNet121, DenseNet169, MobileNetV2, VGG16, and VGG19 were trained over 25 epochs. Training and validating our three chest X-ray datasets. The x-axis represents an epoch and the y-axis a progression. The model training curve. Using training data, it's calculated. Validation curves show whether a model underfits, overfits, or is accurate for a given range of hyperparameter values based on convergence after 25 epochs. Like VGG 19 and VGG 16, extra epochs were needed to converge. All models had low overfitting. Education set convergence equals validation set convergence. In validation, all models were accurate. VGG19 is also accurate. These models have lower loss curves.

Testing of CNN Method

A subset of previously prepared data was used to evaluate the models' performance. Before scoring, a confusion matrix was created. COVID-19 classes confuse some models (table 1). Most models offer a variety. Most models top all three classes. Second-stage training combined model classifications. Stacking methodology uses a matrix to evaluate an evolved model's performance. TP is higher than FP and FN for all classes, according to this classification. Similarly, the FP and FN of healthy and pneumonia are larger than Covid. Examine test results to determine evaluation metrics. Elegant COVID-19 causes confusion. Stacking is the best way to classify X-ray images, according to a study. All lessons had ratios between 0.9 and 1. This version had the best performance compared to others. COVID-19 cases are rarely classified, with other classes near 0, reducing the chance of detecting them from chest X-rays. Most models lost value, except VGG16 and generated. This model calculated best performance rates. DenseNet121, DenseNet169, MobileNetV2, and VGG16 had high range accuracy. VGG19 was most accurate (figures 1 to 11).

Figure 1. Pre-processed chest X-ray images

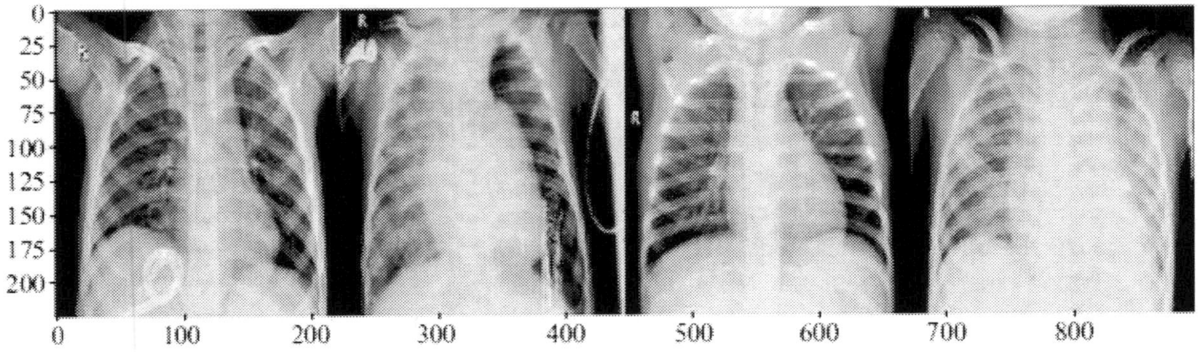

Figure 2. Accuracy and Loss curves acquired by using training and validation for DenseNet121 (a and b)

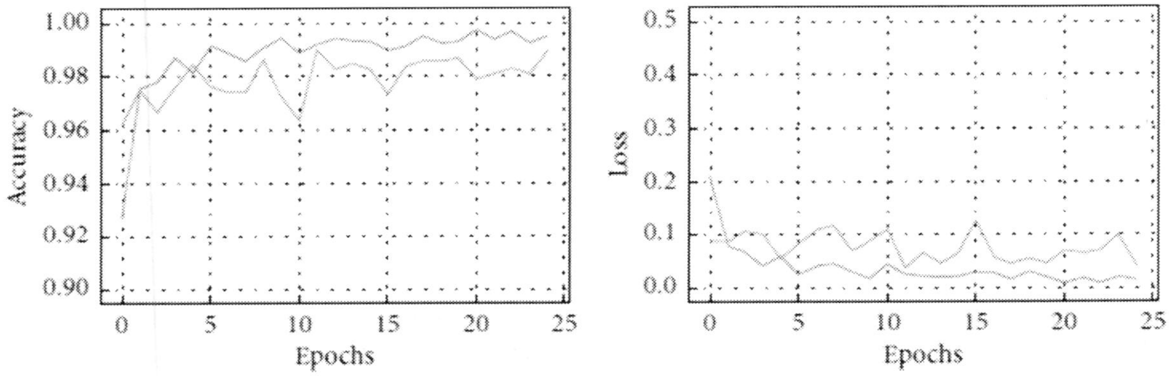

Figure 3. Accuracy and Loss curves acquired by using training and validation for DenseNet169 (a and b)

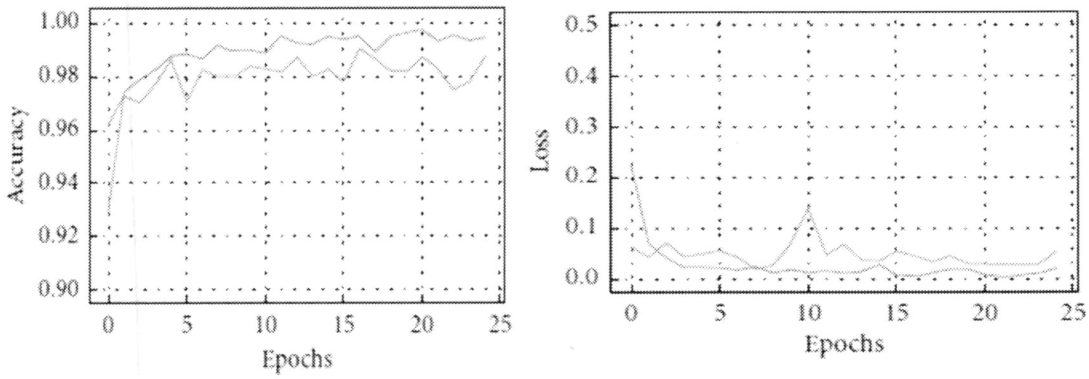

Figure 4. MobileNetV2 training and validation accuracy and loss curves (a and b)

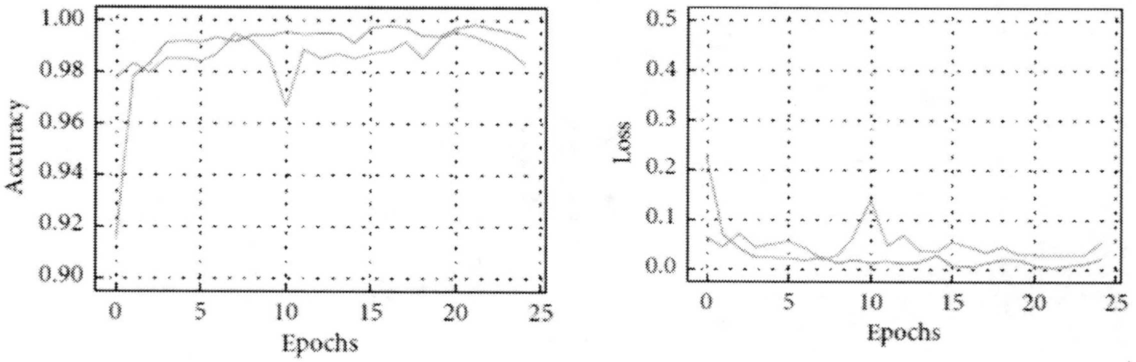

Figure 5. Accuracy and Loss curves acquired by using training and validation for VGG16 (a and b)

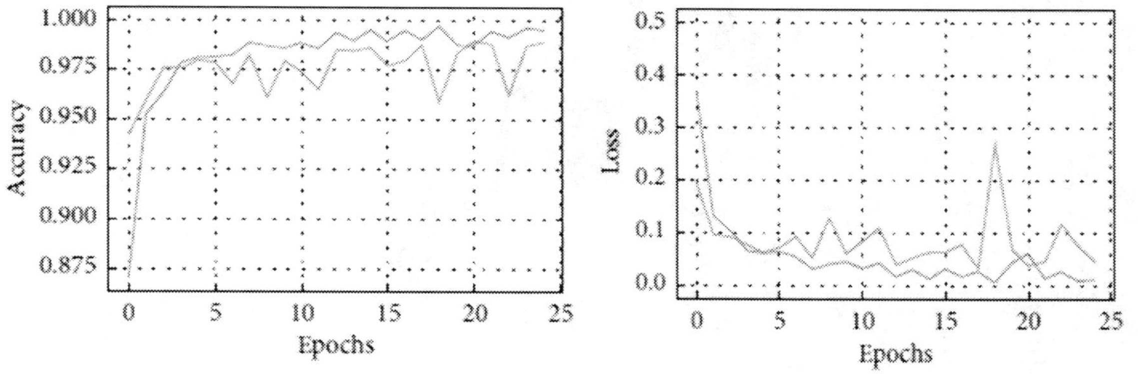

Figure 6. Accuracy and Loss curves acquired by using training and validation for VGG19 (a and b)

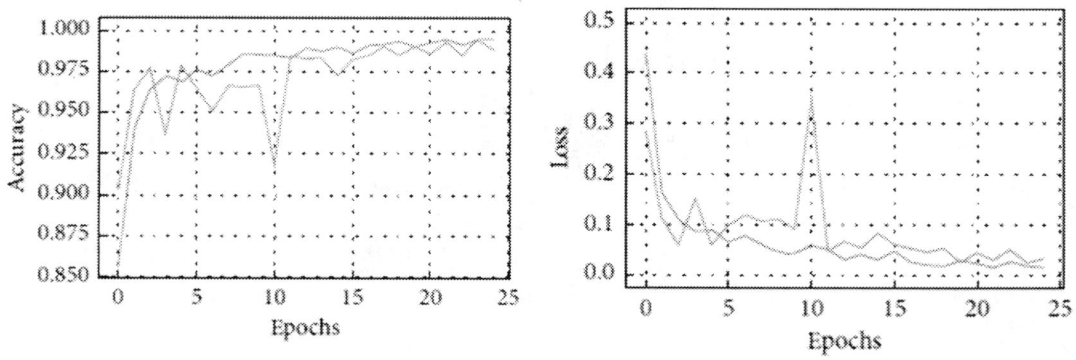

Figure 7. Confusion matrix for DenseNet121

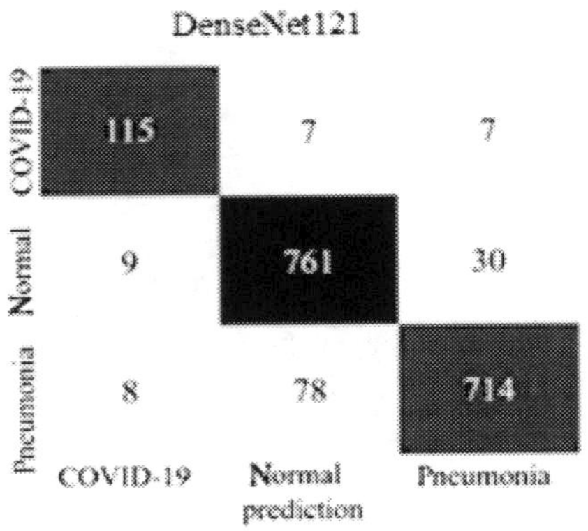

Figure 8. Confusion matrix for DenseNet169

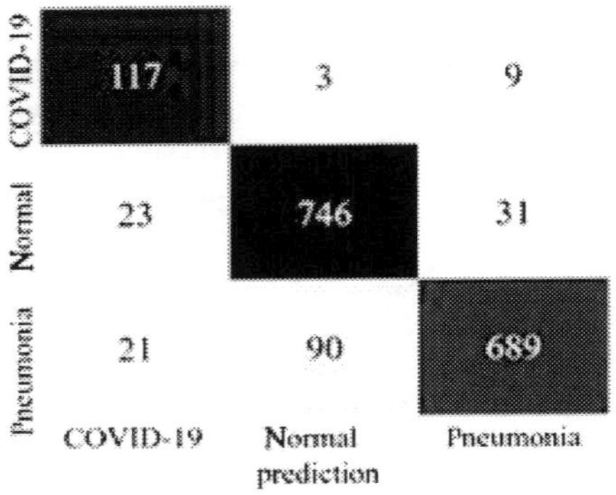

Figure 9. Confusion matrix for MobileNetV2

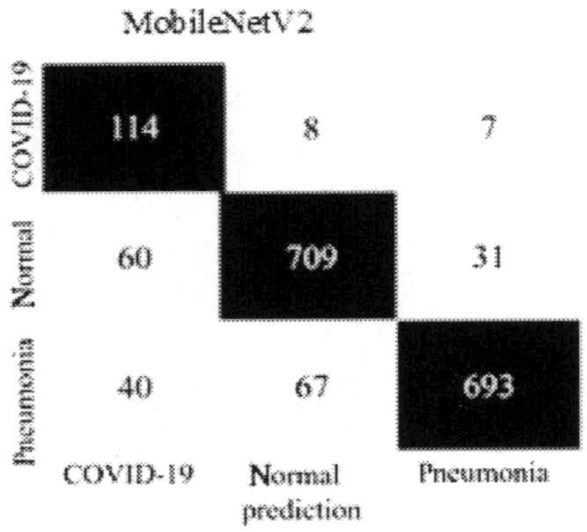

Figure 10. Confusion matrix for VGG16

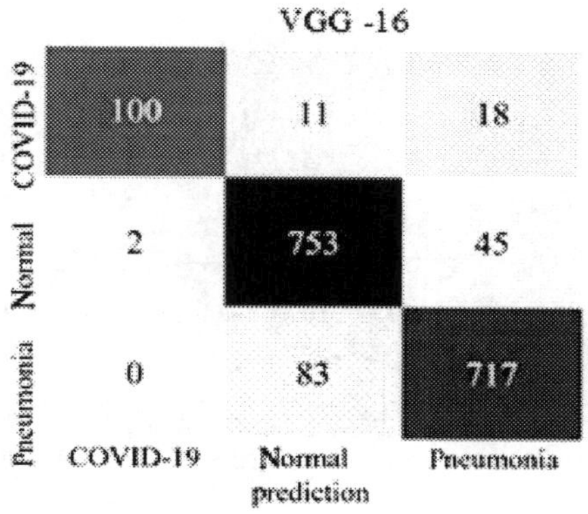

Figure 11. Confusion matrix for VGG19

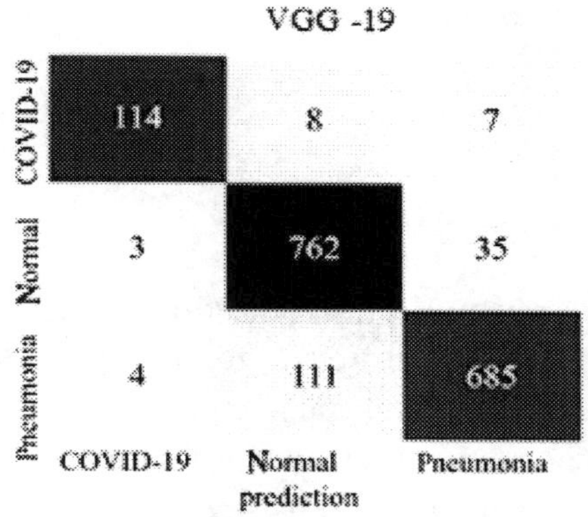

Table 1. Performance Evolution based on Scoring Matrices

Model's	Accuracy in %	Loss in %	Precision in %	Sensitivity in %	Specificity in %	NPV in %
DenseNet121	97.54	5.04	97.46	97.25	98.51	98.55
DenseNet169	96.54	5.89	97.22	95.34	98.58	97.53
MobileNetV2	97.35	5.14	97.41	96.89	97.41	95.44
VGG16	97.74	3.63	97.52	97.61	98.53	97.55
VGG19	98.11	5.60	98.23	97.56	97.62	98.72

DISCUSSION

This research suggests the detection method for the COVID that is based on the stacking method and transfer learning algorithms. These methods were used to build the stack. This system aims to identify COVID-19-infected patients with the most effective algorithm. The five different transfer learning networks of DenseNet121, DenseNet169, VGG16, VGG19 and MobileNetV2 were used as a foundation for the model that was generated. Those are all algorithms that have been trained and tested the usage of the chest X-ray image that had been generated from a variety of different assets. There are three groups represented in this dataset: healthy, COVID-19-impacted, and pneumonia. At the metamodel level, the final prediction model was constructed with the help of KNN. During the KNN algorithm, the predictions made by the fundamental models are integrated to forecast the outcome for patients infected with COVID-19 disease. The value of the loss does not exceed 5% in the vast majority of models. When the value of the loss meter goes up, the values of the other three metrics go down. In this particular research endeavor, every model was successful in achieving a high-value thanks to the measures of specificity and NPV. The proposed diagnostic method performed quite well in comparison to other available options. The PCR test, which is almost universally acknowledged to be the gold standard, is frequently utilized to diagnose COVID-19. Then, by using the concordance rate among the technique and the PCR test, can be able to examine the possibility that our system turns into extensively and widely used throughout the COVID-19 pandemic.

CONCLUSION

This paper aims to propose an effective infection detection method. X-ray images of the chest were used for the COVID-19 diagnostic task. There are five fundamental transfer learning models within the proposed device. Further, COVID-19 detection changed into to be progressed by offering a diagnostic device that employed TL algorithms to extract features from images. This improves the gaining knowledge of the model and permits it to make more consistent predictions. First, organized the dataset for use. It chose deep learning models from the current image classification algorithms. This framework includes a designed head model and trains classifiers on a processed dataset. This test suite found positive results. Above 90% accuracy. To improve accuracy, it chose the most accurate classifiers from the test set and tested the results on two sets (test set and validation set). Based on DenseNet121, DenseNet169, VGG16, VGG19, and MobileNetV2 results. The diagnosis of COVID can be made greater effective through the usage of stacking techniques. When the stacking method was tested on the COVID class, it found average accuracy. And also, this study aims to understand how the stacking method can be used to tackle a critical task such as the diagnosis of COVID-19.

REFERENCES

Li, Y., & Xia, L. (2020). Coronavirus disease 2019 (COVID-19): Role of chest CT in diagnosis and management. *AJR. American Journal of Roentgenology*, *214*(6), 1280–1286. doi:10.2214/AJR.20.22954 PMID:32130038

Liu, Z., Dong, Z., & Liu, D. (2016). Development of a rapid assay to detect the jellyfish Cyanea nozakii using a loop-mediated isothermal amplification method. *Mitochondrial DNA. Part A, DNA Mapping, Sequencing, and Analysis*, *27*(4), 2318–2322. doi:10.3109/19401736.2015.1022762 PMID:25774948

Wang, S. (2020). A fully automatic deep learning system for COVID-19 diagnostic and prognostic analysis. *The European Respiratory Journal, 56*(2). . doi:10.1183/13993003.00775-2020

Toğaçar, M., Ergen, B., & Cömert, Z. (2020). COVID-19 detection using deep learning models to exploit Social Mimic Optimization and structured chest X-ray images using fuzzy color and stacking approaches. *Computers in Biology and Medicine*, *121*(103805), 103805. doi:10.1016/j.compbiomed.2020.103805 PMID:32568679

Wang, L., Lin, Z. Q., & Wong, A. (2020). COVID-Net: A tailored deep convolutional neural network design for detection of COVID-19 cases from chest X-ray images. *Scientific Reports*, *10*(1), 19549. doi:10.103841598-020-76550-z PMID:33177550

Alom, M. Z. (2020). *COVID_MTNet: COVID-19 Detection with Multi-Task Deep Learning Approaches*. https://arxiv.org/abs/2004.03747

Ozturk, T., Talo, M., Yildirim, E. A., Baloglu, U. B., Yildirim, O., & Rajendra Acharya, U. (2020). Automated detection of COVID-19 cases using deep neural networks with X-ray images. *Computers in Biology and Medicine*, *121*(103792), 103792. doi:10.1016/j.compbiomed.2020.103792 PMID:32568675

Elaziz, M. A., Hosny, K. M., Salah, A., Darwish, M. M., Lu, S., & Sahlol, A. T. (2020). New machine learning method for image-based diagnosis of COVID-19. *PLoS One*, *15*(6), e0235187. doi:10.1371/journal.pone.0235187 PMID:32589673

Shan, F. (2020). *Lung infection quantification of COVID-19 in CT images with deep learning*. https://arxiv.org/abs/2003.04655

Gozes, O. (2020). *Rapid AI development cycle for the Coronavirus (COVID-19) pandemic: Initial results for automated detection & patient monitoring using deep learning CT image analysis*. https://arxiv.org/abs/2003.05037

Chowdhury, M. E. H. (2020). *Can AI help in screening Viral and COVID-19 pneumonia?* https://arxiv.org/abs/2003.13145

Farfan, M. J. (2020). Optimizing RT-PCR detection of SARS-CoV-2 for developing countries using pool testing. *Revista Chilena de Infectologia: Organo Oficial de la Sociedad Chilena de Infectologia, 37*(3), 276–280. . doi:10.4067/s0716-10182020000300276

Scohy, A. (2020). Low performance of rapid antigen detection test as frontline testing for COVID-19 diagnosis. *Journal of Clinical Virology, 129*(104455). . doi:10.1016/j.jcv.2020.104455

Asif, S. (2020). *Classification of COVID-19 from Chest X-ray images using Deep Convolutional Neural Networks*. doi:10.1109/ICCC51575.2020.9344870

Qian, Y., Zeng, T., Wang, H., Xu, M., Chen, J., Hu, N., Chen, D., & Liu, Y. (2020). Safety management of nasopharyngeal specimen collection from suspected cases of coronavirus disease 2019. *International Journal of Nursing Sciences*, *7*(2), 153–156. doi:10.1016/j.ijnss.2020.03.012 PMID:32292635

Naseri, M., Heidari, S., Baghfalaki, M., fatahi, N., Gheibi, R., Batle, J., Farouk, A., & Habibi, A. (2017). A new secure quantum watermarking scheme. *Optik (Stuttgart)*, *139*, 77–86. doi:10.1016/j.ijleo.2017.03.091

Naseri, M., Raji, M. A., Hantehzadeh, M. R., Farouk, A., Boochani, A., & Solaymani, S. (2015). A scheme for secure quantum communication network with authentication using GHZ-like states and cluster states controlled teleportation. *Quantum Information Processing*, *14*(11), 4279–4295. doi:10.100711128-015-1107-9

Aoudni, Y., Donald, C., Farouk, A., Sahay, K. B., Babu, D. V., Tripathi, V., & Dhabliya, D. (2022). Cloud security based attack detection using transductive learning integrated with Hidden Markov Model. *Pattern Recognition Letters*, *157*, 16–26. doi:10.1016/j.patrec.2022.02.012

Farouk, A., Alahmadi, A., Ghose, S., & Mashatan, A. (2020). Blockchain platform for industrial healthcare: Vision and future opportunities. *Computer Communications*, *154*, 223–235. doi:10.1016/j.comcom.2020.02.058

Farouk, A., Batle, J., Elhoseny, M., Naseri, M., Lone, M., Fedorov, A., Alkhambashi, M., Ahmed, S. H., & Abdel-Aty, M. (2018). Robust general N user authentication scheme in a centralized quantum communication network via generalized GHZ states. *Frontiers in Physics*, *13*(2), 130306. Advance online publication. doi:10.100711467-017-0717-3

Farouk, A., Zakaria, M., Megahed, A., & Omara, F. A. (2015). A generalized architecture of quantum secure direct communication for N disjointed users with authentication. *Scientific Reports*, *5*(1), 16080. doi:10.1038rep16080 PMID:26577473

Heidari, S., Abutalib, M. M., Alkhambashi, M., Farouk, A., & Naseri, M. (2019). A new general model for quantum image histogram (QIH). *Quantum Information Processing*, *18*(6), 175. Advance online publication. doi:10.100711128-019-2295-5

Metwaly, A. F., Rashad, M. Z., Omara, F. A., & Megahed, A. A. (2014). Architecture of multicast centralized key management scheme using quantum key distribution and classical symmetric encryption. *The European Physical Journal. Special Topics*, *223*(8), 1711–1728. doi:10.1140/epjst/e2014-02118-x

Naseri, M., Abdolmaleky, M., Laref, A., Parandin, F., Celik, T., Farouk, A., Mohamadi, M., & Jalalian, H. (2018). A new cryptography algorithm for quantum images. *Optik (Stuttgart)*, *171*, 947–959. doi:10.1016/j.ijleo.2018.06.113

Zhou, N. R., Liang, X. R., Zhou, Z. H., & Farouk, A. (2016). Relay selection scheme for amplify-and-forward cooperative communication system with artificial noise: Relay selection scheme for amplify-and-forward cooperative communication system with artificial noise. *Security and Communication Networks*, *9*(11), 1398–1404. doi:10.1002ec.1425

Naseri, M., Abdolmaleky, M., Parandin, F., Fatahi, N., Farouk, A., & Nazari, R. (2018). A new quantum gray-scale image encoding scheme. *Communications in Theoretical Physics*, *69*(2), 215. doi:10.1088/0253-6102/69/2/215

Chapter 16
Features Manipulation of Classification and Recognition of Images Under Artificial Intelligence Using CNN Algorithm and LSTM

J. Priyadharshini
Nandha Engineering College, India

E. Padma
Nandha Engineering College, India

S. Prabhadevi
Nandha Engineering College, India

ABSTRACT

The established model provides appropriate picture pixel gaining knowledge in image detection. Additionally, it also affords an alternative solution for item tracking and predicting the usage of deep gaining knowledge of strategies. The proposed technique offers a fine overall performance in photo recognition issues or even outperforms humans in positive cases. Deep learning architectures containing dispensed techniques will become more critical as the scale of datasets increases. Then, it is important to understand which are the most green approaches to carry out distributed education, so as to maximize the throughput of the gadget, while minimizing the accuracy and model regression. This chapter explores features manipulation of classification and recognition of images under artificial intelligence using CNN algorithm and LSTM.

DOI: 10.4018/978-1-6684-6060-3.ch016

INTRODUCTION

Artificial Intelligence

The phrase "artificial intelligence" (AI) refers to a subset of neural networks that fall under the umbrella of "machine learning algorithms" and are known as "artificial neural networks" (ANN). The data in this kind of model are represented through the use of a graphical model that is composed of neurons. ANN is a type of computational system, and its neurons are constructed according to a technique that processes and manipulates data in the same way as a human brain does (Farouk, et al., 2015). The availability of vast amounts of data in the network has led to the development of ANN, which is designed to comprehend the factors that enable outcomes to be favourable (Farouk, et al., 2020).

An input layer, then a number of hidden layers (anything from one to many), and finally, an output layer, make up the feed-forward information of the architecture of neural networks (Farouk, et al., 2018). These layers carry out processing in a methodical manner in order to establish the output of the ultimate system, which is located in the middle of the incoming and outgoing levels (Aoudni, et al., 2022). The incoming information is transformed into useful output information that can be used by the middle layers or hidden layers, which then work on the information before moving on to the next step (Deepika and Prabhu, 2019). The input layer is responsible for providing the middle layers or hidden layers with the incoming information. They are completed with the assistance of connections that are weighted (Heidari, et al., 2019). The information from the intermediate layer is then examined, and the network system is aware of a variety of ways to convey the information to the subsequent output layer based on the facts that it knows about each other (fig.1).

Figure 1. Structure of ANN

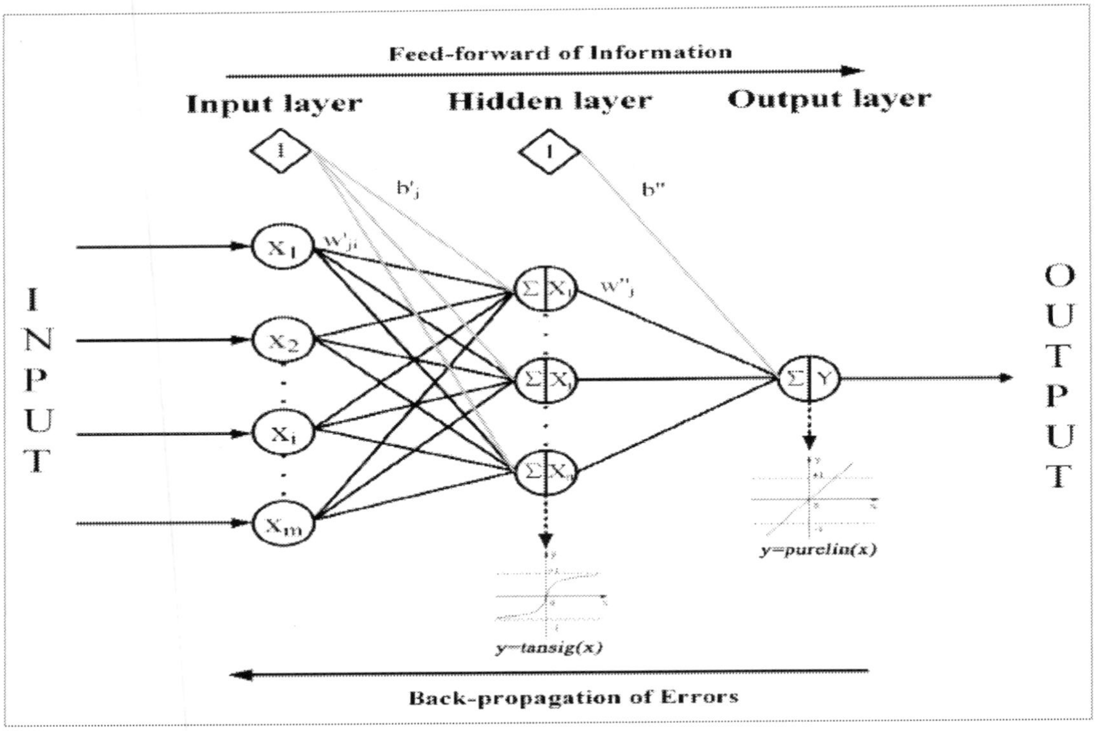

Processing of Image

The concept of system vision is an essential part of the photograph processing field. Research into the topic evolved into a decade-long examination of the issue from the perspective of working from the ground up. This was the endeavour that had been described previously to establish policies that would govern the vision of living organisms.

This method became very successful on certain occasions. A popular description of a system imaginative and prescient in photo processing may be summarized in the following steps:

- Picture seize - The picture is captured either by a digital camera or a comparable tool and digitized.
- Pre-processing -Digitized pictures like_noise reduction and evaluation normalization is changed to emphasize critical functions.
- Segmentation - selection of thrilling capabilities like edges and comparable surfaces.
- Narrative - Removal of radiometric descriptors, photometric descriptors and so forth.
- Categorization - It means to categorize the given objects (fig.2).

Figure 2. Block diagram of an image processing pipeline

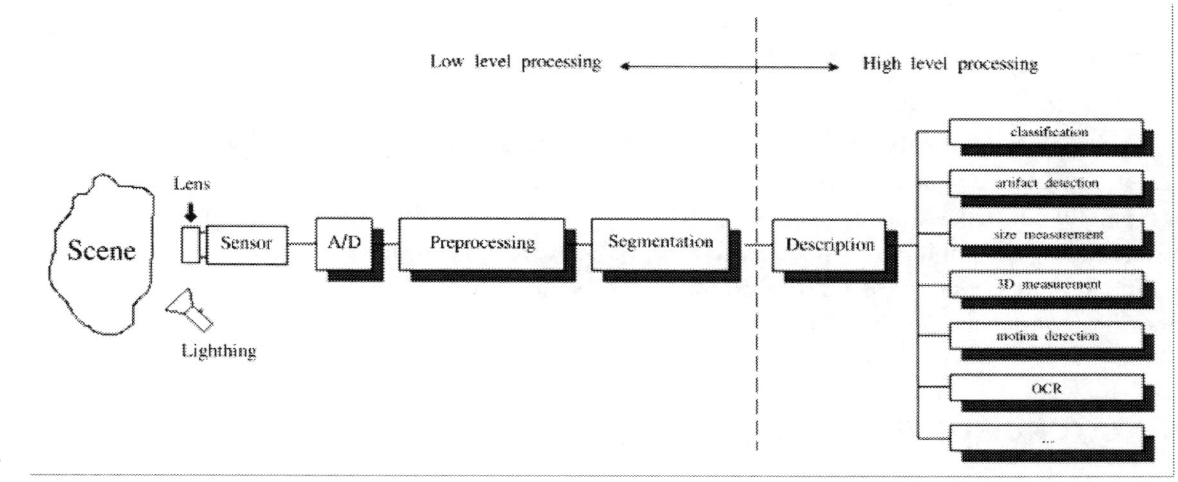

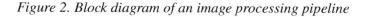

Convolutional Neural Network

Image classification and recognition applications are the focus of CNN, which provides a definition for neural networks. They are almost certainly examples of successful AI models that were inspired by biological phenomena. The design concepts were derived from the field of neuroscience, despite the fact that they were directed by the assistance of a lot more specialized form of fields. They were inspired by a wide variety of subjects, particularly neurobiology, which provided the foundation for their design approaches. It is well known that they have shown to be very successful in the field of image processing; in addition, they have been utilized in natural language and video processing applications in an extremely successful manner. It's usual practise for convolutional networks to have a core structure that's made up of three distinct kinds of layers. Convolutional, pooling, and totally connected are the three layers that make up the whole. Each type of layer implements a unique policy for forward and errors backward signal propagation (fig.3).

Figure 3. Characteristic structure of CNN

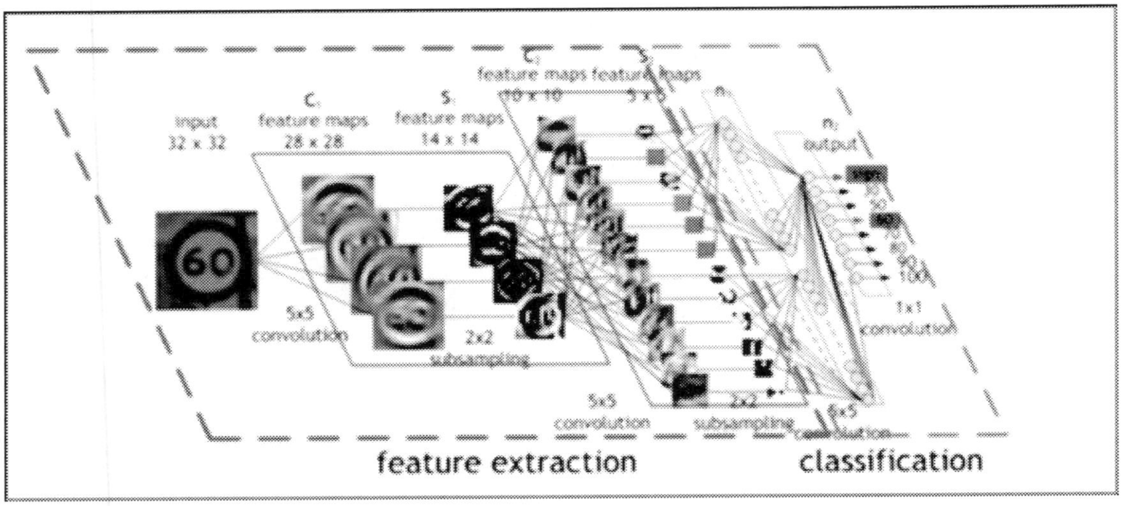

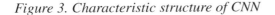

The structure of the different layers should not be built or organized according to any particular criteria, as there are none available. However, with the exception of certain recent developments, CNNs are typically constructed using separate parts. The initial step, which is known as function extraction one and involves combining convolutional and pooling layers, is presented first. The last step, which is the second component and is referred to as a class, is the utilization of fully connected layers. This is demonstrated in discernment chapter one, verse three.

LITERATURE SURVEY

Samadi et al., (2019) proposed a revised deep learning-based method for detecting the images in a changing environment using synthetic aperture radar (SAR) images. In the executed technique, a Deep Belief Network was used as the deep network structure, and the schooling process of this DBN consists of unmonitored function techniques observed via supervised network pleasant-tuning. Generally, the educated DBN outcomes in an alternate map detection which acts as an output. Research on DBNs explains they never provide output without complete information, and there is no proper dataset. The tremendous computational volume in the inefficient simulation is the restriction of deep learning algorithms. So in order to triumph over these limitations, way turned into delivered to greatly lower the computations without compromising the performance of the DBN.

Yu, et al., (2019) proposed recognition of various styles of illness patterns shown in discrete production processes can remarkably lessen the recognition strategies, progressively growth the production system balance and quality. So the overall performance of technical sample recognition (PPR) is stepped forward with the aid of the recognizers. Deep mastering is primarily used in the regions of photo and visible analysis, which gives superb success. But, there are a few simplest techniques available for the application of deep learning in functions getting to know for system management. The author here represented a deep studying technique referred to as a stacked de noising automobile encoder that is referred to as a stacked denoising autoencoder which is called SDAE. This approach is mostly used for developing an SDAE version to learn and recognize the productive capabilities from the procedure alerts and then deploying a powerful PPR through deep community architecture. The effectiveness and reliability of the given process pattern popularity technique are demonstrated and carried out thru a huge simulation dataset.

Santra, A. et al. (2022) proposed the recognition of facial expression is a key step in nonverbal human communication in the field of processor vision. Facial Expression Recognition (FER) structure reflects emotions as well as mental activities, social interaction with people and expressing positive or negative attitudes in general. One of the key challenges in the FER system is the dynamic variation while capturing the image. Convolutional Neural Networks, which is called CNN for recognizing facial expression, has been introduced. The main goal is to classify each facial image into one of the seven facial emotions categories like joy, sorrow, shock, irritation, panic, revulsion and unbiased. CNN can be used to find features like auto-learned from the human face and also classify them. The algorithm is tested on various standard databases like Japanese Female Facial Expressions (JAFFE), which includes 213 images, Cohn-Kanade (CK), which includes 7809 images and Cohn-Kanade (CK+), which includes 10584 images of different facial expressions. Investigational outcomes prove that Convolutional Neural Networks has good performance in recognizing facial expression, which results in 95.30% recognition accuracy on the CK+ database.

Matlani and Shrivastava (2019) currently using wild smoke presently the usage of wild smoke identification making use of gadget primarily based identity technique isn't supplying a good accurateness, so it is not appropriate for correct and reliable prediction. There are various video smoke detection methods that contain minimal lighting fixtures, and the cameras are required to discover the presence of smoke debris in a situation. To conquer and dispose of the challenges, they added a unique rule called deep VGG-Net CNN in order to classify the smoke. The set of rules called the Deep characteristics Synthesis algorithm generates the features for relational datasets. Also, the problems linked to the sluggish convergence are rectified by using hybrid ABC optimization. To manipulate the aggregate of future and historical past elements, a channel called alpha is implemented in the picture elements.

Wang, et al., (2019a) proposed object example detection has won an awful lot of challenges in many real-time programs, mainly in the area of shrewd provider robot. Let us think and consider how robots paint in the actual scenario, and it's far anticipated that the detection technique to be mild one to weigh to allow for the gadget deployment. They have got delivered a technique referred to as BING-Pruned Alexnet (B-PA), which is evolved with very few methods but with a good accuracy level. Their method first makes use of BING to assess boundary containers; by means of lowering neurons and cutting the absolutely linked layers at the Alexnet, they build a pruned network for reputation. For the reason that the examples, for instance, of object detection are low and varied, they extended schooling data by means of combining information augmentation with the synthetic era

Wang, et al., (2020) presents the authors enlisted the subjects from required hospitals. Absolutely, 197 long-term chronically affected alcoholic patients (99 guys, 98 women) and 193 patients who are non-alcoholic manipulate contributors (ninety-seven men, ninety-six ladies) had been registered in their take a look at thru automated diagnostic interview programme model and clinical exam done to check whether the candidates may be registered or left. A scanner named 'Siemens Verio Tim 3.0 T MR' was employed turned into employed to experiment with the registered people. A ten-layer CNN is then proposed for the identity based on the picture, together with 3 other methods named parametric rectified linear unit, normalization and dropout.

Zhe, et al., (2019) proposed which with the aid of explaining the characteristic primarily depends on the method von Misses–Fisher technique, they proposed powerful various other solutions getting to know awt of rules by way of systematically updating the elegance facilities. The proposed gadget gaining knowledge of now not simplest captures the worldwide statistics. However, also provides an exact display of the elegance distribution for the duration of education.

Zhang, et al., (2019) proposed Modern-day system imaginative and prescient systems handcrafted features and no longer get true effects. On this observation, the authors designed a thirteen-layer CNN. Mostly three latest facts augmentation approaches have been used: Gamma correction, photo rotation, and noise injection. Additionally, max pooling is compared with the common pooling technique. The accurate general level of their strategy is 95.95%.

Wang, Y. et al. (2019b) proposed a precise CNN for naming Multi-scale Dilated Convolution of CNN (MsDC), in order to strive present day the originally developed multiscale dilated convolution approach to handle the above-stated problem. The ongoing method provides the contemporary for the filters, which is to combine systematically various multiscale information, not lowering the discipline. Meanwhile, additionally, they make use of residual modern-day approaches to learn residuals at once to hurry up the contemporary technique.

Guo, Z. et al. (2020) proposed the author's here proposed a unique approach to analyzing hepatitis B ailment the usage of Raman spectroscopy with a deep learning model. The blood samples of 498 persons were inflamed with the special kind of virus, and 433 wholesome have were measured. After that, the traits of a couple of scales were maintained and blended through a multiscale fusion approach.

EXISTING SYSTEM

Existing System

The existing machine uses time-tested solutions for the photography class that have been successfully implemented in a variety of real-world scenarios. The software system has a few issues, some of which include insufficient repercussions, poor grouping accuracy, and limited potential for adaptation. The fame of pictures mostly depends on their CNN following a set of rules that, when applied to the software technique, result in the following restrictions: To begin, it is not possible to arrive at an accurate estimate of the intricate characteristics when using the deep learning model. Second, the poor accuracy classifier that is provided by the deep learning technique is not ideal. It has been demonstrated that the deep learning method is capable of achieving better application outcomes in the photograph classification task; however, it does have certain limitations, such as an excessively gradient propagation path and over becoming.

Drawbacks of the Existing System

- The existing device gives a photo classification model which has been widely implemented in many real-time problems; there are a few issues inside the application method, along with insufficient consequences, low grouping accuracy, and weak adaptive ability.
- Photograph Recognition technique involves CNN, which has subsequent problems within some utility processes:
  - It is not feasible to offer approximate complex capabilities in the deep learning approach.
  - The deep studying version provides a low classifier with low accuracy.
- The deep mastering technique has completed better utility final results in the photograph category; it has barriers considering excessive orientation propagation route and over-becoming.

Problem Statement

The approach referred to as photograph reputation and the usage of artificial intelligence is a well-set-up research issue inside the field of computer vision. The goal of the photograph recognition approach is the grouping of detected objects into diverse categorized organizations. There are numerous picture reputation algorithms where the popularity percentage is great. Nowadays, many network-related algorithms depend on a unique sort of image set to design the inner areas of the network.

PROPOSED SYSTEM

Introduction

In this work, a deep mastering method primarily based on the mixture of a CNN and lengthy quick-term reminiscence (LSTM) to recognize an item mechanically from CIFAR-10 dataset pictures. in this proposed gadget, Convolutional Neural community is used for extraction of deep characteristics and LSTM is used for detection using the extracted characteristic. CIFAR-10 is a statistics set containing images of 60,000 colour images. The picture size should be fixed as 32 x 32. It is again further split into 10 classes, and every class carries 6000 pictures (fig.4).

Process Flow Diagram

Figure 4. Process Flow Diagram

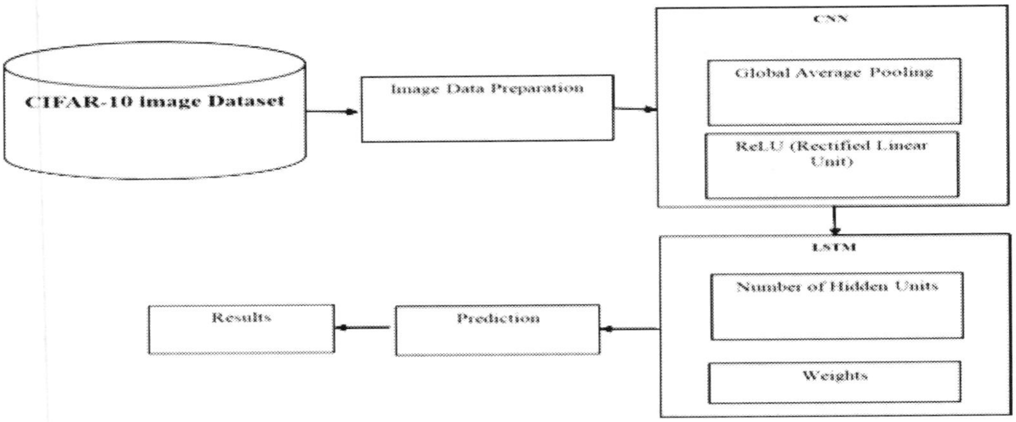

Methodolgy

1. IMAGE DATA PREPARATION
2. CONVOLUTIONAL NEURAL NETWORK MODEL
3. NETWORK STRUCTURE AND IMAGE RECOGNITION
4. LSTM-LONG SHORT-TERM MEMORY NETWORK

Image Data Preparation

Deep techniques to know strategies are, on the whole, used within the modern-day revolution in artificial intelligence for multimedia records analysis. First, picture facts training is executed by way of the CIFAR-10 picture dataset. This dataset is a record set having snapshots of 60,000 shade images. The size of each photograph ought to be 32 × 32 pixels. Its miles are further divided into ten classes, and every class consists of 6000 photos making a complete 60,000. The photograph dataset is divided into 5 training batches, and one takes a look at batch, each with ten thousand snapshots (fig.5).

Figure 5. Example Images from the CIFAR-10 class dataset

However, the dataset CIFAR-10 is a higher picture dataset for evidence of model tasks and continues to be generally used as a standard. In this painting, we aren't aiming at kingdom-of-the-art outcomes for this dataset, nor are we trying out brand new model architecture, but looking at the overall performance given one-of-a-kind training techniques. Consequently, we consider this dataset to be proper sufficient for our wishes, as its size and education instances have to be generalizable to other cases.

Convolutional Neural Network Model

In this module, the convolutional neural network may be broken down into elements:

1. The convolution layers: Takes data from the input
2. Completely related layers: additionally known as dense layers, use information from the convolution layer to generate output.

The data that is sent into the convolution process can have numerous capabilities extracted from them. Edges, traces, and corners make up the low-degree features of the convolutional layers of a computer model. They are obtained in this location. A greater number of layers with a higher degree provide superior stage functions. Convolution of a single kernel with a single input photo results in a single output function; similarly, convolution of H kernels yields H features. The kernel is moved in this direction, from left to right, one component at a time, by beginning in the top-left corner of the input. This process is called left-to-right movement. As soon as it receives a top-right corner, the kernel is moved from left to right by directing one component at a time until it reaches the bottom-right corner. This process is continued until the kernel reaches the highest-right corner.

Long Short Term Memory Network (LSTM)

LSTM, or long short-term memory, is an extension of recurrent neural networks. It is fine at managing time series concerns up to a positive depth and is appropriate for the unique architecture, which conflicts with the disappearance and igniting gradient issues. The information that is provided by LSTM comes from inputs that have already been processed by the hidden state. Unidirectional Long Short-Term Memory (LSTM) only remembers information about the precedent since it only receives inputs based on what it has seen in the past. The inputs are processed using bidirectional LSTM, with one going from the past to the future and the other going in the opposite manner, from the future to the past. The Long short-term memory network that processes backwards to protect information from the future and using the two hidden states are joined at some point to secure data from together history and the future, which is the difference between unidirectional and bidirectional data protection. The result is forceful due to the fact that the Bidirectional LSTM is composed of two LSTM cells in total. The objective of a bidirectional LSTM is to present a result that is not only connected to the information that came before it but also connected to the information that will come after it (figs. 7 to 10).

Network Structure and Image Recognition

The structure of the network can be described below:

- The incoming layer of the Convolutional layer contains 34 feature maps with a [3×3] size image. A rectifier launch function is proposed with a load constraint set to 3 maximum.
- Failure to be set to 20%.
- The Max Pool layer contains 2×2.
- Compress layer.
- Fully connected layer with 502 units with a rectifier launch function.
- Failure to be set to 50%.
- Fully connected outgoing layer with 20 units with a softmax launch function (fig.6)

Figure 6. Network Model

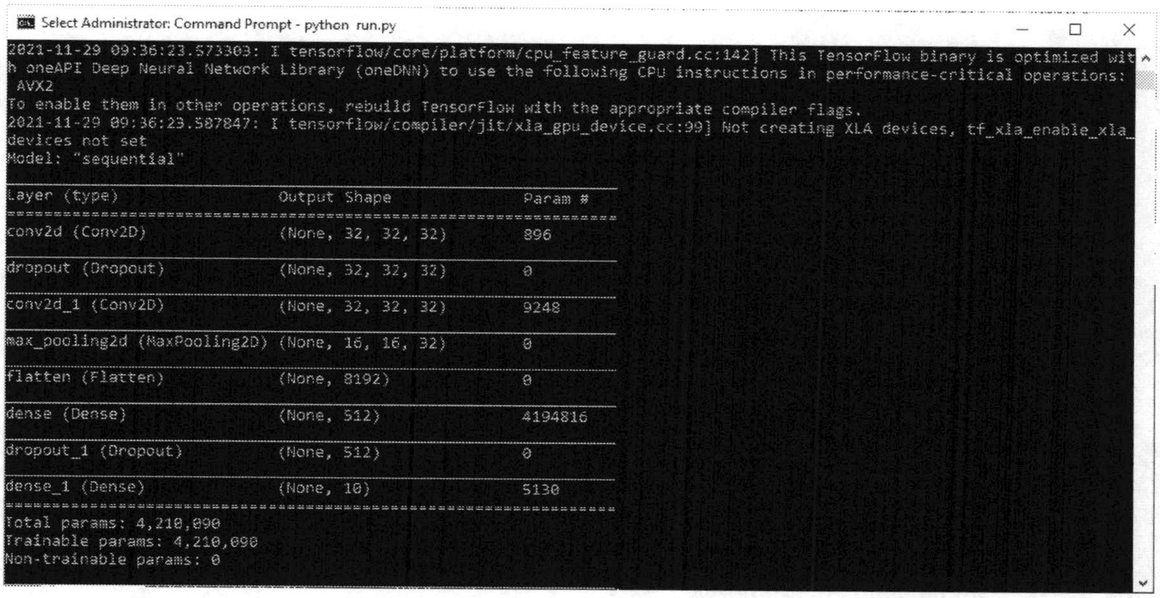

Select Administrator: Command Prompt - python run.py
2021-11-29 09:36:23.573303: I tensorflow/core/platform/cpu_feature_guard.cc:142] This TensorFlow binary is optimized wit
h oneAPI Deep Neural Network Library (oneDNN) to use the following CPU instructions in performance-critical operations:
AVX2
To enable them in other operations, rebuild TensorFlow with the appropriate compiler flags.
2021-11-29 09:36:23.587847: I tensorflow/compiler/jit/xla_gpu_device.cc:99] Not creating XLA devices, tf_xla_enable_xla_
devices not set
Model: "sequential"
Layer (type) Output Shape Param #
conv2d (Conv2D) (None, 32, 32, 32) 896
dropout (Dropout) (None, 32, 32, 32) 0
conv2d_1 (Conv2D) (None, 32, 32, 32) 9248
max_pooling2d (MaxPooling2D) (None, 16, 16, 32) 0
flatten (Flatten) (None, 8192) 0
dense (Dense) (None, 512) 4194816
dropout_1 (Dropout) (None, 512) 0
dense_1 (Dense) (None, 10) 5130
Total params: 4,210,090
Trainable params: 4,210,090
Non-trainable params: 0

RESULT

Figure 7. Input test image

Figure 8. Result of the Input Test image

Figure 9. Result of Image Recognition result

Figure 10. Result of Image Recognition result with accuracy

CONCLUSION AND FUTURE ENHANCEMENT

It is highly advised to employ the hybrid photograph popularity of CNN with LSTM since it has significant effects on the identification of image popularity based entirely on the automated extraction of features from the CIFAR-10 picture dataset. The LSTM architecture makes it possible to gain significant representation capabilities from visual data such as photos. The ongoing method is suitable for characteristic learning and image identification, and it also provides a new method for item tracking and prediction by making use of deep learning algorithms. Both of these applications can benefit from the ongoing method. The approach that was provided achieves a great overall performance in photo reputation difficulties, and in some cases, it even performs better than people do in those same situations. It is going to be exciting to investigate the few applications that use model parallelization rather than data parallelization because of the widespread use of photography in many different sectors. Even though it is said that it does not scale as well as the latter and that the configuration is fairly difficult because operations layers need to be placed manually, it has the potential to be an exciting test. As the network of the cluster is shared amongst all of the jobs, it's far doubtful that slowdowns at some stage in training can be a result of a congested network and to what extent it influences the manner. However, ultimately, we need to evaluate the impact that network congestion has on training times.

REFERENCES

Aoudni, Y., Donald, C., Farouk, A., Sahay, K. B., Babu, D. V., Tripathi, V., & Dhabliya, D. (2022). Cloud security based attack detection using transductive learning integrated with Hidden Markov Model. *Pattern Recognition Letters*, *157*, 16–26. doi:10.1016/j.patrec.2022.02.012

Deepika, M., & Prabhu, M. S.(2019). Cloud Task Scheduling Based on a Two Stage Strategy using KNN Classifier. *International Journal of Latest Engineering Science, 2*(6), 33-39.

Farouk, A., Alahmadi, A., Ghose, S., & Mashatan, A. (2020). Blockchain platform for industrial healthcare: Vision and future opportunities. *Computer Communications*, *154*, 223–235. doi:10.1016/j.comcom.2020.02.058

Farouk, A., Batle, J., Elhoseny, M., Naseri, M., Lone, M., Fedorov, A., ... Abdel-Aty, M. (2018). Robust general N user authentication scheme in a centralized quantum communication network via generalized GHZ states. *Frontiers in Physics*, *13*(2), 1–18.

Farouk, A., Zakaria, M., Megahed, A., & Omara, F. A. (2015). A generalized architecture of quantum secure direct communication for N disjointed users with authentication. *Scientific Reports*, *5*(1), 1–17. doi:10.1038rep16080 PMID:26577473

Guo, Z. (2020). Identification of hepatitis B using Raman spectroscopy combined with gated recurrent unit and multiscale fusion convolutional neural network. *Spectroscopy Letters: An International Journal for Rapid Communication, 53*(4), 277–288. . doi:10.1080/00387010.2020.1737944

Heidari, S., Abutalib, M. M., Alkhambashi, M., Farouk, A., & Naseri, M. (2019). A new general model for quantum image histogram (QIH). *Quantum Information Processing*, *18*(6), 1–20. doi:10.100711128-019-2295-5

Matlani, P., & Shrivastava, M. (2019). Hybrid deep VGG-NET convolutional classifier for video smoke detection. *CMES*, *119*(3), 427–458. doi:10.32604/cmes.2019.04985

Samadi, F., Akbarizadeh, G., & Kaabi, H. (2019). Change detection in SAR images using deep belief network: A new training approach based on morphological images. *IET Image Processing*, *13*(12), 2255–2264. doi:10.1049/iet-ipr.2018.6248

Santra, A., Rai, V., Das, D., & Kundu, S. (2022). Facial Expression Recognition Using Convolutional Neural Network. *International Journal for Research in Applied Science and Engineering Technology*, *10*(5), 1081–1092. doi:10.22214/ijraset.2022.42439

Wang, R., Xu, J., & Han, T. X. (2019a). Object instance detection with pruned Alexnet and extended training data. *Signal Processing Image Communication*, *70*, 145–156. doi:10.1016/j.image.2018.09.013

Wang, S.-H., Muhammad, K., Hong, J., Sangaiah, A. K., & Zhang, Y.-D. (2020). Alcoholism identification via convolutional neural network based on parametric ReLU, dropout, and batch normalization. *Neural Computing & Applications*, *32*(3), 665–680. doi:10.100700521-018-3924-0

Wang, Y., Wang, G., Chen, C., & Pan, Z. (2019b). Multi-scale dilated convolution of convolutional neural network for image denoising. *Multimedia Tools and Applications*, *78*(14), 19945–19960. doi:10.100711042-019-7377-y

Yu, J., Zheng, X., & Wang, S. (2019). A deep autoencoder feature learning method for process pattern recognition. *Journal of Process Control*, *79*, 1–15. doi:10.1016/j.jprocont.2019.05.002

Zhang, Y.-D., Dong, Z., Chen, X., Jia, W., Du, S., Muhammad, K., & Wang, S.-H. (2019). Image based fruit category classification by 13-layer deep convolutional neural network and data augmentation. *Multimedia Tools and Applications*, *78*(3), 3613–3632. doi:10.100711042-017-5243-3

Zhe, X., Chen, S., & Yan, H. (2019). Directional statistics-based deep metric learning for image classification and retrieval. *Pattern Recognition*, *93*, 113–123. doi:10.1016/j.patcog.2019.04.005

Chapter 17
Security Enhancement in Cloud Computing Using CBC Technique

V. Gunasundhari
Nandha Engineering College, India

M. Parvathi
Nandha Engineering College, India

S. Prabhu
Nandha Engineering College, India

ABSTRACT

The data protection mechanism in cloud storage systems is based on two-way factored inversion. With the authors' solution, users can store encrypted communications in the cloud and distribute them to their intended recipients. There is no requirement for the sender to have any other information (public key, certificate, etc.) except from the name of the receiver. There are two things the decoder needs in order to decipher the ciphertext. Your computer's private key is the first. The second is a one-of-a-kind computer-based security system for the individual. The ciphertext cannot be cracked without both keys. The loss or theft of your security device will also cause it to become inoperable. In other words, it can't be utilised to read encrypted messages. A cloud server is an option for this. The sender will not be aware of any of this activity. In the same vein, cloud server reads encrypted Chrome content. The system's practicability is supported by analyses of its safety and efficiency.

INTRODUCTION

In the cloud computing model, data is often stored in pools managed by a third party. Using cloud storage has a number of benefits. The accessibility of information stands out the most. Cloud-based information is always available to anyone with an internet connection. Upkeep tasks in the warehouse, such replacing B. When working with a service provider, it is possible to delegate the task of purchasing more

DOI: 10.4018/978-1-6684-6060-3.ch017

storage space. With cloud storage, customers can benefit from the sharing of data. Emailing large files can be problematic if Alice wants to send them to Bob. Alice then uploads the file to a cloud storage system from which Weave can retrieve it at any moment. Outsourcing information capacity has several advantages, but it also increases the attack surface, which must be considered. In the case of distributed information, for example, the greater the number of storage locations, the greater the risk of unauthorised physical access. With so many people accessing the same storage and network, it's possible for malicious individuals to steal data. This could be the result of careless use, a faulty equipment, or malicious intent.

A promising solution for risk compensation is the use of encryption technology. Encryption allows you to protect your data while it is being sent to and received from your cloud services. In addition, you can protect the data stored by your service provider. Even an incorrect attacker can access the cloud. The data is encrypted so that an attacker cannot get the information in plain text. With asymmetric encryption, the encryption feature uses only public information (such as the recipient's public key or ID) to generate the ciphertext, and the recipient can use the private key to decode the ciphertext. Usually, the foremost helpful encryption mode for sending information is as it does not require symmetric key management encryption.

Enhanced Security Protection

In asymmetric cryptography, the public key or ID is paired with only one corresponding private key. The ciphertext can be unlocked with this key alone. The key is kept in a safe place, like your computer or a server you trust, and is protected with a password. When a server or computer is accessible from the outside of a network, the default security settings should be adequate. This, sadly, is not how things work in the real world. A hacker could potentially compromise a private key without the key owner being aware of it if the machine or server in question is linked to the Internet. For reasons of physical security, the computer storing the user decryption key is changed if the original computer user (that is, the keychain) is missing (for example, if the client walks to the restroom for a while without locking the machine). Users can take advantage of it. Sharing computers is prevalent in workplaces and educational institutions. In a college setting, for instance, it would be useful to have an open computer in a replica data room so that students on the same floor may share information. If the attacker has access to the victim's cloud-stored personal data, then the attacker also gains access to the private key. Therefore, better safeguards are required. Explain why some simplistic methods of bolstering security are not the best bets for reaching your flexibility goals.

Double Encryption

A security device (with an additional key or access code) must be used. This is because the encryption process is iterated twice as fast. Clear text that corresponds to the user's open key or ID is encrypted. And then re-encrypt using the security gadget's public key or number. The utility performs security decryption first during the decryption process. The partially deciphered ciphertext is then sent to the tablet, which uses the user's secret to finish the job. Without both keys, the ciphertext will remain unreadable (private key or security device). It appears that this back-to-basics strategy is bringing us success. Numerous important practical issues remain unresolved. Case in point

- A security device lost by user, the responding ciphertext in the cloud is not permanently decrypt. In short, this approach cannot support the update / undo possibility of a security device.
- The sender wants to know the user's ID / public key as well as security device serial number / public key.
- The method of "identity-based" is completely lost because the sender wants to know the ID and serial number.

The Secret Key Was Divided

Another reliable method is to split the key in half lengthwise. The first half is stored on the computer, while the second half is plugged into the safety device. Just like the over method, this one also requires both halves to decipher the ciphertext. This strategy has proven successful in the past and appears to be able to accomplish our goal. If the attacker doesn't always have access to the full non-public key. In other words, if the private key is split in half, the attacker still has a chance of deciphering it (or at least learning something about the plaintext) in both halves. Usually, this is not what we had expected.

The exists next cryptographic primitive called "leakage-resilient encryption". Even if the private key is leaked to a specific bit, the security is definitely in the scheme, and even if you know these bits, you cannot recover the entire private key. However, the fact that the utilisation of primitive spills can ensure spills from certain bits, there's another reasonable constraint. Assume we portion of the mystery key within the security gadget; shockingly, the gadget was stolen.

The user must have an alternate device to continue decrypting their respective secret key. A simple way is to duplicate the same bits to a new device via a Private Key Generator (PKG) (as in the case of a stolen device). This is very easy to do. However, there are security risks. In case the foe can too delete the computer in the other portion of the mystery key is put away, at that point, it can decode all cipher compared to the casualty client. The most secure way is to debilitate the stolen security gadget. Comparative is online, keeping money. Users need a secure device (and know the password) to connect to the eBanking services. If a reported lost in security device, user will not be able to log in with the old device. Therefore, primitives that are leak resistant cannot provide this security functionality. It is considered the foremost critical standard for two-factor security assurance.

LITERATURE SURVEY

Marwan, et al. (2017) proposed a visual crypto-based method for protecting restorative picture capacity in the cloud. This procedure guarantees security without the requirement for complicated numerical calculations. Results appear that this procedure guarantees the privacy of the information by part the restorative picture into numerous parts. Additionally, we prompt a multi-cloud environment to reduce security threats and beautify execution.

X.Shen, Y.Liu, H.Zhu and L.Wang (2020) proposed a technique based on a multivariate public key cryptosystem using equivalence tests. This paper proposes the main themes of multivariate public key cryptography and equivalence testing (MPKEET), which combines multivariate public key cryptography and equivalence testing to inherit the benefits of each primitive. In addition, the equivalence test calculation proposed in this paper is based on straight lines. It is less demanding to execute than a conspire based on bilinear blending. And our MPKEET theme provides interesting security that can withstand linearisation condition assaults, differential assaults, XL assaults, and assaults on quantum computers when suitable parameters are chosen.

Sankaran, et al., (2018) proposed a technology aimed at developing new key dissemination and encryption mechanisms, especially quantum key dispersion and non-Abel encryption (QKDNAE) for secure capacity and getting to PHR. The outcome of this result evaluates the performance of QAD NAE through a number of damage countermeasures, and its superiority is proved by investigation using existing methods.

An improvement in the calculation of homomorphic encryption using elliptic bending cryptography and the OTP method was investigated by M. K. Sharma and D. Somwanshi (2018). Using elliptic bending cryptographic computation, they generated a tiny key that is as secure as RSA. According to the findings, the implementation is superior to the fundamental calculation in terms of both calculation time and capacity overhead, as well as attack likelihood. The decryption key was protected using one-time passwords in this method.

B. Celiktas, I. Celikbilek and E. Ozdemir (2021) proposed schema builds a key access control topic. This seamlessly passes a hierarchical get to the arrangement to a digital medium. It gives a secure way for all clients of this substance to get to the open cloud from the interior and exterior of the corporate organisations. Important access management topics and ideas for forming Shamir's mystery assistive and polynomial introduction innovation are particularly allowed for classical structures. In addition, by using directed graph topology placement with self-loop, with negligible contemplations when moving business-critical data between open clouds, only users with the appropriate privileges have the same or higher privileges. Making the key accessible to users of key derivation is computationally economical because key overheads such as open and individual capacity prerequisites are decreased to sensible levels. From a security point of view, our subject is unaffected by collaboration assaults and gives key personality security.

A new block cypher developed by R. R. K. Chaudhary and K. Chatterjee (2020) ensures the privacy of data transmitted from such Internet of Things devices. There is a lot of computing work involved and not a lot of energy used by this technique. The final outcome of its practical application suggests that it is both computationally and memory-wise green, while also being incredibly fast, which is great for the task of developing a green cypher.

Singh, et al., (2017) Elliptic bending cryptography for sending encrypted messages from a mechanical human smartphone to another Android smartphone. In addition, it compares Elliptic bend cryptography with the RSA calculation program.

Karthik, Chinnasamy and Deepalakshmi (2017) discovered hybrid technologies that use the symmetric key and symmetric key programs of any algorithm to provide strong security. The proposed technology indicates that the encryption time is more accepted than the existing technology.

Two Efficient and Secure Dynamic Searchable Symmetric Encryption (SEDSSE) Schemes for Medical Cloud Data, H. Li, et al., (2020). They begin by developing a dynamic, searchable symmetric encryption system that can accomplish forward and reverse privacy using safe k-Nearest Neighbor (kNN) and Attribute-Based Encryption (ABE) approaches. Within the realm of dynamic, searchable symmetric encryption, these two security features are crucial and quite demanding.

Ojha, S., & Rajput, V. (2017) Just as the increase in the number of users vs cloud security has been an increasing issue, a lot of work has been done in this area, and they all involve cryptographic approaches, making cloud computing one of the fastest-growing fields of research. To address the limitations of the currently-used method, we employ a cloud-based authentication method that uses AES and MD5 hashes to safeguard user data and login. Our data is encrypted and decrypted upon login, but we are not authenticated at login. Trust alone is not sufficient to guarantee safety.

Supriya and Gurpreet Singh (2013) To protect confidentiality, a number of distinct cryptographic algorithms exist, and the one used typically depends on the needs of the individual user or the security requirements of the business. It examines the pros and cons of a number of popular cryptographic encryption algorithms with respect to a number of carefully selected factors, such as their security level and how efficiently they operate. DES, 3DES, IDEA, CAST128, AES, Blowfish, RSA, ABE, and ECC are just few of the algorithms selected for this task.

The various authentication approaches for mobile cloud computing have been reviewed in depth by Alizadeh et al. (2016). They suggest a new category for authenticators already used in MCC. Next, the merits and flaws of various approaches are examined. We provide a comparative analysis and make suggestions for future study to enhance the implicit authentication under investigation by establishing the cryptographic safety of the recorded usage and action histories.

SYSTEM MODEL

We propose a novel dual-aspect security assurance instrument for information can put away within the cloud. Our component gives the taking after pleasant highlights

1) Our framework is IBE-based instrument. That's the sender, as it were, must know the recipient's ID to send the scrambled information (Ciphertext). No distinctive information about the recipient (e.g. public key, certificates, etc.). At this point, the sender sends the ciphertext to the cloud, and the recipient can download the ciphertext at any time.
2) Our device provides two details of encryption protection to decrypt data stored in the cloud; the client must have two things. start with clients have to store their private keys on their computers. Moment, the client must have an interesting individual security device (USB, Bluetooth, NFC, etc.) used to connect to the computer. The ciphertext can't be decrypted without each part.
3) What's more, our platform makes it possible to retrieve lost security equipment (one of the components). Security is compromised if the device is lost or stolen. Existing ciphertexts will be immediately passed through some algorithms in the cloud to render them indecipherable on this device. The buyer also needs to decrypt his ciphertext using his new or replacement device and secret key. The sender will have no doubt as to which method is being used.

Cryptosystems with Two Secret Keys

There are two distinct families of cryptosystems that both call for two separate private keys. Both CLC and CLC are examples of certificate-based cryptosystems. The first is a certificate-less encryption scheme that has the potential to be more useful. It's like a traditional public key cryptosystem (PKCS#11) fused with the benefits of an identity-based cryptosystem (IBC) (PKI). In order to access their private and public keys, clients like Kin CLC must first select a client secret key. Meanwhile, the specialist (KGC) in the Naming Era generates fractional private keys that match its nature. Decoding or signing in the differentiated period requires the user's private key in addition to the KGC-issued half private key.

Crypto Systems with Online Authority

Intervened encryption was, to begin with, presented for the reason of denying open keys. Each exchange requires a web arbiter called a security arbiter (SEM). SEM, too, gives control of security highlights. In case SEM does not work, you will not be able to trade with public keys. That is, the cancelled client cannot get the collaboration from the SEM. This implies that the repudiated client will not be able to effectively unscramble the ciphertext.

Some time later, the word was refined and made more generic as certificate (SMC) encryption. A user has a private key, a public key, and an ID within the SMC framework. In order to decipher ciphertext or verify a signed communication, the client secret and SEM are necessary. However, the user's public key and associated ID are necessary for signature verification or encryption. The disavowed client cannot issue a signature or unscramble the ciphertext since the SEM is under the jurisdiction of the disavowed institution, which in turn might deny cooperating with the disavowed client.

Accordingly, SMEs should be managed by authoritative means, and they should have a web presence for signature and CHRYTEXT decoding decryption. In addition, it has not been defined. In order to perform the encryption function (or signature verification function), the matching public key must also be known. Consequently, the machine becomes significantly less intelligent and the advantages of having an identity-based system are nullified.

Security Crypto System

The key-separated encryption paradigm was introduced, and variants were proposed. The framework contains a physically secure gadget, but there's a clear restrain. Although long-term keys are stored in this device, the pumpkin secret key is saved by the user with a strong and secure device where the cryptographic calculation is performed. Short-term secrets are updated in individual time periods through dialogue between the client and the base, but the open key does not alter the life of the framework. The client gets a halfway private key from the gadget at the start of each period.

At that point, combine this halfway private key with the private key of the past period to overhaul the private key of the current period. Contrary to our imagination, key-separated cryptosystems require all clients to overhaul their keys on a regular basis. Expensive time synchronisation calculation between clients may be required, which may be practical in many scenarios. A security device is required for the key update process. As soon as the key is updated, signing or decryption algorithms have no longer needed devices inside the same period. Our concept requires a security gadget each time a client endeavours to decode a ciphertext. In addition, the system does not require key updates. Therefore, there is no need to synchronise system-wide.

RESULT AND DISCUSSION

This session gives construction execution comes about and depicts execution or security investigation.

Private Key Generator

Typically, a trust party is dependable for providing private keys for all clients. The RSA cryptosystem is the foremost broadly utilised public key cryptographic calculation in the world. It can be used to encrypt a message without having to replace the private key individually. The RSA calculation can be utilised for open key cryptography and advanced marks. Its security is based on the trouble of applying huge integrability.

Security Device Issuer (SDI)

This is a reliable authority that is responsible for issuing a safety device to each user. This module calls for the consumer to sign in with the device. The device key is crawled and stored in the database to protect each user's incoming data.

Sender

The sender (and maker) of the ciphertext. A person who, as it were, knows the personality of the recipient (email, address, etc.) and knows nothing else related to the recipient. As soon as the sender creates a cryptographic text and sends it to the cloud server, the recipient can be downloaded it.

Receiver

This can be the beneficiary of the ciphertext and features a special ID (such as a mail address). The scrambled content is put away in cloud capacity and can be downloaded by the beneficiary for unscrambling. The beneficiary contains a private key (put away on the computer) and a security gadget (counting touchy data approximately the ID). They are given by PKG. The private key and security gadget both are required to unscramble the ciphertext.

Cloud Server

The cloud server is able to put down all the encoded content (as the recipient downloads the content). When a user reports a lost security gadget (and gets an unused one from PKG), the cloud acts as an intermediary and re-encrypts all past and future ciphertext to coordinate the unused gadget. This means that the old device will be deprecated.

Identity-Based Cryptography

Identity–based One type of open key cryptography uses a publicly available string to represent an individual or organization's private key. You can use a real IP address, email address, or domain name for the beginning of the string (figs. 1 and 2).

Figure 1. Ordinary Data Sharing (Liu, et al., 2016)

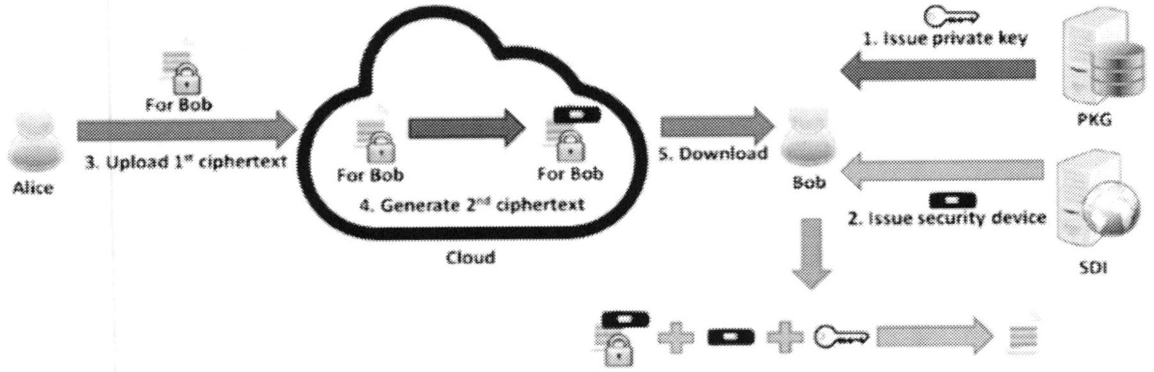

Figure 2. Upgrade ciphertext after issuing an unused security gadget (Liu, et al., 2016)

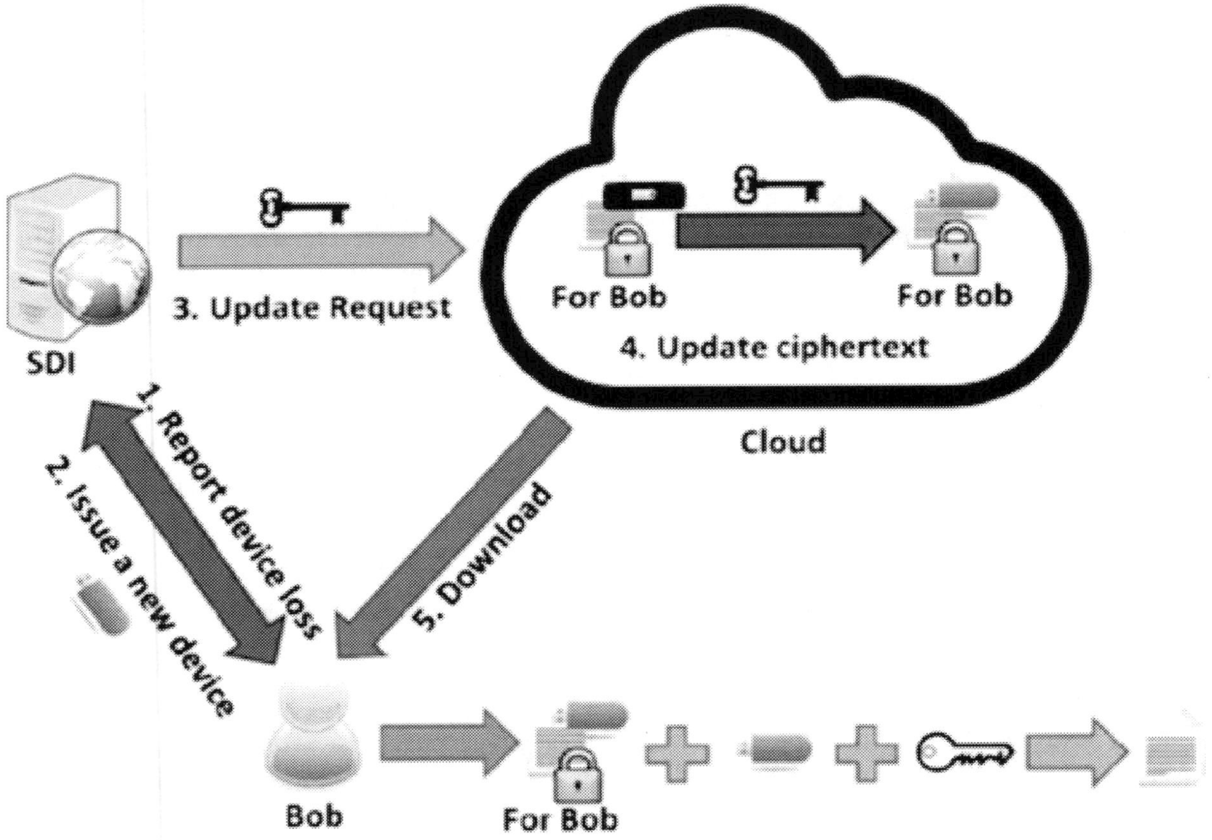

Algorithm Explanation

The RSA calculation contains three fundamental steps. Key era, encryption, and decoding. RSA is an asymmetric key calculation that employments two buttons, private keys and open keys. As the name implies, anyone can get data around the open key, but the private key must be kept a mystery. The thought is that anybody can utilise an open key to scramble a message, but as it were, somebody with the comparing private key can decode the message.

The main function and security of the RSA calculation are based on the truth that the factorisation issue is "troublesome". The only way to break RSA is to find an efficient algorithm to factorise large numbers, but not. On the other hand, the advent of quantum computers has now proven to be the case. Therefore, the advent of quantum computing can kill RSA.

MD5 Algorithm

First, assume you've got a bit message as input, and you need to look for that message bit. Where b may be a non-negative integer. b can be 0, doesnot have to be the number 8, and can be any measure. Think about the written message part like this:

m_0 m_1 ... m_{b-1}

After five steps, the message message process is calculated.

Step 1. Connect the padding bits

The message is "attenuated" (amplified), so a message length (in bits) of 448 corresponds to 512, as a rule. This is a message extended by 64 bits less than 512 bits. Even if the message length is already 448 and modulo 512, it will always be filled. Within the message, one "1" bit is added and then "0" bit is added, and the bit length corresponding to fabric 512 is 448 bit length. From 1 bit to 512 bits are added.

Step 2. Append Length

Finally, a 64-bit representation of b (message length, recently includes squelch bits) is given in the output. If b's exponent is more than 264, which is highly improbable, only the least significant 64 bits of b will be used. (As with the last run, these bytes are represented as two 32-bit words, with the lower word already present.) Having added bits a and b, the total length of the message is now a multiple of 512. This message is exactly 16 (32-bit) words long. The message that n can be a difference of 16 in case m is M.

Step 3. Initialise MD Buffer

The message digest is computed using a four-word buffer (A, B, C, D). In this case, we have four 32-bit registers labelled A, B, C, and D. These registers are set to the next value in the low byte of the hexadecimal number.

word A: 01 25 45 67
word B: 98 ab cd ef
word C: fe dc ba 89
word D: 76 44 32 30

Step 4. Prepare Message In 16-Word Squares

We begin by breaking down the four helper functions, each of which takes 32-bit expressions as input and returns a 32-bit word.

H(X,Y,Z) = X x or Y x or Z

F(X,Y,Z) = XY in ne(X) Z

G(X,Y,Z) = XZ v. Y not(Z)

I(X,Y,Z) = Y xor (X in not(Z))

F conditions each bit location. If X, then Y. XY and not (X)Z never have a 1 in the same bit location, hence F can be defined with +. If X, Y, and Z are independent and unbiased, so will F(X, Y, Z). If the bits X, Y, and Z are independent and unbiased, then G, H, and I (X, Y, Z) are independent and unbiased. H is a bitwise "XOR" or "parity" function. Step employs a sine-created 64-element array T [1... 64]. Let T I equal the integer component of 4294967296 x abs (sin I where I is a radian. Appendix: table elements.

Step 5. Output

Tables A, B, C, and D represent the messages that were returned. In other words, it all begins with the "moo" byte of A and finishes with the "high" byte of D. After this, the MD5 output will be finished. C's citation format places all citations in the bibliography (figs.3 and 4).

Figure 3. Dual Encryption based on user Identity and Device Key

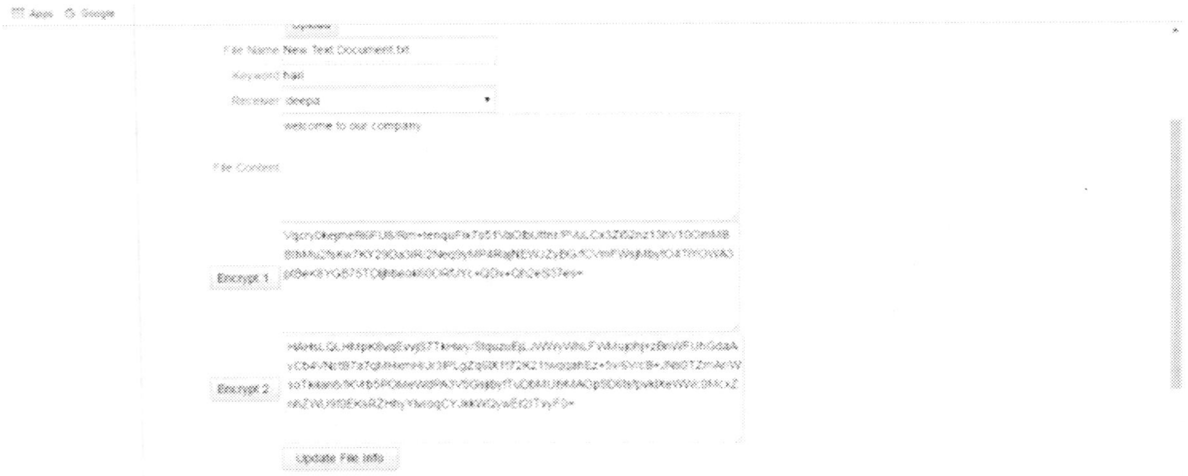

Figure 4. Double Unscrambling based on client Character and Gadget Key

CONCLUSION

This paper described a revolutionary two-factor data protection technique that can be deployed in cloud storage platforms. In the event where both the user's private key and security device are required, the sender of the information is aware of the identity of the information receiver, and the information received can scramble data. Our plan ensures that the gadget will be disavowed and also increases the privacy of the information. That means that the cloud server will secretly provide the matching ciphertext to the device when it is far away. Every step of the process will go off without a hitch. It will be revised to incorporate a discussion of the effectiveness and safety of the system in various use situations.

REFERENCES

Alizadeh, M., Abolfazli, S., Zamani, M., Baharun, S., & Sakurai, K. (2016). Authentication in mobile cloud computing: A survey. *Journal of Network and Computer Applications*, *61*, 59–80. doi:10.1016/j.jnca.2015.10.005

Celiktas, B., Celikbilek, I., & Ozdemir, E. (2021). A higher-level security scheme for key access on cloud computing. *IEEE Access: Practical Innovations, Open Solutions*, *9*, 107347–107359. doi:10.1109/ACCESS.2021.3101048

Chaudhary, R. R. K., & Chatterjee, K. (2020). An efficient lightweight cryptographic technique for IoT based E-healthcare system. In *2020 7th International Conference on Signal Processing and Integrated Networks (SPIN)*. IEEE.

Karthik, C., & Deepalakshmi. (2017). Hybrid cryptographic technique using OTP: RSA. In *2017 IEEE International Conference on Intelligent Techniques in Control, Optimization and Signal Processing (INCOS)*. IEEE.

Li, H., Yang, Y., Dai, Y., Yu, S., & Xiang, Y. (2020). Achieving secure and efficient dynamic searchable symmetric encryption over medical cloud data. *IEEE Transactions on Cloud Computing*, *8*(2), 484–494. doi:10.1109/TCC.2017.2769645

Liu, J. K., Liang, K., Susilo, W., Liu, J., & Xiang, Y. (2016). Two-factor data security protection mechanism for cloud storage system. *IEEE Transactions on Computers*, *65*(6), 1992–2004. doi:10.1109/TC.2015.2462840

Marwan, M., Kartit, A., & Ouahmane, H. (2017). Protecting medical images in cloud using visual cryptography scheme. In *2017 3rd International Conference of Cloud Computing Technologies and Applications (CloudTech)*. IEEE.

Ojha, S., & Rajput, V. (2017). AES and MD5 based secure authentication in cloud computing. In *2017 International Conference on I-SMAC (IoT in Social, Mobile, Analytics and Cloud) (I-SMAC)*. IEEE.

Ruprah, T. S., Kore, V. S., & Mali, Y. K. (2017). Secure data transfer in android using elliptical curve cryptography. In *2017 International Conference on Algorithms, Methodology, Models and Applications in Emerging Technologies (ICAMMAET)*. IEEE. 10.1109/ICAMMAET.2017.8186639

Sharma, M. K., & Somwanshi, D. (2018). Improvement in homomorphic encryption algorithm with elliptic curve cryptography and OTP technique. In *2018 3rd International Conference and Workshops on Recent Advances and Innovations in Engineering (ICRAIE)*. IEEE.

Shen, X., Wang, L., Zhu, H., & Liu, Y. (2020). A multivariate public key encryption scheme with equality test. *IEEE Access: Practical Innovations, Open Solutions*, *8*, 75463–75472. doi:10.1109/ACCESS.2020.2988732

Singh, G., & Supriya, S. (2013). A study of encryption algorithms (RSA, DES, 3DES and AES) for information security. *International Journal of Computers and Applications*, *67*(19), 33–38. doi:10.5120/11507-7224

Thangapandiyan, M., Rubesh Anand, P. M., & Sankaran, K. S. (2018). Quantum key distribution and cryptography mechanisms for cloud data security. In *2018 International Conference on Communication and Signal Processing (ICCSP)*. IEEE. 10.1109/ICCSP.2018.8524298

Chapter 18
Techniques and Applications of Demographic Determinants of Mobile Phone Brand Switching in Attitude Towards Switching and Switching Intentions

Binit Patel
Charotar University of Science and Technology, India

ABSTRACT

The Indian telecom industry is growing at a very rapid pace. Both networking and handset-related technologies are refining day by day and year by year. Even the routine activities are executed by the use of mobile phones. Hence, mobile phones nowadays have become a necessity and not a luxury. Switching has now become a trend. There are demographics that actually suggest the switching behaviour; hence, they need to be identified. The descriptive study was used with a total of 1502 respondents across the state of Gujarat, wherein the respondents were selected using the hybrid sampling method. A structured questionnaire was designed using different items, constructs, and dimensions found in the literature review. The study has developed a regression model that can further help in predicting the switching behaviour of mobile phone users. There are demographics that moderate the relationship between 'switching intention' and 'attitude towards switching'.

INTRODUCTION

The telecom industry in India has developed extensively in the last 20 years. The mobile phone, which was reflected as a luxury product in the past has now become the necessity of an individual's daily life. The global market has estimated about 7.4 billion connections with an estimated world income of about $4.4 trillion in the year 2025. Indian domestic market and the industry are reckless if the growth is considered. The mobile phone industry in India is growing at an unbelievable upward rate and has shown

DOI: 10.4018/978-1-6684-6060-3.ch018

no sign of slowdown even during the pandemic. The telecom industry in India is indeed a booming industry with important players like Apple, Samsung, Xiomi, Oppo, Vivo, Realme, LG, Nokia to name a few. Users expecting more and more as new innovative and pioneering technologies are coming up at a rapid pace. This enables companies to make mobile phones much smarter day by day.

A brand can be defined as 'a distinguishing name and/or symbol, intended to identify a product or producer (Aaker, 1991)'. Brand loyalty is a concept that suggests a repeat purchase of the same brand for the next purchase. It is universally accepted that the cost of getting a new customer is always higher than the cost of serving the existing customer (Fornell & Wernerfelt, 1987). Loyal customers are less likely to switch the brand because they are not much price-sensitive. If the consumers are not much price-sensitive, then they are likely to switch the brand which ignites the company to invest more in the promotions to attract new customers and also loses the future revenue from the switchers (Anisimova, 2007). Customers who are considered loyal to a specific brand are more likely to create a resistance to competing brands. They are also more likely to spread good things about the brand to the prospects available in the market (Delgado-Ballester & Munuera-Alemán, 2001; Dowling & Uncles,1997). Moreover, increased knowledge of the brand creates a more favourable association which generally results in a lower probability of switching the existing brand (Keller, 1993). The companies' primary objective behind the concept of brand loyalty is to generate as much revenue as possible and ultimately increase the customer lifetime value in the long period.

The concept of brand loyalty can always be grilled in the current competitive market structure because competitors keep on modifying the product and offers to be more competitive using the rapid advancement in technology. So, rationally it is not advisable to be loyal all the time as a more competitive offer, improved product, an inexpensive product with more features and benefits are likely to be available during the next purchase of the product category. Sometimes switching can occur due to two different reasons: Firstly, if the current requirements or expectations (in terms of behavioural measures) are not satisfied by the current brand of the product. Secondly, consumers may want to be refreshed or want more variation by experiencing a new brand of the product (McAlister, 1982). Hence, the focus should have to be shifted to brand switching rather than brand loyalty as only limited studies have been conducted on brand switching (Shukla, 2004). This present study is an attempt made to contribute to identifying demographical drivers or factors that drives brand switching.

Many researches in the past considered attitude as a result of the post-purchase response. If the consumers' expectations are met, then they would be satisfied and if performance is below the expectation then they would be dissatisfied. This outcome in terms of satisfaction and dissatisfaction further manipulates the attitude either favourable or unfavourable (Oliver,1989). The conative component includes switching cost which reveals the opportunity cost for switching from the current brand of product to some different brand of product. Attitude is the predecessor of the preference and serves as a reference point for evaluation of the product and the preference can be moderating factor between attitude and the final behaviour. Youjae and Ho (2003) identified that attitudes towards switching affect switching intention differently for different demographic factors like age, gender, occupation, area of residence, income, etc. The study suggests that with increasing age people with the same level of attitude towards switching display different switching intentions. Hence, there is the possibility of having moderating effects of demographic factors on the switching intention. Zeithaml (2008) suggested that females got a high level of involvement while buying a branded product. Ravald and Gronroos (2019), in their study, found that males who were having a high level of satisfaction were more likely to be loyal than a female who had the same level of satisfaction. Petrick (2016) found that lower-income consumers were more likely to switch as they were always looking for the products which gave the best 'Value for Money'. Morgan and Hunt (1994) in their study revealed that age was one of the moderator variables between the switching intention and consumer satisfaction.

The concept of switching behavior is an essential parameter to gain an insight into the factors that affect consumers to switch their current brand of the product. Brand switching is "The replacement or exchange of the current brand with another brand of the product" (Bansal & Taylor, 1999). The switching behavior model given by Keaveney (1995) is vital for understanding the switching behavior in the service industry. The model suggested that pricing is the most important factor that induces switching of services, this is followed by service failures. This can be avoided to stop customer switching (Keaveney, 1995). Colgate & Hedge (2001) claimed that further researches should be done to expand the research area of brand switching behavior. The argument was generated after the conclusion that there is a requirement to have a substantial understanding of why customers are switching a specific brand of a product. Many types of research have been done on why the customers are staying with the same brand which reflects consumer loyalty but it is equally essential to understand why they are not staying with the same brand. As the factors affecting loyalty may not equally impact the switching (Fornell & Birger, 1987). The reasons for the consumers for being with the same brand could be the switching barriers and switching costs as identified by Colgate et. al. (2007). The researcher further renamed these variables as staying reasons. Time and efforts required to search for the new brand of the product, switching cost, absolutely minimal variation in two brands of the product, and the attachment that the consumer has with brands are the four further identified staying reasons. The intention to do something is proven to be used to predict the actual behavior of consumers (Ajzen, 1980). Attitude towards the behavior, behavioral control, and subjective demographic variables are significant in predicting the actual behavior (Ajzen, 1980). Bansal & Taylor (1999) conducted further research and found that attitude towards switching was the single most significant factor which was explaining the switching intention. Moreover, the satisfaction of the consumers with the product was also one of the other determinants which contributes to the prediction of the switching intention.

Zeithaml (2008) suggested that females got a high level of involvement while buying some branded products. Mittal (1995) found that females were more tolerant while purchasing a product with comparatively fewer personal barriers. Wulf and Odekerken (2001) identified the relative importance of gender on the switching intentions of the consumers. Ravald and Gronroos (2019), in their study, found that males who were having a high level of satisfaction were more likely to be loyal than a female who had the same level of satisfaction.

The consumption-related decision is having more impact on consumer income (Reynolds, 1978). The study further suggested that people with high income were more tend to switch the product because of high purchasing power. They do look for much more options available. Further, Walsh et. al (2008) found that the consumers who were having lower income are more likely to repurchase the same brand of the product to avoid search-related and switching costs. Completely contrary to this, Patrick (2016) found that lower-income consumers were more likely to switch as they were always looking for the products which gave the best 'Value for Money'. Morgan and Hunt (1994) in their study revealed that age was one of the moderator variables between the switching intention and consumer satisfaction. In the study it was concluded that with more age, consumers were not processing much information, and hence with limited information, the switching intentions fading. Homburg (2001) suggested that young consumers repurchase intentions are characterized more by their satisfaction level and the age itself. Lambert (2005) identified that older consumers do possess a very little set of consideration and are hence more likely to stick with the brand during the next purchase.

Based on the literature review and researchers' own experience as a mobile phone owner over the years, the conceptual model is derived which may help in predicting the switching intentions. The model needs to be tested further (figure 1).

CONCEPTUAL MODEL

Figure 1. Conceptual Model

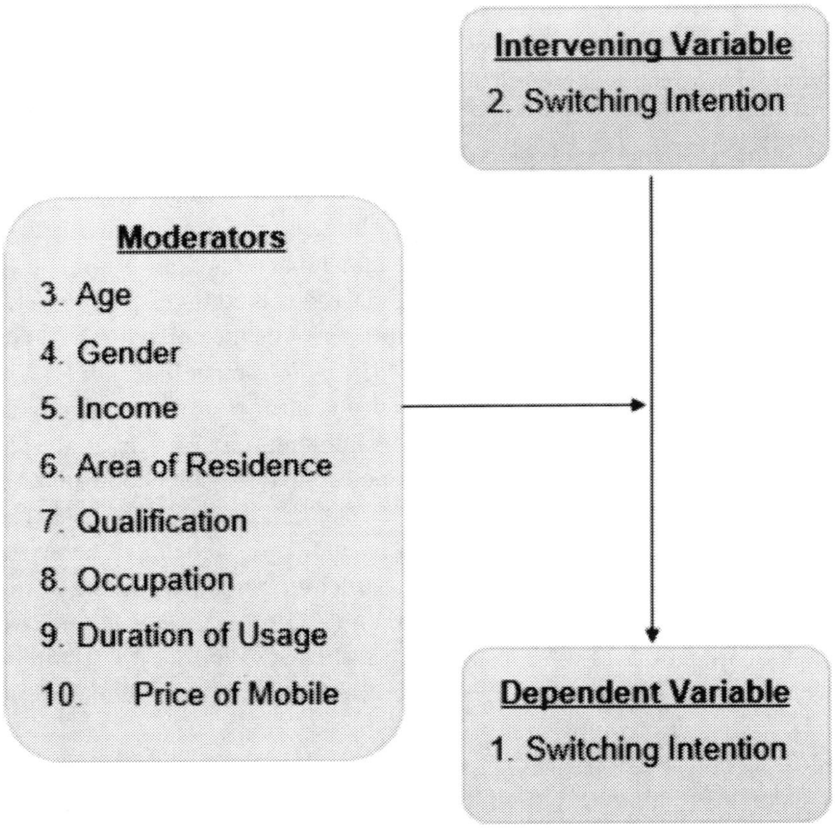

RESEARCH OBJECTIVES

To study the relationship between 'Attitude towards Switching' and 'Switching Intentions':

- Switching intentions are like whether the user is ready to repurchase the same product or going for the switching of a brand. This may be affected by their attitude towards switching. The focus is to identify whether the factor actually contributing to the switching intentions of mobile phone users.

- To study whether any demographical differences exist towards the switching behavior:
- Male may display switching behavior in a certain manner and it may be different from the counterpart. Similarly, the difference may exist income-wise, occupation-wise, qualification-wise, etc. The objective will assess for any potential demographical differences present towards the switching behaviour.

HYPOTHESIS

H1: Demographic variables moderate the relationship between attitude towards switching and switching intentions

METHODOLOGY

A structured questionnaire was used to collect the data from the individual respondents and in total, 1502 respondents were surveyed. To select an individual who owns a mobile phone, stratified sampling was used at the District / City level, and then convenience sampling was used at the respondent level. The size of the population was known as per the census data at the district/city level and hence stratified sampling (10 most populated cities) which is the part of probability sampling was used. No. of mobile phone users in each district/city was not known exactly and therefore convenience sampling which is part of non-probability sampling was used.

Structured questionnaire was used to conduct the study. There were mainly four sections in the instrument. The first was related to the demographic details of the respondents. This section includes information like Age, Gender, Income, Area of Residence, Educational Qualification, and Occupation. The second section is about details about the usage of the mobile phone like how many mobiles, ownership of the first mobile, current mobile phone, price range, etc. The third section consists of the variables/ statements used to measure the satisfaction level related to the current mobile phone brand. The final section included the factors which may affect the switching attitude and also the switching intentions.

DATA ANALYSIS

Table 1. Demographic Details

Age			Gender			Monthly Family Income			
< = 20	233	15.5	Male	764	50.9	< = 20,000	84	5.6	
21 – 30	412	27.4	Female	738	49.1	20,001 – 40,000	414	27.6	
31 – 40	334	22.2				40,001 – 60,000	255	17	
41 – 50	254	16.9				> 60,000	749	49.9	
> 50	269	17.9							

Educational Qualification			Occupation			
SSC	13	0.9	Unemployed	Student	233	15.5
				Homecare	138	9.2
HSC	87	5.8	Service		802	53.4
UG	522	34.8	Business		201	13.4
PG	605	40.3	Farming		128	8.5
Other	275	18.3				

Above table 1 shows the details about the demographic profile of the respondents. Out of the total of 1502 respondents, 233 (15.5%) were from the age group of 20 years and below, 412 (27.4%) were from the age group of age between 21 to 30, 334 (22.2%) of them were from age between 31 to 40 years, 254 (16.9%) were between 41 to 50 years of age, and remaining 269 (17.9%) from the age group of 50 years and above. Considering the gender-wise profile then it is almost 50-50. Total 764 (50.9%) were male respondents and 738 (49.1%) were female respondents out of 1502 aggregate of the respondents. Most (749, 49.9%) of the respondents out of 1502 were having a monthly family income of more than 60,000 rupees. Only 84 (5.6%) of the total respondents were having monthly family income which is less than 20,000 rupees. Seeing the educational background, the majority (522, 40.3%) of the respondents possess post-graduation as their qualification. Only 13 (0.9%) are having SSC as their highest current qualification. 522 (34.8) of the total respondents were holding a UG degree as their current educational qualification. The occupation profile of the respondents suggests that the majority (802, 53.4%) of respondents are having served as their occupation. 201 (13.4%) have their own business, 128 (8.5%) are farmers by profession, 138 (9.2%) of the total respondents were belong to the category of home care, and the remaining 233 (15.5%) were students.

Table 2. Cronbach's Alpha (For Reliability of Scales)

[A]	Attitude towards Switching (ATS) – Cronbach's Alpha = 0.941
1	A good idea
2	Useful
3	Beneficial
4	Wise decision
5	Pleasant
6	Desirable
[B]	**Switching Intention (SI) – Cronbach's Alpha = 0.831**
1	I intend to change my current mobile phone brand in near future
2	I usually search for information about phones of different brand
3	I will definitely wait till next model of same brand is available

Above table 2 shows Cronbach's Alpha for the items used to measure the construct. The value of Cronbach's alpha coefficient is above 0.8 which indicates consistency in the items used to measure the construct.

Table 3. Chi-Square Statistics

Switching Intention Variable	Demographic Variable	df	Sig. Value
Switching Intention	Age	16	0.000
	Gender	4	0.000
	Income	12	0.000
	Area	4	0.000
	Qualification	16	0.000
	Occupation	16	0.000
Switching Intention (As per 3 Preferences)	Age	4	0.000
	Gender	1	0.577
	Income	3	0.000
	Area	1	0.000
	Qualification	4	0.000
	Occupation	4	0.000

As seen in the above table 3, the given variable pairs are having a significant relationship with each other except for 'Switching Intention (As per 3 Preferences)' and 'Gender' as the p-value for the chi-square is 0.577 which is greater than 0.05 (significance level). Therefore, Gender is not having a significant relationship with 'Switching Intention (As per 3 Preferences)'. Further, the exact effect of these demographic variables on 'Switching Intention' is required to be tested.

Table 4. Regression Model

Model Summary				
Model	**R**	**R Square**	**Adjusted R Square**	**Std. Error of the Estimate**
1	.843[a]	.710	.710	.7738
a. Predictors: (Constant), ATS				

ANOVA[a]						
Model		Sum of Squares	df	Mean Square	F	Sig.
1	Regression	2198.668	1	2198.668	3671.799	.000[b]
	Residual	898.198	1500	.599		
	Total	3096.866	1501			
a. Dependent Variable: SI						
b. Predictors: (Constant), ATS						

Coefficients[a]						
Model		Unstandardized Coefficients		Standardized Coefficients	t	Sig.
		B	Std. Error	Beta		
1	(Constant)	.177	.049		3.594	.000
	ATS	.991	.016	.843	60.595	.000
a. Dependent Variable: SI						

It is seen from the above table 4 that about 71% of the variance in 'Switching Intention' is explained by 'Attitude towards Switching' which is the independent variable for the regression model as the r-square value is 0.710. ANOVA test p-value is also 0.000 which suggests that the slope for the regression equation is non-zero. Hence, the independent variable is contributing to the model. The coefficient for 'Attitude towards Switching' is positive and is almost close to 1 which means 'Attitude towards Switching' is more likely to increase the 'Switching Intention' of the users. In other words, if the user has a more inclined attitude towards switching, then the user is likely to develop favorable 'Switching Intention' for the next purchase.

For identification of demographical differences towards the switching behavior, the following model was tested (figure 2):

Figure 2. Moderators between 'Attitude towards Switching' and 'Switching Intention'

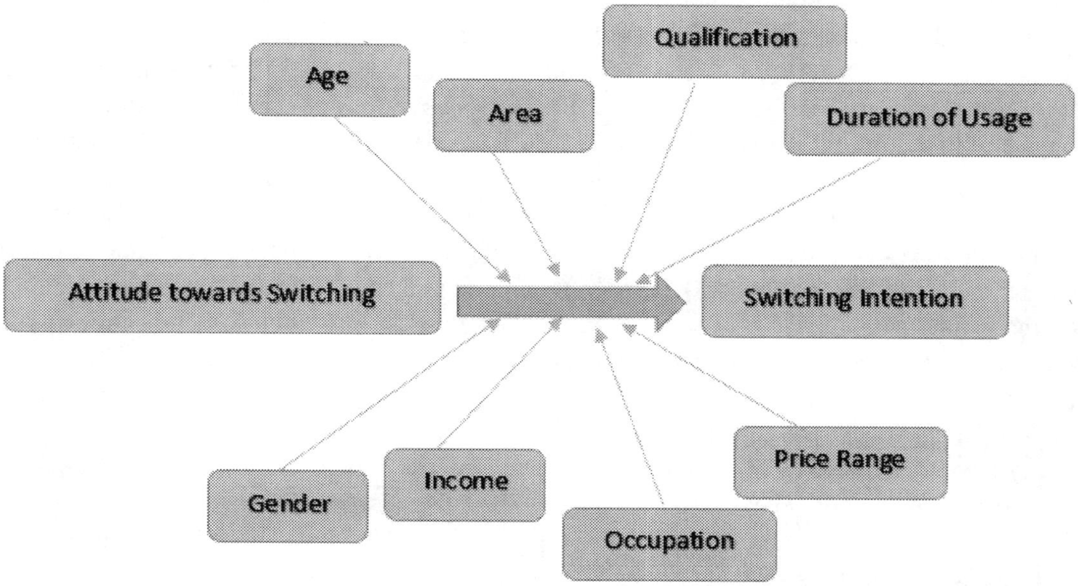

For identification of moderating effect following structure was considered:

- Dependent Variable: Switching Intention
- Independent Variable: Attitude towards Switching
- Moderating Variable: Age, Area, Qualification, Gender, Income, Occupation, Price Range, Duration of Usage

Process Macro (3.5.3) by Andrew F. Hayes was used in SPSS to develop the effect of moderating variables (table 5).

Table 5. Moderation Analysis Results

Sr. No.	Moderator	Model R^2	Coefficient – Interaction Term (X*W)	P-Value	R^2 Change
1	Age	0.7132	0.0382	0.0035	0.0016
2	Gender	0.7258	0.1955	0.0000	0.0069
3	Income	0.7146	-0.0650	0.0000	0.0035
4	Area	0.7175	-0.1644	0.0000	0.0049
5	Qualification	0.7135	0.0242	0.2013	0.0003
6	Occupation	0.7242	0.1457	0.0000	0.0129
7	Duration of Usage	0.7275	0.1483	0.0000	0.0058
8	Price Range	0.7459	-0.0523	0.0000	0.0042

If an interaction effect is considered between 'Age' and 'Attitude towards Switching' then it is significantly impacting the 'Switching Intention' and that too positively as the coefficient of the interaction term is 0.0382 and p-value is also less than 0.05 (significance level). The interaction effect is also contributing about 1% variance for the model additionally. So, it can be concluded that the moderating effect of age is present in the model. Gender having combined (interaction) effect through 'Attitude towards Switching' on 'Switching Intention' as p-value is 0.000. Gender is having a negative coefficient which suggests that males are more likely to switch the current mobile brand compared to females. Further, the interaction effect is contributing about 1% additional variability to the model and is also significant. So, moderating effect of 'Gender' is present in the model. Income is having an interaction effect as the p-value for the interaction term is 0.000. Further, the interaction term is having a negative value which indicates that with the high level of 'Attitude towards Switching', users with low income are more likely to switch to the current mobile phone brand compared to users with high income. Further, the interaction term is adding about 1% variance to the model. Area of residence is having significant moderating effect on 'Switching Intention' of the users as the p-values are 0.000. Further, the coefficient of the interaction term is negative which means as 'Attitude towards Switching' increases, users in the urban area are less likely to switch the current brand of the mobile phone. The interaction effect between 'Qualification' and 'Attitude towards Switching' is not significant as the p-value is 0.2013 which is greater than the value of the significance level. Hence, it can be concluded that 'Qualification' is not having moderating effect between 'Attitude towards Switching' and 'Switching Intention'. 'Occupation' is having an interaction effect on 'Switching Intention' as interaction terms are having p-value less than 0.05 (significance value). So, there exists a moderating effect of 'Occupation' on the model. 'Duration of Usage' and 'Attitude towards Switching' has an interaction effect on 'Switching Intention' as the interaction term is having a p-value of 0.000 which is less than 0.05 (significance value). So, there exists a moderating effect of the 'Duration of Usage' of the current mobile phone brand on the model. 'Price Range' is having an interaction effect on 'Switching Intention' as the p-values are less than 0.05 (significance level). So, there exists a moderating effect of the 'Price Range' of the current mobile phone brand on the model.

FINDINGS

'Attitude towards Switching' is explaining about 71% variance in 'Switching Intention' and is also found to be significant. Considering age of the consumers then, with same level of 'Attitude towards Switching', older users are more likely to switch than younger ones. Males are more likely to switch at lower level of 'Attitude of Switching' than females. But at the higher level of 'Attitude towards Switching' there is no differentiation gender wise. Further, for Income, Users with Lower Income are more likely to switch at any level of 'Attitude towards Switching'. Users from Urban area are more likely to switch at lower level of 'Attitude towards Switching', But, as the level of 'Attitude towards Switching' increases, Users from Semi-Urban area more likely to switch than urban area users. Students are more likely to switch at lower level of 'Attitude towards Switching', but, Business owners are more likely to switch at higher level of 'Attitude towards Switching' than students. Users who are using the same mobile phone from longer period are more likely to switch. Finally, Costlier mobile phone's users are less likely to switch. It was found that Age was not impacting the 'Switching Intention' directly but it was significantly impacting the 'Switching Intention' and that too positively. So, it can be concluded that the moderating effect of age is present in the model.

It can be inferred that 'Gender' has a direct effect on 'Switching Intention' and is also having combined (interaction) effect of 'Gender' and 'Attitude towards Switching' on 'Switching Intention'. It is revealed that the 'Income' is having a direct effect on 'Switching Intention'. It is also having an interaction effect on 'Switching Intention'. It was observed that 'Area' was having a direct effect as well as a significant moderating effect on 'Switching Intention'. Further, 'Occupation' is having a direct and interactive effect on 'Switching Intention'. It was revealed that 'Duration of Usage' was not having a direct effect on 'Switching Intention', but the interaction effect on 'Switching Intention' was present and found to be significant. It is inferred that 'Price Range' was having direct as well as interaction effect on 'Switching Intention' of the mobile phone users. Finally, Age, Gender, Income, Area of Residence, Occupation, Duration of Usage, and Price Range of the Mobile moderate the relationship between 'Attitude towards Switching' and 'Switching Intention'.

CONCLUSION

The study has developed a regression model which can further help in predicting the switching behaviour of mobile phone users. There are demographics such as 'Age', 'Gender', 'Occupation', 'Area of Residence', 'Income' along with 'Price Range' and 'Duration of Usage' moderates the relationship between 'Switching Intention' and 'Attitude towards Switching'. The current study has considered many variables and factors which can explain the variation in the switching behaviour of a mobile phone user. This further requires some additions and refinements. The study can further test the applicability of the model developed from this study using more population representation using sampling for generalization.

REFERENCES

Anisimova, T. A. (2007). The effects of corporate brand attributes on attitudinal and behavioural consumer loyalty. *Journal of Consumer Marketing*, *24*(7), 395–405. doi:10.1108/07363760710834816

Azjen, I., & Fisbein, M. (1980). *Understanding Attitudes and Predicting Social Behaviour*. Prentice Hall.

Bansal & Taylor. (1999). The Service Provider Switching Model (SPSM): A Model of Consumer Switching Behaviour in the Service Industry. *Journal of Service Research*, *2*(2), 200-218.

Colgate, M. R., & Hedge, R. (2001). An Investigation into the Switching Process in Retail Banking Services. *International Journal of Bank Marketing*, *19*(5), 201–212. doi:10.1108/02652320110400888

Delgado-Ballester, E., & Munuera-Aleman, J. L. (2001). Brand trust in the context of consumer loyalty. *European Journal of Marketing*, *35*(11/12), 1238–1258. doi:10.1108/EUM0000000006475

Dowling, G. R., & Uncles, M. (1997, Summer). Do customer loyalty programs really work? *Sloan Management Review*, *38*(4), 71–82.

Fornell & Birger. (1987). Defensive Marketing Strategy by Customer Complaint Management: A Theoretical Analysis. *Journal of Marketing Research*, *24*(4), 337-346.

Fornell, C., & Wernerfelt, B. (1987). Defensive marketing strategy by customer complaint management: A theoretical review. *JMR, Journal of Marketing Research*, *24*(Nov), 337–346. doi:10.1177/002224378702400401

Keaveney, S. M. (1995). Customer Switching Behavior in Service Industries: An Exploratory Study. *Journal of Marketing*, *59*(April), 71–82. doi:10.1177/002224299505900206

Keller, K. L. (1993). Conceptualizing, measuring, and managing customer-based brand equity. *Journal of Marketing*, *57*(Jan), 1–22. doi:10.1177/002224299305700101

McAlister, L. (1982). A dynamic attribute satiation model of variety-seeking behaviour. *The Journal of Consumer Research*, *9*(Sept), 141–150. doi:10.1086/208907

Morgan, R. M., & Hunt, S. D. (1994). The Commitment- Trust Theory of Relationship Marketing. *Journal of Marketing*, *58*(3), 20–38. doi:10.1177/002224299405800302

Morgan, R. M., & Hunt, S. D. (1994). The Commitment- Trust Theory of Relationship Marketing. *Journal of Marketing*, *58*(3), 20–38. doi:10.1177/002224299405800302

Oliver, R. L. (1989). A cognitive model of the antecedents and consequences of satisfaction decisions. *JMR, Journal of Marketing Research*, *17*(Nov), 460–469.

Petrick J. F. (2016). Development of a Multi-Dimensional Scale for Measuring Perceived Value of a Service: Serv Perval Scale. *Journal of Leisure Research*, *34*(2), 119-134.

Petrick, J. F. (2016). Development of a Multi-Dimensional Scale for Measuring Perceived Value of a Service: Serv Perval Scale. *Journal of Leisure Research*, *34*(2), 119-134.

Ravald, A., & Grönroos, C. (2019). The Value Concept and Relationship Marketing. *European Journal of Marketing*, *30*(2), 19–30. doi:10.1108/03090569610106626

Ravald, A., & Grönroos, C. (2019). The Value Concept and Relationship Marketing. *European Journal of Marketing*, *30*(2), 19–30. doi:10.1108/03090569610106626

Shukla, P. (2004). Effect of product usage, satisfaction and involvement on brand switching behavior. *Asia Pacific Journal of Marketing and Logistics*, *16*(4), 82–104. doi:10.1108/13555850410765285

Youjae, Y., & Ho, S. J. (2003). Effects of Loyalty Programs on Value Perception, Program Loyalty and Brand Loyalty. *Journal of the Academy of Marketing Science*, *30*(3), 229–240.

Zeithaml, V. A. (2008). Consumer Perceptions of Price, Quality and Value: A Means-End Model and Synthesis of Evidence. *Journal of Marketing*, *52*(July), 2–22.

Zeithaml, V. A. (2008). Consumer Perceptions of Price, Quality and Value: A Means-End Model and Synthesis of Evidence. *Journal of Marketing*, *52*(July), 2–22.

Chapter 19
Recent Application of Deep Neural Network and Data Augmentation for Classifying Leaf Diseases

R. Angeline
SRM Institute of Science and Technology, India

Raunak Agarwal
SRM Institute of Science and Technology, India

Sidhant Kumar Sidharth
SRM Institute of Science and Technology, India

Pratik Raj Biresh
SRM Institute of Science and Technology, India

ABSTRACT

Vegetable leaves are the main part of the plant and the main source for production of vegetables. The vegetable is high in energy and a superb wellspring of Vitamin C, Vitamin B, potassium-folate, magnesium, and many other nutrients. It also gives iron, phosphorus, and niacin. This natural product has low cholesterol and sodium, which is great for human wellbeing. The species originated in almost all the parts of India but mainly in the northern states. In this chapter, the authors give an overview of leaf boundary examination; recognition of solid, debilitated, or impacted areas of the leaf; and arrangement of leaf sicknesses by involving various techniques for the vegetable plants. It is pivotal and hard for natural eyes to distinguish the specific kind of leaf infection with unaided eyes. Each plant leaf has various side effects of different infections. The calculation intended for one plant doesn't work precisely with another plant's leaf. Particular calculations for the vegetable leaves plant are expected to identify leaf sicknesses alongside the leaf boundary analyzer.

DOI: 10.4018/978-1-6684-6060-3.ch019

INTRODUCTION

The number of people living on this planet is steadily rising and is projected to approach 10 billion by the time the year 2050 comes to a close (Zhang, P. *et al.*, 2011). As a result of a growth in population, the need for food, crops, and other things related to agriculture will steadily increase, and it is anticipated that this demand will increase by around 80 percent by the year 2050. There are also fewer assets accessible, such as water and land, both of which are continuously decreasing owing to factors such as soil erosion and climate change, amongst other factors. In order for the globe to satisfy these objectives, there must be a reduction in the amount of crop loss that is brought on by illnesses that cannot be identified by the model that is now in use (Kia et al., 2005). A unique and empowered method of dealing with cultivating the board, accuracy agribusiness observes, gauges, and breaks down the requirements of distinct fields and harvests. The application of data and information advancements toward the purpose of developing intricate cultivating frameworks is what is meant by the term "shrewd cultivating." Instead of focusing on the stockpiling of information, gaining access to information, and making use of this agricultural business information, the focus is instead placed on the intelligent utilization of the horticulture-related data that has been obtained.

The anticipated model would provide an enhanced method for locating leaf diseases in a plant by making use of a collection of arranged datasets of leaf photos. An image that has been uploaded into the system will be compared to the test image in order to determine whether or not it includes any diseases. In the event that this is not the case, the ailment that afflicts that particular leaf is investigated, and steps toward treating the plant's leaves are taken. In addition, the germs that cause illness have also been linked to the analysis of the photograph that was carried out on the photograph and ensured by experts and academics.

This model provides an accuracy of the results obtained by using a variety of different group sizes, which was improved provisionally with the use of picture segmentation. In order to ensure a productive harvest yield, it is essential in horticulture to identify illnesses as soon as possible. Infectious diseases such as bacterial spot, late curse, septoria leaf spot, and yellow bent leaf all have an effect on the quality of the output. Techniques that are programmed and automated will check in order of plant diseases and will also assist with making a move after identifying the negative effects of leaf illnesses. In this article, we describe a Convolutional Neural Network (CNN) model and a technique based on Learning Vector Quantization for the identification and classification of diseases that affect vegetable leaf tissue.

When attempting to characterize the leaf infection, deep neural networks and data augmentation are two components that are absolutely necessary (Bouchikhi et al., 2013). It is possible to portray profound brain organizations as artificial neural networks (ANN) with multiple layers of complexity between the information layer and the outcome layer. There are many distinct types of brain organization, but most of them involve the same basic components: neurons, synapses, burdens, inclinations, and constraints. These components function similarly to the frontal cortices of humans and can be arranged in a manner similar to that of other ML calculations. The development of computer programmes that can acquire knowledge and make use of it to learn on their own has become the primary focus of the field of machine learning. The concept of "data augmentation" refers to a group of techniques that are used to artificially increase the volume of available data by generating new data of interest from previously collected data. This may involve making minute adjustments to existing data or employing more sophisticated learning models in order to generate new data that is of interest. Ranchers will be assisted in a variety of tasks, including increasing crop yield, through the application of technological developments in farming. The primary focus of this study is on the categorization of leaf diseases that are associated with important staple foods in the Asia Pacific area as well as other parts of the world (Nath, S. *et al.*, 2020). The changes that occur over the course of a lengthy period of time in land usage and the levels of salinity in the soil fundamentally affect the development of harvest yields. In addition, decreased crop yields can be attributed to a number of factors, including odd weather patterns and inefficient practices aimed at forecasting weather trends.

The model that we have suggested provides an enhanced method for locating leaf diseases in a plant by making use of a collection of arranged datasets of leaf images. An image that has been uploaded into the system will be compared to the test image in order to determine whether or not it includes any diseases. If this is not the case, the symptom is categorized as normal, the diseases affecting that leaf are investigated, and the procedure of treating the plant's leaves is begun. In addition, the germs that cause illness are related to the picture analysis that was carried out on the image, which was verified by academics and specialists.

LITERATURE REVIEW

Big Data (BD), Machine Learning (ML), and the Internet of Things (IoT) should have a significant impact on Careful Development in relation to the entire supply chain, particularly for rice production (Zhou et al., 2008). The development aggregate and type of appraisals consistently advanced past the notion that the rising development in IoT gives the rice sharp development framework new capabilities to anticipate alterations and see open entrances. The quality of evaluations received from sensors has a significant impact on both the outer presentation of the appearance systems and the use of ML calculations. Standard crop exhibiting methods are transformed into an optimal advancement of rice sharp development or rice accuracy improvement as a result of the utilization of these three components, which are used plainly to empower all areas of leaf-detection systems in agribusiness.

In this study, we do a framework of the nonstop style appraisals on adroit assessments regulating the period of time that is often spent in the process of producing, specifically in rice creation. We depict the experiences that were gained and the tangled position of the devices that were focusing on the computations in the vegetative leaf sharp turn of events. We do this by focusing on the activities of the contraption gathering in various circumstances, sharp water structure for vegetative leaf, expecting vegetative leaf disease detection assessment, following disease extraction., and focusing on the fine details of the leaf detection portrayal (Frosini and Bassi, 2010). This paper provides something of an arrangement that maps the games denied in rice careful development, the assessments utilized in experiences showing up, and the gadgets taking a gander at up computations used for each side interest denied withinside the get-together and post-conveying levels of the vegetative leaf. Taking into consideration the proposed sorting plan, our ultimate objective is that a green and solid set out some reasonable compromise of a piece of each of these three kinds of progress could be essential in transforming standard rice improvement practises into an immaculate manner of information in rice accuracy development. In conclusion, this research, in addition to providing a summary of the implicating conditions with everything taken into consideration and inventive overhauls closer to the maltreatment of more than one, reasserts withinside the development of monster bits of data in the agricultural industry.

In light of the evaluations of a variety of strategies presented in this research, a fresh-the-box new approach is proposed (Zhou et al., 2010). This method maps three pieces: enormous bits of information, investigation of mechanisms, and cultivation of shrewd vegetal leaf. In this configuration, devices concentrating on assessments that are employed are extremely dependent on the approach that is taken to gain experience. At the same time, the classification of assessments that are necessary is contingent on double the kind of liabilities mentioned in each gathering and subsequent to the production of some piece of fantastic vegetative leaf development. These devices, with a focus on computations, are used to complete the clever experiences supervising inspiration to assist ranchers in coping with liabilities discovered withinside the party and after creation levels (Dalvand, F. *et al.*, 2017). Taking into account the outcomes that were summarised within the focal regions, a device that focuses on computations and sharp progress could be used to work on the general demonstration of the vegetative leaf structure while preserving the torments or expenses that are concerned with the social affair of the vegetative leaf.

Drawbacks

↓ The approach is a bit time-consuming
↓ Narrowly specialized knowledge
↓ Maximizes the complexity of the problem
↓ Prone to Errors
↓ It is not an easy-to-use method.

SYSTEM DESIGN

The results of the segments that were in the previous layer are stored in the convolutional layers. These results include the loads and predispositions that need to be learned (Sun, C. *et al.,* 2021). The pieces that were developed and successfully addressed the information without making any mistakes are the mark of the enhancing effort. A series of numerical cycles are performed in this layer in order to disentangle the component guide from the information image. In addition, the diagram illustrates how the channel moved to start from the upper left corner of the information picture. The upsides of the channel then work to raise the qualities associated with each development, and the resulting additional qualities are the conclusion of this process. The information picture inspires the construction of an additional network of a more manageable scale.

Integrating Extraction: During the process of incorporating extraction, numerous components are eliminated by applying approaches that involve feature extraction. The goal of this endeavour is to depict the regions taking into account the portrayal that was selected. The breaking point is shown by the region's components, such as surface and assortment, and the region is cared to by the cut-off that defines it (Kim, B. S. *et al.*, 2007). This image depicts the area that was wiped out when taking into account the surface, variety, and shape. Although new significant learning algorithms have been presented for the purpose of identifying leaf contamination, current significant learning models such as VGG and ResNet are being employed at this time. One more essential picking-up design has been suggested in this manner to take into consideration the leaf spot thought framework. The primary concept is that the leaf region is where accidental impacts of leaf illness arise, whereas the establishing district does not include any relevant propaganda regarding leaf indisposition. In order to get an understanding of this, two subnetworks have been set up (Garcia-Perez, A. *et al.*, 2011).

The first one is a part division subnetwork, and its purpose in the component map is to add extra distinguishing characteristics to the secluded establishment, leaf areas, and spot localities. The second component is a spot-careful request subnetwork that is used to assemble the precision of the process. The proposed leaf spot idea association is first established by instructing the component division subnetwork with another image set. Within this new image set, the establishment, leaf area, and spot locality are discussed. This is done by connecting the spot-careful gathering subnetwork to the part division subnetwork, which is then pre-arranged precisely on schedule, and later mixed to make the semantic-level spot integrate enlightenment.

Figure 1. System Architecture

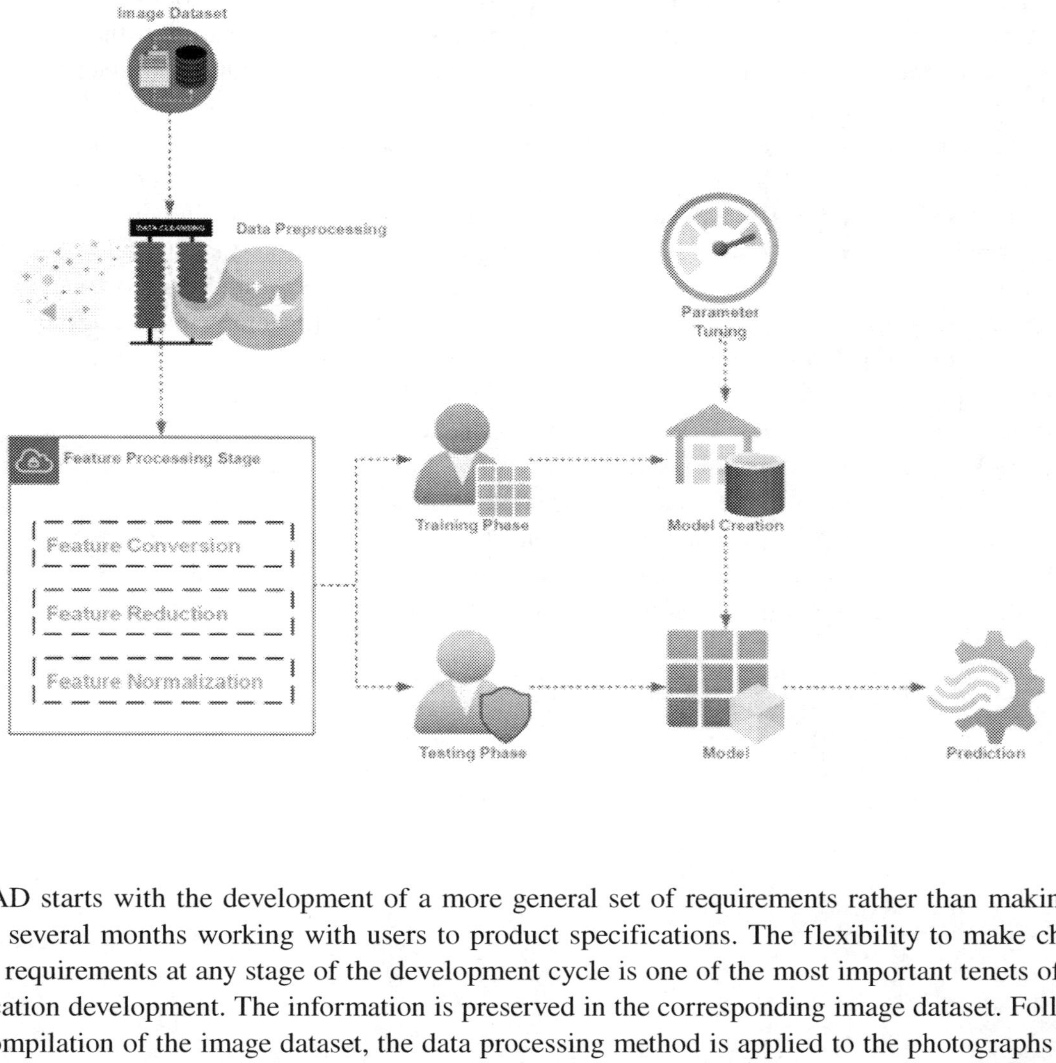

RAD starts with the development of a more general set of requirements rather than making you spend several months working with users to product specifications. The flexibility to make changes to the requirements at any stage of the development cycle is one of the most important tenets of rapid application development. The information is preserved in the corresponding image dataset. Following the compilation of the image dataset, the data processing method is applied to the photographs of the vegetable leaves. The stage of feature processing is reached, and then the training phase and the testing phase are split apart. After passing through the Training phase, the photos were put through model building, and parameter adjustment before the final prediction was made. After going through the training process, the models are applied to the photos before making a final prediction.

IMPLEMENTATION AND EVALUATION

Implementation

During the stage of the Jupyter notebook, the execution was carried out. Jupyter scratchpad has been met with an enthusiastic response in the information science community, to the point where they are gradually replacing Microsoft Word as the default writing environment for research. This is due to the fact that the Jupyter scratchpad is easier to use. The motivation behind the development of the Jupyter scratchpad is to provide a location that is more easily accessible for connection to code that is utilized in carelessly maintained evaluation or informative methods. Because Jupyter scratch pads themselves don't do anything to also investigate or explain strategy directly, devices like Jupyter diaries are less important for learning or educating in a vacuum. This is because Jupyter scratch pads are really just scratch pads. Think about what you hope to do with the help of Jupyter Notebooks before you get started on this model.

Keep in mind your end goal as you work through this example: depending on how you plan to use Jupyter journals, you may have the opportunity to skip over certain sections that are only generally applicable in certain circumstances. Jupyter journal is an open-source, user-friendly web tool that enables users to create and share documents that can include things like intelligent estimations, code, photos, and other such things. Clients are able to combine data, code, and representations into a single notepad, where they can then construct a user-friendly "storey" that they can modify and share with other people. Journals are types of archives that store both computer code (such as Python) and other types of text components such as sections, markdowns, figure 1, joins, and so on. The Jupyter notebook is widely used and recorded, and it provides a user-friendly interface for the creation, modification, and operation of notepads. The scratchpad operates as a web application known as the "Dashboard" or the "Control Board," which displays records that are nearby and enables users to explore journal archives and run snippets of code. The results are formatted in an easy-to-understand manner and displayed on the application.

Figure 2. Taking Database Image as Input

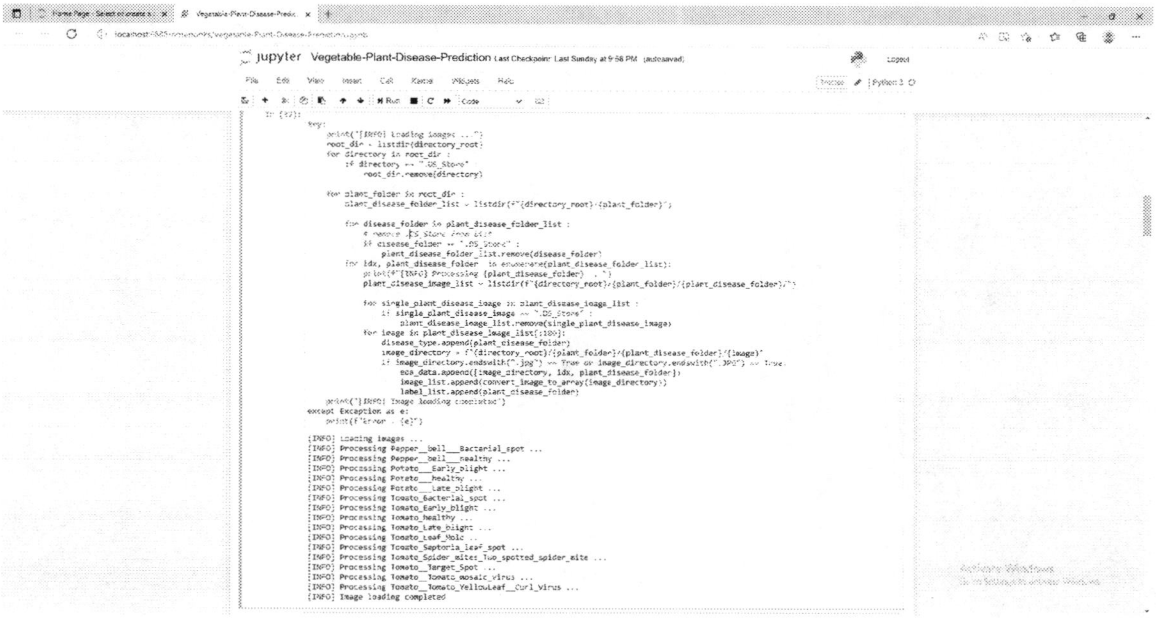

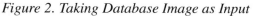

Figure 2 is the image dataset stored in the system. The applied code extracts the image from the dataset and is further processed through the system for final output and prediction.

Figure 3. Disease Found

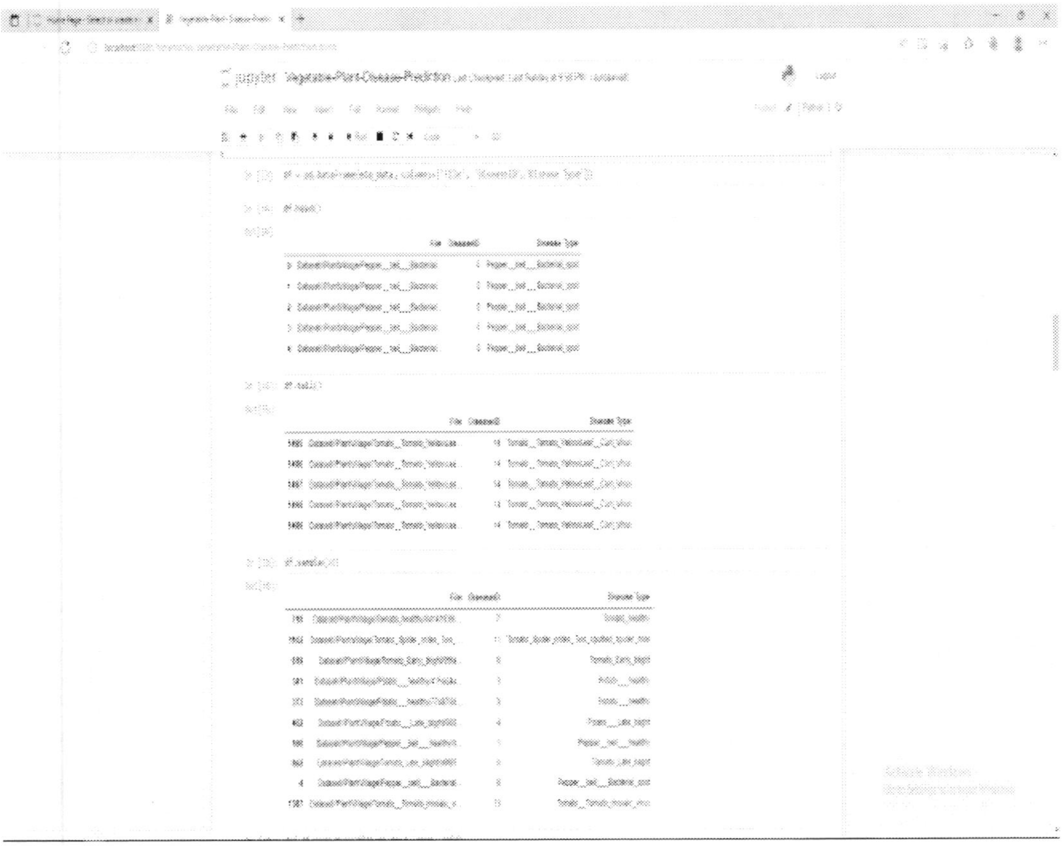

The diseases that were discovered in the input dataset are discussed in Figure 3. This figure also discusses whether or not the leaves have any diseases. The system is able to further identify the types of diseases present thanks to the modules it contains. These diseases manifest themselves differently on the various leaves.

Evaluation

The Jupyter notebook served as the medium for the re-enactment of the suggested structure. Python was used to create the lessons, and the results were saved in Jupyter's scratchpad. In addition to this, photographs of leaves were saved in a dataset so that input could be taken on them with virtually no problems. Using the various coding languages, separate designs were developed. At first, the import of Python work was finished, along with a few default photographs. These pictures were saved to the hard disc and then erased so that major information pictures could be imported after bringing in the essential Python works, the photographs that were captured as information was converted to clusters so that the code could be executed with virtually no difficulties. The images were obtained as a contribution from the root index, the code was run, and the results were obtained depending on the circumstances.

Figure 4. Table Content

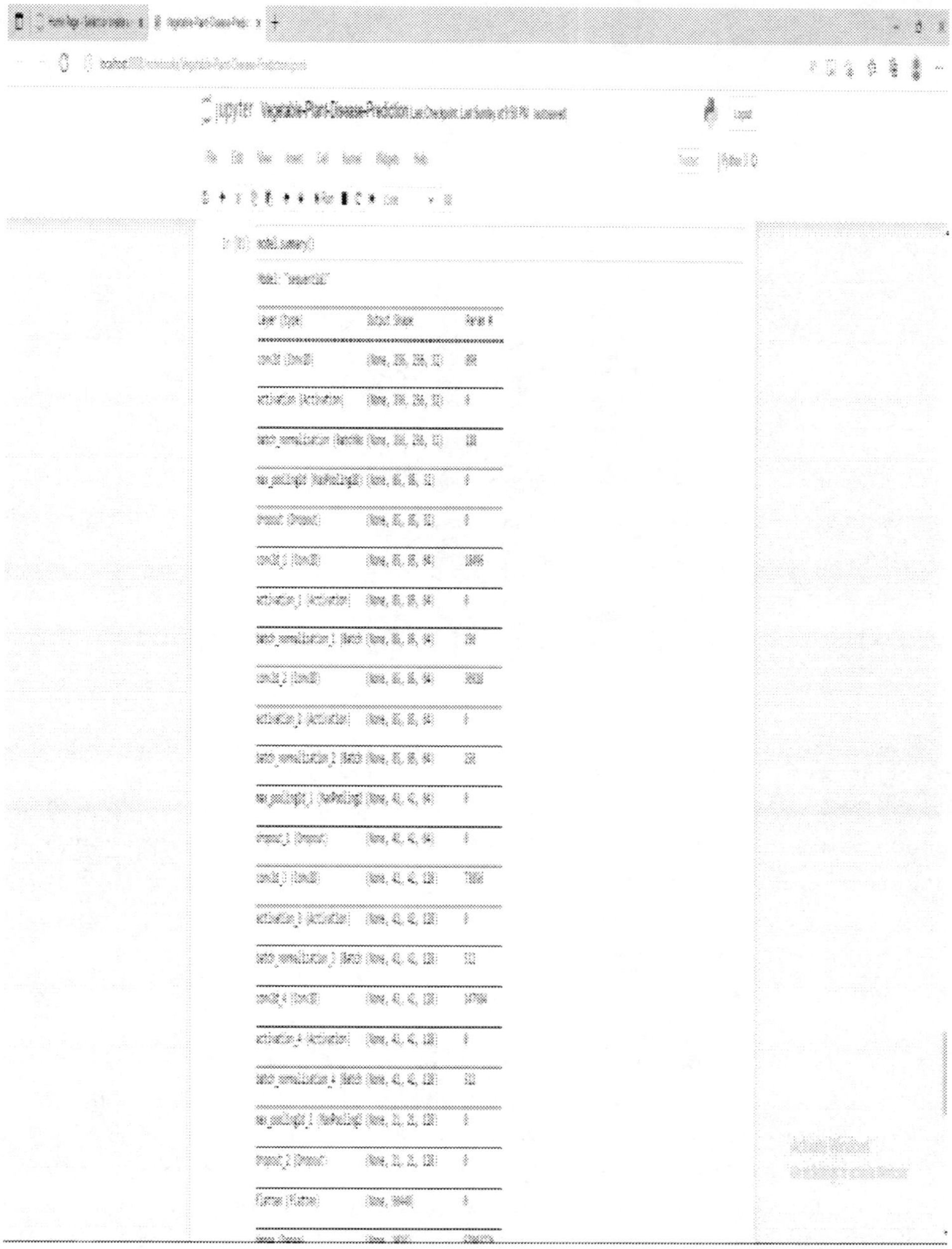

It is necessary to record all of the disorders that were discovered using the tabular format shown in Figure 4. The explanation of the diseases in the form of a table, with respect to the plants to which they are most commonly transmitted, aids in correctly identifying the diseases.

Figure 5. Dataset for leaves

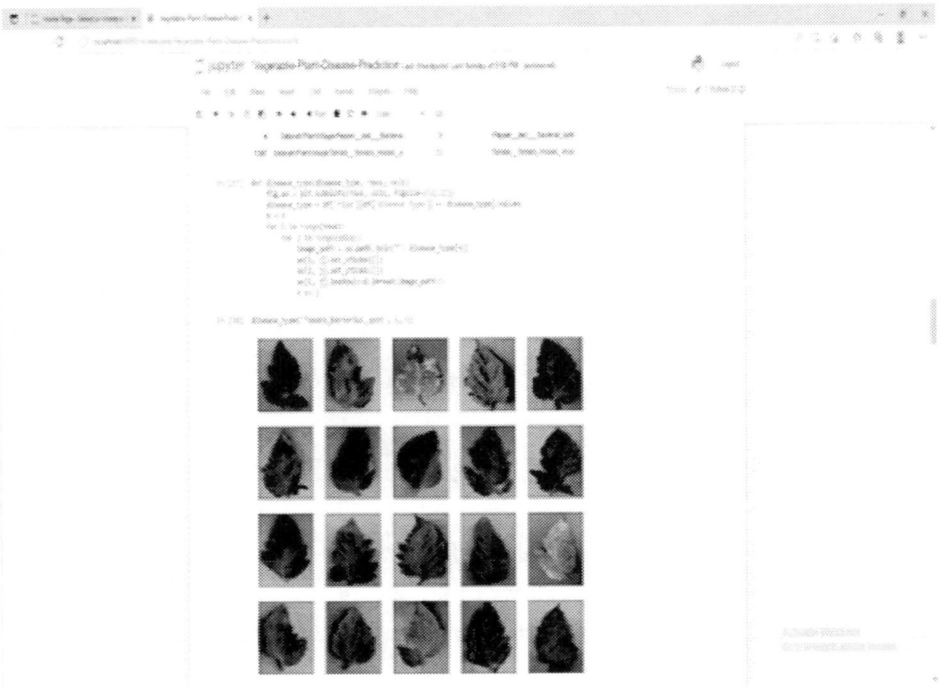

The diseases that were discovered are denoted in the output with various colours, such as blue, green, and red, among others, as shown in Figure 5. This set of leaves is the outcome or output of processing the input data of leaves or it may be the set that is given. In addition to this, the appropriate treatment for the disorders is also presented here.

CONCLUSION

We are interested in expanding this work to include additional categories that are not yet covered in our current review. As an example, we will discuss additional diseases, various features such as mean, deviation, smoothness, and kurtosis and shape features such as locale, edge, minimization and strangeness, and surface features such as imperativeness, entropy, homogeneity, thus fortress hand as well as some other soybean foliar anomalies. The findings also demonstrated that higher-order rates are a consequence of the tone and surface attributes. Additionally, with the help of the trials, we were given the opportunity to establish the minimum height needed for one of our approaches. Despite this, we are able to snap photographs from a variety of perspectives by utilizing a variety of focal points. The purpose of this study is to provide an organized description of the new applications of machine learning calculations and innovative devices for the classification of leaf diseases. In addition, this study proposes a framework that maps vast amounts of information, Deep Neural networks, and agricultural endeavours. The audit study reveals significant benefits to the development of crops that have implemented machine learning procedures and clever gadgets in the crop's dazzling cultivation. These advantages include improved yields and reduced costs. Similarly, as is the case with any investigation, here, in order to facilitate further work, we have additionally compiled the supplementary rules as a result of the findings collected from this survey.

Future Work

As part of our ongoing research, we intend to evaluate the effectiveness of deep neural networks in predicting an increase in the number of diseases observed in plant leaves. In addition to this, we intend to carry out our model using cameras that have a greater variety of functions and a higher resolution. Our model ensures that the results obtained through the application of picture segmentation of varying sizes are accurate to the highest possible degree. Due to the fact that infections have the potential to cause irreparable harm to crops, early disease detection is of the utmost importance. It is important to begin the process of detection as soon as possible so that appropriate treatment and action may be taken with regard to the specific crops. In this paper, we offer a method for the identification of leaf or crop disease that is based on deep neural networks and vector quantization.

REFERENCES

Bouchikhi, E. H. E., Choqueuse, V., & Benbouzid, M. E. H. (2013). Current frequency spectral subtraction and its contribution to induction machines' bearings condition monitoring. *IEEE Transactions on Energy Conversion*, *28*(1), 135–144. doi:10.1109/TEC.2012.2227746

Dalvand, F. (2017). Current noise cancellation for bearing fault diagnosis using time shifting. *IEEE Transactions on Industrial Electronics*, *64*(10), 8138–8147. . doi:10.1109/TIE.2017.2694397

Frosini, L., & Bassi, E. (2010). Stator current and motor efficiency as indicators for different types of bearing faults in induction motors. *IEEE Transactions on Industrial Electronics*, *57*(1), 244–251. . doi:10.1109/TIE.2009.2026770

Garcia-Perez, A. (2011). The application of high-resolution spectral analysis for identifying multiple combined faults in induction motors. *IEEE Transactions on Industrial Electronics*, *58*(5), 2002–2010. . doi:10.1109/TIE.2010.2051398

Kia, S. H., Henao, H., & Capolino, G.-A. (2005). Zoom-MUSIC frequency estimation method for three-phase induction machine fault detection. In *31st Annual Conference of IEEE Industrial Electronics Society*. IEEE. 10.1109/IECON.2005.1569317

Kim, B. S., Lee, S. H., Lee, M. G., Ni, J., Song, J. Y., & Lee, C. W. (2007). A comparative study on damage detection in speed-up and coast-down process of grinding spindle-typed rotor-bearing system. *Journal of Materials Processing Technology*, *187–188*, 30–36. doi:10.1016/j.jmatprotec.2006.11.222

Nath, S., Wu, J., Zhao, Y., & Qiao, W. (2020). Low latency bearing fault detection of direct-drive wind turbines using Stator current. *IEEE Access: Practical Innovations, Open Solutions*, *8*, 44163–44174. doi:10.1109/ACCESS.2020.2977632

Sun, C. (2021). A novel rolling bearing vibration impulsive signals detection approach based on dictionary learning. *IEEE/CAA Journal of Automatica Sinica*, *8*(6), 1188–1198. . doi:10.1109/JAS.2020.1003438

Zhang, P., Du, Y., Habetler, T. G., & Lu, B. (2011). A survey of condition monitoring and protection methods for medium-voltage induction motors. *IEEE Transactions on Industry Applications*, *47*(1), 34–46. doi:10.1109/TIA.2010.2090839

Zhou, W., Habetler, T., & Harley, R. (1982). Bearing fault detection via Stator current noise cancellation and statistical control. *IEEE Transactions on Industrial Electronics*. Advance online publication. doi:10.1109/TIE.2008.2004377

Zhou, W., Habetler, T. G., & Harley, R. G. (2008). Bearing fault detection via Stator current noise cancellation and statistical control. *IEEE Transactions on Industrial Electronics*, *55*(12), 4260–4269. . doi:10.1109/TIE.2008.2005018

Chapter 20
Implementation of Dynamic Gesture Interpretation of Sign Language for Impact on Hearing and Speech Impairment

Judy Flavia B.
SRM Institute of Science and Technology, India

Renuka Thanmai
SRM Institute of Science and Technology, India

Aarthi B.
SRM Institute of Science and Technology, India

Meghana Kesana
SRM Institute of Science and Technology, India

P. Charitharyan
SRM Institute of Science and Technology, India

ABSTRACT

Expression of languages is a basic survival skill to make conversations in this world. To convey thoughts and express themselves vocally and nonverbally, mankind relies on a variety of languages. Hearing-impaired people, on the other hand, are unable to communicate verbally with others. Because sign language communicates one's message through signs using fingers, arms, head, and body, as well as mannerisms, it has become the major means of nonverbal communication for the deaf. Sign recognition is an ideal step in communicating in this non-verbal communication. Much research on languages that signers use and study have been conducted based on their respective regional sign languages such as the American (ASL) and Indian (ISL). Identifying patterns in the nuances of these different non-verbal languages helps us understand what a person is trying to communicate via signs. Since not all gesticulations are universally centralized, a few of them are single-handed; a few others, particularly the majority, use both the hands (or a mix of both).

DOI: 10.4018/978-1-6684-6060-3.ch020

INTRODUCTION

Sign Language is a huge assist in effectively maintaining the social construct of communication. Learning to sign accelerates emotional development, improves attentiveness, and promotes language development (Chen and Zhang, 2016). Understanding the deaf and speech-impaired community is of massive importance (Zhang et al., 2016). To share and hold a meaningful conversation when you do not know sign language is a hurdle we plan to provide a solution to. In this paper, we attempt to contribute a major tool to help us educate ourselves by implementing efficient gesture recognition and pattern recognition software using Artificial intelligence and python using an application with a camera to advocate the importance of accessibility in this society (Zheng et al., 2017).

Nowadays, we are blessed with various tools to help us solve complex problems with simple solutions. Including sign languages in your language skill set will not only make you exceptionally better than most people, as it enhances your cognitive and spatial transformation capabilities, but it will also equip you to handle situations better, making you socially aware and increasing your EQ (M. M. et al., 2019).

Hearing loss strikes almost 5% of the global or 466 million individuals. By 2050, it is anticipated that over 900 million individuals or one out of every ten people, will suffer from hearing impairment (Shenoy et al., 2018). During this apparent rise in disability statistics, we ought to forge a bridge to join the gaps that'll continue to grow between educators and education-seeking individuals with hearing difficulties and hearing imparities (Bhagat et al., 2019). A model that integrates any generic sign language chosen by the regional sign language of choice into a refurbished model that allows two-way communication in real time between a learner and a teacher to aid both parties in better and quick communication, eliminating syntax and semantic difficulties by automatically generating sentence structure instantaneously is a huge step towards progression in the field of languages and artificially intelligent equipped knowledge representation (Nagendraswamy et al., 2016). A World Federation of the Dead study conducted in December 2021 shows that seventy-one countries have officially recognised sign language (Gangadia et al., 2020). The WFD calls for other countries to recognise their sign languages to ensure the inclusion of the deaf and hearing-impaired community (Zhao et al., 2021).

Suppose verbal languages and sign languages are bidirectionally translated (Safeel et al., 2020). In that case, it will remove comprehensive barricades in perception and interpretation, bringing us to the idea of integrating auto-generated captions specially fabricated from a sign language database in a video communication service platform. With the considerable rise of cashing in on telecommunication services over the COVID-19 pandemic, making an update to generate complete sentences instead of just word-to-word translation of signs makes it easy for the communicators to converse with ease while simultaneously also generating normal captions for the party which enables the respective option (Hein et al., 2021). A competent gesture interpreting compression codec application acts as a mediator between the hearing-impaired population and the general public, narrowing the communication gap (Jain et al., 2000).

PROBLEM STATEMENT

Existing systems pave the path for numerous initiatives to infer and analyse sign languages with the help of a sign language dictionary or a mediator. However, implementing real-time motion detection to decipher signs is a task. Technology-based detection of signs is the next step forward to instantaneously comprehending signs at a much faster pace in a more cost-effective and efficient way. Artificially integrated models save time and money otherwise spent on a third party. Manual deciphering also leaves room for human error, which can be minimised when we use a proper model of technology-based interpretation. Prevailing solution models also do not serve convenience in terms of accessibility and time efficiency. These are often unidirectional in terms of communication and not bidirectional. After some proper research, we found out that the main problem was never solved or the solution was inadequate. As two-way cognition is the benchmark for good conversation without any conversational barriers, our goal is to improve the existing system by launching a model with a holistic approach.

EXISTING SYSTEM

Currently, some live signers interpret signs and act as mediators across entertainment, educational platforms and news channels such as Doordarshan. But this practice calls for the expense of several resources that can be minimised with the help of an Artificial intelligent mediator to interpret and translate gestures. Since this method requires no perquisites of sign language knowledge for the passive listener, it is the most effective way of understanding the signer in real-time.

Figure 1. Methods of general acquisition of sign languages

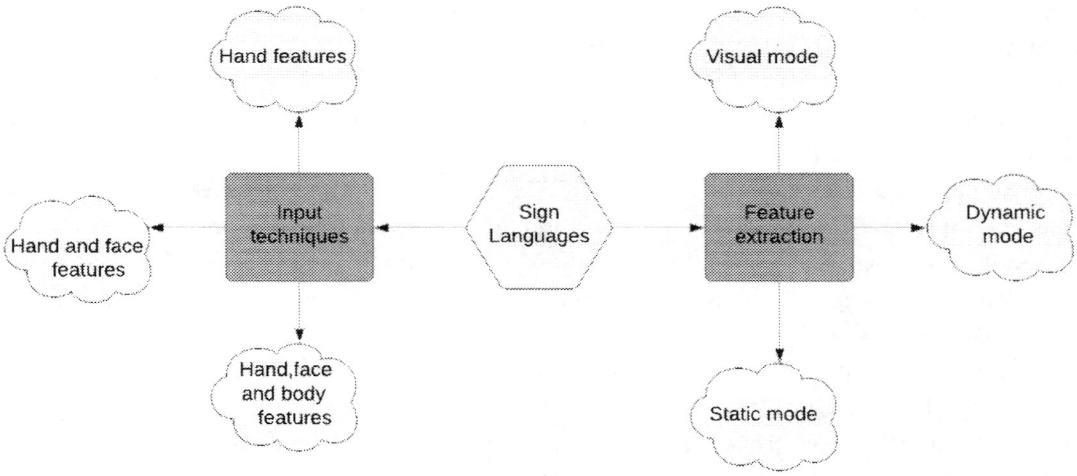

There have been a considerable number of temporary solutions, but nothing for the long run. People only rely on learning the sign language of their region (Indian, British, American, etc.) to communicate with people who are hearing and speaking impaired, which can get complicated and challenging for a new person to master in a short period. Concerning Figure 1, some claim that ASL is harder to learn due to its single-handed system, unlike BSL, which uses double hands for finger spelling. Regardless, these sign languages take the same time to learn and execute.

New updates have been seen in web conferencing platforms such as KUDO, a cloud-based tech that uses language as a source mechanism while translating to multiple languages of choice in real time. However, the language options are limited to a few popular verbal languages worldwide and only one non-verbal language (American sign language). Users are required to schedule a meeting, and live interpreters are available to their respective assigned meet in less than 2 hours. Since this requires the resources of humans at constant disposal, we aim to apply the ideology in a much more technical aspect which is readily available to consumers with limited or no buffer time. This is a great step in the right direction towards diversity and inclusion.

LITERATURE SURVEY

Gunawan et al. (2018); Sarhan and Frintrop (2020) define similarities between Sign Language Recognition and Action Recognition; both attempted to develop one of the top-tier models in Action Recognition, i3d inception, which is also a novel Action Recognition model with very high accuracy. The authors of (PMantas, J., 1987). propose an effective method for recognising isolated sign language words using only RGB data, particularly useful when depth data is unavailable. They used two-stream inflated 3D ConvNets for RGB and optical flow data.

Sharma, P., and Sharma, N. (2019); Du et al., (2018) designed to the RNN, LSTM, and GRU models to recognise gestures. The results show that these methods can accurately recognise hand gestures in real-time, particularly complex gestures. It was discovered that all three models performed similarly, i.e., all people's gestures were correctly predicted.

Borah, S., and Pradhan, R. (2020); Panwar (2012) gestured recognition in the case of static gesture and dynamic, the basic functionality of the gesture recognition system is to recognise gestures that are given as input in the form of images or videos.

Reference paper 15 aims to identify gestures solely based on shape parameters. The flaw in this method is that we have to define some parameters and threshold values by trial and error because it does not take a systematic approach to gesture recognition. The maximum parameter used in this approach is to test the number of images. Are based on the second hypothesis. Gestures are thought to be the most natural and expressive way of interacting with technology.

Using the SVD-PCA approach and a feed-forward artificial neural network, a new method for recognising gestures and body posture is defined and implemented. Various tools recognise the gesture, reveal its meaning, and take the appropriate action based on the meaning of the gesture. The instruments should be able to detect dynamic gestures in various lighting conditions and unprepared environments. Most proposed approaches have many advantages and disadvantages that can be expanded upon by identifying research gaps to improve existing approaches.

PROPOSED METHODOLOGY

As per Figure 2, this is a proposal of an idea to make it easy for an Artificial Intelligence-based approach that combines a technique for the acquisition of data through camera interfacing, image preprocessing through MediaPipe, where the MediaPipe Holistic pipeline combines separate models for the pose, face, and hand components, each optimised for its domain, train the Long Short Term Memory (LSTM) Model which will be used for classifying the sequence data, with the help of TensorFlow as well, which is an open-source software library related to Artificial Intelligence, and to help further we would be using the real-time detection of motion using OpenCV, which will be used for image processing and computer vision tasks. And to top this off, we will be adding a Metadata table in a cloud database where the existing sign language pictures (ASL, ESL, ISL) will be added to help the other models recognise them to give it the dynamic behavior (Fu, K. S., 1976).

Figure 2. Architecture Diagram for our Proposed Methodology

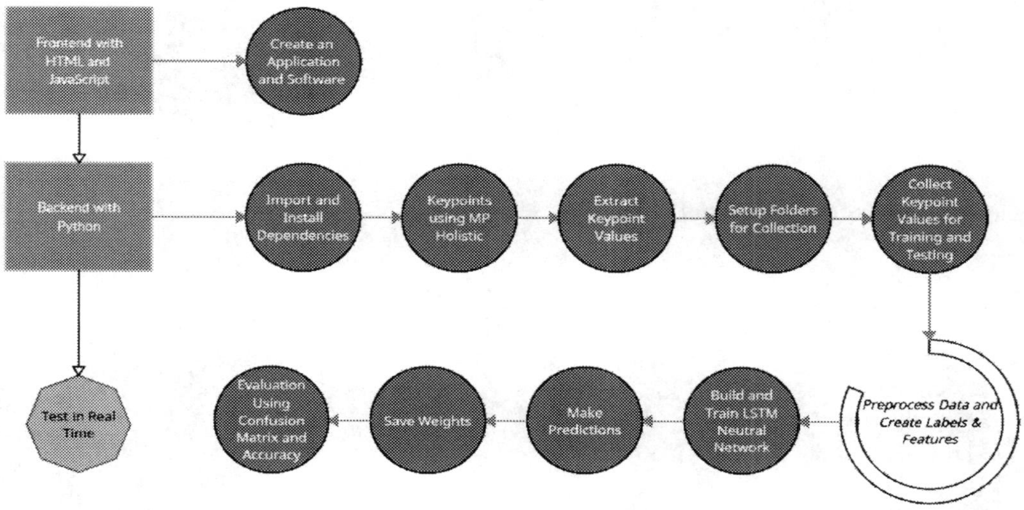

MediaPipe Holistic

MediaPipe Holistic, which provides a topology of the modern human condition that opens up new use cases, includes a new pipeline with improved placement, each real-time face and hand, and less memory transfer between their hypothetical backends, as well as additional support for three-dimensional exchanges depending on trading quality/speed. Concerning Figures 3, 4, and 5, MediaPipe Holistic delivers a combined topology of 540+ key points (33 stops, 21 per hand, and 468 face gestures) and achieves real-time performance on mobile devices when all three components are used together. MediaPipe is available on mobile devices (Android, iOS) and the desktop as part of the overall MediaPipe.

Figure 3. Reference for the working model of MediaPipe Holistic

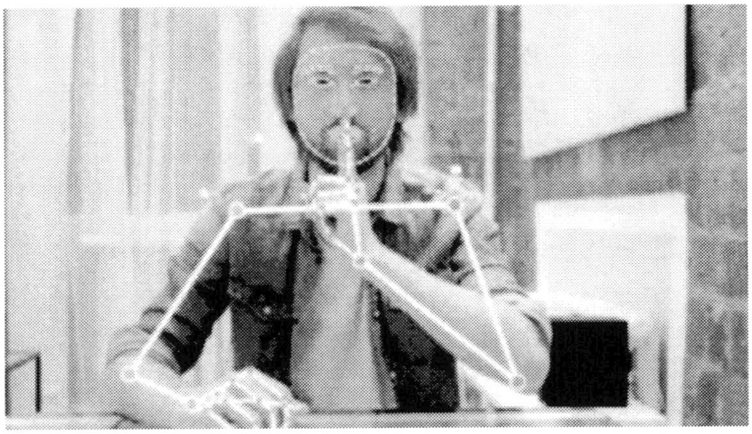

Here is the working model of MediaPipe holistic:

Figure 4. Reference for the working model of MediaPipe Holistic

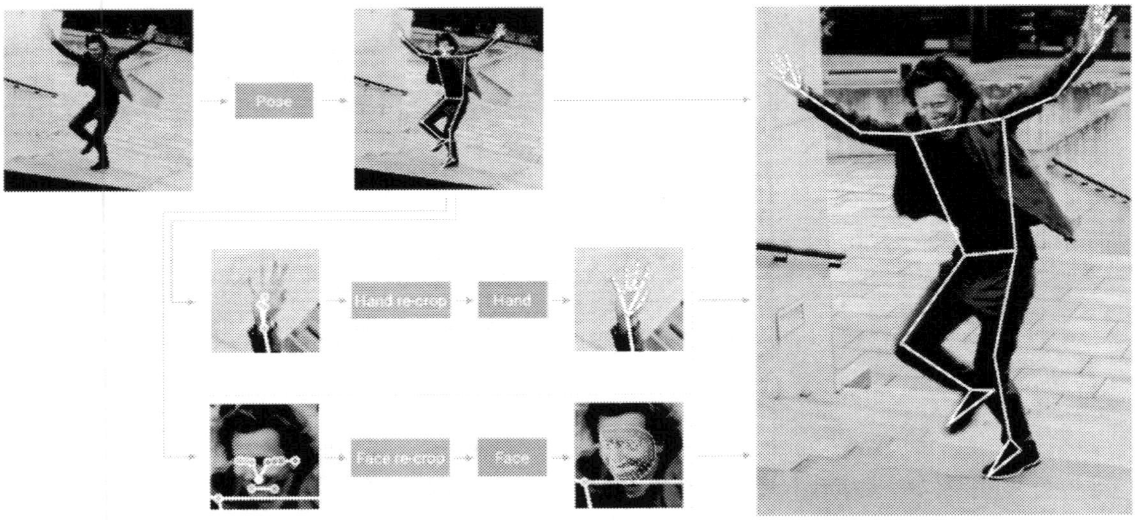

Here is the architectural diagram of MediaPipe Holistic:

Figure 5. Architectural diagram of MediaPipe Holistic

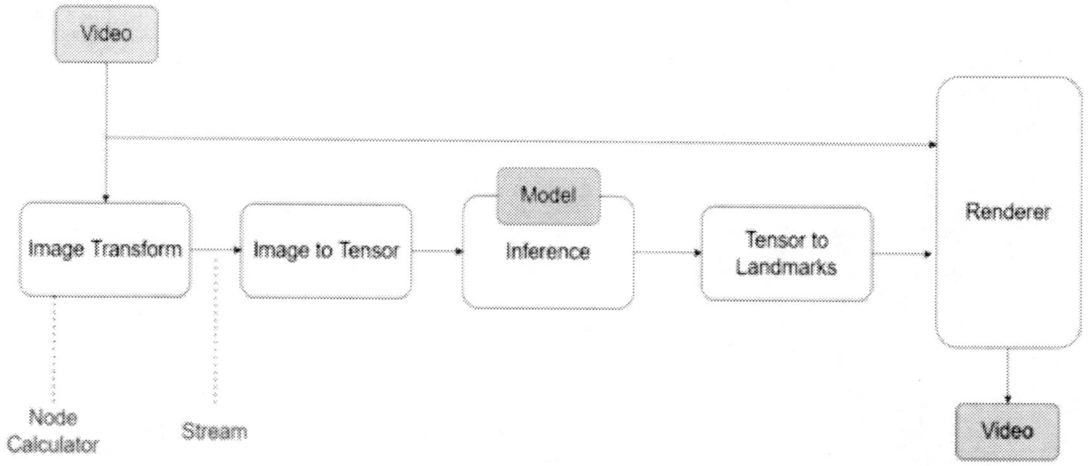

Long Short-Term Memory (LSTM) Model

Long Short-Term Memory (LSTM) is a model that enhances the memory of recurrent neural networks. Recurrent neural networks have short-term memory in that they allow previously determined information to be employed in the current neural network. For immediate tasks, earlier data is used. We can't have a list of all the previously reported information for a nerve node. In RNNs, LSTMs are widely used in neural networks. Their effectiveness should be applied to many sequence modelling problems in many application domains such as video, NLP, geospatial and time series.

Here is Figure 6, a graph for the rates of MediaPipe Holistic's performance compared to general pattern recognition.

Figure 6. Graph for Representation of surge in MediaPipe Holistic (in blue) being chosen over regular Pattern Recognition (in red)

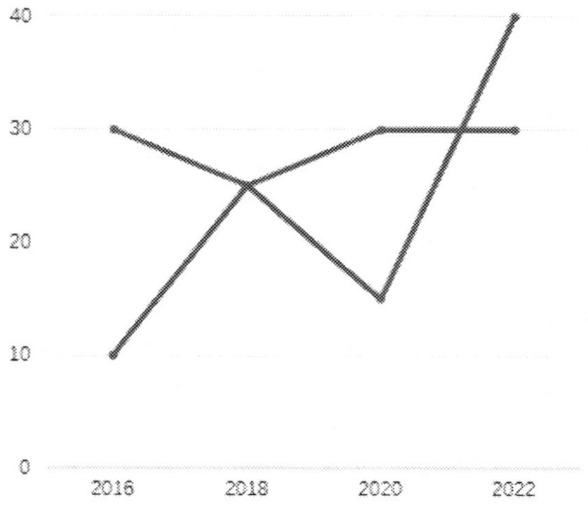

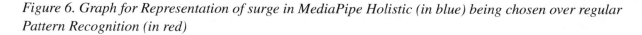

The concept of LSTM is very simple. In Figure 7, Tensorflow uses the same equation to compute and train a neural network.

Figure 7. Computation and training of Neural Network with formulae

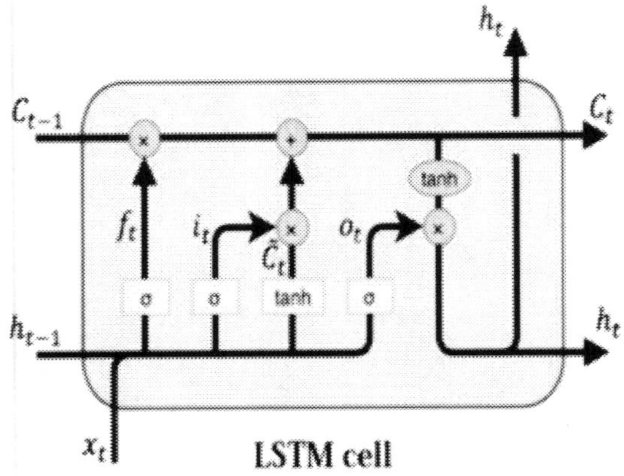

$$i_t = \sigma\left(x_t U^i + h_{t-1} W^i\right)$$
$$f_t = \sigma\left(x_t U^f + h_{t-1} W^f\right)$$
$$o_t = \sigma\left(x_t U^o + h_{t-1} W^o\right)$$
$$\tilde{C}_t = \tanh\left(x_t U^g + h_{t-1} W^g\right)$$
$$C_t = \sigma\left(f_t * C_{t-1} + i_t * \tilde{C}_t\right)$$
$$h_t = \tanh(C_t) * o_t$$

The zero (0) tells me that it's the first layer, W is the weight matrix, and b is the bias vector. Here is Figure 8, the architectural diagram of the LSTM model:

Figure 8. Architectural Diagram of LSTM Model

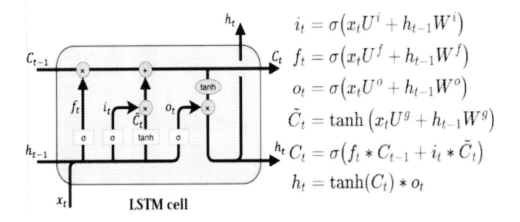

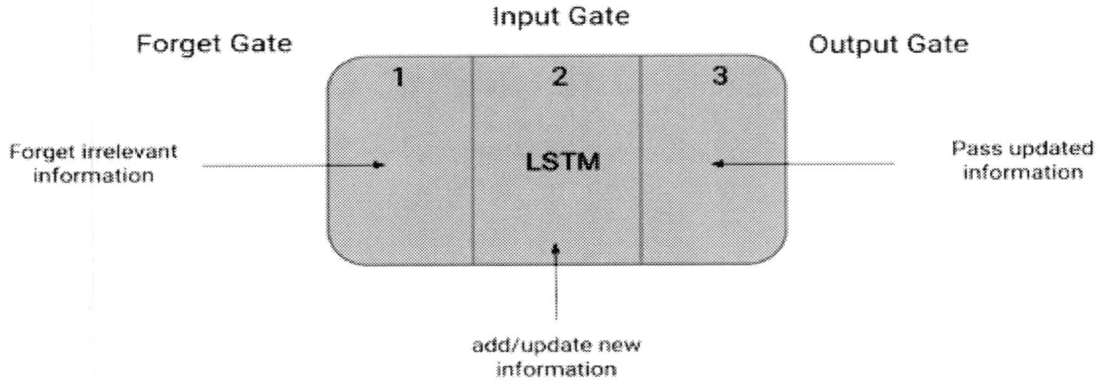

TensorFlow

TensorFlow is free, an end-to-end open-source machine learning platform with a large, flexible ecosystem of tools, libraries, and community resources that allows researchers to push the boundaries of machine learning while allowing developers to quickly build and deploy ML-powered applications.

TensorFlow is a set of workflows allowing beginners and experts to build machine learning models in multiple languages using intuitive, high-level APIs. Developers can use this model on various platforms, including servers, the cloud, mobile and edge devices, browsers, and other JavaScript platforms. It makes it much easier for developers to move from model creation to training and deployment.

We are choosing TensorFlow because it offers easy model building, provides robust machine learning production anywhere, and it sure is powerful experimentation for research.

The exact applied formula is equation (1), which would be softmax:

$$\sigma(x_j) = \frac{e^{x_j}}{\sum_i e^{x_i}} \tag{1}$$

And cross-entropy is equation (2), which would be:

$$H(p,q) = -\sum_{x} p(x) \log q(x)$$

$$d = \sqrt{\sum_{i=1}^{n} (x_i - y_i)^2} \tag{2}$$

where q(x) = Σ (x_j) or (1-Σ (x_j)) depending on whether j is the correct ground truth class or not and p(x) = labels which are then one-hot-encoded. In a cross-entropy equation, p(x) is the true distribution, while q(x) is the distribution obtained from softmax. So, if p(x) is one-hot (and this is so. Otherwise, sparse cross-entropy could not be applied), cross-entropy is just a negative log for the probability of true category.

Here is Figure 9, the architectural diagram of how TensorFlow works:

Figure 9. Architectural Diagram of TensorFlow working system

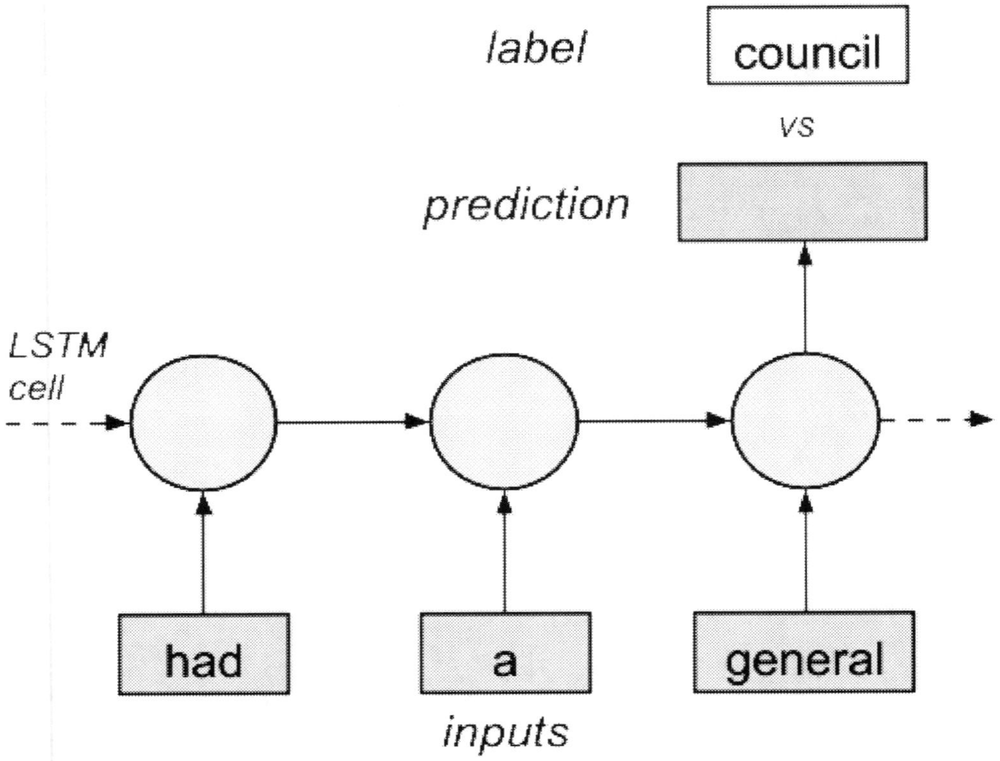

Here is Table 1, a data table for the statistics of Gesture Interpretation Application:

Table 1. Statistics of Gesture Interpretation Application

Particular	Rate
Accuracy	98.99%
Recognition	97.25%
Detection	99.99%
Processing	100%
Output	97.68%

ALGORITHM

With relevance to SVM, this is an improved Point Vector Machine Algorithm, and the following are the steps to be followed:

1. 1: PVM algorithm also predicts the classes. While one class is identified as 1. the other is identified as -1
2. 2: As with all machine learning algorithms, the business problem is transformed into a mathematical equation with unknown variables. By converting the problem into an optimisation problem, these unknowns are discovered. In the case of the PVM classifier, a loss function known as the hinge loss function is used and tweaked to find the maximum margin, as optimisation problems always aim to maximize or minimize something while looking and tweaking for the unknowns.
3. 3: This loss function can also be called a cost function because it has no cost when no class is incorrectly predicted. If this is not the case, error/loss will be calculated. The issue with the current scenario is that there is a trade-off between maximizing the margin and the loss that results if the margin is maximized to an extreme degree. A regularization parameter is added to bring these concepts into theory.
4. 4: Weights are optimised by calculating the gradients using advanced calculus concepts such as partial derivatives, as is the case with most optimisation problems.
5. 5: When there is no error in the classification, the gradients are only updated using the regularization parameter, but the loss function is also used when misclassification occurs.
6. 6: When there is no error in the classification, the gradients are only updated using the regularization parameter, but the loss function is also used when misclassification occurs.

Sample Analysis

This is how the output is to be shown by the software and application:

Figure 10. Sample for 'Hello' with its percentage of recognition

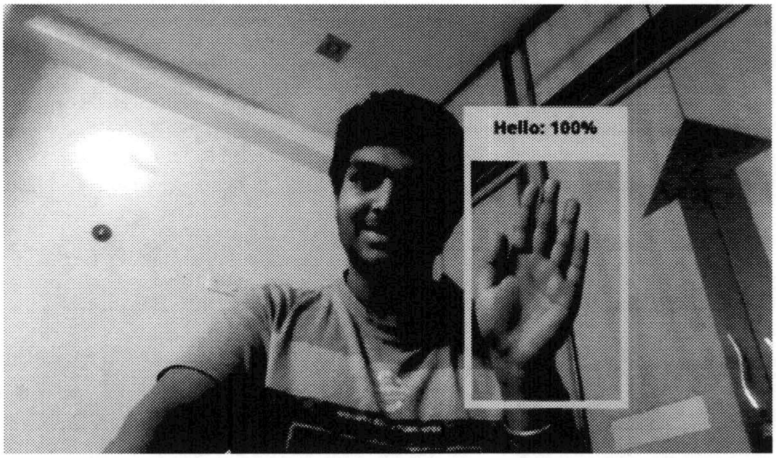

In Figure 10, the sign shown by the human is being recognised by the application with the help of MediaPipe Holistic and Tensorflow, which recognise the pattern. With its dynamic behavior (to Long Short Term Memory) and pre-fed datasets in the cloud, these patterns are recognised and give us an accurate interpretation, where in this case, it is 'Hello'.

Figure 11. Sample for 'I Love You with its percentage of recognition

In Figure 11, the sign shown by the human is being recognised by the application with the help of MediaPipe Holistic and Tensorflow, which recognise the pattern. With its dynamic behavior (to Long Short Term Memory) and pre-fed datasets in the cloud, these patterns are recognised and give us an accurate interpretation, where in this case, it is 'I Love You.

Figure 12. Sample for 'No' with its percentage of recognition

In Figure 12, the sign shown by the human is being recognised by the application with the help of MediaPipe Holistic and Tensorflow, which recognise the pattern. With its dynamic behavior (to Long Short Term Memory) and pre-fed datasets in the cloud, these patterns are recognised and give us an accurate interpretation, where in this case, it is 'No'.

Figure 13. Sample for 'Yes' with its percentage of recognition

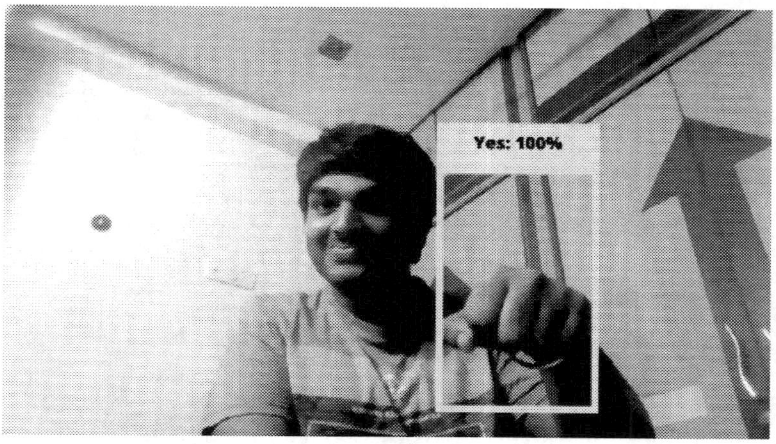

In Figure 13, the sign shown by the human is being recognised by the application with the help of MediaPipe Holistic and Tensorflow, which recognise the pattern. With its dynamic behavior (to Long Short Term Memory) and pre-fed datasets in the cloud, these patterns are recognised and give us an accurate interpretation, where in this case, it is 'Yes'.

Figure 14. Sample for 'Thank You with its percentage of recognition

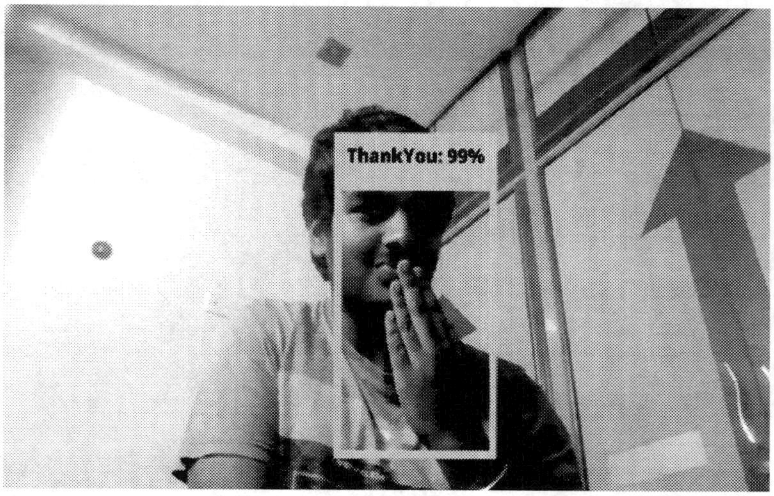

In Figure 14, the sign shown by the human is being recognised by the application with the help of MediaPipe Holistic and Tensorflow, which recognise the pattern. With its dynamic behavior (to Long Short Term Memory) and pre-fed datasets in the cloud, these patterns are recognised and give us an accurate interpretation, where in this case, it is 'Thank You.

Figure 15. Sample for 'Artificial Intelligence with its percentage of recognition

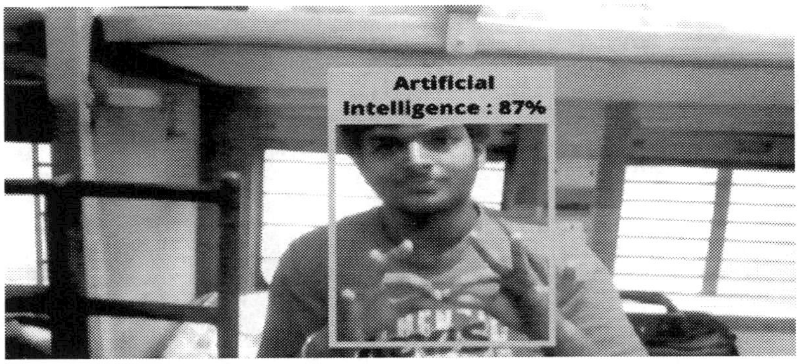

In Figure 15, the sign shown by the human is being recognised by the application with the help of MediaPipe Holistic and Tensorflow, which recognise the pattern. With its dynamic behavior (to Long Short Term Memory) and pre-fed datasets in the cloud, these patterns are recognised and give us an accurate interpretation. In this case, it is 'Artificial Intelligence.

Figure 16. Sample for 'Machine Learning with its percentage of recognition

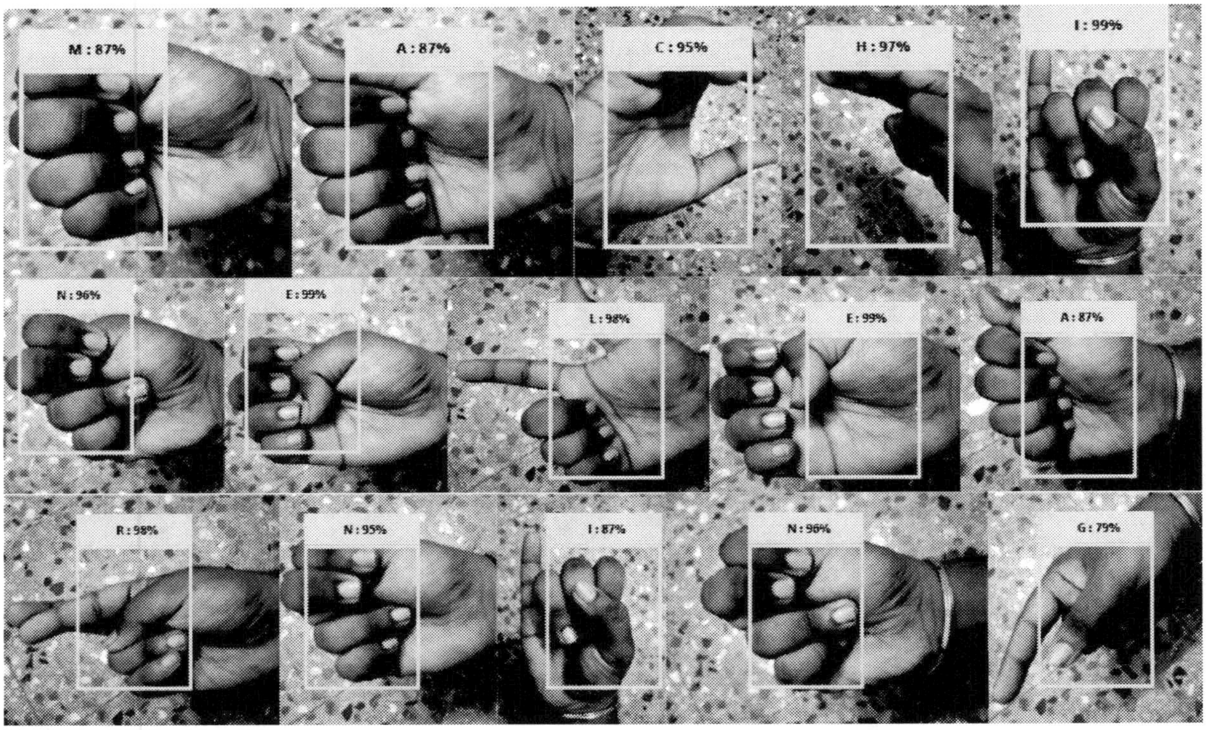

In Figure 16, the sign shown by the human is being recognised by the application with the help of MediaPipe Holistic and Tensorflow, which recognise the pattern. With its dynamic behavior (to Long Short Term Memory) and pre-fed datasets in the cloud, these patterns are recognised and give us an accurate interpretation, where in this case, it is multiple letters to form the word 'Machine Learning' (as not all keywords have a sign).

Figure 17. Sample for 'SQL' with its percentage of recognition

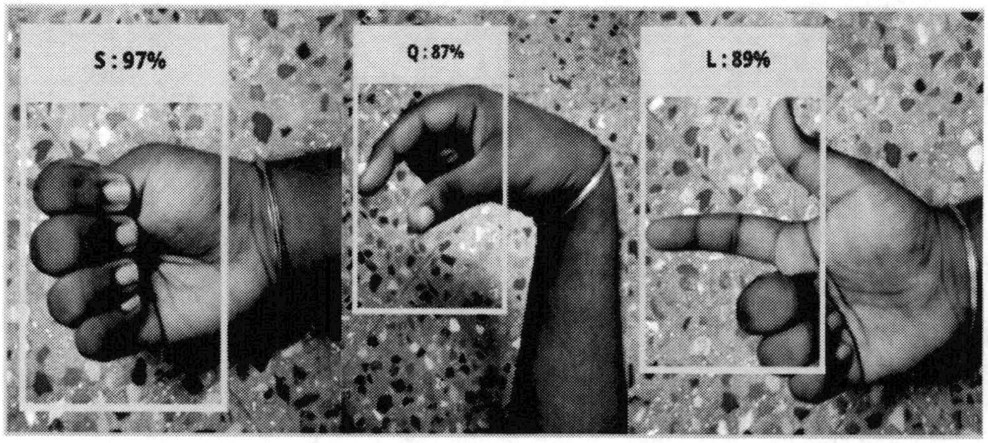

In Figure 17, the sign shown by the human is being recognised by the application with the help of MediaPipe Holistic and Tensorflow, which recognise the pattern. With its dynamic behavior (to Long Short Term Memory) and pre-fed datasets in the cloud, these patterns are recognised and give us an accurate interpretation, where in this case, it is multiple letters to form the word 'SQL' (as not all keywords have a sign).

Figure 18. Sample for 'Minimax Algorithm' with its percentage of recognition

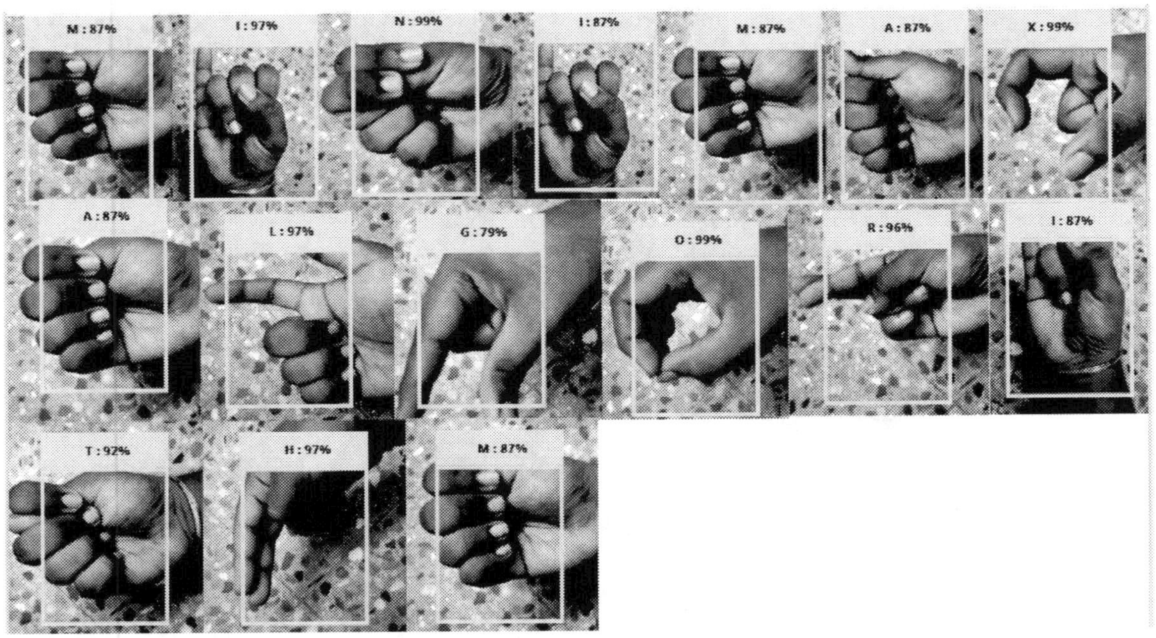

In Figure 18, the sign shown by the human is being recognised by the application with the help of MediaPipe Holistic and Tensorflow, which recognise the pattern. With its dynamic behavior (to Long Short Term Memory) and pre-fed datasets in the cloud, these patterns are recognised and give us an accurate interpretation, where in this case, it is multiple letters to form the word 'MINIMAX ALGORITHM' (as not all keywords have a sign).

CONCLUSION

To conclude, this idea expects to pass with flying colours, especially with the trials done with the program and software. We will be able to use Tensorflow to construct a deep neural network that uses LSTM layers to manage the sequence of key points as part of the model-building process. So far, approaches to detect sign language have been under two schools of thought. The first one is image-based recognition, where the image is understood by detecting and extracting certain key points from an image using either computer vision algorithms or supervised or unsupervised learning techniques (like the Support Vector Machine algorithm). A second way is a sensor-based approach where multiple sensors affixed to the person's body or hands are used to determine finger and hand movement patterns (motion, orientation, and velocity). This application expects to be helpful to people who are deaf and dumb. For further improvements, the ideas are to upgrade and create a proper front-end and backend, add a video-to-voice converter, and vice versa to make this application even more user-friendly.

ACKNOWLEDGMENT

Special thanks to Nicholas Renotte and Y. Rethvick Sriram for being a good help with the idea and programming clarifications.

REFERENCE

Bhagat, N. K., Vishnusai, Y., & Rathna, G. N. (2019). *Indian sign language gesture recognition using image processing and deep learning. In 2019 Digital Image Computing: Techniques and Applications (DICTA)*. IEEE.

Borah, S., & Pradhan, R. (2020). Gesture Recognition Approaches and its Applicability: A Study. In *2020 4th International Conference on Electronics, Communication and Aerospace Technology (ICECA)* (pp. 1458-1463). IEEE.

Chen, Y., & Zhang, W. (2016). Research and implementation of sign language recognition method based on Kinect. In *2016 2nd IEEE International Conference on Computer and Communications (ICCC)* (pp. 1947-1951). IEEE.

Du, T., Ren, X., & Li, H. (2018). Gesture recognition method based on deep learning. In *2018 33rd Youth Academic Annual Conference of Chinese Association of Automation (YAC)* (pp. 782-787). IEEE. 10.1109/YAC.2018.8406477

Fu, K. S. (1976). Pattern recognition and image processing. *IEEE Transactions on Computers*, *100*(12), 1336–1346.

Gangadia, D., Chamaria, V., Doshi, V., & Gandhi, J. (2020). Indian sign language interpretation and sentence formation. In *2020 IEEE Pune Section International Conference (PuneCon)* (pp. 71-76). IEEE. 10.1109/PuneCon50868.2020.9362383

Gunawan, H., Thiracitta, N., & Nugroho, A. (2018). Sign language recognition using modified convolutional neural network model. In *2018 Indonesian Association for Pattern Recognition International Conference (INAPR)* (pp. 1-5). IEEE.

Hein, Z., Htoo, T. P., Aye, B., Htet, S. M., & Ye, K. Z. (2021). Leap Motion based Myanmar Sign Language Recognition using Machine Learning. In *2021 IEEE Conference of Russian Young Researchers in Electrical and Electronic Engineering (ElConRus)* (pp. 2304-2310). IEEE. 10.1109/ElConRus51938.2021.9396496

Islam, M. S., Rahman, M. H., Sassi, R., Rivolta, M. W., & Aktaruzzaman, M. (2019). A new benchmark on American sign language recognition using convolutional neural network. In *2019 International Conference on Sustainable Technologies for Industry 4.0 (STI)* (pp. 1-6). IEEE.

Jain, A. K., Duin, R. P. W., & Mao, J. (2000). Statistical pattern recognition: A review. *IEEE Transactions on Pattern Analysis and Machine Intelligence*, *22*(1), 4–37. doi:10.1109/34.824819

Mantas, J. (1987). Methodologies in pattern recognition and image analysis—A brief survey. *Pattern Recognition*, *20*(1), 1–6. doi:10.1016/0031-3203(87)90012-4

Nagendraswamy, H. S., Kumara, B. C., & Chinmayi, R. L. (2016). Indian sign language recognition: An approach based on fuzzy-symbolic data. In *2016 International Conference on Advances in Computing, Communications and Informatics (ICACCI)* (pp. 1006-1013). IEEE. 10.1109/ICACCI.2016.7732176

Panwar, M. (2012). Hand gesture recognition based on shape parameters. In *2012 International Conference on Computing, Communication and Applications* (pp. 1-6). IEEE. 10.1109/ICCCA.2012.6179213

Safeel, M., Sukumar, T., Shashank, K. S., Arman, M. D., Shashidhar, R., & Puneeth, S. B. (2020). Sign language recognition techniques-a review. In *2020 IEEE International Conference for Innovation in Technology (INOCON)* (pp. 1-9). IEEE.

Sarhan, N., & Frintrop, S. (2020). Transfer learning for videos: From action recognition to sign language recognition. In *2020 IEEE International Conference on Image Processing (ICIP)* (pp. 1811-1815). IEEE. 10.1109/ICIP40778.2020.9191289

Sharma, P., & Sharma, N. (2019). Gesture recognition system. In *2019 4th International Conference on Internet of Things: Smart Innovation and Usages (IoT-SIU)* (pp. 1-3). IEEE. 10.1109/IoT-SIU.2019.8777487

Shenoy, K., Dastane, T., Rao, V., & Vyavaharkar, D. (2018). Real-time Indian sign language (ISL) recognition. In *2018 9th International Conference on Computing, Communication and Networking Technologies (ICCCNT)* (pp. 1-9). IEEE.

Zhang, C., Tian, Y., & Huenerfauth, M. (2016). Multi-modality American sign language recognition. In *2016 IEEE International Conference on Image Processing (ICIP)* (pp. 2881-2885). IEEE. 10.1109/ICIP.2016.7532886

Zhao, K., Zhang, K., Zhai, Y., Wang, D., & Su, J. (2021). Real-time sign language recognition based on video stream. International Journal of Systems. *Control and Communications*, *12*(2), 158–174.

Zheng, L., Liang, B., & Jiang, A. (2017). Recent advances in deep learning for sign language recognition. In *2017 International Conference on Digital Image Computing: Techniques and Applications (DICTA)* (pp. 1-7). IEEE. 10.1109/DICTA.2017.8227483

Chapter 21
Adapting Multi-Temporal Information for Optimized Ship Detection From SAR Image Dataset Using Transfer Learning Application

Deva Hema D.
SRM Institute of Science and Technology, Ramapuram, India

Agnes Faustina
SRM Institute of Science and Technology, Ramapuram, India

E. Aravindhan
SRM Institute of Science and Technology, Ramapuram, India

ABSTRACT

Synthetic aperture radar (SAR) can be reasonably mobile or area-based 2D high-resolution imaging radar. Unlike optical remote sensing, which can add bad climatic conditions and nights, SAR works day and night regardless of climatic conditions and can be used for military and civilian purposes. However, unlike natural images, SAR images duplicate the intensity of electromagnetic backscatter and require specialists to interpret the SAR images. In addition, finding interesting targets in huge human SAR images is tedious and very difficult, justifying the demand for low-cost automated SAR target recognition (ATR). Ways of supporting headed-oriented bounding boxes (OBB) have received progressive attention from researchers. However, most of the recently planned deep learning-based methods for OBB detection meet with the boundary separation downside in angle or aim for regression to attenuate this downside.

DOI: 10.4018/978-1-6684-6060-3.ch021

INTRODUCTION

As an illustration learning technique, the closest regularized mathematical space (NRS) formula is a good tool to get PolSAR Image classification accuracy and speed. However, the existing NRS method uses the colourimetric feature vector of the original PolSAR variance matrix (known as the Hermitian positive definite (HPD) matrix) for input. Matrix structures are not considered, but existing NRS-based methods cannot learn correlations between channels. The max pooling layer is employed to model the spatial relationship of options between one object and another to enhance the spatial feature correlations. To extend the accuracy of the target-recognized victimization rule to beat the limitation in achieving the accuracy of victimization-less attributes. Use the wealthy structure options to attain high recognition accuracy for SAR target recognition. (Z. Huang, Z. Pan, and B. Lei, 2017) In this paper, unlabeled residences have been found. SAR scene snapshots skilled with the stack convolutional autoencoder may be transferred to the SAR target. This is impressive and beneficial in case of a shortage SAR target; however, use a SAR picture without the proper label, such as the traits of numerous supply obligations are preferred or specific It continues to be doubtful if it will likely be dispatched to the SAR target. Transfer among training and validation records from use area matches to weaken hyperspectral image differences in a statistical distribution.

This experiment uses transfer learning to recognise SAR targets. Three convolution and max-pooling layers extract lower attributes. Then local and global aspects are highlighted. Several algorithms improve image quality. His study uses the transfer learning algorithm of the CNN max pooling layer for feature extraction and object classifier, which reduces memory and time.

This study facilitates target detection for lightweight two-stream convolutional neural networks (CNNs) and synthetic aperture radars (SARs). In particular, CNN's dual streaming provides low-level functionality through three alternating layers of convolution and bulk integration. Then follows, the two streams extract local and international features. The process uses the highest level of global integration to produce the most local features. Answer using the capital letters of persuasion. Exclude global features. Finally, combining the two streams to see the target. Therefore, CNN dual broadcasts can learn a wealth of features at many levels to achieve the highest accuracy of SAR detection. In addition, a CNN with two streams is much simpler than other common CNNs.

The results of experiments on the detection and recognition of moving and fixed targets (MSTAR) show that the proposed method improves visual accuracy and significantly shortens the number of model parameters. This paper raises CNN's two-stream targeted SAR (J. Xu et al., 2008). CNN has three segments, two streams. The first half excludes low-level features like integration and bulk integration. Next, two streams merge to extract multilevel characteristics. One broadcast attempts to unleash local features such a convolution layer, global integration layer, and central group layer. This journal will cite this paper. The two streams are integrated into the classification layer in the final phase. The dual loss feature is built to train CNN dual broadcasts. MSTAR dataset test results show that CNN dual broadcast achieves higher detection accuracy than other CNN-based methods (D. Deva Hema, K. Ashok Kumar, 2022). At the same time, CNN is much simpler with two streams. This is because we highlight the potential to extract relevant traits rather than tracking depth when designing neural networks.

High prediction complexity for large datasets Poor Application Performance Maximizes the complexity of the problem Difficult and Less Commonly used Higher correlation in prediction errors.

LITERATURE SURVEY

This article (2020) suggests getting an exact and error-free target (CAD model) when the target cannot be accessed right. This methodology utilized accessible target-related indirect information like two-dimensional designs, photo prints, web purchase representations, and plastic representations. In addition, this methodology presented a way to fix incorrectly created components or artefacts. It is highly scalable because it can undertake enormous amounts of data easily and rapidly. It works very reliably. Unstable and difficult to train. Behavioural patterns cannot be constrained in complex systems.

Y. Zhang et al. (2021) involve traditional target detection and identification methods on high-resolution synthetic aperture radar (SAR); images are normally less accurate and slower, particularly in sizable and complex scenes. The proposed article suggests ways to detect and distinguish targets based on visual attention to eliminate such shortcomings. The effectiveness of distributed optimization of inaccurate models can result in poor or excessive system performance. The amount of calculation involved in this article model training is large.

J. Wang et al. (2020) review of detecting and monitoring transferring objectives with Synthetic Aperture Radar (SAR) records is a frightening challenge that calls for contemporary processing strategies and superior SAR systems. The modern-day method ignores the blessings of the overall monitoring framework. It makes a speciality of the problem of both end-muddle movement goal monitoring and exo-muddle movement goal monitoring. The hassle is solved end-to-end. Superior empirical overall performance Reduces latency and improves detection efficiency.

J. Oh et al. (2021) involve frequent insurance of Earth observations at GEOSABM SAR, giving high-quality blessings in SAR ground transferring goal indications (SARGMTI). Moreover, the speed of the azimuth spectrum on the implementation is greater than the heartbeat repetition frequency (PRF), so the entire spectrum is splitted into numerous subgroups. H. Azimuth spectrum aliasing (ASA). The paper projects method of optimal mastering for brief and green use of extracted functions has the best attractiveness rate. Error-inclined prediction Error correlation faces excessive accuracy and reminiscence challenges.

L. Chen, X. Jiang et al. (2020) proposed Deep notion networks (DBNs) had been carried out for SAR goal detection in recent years because of the creation of numerous restrictions. Still, present DBN algorithms have a few troubles, including excessive schooling epochs, low detection rates, and complicated structures. There is. Therefore, this article endorses a set of rules based on regulated reformation and weighted norm-limited DBN, which is no longer difficult to peer at what is laid low with lowering function reuse.

L. M. Novak et al. (1997) were involved. Deep notion networks (DBNs) that had been carried out for SAR goal detection in recent years because of the creation of numerous restrictions. Still, present DBN algorithms have a few troubles, including excessive schooling epochs, low detection rates, and complicated structures. Therefore, we endorse rules based on guided reconstruction and weighted norm-limited DBN. It's no longer difficult to peer what is laid low with lowering function reuse.

R. Hummel (2000) advises a brand-new CNN-primarily based SAR goal detection community called SPAMNet. This is the posterior possibility of the goal elegance primarily based on Bayes' theorem in phrases of elegance-associated chances and earlier chances. SPAMNet includes subnets. CP subnets are skilled in examining elegance-associated chances. Highly powerful for complicated problems. The loss characteristic is optimized. Excellent studying skills. This technique no longer simply increases schooling time; however, it reduces community stability. Capital and running fees will boom significantly. High reminiscence intake for the duration of construction.

M. Liu et al. (2007) Speckle noise greatly impacts the category of floor objectives in SAR images. This paper proposes a deep network-primarily based category approach to remedy this problem using a two-degree mixed CNN architecture. This consists of speckle elimination subnetworks and category subnetworks. Use the denoised SAR photo of the goal from the speckle elimination subnet as education information. Better self-mastering competencies Fast and efficient, but as correct as present-day algorithms. It may be scaled in share to the quantity of educational information available. Identifying information inconsistencies may be very difficult. Diminishing returns of performance. Inaccurate fashions can bring about negative or immoderate gadget performance.

M. Liu et al. (2013) proposed a transferring goal monitoring approach based on the progressed GM-PHD lter within the round SAR gadget. A multiple-goal monitoring version is set up for the round SAR gadget. The progressed categorized GMPHD Iter with an adaptive goal delivery depth is furnished to recognize the transferring goal monitoring and the residual litter removal concurrently within the SAR image. Reduces the assets used for processing purposes. Effectiveness for allotted optimization Better Self-Learning capabilities. Face demanding situations in each accuracy and reminiscence. Have to go through enormous fine-tuning of the check dataset parameters.

D. Hong et al. (2019) proposed a feature-primarily based speckle discount set of rules to beautify the goal shape whilst suppressing SAR picture interference. By combining low-ranked residences with stable perspective continuity, the proposed (CID: 2) pLSCE set of rules complements goal traits via speckle noise separation, which poses a complex. Sensitive to the traits of education data. High complexity and protection attempt When education a model, it's far very computationally intensive.

N. Yokoya et al. (2019) aim to explain, study and examine the state-of-the-art assessment for computerized goal detection in Synthetic Aperture Radar Images (SAR ATR). The motive isn't to create a complete evaluation of the giant literature but to recognize extraordinary processes to enforce the SARATR machine in a single place. Performance may be included as a characteristic of the machine layout process. It additionally allows SARATR machine layout overall performance and machine overall performance benchmarking, saving time and money.

Qingdong Wanget al. (2016) propose a synthetic aperture radar (SAR) target detection approach that incorporates multiple characteristics and filters. The SAR pictures were quantified using Zernike moments, nuclear principal component analysis (KPCA), and monochromatic signals. The aspects of the SAR target geometries, projector attributes, and decaying visual functions are categorized.

S. Chen et al. (2017) propose a Synthetic Aperture Target Detection (SAR) approach that mixes more than one feature and more than one classifier. Characterize SAR pictures using Zernike moments, kernel fundamental factor analysis (KPCA), and monographic signals. The three features describe the geometry feature, projection feature, and photograph decomposition feature of the SAR goal. It describes the geometry of the goal and has the blessings of invariant translation and rotation. The feature has a clean body which means and displays the info about the goal. The parameters of the check dataset want to be substantially fine-tuned.

J. Pei et al. (2018) propose a brand-new stop-to-stop two-flow fusion community to take complete gain of the diverse traits received from HRRP records and SAR photograph modelling for SAR goal detection. The proposed goal detection technique affords a vast overall performance improvement. There is a decreased pace limit.

S. Tian et al. (2015), a deep era, in addition to the reputation version, is derived primarily based totally on Conditional Variational Auto-encoder (CVAE) and Generative Adversarial Network (GAN). A characteristic area for SAR-ATR is constructed based on the proposed CVAE-GAN version.

ARCHITECTURE DIAGRAM

Project Module and Methodology

The envisioned system is a multiscale network preferred for SAR image capture. This particular type of system is quite advantageous in two facets- Firstly, it enhances the rationality of a structural element, and an MSCM helps to delineate the dimensional relationship dealing with signals flanked by one object and a variant. With this module, combining a feature from different locations, we can achieve equal features. The analysis for this procedure proved effective compared to other similar methods. A key note is that all competitive methods utilize many features in their procedure by incorporating scatter information, image features and polarimetric data. Although the method exercised is the original PolSAR data feature. The proposed system is ensured to be productive even with minimal features.

Figure 1. Detailed architecture diagram of the proposed system

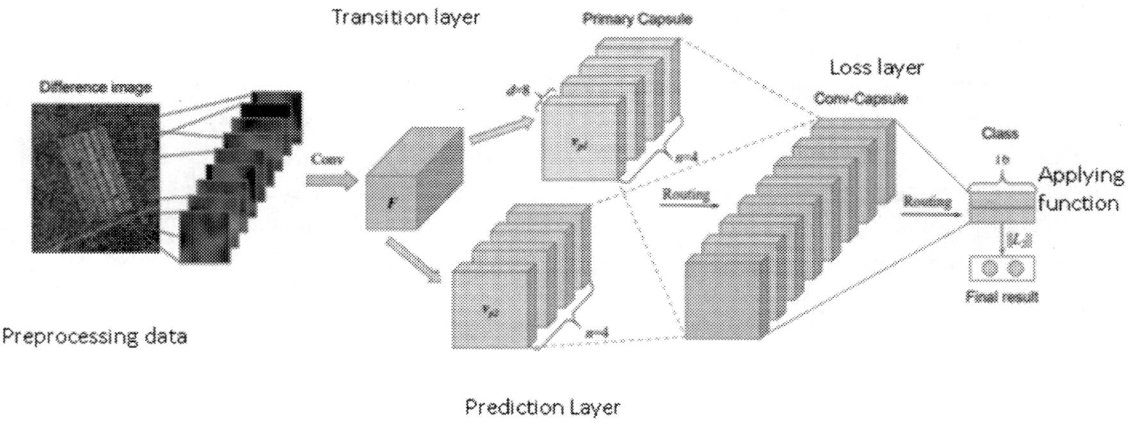

Proposed Methodology

Several deep learning algorithms came into existence to solve real-world problems. Transfer Learning is a popular method in deep learning which enables us to build accurate models within a short timeframe). The architecture diagram of the proposed model is given in Figure 1. The model does not learn from the beginning but relies on the learning patterns identified when solving various problems. That way, we can strengthen our previous insights and prevent beginning from scratch.

During the reuse of a model that has already been trained on a new problem, knowledge is obtained by solving a problem and solving it to another similar problem. There are many advantages of transfer learning; by using minimal datasets, it can achieve good performance with higher accuracy. Also, we can save much time when compared with other algorithms. Transfer learning is particularly very useful when you have a small training dataset.

1. Choose an appropriate learning model.
2. Use Size-Similarity Matrix to classify the problem.
3. Fine-tune the model

This paper offers a light-flowing CNN for the popular Synthetic Aperture Radar (SAR) pre-training model. CNN RST retrieves low-level abilities through three convolution and max-pooling layers. Then, nearby and global abilities are extracted from streams. One employs maximum global pooling to extract nearby skills, whereas the other uses large-stride convolution kernels to extract global skills. Finally, popularity from both streams is pooled. Two-circle CNN can use rich multilevel abilities to boost SAR popularity accuracy.

In pre-trained, the data, which is now connected to grayscale images, is not under the process of detection.

- The image initially has to be reshaped in the required feature extraction. In this model, we apply a transfer learning algorithm for feature extraction from the initial steps. We include feature parameters to the modelling by adding a few layers before. Thus, including and expanding the model's capabilities to interpret the fully extracted features of the data set combinations.
- In the model, the loaded image with the classifier part with the specified shape of images is our new dataset.
- After classifying and categorizing the images accordingly, we use the new available function in Keras API that helps us define a new model with the classifier Flatten layer.
- In the pooling layer and then the Dense connected layer, which predicts the probability.
- The weight of the previous and newly classified models will be trained together for the new dataset (the one with classified features).

First, to calculate the layers of the convolutional layers in Keras API.

- To calculate the output layers, the following formula is used:

$$\text{output} = \frac{\text{input} - \text{kernel size} + 2 * \text{padding}}{\text{stride}} \tag{1}$$

The input layer is classified into three dimensions [x1,x2,x3].To calculate the first layer sigmoid function is applied as the activation layer.

$$a = \sigma\,(Wx + b) \tag{2}$$

- The dimensions of W is {x,y) and dimensions of b(x,z). Therefore we arrive at a confined relational function:

W[L]:(n[L], n[L-1]) (3)

b[L]: (n[L], 1) (4)

- Here, L is the layer, and n[L] is the number of layers.
- The calculation of the convolutional layer is different for different volumes. We generalize the formula of calculating the cube layer and number of param for each filter to:

one cube = k* k*n [l – 1] +1 (5)

total params = one cube * filter num= (k * k * n[l – 1] + 1) * n[l] (6)

Here, k is the kernel size, n[L] is the number of filters in layer L and n[L-1] is the number of filters in layer L-1, which is also the number of channels of the cube.

The new classified dataset model is now set for further feature removal. Further, we extract the image, find the ship detected, and locate the ship's coordinates in the SAR data image.

- First, the function of cutting the removal of unwanted noise features in our dataset, we remove the land and port features, which include soil and tree, house and boundary.
- Second, the function is not near the feature we find and locate the ship we find which is not near the land features. Since there could be a possibility of ships near the boundary and mostly away from the boundary in the far waters. We find and locate the ship and analyze the feature with our dataset.
- After extracting and detecting the ships in the SAR image, we use the show ship function to help us locate the ships in the image with their respective coordinates.

Preprocessing

Normal or logical-mathematical functions for two or more images are optional. Operators are used in stages. The pixel output value depends only on the pixel input value. Therefore, the size of the images should be the same. The big advantage of using math functions is that they are quick and easy to use. As a mathematical operation, logical operations are often used to combine two or more binary images. Sane operators often use digital photography in a somewhat clever way. Convert color images to grayscale to reduce computer complexity: In some cases, losing unnecessary information in your photos can reduce space and computational complexity. For example, convert a color photo to a gray image. This is because, in many cases, no color is needed to recognize and convert the image. Grayscale is enough to see things. Color images accommodate more information than black-and-white images, which adds uncalled complications and can occupy additional memory (the color image has three channels, and converting to grayscale reduces the number of pixels processed). An important obligation inherent in some machine learning algorithms, such as CNN, is the need to scale the images in the database to a compact size. This means the image must be pre-scanned and scored with the same width and length before running the training algorithm. Another common preprocessing method is extending an existing database with a corrupted version of an existing image. Measurements, rotations, and other appropriate changes are common. This extends the database and exposes the neural network to different images. This makes it easier for the model to see things in some way.

Edge Detection

Edges are an important local change in image robustness. Edges usually appear at the boundaries between two different areas in an image. The apparent edge of the image is a straight line between black and white paper. From our view, the black and white pixels are suddenly swapped. If zoomed in on the edges as in the image, we find that the edges between the black and white areas of the image are blurred. The Canny edge detection method uses a series of steps, some of which include other types of edge detection. The function image. Feature. Canny () performs the following steps: Use Gaussian blur (indicated by the Sigma parameter, see Getting Started) to remove stones from the image. (Therefore, do not perform a blur action when performing edge detection for this function.) Sobel edge detection is performed in both x and y dimensions to determine the edge thickness of the image. Sobel edge detection calculates the output of one curve equal to the slope between the light and dark areas of the image. It then determines the height of the other curve, which is interpreted as the pixel position of the edge. The pixel is highlighted but removed because it is far from the edge. This is called non-maximum suppression and results in thinner lines than other methods. Double thresholds are used to determine possible edges. This is where extra softer pixels than necessary, caused by noise and color shifts, are removed. If the number of pixels in the gradient is based on Sobel and the difference is greater than the maximum threshold, it is considered a Solid Edge candidate. It closes when the gradient falls below the minimum. If the gradient is at the center, the pixel is regarded as a candidate pixel with a weak edge. Hysteresis is the final process for edge detection. Here, weak candidate pixels are tested, and if they are attached to solid candidate pixels, they are observed as edge pixels. The remaining weak unconnected candidates are closed.

Ship Detection

Transfer learning is a research problem in the field of machine learning. Retaining the knowledge we have acquired while solving one problem and applying it to another related problem. Transfer learning is about using feature presentations from a pre-trained model, so there is no need to train a new model from scratch. Pre-trained models are usually trained in large databases, a common measure of computer vision. Weights obtained from models can be reused in other computer vision functions. These models can be used directly to create new job predictions or be integrated with the new model training process. Incorporating pre-trained models into the new model reduces training time and a lower standard error. Transfer learning is especially important if you have a small training database. In this case, you can use, for example, to use weights from previously trained models to launch new weight weights. As you will see later, the transfer of reading can also be applied to the problems of processing natural language. During these three comparative processes, most noisy points are caused by vegetation and are incorrectly classified and developed.

RESULT AND DISCUSSION

In this paper, we detect the location of ships in the data and their coordinates. Firstly, the training of the model for the algorithm on the features of the ship and finding the accuracy of the training and testing data. Figure 2 shows the category of a ship. The image is first detected and classified as an object and classified as its class. The original and detected images are given in Figure 3 and Figure 4, respectively. Then the data is trained accordingly. The algorithm takes in the modelled data and discovers the images of the ships and their location coordinates in the image providing details of the ship and coordinates. The resultant images are shown in Figure 5.

In addition, many low-density pixels in the lower right corner are incorrectly separated into high-density. In the proposed method, the final result differentiates between the landscapes and water bodies and recognizes the shape and structure of the ship with the help of the modelled data. Since the clarity of the image is increased, the algorithm's accuracy is high and clear even when using fewer parameters for recognition and a capsule network in transfer learning. By combining the results obtained from OSM and OSD methods, results can be enhanced better. The accuracy and loss graphs are shown in Figure 6 and Figure 7, respectively.

Figure 2. Classified category of ship

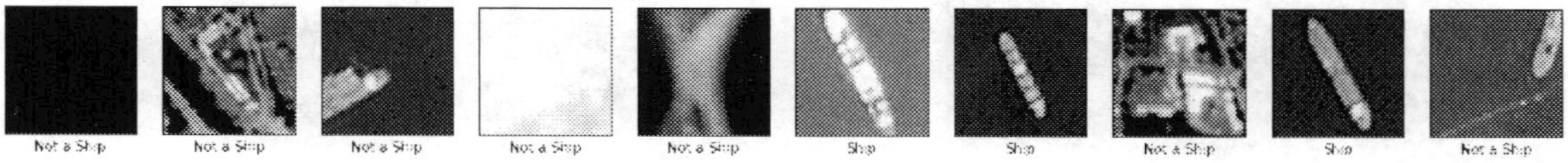

Figure 3. Original image

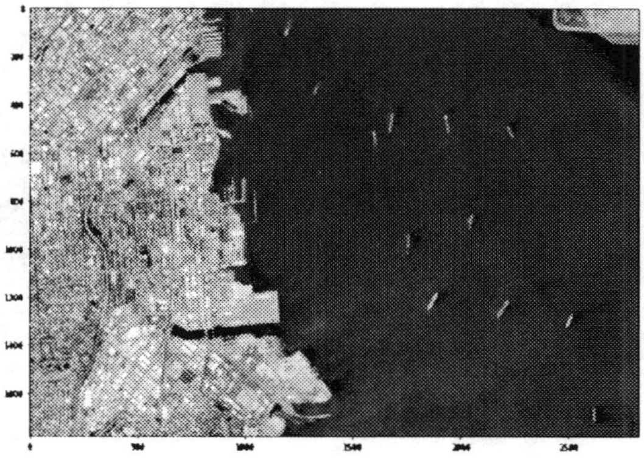

Figure 4. Detected ship images

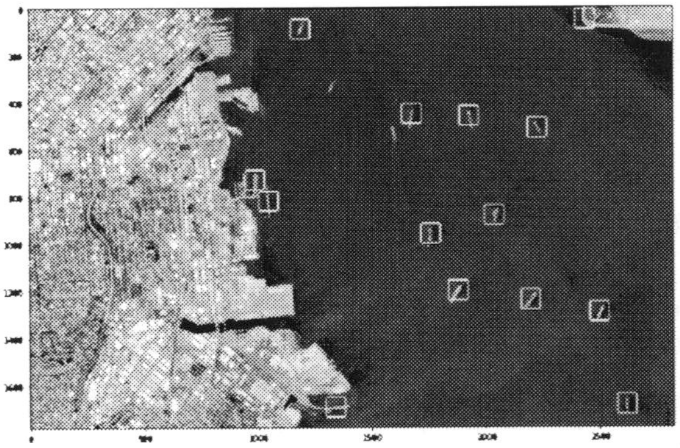

Figure 5. Screenshots of resultant images

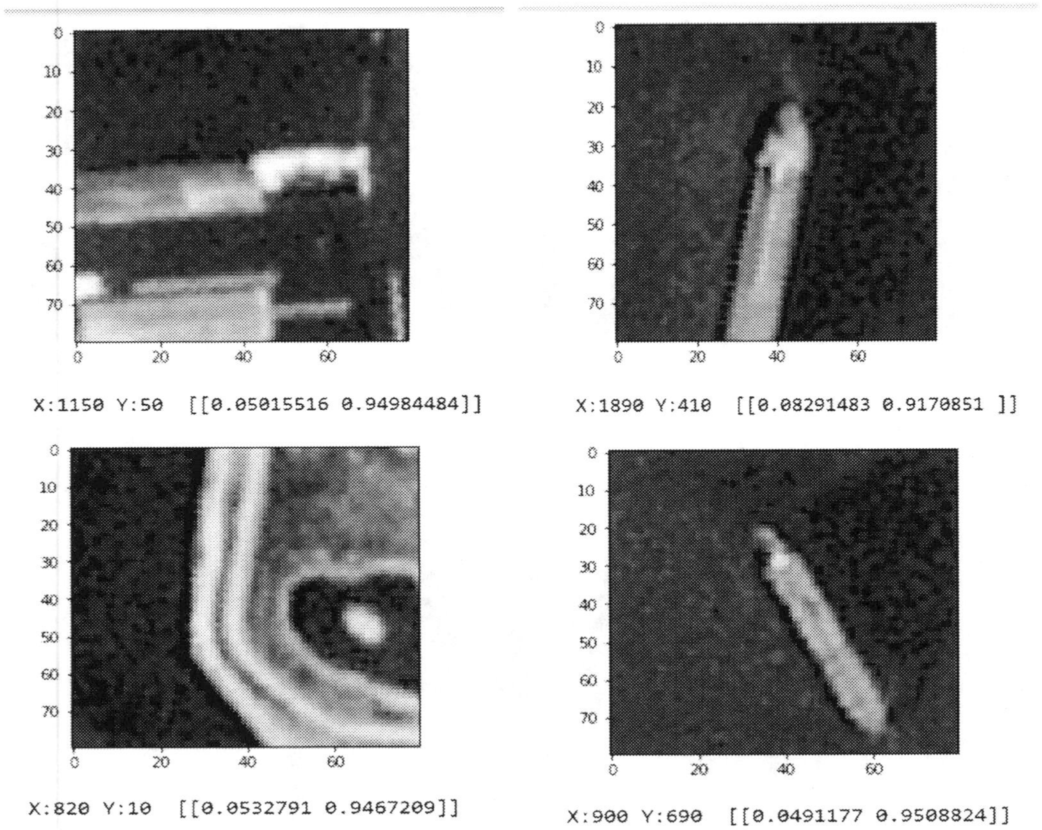

Figure 6. Accuracy graph

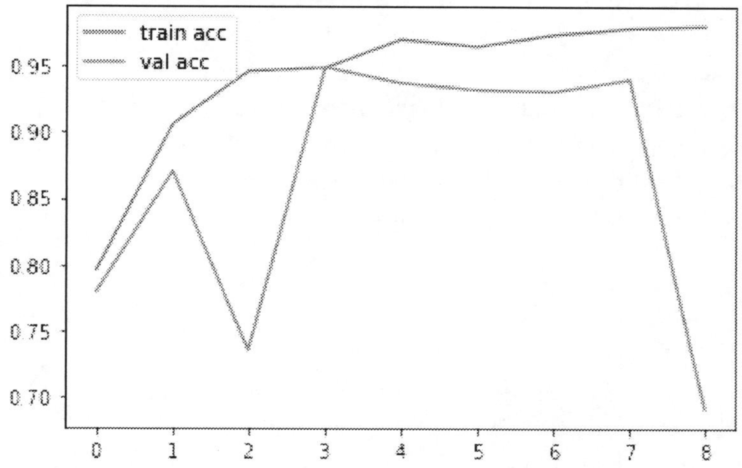

Figure 7. Loss graph

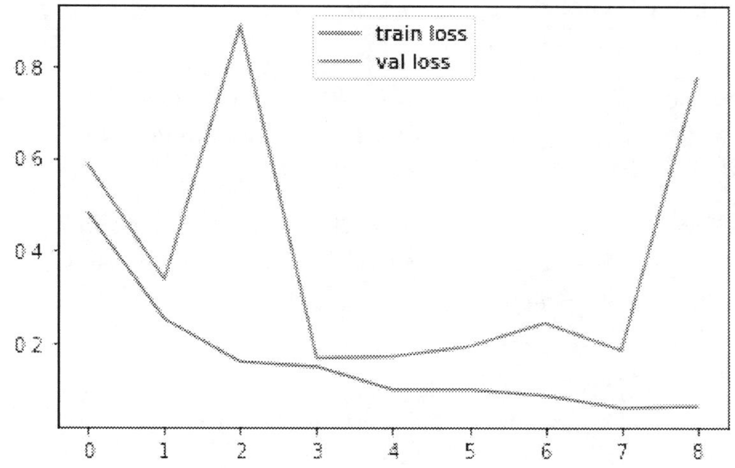

CONCLUSION

In this paper, the multiscale network that is recommended for SAR picture ship recognition is investigated. As was previously said, it is advantageous since it improves the correlations between the spatial features. Equivariant qualities have the potential to serve as the feature component in a variety of different places. The following are some of the highlights from the paper's modules, architecture, and process: The image module brings out the maximum clarity and image structure, which makes it easier when SAR images are modelled for classification and recognition; The use of simple and less parametric classification used in training and testing data maximizes efficiency, accuracy, and time. An image module that brings maximum clarity and structure makes it easier when SAR images are modelled for classification and recognition. When compared to other operational procedures, the constraints are significantly less severe. As a result, the approach that has been proposed helps to achieve higher performance despite having minimal features. We might concentrate on enhancing the increase in the classification and recognition method by adding more important criteria while still preserving a high level of accuracy to bring about future improvements. To build and then change the existing software so it can be used in many research areas in medicine, biotechnology, and social forums.

REFERENCES

Chen, L., Jiang, X., Li, Z., Liu, X., & Zhou, Z. (2020). Feature-Enhanced Speckle Reduction via Low-Rank and Space-Angle Continuity for Circular SAR Target Recognition. *IEEE Transactions on Geoscience and Remote Sensing*, *58*(11), 7734–7752. doi:10.1109/TGRS.2020.2983420

Chen, S., Wang, H., Xu, F., & Jin, Y.-Q. (2016). Target classification using the deep convolutional networks for SAR images. *IEEE Transactions on Geoscience and Remote Sensing*, *54*(8), 4806–4817. doi:10.1109/TGRS.2016.2551720

Deva Hema, D., & Ashok Kumar, K. (2022). Novel algorithm for multivariate time series crash risk prediction using CNN-ATT-LSTM model. *Journal of Intelligent & Fuzzy Systems*, *43*(4), 4201–4213. Advance online publication. doi:10.3233/JIFS-211775

Hong, D., Yokoya, N., Chanussot, J., & Zhu, X. X. (2019). An augmented linear mixing model to address spectral variability for hyperspectral unmixing. *IEEE Transactions on Image Processing*, *28*(4), 19231938. doi:10.1109/TIP.2018.2878958 PMID:30418901

Hong, D., Yokoya, N., Ge, N., Chanussot, J., & Zhu, X. X. (2019). Learnable manifold alignment (LeMA): A semi-supervised cross-modality learning framework for land cover and land use classification. *ISPRS Journal of Photogrammetry and Remote Sensing*, *147*, 193–205. doi:10.1016/j.isprsjprs.2018.10.006 PMID:30774220

Huang, Z., Pan, Z., & Lei, B. (2017). Transfer learning with deep convolutional neural network for SAR target classification with limited labelled data. *Remote Sensing Journal*, *9*(9), 907. doi:10.3390/rs9090907

Hummel, R. (2000). Model-based ATR using synthetic aperture radar. *Proc. Rec. IEEE Int. Radar Conf.*

Liu, M., Wu, Y., Zhang, P., Zhang, Q., Li, Y., & Li, M. (2013). SAR target con- guration recognition using locality preserving property and Gaussian mixture distribution. *IEEE Geoscience and Remote Sensing Letters*, *10*(2), 268272.

Murugan & Durairaj. (2017). Regularization and optimization strategies in deep convolutional neural network. *Computer Vision and Pattern Recognition.*

Novak, L. M., Owirka, G. J., Brower, W. S., & Weaver, A. L. (1997). The auto- Matic target-recognition system in SAIP. *The Lincoln Laboratory Journal*, *10*(2), 187201.

Oh, J., Youm, G.-Y., & Kim, M. (2021). SPAM-Net: A CNN-Based SAR Target Recognition Network With Pose Angle Marginalization Learning. *IEEE Transactions on Circuits and Systems for Video Technology*, *31*(2), 701–714. doi:10.1109/TCSVT.2020.2987346

Pei, J., Huang, Y., Huo, W., Zhang, Y., Yang, J., & Yeo, T.-S. (2018). SAR automatic target recognition based on multiview deep learning framework. *IEEE Transactions on Geoscience and Remote Sensing*, *56*(4), 2196–2210. doi:10.1109/TGRS.2017.2776357

Sun, Y., Liu, Z., Todorovic, S., & Li, J. (2007). Adaptive boosting for SAR automatic target recognition. *IEEE Transactions on Aerospace and Electronic Systems*, *43*(1), 112125. doi:10.1109/TAES.2007.357120

Tian, S., Yin, K., Wang, C., & Zhang, H. (2015). *An SAR ATR method based on scattering center feature and bipartite graph matching*. IETE Tech.

Wang, J., Liu, J., Ren, P., & Qin, C.-X. (2020). A SAR Target Recognition Based on Guided Reconstruction and Weighted Norm-Constrained Deep Belief Network. *IEEE Access: Practical Innovations, Open Solutions*, *8*, 181712–181722. doi:10.1109/ACCESS.2020.3025379

Xu, J., Li, G., Peng, Y.-N., Xia, X.-G., & Wang, Y.-L. (2008). Parametric veloc- its synthetic aperture radar Multi look processing and its applications. *IEEE Transactions on Geoscience and Remote Sensing*, *46*(11), 3488–3502. doi:10.1109/TGRS.2008.2000877

Chapter 22
YOLO v5 and Faster R-CNN Performance Evaluation of Solid Waste in Object Detection Application

Pradeep Kumar T.
Adhiyamaan College of Engineering, India

Lilly Florence M.
Adhiyamaan College of Engineering, India

Fathima G.
Adhiyamaan College of Engineering, India

ABSTRACT

Object detection is a booming technology that is on par with computer vision and image processing in which an object of a specific type is detected in an image or video. Object detection consists of several approaches like Retina-Net, Single Shot MultiBox Detector (SSD), and Faster R-CNN. These approaches are used in object detection with limited data, but these approaches either run in two algorithms or has high execution time; to overcome these limitations, the authors have used the latest version of Yolo with the custom dataset of solid waste. In this algorithm, an image in the solid waste dataset, which was annotated, labelled, pre-processed, and segmented and a build version is created with the yolo model; this version can either be used directly in the code for online execution or downloaded in the local system for offline execution.

DOI: 10.4018/978-1-6684-6060-3.ch022

INTRODUCTION

A Human is capable of recognising the object within the image and locating them in an instant, unlike a machine. The object detection model takes an image or video stream as input to identify known objects and the position of the object within the image. A model in the State-of-art to simulate object detection similar to a human visual system on which scientists are researching for more accurate and fast processing. The object detection method consisted of two stages: Extraction of feature areas in the image; to determining the object class using classification. This method demanded a large amount of computation and consisted of multiple stages. Among Object detection models, YOLO is the best and faster-performing algorithm after Faster R-CNN) because all the essential stages to detect an object was performed using a single neural network.

Convolutional Neural Networks (CNN) such as Regions Proposal Networks (R-CNN), which use Selective Search algorithm and Regions Proposal Networks (RPNs), which were used before YOLO. In Faster R-CNN, from each region, proposal features are extracted using a pooling layer in which multiple stages, computation for each proposal and high disk storage are overcome when compared to Fast R-CNN and R-CNN. YOLO (You Look Only Once) upgraded object detection, in which single regression problem, image pixels to bounding boxes and class probabilities for objects within boxes. The first YOLO model was published in 2016 by Joseph Redmon (Redmon, et al., 2016) in which an N*N grid is formed on the input image, and objects are detected on the grid cell; likewise, all the grid cells containing objects are collected to form bounding box to locate and identify the image. The drawback of first version localisation and recall were overcome in YOLOv2 (2017) algorithm (Joseph Redmon and Ali Farhadi 2016), and multi-label prediction and feature extractor network Darknet53 was a major advantage used in YOLOv3 (2018) (Joseph Redmon and Ali Farhadi, 2018) in which Alexey Bochkovskiy improved mean average precision and number of fps in the current version YOLOv4 in 2020 (Bochkovskiy, et al., 2020). YOLOv5 is scripted in python in which installation and integration are at ease, and focus structure is the additional layer used in the backbone, and the anchor box selection process is included accordingly best anchor box for the dataset is learned and used in training.

LITERATURE SURVEY

The author compared the YOLO method to the Mask R-CNN technique for fish head and tail segmentation (Prasetyo, et al., 2020). The fish's head and tail's physical features are employed to spot its youthfulness. A division technique that isolates in order to do additional research, specific fish body sections must be used in an exceedingly a mechanism for automatically determining the youthfulness of fish. They need to investigate and retrained the dataset. The researcher of the paper studied a technique to acknowledge automobile types supported in depth learning model. Faster-RCNN, YOLO, and SSD (Kim, et al., 2020), which are processed in period of time and have comparatively high accuracy. They have trained every rule through associate automobile coaching dataset and analysed the performance to envision what the optimised model for vehicle kind recognition is.

The author of this paper developed a system called IWASTE (Chen, et al., 2020) that uses films taken by a camera-equipped trash container to detect and classify medical waste. In this pilot study, they used a motion detection-based pre-processing and cut valuable from a video dataset of 4 waste things. In this paper, the R3D+C2D architecture is utilised to identify garbage films by combining features learnt by

2D and 3D CNN. The author of this paper proposed a waste classification system based on Mask Scoring RCNN (Li, et al., 2020). Create a new dataset based on Beijing Municipal Garbage Classification Criteria, use RCNN for mask score for training. This system helps people to segregate their garbage correctly and minimizes the time wasted due to garbage sorting. The test results of the system's garbage classification accuracy are high, and the segmentation recognition efficiency is good.

The objective of this paper (Nagori, et al., 2019) is to spot the styles of waste in India, the character of waste popping out from different cities, the disposal method being employed there, amount of waste that gets dumped at the landfill. This paper justifies the explanation behind expanding the number of landfills in India. Valuable insights are obtained after classifying waste into biodegradable/ non-biodegradable classes and its suitability for disposal or not. The author used: WRC, CSP, CmBN, SAT, Mish activation, Mosaic data augmentation, CmBN, DropBlock regularisation (Bochkovskiy, et al., 2020), and CIoU loss, and mix a number of them to realise on the YOLOv3. The researcher has presented some updates to YOLO and some design changes to form it better. The network which they have trained is precise and fast, but the content is huge. At 320x320 YOLOv3 (Joseph Redmon and Ali Farhadi, 2018), 28.2 mAP is obtained when run at 22 ms, which is as accurate as SSD but thrice faster. The performance is high in the latest version.

The author used Object detection in shelf images (Kumar et al., 2020) to resolve problems in retail sales, for example, by observing the count of objects and matching things. They achieved the detection of objects in shelf pics with in depth learning algorithms. Object and dataset detection algorithms have been reviewed in the literature. Then a pilot study was performed using pictures dataset with YOLO (You Look Only Once) algorithm. The author of this work has selected the more adaptive Surf algorithm to detect feature points and geometric hash algorithm (Guo, et al., 2020) and to achieve target matching in complex environments, which improved the algorithm processing. Object Identification algorithm like you only Look Once (YOLOv3 and YOLOv4) (Ceren Gulra Melek et al., 2019) is presented by the author for traffic and monitoring apps. An input layer with at least one hidden layer and an output layer make up a neural network. Multiple object dataset, which consists of different classes of pics captured during RGB and grayscale images.

IA self-controlled robot app (Supasan,et al., 2018) was used in this work. The robot was able to identify and retrive lightweight solid garbage within a ground area. It consisted of 4 major implantation parts, namely, the Robot Platform, Image Processing Unit, Sensor Component and Collection Arm. A large spinning bush within the collection arm, conveyor belt and can were attached to grab, collect and store the identified waste things, respectively. The robot was put to the test to see how effective it is in lifting lightweight waste and detecting paths. The researcher has introduced YOLO9000 (Joseph Redmon and Ali Farhadi 2016), object identifying real-time system capable of identifying different categories. First, different improvements to YOLO were imposed, novel and used for prior work. On identification tasks, the updated model, YOLOv2, is state-of-the-art. The author of this research offers DeepCounter (Mikami, et al., 2018), a vehicle sensing system which uses deep learning-based picture technology to count the amount of trash bags collected from video. The single-shot multibox detector is used to create and implement a detection-tracking-counting (DTC) algorithm (SSD).

The author used a YOLO (You Only Look Once)-based detection and classification approach (YOLOv2) (Jana, et al., 2018) to improve computation and processing efficiency while also precisely identifying objects in video recordings. Each item the class on which the classifier is trained produces a bounding box and an annotation that describes item type. The GPU (Graphics Processing Unit) is employed in the YOLO-based detection and classification (YOLOv2) to speed up calculation and which was processed at a rate of 40 fps. The fps obtained in work is comparatively very high. The author of the paper is responsible for first introducing YOLO (Ren, et al., 2017); in this work, they framed object detection as a regression problem to spatially separate bounding boxes and associated class probabilities. Bounding boxes and class probabilities are presage in directly from the full pics in an evaluation. The researcher proposed a Region Proposal Network (RPN) (Redmon, et al., 2016) that shares complete set of pic convolutional features with the identification network, that permits region to suggest almost freely. An RPN is a fully convolutional network that anticipate object which has bounds and credibility scores simultaneously. RPNs are trained from start to finish to create high-quality region proposals, which Fast R-CNN uses for detection. The author of this paper proposed a Fast Region-based Conv Network method (Fast R-CNN) for object identification. Fast R-CNN improves prior work to precisely categorise item suggestions using deep conv networks by incorporating many advances that speed up training and testing with which the accuracy is improved.

PROPOSED WORK

Faster R-CNN, Retina-Net, and Single-Shot MultiBox Detector (SSD) are some of the technologies used to detect objects despite the fact these approaches overcome the limitations of data and modeling limitations in object detection, but no longer capable of finding in one algorithm run. YOLOv5 is the latest release of the YOLO algorithm (Redmon, et al., 2016), is a group of complex scale object detection models trained on a custom dataset used for a model to combine multiple models during prediction, by making random changes course on test image like flip, rotate, etc. and optimising hyper-parameters using a genetic algorithm for optimisation.

METHODOLOGY

YOLO (You Only Look Once)

YOLO is an object recognition system that is used to detect discrete objects in a pic. Object detection in this algorithm is achieved by resolving regression problems in YOLO, and the class probabilities of the identified images are noted. In YOLO, conv networks (CNN), which is the most advanced and emerging field in deep learning, detect, locate and classify objects in real time. This algorithm technique is done in one propagation with a neural network, and the CNN is employed to forecast several bounding boxes and class probabilities.

Convolutional Neural Networks (CNN) implemented algorithm consists of three stages for any object detection algorithm:

Backbone - This is a CNN stage that is used to extract and collect image features at different granularities.

Neck - This is a group of layers to combine image features and forward them to the next stage for identification.

Head - In this stage, fused Image features are used to identify the object by forming bounding boxes and classifying them accordingly.

YOLO algorithm uses three strategies to detect, locate and identify the object are as follows:

Residual blocks

The pics are divided into several grids; the dimensions of unique grid are S x S, and Objects that exist within grid cells will be observed by all grid cell.

Regression

The bounding box is an outline of a certain object in the image, and the following elements are present across every bounding box and grid cell in the image:

The bounding box for predicted co-ordinates (px, py, pw, ph)

Bounding box Width (S_w), Bounding box Height (S_h), Center of the square (S_x, S_y) for x and y co-ordinates

Length of a grid cell x co-ordinate, and y co-ordinate (c_x, c_y)

Width and height of predicted Bounding box (w, h)

$S_x = \sigma(px) + c_x$, $S_y = \sigma(py) + c_y$, $S_w = w\ e^{pw}$ and $S_h = h\ e^{ph}$

Intersection over Union (IoU)

In YOLO (Bochkovskiy, et al., 2020), the outline of the object is predicted using IOU and creates an output box. The bounding boxes and their credebility scores are likely with repective to all grid cell. If the guessed bounding box and actual box are similar, the IOU is 1. In this method, bounding boxes that aren't similar to actual boxes are removed.

Combine

The pic is virtually splitted into equal grid cells, and bounding boxes of an object in all the grid cell, along with their credibility scores, is inferenced. To find the classification of each object, the cells estimate correct label. Only one CNN is utilized to make and approximate at the same time. The bounding boxes are predicted by the actual boxes of the objects when the intersection on the link is used. This technique is used to avoid sub-bounding boxes that do not match the properties of the object, such as height and width. The final detection will consist of separate bounding boxes that exactly correspond to the objects.

Faster R-CNN

Faster R-CNNis development of Fast R-CNN and is agile than Fast R-CNN because of the implementation of a Region Proposal Network (RPN) for generating region proposals, and a selective search technique is used to generate region proposals. The first layer represents a binary classifier that generates a confidence score that determines whether the region contains a feature or is part of the background of each region proposition. The second layer represents the bounding box of a region. It uses the ROI Pooling layer in which required values are collected. Faster R-CNN to train RPN and Fast R-CNN while allocating the convolutional layers using three different ways as follows:

Alternating Training

In this stage, RPN is competent to develop region proposals. The weight based on a existing model are initialized based on the shared convolutional layers, and the other weights are randomly initialized on the RPN. The weights of RPN and layers which are shared are tuned once region proposals boxes are produced by RPN. The weights of the layers are initialized with the tuned weights. RPN has trained again once the shared layer tunes its weights, and the process repeats.

Approximate Joint Training

In this stage, the region proposals are originated by the RPN. The region proposal is given to Fast R-CNN without modifying the weights of the layers to locate the object, in which Faster R-CNN weights are fine-tuned after Fast R-CNN results are evaluated. The training time is reduced along with the accuracy.

Non-Approximate Joint Training

In this method, an ROI layer for the weights evaluated in regard to calculate bounding box.

For RPN training, the parameters with respect to the reference box are validated as either +ve or -ve Credibility Score based on Intersection over Union (IoU), as mentioned above. In RPN, IoU is evaluated by finding the ratio between the intersection of the area between theparameters. The positivity of the credit score increases as both boxes close in. The credibility Score is positive if IoU is more than 0.7 and between 0.3 and 0.7 but negative if IoU is less than 0.3. The limitation of Faster R-CNN is that the network used consumes more time to converge one image in which anchors are extracted.

PHASES OF WORK

Phases of the work as shown in Figure 1, dataset assembled with annotating and labelling of images with the respective object names, followed by Pre-processing with isolate object and mosaic augmentation, Yolo and Faster R-CNN implementation with the solid waste dataset, which includes training the model and inference the weights of the same. Concluding with training curves in Tensor board for both the model.

Figure 1. phases of the work

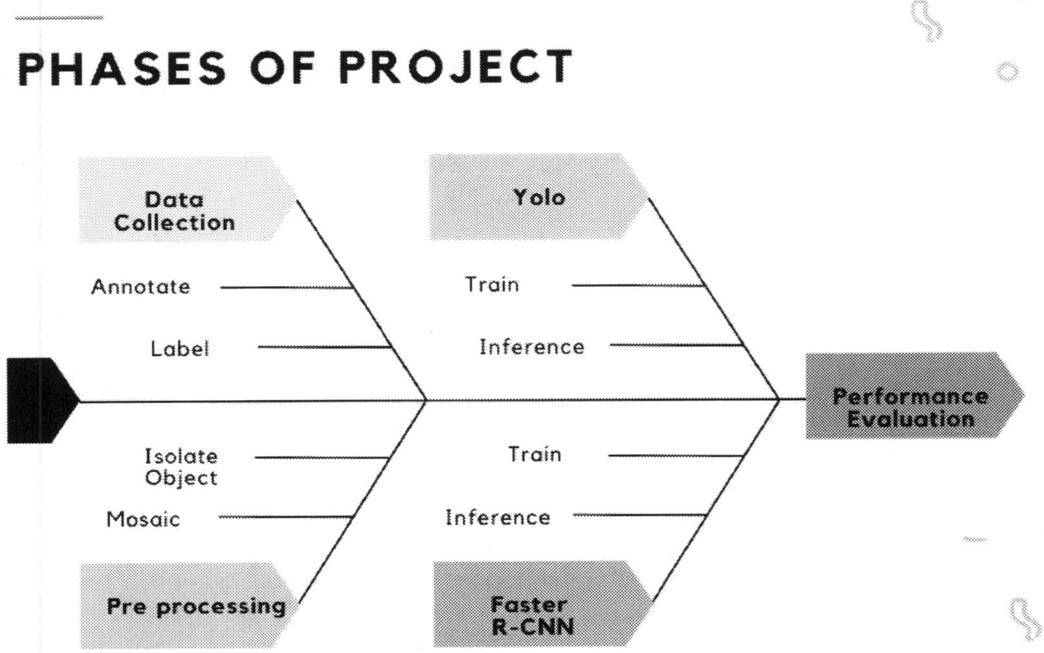

IMPLEMENTATION

YOLO v5

Data Collection

Raw image data are collected from kaggle and other sources. Images that are to be annotated are uploaded in roboflow, and then annotate the images based on the class of the object and labelled them. After annotation, the images in the dataset are split into training, validating and testing sets.

Pre-processing

The images in the dataset undergo auto-orientation and object isolation for necessary images. Along with these pre-processing steps, Mosaic data augmentation is done for better performance of the model in occlusion and translation, as shown in Figure 2.

Figure 2. dataset and its process

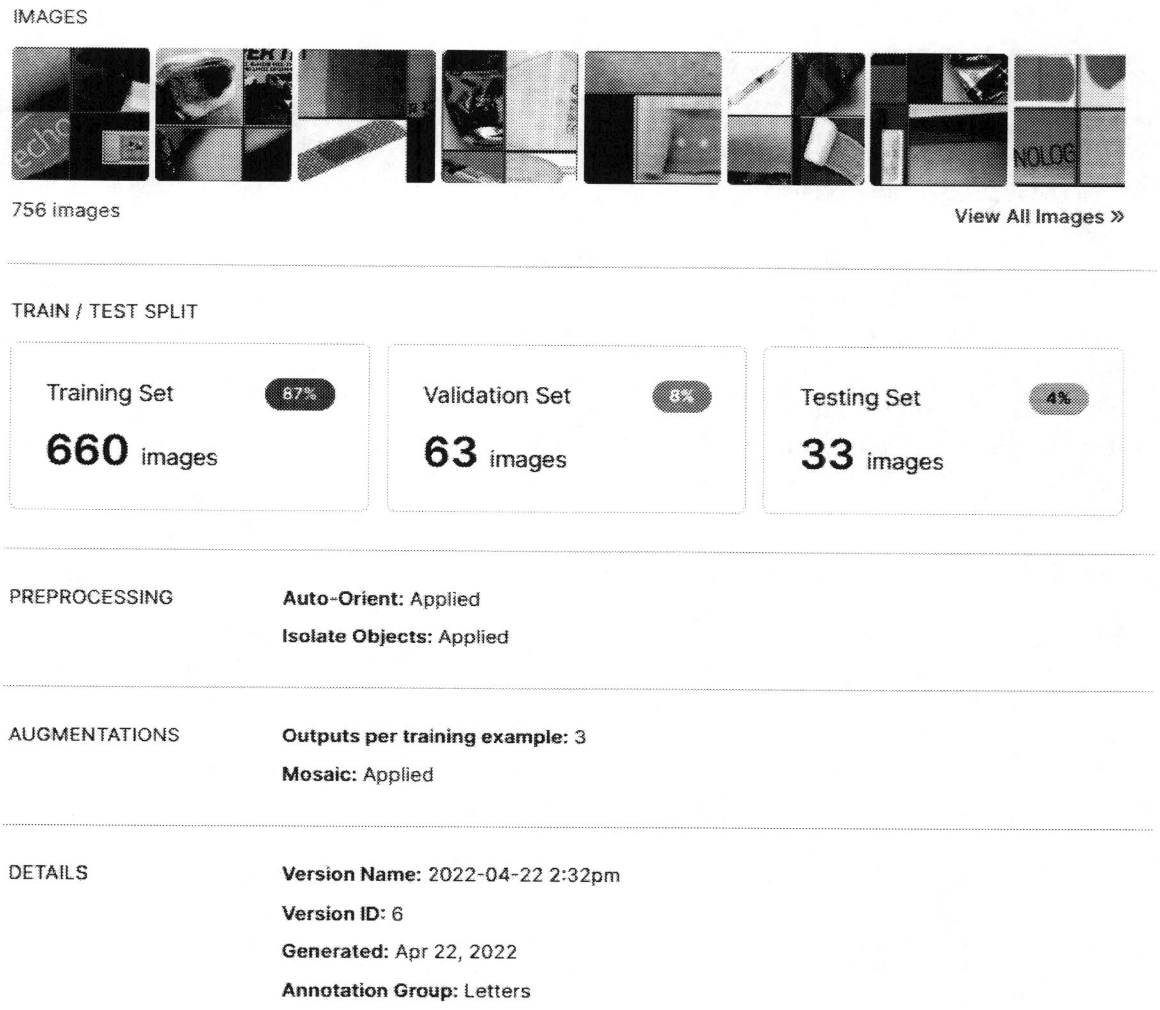

Code Implementation

- Install Requirements:

The required library files are to be downloaded, like numpy, OpenCV, torch, and PyYAML, to train and execute the model. To check whether all these required files are installed, execute the requirements text file and install the files which are not installed.

- Assembling the Dataset:

Import the annotated custom dataset from roboflow and enter the api_key, version of the dataset, workspace, project name and dataset format; all these details can be obtained from dataset export to show the download code.

- Model Configuration:

To use the required yolo model along with its configuration of yolov5s and its layers (backbone, head).

- Training YOLOv5 model using Solid Waste Dataset:

Execute the command to provide it with the epochs, data and weights to train the model on the dataset, as shown in Figure 3.

Epochs: Count of training steps.

Data: Our dataset location is in the "dataset. location".

Weights: assign weights for exchanging.

Figure 3. training yolo for solid waste classification

```
     Epoch   gpu_mem       box       obj       cls    labels  img_size
   144/149     1.63G   0.00793   0.01433  0.003943        63       416: 100% 26/26 [00:13<00:00,  1.86it/s]
               Class    Images    Labels         P         R   mAP@.5 mAP@.5:.95: 100% 2/2 [00:00<00:00,  3.32it/s]
                 all        48        48      0.83     0.921     0.911     0.739

     Epoch   gpu_mem       box       obj       cls    labels  img_size
   145/149     1.63G  0.007716    0.0149  0.002547        48       416: 100% 26/26 [00:14<00:00,  1.86it/s]
               Class    Images    Labels         P         R   mAP@.5 mAP@.5:.95: 100% 2/2 [00:00<00:00,  3.25it/s]
                 all        48        48     0.835     0.922     0.923     0.749

     Epoch   gpu_mem       box       obj       cls    labels  img_size
   146/149     1.63G  0.007668   0.01469  0.002222        73       416: 100% 26/26 [00:13<00:00,  1.87it/s]
               Class    Images    Labels         P         R   mAP@.5 mAP@.5:.95: 100% 2/2 [00:00<00:00,  3.29it/s]
                 all        48        48     0.801     0.942     0.921     0.774

     Epoch   gpu_mem       box       obj       cls    labels  img_size
   147/149     1.63G  0.007549   0.01431  0.003193        61       416: 100% 26/26 [00:13<00:00,  1.86it/s]
               Class    Images    Labels         P         R   mAP@.5 mAP@.5:.95: 100% 2/2 [00:00<00:00,  3.34it/s]
                 all        48        48     0.852     0.918     0.919     0.775

     Epoch   gpu_mem       box       obj       cls    labels  img_size
   148/149     1.63G  0.007433   0.01434  0.003431        50       416: 100% 26/26 [00:13<00:00,  1.86it/s]
               Class    Images    Labels         P         R   mAP@.5 mAP@.5:.95: 100% 2/2 [00:00<00:00,  3.35it/s]
                 all        48        48      0.85     0.914     0.926     0.771

     Epoch   gpu_mem       box       obj       cls    labels  img_size
   149/149     1.63G  0.007413   0.01351  0.002811        74       416: 100% 26/26 [00:13<00:00,  1.87it/s]
               Class    Images    Labels         P         R   mAP@.5 mAP@.5:.95: 100% 2/2 [00:00<00:00,  3.33it/s]
                 all        48        48     0.843     0.915     0.927     0.753

150 epochs completed in 0.631 hours.
Optimizer stripped from runs/train/exp/weights/last.pt, 14.3MB
Optimizer stripped from runs/train/exp/weights/best.pt, 14.3MB

Validating runs/train/exp/weights/best.pt...
Fusing layers...
Model summary: 213 layers, 7020913 parameters, 0 gradients, 15.8 GFLOPs
               Class    Images    Labels         P         R   mAP@.5 mAP@.5:.95: 100% 2/2 [00:01<00:00,  1.65it/s]
                 all        48        48     0.861     0.962     0.965     0.823
            Bandages        48        17      0.85         1     0.951       0.8
           Cardboard        48        18     0.822     0.944     0.959     0.901
               Metal        48         5     0.894         1     0.995     0.896
             Syringe        48         8     0.878     0.905     0.954     0.696
Results saved to runs/train/exp
```

- Evaluate the Performance of YOLOv5 for Custom Dataset:

The performance of yolo on solid waste classification dataset with metrics, train, val.

- Run Inference:

Existing model with their respective checkpoint on contents of the pics folder from Roboflow are inferenced.

Faster R-CNN

Code Implementation

- Required Packages: The required library files are installed, like PyTorch and PyYaml, to train and execute the model; along with it required packages to implement are loaded.
- Configurations: Faster R-CNN support a variety of models in which detectron2 is the model implemented in work, and other pre-trained models and their pipeline configuration files are included in the package as well.
- Import Dataset: The dataset which was annotated, labelled and pre-processed is imported in COCO format with the use of api_key into the implementation. The register of COCO instances is imported from the dataset. The training dataset is shown in Figure 4.

Figure 4. visualising training data

- Training Solid Waste dataset using Faster R-CNN model:

By providing the weight of the model along with batch size per image and number of classifications for the training dataset. All the testing data is executed in 3 layers Bottleneck block, conv2d and frozen batch, as shown in Figure 5.

Figure 5. Training Faster R-CNN

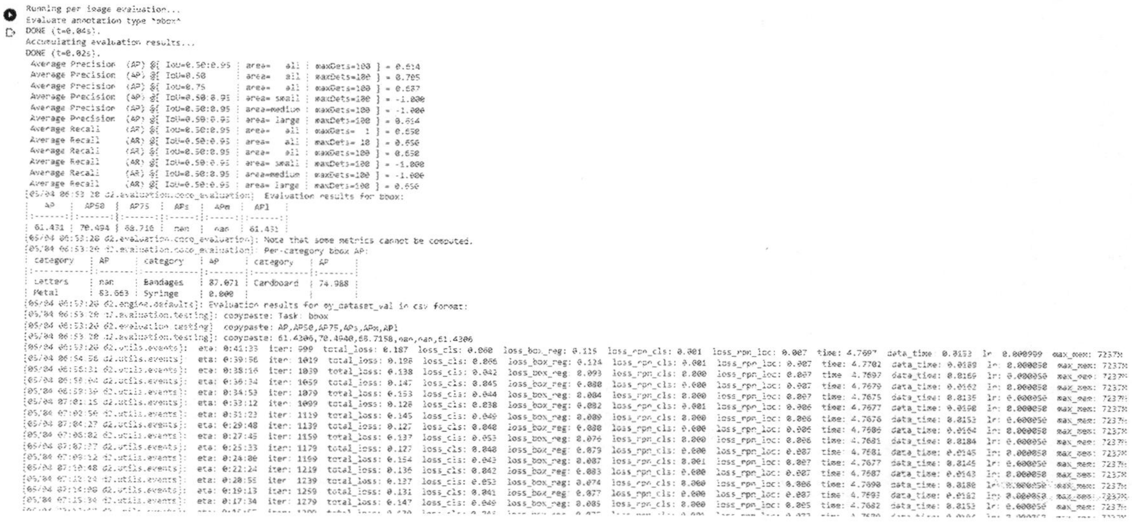

RESULTS

Yolo v5

- The trained weights are inferences on the test set of images which displays the name of the object classified along with its precision, as shown in Figure 6.

Figure 6. inference of yolo on test images

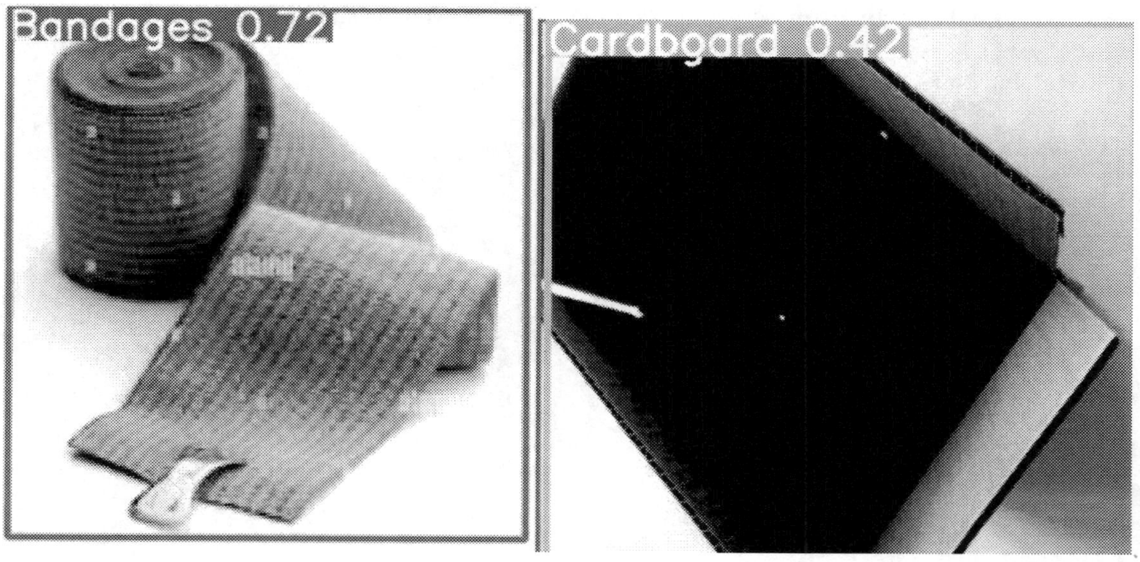

- The performance evaluation of yolov5 on solid waste classification dataset with metrics, training, validation of mean average precision, recall etc., are as shown in Figure 7.

Figure 7. performance evaluation of yolo metrics with mAP and epoch

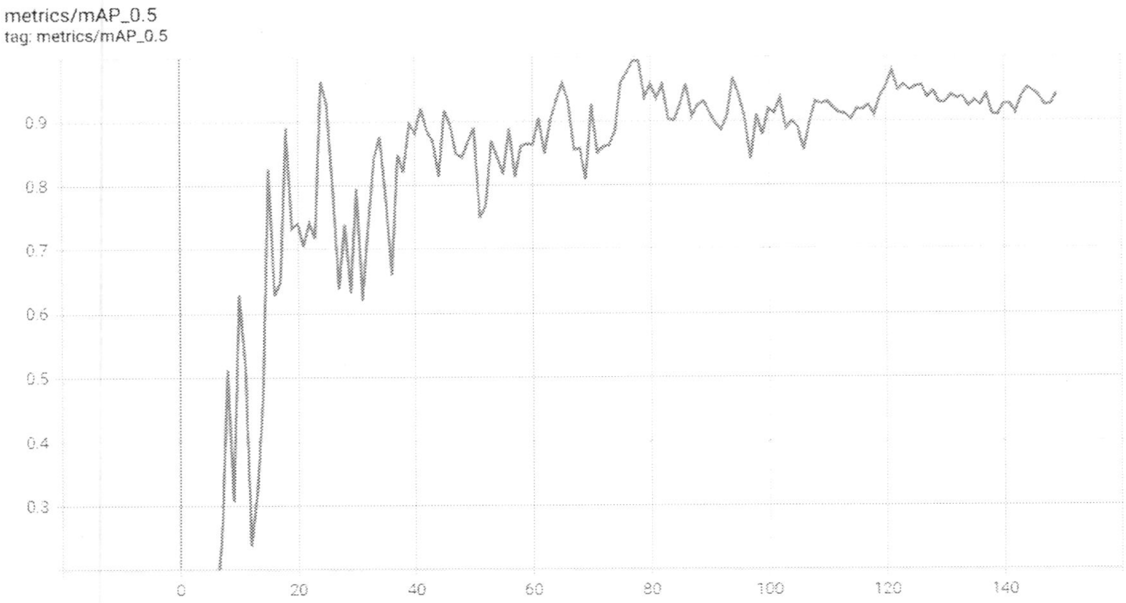

Faster R-CNN

- Using the weights of the model sample, test images are tested, and output with a bounding box along with the accuracy of detecting the object is displayed, as shown in Figure 8.

Figure 8. inference of faster R-CNN on test images

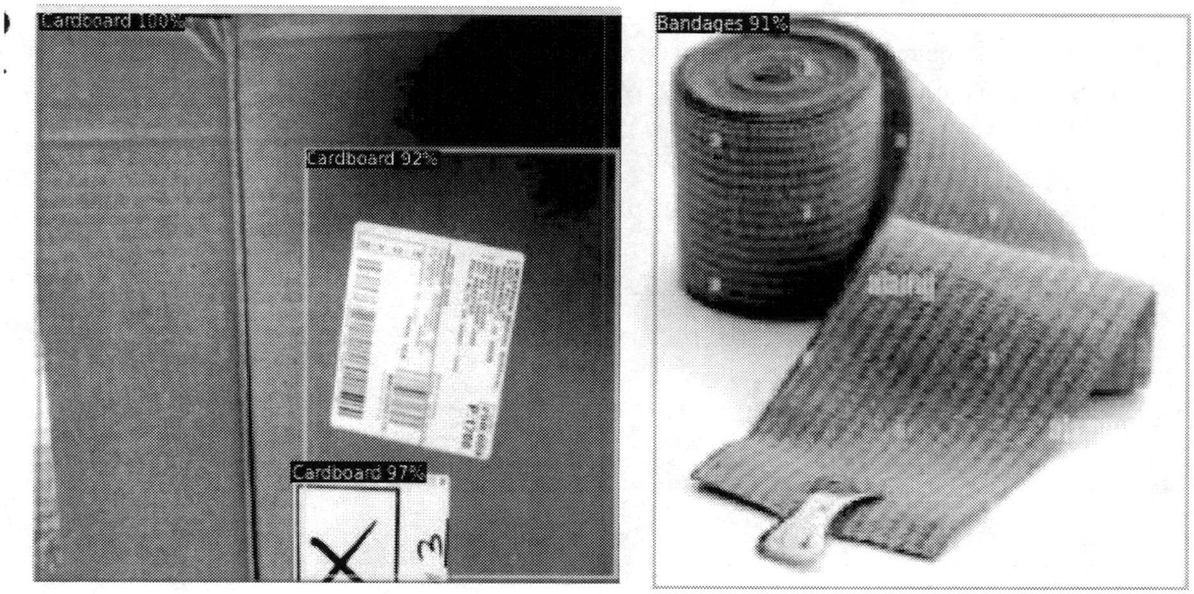

- Based on the AP (Average Precision) on the y-axis and the number of iterations on the x-axis calculated on the solid waste dataset using the Faster R-CNN detectron2 model is shown in Figure 9.

Figure 9. training curves of faster r-CNN with metrics AP and iteration

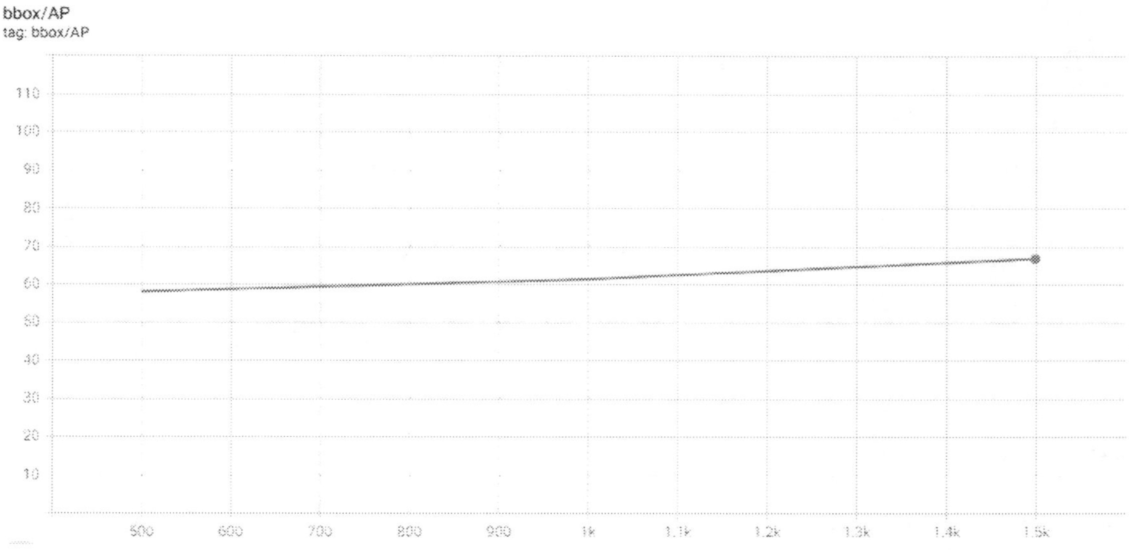

Performance Comparison

- The inference weight is evaluated based on steps 20, 40, 60, till 149 epochs, plotted against mean average precision in which the minimum value is 0.7 and was maxed up to 0.95 using the yolo model for the solid waste dataset as shown in table 1.

Table 1. Evaluation of Yolo model metrics of mean average precision over epochs

YOLO v5	
Step Number	**Map**
20	0.74
40	0.88
60	0.86
80	0.95
100	0.91
120	0.95
140	0.92

- Output is inference, which is evaluated based on steps or iterations of 500, 700, 900 till 1500, plotted against average precision with a gradual rise from an average of 58 using the faster r-CNN model for the solid waste dataset, as shown in the table 2.

Table 2. Evaluation of Faster R-CNN model metrics of average precision over iteration

Faster R-CNN	
Step Number	**AP**
500	58
700	59
900	61
1100	62
1300	65
1500	67

CONCLUSION

This paper presents an image from the solid waste dataset that has been annotated, labelled, pre-processed, and segmented, and a build version has been created with the yolo model. This version can either be used directly in the code for online execution or downloaded in the local system for offline execution. The dataset from roboflow is trained in a single neural network using the yolo technique, and it is then divided based on grids and bounding boxes that are anticipated. These grids and bounding boxes are weighted and biassed in W&B by the estimated probability for each component. Later, respectful weights are inferred together with the test set of data in the solid waste data collection in Tensorboard with metrics like recall, mAP, and others. Similarly, with the same dataset but using the deception2 model configuration for Faster R-CNN, trained models are created. Tensorboard's training curves, complete with accuracy metrics Comparisons are made between the performance of Yolo and a quicker R-CNN whose training curves have been confirmed. The author of this paper has a restricted amount of images in the dataset, which would cause the execution time of faster R-CNN to be lengthened. Additionally, the improvement in accuracy value is modest, but it takes several iteration steps to achieve. The dataset can also be segmented between wet and dry waste, which would be an improvement over its previous iteration and allow for the inclusion of a variety of additional classifications, such as used masks, culinary garbage, and other types of medical waste, amongst others.

REFERENCES

Prasetyo, E., Suciati, N., & Fatichah, C. (2020). A comparison of YOLO and mask R-CNN for segmenting head and tail of fish. In *2020 4th International Conference on Informatics and Computational Sciences (ICICoS).* IEEE.

Kim, J.-A., Sung, J.-Y., & Park, S.-H. (2020). Comparison of faster-RCNN, YOLO, and SSD for real-time vehicle type recognition. In *2020 IEEE International Conference on Consumer Electronics - Asia (ICCE-Asia).* IEEE.

Chen, J., Mao, J., Thiel, C., & Wang, Y. (2020). IWaste: Video-based medical waste detection and classification. *Annual International Conference of the IEEE Engineering in Medicine and Biology Society. IEEE Engineering in Medicine and Biology Society. Annual International Conference*, 5794–5797. 10.1109/EMBC44109.2020.9175645

Li, S., Yan, M., & Xu, J. (2020). Garbage object recognition and classification based on Mask Scoring RCNN. In *2020 International Conference on Culture-Oriented Science & Technology (ICCST).* IEEE. 10.1109/ICCST50977.2020.00016

Nagori, M., Jachak, R. S., & Chaudhari, P. P. (2019). A framework for segregating solid waste by employing the technique of image annotation. In *2019 Second International Conference on Advanced Computational and Communication Paradigms (ICACCP).* IEEE. 10.1109/ICACCP.2019.8882932

Bochkovskiy, A., Wang, C.-Y., & Liao, H.-Y. M. (2020). *YOLOv4: Optimal speed and accuracy of object detection.* https://arxiv.org/abs/2004.10934

Redmon & Farhadi. (2018). *YOLOv3: An Incremental Improvement.* arXiv:1804.02767v1 [cs.CV].

Kumar, Punitha, & Mohana. (2020). YOLOv3 and YOLOv4: Multiple Object Detection for Surveillance Applications. In *2020 Third International Conference on Smart Systems and Inventive Technology (ICSSIT).* IEEE. 10.1109/ICSSIT48917.2020.9214094

Guo, C. L., Lan, H., Ma, Y., Zhu, H., & Sun, K. (2020). The research of garbage classification and recognition based on surf and geometric hashing algorithm. In *2020 IEEE 9th Joint International Information Technology and Artificial Intelligence Conference (ITAIC).* IEEE.

Melek, C. G., Sonmez, E. B., & Albayrak, S. (2019). Object Detection in Shelf Images with YOLO. *IEEE EUROCON 2019-18th International Conference on Smart Technologies*.

Supasan, N. A. I., Kaushalya, W. A. L. U., Maduwantha, S. M. D. P., Yasiru, M. G. A., Wijenayake, S. J. K., Kulathilake, K. A. S. H., & Kohomban, U. (2018). Self-controlled robot for collection of light weight waste in a ground area. In *2018 IEEE International Conference on Information and Automation for Sustainability (ICIAfS)*. IEEE. 10.1109/ICIAFS.2018.8913337

Redmon & Farhadi. (2016). *YOLO9000: Better, Faster, Stronger*. arXiv:1612.08242v1 [cs.CV].

Mikami, K., Chen, Y., Nakazawa, J., Iida, Y., Kishimoto, Y., & Oya, Y. (2018). DeepCounter: Using deep learning to count garbage bags. In *2018 IEEE 24th International Conference on Embedded and Real-Time Computing Systems and Applications (RTCSA)*. IEEE.

Jana, Biswas, & Mohana. (2018). YOLO based Detection and Classification of Objects in video records. In *2018 3rd IEEE International Conference on Recent Trends in Electronics, Information & Communication Technology (RTEICT)*. IEEE.

Ren, S., He, K., Girshick, R., & Sun, J. (2017). Faster R-CNN: Towards real-time object detection with region proposal networks. *IEEE Transactions on Pattern Analysis and Machine Intelligence*, *39*(6), 1137–1149. doi:10.1109/TPAMI.2016.2577031 PMID:27295650

Redmon, J., Divvala, S., Girshick, R., & Farhadi, A. (2016). You only look once: Unified, real-time object detection. In *2016 IEEE Conference on Computer Vision and Pattern Recognition (CVPR)*. IEEE. 10.1109/CVPR.2016.91

Chapter 23
Professional Career Planning and Decision Making Based on SQL Server Data Mining Techniques

Nandhini S.
Sathyabama Institute of Science and Technology, India

S. Parthasarathy
Sathyabama Institute of Science and Technology, India

V. Marimuthu
SRM Institute of Science and Technology, India

ABSTRACT

The world today is facing the fourth industrial revolution – a "revolution of skills." The demand for completely new sets of skills is unprecedented, with the advent of and rapid change in digital technologies. On the other hand, a large population of graduates and professional are struggling to empower themselves with newer skillsets and develop capabilities to achieve competitive edge in building a successful career. There is a need for a platform to bridge the gap between these two market forces so that "the supply meets the demand." This chapter seeks to provide a predictive solution using SQL server data mining techniques that implements Microsoft decision tree data mining algorithm.

INTRODUCTION

SQL Server Data Mining

Data mining is a process of scanning a huge volume of data to find patterns and trends from the data values. Data mining helps organisations to make long-term, data analytics-based decisions that help

DOI: 10.4018/978-1-6684-6060-3.ch023

them to achieve a competitive edge over other organisations (Feng, et al., 2022). Data warehouse stores huge amounts of data over a period of time. A data warehouse is centralized storage that saves data from several different sources and converts that into a standard, multidimensional data model for querying and analysis. For Business Intelligence, OLAP and Data Mining are two complementing technologies. OLAP stands for Online Analytical Processing, and it is a technology that is used to organise and support business intelligence in massive databases (Hajmoosaei, et al., 2011). Instead of performing transactions, OLAP is a database system that has been designed for querying and reporting. OLAP databases are separated into one or more cubes, each of which is organised and customised by a cube administrator to suit your data retrieval and analysis needs. The data warehouse is utilised for both descriptive and diagnostic analysis (what happened) (Why it happened). Business, on the other hand, requires more in-depth examination (Ramadhani, et al., 2021). Predictive Analysis (what will happen) and Prescriptive Analysis (what should happen) can both benefit from data mining (How can we make it happen). In many enterprises, SQL Server is primarily utilised as a storage tool. However, as the demands of many enterprises grow, individuals are turning to SQL Server's various functionalities. SQL Server is being considered for data warehousing. SQL Server has a Data Mining platform that may be used to make data predictions (Farooqui and Mehra, 2018). You may foresee trends, find patterns, define rules and recommendations, identify the series of events in complicated data sets, and get a new view of data by using the data mining algorithms in SQL Server Analysis Services on your data (Hasanika, D. et al., 2021).

SQL Server Data Mining, Integration Services, and Reporting Services to work hand in hand to create an integrated predictive analytics platform that includes data preparation, data transformation, machine learning, and reporting. Neural networks, logistic regression and linear regression, decision trees, and naïve Bayes classifiers are all incorporated and embedded in SQL Server Data Mining. Industry 4.0 is a business terminology that is nowadays used interchangeably with the 4th generation of the industrial revolution (Javad and Asgari, 2021). Industry 4.0 is the collection, storage and utilisation of data and information that are part of the day-to-day operations of any industry. This data is further processed to build a smart industry that constitutes a collection of industrial innovation and collaboration in an inter-connected network of people, processes, services, systems, data and IoT-enabled industrial assets. Digital disruption by industry 4.0 has caused an unprecedented change in the way organisations to work, geo-political dynamics and processes, growth of the contingent workforce and the GIG economy, all leading to a more globalized and integrated way of work. The Covid-19 pandemic has accelerated this shift and brought us to the brink of the "future of work". Such a stipulates the need for maintaining the country's competitive advantage in existing and new sectors and harnessing the demographic bulge to tap into new opportunities. Global MNCs' increasing investments are likely to accentuate the rising demand for skills, expanding the demand-supply imbalance even more (Sharma and Singh, 2021).

As per the data from the "Future of Jobs Survey 2020", employers are expecting that the already existing redundant roles will keep declining from 15.4% of the workforce to 9% (6.4% decline) by the year 2025, while new and emerging professional roles will grow between 7.8% and 13.5% (5.7% growth) out of the total employee base of company resources. Based on this data, by the year 2025, a shift of labour between humans and machines would rearrange 85 million jobs, while new roles of about 97 million suitable for the new categories of labour across humans, machines, and algorithms would have already in place across the 15 industries and 26 economies that are taken for the study. This work will help professionals understand the market demand and help them to scale up and empower themselves with the latest skills and technologies and develop capabilities to achieve a competitive edge in building a successful career.

RELATED WORKS

Data Processing

The goal of data preprocessing is to eliminate unwanted data so that useful information about the attributes can be used for effective modelling. Given the inherent difficulty of data quality, data preparation forms the foundation for legitimate data and is an essential step in conducting data analysis. Before data mining, data preprocessing ensures cleaning, integrating, transforming, and reducing the original data to meet the minimum criteria and specifications that are required by algorithms for knowledge discovery.

Data Cleaning

The practice of deleting data that is incomplete, missing, or redundant is known as data cleaning. There are numerous approaches to building missing values for attributes, including ignoring tuples, utilising a global constant to fill in the gaps, determining the attribute mean value to fill in the gaps, and so on. Fill up the grade records for the courses with the fewest missing courses after deleting the grade records for the courses with the most missing courses. This paper must adhere to the following guidelines: If there are still students with empty course scores, fill them with the course's average value. Delete score records with empty scores in more than two courses. A course with a grade of 0 is considered a student's absence from the exam, and the student's score record is erased.

Data Integration

It is required to integrate comparable courses in order to eliminate data redundancy. Because certain courses are separated into multiple semesters, combining them and using the average score of several semesters as the course score facilitates the reduction of features in future analysis.

Data Transformation

Data transformation is done using the ETL process, which transforms the data from its raw form to the expected form. Here all the data types and schema mapping would happen, and based on that, data is read from the source system and loaded into the destination system. In some cases, the numerical values might have been stored in character data type columns, and while transforming this data record, there could be a situation where the conversion would fail in that the numerical values should be truncated, and only the whole number can be read and loaded.

Data Reduction

Unnecessary data such as credits and class time have been eliminated from the presentation of the result, leaving only the student number and the corresponding course score. To assure the statistical convenience of the final clustered cases, each student record is linked to a serial number.

Building A Mining Model

Data mining uses mathematical modelling in order to identify a set of patterns and trends within data. A data mining approach, by large, is the wholescale synthesis of patterns and trends from the available source dataset. Building a mining model refers to the collection of operations that are carried out in order to comprehend data patterns and covers everything from posing data-related questions to developing a model or structure to answer those questions to deploying these models in a real-world setting. The below diagram illustrates various phases that are in the process, their interconnectivity and the respective Microsoft SQL Server technologies that can be used to finish each phase (figure 1).

Figure 1. Mining Model

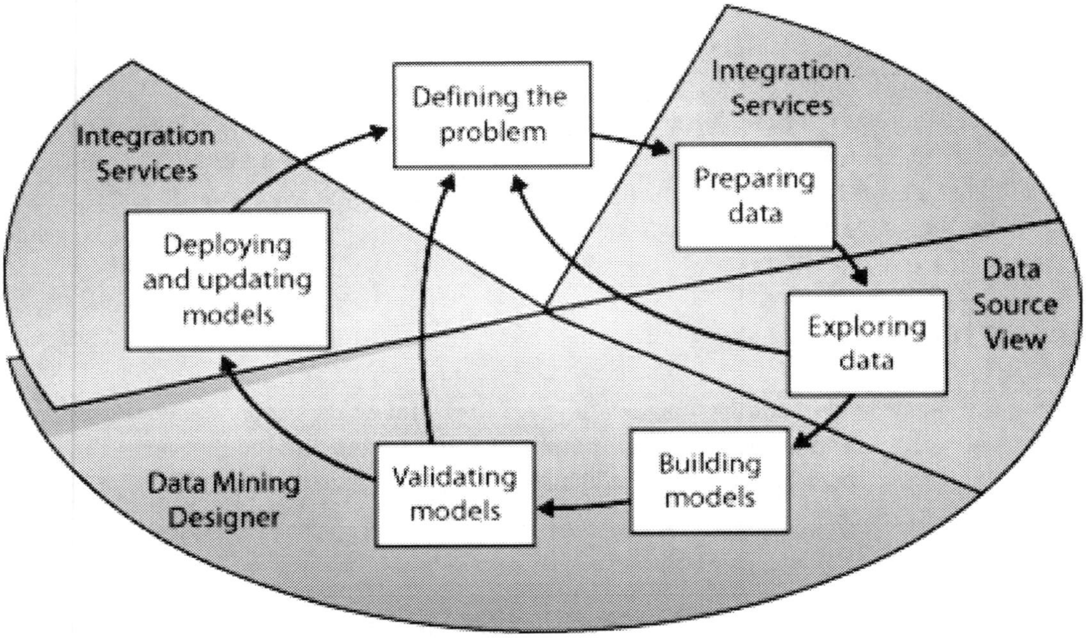

As shown in the diagram above, the process is cyclical in nature, meaning that the task of building a data mining model is dynamic and iterative. After studying the data, it is extremely usual to discover that there is insufficient data to develop acceptable mining models and that more data is required. Alternatively, one may construct numerous models only to discover that they do not effectively address the problem you have specified, necessitating a re-definition of the problem. In this scenario, once the fresh data has become accessible, there is a mandate to refresh the models once they have been created. In order to generate a successful model, each and every phase might have to be iterated several times so as to arrive at an optimal model.

Problem Definition

This step is the initialization phase, where all the business needs are analysed, the scope of the problem is defined, evaluation metrics are identified, and data mining project objectives are set. In simple terms, this step seeks solutions to the fundamental questions that arise when developing a data mining model. To answer these concerns, a data availability study must be conducted, which will look at the needs of business users in terms of available data. In any case, the project design and the architecture have to be re-defined if the data does not meet the expectation of the business demand.

Preparing data

As shown in the diagram, data cleansing and consolidating becomes the next focus area of action items. Data can be dispersed throughout an organisation and saved in various forms, or it can contain irregularities such as incorrect or missing records. The most signification aspect of data cleaning is to find out the hidden similarities and relationships in the data. This also includes finding out the best reliable data sources and deciding on which columns are best for study. Incomplete data, incorrect data, and inputs that appear to be independent but are heavily connected can all affect the model's conclusions in unexpected ways.

Exploring Data

When developing mining models, calculating maximum and minimum values, calculating mean and standard deviations, and assessing the data distribution, a complete grasp of the data is required. Analysing the maximum, minimum, and mean values, for example, may reveal that the data does not provide complete information about your customers or business operations, necessitating the acquisition of more balanced data or a re-evaluation of the criteria. Standard deviations and other distribution metrics are helpful in determining the results' consistency and accuracy. A high standard deviation indicates that you should add more data to your model. The information gathered must be analysed in order to comprehend the business situation. This will lead to the identification of problematic datasets and the creation of a structure to rectify the inaccurate data. To examine the input datasets and discover and correct erroneous or missing data, Microsoft tools such as Master Data Services, SQL Server Data Quality Services, and Data Profiler in Integration Services can be utilised.

Building Models

The mining model is then built using the knowledge gathered during the Exploring Data stage. On the columns of data that are required, a mining structure is developed. The mining structure gets its data only when the model is processed. SQL Server Analysis Services can be utilised to create statistical structures and aggregates from the data, which can be employed for analysis when processing the mining structure. This information is open to any of the mining model that is built on this structure. A data mining model is similar to a placeholder that specifies the input columns, predicted columns, and parameters that simply instruct the algorithm on how to process the data before it is processed. The act of bringing everything together is known as training. It is the process of applying a mathematical model to data in order to detect patterns. The chosen training data, the algorithm, and how the algorithm is configured all justify the patterns observed during the training phase. SQL Server contains a number of algorithms, each of which is chosen depending on the needs of the business to accomplish one or more functions. These models can also be adjusted by changing the input parameters and training dataset, resulting in different outcomes. The goal of these actions is to generate a mining model object that contains summaries and patterns that can be queried, used, or processed further for data prediction. To develop a new model, you can use the Data Mining Wizard in SQL Server Data Tools or the Data Mining Extensions (DMX) language. It's critical to note that the mining structure and model must be updated as the data changes. SQL Server Analysis Services detects data changes and repopulates the mining structure if the source data is dynamically updated.

Exploring and Validating Models

When creating a model, it is a usual practice to build numerous models for a range of input parameters and settings and then test each of them to record and compare the results and ultimately identify the best model which produces the results closest to the problem defined. The training and testing datasets are segregated from the input data so that the performance of all models on the same data may be accurately examined. The training dataset is often used to build the model, while the testing dataset is utilised to evaluate the model's accuracy using prediction queries. As part of the mining model design, this division can be done automatically. The viewers in SQL Server Data Tools' Data Mining Designer can be used to study the trends and patterns discovered by the algorithms. If the results produced from the models do not meet the expectations of the business needs, then the problem statement has to be re-defined, or the incoming dataset has to be re-evaluated.

Deploying and Updating Models

The last step in the data mining process is to deploy the best result-yielding models to a production environment. Once deployed, the following are some of the tasks that can be performed.

- These models are used for forecasts and are subsequently leveraged to make business decisions. SQL Server's DMX language is used to design prediction queries.
- Create content queries to get the model's statistics, rules, and formulae.
- Data mining functionality can be integrated directly into an application.
- SSIS Integration Services packages use these mining models to intelligently divide incoming data into several tables.

DEFINING MINING STRUCTURE

The data is exposed as the source data view by the mining structure. It displays the amount and kind of columns, as well as an optional partition into training and testing sets for mining models. Multiple mining models that share the same domain can be supported by a single mining model.

Data Sources for Mining Structures

Mining structures are defined using columns from a data source view that already exists. A data source view is a shared object that allows you to merge numerous data sources into one. Client applications cannot see the original data sources, but they can edit data types, construct aggregations, and alias columns using the characteristics of the data source view. On the same mining framework, multiple mining models can be developed. For example, you can develop several decision trees and clustering models from a single structure, each of which uses different columns and predicts different qualities. In the form of bindings to the source data, the data mining structure holds the definition of the data source and the columns in it. The mining structure columns are the building blocks of the mining structure. These columns contain details about the data type, content type, and distribution method. The mining structure does not contain information about how columns are utilised in a specific mining model or the type of algorithm used to build a model; this is stated in the mining model itself. Nested tables can also be found in a mining framework. A nested table depicts a one-to-many relationship between a case's entity and its associated characteristics.

Dividing the Data into Training and Testing Sets

One can specify that some of the data be used for training and some for testing while establishing the data for the mining structure. As a result, separating your data before developing a data mining structure is no longer necessary. Instead, when building a model, one might specify that a certain percentage of the data be kept for testing and the remainder for training or a specific number of examples to be employed as the test data set. The mining structure caches the information about the training and testing data sets, allowing the same test set to be applied to all models based on that structure.

Enabling Drill-through

Even if they are not to be employed in a specific mining model, some of the columns can be incorporated into the mining structure. Add a column to the structure but don't provide usage for it, or set the usage flag to Ignore it throughout the analysis and prediction phase. If drill-through has been enabled on the mining model, and if one has the relevant permissions, data highlighted in this way can still be used in queries.

Processing Mining Structures

Until it is processed, a mining structure is nothing more than a metadata store. When SQL Server Analysis Services processes a mining structure, it builds a cache that holds data statistics, information about how continuous attributes is discretised, and other information that is later required by mining models. Instead of storing this summary information, the mining model refers to the data that was cached when the mining structure was performed. As a result, there is no need to reprocess the structure every time a new model is introduced to an old structure; just processing the model is sufficient.

Using Data Mining Models with Mining Structures

A mining model algorithm is applied to the data exposed by a mining structure by means of a data mining model. A mining model is an object that belongs to a specific mining structure and inherits all of the values defined by the mining structure's properties. The model can use all or a subset of the columns contained in the mining structure. A structure can have several copies of a structural column. Multiple copies of a structural column can be added to a model, and each structure column can be given an alias name.

Microsoft Decision Tree Algorithm

An algorithm is a set of heuristics and computations used to create a model from data in data mining (or machine learning). The algorithm examines the data submitted to develop a model, looking for specific patterns or trends. The method iterates over the study's findings to find the best parameters for constructing the mining model. From the entire dataset, these factors are then used to produce actionable patterns and detailed statistics. In predictive modelling, the Microsoft Decision Trees algorithm is a classification and regression approach for both discrete and continuous attributes. The method generates discrete quality predictions based on correlations between input columns in a dataset. It uses the values, known as states, of those columns to anticipate the states of a column that is declared as predictable. The approach looks for input columns that are particularly correlated with the predicted column. The decision tree makes predictions based on this proclivity for a specific outcome. In the case of continuous attributes, linear regression is used to determine where a decision tree splits.

The Principle of the Algorithm

The Microsoft Decision Trees method produces a data mining model by constructing a sequence of splits in the tree. These splits are represented by nodes. The approach adds a node to the model every time an input column is found to be significantly correlated with the predictable column. The algorithm determines a split in a different way depending on whether it is predicting a continuous column or a discrete column. The Microsoft Decision Trees method guides the selection of the most useful attributes by using feature selection. All SQL Server Data Mining techniques employ feature selection to increase performance and analysis quality. It's critical to choose features carefully to avoid wasting processor time on unnecessary properties. When a model gets too sensitive to slight changes in the training data, it becomes overfitted or over-trained, which is a common problem in data mining models. Overfitted models cannot be applied to new data sets. The Microsoft Decision Trees algorithm uses ways to restrict the tree's growth to avoid this problem.

Predicting Discrete Columns

A histogram can be used to show how the Microsoft Decision Trees algorithm generates a tree for a discrete predictable column. A predicted column is plotted against an input column in a histogram. A tree structure is produced as the algorithm adds new nodes to a model.

Predicting Continuous Columns

In the case of a continuous, predictable column, each node is associated with a regression formula. A split happens when the regression formula reaches a point of non-linearity. The Microsoft Decision Trees algorithm looks for generally linear segments of the tree and creates different formulas for them. By this approach, the model performs efficiently in approximating the data.

Data Required for Decision Tree Models

The requirements for a decision tree model are as follows:

- A single key column: Each model must have a single numeric or text column that uniquely identifies each entry. There are no compound keys allowed.
- A predictable column: There must be at least one predictable column. A model can have multiple predictable qualities, and the predictable attributes can be of various sorts, such as numeric or discrete. Processing time can be increased by increasing the number of predictable features.
- Input columns are necessary and can be discrete or continuous. The quantity of input attributes influences the execution time.

Implementation of the Decision Trees Algorithm

The Microsoft Decision Trees algorithm uses Bayesian techniques to train causal interaction models, resulting in approximate posterior distributions for the models. The assumption of likelihood equivalence is used to evaluate the information value of the priors required for learning. Data should not be utilised to identify network topologies that otherwise transmit the same conditional independence statements, according to this concept. For each example, a single Bayesian prior network and a single measure of confidence are assumed. The program then evaluates the relative posterior probability of network structures given the current training data using these previous networks and finally identifies the network structures with the highest posterior probabilities. The Microsoft Decision Trees algorithm calculates the best tree in a number of different methods. Depending on the job, linear regression, classification, or association analysis are some of the methods that could be utilised. A single model can contain many trees expressing different predictable properties. Furthermore, each tree might contain multiple branches depending on the number of attributes and values in the data. The shape and depth of the tree generated in a specific model are determined by the grading system and other criteria. Changes in parameters can impact where the nodes split.

Building the Tree

When the Microsoft Decision Trees algorithm provides a list of possible input values, it employs feature selection to identify the qualities and values that provide the most information while excluding values that are highly rare. The approach also separates data into bins, allowing groupings of values to be treated as a unit to increase performance. A tree is built using the correlations between an input and the intended outcome. After all of the traits have been connected, the algorithm finds the single attribute that most clearly distinguishes the outcomes. The optimal separation point is determined using an equation that calculates information gain. The highest information gain score is used to divide the cases into subsets, which are then analysed recursively by the same technique until the tree cannot be divided any longer.

Discrete and Continuous Inputs

Counting the outcomes per input is as simple as building a matrix and assigning scores to each column when the predictable property is discrete, and the inputs are discrete. The continuous columns' inputs are automatically discretized when the predictable attribute is discrete, and the inputs are continuous. The Discretization Method and Discretization Bucket Count parameters can be used to determine how continuous inputs are discretized. The approach employs linear regression to discover whenever the decision tree splits for continuous attributes. When the predictor is a continuous numeric data type, feature selection is applied to the outputs to reduce the number of possible outcomes and speed up model formation. By changing the MAXIMUM OUTPUT ATTRIBUTES option, the feature selection threshold can be adjusted and increase or decrease the number of potential values.

Scoring Methods and Feature Selection

In the Microsoft Decision Trees approach, three formulas for assessing information gain include Shannon's entropy, Bayesian network with K2 prior, and Bayesian network with a uniform Dirichlet distribution of priors. All three strategies are well-known in the field of data mining. To improve analysis and reduce processing load, all SQL Server Analysis Services data mining algorithms leverage feature selection by default. The strategy for selecting features is determined by the model-building algorithm. The algorithm parameters that control feature selection for a decision trees model are MAXIMUM_INPUT_ATTRIBUTES and MAXIMUM_OUTPUT.

EXPERIMENTAL RESULTS

Dataset Collection and Datawarehouse Load

Two different datasets are collected, viz, the job openings dataset from various job opening advertisements published by corporate companies and the technical certificate courses dataset from advertisements published by industry leaders in conducting certificate exams and awarding certificates. These datasets are collected, formatted, cleansed and transformed into denormalised data by ETL (Extract, Transform and Load) packages developed in SQL Server Integration Services (SSIS). These packages are executed for every new incoming dataset, and they load the transformed data into the Stage table and subsequently are loaded into Data Warehouse (DW) fact tables.

Creating Mining Models In SSAS

Once the dataset is available in Data Warehouse, the next step is to devise a Mining Structure and a Mining Model using SQL Server Analysis Service (SSAS). This requires defining the Mining algorithm as a "Microsoft Decision Tree Algorithm" and specifying the list of input tables or views. While creating the mining structure, it's mandatory to define the "Predictable Column" and "Input Column". The Predictable column is the final output of the execution of the algorithm. SQL Server Data Mining requires defining training datasets as well as test datasets. A training dataset is needed for the algorithm to arrive at the values for "Predictable Column" values. Once all the necessary configurations are completed, the newly created "Mining Structure" is processed, which in turn triggers the SSAS to invoke the mining algorithm and generate the predictions. These are saved and deployed to SSAS under SQL Server for further analysis. Any number of outputs can be generated by changing the input dataset and by altering the Mining structure.

Generating Reports/Charts

These OLAP Cubes are further consumed by the application or SQL Server Reporting Service (SSRS). These reports take a user input dataset comprising of the user's Professional expertise, Technological Platform, the current level of certification etc., and pass on these values are parameters to already generated OLAP cubes and generate the necessary professional career guidance charts. For experimental purposes, user input datasets "DATASET-A" and DATASET-B" are collected from two different professional users ", User-A" and "User-B", respectively, and their professional guidance charts are generated as shown below.

Professional Guidance Chart for Dataset-A (User-A) and DATASET-B (User-B)

Professional career planning and decision-making based on SQL server data mining techniques have performed based on result (figs. 2 to 5).

Figure 2. Job Openings vs Certificates Courses (A)

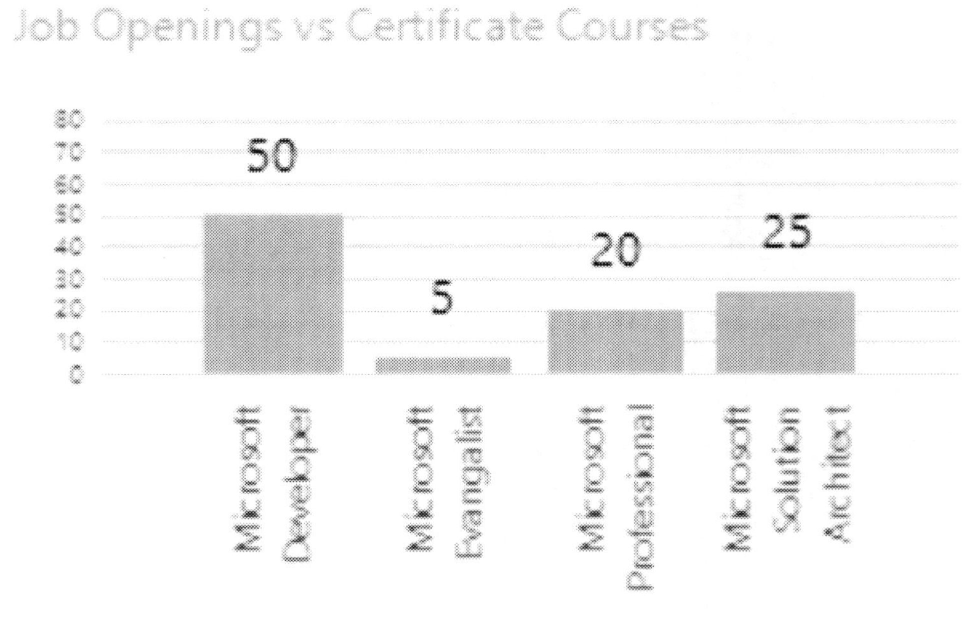

Figure 3. Job Openings vs Certificate Courses (B)

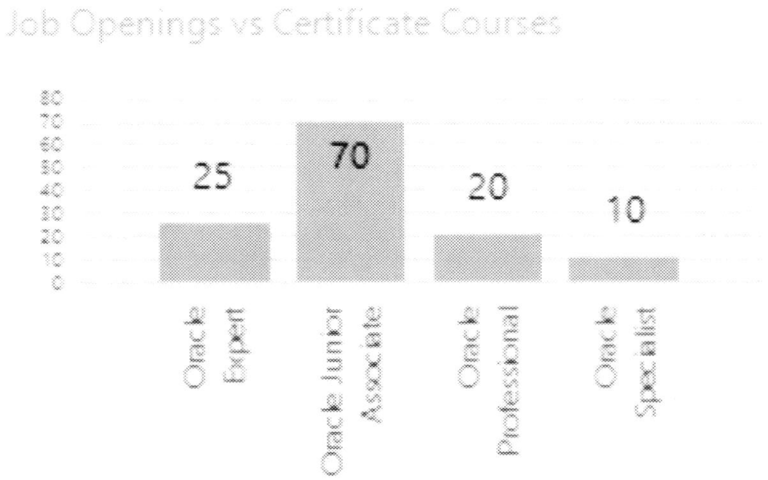

Figure 4. Job Openings vs Certificate Courses (C)

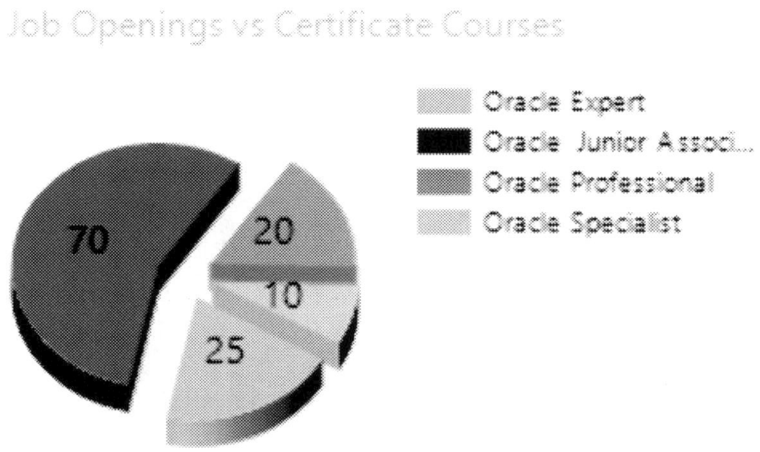

Figure 5. Job Openings vs Certificate Courses (D)

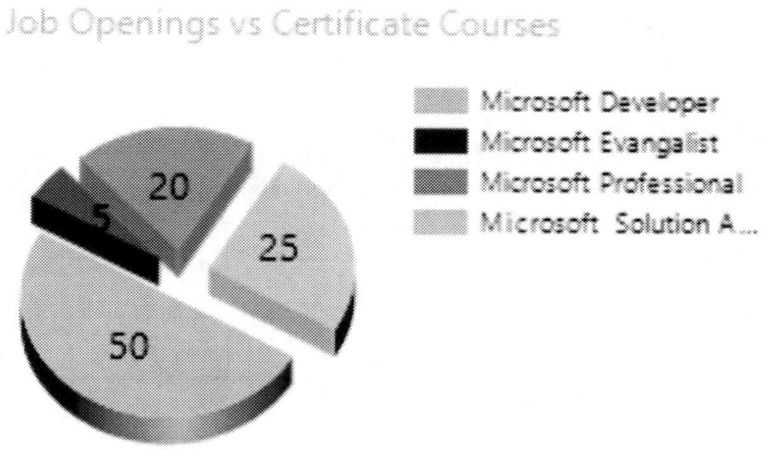

CONCLUSION

The research and projections presented in this paper can help professionals in many different fields make informed decisions about their professional futures. This gives them an advantage and boosts their marketability in the worldwide employment market. However, a sizeable segment of the population, comprising graduates and professionals, is having trouble acquiring cutting-edge knowledge and expanding their abilities in order to gain a marketable competitive edge and build prosperous professions. To make sure that "the supply matches the demand" in the market, a medium between these two antagonistic economic forces is required. This study aims to implement the Microsoft Decision Tree Data Mining Algorithm in SQL Server in order to deliver a predictive solution. Ultimately, it is discovered that the mining model constructed utilising the SQL Server Decision Tree Algorithm has higher credible prediction accuracy, laying the groundwork for providing the greatest potential advice answer to professional careers.

REFERENCES

Farooqui, N. A., & Mehra, R. (2018). Design of A data warehouse for medical information system using data mining techniques. In *2018 Fifth International Conference on Parallel, Distributed and Grid Computing (PDGC)*. IEEE. 10.1109/PDGC.2018.8745864

Feng, G., Fan, M., & Chen, Y. (2022). Analysis and prediction of students' academic performance based on educational data mining. *IEEE Access: Practical Innovations, Open Solutions*, *10*, 19558–19571. doi:10.1109/ACCESS.2022.3151652

Hajmoosaei, A., Kashfi, M., & Kailasam, P. (2011). Comparison plan for data warehouse system architectures. *3rd International Conference on Data Mining and Intelligent Information Technology Applications*, 290–293.

Hasanika, D. (2021). Data mining system for predicting a winning cricket team. In *2021 IEEE 16th International Conference on Industrial and Information Systems (ICIIS)*. IEEE. 10.1109/ICIIS53135.2021.9660702

Javad Shayegan, M., & Asgari Namin, P. (2021). An approach to improve apriori algorithm for extraction of frequent itemsets. In *2021 7th International Conference on Web Research (ICWR)*. IEEE. 10.1109/ICWR51868.2021.9443137

Ramadhani, P. P., Hadi, S., & Rosadi, R. (2021). Implementation of data warehouse in making business intelligence dashboard development using PostgreSQL database and Kimball lifecycle method. In *2021 International Conference on Artificial Intelligence and Big Data Analytics*. IEEE. 10.1109/ICAIBDA53487.2021.9689697

Sharma, A., & Singh, R. K. (2021). An efficient approach to find frequent item sets in large database. In *2021 1st Odisha International Conference on Electrical Power Engineering, Communication and Computing Technology (ODICON)*. IEEE. 10.1109/ODICON50556.2021.9428946

Chapter 24
An Introduction to Audio Manipulation and Generation of a Unified High Performance Recommendation Framework for Netflix

R. Angeline
SRM Institute of Science and Technology, India

Harish Babu M.
SRM Institute of Science and Technology, India

Rehith B.
SRM Institute of Science and Technology, India

Pranav B.
SRM Institute of Science and Technology, India

ABSTRACT

Individual users within the Netflix environment demand flexible and appropriate Netflix operations. In real-time, digital Netflix should be willing to supply appropriate Netflix objects to a user. Collaborative filtering algorithm is used in a large portion of digital recommender systems. These techniques are held back by means of real-time adaptation and need pupils to have prior information. Hence, this proposed research provides an instant recommendation system that is appropriate for complex and changeable contexts. The proposed solution is based on the problem of reinforcement Netflix. The existing method approach can explore the domain to collect information (data) and make use of that information to obtain a judgment. The built strategy is tested by making use of real-world information (data). The suggested system showcases an improved approach called Adaptive Recommendation depending upon digital Netflix style, which uses learners' behavioural data to implement Netflix resource adaption.

DOI: 10.4018/978-1-6684-6060-3.ch024

INTRODUCTION

The rise in popularity of over-the-top (OTT) video has projected a major increase in the need for movie recommendations. As a consequence, finding the right film has become difficult. The usage of recommender systems is one technique to deal with this problem. A content-based recommendation system is a tool that assists consumers in locating interesting products among a huge number of options. Furthermore, in order to recommend favoured movies, a new approach must be developed that is not just focused mostly on the movie itself but also takes the user's opinion into consideration, providing inputs for some further categorization of the readily accessible movies. Recent research has, on the other hand, focused on the accuracy of recommender systems based on movie content rather than the user's input. The purpose of this project is to close that gap. In this regard, movie streamers have been inspired by the success of just such a wide range of recommender systems in online stores in proposing a variety of things. CF, CB filtering, and hybrid filtering make part of frequent methodologies that are involved in recommendation systems. By computing the nearest neighbor of a rating matrix, CF finds unique options from similar viewers' viewpoints. New goods that haven't been reviewed yet as per the user but are to the user's nearest neighbor's interest would be recommended. CB filtering receives recommendations according to item properties. The user will be recommended things with comparable content to the current watching item. Hybrid filtering adds CB plus CF techniques to generate the suggestion. OTT recommender systems, like those in other sectors, can differ in a variety of ways based on the type of object to be suggested (e.g., movies to watch).

Although recommendation engines have been a popular way of recommending things, movie-watching has proven to be a fun way to pass the time. It entails people from comparable social groups who aren't regular movie streamers assisting one another while simultaneously streaming themselves. Help and support from fellow viewers can take numerous forms, including genre sharing. The notion of using normal streamers to promote movie patterns is also well-received. As a result, incorporating a movie watcher-review method that is based upon movie ratings transmitted together into a recommender system, which is what this work has examined, appears promising of exceptional effectiveness. We present an OTT movie recommender system in this research that combines two kinds of recommendation systems: (1) content-based recommendation and (2) suggestion based on frequent streamers' movie ratings. The first suggestion type's goal is to suggest more movie genres that are comparable to the one being seen. It guarantees that the suggested objects are always within the context of the film. The next recommendation type tries to assist customers in choosing a decent movie in order to maximize their leisure time. Happy movie streamers are those who have seen movies that appeal to their tastes and have given them high ratings.

Hence remnants of the work are ordered in a forthcoming manner. Previous works on movie recommendation systems are described in the 'Literature survey' section. The System Description portion shows the general overview of the system and describes the suggested technique, which comprises the recommender framework and arithmetical model for the recommendation of items. Data analysis and results are presented in the 'Methodology' section. This section goes through the specifics of the experimental setup used to evaluate the recommendation process. The 'Implications' section highlights the suggested system's limits as well as the system components that need to be improved. Finally, the 'Conclusion and future efforts' section includes closing thoughts as well as recommendations for future work.

LITERATURE SURVEY

According to Huafeng Liu, social recommendations have become a key element in recommendation systems in terms of holding relationships between users along with their previous activity (Liu, H. et al., 2021). The majority of existing social recommendation techniques solely take into account users' direct social contacts. Researchers recently demonstrated that indirect social links could increase the quality of suggestions while users have very minimal social connections as it can detect the user's group of interest even when no social connection is visible. Separate two-stage techniques have been investigated in the literature, but they are unable to represent the link between less-than-direct relations as well as latent user and item characteristics. The fundamental contribution of this study is to offer InSRMF a new joint recommendation model that uses InSRMF CF over networks and gauging behaviour information. User latent factors can capture users' personal opinions and social group traits simultaneously and seamlessly in our research. We build a parallelism graph vertex method for successfully managing huge-level recommendations information to optimize the InSRMF model. To show the performance of the proposed approach, experiments are done using four datasets. The experimental results suggest that InSRMF can extract the right less direct relations plus increase recommending performances when in contrast to existing methods of testing, particularly for users with minimal neighbors. The aim is on social recommendations in this work, which is rarely investigated but has recently gained attention. We introduced the InSRMF joint model to successfully integrate the social overlaying community spotting plus matrix factorization collaborative filtering in order to improve recommendation performance. Meanwhile, to solve the model, an efficient parallel graph computing approach has been developed.

According to Le Wu, one of the most prominent strategies for developing recommender systems is CF (Wu, L. et al., 2021). To compensate for the lack of data in Collaborative Filtering, social recommendation models have evolved to improve suggestions by using the relation between the interests of users. Motivated by deep learning's enormous success, recommendation systems based on neural networks have also recently demonstrated promising recommendation performance. Despite this, only a few academics have attempted to use neural models to solve the social recommendation problem. To that aim, we provide a neural architecture for a social recommendation that naturally blends the fundamental relation between the structure of social networks and user and item interaction behaviour. In this process, there are two major challenges: How to include the social relation of users' interest throughout this model, and next, to construct a neural-based architecture that captures distinctive aspects of user and item interaction behaviour for a recommender. We create a system called CNSR that has two parts: A social encoding portion and a CNR part, to address these two issues. The user embedding in CNSR is based on an unsupervised deep learning method with social relation regularization that learns each user's social embedding (Li, J. et al., 2021). The user and object word embedding are then fed into a one-of-a-kind neural network that includes a newly developed collaboration layer to simulate both shallow collaboratives plus deeply complicated interaction interactions between people plus items. We also suggest a cooperative learning architecture that allows social encoding and CNR components to complement one another. Finally, substantial experimental findings and real datasets confirm that our suggested approach is effective.

According to Zhenhua Huang, group suggestion is becoming a popular research area and interest in the online network community in recent years (Huang, Z. et al., 2020). Many algorithms based on deep learning are currently being used to educate group preference for objects and anticipate the forthcoming items that groups might be interested in. Despite this, because of the scarce group-item interactions, overall recommendation effectiveness still seems to be inadequate. To address this issue, we present a model, SGRTAB, in this research, which improves the effectiveness and recommendation of groups in online networks. Data preparation (DP) and prototype optimisation are two stages of the SGRTAB model (MO). SGRTAB generates MO inputs and performs three tasks: trying to extract unique features, handling group data via GloVe, as well as making use of users to make a contribution to their own groups in DP. By the concept of transferring plus ensemble learning, SGRTAB may efficiently absorb user preference knowledge into the way of organisational learning. Furthermore, rigorous tests on four datasets show that the suggested SGRTAB method beats current benchmarks and social group recommendations significantly. Through transferring ensemble learning, this study offers SGRTAB as an efficient model for group recommendation.

According to Xiaokang Zhou, Cyber computing is believed to be playing an essential role throughout cyber-related models and applications as a result of the development of many evolving computational paradigms and information transmission technologies (Zhou, X. et al., 2019). They have focused on cyber computing in this paper and present a computational model that incorporates huge-scale choice-making for groups: LSGDM in social recommendations. For social recommendations, a double stage large level decision-making system is proposed: One, a partitioning algorithm modelled on the experts' identification and the impact extending to researchers is developed, and next, a random walk with the algorithm of restart-based is modified to calculate weighed choices for the decision of group aggregating and alternate ranking. Trials with real-world information illustrate the utility as well as the efficiency of the suggested model, which can deliver more credible recommendations to the target researcher.

According to Le Wu, in recent years, image-based social networks have been becoming one of the biggest popular social networking sites (Wu, L. et al., 2020). Understanding user interests in photographs generated by users and giving suggestions has become an important requirement with the massive volume of images posted every day. In fact, numerous hybrid approaches have been presented to improve recommendation performance by combining various types of receiver sides (e.g., picture pictorial depiction, social network) plus user-item previous behaviour (Li, J. et al., 2021). Previous research, however, failed to capture the numerous variables that impact many users' choices in a framework because of the unique qualities of photos generated by users on social platforms. For social contextual imagery recommendation, they suggested a hierarchy of responsive social context systems (HASC). In particular, they have identified social context variables that can influence a user's taste for an image, in addition to online interest modelling: the upload date factor, the influence of social factors, and the owner likeness component.

EXISTING SYSTEM

Presently, the Internet of Things is rapidly exposing the problem of information overload, necessitating research on recommender systems in anticipation of industrial IoT situations. Social recommendations will undoubtedly become a vital function that will provide more accessible personal information services to upcoming consumers as the predominance of various social networks grows. Almost all existing studies, on the other hand, have focused on and quantified correlations involving users' preferences with community relations while ignoring relations between item attributes. It may have an impact on the morphologies of some social groups. This challenge is faced and resolved by the usage of a deep graph neural network-based social recommendation framework (GNN-SoR) (Obeidat et al., 2019). This research proposes a GNN-SoR for forthcoming IoT to address this difficulty. First, the person characteristic space plus item features were encoded using a graph neural network method as two graph networks. The missing rate values in the user and item rating matrix are then filled in by embedding two encoded spaces within two latent factors of matrix factorization. Finally, a significant number of projects were carried out in three datasets to validate the recommended GNNSoR's performance and accuracy (Guo et al., 2021). IoT is becoming an essential component of people's daily lives in the approaching 5G age, particularly in numerous social and leisure activities. The above study is able to look at the use of SoR for upcoming IoT users. To represent features using SoR, the research takes advantage of item-attribute correlations and presents the GNN-SoR framework. First, the user-object featured spaces are aggregated as a double graph network, which is then embedded using the graphical neural network approach. The rating values missing in the user and item rating matrix are then filled in by embedding two encoded spaces inside a double latent element on matrix factorization (Zhao, Z. et al., 2016). Ultimately, a significant number of tests are performed in three datasets and confirm the suggested GNN-efficiency SoR's and stability.

Drawbacks of the Existing System

Existing methods provide an ineffective movie recommendation solution. This system has a major impact on capital and running costs. When used on a big-scale parallel computing system, it suffers endlessly, and the system is prone to errors. The techniques used are not equipped to handle greater data sets, which causes the system to become more complicated and have more dimensions.

PROPOSED METHODOLOGY

The proposed method uses a clustering algorithm on the movie's dataset, and this step is essential to categorize similar users to similar clusters upon their previous behaviour and history. The used cluster algorithm and Euclidean distance are used to gauge the likeness between movies. Movie mining - This part is very important in our recommendation system. Data mining techniques are used to get AR, and the movie dataset is built by linking each movie to one of the items and every user to one of a transaction. The suggested system uses a couple of algorithms in this phase: Algorithm AR Mining is used for every cluster made from the previous phase; it uses movie transaction data which holds 'transactionId' and maps to each and every user set of the items. Frequent sequence mining is to be used to discover patterns that have specific arrangements; hence assembly of movies is required to be applied to the algorithm. Watched movies are ordered for each user based on parameters in the original dataset. AR created in the previous stage will be used for movie recommendations.

ARCHITECTURE DIAGRAM

Figure 1. Detailed Architecture of the proposed system

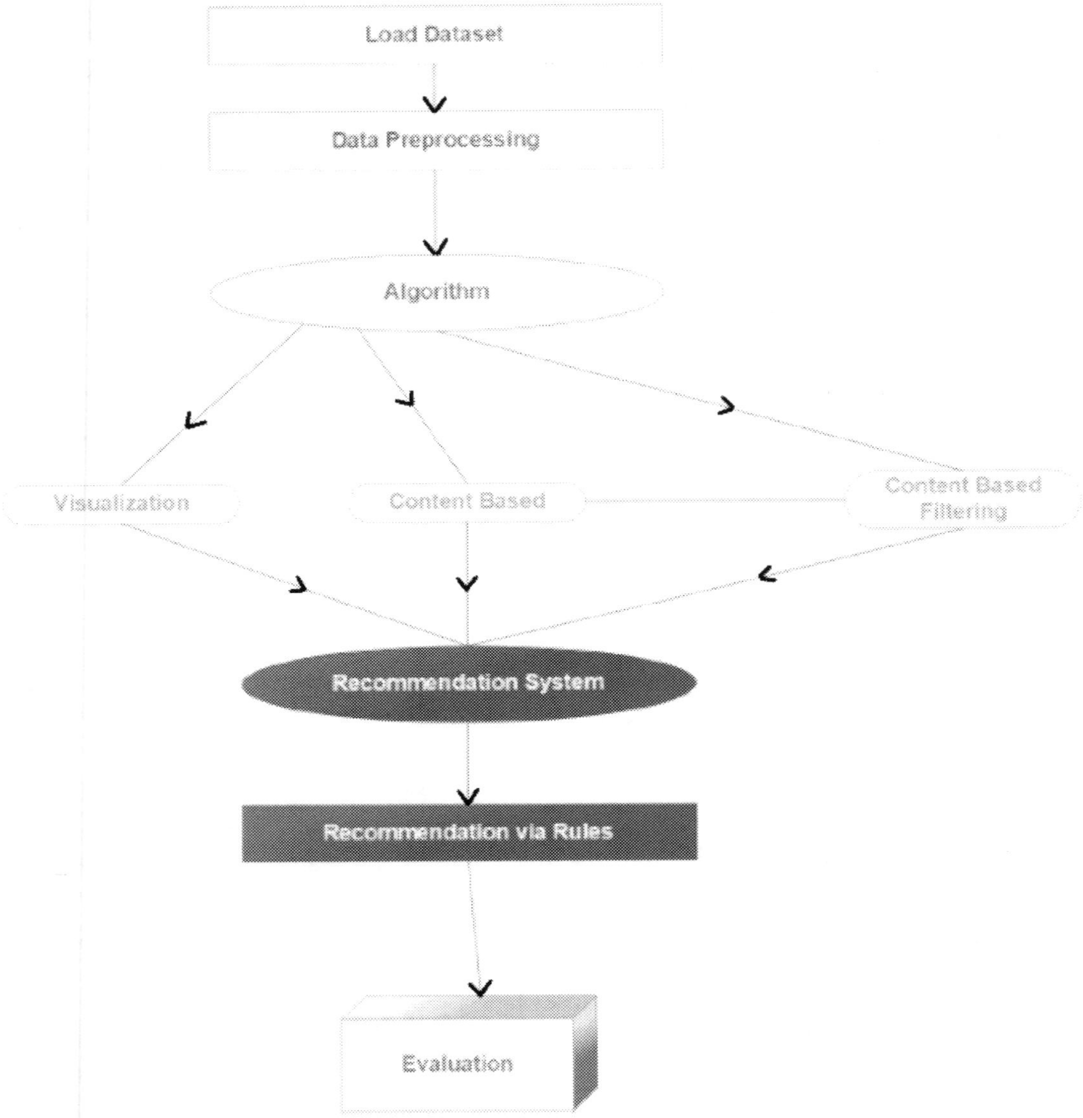

The architecture diagram states the flow of the system carried out to perform the task (fig.1). The dataset is first loaded then the data that is passed to the system is then pre-processed. Later the data is sent to the algorithm, and this algorithm performs content-based filtering of the availability of data, and then the recommendation rules over the data for the recommendation are applied, and the output is obtained.

PROJECT MODULES

Module 1: Exploratory Data Analysis

This data analysis is always categorized in 2 ways. First, it states that any approach can be split into non-graphical or graphical. Next, it states that any approach can be divided into univariate or multivariate. The approach that falls under Non-Graphical methods always indulges computation of summary statistics; on the other hand, graphical methods clearly summarize the information which is available in a graphical representation. A one-time investigation of the relationship among single parameters is carried out in the univariate method, whereas in the multivariate, a parallel investigation of the relationship is carried out over two or more variables. Commonly, a multivariate is known as bivariate, but three or even more variables may be included on rare occasions. Before completing a multivariate EDA, it is nearly often a good idea to run a univariate EDA from each of the aspects of the multivariate EDA.

Module 2: Preprocessing

The process of pre-processing is carried out for the removal of any consequences of modest study errors. Collections are divided into multiple intervals by replacing them with categorical values. Indicator variables: This is used to turn categorized information into values in Boolean. If the resultant that is obtained contains any over two values, yt should be cut down in such a way that it contains one value. For centralizing information on a single feature, the mean of the values should be taken off from all the available values. We would divide the cantered characteristic by both the standard deviation to scale the data. In regard to the categorical feature set, labels provide textual labels, including both ordinal and nominal features. Certain labels might well have order connected with them (ordinal features), while others may not (nominal features). To ensure that such a learning algorithm reads the features correctly, it is critical to encoding labels accurately in numerical form as part of data preparation. The Label Encoder class of the sklearn. The pre-processing module is used to encrypt labels of categorical attributes in the next section. The process which is carried out for manipulating all the available word labels to Arithmetical representation so that an algorithm could interpret is coated as Label encoding.

Module 3: Prediction

Whenever a huge dataset is projected, the ideal approach that should be followed up to state the model is effective the model should contain a train and test split data; this can make the accuracy of the resultant model have huge accuracy over any inputs passed to it. Validation of the data from the dataset is done while training the data, which is why a training split is necessary. The train split is not actually for training the model, but the inputs are fed into the model, and the model carries out the process of comparing the fed input with the predicted values. Each model becomes much more effective if it contains a machine-learning model, and that could be built by using the available training split. The second split of the dataset is called as test dataset, and this is used to validate the model by bringing out the accuracy of the model's prediction. By default, the application doesn't consider the original order of the data. It chooses data randomly to make the test and training splits, which is usually a desired feature in real-world applications to prevent information preparation artifacts. The model uses the KNN algorithm, which represents the quantity of nearest neighbors. Let's take an example of two instances where K is often an odd integer. The algorithm is called the nearest neighbor whenever K is1. This scenario is the simplest. You must first locate only one nearest star to P1 and afterwards apply that label of such nearest point to P1. Assume P1 is indeed the point for which the label must forecast. As the algorithm states finding the nearest point to the P1 is important, which helps to categorize all the points available. The classification is done based on the votes obtained by each point purely depending on the K neighbors. Each item votes for its class, and the votes are mostly determined by the prediction of the class. The distance between similar places is calculated using distance metrics like Manhattan distance, Euclidean distance, Minkowski distance, and Hamming distance (Kulkarni et al., 2022).

RESULTS

Proposed a system for recommending online movies to users based on similarities and differences between the target viewer and other viewers. Data mining methods are employed to construct movie rules using AR algorithms, and a covering measure is used to measure the recommender's performance. We concluded that grouping data into similar clusters ended in increased coverage values rather than constructing rules that covered the entire data through the trials. Cluster datasets have a substantial impact on performance, and choosing heavy covering within the recommender system results in superior end products.

Figure 2. Feeding Movie dataset

```
In [13]: movies.head(2)
Out[13]:
```

	movieId	title	genres
0	1	Toy Story (1995)	Adventure|Animation|Children|Comedy|Fantasy
1	2	Jumanji (1995)	Adventure|Children|Fantasy

Table 1 shows a sample of the available movie dataset, which is meant to be passed to the recommender to yield a recommended output for the user based on the similarities; this dataset contains movie details like movieID, title and genres.

Figure 3. Feeding rating dataset

```
In [14]: ratings.head(2)
Out[14]:
```

	userId	movieId	rating	timestamp
0	1	2	3.5	2005-04-02 23:53:47
1	1	29	3.5	2005-04-02 23:31:16

Table 2 shows a sample of the available rating dataset, which is meant to be passed to the recommender to yield a recommended output for the user based on the similarities; this dataset contains movie ratings, userid, movieID and their timestamp.

Figure 4. Feeding tag dataset

```
In [15]: tags.head(2)
Out[15]:
```

	userId	movieId	tag	timestamp
0	18	4141	Mark Waters	2009-04-24 18:19:40
1	65	208	dark hero	2013-05-10 01:41:18

Table 3 shows a sample of the available tag dataset, which is meant to be passed to the recommender to yield a recommended output for the user based on the similarities this dataset contains movie userid, movieid, tag and timestamps.

Figure 5. Cleaning the fed dataset

```
In [16]: movies['genres'] = movies['genres'].str.replace('|', ' ')

In [17]: movies.head()

Out[17]:
```

	movieId	title	genres
0	1	Toy Story (1995)	Adventure Animation Children Comedy Fantasy
1	2	Jumanji (1995)	Adventure Children Fantasy
2	3	Grumpier Old Men (1995)	Comedy Romance
3	4	Waiting to Exhale (1995)	Comedy Drama Romance
4	5	Father of the Bride Part II (1995)	Comedy

Table 4 shows a method of cleaning the available dataset, and that dataset is later fed to the system for making effective recommendations. This dataset contains movieid, titles and genres.

Figure 6. Grouping UserId with respect to ratings

```
In [21]: ratings_t = ratings.groupby('userId').filter(lambda x: len(x) > 80)
         ratings_t

Out[21]:
```

	userId	movieId	rating	timestamp
0	1	2	3.5	2005-04-02 23:53:47
1	1	29	3.5	2005-04-02 23:31:16
2	1	32	3.5	2005-04-02 23:33:39
3	1	47	3.5	2005-04-02 23:32:07
4	1	50	3.5	2005-04-02 23:29:40
...	...	...	...	...
20000258	138493	68954	4.5	2009-11-13 15:42:00
20000259	138493	69526	4.5	2009-12-03 18:31:48
20000260	138493	69644	3.0	2009-12-07 18:10:57
20000261	138493	70286	5.0	2009-11-13 15:42:24
20000262	138493	71619	2.5	2009-10-17 20:25:36

16817989 rows × 4 columns

Table 5 shows the grouping done over the available dataset that is meant to be fed to the system to provide an effective and efficient recommendation over the similarities between the movies.

Figure 7. Merging the mixed datasets over movieID

```
In [30]: mixed = pd.merge(movies, tags, on='movieId', how = 'left')
         mixed.head()
Out[30]:
```

	movieId	title	genres	userId	tag
0	1	Toy Story (1995)	Adventure Animation Children Comedy Fantasy	1644.0	Watched
1	1	Toy Story (1995)	Adventure Animation Children Comedy Fantasy	1741.0	computer animation
2	1	Toy Story (1995)	Adventure Animation Children Comedy Fantasy	1741.0	Disney animated feature
3	1	Toy Story (1995)	Adventure Animation Children Comedy Fantasy	1741.0	Pixar animation
4	1	Toy Story (1995)	Adventure Animation Children Comedy Fantasy	1741.0	TÃ©a Leoni does not star in this movie

Table 6 shows how the all-available datasets are merged to obtain metadata over movieid that is fed to the system to obtain an effective and efficient recommendation.

Figure 8. Final Metadata

```
In [33]: Final.head()
Out[33]:
```

	movieId	title	genres	tag	metadata
0	1	Toy Story (1995)	Adventure Animation Children Comedy Fantasy	Watched computer animation Disney animated fea...	Watched computer animation Disney animated fea...
1	2	Jumanji (1995)	Adventure Children Fantasy	time travel adapted from:book board game child...	time travel adapted from:book board game child...
2	3	Grumpier Old Men (1995)	Comedy Romance	old people that is actually funny sequel fever...	old people that is actually funny sequel fever...
3	4	Waiting to Exhale (1995)	Comedy Drama Romance	chick flick revenge characters chick flick cha...	chick flick revenge characters chick flick cha...
4	5	Father of the Bride Part II (1995)	Comedy	Diane Keaton family sequel Steve Martin weddin...	Diane Keaton family sequel Steve Martin weddin...

Table 7 states the final metadata obtained by merging all the available datasets; this is the final dataset that is fed to the system for the recommendation to be carried out.

Figure 9. Plotting Graph on Cumulative percent of variance against singular value components

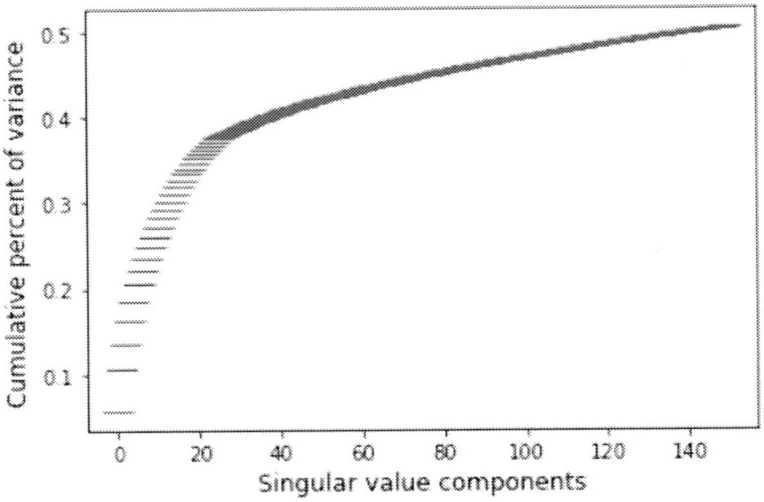

Figure 9 shows that a graph is plotted against the cumulative percent of variance and singular value components to showcase the effectiveness of the system.

Figure 10. Final Recommender

```
In [55]: recommender('Jumanji (1995)', mat_movies_users, model_knn,20)

         Movie Selected:  Jumanji (1995) Index:  1
         Searching for recommendations.....
         1                                         NaN
         360                       Lion King, The (1994)
         470                  In the Line of Fire (1993)
         357               It Could Happen to You (1994)
         490                   Executive Decision (1996)
         574                     Princess Caraboo (1994)
         751                                Heavy (1995)
         709    Halfmoon (Paul Bowles - Halbmond) (1995)
         370                          Richie Rich (1994)
         576               Métisse (Café au Lait) (1993)
         349                           Crow, The (1994)
         373                               Speed (1994)
         148                           Apollo 13 (1995)
         575                 Celluloid Closet, The (1995)
         311             Secret of Roan Inish, The (1994)
         203                     Unstrung Heroes (1995)
         337                    Double Happiness (1994)
         583             Terminator 2: Judgment Day (1991)
         628                      Family Thing, A (1996)
         580                          Home Alone (1990)
         Name: title, dtype: object
```

Table 8 shows the final recommender that is built using all the data mining and deep learning techniques that now can serve the use in producing an effective and efficient recommendation over the similarities among the movies.

CONCLUSION

A high-performance recommendation system has been discussed. We have developed the concept of a movie recommendation system that makes suggestions for users regarding movies to watch based on the similarities and differences that exist between the intended user and other users. In order to develop the courses and rules, data mining techniques were utilised, and coverage measurement was applied in order to evaluate the effectiveness of the suggestions. In the course of the studies, it was discovered that grouping datasets into subsets with comparable characteristics tended to produce higher coverage values, in contrast to the practice of constructing rules to cover the full dataset. Both clustering the dataset and selecting high coverage have enhanced the outcomes of the recommender system. The clustering of the dataset has had a considerable effect on the performance. The recommendation system could be expanded to cover other forms of entertainment, such as television shows and music. Additionally, the existing system could be improved to enable a variety of other methods of gauging a user's interests based on their preferences on social media or their activities on other external websites in order to provide better recommendations. These are all possible works for the future, and they could include the following: not limiting the recommendation system to movies alone.

REFERENCES

Guo, S., Li, X., & Mu, Z. (2021). Adversarial machine learning on social network: A survey. *Frontiers in Physics*, *9*, 766540. Advance online publication. doi:10.3389/fphy.2021.766540

Huang, Z., Ni, J., Yao, J., Xu, X., Zhang, B., Chen, Y., Tan, N., & Xue, C. (2020). Social Group Recommendation With TrAdaBoost. *IEEE Transactions on Computational Social Systems*, *7*(5), 1278–1287. doi:10.1109/TCSS.2020.3009721

Kulkarni, A., Shivananda, A., & Kulkarni, A. (2022). Named-entity recognition using CRF and BERT. In Natural Language Processing Projects. Apress.

Li, J., Wu, L., Hong, R., & Hou, J. (2021). Random walk based distributed representation learning and prediction on Social Networking Services. *Information Sciences*, *549*, 328–346. doi:10.1016/j.ins.2020.10.045

Liu, H., Jing, L., Yu, J., & Ng, M. K. (2021). Social recommendation with learning personal and social latent factors. *IEEE Transactions on Knowledge and Data Engineering*, *33*(7), 2956–2970. doi:10.1109/TKDE.2019.2961666

Obeidat, R., Duwairi, R., & Al-Aiad, A. (2019). A collaborative recommendation system for online courses recommendations. In *2019 International Conference on Deep Learning and Machine Learning in Emerging Applications (Deep-ML)*. IEEE. 10.1109/Deep-ML.2019.00018

Wu, L., Chen, L., Hong, R., Fu, Y., Xie, X., & Wang, M. (2020). A hierarchical attention model for social contextual image recommendation. *IEEE Transactions on Knowledge and Data Engineering*, *32*(10), 1854–1867. doi:10.1109/TKDE.2019.2913394

Wu, L., Sun, P., Hong, R., Ge, Y., & Wang, M. (2021). Collaborative Neural Social Recommendation. *IEEE Transactions on Systems, Man, and Cybernetics. Systems*, *51*(1), 464–476. doi:10.1109/TSMC.2018.2872842

Zhao, Z., Lu, H., Cai, D., He, X., & Zhuang, Y. (2016). User preference learning for online social recommendation. *IEEE Transactions on Knowledge and Data Engineering*, *28*(9), 2522–2534. doi:10.1109/TKDE.2016.2569096

Zhou, X., Liang, W., Huang, S., & Fu, M. (2019). Social recommendation with large-scale group decision-making for cyber-enabled online service. *IEEE Transactions on Computational Social Systems*, *6*(5), 1073–1082. doi:10.1109/TCSS.2019.2932288

Chapter 25
Practical Approaches to Machine Learning for 5G and Beyond Wireless Network

M. M. Kamruzzaman
https://orcid.org/0000-0001-8464-1523
Jouf University, Saudi Arabia

Md Altab Hossin
Chengdu University, China

Ibrahim Alrashdi
Jouf University, Saudi Arabia

ABSTRACT

Wireless communication is now the market segment that is expanding the fastest, and this is because it can offer ubiquitous access to a wide range of applications and services at very low costs. This issue makes it difficult to analyze energy consumption and maximize that energy. Additionally, it might raise certain financial and environmental issues. Modern energy service companies are working to develop and implement energy solutions using cutting-edge technologies. Machine learning is overemphasized by all data scientists while being a widely used technology in the fields of advanced sciences. Automated decision-making is the foundation for advanced machine learning features. It has been noted that every industry is attempting to adopt and utilize machine learning and artificial intelligence in order to reduce reliance on humans. As the field of information technology continues to advance quickly, developers are working to incorporate machine learning for energy management in wireless systems.

DOI: 10.4018/978-1-6684-6060-3.ch025

INTRODUCTION

The fastest-growing segment in today's era is wireless communication, and the reason is that it is highly cost-effective and it can provide pervasive access to a profusion of applications and services. The main support for the foregoing growth is the mobile cellular network. In the 21st century, there are more mobile subscribers than the population. Seven thousand six hundred million number was recorded in 2019, and it grew at 5% in 2021, which is 9000 million subscribers. Furthermore, with the increasing number of mobile subscribers, there is an increase in data traffic that is being produced by the connecting device (A. Desai et al., 2022) and (Singh (Mehtab et al., ener2022). The increase is ten times higher due to the expansion in augmented reality, virtual reality and video streaming, and many more, which are bandwidth-intensive applications. With this increase in data traffic, it becomes hard for operators and managers to manage tons of data (Sesto-Castilla et al., 2019). This problem leads to challenges in analyzing energy consumption and optimizing that energy. Moreover, it can increase costs and raise some environmental concerns. For that reason, nowadays, energy service companies are engaged in building and implementing energy solutions with the help of emerging technologies. They are finding different ways for how energy consumption can be managed effectively by which costs can be reduced, risks can be mitigated, and environmental concerns can be addressed (Feng, 2022). By finding innovative ways through machine learning, companies will become able to manage the energy in mobile networks.

In the present digital age, machine learning has become a hot topic in information technology and, admittedly, a hidden and central part of all lives. Machine learning is a part of artificial intelligence in which algorithm study is explored, data is learned, and predictions are made based on that data (Omer, 2019). With the increase in data traffics, smart data analysis is becoming more ubiquitous for technological progress. The science of machine learning brings a vast number of applications to solve current problems and explore better solutions (Vishwanathan, 2010). Thus, machine learning has also proven helpful in managing energy in wireless mobile networks.

An extensive amount of data is needed to work in machine learning, and this data comes from billion sensors that are continuously coming online in the internet of things (IoT). The internet of things is an intensive technology and helps machine learning to make better artificial intelligence. Internet of things communications is leveraged to make improvements in energy management (Suykens, 2014). To amplify the quality of human life Internet of things implement mobile computations, applications, and wireless communications. Communication's structure of the wireless network is defined by mathematical models. Ongoing data is collected, analyzed, and shared with the help of connected tools such as devices, intelligent wireless communications, and mobiles. Through this deployment, huge factories and computing systems get an insight into how to utilize energy (Feng, 2022). Internet of things systems and wireless connections are achieving rapid development, and with that change, a solution has emerged, which is energy-efficient mobile computing that processes the data of internet of things devices. In this process, the internet of things devices transmit the data, which is formed on physical servers that are present in centres of could data and intermediate computing nodes. There are certain limitations of the internet of things, such as energy-saving, the dynamic nature of IoT devices, and its unpredictable environment. This is why machine learning methods help the internet of things by providing a clear path of accuracy that increases the performance of IoT's infrastructure so that it can forecast energy consumption and power production in computing systems and mobile networks (Feng, 2022). Hence, the above-mentioned points indicate the importance of the internet of things in managing energy in electrical devices.

The aim of this research is to explore various ways to manage energy in wireless mobile networks with the help of machine learning. This research has great significance in this digital age as it not only helps consumers to get a better experience but provides a huge insight to software companies, factories, utilities, and other players so that there be efficient energy management systems in wireless mobile connections. This study also explores the different techniques of machine learning by management processes of the 5G network that can be improved. The analysis of intensive data will enable intelligent systems to predict the future nature of the network through which companies can make rational decisions. The application of machine learning techniques will allow for saving energy through intelligence.

LITERATURE REVIEW

Machine learning can be described as a form of Artificial Intelligence that is used to forecast new results based on previously existing data or the results without being specifically implemented to create or programmed to achieve these results. Integrating artificial intelligence tools like machine language in network management enables networkers to forecast the amount of flow of traffic on a certain network in the near future. Besides that, it also helps in maintaining security measures and getting better data analytics.

The application of Machine Learning in network management firstly helps in predicting fault failures, which helps in mitigating the risk of failure. Besides that, Machine Learning also helps in leveraging performance and quality management, e.g., by forecasting the traffic load, which can prevent compromising on the quality of service provided. Machine Learning is also now widely used for security management as it helps to identify the pattern of misuse detection, which can help in the prevention of networks from those attacks. Moreover, Machine Learning can also help maintain the data for accounting management by ensuring that the data collected is accurate and authentic and by detecting fraud from that data (Sara Ayoubi, 2018). However, the incorporation of Machine Learning is yet to be explored by different companies in the accounting sector.

In a survey, Machine Learning application in the Self Organizing Networks (SON) during the past 15 years was provided. According to Klaine et al. (2017), the deployment of Machine Learning will be essential to be up-to-date with the ever-innovating, autonomous and intelligent future that is flooding through the technologies in the present and future. And as the paradigm is shifting more toward technologies in the future enormous not only human but machine data will be needed to monitor and managed, which will not be possible without the use of ML.

Machine learning also helps in Energy Efficiency Optimization. According to Ali Imran et al. (2019), machine learning facilitates the optimization of energy efficiency as it offers the options to manage resource allocations by using previously collected data and optimizing various network instalments. Besides that, the author also states that although deploying Machine Learning solves the automation of complex and enormous data, it still needs to be made more technologically efficient. This may include bringing efficiency in the decision-making power and working towards making it a more decentralized system for ML to meet the increasing future demands.

In another research, the author enlightens the deployment of machine learning in the 5Gs and other networks. According to Challita et al. (2020), the incorporation of these techniques in network development can help in cost reduction, as well as in improving the performance of energy management for mobile network companies. He argued that there is a need to further research on the importance of the development of the Machine Learning architecture to maintain an end-to-end communication system that conserves energy and reduces costs.

The Wireless Internet Service Provider (WIPS) also integrates Artificial intelligence like Machine Learning to ensure that they meet the customers' needs and expectations to stay ahead of the competition in the wireless communication market. According to Vamvakas et al. (2017), the customers opt for the mechanism that uses Machine Learning. Hence, to meet the Quality Of Service (QOS) demands of the customers, a power control game was introduced among the customers by the WIPS. Through the use of quality optimization methods based on machine learning, mobile networks can be made more efficient in energy consumption while enhancing the quality of networks.

CHALLENGES

Wireless mobile networks or communication is considered one of the developing segments of digital communication. It is mainly due to its cost-effective features and applications. Energy management in wireless mobile networks is very important for stringent sensor nodes. Mostly, all these nodes are attached to powered batteries (Baier, Jöhren & Seebacher 2019). All the data scientist gives too much importance to machine learning as it is one of the popular technology in the advanced sciences. Advanced features of machine learning technologies are based on the automated decision-making process. It has been observed that every industry is trying to adopt and implement Artificial Intelligence and machine learning to minimize human dependency. Developers are trying to implement machine learning for energy management in the wireless as rapid development in the field of information technology and machine learning is creating many opportunities, but there are some concerns and challenges that arise due to the implementation of machine learning (Challita, Ryden & Tullberg, 2020). It is a common perception that machine learning saves the resources such as time and money; however, there are many issues regarding data quality, data sharing, memory limitation and device power, deployment issues and training complexities that arise with the implementation of the machine learning for the energy management in the wireless networks. Quality of service is a crucial component of any business operation. In the recent world, with the advancement in technology, no one wants to compromise on the quality of any services. It has been seen that there is a higher probability of quality affection due to the implementation and adoption of machine learning (Mahakud et al., 2016). Some of the main challenges regarding machine learning for energy management within wireless mobile networks are given below.

QUALITY OF SERVICE

Machine learning in the energy management of the wireless communication system leads to challenges in terms of efficiently utilizing the limited network resources to attain a higher quality of services (Hou, 2020). The demand response of the smart grid technologies has played a crucial role in the improvement of reliability and overall cost reduction; that is why implementation of the demand response on the industry level is required (Lu et al., 2020). But these demand responses are based on past data, which affects the overall quality of the service because, in the traditional way of response, the reactions depend on the updated data. That is why the traditional approach of demand response is considered more appropriate (Lu et al., 2020). However, the overall financial cost and energy consumption increases with the implementation of machine learning for the purpose of energy management in wireless mobile networks. It was also seen that battery capacity is also one of the hurdles in the improvement of the overall quality of service. Energy efficiency is one of the important factors in the design of the wireless mobile network. The main aim is to save as many resources as possible. Improvement of the Quality of Service (QOS) is considered a challenging task with the implementation of machine learning (Hou, 2020).

INSECURE PROCESS

Data insecurity is one of the biggest challenges that arise in the management of energy in wireless mobile networks through machine learning (Kamruzzaman, 2022). That is the reason the accuracy of the processes is affected badly. The incorporation of sensor and communication technologies in the power structures, identified as the smart grid, has the ability to transform the model of the production, supply, monitoring, and control of energy. But securing the smart grid is considered one of the challenging tasks (Babar, Tariq & Jan 2020). Interface management and advanced energy management are considered useful approaches for the optimization of energy utilization, but there is a huge difference between the management of the operation from traditional to advanced models (Babar, Tariq & Jan 2020). Wireless networks enhance the risks of false BSs, jamming attacks and eavesdropping. But implementation of AI and machine learning increases security and cyber threats. There is also the probability of misleading the training data, which consequently affects the overall operations. However, building and creating the appropriate database is also a challenging task for energy management in wireless mobile networks, but on the other side, it is a time taking process as the collection of the complete data is a difficult step (Challita, Ryden & Tullberg, 2020).

INEFFICIENT ENERGY MANAGEMENT

Machine learning in wireless mobile networks leads to inefficient energy management, especially on a large scale. Low-powered devices resist the energy storage in their batteries, and consequently, limitations and shortcomings bring new and complicated challenges to energy optimization with the growth in Information technology and machine learning (Du et al., 2020). Artificial Intelligence and Machine learning-based energy management techniques only need past and present data about the energy arrival for the improvement of communication performance. Due to this, energy-harvesting technologies have been used to harvest energy from potential sources (MM Kamruzzaman &Omar Alruwaili). However, controllable energy is used, which is filled with the battery's capacity. This will lead to overall uncertainty. Hence the implication of machine learning and Artificial Intelligence for energy management in wireless mobile networks can lead to uncertainty due to inefficient energy management (Du et al., 2020).

CENTRALIZED DATA MANAGEMENT

The main aim of Artificial Intelligence is to eliminate complexity through innovation. Machine learning is a subset or component of Artificial Intelligence. Its job is to automatically take a decision based on the available data that was collected from previous operations (Mahakud et al., 2016). The importance of centralized machine data has increased as it requires a series of data for a quick and appropriate response (Moysiadis, Sarigiannidis, & Moscholios, 2018). Traditionally machine learning for the Internet of Things has been done by uploading the series of data to the cloud train in a generic form that can be shared, implemented and applied to all devices simultaneously (Moysiadis, Sarigiannidis, & Moscholios, 2018). However, it requires a series of updated centralized data for the appropriate machine learning so that it can automatically operate as per the desire. The main aim of the Wireless sensor network is to detect important information from the environment based on the deployed application and to send it to the base section for the appropriate action (Mahakud et al., 2016). In this way, sensor nodes communicate with each other. During the collection of the detected data, the data is directly transmitted to the base station. So all these operations require complete centralized data. That is why the collection of standardized or centralized data for energy management in wireless mobile networks is one of the biggest challenges that arise with the implementation of machine learning and Artificial Intelligence (Mahakud et al., 2016).

Moreover, most researchers and developers agree on the point that machine learning brings efficiency into day-to-day operations, which is why there is a need to overcome these challenges through targeted market research and innovation.

USE CASES

At the global level, mobile communication companies are becoming increasingly interested in technology that helps more energy-efficient infrastructure development for commercial, environmentally friendly, and legislative considerations. One such case is Ericson company claims that research activities at Ericsson have been incredibly helpful in identifying ways to reduce energy usage in wireless mobile carriers. Despite retaining a constantly good QoE due to their considerable knowledge of network management and optimizations, the new initiatives seem highly important. There is a requirement for precise prediction models that enable Ericsson to anticipate when such modifications can be performed in advance, given that certain configuration adjustments might take longer to have influence than others (Vandikas et al., 2021). Thus, prospective interruption to the overall operations of the system could be minimized. An ideal approach could be regarded as one of the feasible ways meant to lower energy usage on Ericson's infrastructure components' existing performance for wireless communication. Considering the new technology, Ericson has created the end-to-end (E2E) energy optimization paradigm, which includes the power systems, nodes, and network level. Figure 1 depicts Ericson's idea and emphasizes the energy suggestion mechanism that it has formed for wireless communication.

Figure 1. End-to-end energy optimization from the power system to the node to the network (www.ericsson.com)

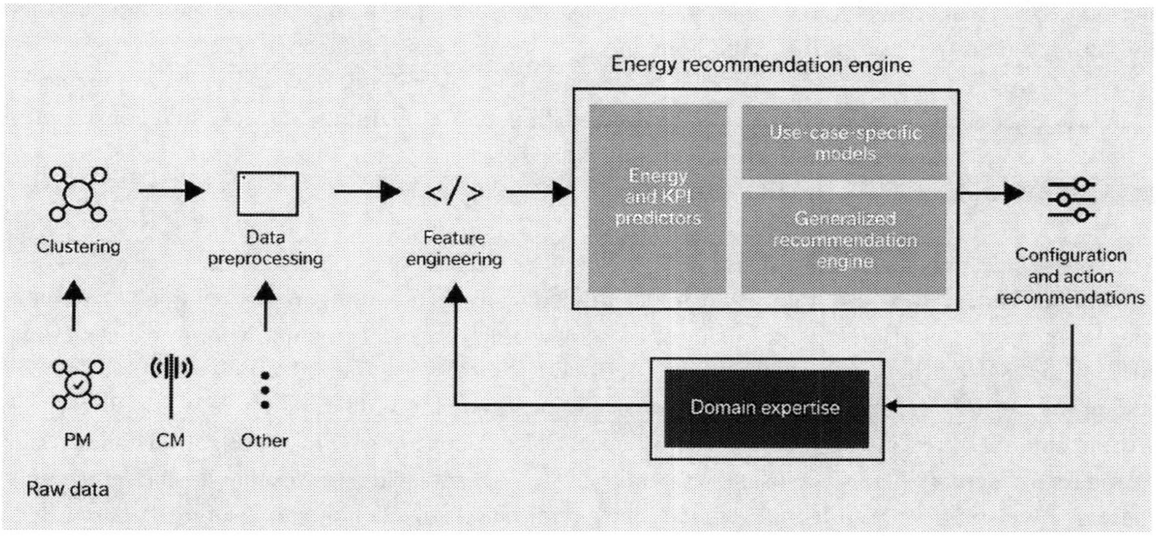

When telecom facilities were constructed, they were often set up with specific criteria, such as the number of cells and the sorts of hardware units (which indicate frequency bands), among others. After the deployment of new components from several manufacturers, there may be a concern with the software or hardware that necessitates reconfiguration. For the comparable quantity of traffic, gradual adjustments and various settings may result in varying energy consumption values, with some instances seeing a favourable while many others may not be in favour. The cellular mobile data collection that Ericson used contains dozens of configuration variables for the communication industry. It usually comprises installed hardware types as well as the settings for each radio cell's frequency in the DL and UL directions. Instead of concentrating on one configuration modification at a period, Ericson was able to propose several adjustments utilizing this data. The result of the energy optimization engine is a collection of modifications to a related node's configuration attributes (Vandikas et al., 2021). While only concentrating on isolated fine-tuning on a per-node level, which could exert an impact on adjacent nodes, the ultimate output highlights the optimization that takes place between various nodes and configurations. This gave rise to forming of two use cases for effective wireless communication mediums.

Use Case No. 1: Radio Signal Interference Detection

Usually, there is a chance that cells will interfere with one another at various frequencies. Many other things can cause interference, including environmental conditions and having many customers using one particular device, especially when they become connected to the cell edge. Power consumption is significantly impacted by interference in addition to QoS. Radio signal interference is recognized as a major issue that is challenging to overcome, despite the fact that modern radio innovation is designed to manage interference in a fashion such as to prevent unwanted emissions. In addition to this, different approaches are employed to restrict interference in the network. Ericsson's energy suggestion engine identifies the nodes that have significant interference and low energy efficiency by introducing clusters and subdividing the problem. The user case's left side displays a split of radio signal interference into four groups. Ericsson believes that future work will focus on the potential for upgrading the nodes titled other nodes. Ericsson can conserve energy by suggesting actions for the interference cells (such as locking them) to take in order to prevent the high energy-consumption condition by modelling the network traffic load, used energy, and other Interference-related KPIs (Vandikas et al. 2021). Consequently, the cell interference factors are distinct and associated with network operation and resource consumption.

Use Case No. 2: PSU Load Utilization

A radio base station is made up of many PSUs that power the radio equipment. The use case shows how frequently PSUs in radio base stations are underutilized. Active PSUs that are not being used frequently could be operating inefficiently and using more power than necessary owing to power dissipation. It must be emphasized that the load affects PSU efficiency. Ericsson grouped nodes based on their PSU load, number of PSUs, relationship to radio network engagement, number of active users, PRB utilization, and amount of registered customers in order to select nodes for PSU load utilization enhancement. Ericson focussed on PSUs whose usage was under 50%. Ericsson also believes that it is better to suggest dynamic power-supply control strategies like putting idle PSUs in sleep mode or shutting them off. The load placed on the PSU output has a significant impact on its efficiency. One percent can be saved by putting one of the system's PSUs in sleep mode (Vandikas et al., 2021). Additionally, the PSUs that are still in service can save an extra 1% thanks to enhanced usage and operational performance (figure 2).

Figure 2. Ericsson's radio signal interference detection and PSU load utilization (www.ericsson.com)

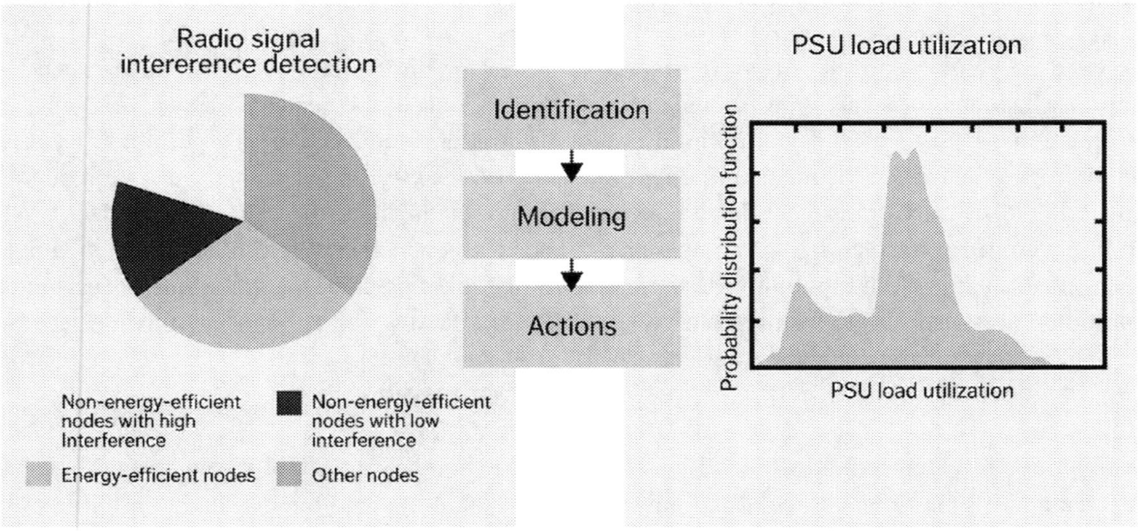

Enhancing network energy efficiency is one of Ericsson's main objectives. The best strategy to accomplish comprehensive energy savings is to employ a comprehensive energy optimization strategy. It is because Ericsson can ensure that any developments made at one level are not ignored by increasing energy usage. An artificial intelligence-powered energy recommendation engine powers the end-to-end (E2E) energy optimization idea. However, using the particular interfaces that may dynamically tune the nodes having zero user involvement, this method has a significant deal of promise for automation. Without additional hardware, it can be entirely software-based. The energy recommendation engine examines pertinent data to determine how to fine-tune node configurations to lower energy consumption without compromising QoE. According to recent research, this technique can result in total E2E efficiency gains of up to 10% for radio cells and up to 2% for PSU optimization (encompassing radio variants). In addition to creating a generalized engine for energy suggestions, Ericson is also creating use-case-specific suggestions for various problems, especially for its basic mobile features for wireless communication (Vandikas, 2021). Ericson employed predictive models in the two use cases designers have so far researched to identify situations where PSUs are underutilized and to identify interference that can result in unusual energy consumption.

CONCLUSION

This study aimed to help the telecommunication sector create effective energy management systems for wireless mobile connections. The various machine learning approaches that can be used to manage the 5G and beyond network management operations are also explored in this study. It has been analyzed that the intelligent system is effective in forecasting the future structure of the network by analyzing extensive data, allowing businesses to make informed decisions. The use of machine learning techniques can allow intelligent energy conservation. This study focuses on the internet of things, which facilitates data collection for machine learning. Wireless communication is now the market segment that is expanding the fastest, and this is because it can offer ubiquitous access to a wide range of applications and services at very low costs. This issue makes it difficult to analyze energy consumption and maximize that energy. Additionally, it might raise certain financial and environmental issues. Contemporary energy service companies are working to develop and implement energy solutions using cutting-edge technologies. They are exploring several strategies for properly managing energy use in order to save costs, decrease hazards, and address environmental concerns. Service quality, vulnerable procedures, ineffective energy management, centralized data management, and deployment of machine learning are some of the challenges regarding machine learning for energy management. Analysis has been conducted using two use cases of Ericsson. By adding clusters and segmenting the issue, Ericsson's energy recommendation engine pinpoints the nodes that have severe interference and low energy efficiency. Additionally, in order to optimize node topologies and reduce energy usage without sacrificing QoE, the energy recommendation engine looks at relevant data. Accordingly, it has been determined that utilizing machine learning to manage energy in wireless mobile networks can be very effective.

REFERENCES

Ali Imran, M., Flávia dos Reis, A., Brante, G., Valente Klaine, P., & Souza, D. (2019). Machine Learning in Energy Efficiency Optimization. Machine Learning for Future Wireless Communications. doi:10.1002/9781119562306.ch6

Ayoubi, S. (2018, January). *Machine Learning for Cognitive Network Management*. Retrieved July 4, 2022, from https://www.researchgate.net/publication/320540444_Machine_Learning_for_Cognitive_Network_Management

Babar, M., Tariq, M. U., & Jan, M. A. (2020). Secure and resilient demand side management engine using machine learning for IoT-enabled smart grid. *Sustainable Cities and Society*, *62*, 102370. doi:10.1016/j.scs.2020.102370

Baier, L., Jöhren, F., & Seebacher, S. (2019, June). Challenges in the Deployment and Operation of Machine Learning in Practice. ECIS.

Challita, U., Ryden, H., & Tullberg, H. (2020). When machine learning meets wireless cellular networks: Deployment, challenges, and applications. *IEEE Communications Magazine*, *58*(6), 12–18. doi:10.1109/MCOM.001.1900664

Cohen, P. (2022). *Vodafone unveils new trans-EU network performance platform*. Retrieved from https://rcrwireless.com/20220509/featured/vodafone-unveils-new-trans-eu-network-performance-platform

Desai, Kulkarni, J., Kamruzzaman, M. M., Hubalovsky, S., Hsu, H.-T., & Ibrahim, A. A. (2022). Interconnected CPW Fed Flexible 4-Port MIMO Antenna for UWB, X, and Ku Band Applications. *IEEE Access: Practical Innovations, Open Solutions*, *10*, 57641–57654. doi:10.1109/ACCESS.2022.3179005

Du, J., Jiang, C., Wang, J., Ren, Y., & Debbah, M. (2020). Machine learning for 6G wireless networks: Carrying forward enhanced bandwidth, massive access, and ultrareliable/low-latency service. *IEEE Vehicular Technology Magazine*, *15*(4), 122–134. doi:10.1109/MVT.2020.3019650

Espanol. (2021). *Ericsson partners with Vodafone to power new 5G lab in Spain*. Retrieved from https://www.ericsson.com/en/news/3/2021/ericsson-partners-with-vodafone-to-power-new-5g-lab-in-spain

Feng, Y. (2022, March 29). Bank Green Credit Risk Assessment and management by Mobile Computing and Machine Learning Neural Network under the efficient wireless communication. *Wireless Communications and Mobile Computing*. Retrieved July 1, 2022, from https://www.hindawi.com/journals/wcmc/2022/3444317/

Hou, Y. (2020). *Evaluation of energy efficiency in mobile cellular networks using a fluid modeling framework* [Doctoral dissertation]. Université Paris-Saclay.

Kamruzzaman, M. M. (2022). 6G wireless communication assisted security management using cloud edge computing. *Expert Systems: International Journal of Knowledge Engineering and Neural Networks*, *13061*. Advance online publication. doi:10.1111/exsy.13061

Kamruzzaman, M. M., & Alruwaili, O. (2022). Energy efficient sustainable Wireless Body Area Network design using network optimization with Smart Grid and Renewable Energy Systems. *Energy Reports*, *8*(November), 3780–3788. doi:10.1016/j.egyr.2022.03.006

Klaine, P. V., Imran, M. A., Onireti, O., & Souza, R. D. (2017). A survey of machine learning techniques applied to self-organizing cellular networks. *IEEE Communications Surveys and Tutorials*, *19*(4), 2392–2431. doi:10.1109/COMST.2017.2727878

Lu, R., Li, Y. C., Li, Y., Jiang, J., & Ding, Y. (2020). Multi-agent deep reinforcement learning based demand response for discrete manufacturing systems energy management. *Applied Energy*, *276*, 115473. doi:10.1016/j.apenergy.2020.115473

Mahakud, R., Rath, S., Samantaray, M., Sinha, B., Priya, P., Nayak, A., & Kumari, A. (2016). Energy management in wireless sensor network using pegasis. *Procedia Computer Science*, *92*, 207–212. doi:10.1016/j.procs.2016.07.347

McCaskill, S. (2021). *Network automation is 'essential' to Vodafone's bid to become a true technology company*. Retrieved from https://www.techradar.com/news/network-automation-is-essential-to-vodafones-bid-to-become-a-true-technology-company

Mehtab, S. (2022). *Design of a High-Speed OFDM-SAC-OCDMA-Based FSO System Using EDW Codes for Supporting 5G Data Services and Smart City Applications. Frontiers in Physics* , 10. doi:10.3389/fphy.2022.934848

Melero, M. J. (2022). *Network experience: Why performance partnerships are crucial*. Retrieved from https://www.ericsson.com/en/blog/2022/2/partnership-new-telecom-era-vodafone-ericsson

Morris, I. (2021). *Ericsson bags 5G 'core' deal with Vodafone UK*. Retrieved from https://www.lightreading.com/5g/ericsson-bags-5g-core-deal-with-vodafone-uk/d/d-id/770266?videoId=6279364677001

Moysiadis, V., Sarigiannidis, P., & Moscholios, I. (2018). Towards distributed data management in fog computing. *Wireless Communications and Mobile Computing*, *2018*, 2018. doi:10.1155/2018/7597686

Omer, O. (2019, December 2). *Introduction to machine learning the Wikipedia Guide*. Retrieved July 1, 2022, from https://www.academia.edu/41157657/Introduction_to_Machine_Learning_The_Wikipedia_Guide

Sesto-Castilla, D., Garcia-Villegas, E., Lyberopoulos, G., & Theodoropoulou, E. (2019). Use of machine learning for energy efficiency in present and future mobile networks. *2019 IEEE Wireless Communications and Networking Conference (WCNC)*. 10.1109/WCNC.2019.8885478

Suykens, J. A. (2014). Introduction to machine learning. In *Academic Press Library in Signal Processing* (Vol. 1, pp. 765–773). Elsevier.

Sze, V., Chen, Y. H., Emer, J., Suleiman, A., & Zhang, Z. (2017, April). Hardware for machine learning: Challenges and opportunities. In *2017 IEEE Custom Integrated Circuits Conference (CICC)* (pp. 1-8). IEEE. 10.1109/CICC.2017.7993626

Valera, M., Guo, Z., Kelly, P., Matz, S., Cantu, V. A., Percus, A. G., Hyman, J. D., Srinivasan, G., & Viswanathan, H. S. (2018). Machine learning for graph-based representations of three-dimensional discrete fracture networks. *Computational Geosciences*, *22*(3), 695–710. doi:10.100710596-018-9720-1

Vamvakas, P., Tsiropoulou, E. E., & Papavassiliou, S. (2017). Dynamic Provider Selection & Power Resource Management in competitive wireless communication markets. *Mobile Networks and Applications*, *23*(1), 86–99. doi:10.100711036-017-0885-y

Vandikas, K., Hallberg, H., Ickin, S., Nyström, C., Sanders, E., Gorbatov, O., & Eleftheriadis, L. (2021). *Ensuring energy-efficient networks with artificial intelligence*. Retrieved from https://www.ericsson.com/en/reports-and-papers/ericsson-technology-review/articles/ensuring-energy-efficient-networks-wi
th-ai

Compilation of References

Adil, M., Khan, M. K., Jadoon, M. M., Attique, M., Song, H., & Farouk, A. (2022b). An AI-enabled Hybrid lightweight Authentication Scheme for Intelligent IoMT based Cyber-Physical Systems. *IEEE Transactions on Network Science and Engineering*, 1. doi:10.1109/TNSE.2022.3159526

Maniccam, S. S., & Bourbakis, N. G. (2004). Image and video encryption using SCAN patterns. *Pattern Recognition, 37*(4), 725–737. doi:10.1016/j.patcog.2003.08.011

Mustafaraj, E., & Metaxas, P. T. (2017). The fake news spreading plague: Was it preventable? *Proceedings of the 2017 ACM on Web Science Conference*. ACM. 10.1145/3091478.3091523

Silverstone, H., & Davia, H. R. (2005b). *Fraud 101: Techniques and strategies for detection*. John Wiley & Sons.

Tian, Y. W., Li, T. L., Zhang, L., & Wang, X. J. (2010). Diagnosis method of cucumber disease with hyperspectral imaging in green house. *Nongye Gongcheng Xuebao (Beijing)*, *26*(5), 202–206.

Adil, M., Khan, M. K., Jamjoom, M., & Farouk, A. (2021c). MHADBOR: AI-enabled Administrative Distance based Opportunistic Load Balancing Scheme for an Agriculture Internet of Things Network. *IEEE Micro*.

Conroy, N. K., Rubin, V. L., & Chen, Y. (2015). Automatic deception detection: Methods for finding fake news: Automatic Deception Detection: Methods for Finding Fake News. *Proceedings of the Association for Information Science and Technology*, *52*(1), 1–4. doi:10.1002/pra2.2015.145052010082

Deepika, S. (2019). Cloud Task Scheduling Based on a Two Stage Strategy using KNN Classifier. *International Journal of Latest Engineering Science, 2*(6), 33-39.

Ma, C., Yan, Z., & Chen, C. W. (2019). Scalable access control for privacy-aware media sharing. *IEEE Transactions on Multimedia*, *21*(1), 173–183. doi:10.1109/TMM.2018.2851446

Prasad, S., Peddoju, S. K., & Ghosh, D. (2016). Multi-resolution mobile vision system for plant leaf disease diagnosis. *Signal, Image and Video Processing*, *10*(2), 379–388. doi:10.100711760-015-0751-y

Xiong, F., Chapple, L., & Yin, H. (2018). The use of social media to detect corporate fraud: A case study approach. *Business Horizons*, *61*(4), 623–633. doi:10.1016/j.bushor.2018.04.002

Adil, M., Song, H., Ali, J., Jan, M. A., Attique, M., Abbas, S., & Farouk, A. (2021d). EnhancedAODV: A Robust Three Phase Priority-based Traffic Load Balancing Scheme for Internet of Things. *IEEE Internet of Things Journal*.

Joseph, F.J.J (2023). Time series forecast of Covid 19 Pandemic Using Auto Recurrent Linear Regression. *Journal of Engineering Research*.

Maniraj S. P, Shettigar, R., Kannadasan, B., & Prabhu, S. (2021). Artificial Intelligence Application in Human Resource Development. *International Journal of Biology, Pharmacy and Allied Sciences, 10*(11), 1089-1100.

Potthast, M., Kiesel, J., Reinartz, K., Bevendorff, J., & Stein, B. (2018). A stylometric inquiry into hyperpartisan and fake news. *Proceedings of the 56th Annual Meeting of the Association for Computational Linguistics* (Volume 1: Long Papers). Association for Computational Linguistics. 10.18653/v1/P18-1022

Zhang, S. W., Shang, Y. J., & Wang, L. (2015). Plant disease recognition based on plant leaf image. *J Anim Plant Sci*, *25*(3), 42–45.

Zhao Q., Chen K., Li T., et al., (2018). Detecting telecommunication fraud by understanding the contents of a call. *Cybersecurity, 1*(8).

Al Shraah, A., Abu-Rumman, A., Alqhaiwi, L. A., & Alsha'ar, H. (2022). The impact of sourcing strategies and logistics capabilities on organizational performance during the COVID-19 pandemic: Evidence from Jordanian pharmaceutical industries. *Uncertain Supply Chain Management*, *10*(3), 1077–1090. doi:10.5267/j.uscm.2022.2.004

Barbedo, J. G. A. (2013). Digital image processing techniques for detecting, quantifying and classifying plant diseases. *SpringerPlus*, *2*(1), 660–672. doi:10.1186/2193-1801-2-660 PMID:24349961

Joseph, F. J. J. (2022b). IoT Based Aquarium Water Quality Monitoring and Predictive Analytics Using Parameter Optimized Stack LSTM. In *International Conference on Information Technology (InCIT)*. IEEE

Klein, D. O., & Wueller, J. R. (2018). Fake News: A legal perspective. *Australasian Policing*, *10*(2). doi:10.3316/informit.807638896756480

Al Shraah, A., Irtaimeh, H. J., & Rumman, M. A. (2013). The Strategic Human Resource Management Practices in Implying Total Quality Management (TQM): An Empirical Study on Jordanian Banking Sector. *International Journal of Management*, *4*(5), 179–190.

Jian, Z., & Wei, Z. (2010). Support vector machine for recognition of cucumber leaf diseases. In*: Proceedings of the international conference on advanced computer control (ICACC),* Patiala, India, pp 264–266.

Rubin, V., Conroy, N., Chen, Y., & Cornwell, S. (2016). Fake news or truth? Using satirical cues to detect potentially misleading news. *Proceedings of the Second Workshop on Computational Approaches to Deception Detection*. Association for Computational Linguistics. 10.18653/v1/W16-0802

Rustam, F., Khalid, M., Aslam, W., Rupapara, V., Mehmood, A., & Choi, G. S. (2021). A performance comparison of supervised machine learning models for Covid-19 tweets sentiment analysis. *PLoS One*, *16*(2), e0245909. doi:10.1371/journal.pone.0245909 PMID:33630869

Aoudni, Y., Donald, C., Farouk, A., Sahay, K. B., Babu, D. V., Tripathi, V., & Dhabliya, D. (2022). Cloud security based attack detection using transductive learning integrated with Hidden Markov Model. *Pattern Recognition Letters*, *157*, 16–26. doi:10.1016/j.patrec.2022.02.012

Asfarian, A., Herdiyeni, Y., Rauf, A., & Mutaqin, K. H. (2014). A computer vision for rice disease identification to support integrated pest management Crop. *Prot*, *61*, 103–104.

Balmas, M. (2014). When fake news becomes real: Combined exposure to multiple news sources and political attitudes of inefficacy, alienation, and cynicism. *Communication Research*, *41*(3), 430–454. doi:10.1177/0093650212453600

Rupapara, V., Rustam, F., Shahzad, H. F., Mehmood, A., Ashraf, I., & Choi, G. S. (2021). Impact of SMOTE on Imbalanced Text Features for Toxic Comments Classification using RVVC Model. *IEEE Access: Practical Innovations, Open Solutions*, *9*, 1–1. doi:10.1109/ACCESS.2021.3083638

Chen, Y., Wang, J., Xia, R., Zhang, Q., Cao, Z., & Yang, K. (2019). The visual object tracking algorithm research based on adaptive combination kernel. *Journal of Ambient Intelligence and Humanized Computing*, *10*(12), 4855–4867. doi:10.100712652-018-01171-4

Devani, D., & Patel, M. (2022). Stock market (BSE) prediction using unsupervised sentiment analysis and LSTM: A hybrid approach,. in *Proceedings of the 2nd International Conference on Recent Trends in Machine Learning, IoT, Smart Cities and Applications. Singapore: Springer Nature Singapore,* pp. 79–87. Springer. 10.1007/978-981-16-6407-6_8

Jin, Z., Cao, J., Zhang, Y., & Luo, J. (2016). News Verification by Exploiting Conflicting Social Viewpoints in Microblogs. *Proceedings of the AAAI Conference on Artificial Intelligence*, *30*(1). doi:10.1609/aaai.v30i1.10382

Rupapara, V., Narra, M., Gunda, N. K., Gandhi, S., & Thipparthy, K. R. (2021). Maintaining social distancing in pandemic using smartphones with acoustic waves. *IEEE Transactions on Computational Social Systems*, 1–7. doi:10.1109/TCSS.2021.3092942

Brewer, P. R., Young, D. G., & Morreale, M. (2013). The impact of real news about "fake news": Intertextual processes and political satire. *International Journal of Public Opinion Research*, *25*(3), 323–343. doi:10.1093/ijpor/edt015

Chen, L., & Yuan, Y. (2019). Agricultural disease image dataset for disease identification based on machine learning. In J. Li, X. Meng, Y. Zhang, W. Cui, & Z. Du (Eds.), Lecture Notes in Computer Science: Vol. 11473. *Big scientific data management. BigSDM 2018*. Springer. doi:10.1007/978-3-030-28061-1_26

Farouk, A., Alahmadi, A., Ghose, S., & Mashatan, A. (2020). Blockchain platform for industrial healthcare: Vision and future opportunities. *Computer Communications*, *154*, 223–235. doi:10.1016/j.comcom.2020.02.058

Pattana-Anake, V., Danphitsanuparn, P., & Joseph, F. J. J. (2021, February). BettaNet: A Deep Learning Architecture for Classification of Wild Siamese Betta Species. *IOP Conference Series. Materials Science and Engineering*, *1055*(1), 012104. doi:10.1088/1757-899X/1055/1/012104

Farouk, A., Batle, J., Elhoseny, M., Naseri, M., Lone, M., Fedorov, A., & Abdel-Aty, M. (2018). Robust general N user authentication scheme in a centralised quantum communication network via generalised GHZ states. *Frontiers in Physics*, *13*(2), 1–18.

Lu, Y., Yi, S., Zeng, N., Liu, Y., & Zhang, Y. (2017). Identification of rice diseases using deep convolutional neural networks. *Neurocomputing*, *267*, 378–384. doi:10.1016/j.neucom.2017.06.023

Rubin, V. L., Chen, Y., & Conroy, N. K. (2015). Deception detection for news: Three types of fakes: Deception Detection for News: Three Types of Fakes. *Proceedings of the Association for Information Science and Technology*, *52*(1), 1–4. doi:10.1002/pra2.2015.145052010083

Upadhyay, S., Dave, D., & Sharma, G. (2016). *"Image encryption by using block-based symmetric transformation algorithm (international data encryption algorithm)," in Advances in Intelligent Systems and Computing*. Springer Singapore.

Farouk, A., Zakaria, M., Megahed, A., & Omara, F. A. (2015). A generalised architecture of quantum secure direct communication for N disjointed users with authentication. *Scientific Reports*, *5*(1), 1–17. doi:10.1038rep16080 PMID:26577473

Park, Y.-H., & Choi, H.-S. (2015a). A trend and prospect of news media through mobile news application. *International Journal of Multimedia and Ubiquitous Engineering*, *10*(7), 11–22. doi:10.14257/ijmue.2015.10.7.02

Xing, L., Li, L., Gong, J., Ren, C., Liu, J., & Chen, H. (2018). Daily soil temperatures predictions for various climates in united states using data-driven model. *Energy*, *160*, 430–440. doi:10.1016/j.energy.2018.07.004

Yousaf, A., Umer, M., Sadiq, S., Ullah, S., Mirjalili, S., Rupapara, V., & Nappi, M. (2021). Emotion Recognition by Textual Tweets Classification Using Voting Classifier (LR-SGD). *IEEE Access: Practical Innovations, Open Solutions*, *9*, 6286–6295. doi:10.1109/ACCESS.2020.3047831

Abdolmaleky, M., Naseri, M., Batle, J., Farouk, A., & Gong, L. H. (2017). Red-Green-Blue multi-channel quantum representation of digital images. *Optik (Stuttgart)*, *128*, 121–132. doi:10.1016/j.ijleo.2016.09.123

Andreassen, R. (2021). Social media surveillance, LGBTQ refugees and asylum: How migration authorities use social media profiles to determine refugees as "genuine" or "fraud". *First Monday*, *26*, 1–4. doi:10.5210/fm.v26i1.10653

Dhanush, S., Mohanraj, S. C., Sruthi, V. S., Cloudin, S., & Joseph, F. J. J. (2022). CODEDJ-Private Permissioned Blockchain Based Digital Wallet with Enhanced Security. *International Conference on Bio-Neuro Informatics Models and Algorithms*. IEEE.

Kanade, P. A. (2020). Machine learning model for stock market prediction. *International Journal for Research in Applied Science and Engineering Technology*, *8*(6), 209–216. doi:10.22214/ijraset.2020.6030

Rehman, F. U., Kalsoom, M., Adnan, M., Toor, M., & Zulfiqar, A. (2020). "Plant growth promoting rhizobacteria and their mechanisms involved in agricultural crop production: A review." SunText Rev. *Biotechnol*, *1*(2), 1–6.

Shu, K., Sliva, A., Wang, S., Tang, J., & Liu, H. (2017). Fake news detection on social media: A data mining perspective. *SIGKDD Explorations: Newsletter of the Special Interest Group (SIG) on Knowledge Discovery & Data Mining, 19*(1), 22–36. doi:10.1145/3137597.3137600

Guo, Y., Han, S., Shen, C., Li, Y., Yin, X., & Bai, Y. (2018). An adaptive SVR for high-frequency stock price forecasting. *IEEE Access: Practical Innovations, Open Solutions*, *6*, 11397–11404. doi:10.1109/ACCESS.2018.2806180

Samadianfard, S., Asadi, E., Jarhan, S., Kazemi, H., Kheshtgar, S., Kisi, O., Sajjadi, S., & Manaf, A. A. (2018). Wavelet neural networks and gene expression programming models to predict short-term soil temperature at different depths. *Soil & Tillage Research*, *175*, 37–50. doi:10.1016/j.still.2017.08.012

Ward, A., & … . (1997). *Naive realism in everyday life: Implications for social conflict and misunderstanding. Values and knowledge, Publisher: Lawrence Erlbaum AssociatesEditors: Terrance Brown, Edward S.* Reed, Elliot Turiel.

Gurav, U., & Sidnal, N. (2018). Predict stock market behavior: Role of machine learning algorithms. In Intelligent Computing and Information and Communication. Springer.

Nickerson, R. S. (1998). Confirmation bias: A ubiquitous phenomenon in many guises. *Review of General Psychology*, *2*(2), 175–220. . doi:10.1037/1089-2680.2.2.175

Sanikhani, H., Deo, R. C., Yaseen, Z. M., Eray, O., & Kisi, O. (2018). Non-tuned data intelligent model for soil temperature estimation: A new approach. *Geoderma*, *330*, 52–64. doi:10.1016/j.geoderma.2018.05.030

Heidari, S., Abutalib, M. M., Alkhambashi, M., Farouk, A., & Naseri, M. (2019). A new general model for quantum image histogram (QIH). *Quantum Information Processing*, *18*(6), 1–20. doi:10.100711128-019-2295-5

Nyhan, B., & Reifler, J. (2010). When corrections fail: The persistence of political misperceptions. *Political Behavior*, *32*(2), 303–330. doi:10.100711109-010-9112-2

Salam, A., & Shah, S. (2019). Internet of things in smart agriculture: Enabling technologies. In *5th World Forum on Internet of Things (WF-IoT)*, pp. 692-695. IEEE.

Ahmed, N., De, D., & Hussain, I. (2018). Internet of Things (IoT) for smart precision agriculture and farming in rural areas. *IEEE Internet of Things Journal*, *5*(6), 4890–4899. doi:10.1109/JIOT.2018.2879579

Al-Naif, K. L. & Al Shraah A. E. M. (2018). Working capital management and profitability: Evidence from Jordanian mining and extraction industry sector. *IUG Journal of Economics and Business, 2*(1), pp 42-60.

Kahneman, D., & Tversky, A. (2013). Prospect theory: An analysis of decision under risk. In *Handbook of the Fundamentals of Financial Decision Making* (pp. 99–127). World Scientific. doi:10.1142/9789814417358_0006

Khan, W., Ghazanfar, M. A., Azam, M. A., Karami, A., Alyoubi, K. H., & Alfakeeh, A. S. (2022). Stock market prediction using machine learning classifiers and social media, news. *Journal of Ambient Intelligence and Humanized Computing, 13*(7), 3433–3456. doi:10.100712652-020-01839-w

Raj, J. S., & Vijitha Ananthi, J. (2019). Automation using IoT in greenhouse environment. *Journal of Information Technology, 1*(01), 38–47.

Tversky, A., & Kahneman, D. (2016). Advances in prospect theory: Cumulative representation of uncertainty. In *Readings in Formal Epistemology* (pp. 493–519). Springer International Publishing. doi:10.1007/978-3-319-20451-2_24

Ferrara, E., Varol, O., Davis, C., Menczer, F., & Flammini, A. (2016). The rise of social bots. *Communications of the ACM, 59*(7), 96–104. doi:10.1145/2818717

Mendonça, R. V., Silva, J. C., Rosa, R. L., Saadi, M., Rodriguez, D. Z., & Farouk, A. (2021). A lightweight intelligent intrusion detection system for industrial internet of things using deep learning algorithm. *Expert Systems: International Journal of Knowledge Engineering and Neural Networks*, 12917.

Vijayakumar, T., & Vinothkanna, R. (2020). Mellowness Detection of Dragon Fruit Using Deep Learning Strategy [JIIP]. *Journal of Innovative Image Processing, 2*(01), 35–43. doi:10.36548/jiip.2020.1.004

Adeyemi, O., Grove, I., Peets, S., Domun, Y., & Norton, T. (2018). Dynamic Neural Network Modelling of Soil Moisture Content for Predictive Irrigation Scheduling. *Sensors (Basel), 18*(10), 3408. doi:10.339018103408 PMID:30314346

B, J. M. (2018). *Fake news: Real lies, affecting real people*. Createspace Independent Publishing Platform.

Metwaly, A. F., Rashad, M. Z., Omara, F. A., & Megahed, A. A. (2014). Architecture of multicast centralised key management scheme using quantum key distribution and classical symmetric encryption. *The European Physical Journal. Special Topics, 223*(8), 1711–1728. doi:10.1140/epjst/e2014-02118-x

Del Vicario, M., Vivaldo, G., Bessi, A., Zollo, F., Scala, A., Caldarelli, G., & Quattrociocchi, W. (2016). Echo chambers: Emotional contagion and group polarization on Facebook. *Scientific Reports, 6*(1), 37825. doi:10.1038rep37825 PMID:27905402

Gao, P., Xie, J., Yang, M., Zhou, P., Chen, W., Liang, G., Chen, Y., Han, X., & Wang, W. (2021). Improved Soil Moisture and Electrical Conductivity Prediction of Citrus Orchards Based on IoT Using Deep Bidirectional LSTM. *Agriculture, 11*(7), 635. doi:10.3390/agriculture11070635

Naseri, M., Abdolmaleky, M., Laref, A., Parandin, F., Celik, T., Farouk, A., Mohamadi, M., & Jalalian, H. (2018a). A new cryptography algorithm for quantum images. *Optik (Stuttgart), 171*, 947–959. doi:10.1016/j.ijleo.2018.06.113

Naseri, M., Abdolmaleky, M., Parandin, F., Fatahi, N., Farouk, A., & Nazari, R. (2018b). A new quantum gray-scale image encoding scheme. *Communications in Theoretical Physics, 69*(2), 215. doi:10.1088/0253-6102/69/2/215

Quattrociocchi, W., Scala, A., & Sunstein, C. R. (2016). Echo chambers on Facebook. SSRN Electronic Journal. doi:10.2139/ssrn.2795110

Naseri, M., Heidari, S., Baghfalaki, M., Gheibi, R., Batle, J., Farouk, A., & Habibi, A. (2017). A new secure quantum watermarking scheme. *Optik (Stuttgart), 139*, 77–86. doi:10.1016/j.ijleo.2017.03.091

Paul, C., & Matthews, M. (2016). The Russian "firehose of falsehood" propaganda model. *Rand Corporation*, *2*(7), 1–10.

Abulkasim, H., Alsuqaih, H. N., Hamdan, W. F., Hamad, S., Farouk, A., Mashatan, A., & Ghose, S. (2019). Improved dynamic multiparty quantum private comparison for next-generation mobile network. *IEEE Access: Practical Innovations, Open Solutions*, *7*, 17917–17926. doi:10.1109/ACCESS.2019.2894101

Ana Ruxandra, M. I. C. U., Tudor, V., & Dumitru, E. A. (2018). *Researches on the Capacity of Marketing Agricultural Crop Production in the South-West Oltenia Region*. SCIENTIFIC PAPERS.

Brancik, K.C. *Insider computer fraud: an in-depth framework for detecting and defending against insider attacks.* CRC Press.

Ishaq, A., Sadiq, S., Umer, M., Ullah, S., Mirjalili, S., Rupapara, V., & Nappi, M. (2021). Improving the Prediction of Heart Failure Patients' Survival Using SMOTE and Effective Data Mining Techniques. *IEEE Access: Practical Innovations, Open Solutions*, *9*, 39707–39716. doi:10.1109/ACCESS.2021.3064084

Torres, P. E. P. (2019). Stock market data prediction using machine learning techniques. In Advances in Intelligent Systems and Computing. Springer International Publishing.

Wakefield, J. (2016, June 14). Social media "outstrips TV" as news source for young people. *BBC News*. https://www.bbc.com/news/uk-36528256

Naseri, M., Raji, M. A., Hantehzadeh, M. R., Farouk, A., Boochani, A., & Solaymani, S. (2015). A scheme for secure quantum communication network with authentication using GHZ-like states and cluster states controlled teleportation. *Quantum Information Processing*, *14*(11), 4279–4295. doi:10.100711128-015-1107-9

Zajonc, R. B. (1968). Attitudinal effects of mere exposure. *Journal of Personality and Social Psychology*, *9*(2, Pt.2), 1–27. doi:10.1037/h0025848

Reshma, R. (2021). Stock market prediction using machine learning techniques. In Advances in Parallel Computing Technologies and Applications. IOS Press.

Zajonc, R. B. (2001). Mere exposure: A gateway to the subliminal. *Current Directions in Psychological Science*, *10*(6), 224–228. doi:10.1111/1467-8721.00154

Gentzkow, M., Shapiro, J. M., & Stone, D. F. (2015). Media bias in the marketplace: Theory, in Handbook of media economics. Elsevier, 623-645.

Feldman, R., & Sanger, J. (2006). Text Mining Preprocessing Techniques. In *The Text Mining Handbook* (pp. 57–63). Cambridge University Press. doi:10.1017/CBO9780511546914.004

Karuppusamy, S., & Singaravel, G. (2019). *Investigation Analysis for Software Fault Prediction using Error Probabilities and Integral Methods* (Vol. 13). Applied Mathematics & Information Sciences An International Journal.

Forman, G. (2003). An extensive empirical study of feature selection metrics for text classification. *Journal of Machine Learning Research*, *3*, 1289–1305.

Zhou, N. R., Liang, X. R., Zhou, Z. H., & Farouk, A. (2016). Relay selection scheme for amplify-and-forward cooperative communication system with artificial noise. *Security and Communication Networks*, *9*(11), 1398–1404. doi:10.1002ec.1425

Guyon, I., & Elisseeff, A. (2003). An introduction to variable and feature selection. *Journal of Machine Learning Research*, *3*, 1157–1182.

Zhu, F., Zhang, C., Zheng, Z., & Farouk, A. (2021). Practical Network Coding Technologies and Softwarization in Wireless Networks. *IEEE Internet of Things Journal*, *8*(7), 5211–5218. doi:10.1109/JIOT.2021.3056580

Guyon, I., Weston, J., Barnhill, S., & Vapnik, V. (2002). Gene selection for cancer classification using support vector machines. *Machine Learning*, *46*(1/3), 389–422. doi:10.1023/A:1012487302797

Kyriakopoulou, A., & Kalamboukis, T. (2007). Using clustering to enhance text classification. *Proceedings of the 30th Annual International ACM SIGIR Conference on Research and Development in Information.* ACM Press. 10.1145/1277741.1277918

Chen, Y., Conroy, N. J., & Rubin, V. L. (2015). Misleading online content: recognizing clickbait as "false news". In *Proceedings of the 2015 ACM on workshop on multimodal deception detection.* ACM. 10.1145/2823465.2823467

Fürnkranz, J. (1998). A study using n-gram features for text categorization. Austrian Research Institute for Artificial Intelligence, 1–10.

Abulkasim, H., Farouk, A., Alsuqaih, H., Hamdan, W., Hamad, S., & Ghose, S. (2018). Improving the security of quantum key agreement protocols with single photon in both polarisation and spatial-mode degrees of freedom. *Quantum Information Processing*, *17*(11), 1–11. doi:10.100711128-018-2091-7

Coderre, D. (2009). *Fraud analysis techniques using ACL.* John Wiley & Sons.

Irfan Ramzan Parry, Surinder Singh Khurana, Munish Kumar, Ali A. Altalbe (2020). Time Series Data Analytics of Stock Price Movement using Machine Learning Techniques. *Time.*

Joseph, A. J. J., Joseph, F. J. J., Stanislaus, O. M., & Das, D. (2022a). *Classification methodologies in healthcare, Evolving Predictive Analytics in Healthcare: New AI techniques for real-time interventions.* IET.

Wikipedia contributors. (2022, November 18). Pizzagate conspiracy theory. *Wikipedia.* http://en.wikipedia.org/w/index.php?title=Pizzagate_conspiracy_theory&oldid=1122678316

Wiréhn, L. (2018). Nordic agriculture under climate change: A systematic review of challenges, opportunities and adaptation strategies for crop production. *Land Use Policy*, *77*, 63–74. doi:10.1016/j.landusepol.2018.04.059

Afroz, S., Brennan, M., & Greenstadt, R. (2012). Detecting hoaxes, frauds, and deception in writing style online. *Symposium on Security and Privacy*. IEEE. 10.1109/SP.2012.34

Gupta, A. (2013). Faking sandy: characterizing and identifying fake images on twitter during hurricane sandy. In *Proceedings of the 22nd international conference on World Wide Web.* ACM. 10.1145/2487788.2488033

Jin, Z., Cao, J., Zhang, Y., Zhou, J., & Tian, Q. (2017). Novel visual and statistical image features for microblogs news verification. *IEEE Transactions on Multimedia*, *19*(3), 598–608. doi:10.1109/TMM.2016.2617078

Yang, F., Liu, Y., Yu, X., & Yang, M. (2012). Automatic detection of rumor on Sina Weibo. *Proceedings of the ACM SIGKDD Workshop on Mining Data Semantics*. ACM Press. 10.1145/2350190.2350203

Ma, J., Gao, W., Wei, Z., Lu, Y., & Wong, K.-F. (2015). Detect rumors using time series of social context information on microblogging websites. *Proceedings of the 24th ACM International on Conference on Information and Knowledge Management.* ACM Press. 10.1145/2806416.2806607

Kwon, S., Cha, M., Jung, K., Chen, W., & Wang, Y. (2013). Prominent features of rumor propagation in online social media. *13th International Conference on Data Mining*. IEEE.

Tacchini, E., Ballarin, G., Della Vedova, M. L., Moret, S., & de Alfaro, L. (2017). Some like it hoax: Automated fake news detection in social networks. https://arxiv.org/abs/1704.07506

Ruchansky, N., Seo, S., & Liu, Y. (2017). CSI: A hybrid deep model for fake news detection. https://arxiv.org/abs/1703.06959 doi:10.1145/3132847.3132877

Kotteti, C. M. M., Dong, X., Li, N., & Qian, L. (2018). Fake news detection enhancement with data imputation. *2018 IEEE 16th Intl Conf on Dependable, Autonomic and Secure Computing, 16th Intl Conf on Pervasive Intelligence and Computing, 4th Intl Conf on Big Data Intelligence and Computing and Cyber Science and Technology Congress(DASC/PiCom/DataCom/CyberSciTech)*. IEEE.

Mikolov, T., Chen, K., Corrado, G., & Dean, J. (2013). Efficient estimation of word representations in vector space. https://arxiv.org/abs/1301.3781

Abulkasim, H., Farouk, A., Hamad, S., Mashatan, A., & Ghose, S. (2019). Secure dynamic multiparty quantum private comparison. *Scientific Reports*, *9*(1), 1–16. doi:10.103841598-019-53967-9 PMID:31780675

Diaz-Granados, M., Diaz-Montes, J., & Parashar, M. (2015). Investigating insurance fraud using social media. *Big Data*, 1344–1349.

Joseph, F. J. J. (2019). Twitter based outcome predictions of 2019 indian general elections using decision tree. In *4th International Conference on Information Technology (InCIT)* (pp. 50-53). IEEE. 10.1109/INCIT.2019.8911975

Ray, R. L., Fares, A., & Risch, E. (2018). Effects of drought on crop production and cropping areas in Texas. *Agricultural & Environmental Letters*, *3*(1), 170037. doi:10.2134/ael2017.11.0037

Verma, J. P, Tanwar, S., Garg, S., Gandhi, I., & Bachani, N. (2019). Evaluation of Pattern Based Customized Approach for Stock Market Trend Prediction With Big Data and Machine Learning Techniques. *International Journal of Business Analytics (IJBAN), 6*(3), pages 1-15.

Pennington, J., Socher, R., & Manning, C. (2014). Glove: Global vectors for 356 word representation. In *Proceedings of the 2014 conference on empirical methods in natural*. ACL Anthology. 10.3115/v1/D14-1162

Thorne, J. (2018). Fever: a large-scale data-set for fact extraction and verification.

Chen, D., Fisch, A., Weston, J., & Bordes, A. (2017). Reading Wikipedia to answer open-domain questions. *Proceedings of the 55th Annual Meeting of the Association for Computational Linguistics* (Volume 1: Long Papers). Association for Computational Linguistics. 10.18653/v1/P17-1171

Ferreira, W., & Vlachos, A. (2016). Emergent: a novel data-set for stance classification. *Proceedings of the 2016 Conference of the North American Chapter of the Association for Computational Linguistics: Human Language Technologies*. Association for Computational Linguistics. 10.18653/v1/N16-1138

Merryton, A. R., & Augasta, G. (2020). A survey on recent advances in machine learning techniques for fake news detection. *Test Eng. Manag*, *83*, 11572–11582.

Meserole, C. (2022). *How Misinformation Spreads on Social Media—and What to Do About It*. Brookings. https://www.brookings.edu/blog/order-from-chaos/2018/05/09/how-misinformation-spreads-on-social-media-and-what-to-do-about-it/

Ikonomakis, M., Kotsiantis, S., & Tampakas, V. (2005). Text classification using machine learning techniques. *WSEAS Transactions on Computers*, *4*(8), 966–974.

Kim, S.-B., Rim, H.-C., Yook, D., & Lim, H.-S. (2002). Effective methods for improving naive Bayes text classifiers. In *Lecture Notes in Computer Science* (pp. 414–423). Springer Berlin Heidelberg.

Schneider, K.-M. (2005). Techniques for improving the performance of naive Bayes for text classification. In *Computational Linguistics and Intelligent Text Processing* (pp. 682–693). Springer Berlin Heidelberg. doi:10.1007/978-3-540-30586-6_76

Kłopotek, M. A., & Woch, M. (2003). Very large Bayesian networks in text classification. *International Conference on Computational Science*. Springer 10.1007/3-540-44860-8_41

Abu-Rumman, A., & Qawasmeh, R. (2022, December 06). And Qawasmeh, R (2021). "Assessing international students' satisfaction of a Jordanian university using the service quality model. *Journal of Applied Research in Higher Education, 14*(4), 1742–1760. doi:10.1108/JARHE-05-2021-0166

Glazer, J. V., MacDonnell, K., Frederick, C., Ingersoll, K., & Ritterband, L. M. (2021, September 25). Liar! Liar! Identifying eligibility fraud by applicants in digital health research. *Internet Interventions: the Application of Information Technology in Mental and Behavioural Health, 25*, 100401. doi:10.1016/j.invent.2021.100401 PMID:34094883

Joseph, F. J. J. (2022c). IoT-Based Unified Approach to Predict Particulate Matter Pollution in Thailand. *The Role of IoT and Blockchain: Techniques and Applications*, 145-151.

Mee, C. Y., Balasundram, S. K., & Hanif, A. H. M. (2017). Detecting and monitoring plant nutrient stress using remote sensing approaches: A review. *Asian Journal of Plant Sciences, 16*, 1–8.

Umer, M., Awais, M., & Muzammul, M. (2019). Stock market prediction using machine learning(ML)algorithms. *Adcaij Advances In Distributed Computing And Artificial Intelligence Journal, 8*(4), 97–116. doi:10.14201/ADCAIJ20198497116

Shanahan, J. G., & Roma, N. (2003). Improving SVM text classification performance through threshold adjustment. In *Machine Learning: ECML 2003* (pp. 361–372). Springer Berlin Heidelberg. doi:10.1007/978-3-540-39857-8_33

Johnson, D. E., Oles, F. J., Zhang, T., & Goetz, T. (2002). A decision-tree-based symbolic rule induction system for text categorization. *IBM Systems Journal, 41*(3), 428–437. doi:10.1147j.413.0428

Kamath, C. N., Bukhari, S. S., & Dengel, A. (2018). Comparative study between traditional machine learning and deep learning approaches for text classification. *Proceedings of the ACM Symposium on Document Engineering*. ACM. 10.1145/3209280.3209526

Rosenblatt, F. (1961). *Principles of neurodynamics. perceptrons and the theory of brain mechanisms.* Armed Services Technical Information Agency.

Leudar, I. (1989). James L. McClelland, David Rumelhart and the PDP Research Group, Parallel distributed processing: explorations in the microstructure of cognition. Vol. 1. Foundations. Vol. 2. Psychological and biological models. Cambridge MA: M.I.T. Press, 1987. *Journal of Child Language, 16*(2), 467–470. doi:10.1017/S0305000900010631

Pedregosa, F., Varoquaux, G., Gramfort, A., Michel, V., Thirion, B., Grisel, O., & Duchesnay, É. (2012). Scikit-learn: Machine Learning in Python. https://arxiv.org/abs/1201.0490

Bharadwaj, P., & Shao, Z. (2019). Fake news detection with semantic features and text mining. *International Journal on Natural Language Computing, 8*(3), 17–22. doi:10.5121/ijnlc.2019.8302

Abu-Rumman, A. (2021). Effective Knowledge Sharing: A Guide to the Key Enablers and Inhibitors. In D. Tessier (Ed.), *Handbook of Research on Organizational Culture Strategies for Effective Knowledge Management and Performance* (pp. 133–156). IGI Global. doi:10.4018/978-1-7998-7422-5.ch008

Joseph, F. J. J., & Auwatanamongkol, S. (2016). A crowding multi-objective genetic algorithm for image parsing. *Neural Computing & Applications, 27*(8), 2217–2227. doi:10.100700521-015-2000-2

Khan, A. T., Cao, X., Li, S., Katsikis, V. N., Brajevic, I., & Stanimirovic, P. S. (2021). Fraud detection in publicly traded US firms using beetle antennae search: A machine learning approach. *Expert Systems with Applications*, 116–148.

Nabipour, M., Nayyeri, P., Jabani, H., S, S., & Mosavi, A. (2020). Predicting stock market trends using machine learning and deep learning algorithms via continuous and binary data; A comparative analysis. *IEEE Access: Practical Innovations, Open Solutions*, *8*, 150199–150212. doi:10.1109/ACCESS.2020.3015966

Saddik, A., Latif, R., El Ouardi, A., & Elhoseney, M. (2021). VSSAgri: A Vegetation Surveillance System for precision Agriculture application. In *E3S Web of Conferences* (Vol. 297, p. 01054). EDP Sciences. doi:10.1051/e3sconf/202129701054

Adil, M., Ali, J., Attique, M., Jadoon, M. M., Abbas, S., Alotaibi, S. R., & Farouk, A. (2021a). Three Byte-Based Mutual Authentication Scheme for Autonomous Internet of Vehicles. *IEEE Transactions on Intelligent Transportation Systems*.

Carvajal-Yepes, M., Cardwell, K., Nelson, A., Garrett, K. A., Giovani, B., Saunders, D. G., Kamoun, S., Legg, J. P., Verdier, V., Lessel, J., Neher, R. A., Day, R., Pardey, P., Gullino, M. L., Records, A. R., Bextine, B., Leach, J. E., Staiger, S., & Tohme, J. (2019). A global surveillance system for crop diseases. *Science*, *364*(6447), 1237–1239. doi:10.1126cience.aaw1572 PMID:31249049

Higgins, A., McIntire, M., & Dance, G. J. (2016, November 25). Inside a fake news sausage factory: 'this is all about income.' *The New York Times*. https://www.nytimes.com/2016/11/25/world/europe/fake-news-donald-trump-hillary-clinton-georgia.html

Matti, T. (2014). Financial fraud detection using social media crowdsourcing. *33rd International Performance Computing and Communications Conference, IPCCC 2014.* (pp. 2). IEEE. 10.1109/PCCC.2014.7017023

Prabhu, S., Sengottaiyan, N., & And Geetha, B. G. (2019). Self Adaptive Approaches to Probability Distribution of Data Analytics in Cloud Computing Resource Services for Infrastructure Hybrid Models. *Applied Mathematics & Information Sciences*, *13*(S1, No: S1), 437–446. doi:10.18576/amis/13S147

Srisook, N., Tuntoolavest, O., Danphitsanuparn, P., Pattana-anake, V., & Joseph, F. J. J. (2022). Convolutional Neural Network Based Nutrient Deficiency Classification in Leaves of Elaeis guineensis Jacq. *International Journal of Computer Information Systems and Industrial Management Applications*, *14*, 19–27.

Adil, M., Attique, M., Khan, M. M., Ali, J., Farouk, A., & Song, H. (2022a). HOPCTP: A Robust Channel Categorization Data Preservation Scheme for Industrial Healthcare Internet of Things. *IEEE Transactions on Industrial Informatics*, *18*(10), 7151–7161. doi:10.1109/TII.2022.3148287

Jain, S. & Kain, M. (2018). Prediction for Stock Marketing Using Machine Learning. *International Journal IJRITCC, 6*(4).

Mergel, I., & Greeves, B. (2012). *Social media in the public sector field guide: Designing and implementing strategies and policies*. John Wiley & Sons.

Sadiq, S., Umer, M., Ullah, S., Mirjalili, S., Rupapara, V., & Nappi, M. (2021). Discrepancy detection between actual user reviews and numeric ratings of Google App store using deep learning. *Expert Systems with Applications*, *115111*, 115111. doi:10.1016/j.eswa.2021.115111

Soll, J. (2016, December 18). The long and brutal history of fake news. *POLITICO Magazine*. https://www.politico.com/magazine/story/2016/12/fake-news-history-long-violent-214535/

Story, D., Kacira, M., Kubota, C., Akoglu, A., & An, L. (2010). Lettuce calcium deficiency detection with machine vision computed plant features in controlled environments. *Computers and Electronics in Agriculture*, *74*(2), 238–243. doi:10.1016/j.compag.2010.08.010

Adil, M., Jan, M. A., Mastorakis, S., Song, H., Jadoon, M. M., Abbas, S., & Farouk, A. (2021b). Hash-MAC-DSDV: Mutual Authentication for Intelligent IoT-Based Cyber-Physical Systems. *IEEE Internet of Things Journal.*

Allcott, H., & Gentzkow, M. (2017). Social media and fake news in the 2016 election. *The Journal of Economic Perspectives: A Journal of the American Economic Association, 31*(2), 211–236. . doi:10.1257/jep.31.2.211

Kompella, S., & Chilukuri, K. C. (2019). Stock market prediction using machine learning methods. *International Journal Of Computer Engineering And Technology, 10*(3). doi:10.34218/IJCET.10.3.2019.003

Pattana-anake, V., & Joseph, F. J. J. (2022). Hyper Parameter Optimization of Stack LSTM Based Regression for PM 2.5 Data in Bangkok, In *International Conference on Business and Industrial Research (ICBIR).* IEEE 10.1109/ICBIR54589.2022.9786465

Semary, N. A., Tharwat, A., Elhariri, E., & Hassanien, A. E. (2015). Fruitbased tomato grading system using features fusion and support vector machine. In D. Filev, (Ed.), *Intelligent Systems'(2014). AISC* (Vol. 323, pp. 401–410). Springer. doi:10.1007/978-3-319-11310-4_35

Silverstone, H., & Davia, H. R. (2005a). Techniques and Strategies for Detection (2nd ed.). John Wiley & Sons, Inc.

Ali Imran, M., Flávia dos Reis, A., Brante, G., Valente Klaine, P., & Souza, D. (2019). Machine Learning in Energy Efficiency Optimization. Machine Learning for Future Wireless Communications. doi:10.1002/9781119562306.ch6

Alizadeh, M., Abolfazli, S., Zamani, M., Baharun, S., & Sakurai, K. (2016). Authentication in mobile cloud computing: A survey. *Journal of Network and Computer Applications, 61*, 59–80. doi:10.1016/j.jnca.2015.10.005

Alliance, C. S. (2014). *Cloud usage: Risks and opportunities report* https://downloads.cloudsecurityalliance.org/initiatives/collaborate/netskope/Cloud_Usage_Risks_and_ Opportunities _Survey_Report.pdf

Alom, M. Z. (2020). *COVID_MTNet: COVID-19 Detection with Multi-Task Deep Learning Approaches.* https://arxiv.org/abs/2004.03747

Alrashdi, I. (2019). AD-IoT: Anomaly detection of IoT cyberattacks in smart city using machine learning. In *2019 IEEE 9th Annual Computing and Communication Workshop and Conference (CCWC).* IEEE. 10.1109/CCWC.2019.8666450

Anandamurugan, S., & Abirami, T. (2017). Anti-predator adaptation shuffled frog leap algorithm to improve network lifetime in wireless sensor network. *Wireless Personal Communications, 94*(4), 2031–2042. doi:10.100711277-016-3354-1

Anderegg, L., & Eidenbenz, S. (2003). Ad hoc-VCG: A Truthful and Cost-Efficient Routing Protocol for Mobile ad hoc Networks with Selfish Agents. *Proceedings of the Annual International Conference on Mobile Computing and Networking, MOBICOM*, 245–259. 10.1145/938985.939011

Anisimova, T. A. (2007). The effects of corporate brand attributes on attitudinal and behavioural consumer loyalty. *Journal of Consumer Marketing, 24*(7), 395–405. doi:10.1108/07363760710834816

Ari, A. A. A., Yenke, B. O., Labraoui, N., Damakoa, I., & Gueroui, A. (2016). A power efficient cluster-based routing algorithm for wireless sensor networks: Honeybees swarm intelligence based approach. *Journal of Network and Computer Applications, 69*, 77–97. doi:10.1016/j.jnca.2016.04.020

Asif, S. (2020). *Classification of COVID-19 from Chest X-ray images using Deep Convolutional Neural Networks.* doi:10.1109/ICCC51575.2020.9344870

Aversano, L., Bernardi, M. L., Cimitile, M., Pecori, R., & Veltri, L. (2021). Effective anomaly detection using deep learning in IoT systems. *Wireless Communications and Mobile Computing, 2021*, 1–14. doi:10.1155/2021/9054336

Avgerou, C., Masiero, S., & Poulymenakou, A. (2019). Trusting e-voting amid experiences of electoral malpractice: The case of Indian elections. *Journal of Information Technology*, *34*(3), 263–289. doi:10.1177/0268396218816199

Ayoubi, S. (2018, January). *Machine Learning for Cognitive Network Management*. Retrieved July 4, 2022, from https://www.researchgate.net/publication/320540444_Machine_Learning_for_Cognitive_Network_Management

Azjen, I., & Fisbein, M. (1980). *Understanding Attitudes and Predicting Social Behaviour*. Prentice Hall.

Babar, M., Tariq, M. U., & Jan, M. A. (2020). Secure and resilient demand side management engine using machine learning for IoT-enabled smart grid. *Sustainable Cities and Society*, *62*, 102370. doi:10.1016/j.scs.2020.102370

Baier, L., Jöhren, F., & Seebacher, S. (2019, June). Challenges in the Deployment and Operation of Machine Learning in Practice. ECIS.

Bala, K., Chandra Sekar, A., Baskar, M., & Paramesh, J. (2019). An efficient multi- level intrusion detection system for mobile ad-hoc network using clustering technique. *International Journal of Engineering and Advanced Technology*, *8*(6), 1977–1985. doi:10.35940/ijeat.F8291.088619

Balas-Timar, D., & Lile, R. (2015). The story of Goldilocks told by organisational psychologists. *Procedia: Social and Behavioral Sciences*, *203*, 239–243. doi:10.1016/j.sbspro.2015.08.288

Bansal & Taylor. (1999). The Service Provider Switching Model (SPSM): A Model of Consumer Switching Behaviour in the Service Industry. *Journal of Service Research*, *2*(2), 200-218.

Bhagat, N. K., Vishnusai, Y., & Rathna, G. N. (2019). *Indian sign language gesture recognition using image processing and deep learning. In 2019 Digital Image Computing: Techniques and Applications (DICTA)*. IEEE.

Bhavana, D., Kishore Kumar, K., Rajesh, V., Swetha Sree, M., Mounika, D., & Bhavana, N. (2019). Deep learning for pixel-level image fusion using CSR technique. *International Journal of Recent Technology and Engineering*, *8*(2), 792-797.

Bochkovskiy, A., Wang, C.-Y., & Liao, H.-Y. M. (2020). *YOLOv4: Optimal speed and accuracy of object detection*. https://arxiv.org/abs/2004.10934

Borah, S., & Pradhan, R. (2020). Gesture Recognition Approaches and its Applicability: A Study. In *2020 4th International Conference on Electronics, Communication and Aerospace Technology (ICECA)* (pp. 1458-1463). IEEE.

Bouchikhi, E. H. E., Choqueuse, V., & Benbouzid, M. E. H. (2013). Current frequency spectral subtraction and its contribution to induction machines' bearings condition monitoring. *IEEE Transactions on Energy Conversion*, *28*(1), 135–144. doi:10.1109/TEC.2012.2227746

Celiktas, B., Celikbilek, I., & Ozdemir, E. (2021). A higher-level security scheme for key access on cloud computing. *IEEE Access: Practical Innovations, Open Solutions*, *9*, 107347–107359. doi:10.1109/ACCESS.2021.3101048

Challita, U., Ryden, H., & Tullberg, H. (2020). When machine learning meets wireless cellular networks: Deployment, challenges, and applications. *IEEE Communications Magazine*, *58*(6), 12–18. doi:10.1109/MCOM.001.1900664

Chaudhary, R. R. K., & Chatterjee, K. (2020). An efficient lightweight cryptographic technique for IoT based E-healthcare system. In *2020 7th International Conference on Signal Processing and Integrated Networks (SPIN)*. IEEE.

Chen, J., Mao, J., Thiel, C., & Wang, Y. (2020). IWaste: Video-based medical waste detection and classification. *Annual International Conference of the IEEE Engineering in Medicine and Biology Society. IEEE Engineering in Medicine and Biology Society. Annual International Conference*, 5794–5797. 10.1109/EMBC44109.2020.9175645

Chen, N., & Chen, Y. (2022). Anomalous vehicle recognition in Smart Urban traffic monitoring as an edge service. *Future Internet, 14*(2), 54. doi:10.3390/fi14020054

Chen, Y., & Zhang, W. (2016). Research and implementation of sign language recognition method based on Kinect. In *2016 2nd IEEE International Conference on Computer and Communications (ICCC)* (pp. 1947-1951). IEEE.

Cheng, H., Yang, S., & Wang, X. (2012). Immigrants-enhanced multi-population genetic algorithms for dynamic shortest path routing problems in mobile ad hoc networks. *Applied Artificial Intelligence, 26*(7), 673–695. doi:10.1080/08839514.2012.701449

Chen, L., Jiang, X., Li, Z., Liu, X., & Zhou, Z. (2020). Feature-Enhanced Speckle Reduction via Low-Rank and Space-Angle Continuity for Circular SAR Target Recognition. *IEEE Transactions on Geoscience and Remote Sensing, 58*(11), 7734–7752. doi:10.1109/TGRS.2020.2983420

Chen, S., Wang, H., Xu, F., & Jin, Y.-Q. (2016). Target classification using the deep convolutional networks for SAR images. *IEEE Transactions on Geoscience and Remote Sensing, 54*(8), 4806–4817. doi:10.1109/TGRS.2016.2551720

Chowdhury, M. E. H. (2020). *Can AI help in screening Viral and COVID-19 pneumonia?* https://arxiv.org/abs/2003.13145

Chugh, S., & Baweja, V. R. (2020). Data mining application in segmenting customers with clustering. In *2020 International Conference on Emerging Trends in Information Technology and Engineering (ic-ETITE)*. IEEE. 10.1109/ic-ETITE47903.2020.259

Cloud computing - statistics on the use by enterprises. (n.d.). Retrieved November 2, 2022, from Europa.eu website: https://ec.europa.eu/eurostat/statistics-explained/index.php/Cloud_computing_-_statistics_on_the_use_by_enterprises

Cohen, P. (2022). *Vodafone unveils new trans-EU network performance platform*. Retrieved from https://rcrwireless.com/20220509/featured/vodafone-unveils-new-trans-eu-network-performance-platform

Colgate, M. R., & Hedge, R. (2001). An Investigation into the Switching Process in Retail Banking Services. *International Journal of Bank Marketing, 19*(5), 201–212. doi:10.1108/02652320110400888

Dalvand, F. (2017). Current noise cancellation for bearing fault diagnosis using time shifting. *IEEE Transactions on Industrial Electronics, 64*(10), 8138–8147. . doi:10.1109/TIE.2017.2694397

Deepika, M., & Prabhu, M. S.(2019). Cloud Task Scheduling Based on a Two Stage Strategy using KNN Classifier. *International Journal of Latest Engineering Science, 2*(6), 33-39.

Delgado-Ballester, E., & Munuera-Aleman, J. L. (2001). Brand trust in the context of consumer loyalty. *European Journal of Marketing, 35*(11/12), 1238–1258. doi:10.1108/EUM0000000006475

Demeter, E., Rad, D., & Balas, E. (2021). Schadenfreude and General Anti-Social Behaviours: The Role of Violent Content Preferences and Life Satisfaction. BRAIN. *Broad Research in Artificial Intelligence and Neuroscience, 12*(2), 98–111. doi:10.18662/brain/12.2/194

Deng, H., Qin, Z., Wu, Q., Guan, Z., Deng, R. H., Wang, Y., & Zhou, Y. (2020). 'Identity-based encryption transformation for flexible sharing of encrypted data in public cloud. *Trans. Inf. Forensics Security, 15*, 3168–3180. doi:10.1109/TIFS.2020.2985532

Desai, Kulkarni, J., Kamruzzaman, M. M., Hubalovsky, S., Hsu, H.-T., & Ibrahim, A. A. (2022). Interconnected CPW Fed Flexible 4-Port MIMO Antenna for UWB, X, and Ku Band Applications. *IEEE Access: Practical Innovations, Open Solutions, 10*, 57641–57654. doi:10.1109/ACCESS.2022.3179005

Deva Hema, D., & Ashok Kumar, K. (2022). Novel algorithm for multivariate time series crash risk prediction using CNN-ATT-LSTM model. *Journal of Intelligent & Fuzzy Systems*, *43*(4), 4201–4213. Advance online publication. doi:10.3233/JIFS-211775

Domingo-Ferrer, J., Farràs, O., Ribes-González, J., & Sánchez, D. (2019). Privacy-preserving cloud computing on sensitive data: A survey of methods, products and challenges. *Computer Communications*, *140–141*, 38–60. doi:10.1016/j.comcom.2019.04.011

Dowling, G. R., & Uncles, M. (1997, Summer). Do customer loyalty programs really work? *Sloan Management Review*, *38*(4), 71–82.

Du, T., Ren, X., & Li, H. (2018). Gesture recognition method based on deep learning. In *2018 33rd Youth Academic Annual Conference of Chinese Association of Automation (YAC)* (pp. 782-787). IEEE. 10.1109/YAC.2018.8406477

Du, J., Jiang, C., Wang, J., Ren, Y., & Debbah, M. (2020). Machine learning for 6G wireless networks: Carrying forward enhanced bandwidth, massive access, and ultrareliable/low-latency service. *IEEE Vehicular Technology Magazine*, *15*(4), 122–134. doi:10.1109/MVT.2020.3019650

Dutt, A. (2015). Clustering algorithms applied in educational data mining. *International Journal of Information and Electronics Engineering*. . doi:10.7763/IJIEE.2015.V5.513

Elaziz, M. A., Hosny, K. M., Salah, A., Darwish, M. M., Lu, S., & Sahlol, A. T. (2020). New machine learning method for image-based diagnosis of COVID-19. *PLoS One*, *15*(6), e0235187. doi:10.1371/journal.pone.0235187 PMID:32589673

Espanol. (2021). *Ericsson partners with Vodafone to power new 5G lab in Spain*. Retrieved from https://www.ericsson.com/en/news/3/2021/ericsson-partners-with-vodafone-to-power-new-5g-lab-in-spain

Faizan, M., F, M., Ismail, S., & Sultan, S. (2020). Applications of clustering techniques in data mining: A comparative study. *IJACSA*, *11*(12). Advance online publication. doi:10.14569/IJACSA.2020.0111218

Fanian, F., & Kuchaki Rafsanjani, M. (2018). Memetic fuzzy clustering protocol for wireless sensor networks: Shuffled frog leaping algorithm. *Applied Soft Computing*, *71*, 568–590. doi:10.1016/j.asoc.2018.07.012

Farfan, M. J. (2020). Optimizing RT-PCR detection of SARS-CoV-2 for developing countries using pool testing. *Revista Chilena de Infectologia: Organo Oficial de la Sociedad Chilena de Infectologia, 37*(3), 276–280. . doi:10.4067/s0716-10182020000300276

Farooqui, N. A., & Mehra, R. (2018). Design of A data warehouse for medical information system using data mining techniques. In *2018 Fifth International Conference on Parallel, Distributed and Grid Computing (PDGC)*. IEEE. 10.1109/PDGC.2018.8745864

Farouk, A., Batle, J., Elhoseny, M., Naseri, M., Lone, M., Fedorov, A., ... Abdel-Aty, M. (2018). Robust general N user authentication scheme in a centralized quantum communication network via generalized GHZ states. *Frontiers in Physics*, *13*(2), 1–18.

Farouk, A., Batle, J., Elhoseny, M., Naseri, M., Lone, M., Fedorov, A., Alkhambashi, M., Ahmed, S. H., & Abdel-Aty, M. (2018). Robust general N user authentication scheme in a centralized quantum communication network via generalized GHZ states. *Frontiers in Physics*, *13*(2), 130306. Advance online publication. doi:10.100711467-017-0717-3

Feng, Y. (2022, March 29). Bank Green Credit Risk Assessment and management by Mobile Computing and Machine Learning Neural Network under the efficient wireless communication. *Wireless Communications and Mobile Computing*. Retrieved July 1, 2022, from https://www.hindawi.com/journals/wcmc/2022/3444317/

Feng, G., Fan, M., & Chen, Y. (2022). Analysis and prediction of students' academic performance based on educational data mining. *IEEE Access: Practical Innovations, Open Solutions*, *10*, 19558–19571. doi:10.1109/ACCESS.2022.3151652

Fornell & Birger. (1987). Defensive Marketing Strategy by Customer Complaint Management: A Theoretical Analysis. *Journal of Marketing Research*, *24*(4), 337-346.

Fornell, C., & Wernerfelt, B. (1987). Defensive marketing strategy by customer complaint management: A theoretical review. *JMR, Journal of Marketing Research*, *24*(Nov), 337–346. doi:10.1177/002224378702400401

Frosini, L., & Bassi, E. (2010). Stator current and motor efficiency as indicators for different types of bearing faults in induction motors. *IEEE Transactions on Industrial Electronics*, *57*(1), 244–251. . doi:10.1109/TIE.2009.2026770

Fu, K. S. (1976). Pattern recognition and image processing. *IEEE Transactions on Computers*, *100*(12), 1336–1346.

Fusco, F., Lunesu, M. I., Pani, F. E., & Pinna, A. (2018). Crypto-voting, a Blockchain based e-Voting System. In KMIS (pp. 221-225). doi:10.5220/0006962102230227

Gangadia, D., Chamaria, V., Doshi, V., & Gandhi, J. (2020). Indian sign language interpretation and sentence formation. In *2020 IEEE Pune Section International Conference (PuneCon)* (pp. 71-76). IEEE. 10.1109/PuneCon50868.2020.9362383

Garcia-Perez, A. (2011). The application of high-resolution spectral analysis for identifying multiple combined faults in induction motors. *IEEE Transactions on Industrial Electronics*, *58*(5), 2002–2010. . doi:10.1109/TIE.2010.2051398

Goel, N. (2019). Implementing cluster analysis on an E-learning website. *Vivekananda Journal of Research*, *8*(2), 158–170.

Goyal, P., Parmar, V., & Rishi, R. (2011). Manet: Vulnerabilities, challenges, attacks, application. *IJCEM International Journal of Computational Engineering & Management*, *11*, 32–37.

Gozes, O. (2020). *Rapid AI development cycle for the Coronavirus (COVID-19) pandemic: Initial results for automated detection & patient monitoring using deep learning CT image analysis*. https://arxiv.org/abs/2003.05037

Guiamalon, T. S. (2022a). Social And Economic Development: State Universities And Colleges' (Suc's) Contribution Creativity Skills Of The Students In Recycling. *Globus Journal of Progressive Education: A Refereed Research Journal*, *12*(1), 104-110.

Guiamalon, T., Sandigan, D. A., & Dilna, S. G. (2022b). The impact of Alternative Learning System in Cotabato Division: A case study. *International Journal of Scientific Research and Management*, *10*(4), 1–5. . doi:10.18535/ijsrm/v10i4.el01

Gunawan, H., Thiracitta, N., & Nugroho, A. (2018). Sign language recognition using modified convolutional neural network model. In *2018 Indonesian Association for Pattern Recognition International Conference (INAPR)* (pp. 1-5). IEEE.

Guo, C. L., Lan, H., Ma, Y., Zhu, H., & Sun, K. (2020). The research of garbage classification and recognition based on surf and geometric hashing algorithm. In *2020 IEEE 9th Joint International Information Technology and Artificial Intelligence Conference (ITAIC)*. IEEE.

Guo, Z. (2020). Identification of hepatitis B using Raman spectroscopy combined with gated recurrent unit and multiscale fusion convolutional neural network. *Spectroscopy Letters: An International Journal for Rapid Communication*, *53*(4), 277–288. . doi:10.1080/00387010.2020.1737944

Guo, S., Li, X., & Mu, Z. (2021). Adversarial machine learning on social network: A survey. *Frontiers in Physics*, *9*, 766540. Advance online publication. doi:10.3389/fphy.2021.766540

Gupta, G. P., & Jha, S. (2018). Integrated Clustering and routing protocol for wireless sensor networks using cuckoo and harmony search based meta-heuristic techniques. *Engineering Applications of Artificial Intelligence*, *68*, 101–109. doi:10.1016/j.engappai.2017.11.003

Gushchina, O. M., & Ochepovsky, A. V. (2020). Data mining of students' behavior in E-learning system. *Journal of Physics: Conference Series*, *1553*(1), 012027. doi:10.1088/1742-6596/1553/1/012027

Haeberlen & Dupre. (2012). *Cloud computing. benefits, risks and recommendations for information security (rev. b)*. European Network and Information Security Agency.

Hajmoosaei, A., Kashfi, M., & Kailasam, P. (2011). Comparison plan for data warehouse system architectures. *3rd International Conference on Data Mining and Intelligent Information Technology Applications*, 290–293.

Hardwick, F. S., Gioulis, A., Akram, R. N., & Markantonakis, K. (2018). E-voting with blockchain: An e-voting protocol with decentralisation and voter privacy. In *2018 IEEE International Conference on Internet of Things (iThings) and IEEE Green Computing and Communications (GreenCom) and IEEE Cyber, Physical and Social Computing (CPSCom) and IEEE Smart Data (SmartData)* (pp. 1561-1567). IEEE.

Harnik, D., Pinkas, B., & Shulman-Peleg, A. (2010). Side channels in cloud services: Deduplication in cloud storage. *IEEE Security and Privacy*, *8*(6), 40–47. doi:10.1109/MSP.2010.187

Hasanika, D. (2021). Data mining system for predicting a winning cricket team. In *2021 IEEE 16th International Conference on Industrial and Information Systems (ICIIS)*. IEEE. 10.1109/ICIIS53135.2021.9660702

Hassija, V., Chamola, V., Saxena, V., Jain, D., Goyal, P., & Sikdar, B. (2019). A survey on IoT security: Application areas, security threats, and solution architectures. *IEEE Access: Practical Innovations, Open Solutions*, *7*, 82721–82743. doi:10.1109/ACCESS.2019.2924045

Hein, Z., Htoo, T. P., Aye, B., Htet, S. M., & Ye, K. Z. (2021). Leap Motion based Myanmar Sign Language Recognition using Machine Learning. In *2021 IEEE Conference of Russian Young Researchers in Electrical and Electronic Engineering (ElConRus)* (pp. 2304-2310). IEEE. 10.1109/ElConRus51938.2021.9396496

Hemasundara Rao, C., Naganjaneyulu, P.V., & Satyaprasad, K. (2019). Automatic classification breast masses in mammograms using fusion technique and FLDA analysis. *International Journal of Innovative Technology and Exploring Engineering*, *8*(5), 1061-1071.

Hinds, A., Ngulube, M., Zhu, S., & Al-Aqrabi, H. (2013). A review of routing protocols for mobile ad-hoc networks (manet). *International Journal of Information and Education Technology (IJIET)*, *3*(1), 1–5. doi:10.7763/IJIET.2013.V3.223

Hjálmarsson, F. Þ., Hreiðarsson, G. K., Hamdaqa, M., & Hjálmtýsson, G. (2018). Blockchain-based e-voting system. In *2018 IEEE 11th international conference on cloud computing (CLOUD)* (pp. 983-986). IEEE. 10.1109/CLOUD.2018.00151

Hong, D., Yokoya, N., Chanussot, J., & Zhu, X. X. (2019). An augmented linear mixing model to address spectral variability for hyperspectral unmixing. *IEEE Transactions on Image Processing*, *28*(4), 19231938. doi:10.1109/TIP.2018.2878958 PMID:30418901

Hong, D., Yokoya, N., Ge, N., Chanussot, J., & Zhu, X. X. (2019). Learnable manifold alignment (LeMA): A semi-supervised cross-modality learning framework for land cover and land use classification. *ISPRS Journal of Photogrammetry and Remote Sensing*, *147*, 193–205. doi:10.1016/j.isprsjprs.2018.10.006 PMID:30774220

Hou, Y. (2020). *Evaluation of energy efficiency in mobile cellular networks using a fluid modeling framework* [Doctoral dissertation]. Université Paris-Saclay.

Huang, Z., Ni, J., Yao, J., Xu, X., Zhang, B., Chen, Y., Tan, N., & Xue, C. (2020). Social Group Recommendation With TrAdaBoost. *IEEE Transactions on Computational Social Systems*, *7*(5), 1278–1287. doi:10.1109/TCSS.2020.3009721

Huang, Z., Pan, Z., & Lei, B. (2017). Transfer learning with deep convolutional neural network for SAR target classification with limited labelled data. *Remote Sensing Journal*, *9*(9), 907. doi:10.3390/rs9090907

Huiyao, A., Xicheng, L., & Wei, P. (2004). *A cluster-based multipath routing for MANET*. Computer School, National University of Defense Technology.

Hummel, R. (2000). Model-based ATR using synthetic aperture radar. *Proc. Rec. IEEE Int. Radar Conf.*

Hussain, S. S., Reddy, E. S. C., Akshay, K. G., & Akanksha, T. (2021). Fraud Detection in Credit Card Transactions Using SVM and Random Forest Algorithms. In *2021 Fifth International Conference on I-SMAC (IoT in Social, Mobile, Analytics and Cloud) (I-SMAC)* (pp. 1013-1017). IEEE.

Inthiyaz, S., Madhav, B. T. P., & Kishore, P. V. V. (2018). Flower image segmentation with PCA fused colored covariance and gabor texture features based level sets. *Ain Shams Engineering Journal*, *9*(4), 3277–3291. doi:10.1016/j.asej.2017.12.007

Islam, M. S., Rahman, M. H., Sassi, R., Rivolta, M. W., & Aktaruzzaman, M. (2019). A new benchmark on American sign language recognition using convolutional neural network. In *2019 International Conference on Sustainable Technologies for Industry 4.0 (STI)* (pp. 1-6). IEEE.

Jabeur, N. (2016). A firefly-inspired micro and macro clustering approach for wireless sensor networks. *Procedia Computer Science*, *98*, 132–139. doi:10.1016/j.procs.2016.09.021

Jain, A. K., Duin, R. P. W., & Mao, J. (2000). Statistical pattern recognition: A review. *IEEE Transactions on Pattern Analysis and Machine Intelligence*, *22*(1), 4–37. doi:10.1109/34.824819

Jana, Biswas, & Mohana. (2018). YOLO based Detection and Classification of Objects in video records. In *2018 3rd IEEE International Conference on Recent Trends in Electronics, Information & Communication Technology (RTEICT)*. IEEE.

Javad Shayegan, M., & Asgari Namin, P. (2021). An approach to improve apriori algorithm for extraction of frequent itemsets. In *2021 7th International Conference on Web Research (ICWR)*. IEEE. 10.1109/ICWR51868.2021.9443137

Kaaniche, N., & Laurent, M. (2014). A secure client side deduplication scheme in cloud storage environments. In *2014 6th International Conference on New Technologies, Mobility and Security (NTMS)*. IEEE. 10.1109/NTMS.2014.6814002

Kaaniche, N., & Laurent, M. (2017). Data security and privacy preservation in cloud storage environments based on cryptographic mechanisms. *Computer Communications*, *111*, 120–141. doi:10.1016/j.comcom.2017.07.006

Kamruzzaman, M. M. (2022). 6G wireless communication assisted security management using cloud edge computing. *Expert Systems: International Journal of Knowledge Engineering and Neural Networks*, *13061*. Advance online publication. doi:10.1111/exsy.13061

Kamruzzaman, M. M., & Alruwaili, O. (2022). Energy efficient sustainable Wireless Body Area Network design using network optimization with Smart Grid and Renewable Energy Systems. *Energy Reports*, *8*(November), 3780–3788. doi:10.1016/j.egyr.2022.03.006

Karthik, C., & Deepalakshmi. (2017). Hybrid cryptographic technique using OTP: RSA. In *2017 IEEE International Conference on Intelligent Techniques in Control, Optimization and Signal Processing (INCOS)*. IEEE.

Karthikeswaran, D. (2012). A pattern based framework for privacy preservation through association rule mining. *IEEE-International Conference On Advances In Engineering, Science And Management (ICAESM -2012),* 816–821.

Karthikeyan, B., Kanimozhi, N., & Ganesh, S. H. (2014). Analysis of reactive AODV routing protocol for MANET. *World Congress on Computing and Communication Technologies*, 264–267 10.1109/WCCCT.2014.70

Kaur, M. (2013). Cluster analysis of behavior of E-learners. *International Journal of Soft Computing and Engineering*, *3*(2), 344–346.

Keaveney, S. M. (1995). Customer Switching Behavior in Service Industries: An Exploratory Study. *Journal of Marketing*, *59*(April), 71–82. doi:10.1177/002224299505900206

Keller, K. L. (1993). Conceptualizing, measuring, and managing customer-based brand equity. *Journal of Marketing*, *57*(Jan), 1–22. doi:10.1177/002224299305700101

Khan, M. A. (2016). A survey of security issues for cloud computing. *Journal of Network and Computer Applications*, *71*, 11–29. doi:10.1016/j.jnca.2016.05.010

Khor, E. T. (2021). A learning analytics approach using clustering data mining for learners profiling to extrapolate e-learning behaviours. In T. Bastiaens (Ed.), *Proceedings of Innovate Learning Summit 2021 Online* (pp. 59-64). Association for the Advancement of Computing in Education (AACE). https://www.learntechlib.org/primary/p/220271

Kia, S. H., Henao, H., & Capolino, G.-A. (2005). Zoom-MUSIC frequency estimation method for three-phase induction machine fault detection. In *31st Annual Conference of IEEE Industrial Electronics Society*. IEEE. 10.1109/IECON.2005.1569317

Kim, J.-A., Sung, J.-Y., & Park, S.-H. (2020). Comparison of faster-RCNN, YOLO, and SSD for real-time vehicle type recognition. In *2020 IEEE International Conference on Consumer Electronics - Asia (ICCE-Asia)*. IEEE.

Kim, B. S., Lee, S. H., Lee, M. G., Ni, J., Song, J. Y., & Lee, C. W. (2007). A comparative study on damage detection in speed-up and coast-down process of grinding spindle-typed rotor-bearing system. *Journal of Materials Processing Technology*, *187–188*, 30–36. doi:10.1016/j.jmatprotec.2006.11.222

Kiran, R., & Kumar, D. K. R. A. (2020). Adaptive upgradation of personalized E-learning portal using data mining. *International Journal of Innovative Technology and Exploring Engineering*, *10*(1), 224–227. doi:10.35940/ijitee.A8167.1110120

Klaine, P. V., Imran, M. A., Onireti, O., & Souza, R. D. (2017). A survey of machine learning techniques applied to self-organizing cellular networks. *IEEE Communications Surveys and Tutorials*, *19*(4), 2392–2431. doi:10.1109/COMST.2017.2727878

Kousiga, T., & Shanmuga Vadivu, R. (2019). Survey on hierarchical clustering algorithms in data mining. *International Journal of Scientific Development and Research*, *4*(9), 1–3.

Kshetri, N., & Voas, J. (2018). Blockchain-enabled e-voting. *IEEE Software*, *35*(4), 95–99. doi:10.1109/MS.2018.2801546

Kulkarni, A., Shivananda, A., & Kulkarni, A. (2022). Named-entity recognition using CRF and BERT. In Natural Language Processing Projects. Apress.

Kulkarni, D. (2021). Leveraging blockchain technology in the education sector. *Turkish Journal of Computer and Mathematics Education*, *12*(10), 4578–4583.

Kumar, Punitha, & Mohana. (2020). YOLOv3 and YOLOv4: Multiple Object Detection for Surveillance Applications. In *2020 Third International Conference on Smart Systems and Inventive Technology (ICSSIT)*. IEEE. 10.1109/ICSSIT48917.2020.9214094

Kumar, P., & Kumar, S., & Alphonse. (2018). Attribute based encryption in cloud computing: A survey, gap analysis, and future directions. *Journal of Network and Computer Applications*, *108*, 37–52. doi:10.1016/j.jnca.2018.02.009

Kumer, S. A., & Srivatsa, S. K. (2019). An implementation of futuristic deep learning neural network in satellite images for hybrid image fusion. *International Journal of Recent Technology and Engineering*, *8*(1), 484–487.

Li, H., Yang, Y., Dai, Y., Yu, S., & Xiang, Y. (2020). Achieving secure and efficient dynamic searchable symmetric encryption over medical cloud data. *IEEE Transactions on Cloud Computing*, *8*(2), 484–494. doi:10.1109/TCC.2017.2769645

Li, J., Chen, X., Huang, X., Tang, S., Xiang, Y., Hassan, M. M., & Alelaiwi, A. (2015). Secure distributed deduplication systems with improved reliability. *IEEE Transactions on Computers*, *64*(12), 3569–3579. doi:10.1109/TC.2015.2401017

Li, J., Wu, L., Hong, R., & Hou, J. (2021). Random walk based distributed representation learning and prediction on Social Networking Services. *Information Sciences*, *549*, 328–346. doi:10.1016/j.ins.2020.10.045

Li, S., Yan, M., & Xu, J. (2020). Garbage object recognition and classification based on Mask Scoring RCNN. In *2020 International Conference on Culture-Oriented Science & Technology (ICCST)*. IEEE. 10.1109/ICCST50977.2020.00016

Liu, H., Jing, L., Yu, J., & Ng, M. K. (2021). Social recommendation with learning personal and social latent factors. *IEEE Transactions on Knowledge and Data Engineering*, *33*(7), 2956–2970. doi:10.1109/TKDE.2019.2961666

Liu, J. K., Liang, K., Susilo, W., Liu, J., & Xiang, Y. (2016). Two-factor data security protection mechanism for cloud storage system. *IEEE Transactions on Computers*, *65*(6), 1992–2004. doi:10.1109/TC.2015.2462840

Liu, M., Wu, Y., Zhang, P., Zhang, Q., Li, Y., & Li, M. (2013). SAR target con- guration recognition using locality preserving property and Gaussian mixture distribution. *IEEE Geoscience and Remote Sensing Letters*, *10*(2), 268272.

Liu, Z., Dong, Z., & Liu, D. (2016). Development of a rapid assay to detect the jellyfish Cyanea nozakii using a loop-mediated isothermal amplification method. *Mitochondrial DNA. Part A, DNA Mapping, Sequencing, and Analysis*, *27*(4), 2318–2322. doi:10.3109/19401736.2015.1022762 PMID:25774948

Li, Y., & Xia, L. (2020). Coronavirus disease 2019 (COVID-19): Role of chest CT in diagnosis and management. *AJR. American Journal of Roentgenology*, *214*(6), 1280–1286. doi:10.2214/AJR.20.22954 PMID:32130038

Lumapenet, H. T., & Usop, M. P. (2022). School Readiness towards the Delivery of Learning in the New Normal. *International Journal of Early Childhood Special Education, 14*(3), 2629-2637.

Lu, R., Li, Y. C., Li, Y., Jiang, J., & Ding, Y. (2020). Multi-agent deep reinforcement learning based demand response for discrete manufacturing systems energy management. *Applied Energy*, *276*, 115473. doi:10.1016/j.apenergy.2020.115473

Mahakud, R., Rath, S., Samantaray, M., Sinha, B., Priya, P., Nayak, A., & Kumari, A. (2016). Energy management in wireless sensor network using pegasis. *Procedia Computer Science*, *92*, 207–212. doi:10.1016/j.procs.2016.07.347

Mantas, J. (1987). Methodologies in pattern recognition and image analysis—A brief survey. *Pattern Recognition*, *20*(1), 1–6. doi:10.1016/0031-3203(87)90012-4

Marina, M. K., & Das, S. R. (2001). On-demand multipath distance vector routing in ad hoc networks. *Proceedings of the Ninth International Conference on Network Protocols (ICNP)*, 14–23. 10.1109/ICNP.2001.992756

Marwan, M., Kartit, A., & Ouahmane, H. (2017). Protecting medical images in cloud using visual cryptography scheme. In *2017 3rd International Conference of Cloud Computing Technologies and Applications (CloudTech)*. IEEE.

Matlani, P., & Shrivastava, M. (2019). Hybrid deep VGG-NET convolutional classifier for video smoke detection. *CMES*, *119*(3), 427–458. doi:10.32604/cmes.2019.04985

McAlister, L. (1982). A dynamic attribute satiation model of variety-seeking behaviour. *The Journal of Consumer Research*, *9*(Sept), 141–150. doi:10.1086/208907

McCaskill, S. (2021). *Network automation is 'essential' to Vodafone's bid to become a true technology company*. Retrieved from https://www.techradar.com/news/network-automation-is-essenti al-to-vodafones-bid-to-become-a-true-technology-company

Mehtab, S. (2022). *Design of a High-Speed OFDM-SAC-OCDMA-Based FSO System Using EDW Codes for Supporting 5G Data Services and Smart City Applications. Frontiers in Physics* , 10. doi:10.3389/fphy.2022.934848

Melek, C. G., Sonmez, E. B., & Albayrak, S. (2019). Object Detection in Shelf Images with YOLO. *IEEE EUROCON 2019-18th International Conference on Smart Technologies.*

Melero, M. J. (2022). *Network experience: Why performance partnerships are crucial.* Retrieved from https://www.ericsson.com/en/blog/2022/2/partnership-new-telecom-era-vodafone-ericsson

Mikami, K., Chen, Y., Nakazawa, J., Iida, Y., Kishimoto, Y., & Oya, Y. (2018). DeepCounter: Using deep learning to count garbage bags. In *2018 IEEE 24th International Conference on Embedded and Real-Time Computing Systems and Applications (RTCSA).* IEEE.

Morgan, R. M., & Hunt, S. D. (1994). The Commitment- Trust Theory of Relationship Marketing. *Journal of Marketing, 58*(3), 20–38. doi:10.1177/002224299405800302

Morris, I. (2021). *Ericsson bags 5G 'core' deal with Vodafone UK.* Retrieved from https://www.lightreading.com/5g/ericsson-bags-5g-core-deal-with-vodafone-uk/d/d-id/770266?videoId=6279364677001

Moysiadis, V., Sarigiannidis, P., & Moscholios, I. (2018). Towards distributed data management in fog computing. *Wireless Communications and Mobile Computing, 2018*, 2018. doi:10.1155/2018/7597686

Murugan & Durairaj. (2017). Regularization and optimization strategies in deep convolutional neural network. *Computer Vision and Pattern Recognition.*

Nagendraswamy, H. S., Kumara, B. C., & Chinmayi, R. L. (2016). Indian sign language recognition: An approach based on fuzzy-symbolic data. In *2016 International Conference on Advances in Computing, Communications and Informatics (ICACCI)* (pp. 1006-1013). IEEE. 10.1109/ICACCI.2016.7732176

Nagori, M., Jachak, R. S., & Chaudhari, P. P. (2019). A framework for segregating solid waste by employing the technique of image annotation. In *2019 Second International Conference on Advanced Computational and Communication Paradigms (ICACCP).* IEEE. 10.1109/ICACCP.2019.8882932

Nath, S., Wu, J., Zhao, Y., & Qiao, W. (2020). Low latency bearing fault detection of direct-drive wind turbines using Stator current. *IEEE Access: Practical Innovations, Open Solutions, 8*, 44163–44174. doi:10.1109/ACCESS.2020.2977632

Nayak, S. R., Mishra, J., & Palai, G. (2018). A modified approach to estimate fractal dimension of gray scale images. *Optik (Stuttgart), 161*, 136–145. doi:10.1016/j.ijleo.2018.02.024

Novak, L. M., Owirka, G. J., Brower, W. S., & Weaver, A. L. (1997). The auto- Matic target-recognition system in SAIP. *The Lincoln Laboratory Journal, 10*(2), 187201.

Obeidat, R., Duwairi, R., & Al-Aiad, A. (2019). A collaborative recommendation system for online courses recommendations. In *2019 International Conference on Deep Learning and Machine Learning in Emerging Applications (Deep-ML).* IEEE. 10.1109/Deep-ML.2019.00018

Oh, J., Youm, G.-Y., & Kim, M. (2021). SPAM-Net: A CNN-Based SAR Target Recognition Network With Pose Angle Marginalization Learning. *IEEE Transactions on Circuits and Systems for Video Technology, 31*(2), 701–714. doi:10.1109/TCSVT.2020.2987346

Ojha, S., & Rajput, V. (2017). AES and MD5 based secure authentication in cloud computing. In *2017 International Conference on I-SMAC (IoT in Social, Mobile, Analytics and Cloud) (I-SMAC).* IEEE.

Oliver, R. L. (1989). A cognitive model of the antecedents and consequences of satisfaction decisions. *JMR, Journal of Marketing Research, 17*(Nov), 460–469.

Omer, O. (2019, December 2). *Introduction to machine learning the Wikipedia Guide*. Retrieved July 1, 2022, from https://www.academia.edu/41157657/Introduction_to_Machine_Learning_The_Wikipedia_Guide

Ozturk, T., Talo, M., Yildirim, E. A., Baloglu, U. B., Yildirim, O., & Rajendra Acharya, U. (2020). Automated detection of COVID-19 cases using deep neural networks with X-ray images. *Computers in Biology and Medicine*, *121*(103792), 103792. doi:10.1016/j.compbiomed.2020.103792 PMID:32568675

Padmini, G. R., Rajesh, O., Raghu, K., Sree, N. M., & Apurva, C. (2021, March). Design and Analysis of 8-bit ripple Carry Adder using nine Transistor Full Adder. In *2021 7th International Conference on Advanced Computing and Communication Systems (ICACCS)* (Vol. 1, pp. 1982-1987). IEEE.

Panwar, M. (2012). Hand gesture recognition based on shape parameters. In *2012 International Conference on Computing, Communication and Applications* (pp. 1-6). IEEE. 10.1109/ICCCA.2012.6179213

Patel, D. N., Patel, S. B., Kothadiya, H. R., Jethwa, P. D., & Jhaveri, R. H. (2014). A survey of reactive routing protocols in MANET. *International Conference on Information Communication and Embedded Systems (ICICES2014)*, 1–6. 10.1109/ICICES.2014.7033833

Pei, J., Huang, Y., Huo, W., Zhang, Y., Yang, J., & Yeo, T.-S. (2018). SAR automatic target recognition based on multiview deep learning framework. *IEEE Transactions on Geoscience and Remote Sensing*, *56*(4), 2196–2210. doi:10.1109/TGRS.2017.2776357

Peter, K. J. (2011). Improving ATM security via face recognition. In *2011 3rd International Conference on Electronics Computer Technology*. IEEE. 10.1109/ICECTECH.2011.5942118

Petrick J. F. (2016). Development of a Multi-Dimensional Scale for Measuring Perceived Value of a Service: Serv Perval Scale. *Journal of Leisure Research*, *34*(2), 119-134.

Petrick, J. F. (2016). Development of a Multi-Dimensional Scale for Measuring Perceived Value of a Service: Serv Perval Scale. *Journal of Leisure Research*, *34*(2), 119-134.

Prabhu, S., Sengottaiyan, N., & Geetha, B. G. (2019). Self-adaptive approaches to probability distribution of data analytics in cloud computing resource services for infrastructure hybrids models. Applied Mathematics &. *Information Sciences*, *13*(S1), 437–446. doi:10.18576/amis/13s147 1

Prasetyo, E., Suciati, N., & Fatichah, C. (2020). A comparison of YOLO and mask R-CNN for segmenting head and tail of fish. In *2020 4th International Conference on Informatics and Computational Sciences (ICICoS)*. IEEE.

Priya. (2021). Robust attack detection approach for IIoT using ensemble classifier. *Computers, Materials & Continua*, *66*(3), 2457–2470. . doi:10.32604/cmc.2021.013852

Qian, Y., Zeng, T., Wang, H., Xu, M., Chen, J., Hu, N., Chen, D., & Liu, Y. (2020). Safety management of nasopharyngeal specimen collection from suspected cases of coronavirus disease 2019. *International Journal of Nursing Sciences*, *7*(2), 153–156. doi:10.1016/j.ijnss.2020.03.012 PMID:32292635

Qiu, F., Zhang, G., Sheng, X., Jiang, L., Zhu, L., Xiang, Q., Jiang, B., & Chen, P. (2022). Predicting students' performance in e-learning using learning process and behaviour data. *Scientific Reports*, *12*(1), 453. doi:10.103841598-021-03867-8 PMID:35013396

Rad, D., Balas, E., Ignat, S., Rad, G., & Dixon, D. (2020). A Predictive Model of Youth Bystanders' Helping Attitudes. *Revista romaneasca pentru educatie multidimensionala-Journal for Multidimensional Education*, *12*(1Sup2), 136-150.

Rad, D., Dughi, T., & Demeter, E. (2019). The Dynamics of the Relationship between Humor and Benevolence as Values. *Revista romaneasca pentru educatie multidimensionala-Journal for Multidimensional Education, 11*(3), 201-212.

Rad, D., & Balas, V. E. (2020). A Novel Fuzzy Scoring Approach of Behavioural Interviews in Personnel Selection. BRAIN. *Broad Research in Artificial Intelligence and Neuroscience, 11*(2), 178–188. doi:10.18662/brain/11.2/81

Rafaeli, S., & Hutchison, D. (2003). A survey of key management for secure group communication. *ACM Computing Surveys, 35*(3), 309–329. doi:10.1145/937503.937506

Raja, M., Srinivasan, K., & Syed-Abdul, S. (2019). Preoperative Virtual Reality Based Intelligent Approach for Minimising Patient Anxiety Levels. *2019 IEEE International Conference on Consumer Electronics - Taiwan, ICCE-TW 2019*, art.no. 8991754.

Raja, C., & Balaji, L. (2019). An automatic detection of blood vessel in retinal images using convolution neural network for diabetic retinopathy detection. *Pattern Recognition and Image Analysis, 29*(3), 533–545. doi:10.1134/S1054661819030180

Raja, M., & Lakshmi Priya, G. G. (2020). Factors Affecting the Intention to Use Virtual Reality in Education. *Psychology and Education, 57*(9), 2014–2022.

Raja, M., & Lakshmi Priya, G. G. (2022). Using Virtual Reality and Augmented Reality with ICT Tools for Enhancing quality in the Changing Academic Environment in COVID-19 Pandemic: An Empirical Study. *Studies in Computational Intelligence, 1019*, 467–482. doi:10.1007/978-3-030-93921-2_26

Raja, M., & Priya, G. G. L. (2021a). An Analysis of Virtual Reality Usage through a Descriptive Research Analysis on School Students' Experiences: A Study from India. *International Journal of Early Childhood Special Education, 13*(2), 990–1005. doi:10.9756/INT-JECSE/V13I2.211142

Raja, M., & Priya, G. G. L. (2021b). Conceptual Origins, Technological Advancements, and Impacts of Using Virtual Reality Technology in Education. *Webology, 18*(2), 116–134. doi:10.14704/WEB/V18I2/WEB18311

Ramadhani, P. P., Hadi, S., & Rosadi, R. (2021). Implementation of data warehouse in making business intelligence dashboard development using PostgreSQL database and Kimball lifecycle method. In *2021 International Conference on Artificial Intelligence and Big Data Analytics*. IEEE. 10.1109/ICAIBDA53487.2021.9689697

Ramapatruni, S. (2019). Anomaly detection models for smart home security. In *2019 IEEE 5th Intl Conference on Big Data Security on Cloud (BigDataSecurity), IEEE Intl Conference on High Performance and Smart Computing, (HPSC) and IEEE Intl Conference on Intelligent Data and Security (IDS)*. IEEE. 10.1109/BigDataSecurity-HPSC-IDS.2019.00015

Ramirez, Brill, Ohlhausen, Wright, & McSweeny. (2014). *Data brokers: A call for transparency and accountability*. US Federal Trade Commission.

Rashid, M. M., Kamruzzaman, J., Hassan, M. M., Imam, T., & Gordon, S. (2020). Cyberattacks detection in IoT-based smart city applications using machine learning techniques. *International Journal of Environmental Research and Public Health, 17*(24), 9347. doi:10.3390/ijerph17249347 PMID:33327468

Ravald, A., & Grönroos, C. (2019). The Value Concept and Relationship Marketing. *European Journal of Marketing, 30*(2), 19–30. doi:10.1108/03090569610106626

Reddy, D. K., Behera, H. S., Nayak, J., Vijayakumar, P., Naik, B., & Singh, P. K. (2021). Deep neural network based anomaly detection in Internet of Things network traffic tracking for the applications of future smart cities. *Transactions on Emerging Telecommunications Technologies, 32*(7). Advance online publication. doi:10.1002/ett.4121

Redmon & Farhadi. (2016). *YOLO9000: Better, Faster, Stronger*. arXiv:1612.08242v1 [cs.CV].

Redmon & Farhadi. (2018). *YOLOv3: An Incremental Improvement*. arXiv:1804.02767v1 [cs.CV].

Redmon, J., Divvala, S., Girshick, R., & Farhadi, A. (2016). You only look once: Unified, real-time object detection. In *2016 IEEE Conference on Computer Vision and Pattern Recognition (CVPR)*. IEEE. 10.1109/CVPR.2016.91

Ren, S., He, K., Girshick, R., & Sun, J. (2017). Faster R-CNN: Towards real-time object detection with region proposal networks. *IEEE Transactions on Pattern Analysis and Machine Intelligence*, *39*(6), 1137–1149. doi:10.1109/TPAMI.2016.2577031 PMID:27295650

Risnanto, S., Abd Rahim, Y., Mohd, O., & Abdurrohman, A. (2022). *E-Voting: Technology Requirements Mapping*. Academic Press.

Robinson, Y. H., & Rajaram, M. (2015). Energy-aware multipath routing scheme based on particle swarm optimization in mobile ad hoc networks. *TheScientificWorldJournal*, *284276*, 1–9. Advance online publication. doi:10.1155/2015/284276 PMID:26819966

Rodriguez-Galiano, V. F., Ghimire, B., Rogan, J., Chica-Olmo, M., & Rigol-Sanchez, J. P. (2012). An assessment of the effectiveness of a random forest classifier for land-cover classification. *ISPRS Journal of Photogrammetry and Remote Sensing*, *67*, 93–104. doi:10.1016/j.isprsjprs.2011.11.002

Roman, A., Rad, D., Egerau, A., Dixon, D., Dughi, T., Kelemen, G., Balas, E., & Rad, G. (2020). Physical Self-Schema Acceptance and Perceived Severity of Online Aggressiveness in Cyberbullying Incidents. *Journal of Interdisciplinary Studies in Education*, *9*(1), 100–116. doi:10.32674/jise.v9i1.1961

Ruprah, T. S., Kore, V. S., & Mali, Y. K. (2017). Secure data transfer in android using elliptical curve cryptography. In *2017 International Conference on Algorithms, Methodology, Models and Applications in Emerging Technologies (ICAMMAET)*. IEEE. 10.1109/ICAMMAET.2017.8186639

Saba, S. S., Sreelakshmi, D., Sampath Kumar, P., Sai Kumar, K., & Saba, S. R. (2020). Logistic regression machine learning algorithm on MRI brain image for fast and accurate diagnosis. *International Journal of Scientific and Technology Research*.

Safeel, M., Sukumar, T., Shashank, K. S., Arman, M. D., Shashidhar, R., & Puneeth, S. B. (2020). Sign language recognition techniques-a review. In *2020 IEEE International Conference for Innovation in Technology (INOCON)* (pp. 1-9). IEEE.

Sahu, N. K., & Mukherjee, I. (2020). Machine Learning based anomaly detection for IoT Network: (Anomaly detection in IoT Network). In *2020 4th International Conference on Trends in Electronics and Informatics (ICOEI)*. IEEE. 10.1109/ICOEI48184.2020.9142921

Samadi, F., Akbarizadeh, G., & Kaabi, H. (2019). Change detection in SAR images using deep belief network: A new training approach based on morphological images. *IET Image Processing*, *13*(12), 2255–2264. doi:10.1049/iet-ipr.2018.6248

Santra, A., Rai, V., Das, D., & Kundu, S. (2022). Facial Expression Recognition Using Convolutional Neural Network. *International Journal for Research in Applied Science and Engineering Technology*, *10*(5), 1081–1092. doi:10.22214/ijraset.2022.42439

Sarhan, N., & Frintrop, S. (2020). Transfer learning for videos: From action recognition to sign language recognition. In *2020 IEEE International Conference on Image Processing (ICIP)* (pp. 1811-1815). IEEE. 10.1109/ICIP40778.2020.9191289

Sarkar, S., & Datta, R. (2013). A game theoretic model for stochastic routing in self-organized MANETs. *Proceedings of the IEEE Wireless Communications and Networking Conference (WCNC)*, 1962–1967. 10.1109/WCNC.2013.6554865

Sarkar, S., & Datta, R. (2016). A secure and energy-efficient stochastic multipath routing for self-organized mobile ad hoc networks. *Ad Hoc Networks*, *37*, 209–227. doi:10.1016/j.adhoc.2015.08.020

Sastry, A. S. C. S., Geetesh, S., Sandeep, A., Varenya, V. V., Kishore, P. V. V., Kumar, D. A., & Kumar, M. T. K. (2019). Fusing spatio-temporal joint features for adequate skeleton based action recognition using global alignment kernel. *International Journal of Engineering and Advanced Technology*, *8*(4), 749–754.

Savic, M., Lukic, M., Danilovic, D., Bodroski, Z., Bajovic, D., Mezei, I., Vukobratovic, D., Skrbic, S., & Jakovetic, D. (2021). Deep learning anomaly detection for cellular IoT with applications in smart logistics. *IEEE Access: Practical Innovations, Open Solutions*, *9*, 59406–59419. doi:10.1109/ACCESS.2021.3072916

Scohy, A. (2020). Low performance of rapid antigen detection test as frontline testing for COVID-19 diagnosis. *Journal of Clinical Virology, 129*(104455). . doi:10.1016/j.jcv.2020.104455

Sesto-Castilla, D., Garcia-Villegas, E., Lyberopoulos, G., & Theodoropoulou, E. (2019). Use of machine learning for energy efficiency in present and future mobile networks. *2019 IEEE Wireless Communications and Networking Conference (WCNC)*. 10.1109/WCNC.2019.8885478

Shaheen, S. H., Yousaf, M., & Jalil, M. (2017). Temper proof data distribution for universal verifiability and accuracy in electoral process using blockchain. In *2017 13th International Conference on Emerging Technologies (ICET)* (pp. 1-6). IEEE. 10.1109/ICET.2017.8281747

Shahzad, B., & Crowcroft, J. (2019). Trustworthy electronic voting using adjusted blockchain technology. *IEEE Access: Practical Innovations, Open Solutions*, *7*, 24477–24488. doi:10.1109/ACCESS.2019.2895670

Shakya, D. S., & Smys, D. (2020). Anomalies detection in fog computing architectures using deep learning. *Journal of Trends in Computer Science and Smart Technology*, *2*(1), 46–55. doi:10.36548/jtcsst.2020.1.005

Shan, F. (2020). *Lung infection quantification of COVID-19 in CT images with deep learning*. https://arxiv.org/abs/2003.04655

Shan, Z., Ren, K., Blanton, M., & Wang, C. (2019). Practical secure computation outsourcing: A survey. *ACM Computing Surveys*, *51*(2), 1–40. doi:10.1145/3158363

Sharma, A., & Singh, R. K. (2021). An efficient approach to find frequent item sets in large database. In *2021 1st Odisha International Conference on Electrical Power Engineering, Communication and Computing Technology (ODICON)*. IEEE. 10.1109/ODICON50556.2021.9428946

Sharma, M. K., & Somwanshi, D. (2018). Improvement in homomorphic encryption algorithm with elliptic curve cryptography and OTP technique. In *2018 3rd International Conference and Workshops on Recent Advances and Innovations in Engineering (ICRAIE)*. IEEE.

Sharma, P., & Sharma, N. (2019). Gesture recognition system. In *2019 4th International Conference on Internet of Things: Smart Innovation and Usages (IoT-SIU)* (pp. 1-3). IEEE. 10.1109/IoT-SIU.2019.8777487

Shenoy, K., Dastane, T., Rao, V., & Vyavaharkar, D. (2018). Real-time Indian sign language (ISL) recognition. In *2018 9th International Conference on Computing, Communication and Networking Technologies (ICCCNT)* (pp. 1-9). IEEE.

Shen, X., Wang, L., Zhu, H., & Liu, Y. (2020). A multivariate public key encryption scheme with equality test. *IEEE Access: Practical Innovations, Open Solutions*, *8*, 75463–75472. doi:10.1109/ACCESS.2020.2988732

Shukla, P. (2004). Effect of product usage, satisfaction and involvement on brand switching behavior. *Asia Pacific Journal of Marketing and Logistics*, *16*(4), 82–104. doi:10.1108/13555850410765285

Singh, A., & Chatterjee, K. (2017). Cloud security issues and challenges: A survey. *Journal of Network and Computer Applications*, *79*, 88–115. doi:10.1016/j.jnca.2016.11.027

Singh, G., & Supriya, S. (2013). A study of encryption algorithms (RSA, DES, 3DES and AES) for information security. *International Journal of Computers and Applications*, *67*(19), 33–38. doi:10.5120/11507-7224

Singh, O., Singh, J., & Singh, R. (2018). Multi-level trust based intelligence intrusion detection system to detect the malicious nodes using elliptic curve cryptography in MANET. *Cluster Computing*, *21*(1), 51–63. doi:10.100710586-017-0927-z

Singh, S., Jeong, Y.-S., & Park, J. H. (2016). A survey on cloud computing security: Issues, threats, and solutions. *Journal of Network and Computer Applications*, *75*, 200–222. doi:10.1016/j.jnca.2016.09.002

Subba, B., Biswas, S., & Karmakar, S. (2016). "Intrusion detection in mobile ad hoc Networks: Bayesian game formulation. *EngSciTechnol. Engineering Science and Technology, an International Journal*, *19*(2), 782–799. doi:10.1016/j.jestch.2015.11.001

Sun, C. (2021). A novel rolling bearing vibration impulsive signals detection approach based on dictionary learning. *IEEE/CAA Journal of Automatica Sinica*, *8*(6), 1188–1198. . doi:10.1109/JAS.2020.1003438

Sun, Y., Liu, Z., Todorovic, S., & Li, J. (2007). Adaptive boosting for SAR automatic target recognition. *IEEE Transactions on Aerospace and Electronic Systems*, *43*(1), 112125. doi:10.1109/TAES.2007.357120

Supasan, N. A. I., Kaushalya, W. A. L. U., Maduwantha, S. M. D. P., Yasiru, M. G. A., Wijenayake, S. J. K., Kulathilake, K. A. S. H., & Kohomban, U. (2018). Self-controlled robot for collection of light weight waste in a ground area. In *2018 IEEE International Conference on Information and Automation for Sustainability (ICIAfS)*. IEEE. 10.1109/ICIAFS.2018.8913337

Suykens, J. A. (2014). Introduction to machine learning. In *Academic Press Library in Signal Processing* (Vol. 1, pp. 765–773). Elsevier.

Sze, V., Chen, Y. H., Emer, J., Suleiman, A., & Zhang, Z. (2017, April). Hardware for machine learning: Challenges and opportunities. In *2017 IEEE Custom Integrated Circuits Conference (CICC)* (pp. 1-8). IEEE. 10.1109/CICC.2017.7993626

Taha, A., Alsaqour, R., Uddin, M., Abdelhaq, M., & Saba, T. (2017). Energy efficient multipath routing protocol for mobile ad-hoc network using the ftness function. *IEEE Access: Practical Innovations, Open Solutions*, *5*, 10369–10381. doi:10.1109/ACCESS.2017.2707537

Tang, J., Cui, Y., Li, Q., Ren, K., Liu, J., & Buyya, R. (2017). Ensuring security and privacy preservation for cloud data services. *ACM Computing Surveys*, *49*(1), 1–39. doi:10.1145/2906153

Thangapandiyan, M., Rubesh Anand, P. M., & Sankaran, K. S. (2018). Quantum key distribution and cryptography mechanisms for cloud data security. In *2018 International Conference on Communication and Signal Processing (ICCSP)*. IEEE. 10.1109/ICCSP.2018.8524298

Tian, S., Yin, K., Wang, C., & Zhang, H. (2015). *An SAR ATR method based on scattering center feature and bipartite graph matching*. IETE Tech.

Toğaçar, M., Ergen, B., & Cömert, Z. (2020). COVID-19 detection using deep learning models to exploit Social Mimic Optimization and structured chest X-ray images using fuzzy color and stacking approaches. *Computers in Biology and Medicine*, *121*(103805), 103805. doi:10.1016/j.compbiomed.2020.103805 PMID:32568679

Uddin, M., Rahman, A. A., Alarifi, A., Talha, M., Shah, A., Iftikhar, M., & Zomaya, A. (2012). Improving performance of mobile ad hoc networks using efficient tactical on demand distance vector (TAODV) routing algorithm. *International Journal of Innovative Computing, Information, & Control*, *8*(6), 4375–4389.

Valera, M., Guo, Z., Kelly, P., Matz, S., Cantu, V. A., Percus, A. G., Hyman, J. D., Srinivasan, G., & Viswanathan, H. S. (2018). Machine learning for graph-based representations of three-dimensional discrete fracture networks. *Computational Geosciences*, *22*(3), 695–710. doi:10.100710596-018-9720-1

Vamvakas, P., Tsiropoulou, E. E., & Papavassiliou, S. (2017). Dynamic Provider Selection & Power Resource Management in competitive wireless communication markets. *Mobile Networks and Applications*, *23*(1), 86–99. doi:10.100711036-017-0885-y

Vandikas, K., Hallberg, H., Ickin, S., Nyström, C., Sanders, E., Gorbatov, O., & Eleftheriadis, L. (2021). *Ensuring energy-efficient networks with artificial intelligence*. Retrieved from https://www.ericsson.com/en/reports-and-papers/ericsson-technology-review/articles/ensuring-energy-efficient-networks-wi
th-ai

Venkatesan, T. P., Rajakumar, P., & Pitchaikkannu, A. (2014). Overview of Proactive Routing protocols in MANET. *Fourth International Conference on Communication Systems and Network Technologies*, 173–177. 10.1109/CSNT.2014.42

Vijayalakshmi, C. (2020). Convergent dispersal: Toward storage-efficient security in a cloud-of-clouds. *International Journal for Research in Applied Science and Engineering Technology*, *8*(4), 541–547. doi:10.22214/ijraset.2020.4087

Wang, S. (2020). A fully automatic deep learning system for COVID-19 diagnostic and prognostic analysis. *The European Respiratory Journal, 56*(2). . doi:10.1183/13993003.00775-2020

Wang, C. (2010). A novel encryption scheme for data deduplication system. In *2010 International Conference on Communications, Circuits and Systems (ICCCAS)*. IEEE. 10.1109/ICCCAS.2010.5581996

Wang, J., Liu, J., Ren, P., & Qin, C.-X. (2020). A SAR Target Recognition Based on Guided Reconstruction and Weighted Norm-Constrained Deep Belief Network. *IEEE Access: Practical Innovations, Open Solutions*, *8*, 181712–181722. doi:10.1109/ACCESS.2020.3025379

Wang, L., Lin, Z. Q., & Wong, A. (2020). COVID-Net: A tailored deep convolutional neural network design for detection of COVID-19 cases from chest X-ray images. *Scientific Reports*, *10*(1), 19549. doi:10.103841598-020-76550-z PMID:33177550

Wang, R., Xu, J., & Han, T. X. (2019a). Object instance detection with pruned Alexnet and extended training data. *Signal Processing Image Communication*, *70*, 145–156. doi:10.1016/j.image.2018.09.013

Wang, S.-H., Muhammad, K., Hong, J., Sangaiah, A. K., & Zhang, Y.-D. (2020). Alcoholism identification via convolutional neural network based on parametric ReLU, dropout, and batch normalization. *Neural Computing & Applications*, *32*(3), 665–680. doi:10.100700521-018-3924-0

Wang, Y., Wang, G., Chen, C., & Pan, Z. (2019b). Multi-scale dilated convolution of convolutional neural network for image denoising. *Multimedia Tools and Applications*, *78*(14), 19945–19960. doi:10.100711042-019-7377-y

Westin, A. (1967). *Privacy and Freedom*. Atheneum.

Wu, L., Chen, L., Hong, R., Fu, Y., Xie, X., & Wang, M. (2020). A hierarchical attention model for social contextual image recommendation. *IEEE Transactions on Knowledge and Data Engineering*, *32*(10), 1854–1867. doi:10.1109/TKDE.2019.2913394

Wu, L., Sun, P., Hong, R., Ge, Y., & Wang, M. (2021). Collaborative Neural Social Recommendation. *IEEE Transactions on Systems, Man, and Cybernetics. Systems*, *51*(1), 464–476. doi:10.1109/TSMC.2018.2872842

Xu, J., Li, G., Peng, Y.-N., Xia, X.-G., & Wang, Y.-L. (2008). Parametric veloc- its synthetic aperture radar Multi look processing and its applications. *IEEE Transactions on Geoscience and Remote Sensing*, *46*(11), 3488–3502. doi:10.1109/TGRS.2008.2000877

Yadav, A. K., & Tripathi, S. (2017). QMRPRNS: Design of QoS multicast routing protocol using reliable node selection scheme for MANETs. *Peer-to-Peer Networking and Applications*, *10*(4), 897–909. doi:10.100712083-016-0441-8

Yannam, A. (2019). Trust aware intrustion detection system to defend attacks in MANET. *International Journal of Innovative Technology and Exploring Engineering*, *8*(6), 1298–1306.

Yavuz, A. A., Alagöz, F., & Anarim, E. (2010). A new Multi-Tier adaptive military MANET security protocol using hybrid cryptography and signcryption. *Turkish Journal of Electrical Engineering and Computer Sciences*, *18*, 1–22. doi:10.3906/elk-0904-6

Youjae, Y., & Ho, S. J. (2003). Effects of Loyalty Programs on Value Perception, Program Loyalty and Brand Loyalty. *Journal of the Academy of Marketing Science*, *30*(3), 229–240.

Yu, J., Zheng, X., & Wang, S. (2019). A deep autoencoder feature learning method for process pattern recognition. *Journal of Process Control*, *79*, 1–15. doi:10.1016/j.jprocont.2019.05.002

Zahedi, Z. M., Akbari, R., Shokouhifar, M., Safaei, F., & Jalali, A. (2016). Swarm intelligence based fuzzy routing protocol for clustered wireless sensor networks. *Expert Systems with Applications*, *55*, 313–328. doi:10.1016/j.eswa.2016.02.016

Zeithaml, V. A. (2008). Consumer Perceptions of Price, Quality and Value: A Means-End Model and Synthesis of Evidence. *Journal of Marketing*, *52*(July), 2–22.

Zervoudakis, K., & Tsafarakis, S. (2020). A mayfly optimization algorithm. *Computers & Industrial Engineering*, *145*, 106559. doi:10.1016/j.cie.2020.106559

Zhang, C., Tian, Y., & Huenerfauth, M. (2016). Multi-modality American sign language recognition. In *2016 IEEE International Conference on Image Processing (ICIP)* (pp. 2881-2885). IEEE. 10.1109/ICIP.2016.7532886

Zhang, P., Du, Y., Habetler, T. G., & Lu, B. (2011). A survey of condition monitoring and protection methods for medium-voltage induction motors. *IEEE Transactions on Industry Applications*, *47*(1), 34–46. doi:10.1109/TIA.2010.2090839

Zhang, Y.-D., Dong, Z., Chen, X., Jia, W., Du, S., Muhammad, K., & Wang, S.-H. (2019). Image based fruit category classification by 13-layer deep convolutional neural network and data augmentation. *Multimedia Tools and Applications*, *78*(3), 3613–3632. doi:10.100711042-017-5243-3

Zhao, K., Zhang, K., Zhai, Y., Wang, D., & Su, J. (2021). Real-time sign language recognition based on video stream. International Journal of Systems. *Control and Communications*, *12*(2), 158–174.

Zhao, Z., Lu, H., Cai, D., He, X., & Zhuang, Y. (2016). User preference learning for online social recommendation. *IEEE Transactions on Knowledge and Data Engineering*, *28*(9), 2522–2534. doi:10.1109/TKDE.2016.2569096

Zheng, L., Liang, B., & Jiang, A. (2017). Recent advances in deep learning for sign language recognition. In *2017 International Conference on Digital Image Computing: Techniques and Applications (DICTA)* (pp. 1-7). IEEE. 10.1109/DICTA.2017.8227483

Zhe, X., Chen, S., & Yan, H. (2019). Directional statistics-based deep metric learning for image classification and retrieval. *Pattern Recognition*, *93*, 113–123. doi:10.1016/j.patcog.2019.04.005

Zhou, W., Habetler, T. G., & Harley, R. G. (2008). Bearing fault detection via Stator current noise cancellation and statistical control. *IEEE Transactions on Industrial Electronics*, *55*(12), 4260–4269. . doi:10.1109/TIE.2008.2005018

Zhou, W., Habetler, T., & Harley, R. (1982). Bearing fault detection via Stator current noise cancellation and statistical control. *IEEE Transactions on Industrial Electronics*. Advance online publication. doi:10.1109/TIE.2008.2004377

Zhou, X., Liang, W., Huang, S., & Fu, M. (2019). Social recommendation with large-scale group decision-making for cyber-enabled online service. *IEEE Transactions on Computational Social Systems*, *6*(5), 1073–1082. doi:10.1109/TCSS.2019.2932288

About the Contributors

Ahmed J. Obaid is in the Department of Computer Science, Faculty of Computer Science and Mathematics, University of Kufa, Iraq.

Ghassan H. Abdul-Majeed is a full professor at the University of Baghdad, works as a consultant for improving the research dimension of the University in Scopus and ranking systems. He received his PhD in Petroleum Engineering at University of Baghdad in 1997 with excellent degree. The topic of his dissertation was A Comprehensive Mechanistic Model for Vertical and Inclined Two-Phase Flow. From 2004 to 2013, he became the head of the computer center of Baghdad University. During this period, the computer center became the best training center in Iraq, also during his management; he got several international certificates from Cisco, MS and other computer companies. He also performed a research school in computer networks. He published 32 technical papers in reputable journals in the fields of petroleum engineering and information technology. His research interest: Two-Phase Flow, Modeling and Simulation in Petroleum Engineering, Computer Networks. He is a member in international journal and conference comities. He was supervisor and examiner for many Master's and Ph.D. students. He has many publications in international and ISI journals and conferences.

Adriana Burlea-Schiopoiu currently works at the Department of Management, Marketing and Business Administration, University of Craiova. Adriana does research in Behavioural Economics, Business Administration and Business Ethics. Their current project is 'Corporate Social Responsibility'.

Parul Agarwal is associated with Jamia Hamdard since 2002. She is currently an Associate Professor in the Department of Computer Science and Engineering. Her area of specialization include Fuzzy Data Mining, Cloud Computing, and Soft Computing. Her particular interest includes Sustainable Computing and its applications in Agriculture, transportation and health care. She has published several papers in reputed and SCI, Scopus and Elsevier indexed journals and many book chapters published by CRC press, Springer, IGI-Global are to her credit. She has chaired several sessions of International/ National Conferences of repute. Having Google Scholar Citations of more than 100, h-Index 5 and i-10 as 4. Currently, several PhD. Scholars are working under her supervision. Member of several committees at university level and membership of several professional bodies like ISTE, IEEE are to her credit.

* * *

Muruganantham A. is serving as the Associate Professor in the Department of Computer Science at Kristu Jayanti College (Autonomous), Bangalore. He has 25 years in the field of education holding various academic roles. He has pursued his research in web mining. Exceptional track record of research success with multiple published articles. His expertise and interests are in Web mining, Data mining, Object-oriented Programming, Middleware Technologies and various high-level programming languages. He has won the Teacher Innovation Award from ZIIEI in the year 2019, Won Educator Excellence Award from Vendant Foundation, Leading Educationist of India Award 2022 from Friendship Forum and his achievements are listed in Asian Biographies website. Highly committed person who goes beyond the call of duty and inspires students to pursue academic and personal excellence.

Nadia Al Zubaidy is Assistance Lecturer at college of College of Science, Mustansiriyah University, Iraq. She Holds a Master degree in Computer Science with specialization in software engineering. Her research areas are Software Engineering, Artificial Intelligent, Internet of Things.

Ibrahim Alrashdi received the M.S. degree in Computer Science from Western Illinois University, IL, USA, in 2013, the Ph.D. degree in Computer Science and Informatics from Oakland University, MI, USA, in 2019. He is currently an Assistant Professor in the Department of Computer Science at Jouf University. His research interests include the Internet of Things, Cybersecurity, Cloud computing, and Artificial intelligence. He is a member of the IEEE and ACM.

Rekha Baghel joins Ajay Kumar Garg Engineering College Ghaziabad in the Department of CSE. Prior to coming to Ajay Kumar Garg Engineering College she was an assistant professor at Galgotias College of Engineering and technology Greater Noida. She received her BE in CSE from Institute of Engineering and Technology, Agra and M. Tech from National Institute of Technology, Jalandhar. Her primary research interests are in the field of Sentiment Analysis, Machine Learning, Data Mining.

Arun Singh Chouhan is working as Associate Professor in Department of Computer Science & Engineering Cyber Security in Malla Reddy University, Hyderabad. He is having 14 years of experience in Research and Teaching. He is expert in Cloud Computing, Cyber Security and Artificial Intelligence. He is having many International Parents and National Parents & Copyright. He is member of Fellow IETE,CSI India, CSTA, New York, IEEE, IAENG, Hong Kong, MIRLABS (USA), UACEE (USA). He is certified from Cloud University, USA and ISTQB, Germany.

Rosy Salomi Victoria D. received the M.E. degree in Computer Science and Engineering from Sathyabama University, in 2003. She obtained Ph.D. from Anna University, Chennai in 2015. Currently, she is an Associate Professor at St. Joseph's College of Engineering. Her interests are in Computer Networks, Image Processing, object Oriented Analysis and Design and Distributed systems. She published papers nearly in 15 journals.

Fathima G. has obtained her B.E. degree in Computer Science and Engineering from Thiagarajar College of Engineering, Madurai in the year 1994. She obtained her M.E. degree in Computer Science from R.E.C. (currently N.I.T), Tiruchirapalli in the year 2003. Obtained her Doctoral Degree in Computer Science from Anna University, Chennai in the year 2012. She has teaching Experience of 22+ years and 12+ years of administrative experience. Has published 16 papers in International Journals and presented 17 papers in various International/National Conferences. Organized several technical symposiums, workshops, National Conferences and FDPs for benefit of students, research scholars, and Faculties. Her areas of interest include Computer Networks, Mobile Ad Hoc Networks, Cryptography and Data mining. She has received appreciation award from EMC2 and Infosys for her contribution to EMC Academic Alliance program and Infosys Campus connect Foundation program. She is involved in research projects sponsored by UGC, AICTE and TNSCST. She is currently working as Prof & Head of Department of Computer Science and Engineering at Adhiyamaan College of Engineering, Hosur.

Lilly Florence M. is working as Professor in Department of CSE at Adhiyamaan College of Engineering, her current research area is machine learning,deep learning and cloud computing.

Makki Mohialden is a lecturer at College of Science, Mustansiriyah University, Iraq. She Holds a Master degree in Computer Science with specialization in Software Engineering. Her research areas are Software Engineering, Artificial Intelligent, Internet of Things and Cloud Computing. She is Head of Computer Center in the College of Science.

P. L. Rajarajeswari received B.E. degree in the department of Computer Science and Engineering from Bharathidasan University, Saranathan College of Engineering, Trichy, India in the year 2003,M.E. degree in Computer Science and Engineering from Anna University, VLB Janakiammal College of Engineering and Technology, Coimbatore - India in the year 2010 and received her Ph.D. degree in Information and Communication Engineering from Anna University, Chennai, Tamil Nadu, India in the year 2017. Her academic experience in teaching field is around 16 years. She had published around 20 research papers indexed in SCI, Scopus, Web of science and UGC care approved journals. She has also published 2 patents. She has authored a book entitled "Fundamentals of Mobile and Pervasive Computing" and also an active life time member of ISTE. Her areas of interest include Wireless Sensor Networks, Wireless Communication and IOT. She had also delivered many guest lectures to the students of various Engineering colleges. Presently, she is designated as Associate Professor in the Department of Computer Science and Engineering in Saranathan College of Engineering, Trichy.

Venkatasubramanian S. received the B.E. degree in Electronics and Communication from Bharathidasan University and M.E. degree in Computer science from Regional Engineering College, Trichy. He has 24 years of teaching experience. He is currently pursuing doctoral research in mobile Ad hoc networks. His areas of interest include mobile networks, Network Security and software Engineering. He has published 29 papers in the international journals and 15 papers in international conference. He has also registered three patents. At present he is working as an Associate Professor in Department of CSBS at Saranathan college of Engineering, Trichy, India. He has also authored books on "Software Engineering" and and "python programming". He is the receiver of the Global teacher award from AKS academy and Dr. Sarvepalli Radhakrishnan lifetime achiever national award.

Aswin Kumer S. V. graduated in Electronics and Communication Engineering from Pallavan College of Engineering, Kanchipuram in April 2008 and received his Master's degree in Embedded System Technology SRM University, Kanchipuram in May 2012. He received his doctoral degree for the implementation of image fusion using Artificial Neural Network from SCSVMV (Deemed to be University), Enathur in February 2019. He is working as an Associate Professor in Department of Electronics and Communication Engineering at KLEF (Deemed to be University), Guntur. He has more than 14 years of teaching experience. His areas of interest are Digital Communication and Digital Signal Processing.

Index

F

G

H

I

K

L

M

N

P

R

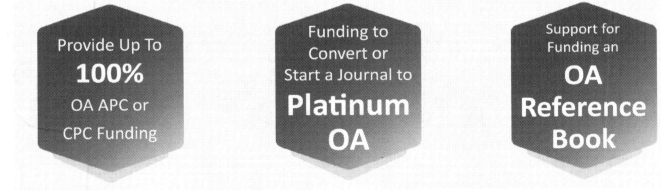

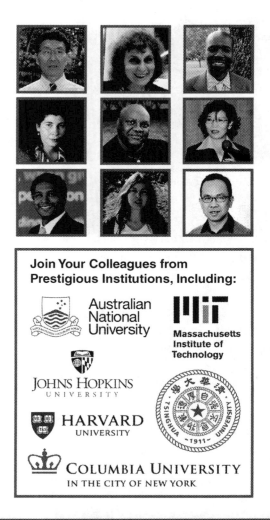